Sex & Gender

Sex & Gender

An Introduction

FOURTH EDITION

Hilary M. Lips
Radford University

Mayfield Publishing Company
Mountain View, California
London • Toronto

Library of Congress Cataloging-in-Publication Data

Lips, Hilary M.
    Sex and gender : an introduction / Hilary M. Lips. — 4th ed.
      p. cm.
    Includes bibliographical references and index.
    ISBN 0–7674–1614–7
    1. Sex role. 2. Sex differences (Psychology)   I. Title

HQ1075.L58 2000
305.3—dc21

                    00-022061
                    CIP

Manufactured in the United States of America
10   9   8   7   6   5   4   3   2   1

Mayfield Publishing Company
1280 Villa Street
Mountain View, California 94041

Sponsoring editor, Franklin C. Graham; production editor, Windy Johnson; manuscript editor, Kay Mikel; design manager, Jean Mailander; cover designer, Ann L. Vestal; manufacturing manager, Randy Hurst. The text was set in 10/12 Galliard Roman by Carlisle Communications, Inc., and printed on 45# Chromatone Matte by Banta Book Group.

For Jennifer, Hilary, and Leif
in the trust that your talents and strengths,
unfettered by notions of femininity and masculinity,
will shape what you choose and seek

Contents

PART II   Behavior & Experience:
Female–Male Similarities & Differences

CHAPTER 13
Issues in the Workplace
by Hilary Lips and Nina Colwill   395

CHAPTER 14
Justice, Equity, & Social Change   425

Preface

This fourth edition of *Sex & Gender* goes to press as we celebrate the turn of the century. Despite the flood of millennial prophecies and retrospectives currently choking the airwaves, and the number of commentators competing to name the most important events and people of the 1900s, little attention has been paid to the changes that have been wrought over the 20th century in female–male relationships, in the ways women and men think of themselves and each other, and in the societal norms for feminine and masculine behavior. This omission is surprising given the changes that have occurred. For example, at the beginning of the 1900s, women did not have the right to vote in any country except New Zealand. With the exception of a few strong monarchs, such as Queen Victoria, women had been largely absent from high-profile political leadership positions. They had, until the last few years of the 19th century, been barred from institutions of higher education and were believed to be unsuited for great intellectual efforts. Women regularly died in childbirth, often as a result of a pregnancy they did not choose but were powerless to prevent.

Today women hold voting rights in most nations of the world and have held the roles of president or prime minister in more than 30 countries. Women have gained access to higher education in large numbers, currently making up the majority of university students in the United States. Advances in medical technology and changes in the laws surrounding contraception and abortion have made unwanted pregnancies less inevitable and far less dangerous, allowing choices for women that were unthinkable 100 years ago.

Yet, in the face of so many transitions, one thing has changed little: the notion that gender is an important dimension in human life, that it is a category to be reckoned with. The division of the human race into females and males has, in many ways, assumed an importance that overshadows other divisions. From culture to culture, the male–female distinction has been assigned meanings and significance that have implications for work, family, leisure, and ritual—virtually all aspects of social life. Yet it is only within fairly recent history that we have begun to stand back from and question the meaning that cultures have placed on femaleness and maleness, femininity and masculinity. It is this process of questioning that both leads to and is nourished by the study of sex and gender.

The study of the differences and similarities between women and men is compelling for both its personal and its political implications. Issues of femininity and masculinity are emphasized strongly in our culture and can be important aspects of individual identity and self-concept. But such issues go far beyond questions of personal self-awareness. Feminist scholarship over the last three decades has made it increasingly apparent that beliefs about the differences and similarities between women and men are both rooted in and help to perpetuate particular social and political arrangements. To appreciate both the personal and political dimensions of gender, it is useful to examine what we know and do not know about the similarities and differences between women and men, where that knowledge comes from, and how that knowledge may itself be shaped and limited by cultural perceptions of femininity and masculinity. It is precisely to this type of examination that this book is dedicated.

Any one person's attempt to summarize a body of knowledge must necessarily reflect her own values and biases; this book is no exception to that rule. As a feminist social psychologist, I have a conviction that many of the differences in the ways female and male human beings behave can be traced to social factors such as stereotyping, self-fulfilling prophecy, conformity to social pressure, expectancy effects, and different socialization practices for the two genders. Furthermore, although I believe empirical research—research that tests theories against observable facts—is one of the best tools for unmasking and discrediting false assumptions and inaccurate stereotypes about sex and gender, I am also well aware that researchers shape their own truths to some extent and that the biases built into the research process itself affect investigators' findings and can perpetuate faulty theories and sexist interpretations of data. Thus, this book emphasizes empirical research but takes a critical approach to that research.

Knowledge is gathered and opinions formed in a social context. Early research on male–female differences took place in a context in which, for instance, it was often taken for granted that women's chief purpose in life was to bear children and that men were naturally better suited than women to take on public roles outside the family. Had I written this book 30 years ago, it would have been difficult to find and include a substantial amount of research that examined the social underpinnings of gender roles or challenged the assumption that sex differences in temperament were the inevitable outcome of the anatomical and physiological differences between females and males. It is largely under the impetus provided by the feminist movement that social scientists have begun to consider gender as something that is socially constructed rather than biologically inevitable. Yet our present social context continues to limit the study and understanding of sex and gender, and important gaps remain in the information that is available. Two of these gaps have been particularly noticeable to me as I compiled information for this book. The first is the small proportion of research on sex and gender that focuses on, or even includes, perspectives other than those of White, middle-class females and males. Most of the research is based at universities, and universities have been much more accessible to this group than to any other. This gap is hardly cause for surprise, but it is cause for concern. If we shape our "feminine" or "masculine" behavior largely in response to social cues and social pressure, it stands to reason that, to the extent that different groups emphasize or are subjected to different patterns of social cues and social pressure, femininity or masculinity in those groups will be associated with different experiences and behavior. For example, although some commonalties certainly exist, the female experience may differ in important ways for African American women, Asian American women, and European American women in the United States; the male experience may differ in important ways for Native American men or for men of Indo-Pakistani or European descent in Canada. Where possible in this book I have tried to include information that broadens the perspective on gender beyond that of White middle-class culture. Such inclusiveness has been easier in this fourth edition because of a burgeoning emphasis on diversity in feminist scholarship. However, information on every group for every topic is not readily available.

A second gap in the knowledge base about sex and gender stems from a tendency on the part of social scientists to ignore the experience of anyone who is not heterosexual. Thus, research on the development of sexual feelings and relationships, and research on couples and families, has until recently all but ignored the experiences of lesbians and gay men and bisexual and transgendered individuals. Although gaps still remain in this area, some excellent studies now exist. I have tried to include this perspective wherever information is available.

The book is divided into three parts. Part One, Myths, Theories, and Research, focuses on the stereotypes of femininity and masculinity and on the ways theory and research in psychology and the other social sciences have been influenced by and have affected these stereotypes. Part Two, Behavior and Experience: Female–Male Similarities and Differences, pits the gender stereotypes against the research evidence. It examines the evidence for male–female similarities and differences in a wide range of domains, from aggression to altruism, from mathematical performance to sexuality, from the experience of reproduction to mental and physical health. Throughout this section, the emphasis is on evaluating the evidence for gender differences and where differences appear, on trying to understand the reasons for them. Part Three, Sex and Gender in Social Relationships, examines the reciprocal links between gender roles and the structure of relationships, in the social world, from friendships to families, and from work relationships to politics and law. This section stresses the position of individuals in their social context. Feminine and masculine gender roles are not simply sets of qualities developed by individuals; they are part of the rules of a social system in which these individuals live. Built into that system is a hierarchy in which males, in general, have more power than females. The power difference cannot be ignored, and it is not easy for an individual to break away from it or to change it. Its consequences can be very negative for women, and there are negative side effects for men as well. An understanding of how gender, as an aspect of social relationships, is a reflection of a status hierarchy in which males outrank females leads back to an understanding of why gender stereotypes are the way they are, thus completing the circle that was begun in the first chapter of the book.

A primary emphasis of this fourth edition is to evaluate and resituate the major issues of every chapter in the context of the most current research literature. Strangely, one of the most important reasons for doing this is not due to advances in gender equity or understanding in the late 1990s, but rather the necessity to document via the most recent sources the lack of such advances. In business, in education, in politics, and in media stereotyping of females and males, women and men still receive different messages and are encouraged in different directions. Men are disproportionately represented in political leadership positions, in corporate boardrooms, and at the top levels of academic institutions. Little girls still encounter more barriers than do little boys when they explore mathematics, science, or computing. Rape and sexual harassment continue to be major issues confronting women in their daily environments—including on college campuses. The research I reviewed for this edition makes it abundantly clear that we must continue to pay attention to gender-related issues.

On a more positive note, frequent revisions of this book are necessary because of the explosion in scholarship on gender in recent years. Many issues have been rethought and reanalyzed: Are sex and gender really two different things? How malleable is gender identity? Should we emphasize gender differences, or is that the wrong question? When should we call a gender difference "small"? Are women really "nonaggressive," or does that label stem from stereotyping? How does subtle or "modern" sexism work on its targets? It is heartening to see the attention researchers are paying to these questions; it is difficult for an author to keep up with and include all the important scholarship being generated. And, of course, not everything has been included. This edition does, however, convey some of the flavor of the interesting data-gathering and debate that have focused on gender in the last three years.

Many people have provided me with help and encouragement. I thank the following people for insightful comments and suggestions on all or part of the manuscript or proposal for the first edition: Katherine Schultz, Dena Davidson, Nina Colwill, Jane Prather, Rhona Steinberg, Jeanne Kohl, Jeanne Maracek, Anne Peplau, and Ann Costain. Nina Colwill, my coauthor for Chapter 13 (Issues in the Workplace), provided welcome expertise and inspiration on many occasions. A book that she and I coauthored more than two decades ago, *The Psychology of Sex Differences,* provided some of the groundwork for this one, and I am indebted to her for the ideas that have been carried over from that earlier work to this. For the second edition, I extend my circle of thanks to include the following reviewers: Judy Rollins Bohannon, East Carolina University; Claire Etaugh, Bradley University; Lisa Judd, Winona State University; Faye D. Pascak-Craig, Marian College; Gwendolyn T. Sorrell, Texas Tech University; Michael R. Stevenson, Ball State University; Gail A. Thoen, University of Minnesota; Mary Roth Walsh, Harvard University. For the third edition, I thank the following reviewers: Cathleen Callahan, John Carroll University; Claire Etaugh, Bradley University; and John R. McCarthy, University of Albany, State University of New York. Finally, for this fourth edition, I thank reviewers Kristine Anthis, University of Nebraska, Omaha; Mary M. Brazier, Loyola University New Orleans; Barbara Peters, Southampton College; Gwendolyn T. Sorell, Texas Tech University; Gail A. Thoen, University of Minnesota.

I am grateful to Frank Graham, my sponsoring editor at Mayfield Publishing Company, for his support, suggestions, and encouragement through all editions. In the editing and production of this fourth edition, I have much appreciated the careful help of Kay Mikel, Windy Johnson, and Martha Granahan. The students who have worked with me at Radford University's Center for Gender Studies have been an important source of inspiration and support as I worked through this edition. In particular, I thank Ginger Hudson and Melanie Rogers for helping me remember the reasons I was working so hard on this project. My students and colleagues in the Psychology Department and the Women's Studies Program also deserve thanks for sharing their ideas with me and keeping me on my toes. Finally, I am deeply indebted to Wayne Andrew for his patience and care, his ideas and encouragement, the many late nights, and for help in a multitude of ways large and small.

CHAPTER 1

Masculinity & Femininity

Myths & Stereotypes

Jazz musician Billy Tipton lived life as a man, developed a thriving public career, married, adopted three sons, and spent a lifetime playing piano and saxophone in nightclubs. In death, at age 74, Billy Tipton was revealed to be a woman. In life, Tipton's secret was kept from everyone but his spouse, who said that Tipton had taken on a male identity to remove barriers to a musical career. Tipton's sons, as well as his former musician colleagues, were surprised and shocked to learn that he was female. "I'm just lost," said one son. "He'll always be Dad, but I think that he should have left something behind for us, something that would have explained the truth" ("Jazzman," 1989, p. 3A).

Ms. magazine carried a story about an "electronic imposter" (Van Gelder, 1985). This individual, a man, had presented himself as a woman on one of the large computer communication networks and had interacted for months with other users of the network under this assumed identity. When his deception was unmasked, the man's electronic "pen pals" were furious and hurt, not only because he had lied to them but also because they felt they had been tricked into relating to him in ways that they would not have done had they known he was male.

These stories are two of many possible illustrations of the force with which the dimension "male–female" affects our perceptions of and reactions to other people. The discovery that someone with whom we have interacted is female when we supposed her to be male, or male when we supposed him to be female, is upsetting. Even when communicating by means of words typed on a screen, it is unnerving to be uncertain of the sex of the person on the other end of the conversation. The labels "female" and "male" carry powerful associations about what to expect from the person to whom they are applied. We use the information the labels provide to guide our behavior toward other people and to interpret their behavior toward us. We also use the label applied to ourselves to create guidelines for our own activities. Not sure whether you believe this? Ask yourself these questions: If I heard footsteps behind me in a lonely, dark alley, would I care whether they were those of a man or a woman? If I were boarding a transatlantic flight and found that the pilot was a woman, would I feel a touch of extra anxiety? If a bright, articulate male friend decided to postpone finishing college in order to get married and raise children, would I be more surprised than if a bright, articulate female friend made the same decision? More disapproving? If you can give an unhesitating "no" to all of these questions, it is just possible that you have evaded the effects of the stereotyping on the basis of sex that is prevalent in North American society. Most of us, however, have not.

Sex stereotypes are socially shared beliefs that certain qualities can be assigned to individuals based on their membership in the female or male half of the human race. Stereotyping individuals can proceed on the basis of race, age, religion, height, social class, or any other distinction that can be used to divide people into groups. Sex stereotyping, though, has the relatively unique aspect of being based on a distinction that divides human beings into two groups: male or female. A result of this situation seems to be that many of our sex stereotypes are based on the notion of opposites. Indeed, our custom of referring to "the opposite sex" in discussions of female–male relationships springs from this tradition. In various cultures, the nature of the opposites has been specified. In some, the male principle has been represented by the sun, the female by the moon; the male by rationality and logic, the female by emotion and intuition; the male by light and clarity, the female by darkness, mystery, and magic. Some researchers now suggest that the notion of the two sexes as opposites, and of femininity and masculinity as two opposing poles on a continuum, may be one of the basic organizing principles human beings have learned to use when thinking about gender (Deaux & Lewis, 1984; Foushee, Helmreich, & Spence, 1979). It is not necessarily natural to think of women and men as opposites, however. Historians have noted that in Western culture the "opposites" tradition succeeded an equally strong "hierarchical" one in which women and men were considered to be similar, with women less advanced than men along the same continuum of perfection (Laqueur, 1990).

An implication of stereotyping two groups as polar opposites is that any movement away from the stereotype of one group is, by definition, a movement toward that of the other group. For instance, a man who acts less rational than the male stereotype is seen not only as less masculine but as more feminine; a woman who acts less emotional than the female stereotype is viewed not only as less feminine but as more masculine. Thus it is that, for example, women doing competent intellectual work have been told "You think like a man," and men showing reluctance to enter dangerous situations have been taunted with the epithet "old woman."

Another implication of the opposing stereotypes of masculinity and femininity is the notion that women and men should be separate from each other in a variety of contexts. A lone male or female in the midst of a group of the other sex is often made to feel like an invader or is obviously excluded, and individuals may scrupulously avoid situations they feel are geared for the other sex. The ludicrous lengths to which such avoidance may be carried were demonstrated in an old episode of the television show *Candid Camera.* The crew labeled two adjacent telephone booths with the signs Men and Women, placed a man in the "men's" booth, and waited to see what would happen as male passersby came along wanting to make a phone call. Remarkably, men ignored the empty "women's" phone booth and paced around impatiently waiting for their turn to use the one labeled "Men."

Another example that reflects both the arbitrariness of gender stereotypes and the phobia about violating them is provided by Tonkinson (1974), writing about the Aboriginal people of Australia. He tells of encountering a group of rural Aboriginal men who had been given some used clothing by a White station owner traveling through the area: "When our patrol arrived at the spot, the men in the group were wearing not only the trousers they had been given, but also the dresses. Our Aboriginal guide was quite embarrassed and quickly informed the men of their mistake; within seconds they discarded the female attire" (p. 104). To these men, who had not grown up with Western European customs, wearing dresses seemed just as appropriate as wearing pants—*until* the dresses were labeled as "for women."

THE SOCIAL CONTEXT OF STEREOTYPES

Stereotypes about women and men, like stereotypes about ethnic, racial, religious, or other groups, do not exist in a social vacuum. To understand why stereotypes persist in a particular form, it is necessary to know something about the social relations between the groups in question. In the case of women and men, many cultures, including our own, have a long history of a hierarchical relationship between the groups: Men have held more social power than women; men have been dominant and women subordinate (for comprehensive overviews of power and gender, see Lipman-Blumen, 1984, and Lips, 1991). One function of stereotypes is to bolster the status quo, so it is not surprising that dominant groups are stereotypically credited with more competence and intelligence than subordinate groups are, and that groups with low social power are more likely to be stereotyped as emotional and incompetent than their higher power counterparts are. This pattern, which can be seen in the stereotypes for Blacks and Whites in the United States, and for francophone and anglophone Canadians, is also evident in stereotypic beliefs about women and men. Indeed, stereotypes are often perpetuated simply because they justify prejudice against a subordinate group.

Stereotyping and prejudice involve dynamic processes, not just static collections of beliefs and evaluations. People who lack power and who are victims of prejudice actually develop qualities that are due to the prejudice and serve, in a self-fulfilling way, to reinforce it (Allport, 1954). They may, for instance, identify with the dominant group and accept that group's negative evaluation of their own group. Thus, for example, a woman may say that she does not like other women and that she finds men more interesting than women. In the discussion of stereotyping that follows, and indeed for the remainder of this book, it is important to remember that the behaviors and traits attributed to women and men have been observed in particular social contexts—contexts in which men have, in many ways, held greater social power than women have.

Because stereotypic views of females and males are dynamic and depend on social context, sex stereotypes and ideals of femininity and masculinity are likely to vary somewhat across social/cultural groups and historical periods. For a White woman in the American South of the 1950s, femininity might mean emphasizing one's frailty and forswearing smoking on the street. For an African American urban woman in the United States in the 1990s, the notions of acceptably "feminine" behavior might be quite different. For a contemporary middle-class Japanese man in Tokyo, masculinity might involve working an intense 80-hour week without complaint, rarely taking vacations, and squeezing in time with his family when he can. For his North American counterpart, however, masculinity might imply having the leisure and means to do things with his family. Thus, there is no *single* stereotype of masculinity or of femininity. Rather, these constructs are specific to time and place and are continually being reworked and their boundaries renegotiated. Moveable though the boundaries are in theory, however, we often experience them as daunting in our own culture, time, and place. We sense that transgressing them may involve negative reactions from others.

SEX OR GENDER: MORE THAN A QUESTION OF TERMINOLOGY?

In the past, the words *sex* and *gender* were often used interchangeably. However, many psychologists, stimulated by an appeal from Rhoda Unger (1979), adopted more precise definitions of the two terms. **Sex** was used to refer to a person's biological maleness or femaleness, **gender** to the nonphysiological aspects of being female or male—the cultural expectations for femininity and masculinity. The distinction seemed a useful one because it kept us focused on the fact that many female–male differences in behavior or experience do not spring naturally or automatically from biological differences between the sexes.

No clean, absolute separation of "sex" and "gender" is possible, however. Cultural expectations for women and men (gender) are not separable from observations about women's and men's physical bodies (sex). Thus, cultural constructions of gender include sex, in some sense. Conversely, history illustrates that even the most obvious biological "facts" about sex are susceptible to misperception and misinterpretation when they violate investigators' assumptions about gender. For example, the distinguished anatomist Herophilus of Alexandria, working under the assumption that women were essentially unperfected men, "saw" in his dissections of human bodies that women had testes with seminal ducts that connected to the neck of the bladder, just as men did (Laqueur, 1990). What he saw were ovaries and Fallopian tubes—which clearly do *not* connect to the bladder. However, his expectation that women and men should be anatomically similar guided his perceptions, encouraging him to see similarities even where the evidence favored differences. Thus, our understanding of biological sex differences is likely to be shaped by our culture's notions of gender.

We cannot, then, use the terms *sex* and *gender* to represent separate, nonoverlapping concepts. Often we do not know whether a particular difference between females and males arises from biology or culture. In fact, what we do know is that many differences are the result of biology–environment interactions (Hyde, 1994; Unger & Crawford, 1993). In this book, *gender* is used as the more inclusive term when discussing female–male differences that may be caused by any combination of environment and biology. *Sex* is reserved for discussions of anatomy and the classification of individuals based on their anatomical category. *Gender* is also used as a label for the system of expectations held by societies with respect to feminine and masculine roles.

"SUGAR AND SPICE" OR "SNIPS AND SNAILS": THE CONTENT OF GENDER STEREOTYPES

Personality Traits

Aggressive. Sensitive. Ambitious. Emotional. Which of these adjectives would you say are typically associated with men? With women? It is on questions such as these that much of our knowledge of the content of gender stereotypes is based.

More than two decades ago, two researchers asked students at an American university to categorize 300 adjectives as being typically associated with women or men (J. E. Williams & Bennett, 1975). Seventy-five percent of the students agreed on 30 adjectives describing women and 33 describing men. These adjectives are shown in Table 1.1. They are not atypical of the findings of current research on gender stereotypes (B. P. Allen, 1995; C. L. Martin, 1987). Researchers in Canada (Edwards & Williams, 1980), Britain (Burns, 1977), and India (Gupta, 1991) have found similar if not identical patterns, and a study of gender stereotyping in 30 countries has shown considerable cross-cultural uniformity in these descriptions (J. E. Williams & Best, 1982, 1990). Studies of adults in 25 countries showed a core of adjectives that were agreed on as typical of women and men by 75% of the countries studied and that 6 (out of a possible 300) items were associated with men in every country: *adventurous, dominant, forceful, independent, masculine,* and *strong* (J. E. Williams & Best, 1990). Only 3 items were associated with women in every country: *sentimental, submissive,* and *superstitious.* When Williams and Best scaled the items for affective meaning along the dimensions of favorability, strength, and activity, they found that in all countries the male stereotype items were more active and stronger, and the female stereotype items were more passive and weaker.

Some cross-cultural differences in gender stereotypes have been noted. Block (1973) found that American students, both male and female, were more likely than their counterparts in England, Sweden, Denmark, Finland, and Norway to endorse agentic (goal-oriented, focused on individual success and achievement) adjectives such as *adventurous, assertive,* and *ambitious* in their description of both the masculine and the feminine ideals, whereas Lii and Wong (1982) found American students more likely than Chinese students to use agentic and competent attributes to describe the feminine stereotype. These respondents are describing their societies' stereotypes, and as such the findings describe the extent to which people in various parts of the world *know* the male and female stereotypes, not necessarily the extent to which they actually *believe* them to be true.

Table 1.1   Adjectives stereotypically associated with women and men (based on Williams & Bennett, 1975)

Women

Affected	Feminine	Prudish
Affectionate	Fickle	Rattlebrained
Appreciative	Flirtatious	Sensitive
Attractive	Frivolous	Sentimental
Charming	Fussy	Softhearted
Complaining	Gentle	Sophisticated
Dependent	High-strung	Submissive
Dreamy	Meek	Talkative
Emotional	Mild	Weak
Excitable	Nagging	Whiny

Men

Adventurous	Disorderly	Realistic
Aggressive	Dominant	Robust
Ambitious	Enterprising	Self-confident
Assertive	Forceful	Severe
Autocratic	Handsome	Stable
Boastful	Independent	Steady
Coarse	Jolly	Stern
Confident	Logical	Strong
Courageous	Loud	Tough
Cruel	Masculine	Unemotional
Daring	Rational	Unexcitable

Although the existence of both female and male stereotypes can be demonstrated, the male stereotype seems to be the more rigidly defined of the two. When 400 undergraduates were asked to use lists of trait and appearance adjectives to describe personal (How do you personally see males?), social (How does society view males?), and ideal (How do you see the ideal male?) views of males and females, all three perspectives on males were more stereotypic than the comparable perspectives on females (Hort, Fagot, & Leinbach, 1990). An important component of the masculine stereotype seems to be a belief that males do not express the emotions they feel (Fabes & Martin, 1991).

In trying to describe the themes inherent in gender stereotypes, psychologists have relied on a dichotomy first proposed by two family sociologists: instrumentality versus expressiveness (T. Parsons & Bales, 1955). The masculine stereotype is said to be characterized by expectations of **instrumentality:** an orientation toward action, accomplishment, and leadership. The feminine stereotype combines attributes that add up to **expressiveness:** an orientation toward emotion and relationships. Congruent with this pattern are the findings of Broverman, Vogel, Broverman, Clarkson, and Rosenkrantz (1972) and McKee and Sherriffs (1957), who noted that the most highly valued male-stereotyped traits formed a "competency" cluster, whereas the most highly valued female-stereotyped traits formed a "warmth–expressiveness" cluster. Although this dichotomy focuses only on positive qualities and fails to capture completely the stereotypic beliefs about female–male differences (for example, the masculine traits "loud" and "disorderly" do not really seem to depict instrumentality, whereas the feminine traits "weak" and "whiny" bear no obvious relation to expressiveness), it does help to provide a framework for studying these stereotypes. But how is such study carried out? What do researchers really mean when they claim to have delineated the existence of a certain stereotype about a particular group among members of a particular population?

Measuring Stereotypes

Researchers using key attributes to define masculinity and femininity may end up with findings that overestimate the strength of stereotypes and underestimate the overlap in the popular perceptions of females and males. The question comes with a built-in assumption that each adjective may be classified as more typical of either women or men. People answering such a question are thus subtly encouraged to provide stereotypic answers, and the results may yield an exaggerated view of the stereotypes. Moreover, respondents in these studies have usually been asked to indicate whether certain traits are "typically associated" with women or men, not whether they personally believe a particular set of adjectives actually reflects what women and men are like. Finally, a fact often overlooked in discussions of stereotypes is that the average ratings obtained for males and females in these studies, although significantly different from each other, do not usually represent opposite extremes. For instance, on a 10-point scale ranging from passive (1) to active (10), males might be rated at 7.2 and females at 6.1. Indeed, the mean ratings of males and females on such scales rarely fall on opposite sides of the midpoint (Spence, Helmreich, & Stapp, 1974).

Researchers using different methods to assess stereotypes have found less evidence for their pervasiveness and for their bipolarity. When measures are used that allow respondents to describe males and females on the basis of overlapping as well as differentiating characteristics, subjects indicate that the "most feminine" and "most masculine" persons they can imagine possess many of the same desirable traits (Jenkin & Vroegh, 1969).

Stereotypes are more than catalogues of adjectives, and researchers now recognize that, for example, some "masculine" adjectives are considered more representative of the category *Men* than others are. Studies using a method that allows participants to rate the degree to which traits characterize both the typical woman and the typical man suggest a tendency for the clusters of traits seen to characterize each to overlap (De Lisi & Soundranayagam, 1990). These studies are based on the idea that gender stereotypes represent natural language categories composed of "core" or **prototypical traits** (the clearest examples of each category) surrounded by peripheral traits (those less strongly associated with each category). The core traits for women generally belong to a niceness/nurturance dimension, whereas those for men belong to a potency/power dimension. Overlap between the two categories is seen in that core adjectives for one gender tend to fall in the periphery for the other gender. One intriguing finding is that female respondents add to the niceness/nurturance qualities that constitute the female core a second group of adjectives: *capable, competent, dependable, intelligent,* and *responsible.* Male respondents do not include these adjectives in the female core; rather, they tend to add *attractive, good-looking, sexy,* and *soft* (De Lisi & Soundranayagam, 1990).

When people describe women and men according to gender stereotypes, are they overestimating the differences, seeing differences that do not exist, or giving an accurate report of real gender differences? To find out, some researchers have examined gender stereotypes using a ratio method (B. P. Allen, 1995; C. L. Martin, 1987). For each trait on a list, respondents are asked to estimate the proportion of men and women who have the trait, and also to report on whether they themselves possess the trait. Using this method, both C. L. Martin (1987) and B. P. Allen (1995) found that people tend to overestimate the differences between women and men in comparison to the differences between women and men in their self-reports. In contrast, Janet Swim (1994) compared respondents' estimates of gender differences to research findings of behavioral gender differences on the same traits. She found that, compared with past research results rather than self-reports, her respondents tended to be accurate or to underestimate gender differences rather than to overestimate them.

There is considerable controversy in the field of psychology about the appropriate criteria to use when measuring the accuracy of stereotypes. Researchers will no doubt continue to produce conflicting findings about the extent to which people's perceptions of group differences between women and men parallel or exaggerate "real" differences, especially since the "real" differences can change across time and place. As Swim (1994) notes, it is important to remember that even if people have a roughly accurate idea of the direction and size of gender differences on particular traits, it does not mean they understand the reasons for the differences or that they will apply the knowledge accurately to individual women and men. In Swim's research, her respondents underestimated the power of particular situations to produce gender differences. Yet research shows that the appearance of gender differences in behavior often seems to depend heavily on the social context (e.g., Maccoby, 1990).

BEYOND PERSONALITY TRAITS: THE MANY FACES OF GENDER STEREOTYPES

If you had to choose the qualities that most clearly make people seem "feminine" or "masculine" to you, would you focus on personality traits? Or might you concentrate instead on other things about the person: physical appearance, perhaps, or certain behaviors, occupation, or sexual preference? In recent years, researchers have come to realize that gender stereotypes are multifaceted, encompassing a variety of expectations about how people will look, act, think, and feel. Moreover, it is becoming apparent that there is more than a single "typical" male and female; rather, many people hold sets of stereotypes about different "types" of males and females.

Kay Deaux and Laurie Lewis (1984) showed that a number of separate **components of gender stereotypes** can be identified: traits, role behaviors, occupations, and physical appearance—each of which has a masculine and a feminine version. Their research suggests that people see these components as able to vary independently to some extent. For example, a person could have a very masculine appearance but not necessarily be in a masculine occupation or show a lot of masculine personality traits. However, they have also demonstrated that information about one component influences people's assumptions about the others, in the absence of conflicting information (Deaux & Lewis, 1984). For a hypothetical person, they gave participants a sex label (male or female) and information about specific role behaviors (masculine, feminine, or mixed) and asked the participants to estimate the likelihood that the person possessed particular masculine and feminine traits, pursued particular male- or female-associated occupations, and was heterosexual or homosexual. For example, participants were given the following description: "A woman has been described in terms of the following characteristics and behaviors: source of emotional support, manages the house, takes care of children, responsible for decorating the house. Consider these characteristics carefully and think about what type of woman this would be." The participants concluded that this woman was more likely to show feminine traits such as emotionality, gentleness, and understanding of others and to be in a feminine occupation such as occupational therapist or elementary school teacher than to show masculine traits or be in a masculine occupation. They also indicated a high probability that the woman was heterosexual. In general, the participants apparently relied more heavily on the information they were given about role behaviors than on the male–female labels to estimate the probability of masculine or feminine traits or occupations. A person described in terms of the masculine role behaviors—head of household, financial provider, a leader, and responsible for household repairs—was judged much more likely to possess masculine traits such as independence, activity, and competitiveness, and to be in male-associated occupations such as truck driver, insurance agent, or urban planner than was a person described in terms of female role behaviors, regardless of whether the person was labeled female or male. Also noteworthy is the finding that role behavior that is counterstereotypic for an individual's biological sex is linked to speculation that the person is homosexual. When feminine role behaviors were described for a hypothetical man, the estimated probability of homosexuality reached 40%. It is clear that gender stereotypes and stereotypes about homosexuality are linked, despite the lack of evidence that a person's sexual preference is related to gender-role behavior.

In a follow-up experiment, these researchers found that physical appearance cues (masculine: tall, strong, sturdy, broad-shouldered; feminine: quiet voice, dainty, graceful, soft) always outweighed sex labels when participants were making inferences about a hypothetical person's traits, occupation, or role behaviors. Other researchers have subsequently found that the masculinity or femininity of facial appearance can have an impact on judgments about a person's sexual orientation: Individuals with feminine male faces and masculine female faces were more likely than others to be judged as gay or lesbian (Dunkle & Francis, 1990). Indeed, it is quite likely that appearance is a core aspect of gender stereotyping, judging by the level of dismay that greets deviations from "appropriate" feminine and masculine physiques. It is instructive to note that a common reaction to female bodybuilders, for example, is not to marvel at their achievement of a muscular body but to bemoan their lack of feminine appearance. In the women's bodybuilding championship depicted in the documentary film *Pumping Iron II,* the woman with the biggest, most well-defined muscles was given low scores because she "didn't look like a woman," despite one judge's argument that penalizing a contestant for having muscles that were too big was akin to telling a female skier that she would be disqualified if she went too fast! It is becoming clear that people's ideas about gender are composed of several dimensions and that specific information about a person's characteristics can be more important in setting expectations about that person than is the knowledge that she or he is female or male.

The research just described underscores another important point: Despite our tendency to think of females and males as opposites, stereotyping by sex is not an all-or-nothing affair. Clearly, respondents do not believe that *only* males can be aggressive, drive trucks, or act as leaders, nor that *only* females can be nurturant, have

Table 1.2   Probability judgments of male and female
stereotypic characteristics (adapted from Deaux, 1984)

	Judgment[a]	
Characteristic	Men	Women
Trait		
Independent	.78	.58
Competitive	.82	.64
Warm	.76	.77
Emotional	.56	.84
Role behavior		
Financial provider	.83	.47
Takes initiative with opposite sex	.82	.54
Takes care of children	.50	.85
Cooks meals	.42	.83
Physical characteristic		
Muscular	.64	.36
Deep voice	.73	.30
Graceful	.45	.68
Small-boned	.39	.62

[a]Subjects' estimate of the probability that the average person of either
sex would possess a characteristic.

soft voices, and be elementary school teachers. Rather, the stereotypes are an expression of the perceived *probability* that a person will have certain qualities, given that she or he is female or male. Table 1.2 shows the probability judgments that subjects made about whether men and women would have particular characteristics. Although a higher probability is given to the possession of stereotypic characteristics by men and women, the table shows that there is always some acknowledged probability that each characteristic could be displayed by an individual of either sex.

One final note on the complexity of gender stereotypes: Not only do they seem to be made up of different components, they also seem to be organized in terms of specific *types* of men and women (Coats & Smith, 1999; Six & Eckes, 1991). Researchers find that respondents can quite easily list several types of women and men, along with descriptions that differentiate among the types. Sample types of males obtained from respondents in one study included the career man (well-dressed, self-confident, calculating, materialistic, eloquent), and the softy (sympathetic, can show weakness, sensitive, unconventional, frank), along with such others as the egoist, the intellectual, the macho type, the cool type, and the playboy. Female types included the feminist (self-confident, cunning, intolerant, doesn't show feelings) and the housewife (unattractive, "good girl," obsequious, selfless, no interests of her own), along with such others as the society lady, the maternal type, the vamp, and the secretary (Six & Eckes, 1991).

Even when gender stereotypes have been narrowed down to such subtypes of women and men, they are still likely to vary in response to the examples of such subtypes that an individual has recently observed. Coates and Smith (1999) found that, depending on which of two examples of gender subtypes they showed to their research participants, participants listed different characteristics as descriptive of those subtypes. For example, participants who had, earlier in the study, been asked to fill out questionnaires about either television character Murphy Brown or news anchor Connie Chung (both examples of the female subtype "professional woman") later provided different descriptions of the professional woman subtype. People who had been asked to think about Murphy Brown later described the subtype "professional woman" as higher on an index of characteristics that included independent, dedicated, unfriendly, opinionated, impolite, and insensitive than did participants who had earlier been asked to think about Connie Chung. Similarly, participants who earlier had been asked to think about either tennis star Andre Aggasi or boxing great Muhammad Ali gave different ratings on a list of characteristics for the subtype "athletic man." Those who had answered questions about Andre Aggasi later described the athletic man subtype as more outgoing, attractive, feminine, sexual, confident, conceited, and less aggressive than did those who had answered questions about Muhammad Ali. It appears that the exemplars of a particular subtype a person has seen lately affect the way that person thinks about that category of individuals.

DIFFERENT AND UNEQUAL?
THE EVALUATIVE ASPECTS OF GENDER STEREOTYPES

Stereotypes imply only beliefs about group differences and are not necessarily accompanied by positive or negative judgments about the groups in question, but there is some evidence that such evaluative judgments *do* accompany gender stereotypes. The negative evaluation of persons or their activities because they belong to a particular group is known as **prejudice,** and the brand of prejudice that is based on a person's sexual category is called **sexism.** By definition, sexism can be used against either females or males; both women and men can be judged harshly, not be taken seriously, or be deprived of opportunities *because* they are women or *because* they are men.

The evidence that sexism plays a role in reactions to and treatment of women is long-standing and comprehensive. One need not be familiar with the psychological research literature to detect evidence of sexism either in our history or in our everyday lives. For years, women in the United States and Canada (among other countries) were denied the vote, denied equal access to higher education, and routinely and openly discriminated against in hiring and salary. Women who fought their way into institutions of higher education found that, when they had completed the requirements for advanced degrees, those degrees were withheld (Furomoto & Scarborough, 1986). Women who marched in public protest over their lack of voting rights were beaten by police and imprisoned in the United States and in Britain. Popular stereotypes of women emphasized their helplessness and compared them to children, and such views were enshrined in a multitude of laws and legal practices that restricted women's access to jobs and required a woman to have the permission of her husband or father to apply for a loan, own property, or change her name. The length and bitterness of the struggle for women's suffrage in so many countries, the necessity for

Canadian women in the 1920s to go to court to have women declared "persons" under the law,* and the continuing controversy over issues such as equal pay for work of equal value and equal access to work bear strong testimony to the pervasiveness of sexism in the treatment of women.

Does all this mean that people don't like women as much as men? Not necessarily. In fact, researchers have found that women are evaluated more favorably than men—perhaps because women are stereotyped as more likely to be helpful, gentle, and understanding (Eagly, Mladinic, & Otto, 1991). In fact, recent research tends to show a "women are wonderful" effect. Both women and men evaluate women more favorably than men (Eagly & Mladinic, 1989; 1994), but there are two important qualifications to this finding. First, favorability ratings can vary dramatically, depending on what *kind* of woman is on the mind of the evaluator. One study showed, for example, that among right-wing authoritarian respondents women were evaluated most negatively when they were viewed as "feminists" but most positively when they were viewed as housewives (Haddock & Zanna, 1994). Second, being liked apparently does not necessarily translate into being respected or being treated fairly.

Researchers have found that discrimination against women can be based on ambivalence, not just hostility toward women (Glick & Fiske, 1997). Men who have ambivalent, or mixed, feelings about women may display two different kinds of sexism: **hostile sexism** (dominance-oriented paternalism, derogatory beliefs about women, and heterosexual hostility) and **benevolent sexism** (protective paternalism, idealization of women, and desire for intimate relations). Even though the latter type of sexism sounds more positive, it still acts as a justification for keeping women in subordinate positions and traditional roles. Men who score high on the Ambivalent Sexism Inventory, which measures the hostile and benevolent components of sexism, are more likely than nonsexist men to classify women into polarized subgroups: those that belong on a "pedestal" and those that belong in the "gutter" (Glick, Diebold, Bailey-Werner, & Zhu, 1997). Yet women tend to underestimate the likelihood that benevolent and hostile sexism could exist in the same person, and many women fall into the trap of "wanting it both ways": approving of benevolent sexism while condemning hostile sexism (Kiliansky & Rudman, 1998).

Not all sexism is obvious. In fact, since so many people are aware of the disapproval that may greet the expression of gender stereotypes, they often express such stereotypes in subtle ways. Researchers in the United States and Canada have identified a constellation of attitudes they label **modern sexism** (Swim, Aikin, Hall, & Hunter, 1995) or **neosexism** (Tougas, Brown, Beaton, & Joly, 1995). Old-fashioned sexism openly endorsed stereotypic judgments about and differential treatment of women and men. Modern sexism is more subtle and is characterized by a denial that

*In 1927, a group of prominent Canadian feminists known as the Famous Five (Henrietta Muir Edwards, Emily Murphy, Louise McKinney, Irene Parlby, and Nellie McClung) petitioned Parliament for an interpretation of a clause in the Constitution that referred to the eligibility of "persons" for appointments to the Senate. The Supreme Court of Canada ruled that women were not to be considered as persons under this clause and so did not qualify for Senate appointments. This decision was reversed by Britain's Privy Council in 1929—an event that is still celebrated by Canadian feminists on "Persons Day" in October. The "Women Are Persons" monument, comprising bronze statues of the five women celebrating their victory, is to be placed on Parliament Hill on October 18, 2000. It will be the first statue in that location that does not commemorate either royalty or a prime minister of Canada.

women are still targets of discrimination, by antagonism toward women's demands, and by a lack of support for policies designed to improve women's status. Men who hold neosexist attitudes are more likely to show a pro-male bias in the evaluation of competence and are less likely to support women (Beaton, Tougas, & Joly, 1996).

What of sexism in the treatment of men? Although men are privileged over women in many respects, they can also be victims of sexist assumptions. Sexism cuts both ways; for example, the other side of the prejudiced attitude that bars women from combat positions in the military is the attitude that it is somehow less upsetting to have male soldiers killed than to have female soldiers killed. Small but active organizations of men have identified ways in which stereotypic expectations of men can result in negative consequences for them. Men's organizations—both liberal, feminist (e.g., National Organization for Changing Men) and conservative, masculinist (e.g., National Congress for Men)—note that the stereotype of men as tough, unemotional, and aggressive can result in harsh treatment of men and in male alienation. They cite, albeit from differing perspectives, society's lack of support for fathering, the expectation that men will do the fighting and dying in wartime, and ways in which the protector and provider roles have damaged and dehumanized men (C. W. Franklin, 1988).

With respect to the evaluation of men, some research shows that men may be more rigid than women in their insistence on stereotypical masculinity. Male college students describe the "ideal" man in more stereotypic terms than female students do (Hort, Fagot, & Leinbach, 1990). Moreover, when female college students were given the opportunity to "listen in" on scripted interviews in which the male interviewees portrayed either traditional masculine or nontraditional, androgynous roles, they consistently rated the nontraditional male more favorably (more appropriate, likeable, moral, adaptive, conscientious, tactful, reliable, and less conventional, conceited, and jealous) than his traditional counterpart (Cramer, Dragna, Cupp, & Stewart, 1991).

Sexism in the Evaluation of Work

One of the most obvious manifestations of sexism directed against women is undervaluing their work. In a now classic study, P. H. Goldberg (1968) gave college women articles to evaluate that were supposedly written by a woman or a man. The same article was rated more favorably when attributed to a man than to a woman, leading Goldberg to suggest that women were prejudiced against other women. Similar research carried out years later by Paludi and Strayer (1985) indicates that a pro-male bias can still be found, in both men and women, in reactions to written work. They asked 300 women and men to evaluate an article that was supposedly written by a man, a woman, an author with a sexually ambiguous name, or an anonymous author. The articles used were chosen to represent areas of stereotypically masculine expertise (politics), stereotypically feminine expertise (the psychology of women), or a neutral field (education). Raters judged the articles, even in the feminine and neutral fields, to be better written, more insightful, more persuasive, and higher in overall quality when they were told they were written by a man. Moreover, when presented with the "neutral" article attributed to either an anonymous author or to one whose name was sexually ambiguous, most respondents thought that the author was a man—and rated the article more favorably than did those few who assumed the author was a woman. Such a tendency to evaluate men's work more favorably than women's is not always found; however, when differences in evaluation are found, they tend to favor men (Top, 1991). An antifemale bias is most likely to occur in domains that are stereotypically masculine when gender-neutral (rather than feminine or masculine) material is being rated, when subjects have less information about the people being rated, and when subjects are rating a job application or résumé rather than material such as written work or a biography (Swim, Borgida, Maruyama, & Myers, 1989).

Prejudice against women is more likely to be found in studies outside the lab, in which respondents believe their ratings have real consequences (Top, 1991). Job applications seem particularly likely to trigger prejudiced evaluations. Although this effect is not always found, experimental studies of the impact of gender and qualifications on hiring recommendations show that males tend to be preferred over females (Harvie, Marshal-McCaskey, & Johnston, 1998; Olian, Schwab, & Haberfeld, 1988; Powell, 1987). For example, when confronted with male and female applicants with equivalent qualifications, studies have demonstrated that respondents favored the male over the female applicants for positions in university-level psychology teaching (Bronstein, Black, Pfenning, & White, 1986), newswriting (Etaugh & Kasley, 1981), sports photography (Heilman, Martell, & Simon, 1988), accounting (Zickmund, Hitt, & Pickens, 1978), and Congress (E. J. Katz & Madden, 1984). In addition to unfavorable judgments of performance, women receive other negative evaluations with respect to their competence: Their success is often devalued by being explained as "luck," and competent women are sometimes described as "unfeminine" and as less likeable than competent men (Lott, 1985).

Clearly, the stereotypes about women as a group pave the way for the inference that women will not perform as well as men in a variety of arenas. Such an inference can be countered, however, by specific information about a job applicant—information that preempts stereotypic characterization. A review of available studies shows that when specific, unambiguous information of direct relevance to job performance is presented about applicants, it tends to undermine discrimination against women (Tosi & Einbender, 1985).

Perhaps the reason for discrimination against women is not simply bias against women but bias against people behaving, or trying to behave, in ways incongruent with gender stereotypes. After all, all of the activities just mentioned, from writing articles to accounting, demand professional, competent, instrumental behavior—a type of behavior that forms part of the masculine stereotype. If the job or task in question requires more expressive than instrumental qualities or is classified as more suitable for a woman than a man, would men be the victims of discrimination? Some researchers suggest that they would. Professional personnel consultants judging the suitability of applicants for two male sex-typed jobs (automobile salesperson, hardware shipping and receiving clerk), two female sex-typed jobs (telephone operator, receptionist), and two neutral jobs (motel desk clerk, darkroom assistant) judged male and female applicants as more suitable for their respective sex-typed occupations and showed no significant preference for male or female applicants on the neutral jobs (Cash, Gillen, & Burns, 1977). Kalin, Stoppard, and Burt (1980) found similar results using a greater number and variety of sex-typed occupations.

A more elaborate theory of how gender stereotypes influence perceived suitability for particular jobs has been proposed by Felicia Pratto and her colleagues (Pratto, Sidanius, & Siers, 1997). They argue that women are stereotyped as holding values that are hierarchy-attenuating (challenging to the often male-dominated organizational power structure) whereas men are assumed to hold values that are hierarchy-enhancing (supportive of the power structure). Thus, managers are likely to hire women and men for jobs that seem to fit these value systems: women for jobs that require the person to try to change the system or help people who have been marginalized in the system, and men for jobs that require the person to support and strengthen the status quo. Indeed, when given the task of placing applicants in positions with different levels of hierarchy-attenuating or -enhancing features, participants favored women for the hierarchy-attenuating jobs and men for the hierarchy-enhancing jobs. This pattern held, even when the applicants' résumés showed a consistent violation of the stereotypes.

Once a person is actually *in* a job, performance evaluations may also be influenced by gender stereotypes. Female leaders are most likely to be evaluated less favorably than their male counterparts when they use a masculine leadership style (Eagly, Makhijani, & Klonsky, 1992). However, for women, negative evaluations are not always associated with behaving in counterstereotypic ways. In some stereotypical masculine occupations, women who behave in masculine ways are evaluated more highly than men (D. P. Moore, 1984), and women who behave in feminine ways are evaluated less favorably. For example, women police officers who adopt a feminine style often have negative work reputations among their colleagues (Wexler, 1985). Clearly, conformity to gender expectations plays a role in how individuals are evaluated, but conformity to the demands of a particular job can also play a part.

Where do gender expectations come from? Alice Eagly and Valerie Steffen (1984) have shown that they come, in part, from the very way women and men are distributed into social roles. We seem to be caught in a vicious circle: We expect women and men to be different because we observe that they tend to do different things, and this very expectation then leads us to react negatively to those whose behavior does not match our original observations. Moreover, our expectations encompass not only stereotypical differences between women and men but also a hierarchy of occupational roles. Mary Ann Cejka and Alice Eagly (1999) examined the relationship between the distribution of women and men in 80 occupations and research participants' beliefs that six dimensions of gender-stereotypic qualities contribute to success in these occupations. They found that participants' beliefs that an occupation demanded feminine or masculine physical or personality traits predicted the extent to which that occupation was female- or male-dominated. Moreover, participants' beliefs that occupations required masculine personality or cognitive characteristics for success predicted the prestige of occupations.

Can competence in a "gender-inappropriate" endeavor ever work to one's advantage? Some researchers argue that persons presented as very competent in a field that is extremely unusual for their gender can be *overevaluated*. In one study, females identified as finalists in a football photography contest (a strongly male sex-typed field) were judged as more competent than male finalists in the same contest, but a similar overevaluation of females did not occur in the more moderately male sex-typed field of tennis photography (Heilman et al., 1988). In a similar vein, raters awarded the highest presentation marks, among two female and two male speakers, to a man who spoke on a strongly female sex-typed topic: "sex bias in the counseling of women" (Gilbert, Lee, & Chiddix, 1981). At least under some conditions, women who are good at "men's" work and men who are good at "women's" work are the beneficiaries of more positive evaluations than their more traditional counterparts are. What is going on here? Researchers speculate that when behavior contrasts so sharply with stereotypical expectations that it exceeds a critical threshold it creates a boomerang effect (Weber & Crocker, 1983). The individual is characterized as an exception who does not fit the stereotype, or as a member of a "subtype" of the larger group ("career woman," "sensitive man") whose qualities are different from those of the larger group. These individuals may be given positive evaluations simply because their good performance is so surprising for their gender—gender bias works *for* them instead of against them.

Unfortunately for people entering nontraditional jobs, they cannot usually count on this positive effect of gender bias. Such an effect occurs, at least with respect to women, under very specific conditions: Information about high performance ability must be present, and the job in question must be very atypical for a woman to pursue (Heilman et al., 1988). When these conditions are not met, gender bias works *against* women pursuing nontraditional occupations.

One of the clearest illustrations that the prejudice against women involves something more than their perceived suitability to do particular work is the fact that occupations undergoing a transition from being dominated by men to being dominated by women lose status, sometimes drastically. When secretarial positions were held mainly by men, they were reasonably high-status positions, whose occupants had reasonable chances for advancement (Davies, 1975). Now that virtually all secretaries are women, the job is low-status and often a dead end. A similar pattern has been noted for bank tellers (Prather, 1971) and teachers (Oppenheimer, 1970). In a laboratory demonstration of this phenomenon, Touhey (1974) gave participants descriptions of five high-status professions: architect, college professor, lawyer, physician, and scientist. On the information sheet describing each profession, half the participants were told that the percentage of women in the profession was expected to remain stable and low for the next 25 to 30 years. The other half were told that the percentage of women would increase dramatically over the same time period. When told to expect an increasing proportion of women in the professions, participants consistently rated them lower in prestige. Congruent with this result is Glick's (1991) finding of a positive relationship between raters' perceptions that masculine traits were required for a job and the prestige and salary they assigned to that job. He also found that the greater the percentage of women raters perceived to be in an occupational category, the lower the salary they assigned to that occupation. A more recent study shows that not only are masculine personality traits linked to occupational prestige, virtually *all* highly prestigious jobs are male-dominated (Glick, Wilk, & Perreault, 1995).

Worry over the potential decline in personal or institutional status associated with an increase in the number of women may explain some aspects of men's resistance to such an increase. This resistance has been documented in cases ranging from private golf clubs (e.g., MacLean, 1991) to state universities (e.g., E. Greene, 1987; Henderson & Baker, 1990). For example, at the University of North Carolina, concern over the fact that female students had become a majority led some trustees to propose changing the weights for admission criteria to restore the male majority (E. Greene, 1987).

It is safe to conclude that although both women and men are subject to the restrictions of gender stereotypes, the masculine stereotype is associated with higher status. Moreover, although members of either sex may suffer discrimination based on views that their gender renders them unsuitable for a task or position, women are the targets of more discrimination in this respect than men. Not only are almost all the high-status jobs defined as more suitable for men, but high-status jobs that become female-dominated quickly lose their prestige.

GENDER AND OTHER STEREOTYPES: RACE, CLASS, AGE, APPEARANCE, SEXUAL ORIENTATION, DISABILITY

When someone completing a questionnaire to measure male–female stereotyping is asked about the "typical" woman or man, what kind of person do you suppose comes to that individual's mind? An elderly Black woman? A middle-aged Native American man confined to a wheelchair? A young woman who has trouble finding stylish clothing because she weighs 200 pounds? Most likely, the image is influenced by the person's tendency to define "typical" with reference to him- or herself and to the people most visible in the environment. Probably, as Hope Landrine (1985) suggests, research participants cannot imagine a woman (or man) "without attributing a race, a social class, an age, and even a degree of physical attractiveness to the stimulus" (p. 66). The image among North American college students, whose responses have formed much of the basis for research on gender stereotypes, is likely to be of someone who is relatively young, White, able bodied, neither too fat nor too thin, neither too short nor too tall, and of average physical attractiveness. Thus, our studies of the stereotypes that accompany gender are most likely limited by their reliance on generalizations that systematically exclude groups such as old people, Blacks, Latinos, native peoples, Asians, disabled people, fat people, lesbians and gay men, and people whose appearance diverges markedly from the norm. In holding to gender stereotypes based on the so-called typical man or woman, it is also likely that our society creates added difficulties for individuals already victimized by racism, ageism, an intolerance of difference, or society's obsession with attractiveness and thinness.

Gender Stereotypes and Race

Researchers have tried to understand the interactive workings of racism and sexism by comparing the experiences of different gender–race groups. It has been noted, for example, that the forms of racism directed at Black women and Black men may differ, and that sexism may be expressed toward and experienced by a woman differently as a function of her race (A. Smith & Stewart, 1983). Nonetheless, only a small percentage of articles in psychological journals concerned with issues of sex and gender has focused on Black women (Thomas & Miles, 1995). An examination of gender stereotypes cannot ignore the way race and gender stereotypes interact, or the ways in which different racial groups may differ in the images and ideals they hold for femininity and masculinity.

FEMININITY   In an attempt to determine whether the often-reported stereotype of women is actually just a stereotype of middle-class White women, Landrine (1985) asked undergraduates to describe the stereotype of each of four groups of women—

Black and White middle-class women and Black and White lower-class women—based on a list of 23 adjectives. She found that although the stereotypes differed significantly by both race and social class, with White women and middle-class women being described in ways most similar to the dominant culture's traditional stereotypes of women, all four groups were rated in ways consistent with this feminine stereotype. White women were described more often than Black women by the most stereotypical terms: *dependent, emotional,* and *passive.* However, both groups were rated similarly on many other adjectives: *ambitious, competent, intelligent, self-confident,* and *hostile,* for example. The findings suggest that race and social class are implicit in what have been described as gender stereotypes but that a set of expectations for women transcends these variables to some extent.

According to the stereotypes held by the dominant White society, Black women may be judged as less "feminine" than White women. The history of Black women in the United States makes it clear that they have not, as a group, been conditioned toward the helpless, delicate, even frail image of femininity so often cultivated in their White counterparts. As slaves, women were expected to endure backbreaking physical labor and hardships and were denied the security in their marital lives that White women took for granted. Angela Davis (1981) notes that, under slavery, Black women constructed a definition of womanhood that included "hard work, perseverance and self-reliance, a legacy of tenacity, resistance and an insistence on sexual equality" (p. 29). Long after slavery ended, Black women continued a tradition of hard work that is at odds with any stereotypically feminine notions of helplessness or dependence. Of all American married women, African American women have consistently been the most likely to be in the paid labor force, as illustrated in Figure 1.1. Before the passage of the Civil Rights Act of 1964 made it illegal to discriminate in hiring on the basis of race, African American women were often restricted to the lowest paid and most physically demanding jobs. In the United States in 1950, 42% of Black women were employed as domestic workers; by 1980 that number had dropped to 5% (Amott & Matthaei, 1991).

According to some African American women theorists, another legacy among American Black women that sets them apart from White models of femininity is their strong tradition of speech rather than silence, of oratory, preaching, and storytelling rather than subservient listening (P. H. Collins, 1991). One view within the African American community is that "blacks have withstood the long line of abuses perpetrated against them ever since their arrival in this country mainly because of the black woman's fortitude, inner wisdom, and sheer ability to survive" (Terrelonge, 1989, p. 556). Indeed, a persistent stereotype of Black women in the social science literature encompasses strength, self-reliance, and a strong achievement orientation (Fleming, 1983a; Greene, 1994a). However, Black women have also been stereotyped as sexually promiscuous, sexually aggressive, and morally loose (Greene, 1994a).

Fleming (1983b) documented the existence of a "Black matriarchy" theory among social scientists, which suggests that Black women are more dominant, assertive, and self-reliant than Black men. Although such a stereotype may appear positive at first glance, the narrow labeling of Black women's strengths as "matriarchal" represents a refusal to conceptualize strong women in anything but a family context. Moreover, there has been a tendency to blame Black women's strong, assertive behavior for some of the problems experienced by Black men—a tendency that surely reflects stereotypic notions

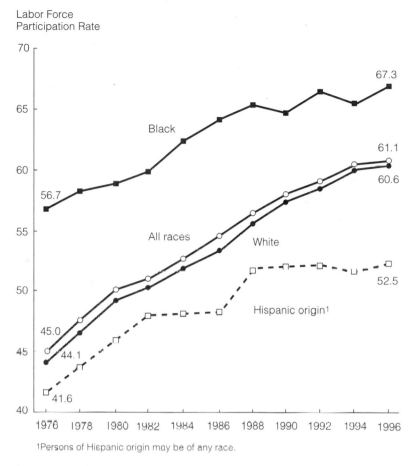

Labor Force
Participation Rate

Figure 1.1 Labor Force Participation Rates of Married Women by Race and Hispanic Origin, 1976–1996

Source: From Costello, Miles, & Stone (1998). *American women, 1999–2000: A century of change—what's next?*, p. 294.

about what kinds of behavior are "proper" for women. Fleming and others (e.g., Dugger, 1991; Staples, 1978) argue that the Black matriarchy theory is a myth based largely on flawed or misleading evidence. Fleming suggests that this particular stereotype may have arisen from the fact that "their long history of instrumentality in the service of family functioning may well have built in black women an air of self-reliance that arouses further stereotyping among those (largely white) social scientists more accustomed to white traditional norms for women" (Fleming, 1983a, p. 43). Indeed, P. H. Collins (1990) argues that the image of the Black matriarch has been and is held up to all women as a symbol of the problems associated with a rejection of "appropriate" gender norms: "Aggressive, assertive women are penalized—they are abandoned by their men, end up impoverished, and are stigmatized as being unfeminine" (p. 75).

In contrast to Black women, Latinas (a group that includes Mexican Americans, Puerto Ricans, Cubans, and women from Central and South America and the

Caribbean) have traditionally faced cultural ideals of femininity that glorified mother-hood, subservience to men, and long-suffering endurance (Garcia, 1991; Ginorio, Gutiérrez, Cauce, & Acosta, 1995). A woman was supposed to gain fulfillment by loving and supporting her husband and nurturing her children, and her place was unquestionably in the home (Astrachan, 1989). Historically, this ideal was fostered by the Catholic church, which played a large role in colonizing what is now South and Central America and the American Southwest. The church taught women to venerate the Virgin Mary and to emulate her by being silent, submissive, altruistic, and self-denying (Almquist, 1995). In recent years, however, these ideals have begun to change. For example, Mexican American women have taken on new roles, and their rate of participation in the labor force, while still lower than that of Anglos, has been increasing rapidly. In addition, a vocal Chicana feminist movement has emerged (Garcia, 1991; Segura & Pesquera, 1995). This movement, reflecting the values of Mexican American culture, has incorporated a positive valuing rather than a rejection of the roles of wife and mother along with the acceptance of broader roles for women.

One of the reasons for race-related differences in gender-role attitudes is that members of different racial groups frequently live in different social conditions. For example, in the United States, Black women have been more likely than White women to have to work for economic reasons; thus, working for wages has been a normative aspect of their womanhood. For White women, however (and perhaps even more for Latina women, who have only recently joined the labor force in such large numbers), the movement into paid work is more likely to provoke a questioning of traditional views of gender because it represents a break with past traditions (Dugger, 1991).

MASCULINITY   The interaction of masculinity stereotypes with race is similarly complex. Black, White, and Latino males in the United States, for example, hold and face differing, though overlapping, images of what it means to be masculine. The differences probably stem as much or more from variations in the social structural conditions currently facing the three groups than from their differing cultural heritage (Baca Zinn, 1989).

The status of Black males in American society has been in flux for the last several decades. Long after legal racial segregation ended, the effects of racism are still extremely obvious in the White society's treatment of Black men. For example, Black men have often been referred to not as "men," but as "boys." Some writers have argued that it was not until the advent of the Black Power movement in the late 1960s that adult Black males were recognized as "men" by most of American society (C. W. Franklin, 1984; Poussaint, 1982). As a group, Black males currently live a hazardous existence as they try to maintain the competitive, success-oriented, aggressive aspects of masculinity in the face of discrimination and a lack of economic opportunities to pursue the "protector/provider" role. The result, according to some authors, is channeling attempts to be masculine into a cluster of behaviors that emphasize physical toughness, violence, and risk-taking, especially among *young* Black men (C. W. Franklin, 1984). A tragic result is that the death rate from violence is frighteningly high in this group. Homicide is the leading cause of death among young American Black men; they are far more likely than any other age/gender/race group to be victims and perpetrators of homicide (U.S. Department of Justice, 1998).

Richard Majors (1989) writes of the "Cool Pose," a cultural signature adopted by many Black males as a mechanism for survival and social competence. A set of poses and postures displays elements of control, toughness, and detachment that symbolize strength, pride, and a refusal to show hurt or weakness—especially to outsiders. According to Majors, "coolness" is also displayed through the "expressive lifestyle." The style is manifested in creative, even flamboyant, performances in arenas ranging from the street to the basketball court to the pulpit: performances that say "You can't copy me." The Cool Pose, an aggressive assertion of masculinity, guards these males' pride and dignity but may be costly to relationships when it blocks the expression of emotions or needs.

Latino men have also developed a tradition that places strong importance on masculinity—sometimes expressed in an ideology of male dominance labeled "machismo." Machismo, Oliva Espín (1997) notes, "is nothing but the Hispanic version of the myth of male superiority supported by most cultures" (p. 89). Although some have argued that machismo is a myth used to negatively stereotype Latinos and rationalize their lack of success in the dominant society, there seems little doubt that a male-dominant ideology of masculinity has played an important role in relations between Latinos and Latinas (Espín, 1997; Garcia, 1991). The core aspect of machismo is men's dominance over women. The stereotypical macho male expects to be considered the head of his household and demands deference and respect from his wife and children. He may feel strongly that his wife's place is in the home and that his manhood is demonstrated by the number of children he has (Astrachan, 1989). A Chicano man may behave in an aggressive, macho way partly as "a conscious rejection of the dominant society's definition of Mexicans as passive, lazy, and indifferent" (Baca Zinn, 1989, p. 95). Yet machismo appears to be, in its own way, a public pose. Researchers find that actual decision making in Chicano families is as likely to be egalitarian as male-dominant and that Chicano fathers are nurturant and expressive rather than distant and authoritarian with their young children. Even in egalitarian families, however, patriarchal ideology is strong, as expressed in statements that the father is the head of the house, the boss, the one in charge (Baca Zinn, 1989). Baca Zinn suggests that patriarchal ideology is associated with family solidarity and that perhaps "the father's authority is strongly upheld because family solidarity is important in a society that excludes and subordinates Chicanos" (p. 95).

It is possible that in a society that values masculinity over femininity, gender may take on a special significance for men of color and other men who have little access to socially valued roles. They may emphasize and act out the toughness and dominance aspects of masculinity, both as a defense against putdowns from the larger society and because "being male is one sure way to acquire status when other roles are systematically denied" (Baca Zinn, 1989, p. 94).

STEREOTYPING WITHIN GROUPS   Studies of gender stereotyping and gender-role attitudes within racial groups other than Whites show mixed results (e.g., Lyson, 1986; Smith & Midlarsky, 1985). A review of research on Black gender roles finds some studies in which Blacks are more egalitarian in their gender-role attitudes than Whites are, some in which the opposite is found, and some in which gender attitudes among Blacks do not fit neatly into the egalitarian/traditional distinction that has been useful for Whites (Hatchett & Quick, 1983). O'Leary and Harrison (1975), comparing the gender stereotypes of Black and White women and men, found that Blacks endorsed fewer items that discriminated between the sexes than Whites did, and that Black respondents were less likely than Whites to devalue females on stereotypic grounds. White respondents of both sexes rated the White woman more negatively than Black respondents rated the Black woman. When a sample of Black and White male and female university students were asked to rate various qualities as characteristic of their "ideal man," the Black males placed significantly higher emphasis on aggressiveness than the other groups did (Cazenave & Leon, 1987). Black males also ranked highest among the groups in their rating of being comfortable with children as an ideal male quality. White females ranked highest among the groups in their rating of warmth and gentleness as essential characteristics of an ideal man. In a comparison of the gender-role attitudes of American Black and White women, Dugger (1991) found that Black women more often rejected culturally dominant views of the female role. For example, they were more likely than their White counterparts to indicate that they noticed sex discrimination; supported the women's movement; admired intelligent, outspoken women; and accepted nontraditional family structures. But these same Black women were *more* likely than White women to accept that girls and boys should be brought up to be feminine and masculine, respectively.

Interpreting group comparisons that are based on the endorsement of particular items, such as "feminine," "independent," or "passive," must be done with caution. Hope Landrine and her colleagues (Landrine, Klonoff, & Brown-Collins, 1995) showed that even when diverse groups of women rate themselves identically on such terms what they actually mean by the terms may be quite different. Their samples of European American women and Women of Color did not differ in how strongly they agreed that the terms *passive, assertive,* and *feminine* described themselves. However, the groups did differ significantly in the definitions they chose for these three terms. For example, the largest percentage of Women of Color, when asked to choose a definition for the term *passive,* selected "am laid back/easy-going," whereas the largest percentage of European American women chose "don't say what I really think." Thus, it may be quite difficult to interpret data comparing the gender stereotypes of different groups.

Gender Stereotypes and Social Class

In a television advertisement for plastic wrap, a male chef—obviously very refined, very "cultured"—is shown debating what brand of wrap to use for his creation. In the background, a pudgy man in coveralls and a dirty face waits to take the package. The chef asks, appalled, "Is he going to *touch* it?," then hurriedly decides, presumably to avoid contamination of his food, to use the advertised brand of wrap. In this example, the two men are stereotyped according to social class: the chef (clearly portrayed as middle-class) is apparently educated, intelligent, and sensitive, and has an appreciation of the finer things in life; the man in coveralls (presumably a working-class man) is portrayed as dumb and dirty. The pro-middle-class bias is obvious, as is the observation that the notion of masculinity embodied in the two portrayals is quite different.

Social class is measured through socioeconomic indicators such as education, income, and occupation. The stereotypes applied to women and men differ somewhat according to their perceived social class. For example, one study among middle-class college students found that the stereotype of lower-class women was significantly higher than that of middle-class women for the traits *confused, dirty, hostile, illogical, impulsive, incoherent, inconsiderate, irresponsible,* and *superstitious* (Landrine, 1985). Working-class males, in the view of many middle-class social scientists, have been stereotyped as exemplars of old-fashioned, defiant, aggressive masculinity (Ehrenreich, 1983).

Members of different social classes may differ in their notions of masculinity and femininity. Lillian Rubin (1976) argues that professional men, with more access to status and prestige outside the home, are more able than working-class men to assume a less authoritarian role within the family. Anthony Astrachan (1989) suggests, however, that the apparent differences between middle-class and working-class men may be partly just a matter of honesty:

> Blue-collar men feel the contradiction between their physical power and their place at the bottom of the male hierarchy, and they are more obvious than men in other classes about their need to treat women as underlings to compensate. They are more honest, or quicker to voice their anger and their fear, about changes in the balance of power and in sex roles, at work and at home. (p. 63)

Finally, Barbara Ehrenreich (1983) warns that

> patterns of working-class behavior may be formed, in part, in response to middle-class behavior and observation. . . . The middle-class "gaze" . . . can be an uncomfortable one—associated, in lower classes, with workplace supervision and negative judgments by teachers and other authorities. What appears to be a lack of "interpersonal skills" can be a withdrawal from middle-class discourse; what looks like residual "physical aggression" can be actual and ongoing hostility; and . . ."working-class male chauvinism" might be an expression of class, rather than gender, antagonism. (p. 135)

Because people can move between social classes, it is easier to understand group differences if social class is considered a dynamic variable rather than a static category (Cazenave, 1984). Such a perspective allows researchers to recognize, for example, that what may appear at first to be racial differences are probably attributable to social class. For example, one study of Black and White American men's conception of the "ideal man" found differences between the White and Black middle-class samples. The Black sample placed more emphasis on, among other things, being aggressive and competitive, being successful at work, protecting one's family, and self-confidence (Cazenave, 1984). The researcher notes that many of the White men in the sample had been born into the middle class and were thus likely to take its advantages for granted, but many of the Black men were first-generation middle class and so still felt a sense of struggling to "make it." He argues that "in the quest for upward mobility, middle-class blacks may embrace traditional gender-role prescriptions, which more established and secure middle-class whites feel secure in relinquishing" (Cazenave & Leon, 1987, p. 246).

In a similar vein, a study of the well-being of employed professional and managerial women found that women from working-class families had received far less financial and informational support from their families in the transition from high school to college than had those from middle-class families (Cannon, Higginbotham, & Leung, 1991). The typical Black woman volunteer for the study had been raised in a working-class family, and the typical White woman volunteer had been raised in a middle-class family. If the researchers had not attended to the social-class background of the women, it would have appeared simply that Black families gave less support to their daughters than White families did to theirs.

Gender Stereotypes and Age

The stereotypes of femininity and masculinity seem to apply most strongly to the young. There is scattered evidence that both women and men describe themselves in less stereotypic terms as they age (Cooper & Guttmann, 1987; Farrell & Rosenberg, 1981). Older men rate older women as more active, involved, hardy, and stable than themselves (Kahana & Kahana, 1970). There are some indications that women become more powerful as they move into older adulthood (A. Friedman, 1987; Helson & Mitchell, 1990). Some investigators note that men at midlife appear more interested in close relationships and are less caught up in competition and achievement strivings than younger men are (J. Moreland, 1980). There is, however, little evidence that self-reported investment in male or female role behavior changes between young adulthood and midlife (B. E. Carlson & Videka-Sherman, 1990).

Perhaps gender stereotypes become less pronounced for older people because age stereotypes replace them. For example, elderly women are often assumed to be disabled in some way (Healey, 1993). In one study in which respondents were asked to list the traits of 35-year-old and 65-year-old women and men, age stereotypes were more evident than gender stereotypes. Respondents described 65-year-old women and men similarly as *lonely, hard of hearing, rigid, experienced,* and *interesting* (Kite, Deaux, & Miele, 1991). One of the widely accepted stereotypes about the elderly is that they are no longer interested in sexuality (Kay & Neelley, 1982). But sexuality is one of the major underpinnings of social expectations about gender. One of the main reasons for a heterosexual man to be masculine is to be sexually attractive to women, and vice versa. If sexuality becomes irrelevant, so, in a sense, do masculinity and femininity. Although studies show that sexuality is *not,* in fact, irrelevant to older people (e.g., W. H. Masters & Johnson, 1966), perhaps one accidentally beneficial consequence of the myth is that it is a partial release from the restrictions of gender stereotypes.

Many writers have noted a "double standard" of aging, however, that places older women at a disadvantage with respect to older men (I. P. Bell, 1989). In contemporary North American society, much of a woman's worth is defined in terms of her physical attractiveness to men. The aging woman may find that, along with her "femininity," she is losing her value as a person. The changes in physical appearance that accompany aging, which are often considered acceptable or even "distinguished" in men, move women farther and farther from current definitions of female beauty. One study found that ratings of an individual's attractiveness decreased with age when the individual was a woman but not when the individual was a man (Mathes, Brennan, Haugen, & Rice, 1985). An examination of 100 top-grossing popular films from the 1940s to 1980s found that in these movies older female characters were underrepresented and more negatively portrayed than older males (Bazzini, McIntosh, Smith, Cook, et al., 1997). On the whole, these aging women were portrayed as unattractive, unfriendly and unintelligent—hardly positive images!

For women, who often have few other sources of power and prestige than their attractiveness, these changes can signify a slide into decreasing social worth. Older men, who are less likely to have to rely on their appearance for power and prestige, may have wider access to sources of social worth—through occupational achievement, money, and even relationships with younger women.

Gender Stereotypes and Appearance

Psychologists have become increasingly aware that physical appearance is a critical aspect of stereotyping. In terms of gender stereotypes, physical appearance may have strong implications for how masculine or feminine a person is thought to be. Many a tall, broad-shouldered woman has slouched and crouched through life in a futile effort to appear petite and "feminine," and many a short man has quietly cursed his diminutive stature because it seemed to detract from his ability to project a "masculine" image.

Although physical appearance is important to both males and females, beauty is generally defined as a peculiarly feminine attribute, and preoccupation with one's appearance is seen as part of the feminine stereotype (R. Freedman, 1986; Rodin, Silberstein, & Striegel-Moore, 1985). In an exploration of the concept of femininity, Susan Brownmiller (1984) illustrates the powerful role played by physical appearance in cultural definitions of femininity. In various times and places, aspects of the female anatomy have become supposed signals of how feminine and how sexual a woman is. For example, she notes the way that others react to a young woman's breast development: "Parents and relatives mark their appearance as a landmark event, schoolmates take notice, girlfriends compare, boys zero in; later a husband, a lover, a baby expect a proprietary share. No other part of the human anatomy has such semipublic, intensely private status" (pp. 40–41). Why all the fuss? Brownmiller argues that breasts are used as a prime cue to a woman's sexuality. She notes the myth that a flat-chested woman is nonsexual and that a woman with large breasts is flaunting her sexuality and seeking attention. Small wonder that women sometimes become intensely self-conscious about this part of their anatomy.

Stereotypical masculinity, too, is reflected in physical appearance, particularly in strength and muscularity. Men, like women, are not immune to concerns about how their bodies will be judged—but, perhaps because concern with one's appearance is supposed to be a feminine quality, it seems less acceptable for them to talk about it. Nonetheless, muscles are equated with masculinity, and entrepreneurs have made fortunes playing on men's insecurity about their bodies. Bernarr Macfadden, originator of the physical culture movement of the 1900s, warned men that they must choose "whether you shall be a strong virile animal . . . or a miserable little crawling worm" (quoted in Glassner, 1989), and Charles Atlas enticed thousands of men into his exercise program in the 1950s with the promise: "I manufacture weaklings into MEN."

Studies show that up to 95% of men express dissatisfaction with some aspect of their bodies, most frequently with their chest, weight, and waist (Mishkind, Rodin, Silberstein, & Striegel-Moore, 1987). The overwhelming majority of men studied say they would prefer to be of well-proportioned, average build rather than thin or fat. Most say their ideal would be a muscular, mesomorphic body—characterized by well-developed chest and arm muscles, broad shoulders, and a narrow waist (Tucker, 1982). Thinning hair is also a source of much anxiety for many men (Franzoi, Anderson, & Frommelt, 1990).

Perhaps no aspect of appearance is the cause of more grief in our own society right now than weight. Dieting has become a North American obsession, particularly for women (Brownell & Rodin, 1994). When female Canadian university students were asked what kinds of activities or situations would make them feel less feminine, by far the most frequently checked item was "being overweight," which was endorsed by more than 50% of the sample (Lips, 1986a). So highly charged is the issue of weight for women that, according to Hatfield and Sprecher (cited in Rodin et al., 1985), women respondents in the early Kinsey surveys of sexual practices were more embarrassed when asked their weight than when asked "How often do you masturbate?" or "Have you ever had a homosexual affair?"

Research shows that physical attractiveness is a more central part of the self-concept for women than for men (Jackson, Sullivan, & Rostker, 1988). Moreover, a test of a sample of college undergraduates indicated that weight and body shape, although important to men, were the *central* determinants of women's perception of their physical attractiveness (Rodin & Striegel-Moore, 1984; Stake & Lauer, 1987). Self-perceived heavy weight is linked to feelings of low self-esteem—and the link is stronger among women than among men (C. T. Miller & Downey, 1999). College women report a greater discrepancy between their actual and ideal body image than men do (Fallon & Rozin, 1985). College women are not alone in their concern. A representative survey of 803 adult women in the United States demonstrated high levels of body dissatisfaction, with nearly half the women reporting overall negative evaluations of their appearance (Cash & Henry, 1995). These women also reported a preoccupation with being or becoming overweight. These levels of body dissatisfaction among women are substantially higher than those found in a large survey taken a decade ago (Cash, Winstead, & Janda, 1986).

An interesting finding that emerged from the representative survey was a difference in body satisfaction between African American women and their White Anglo and Hispanic counterparts. African American women held more positive body images and were less concerned with being or becoming overweight. These findings parallel others in which African American women report more positive feelings toward their bodies than do European American women (S. M. Harris, 1994, 1995). African American women, like other women of color in North America, live in a culture in which the predominant images of feminine beauty presented in the media are White (K. Russell, Wilson, & Hall, 1992). Do these findings of less body dissatisfaction among African American women mean they are successfully resisting the notion that they should match these images? The answer may be complicated. Some research shows that African American women with a strong positive racial identity are likely to report less dissatisfaction with their bodies (S. M. Harris, 1995). This finding seems to point to successful resistance. Other research shows, however, that weight-related factors *are* linked to body dissatisfaction among African American women (S. M. Harris, 1995; Rozin & Fallon, 1988). It is possible that the measures of body image satisfaction are interpreted differently by African American and European American women; however, more research is necessary before such a conclusion can be reached.

Women's concern about their body shape and size can be so profound that it pre-occupies them and interferes with their performance at school or elsewhere. Barbara Fredrickson and her colleagues (Fredrickson, Roberts, Noll, Quinn, & Twenge, 1998) asked female and male undergraduate students in their lab to put on either a sweater or a swimsuit and then to complete a questionnaire that measured body shame and to take a math test. Women wearing swimsuits often reported feeling shame and disgust with their bodies, whereas men reported simply that they found the situation "silly." More disturbing, however, women wearing bathing suits tended to score much lower than men on the math test—a difference that was considerably narrower when participants were attired in sweaters. It appears that when wearing swimsuits the women were so distracted by disturbing thoughts about their bodies that they could not concentrate on the math problems. Men, by contrast, found the situation funny rather than disturbing and were easily able to turn their attention to math.

Women have good reason to be concerned about their weight and shape as obesity seems to trigger more negative evaluations for women than for men. Researchers who showed silhouettes of fat and thin women and men to hundreds of passersby at a summer fair found that fat men were rated significantly less negatively than fat women were; thin women were rated less negatively than their male counterparts (Spigelman & Schultz, 1981). Furthermore, women who are "marketing themselves" for a male partner receive a consistent message that appearance, especially thinness, is a crucial selling point. Males placing personal ads for dating relationships in singles magazines and newspapers are more likely than women to emphasize the desired partner's physical appearance (S. Davis, 1990; J. E. Smith, Waldorf, & Trembath, 1990) and are far more likely than females (33.6% versus 2.2%) to specify that they are looking for someone who is thin (J. E. Smith et al., 1990).

Gender Stereotypes and Sexual Orientation

As just noted, gender stereotypes are linked with social notions of sexuality: A "feminine" woman is supposed to be attractive to men, a "masculine" man is thought to be desirable to women. A major aspect of the stereotypes surrounding gay and lesbian individuals is that they do not fit the accepted stereotypes for their own gender. According to the dubious logic of stereotypes, a really feminine woman would not be sexually attracted to other women; a "real" man would not be sexually attracted to other men. Thus, in a reversal of gender stereotypes, lesbians are often characterized as masculine, and gay men are described as feminine. We have already seen that facial and other physical features that are stereotyped as feminine are linked, when found in males, with attributions of homosexuality, as are masculine features when found in females.

Stereotyped views of lesbian women often center on the notion that lesbians are not feminine. In one study, the predominant stereotypes of lesbian women included an aura of masculinity and the idea that lesbians would try to seduce heterosexual women (Eliason, Donelan, & Randall, 1992). In another, heterosexual college students rated lesbians as significantly less attractive, more insecure, more masculine, less loving, less emotional, less stable, and less mentally healthy than a sample of lesbians rated themselves (Viss & Burn, 1992). The stereotype of gay men incorporates the notion of femininity (Deaux & Lewis, 1984) and also shares with the lesbian stereotype the notion of instability (Simon, Glässner-Bayerl, & Stratenwerth, 1991).

Lesbian and gay male relationships are also stereotyped, often as mimicking heterosexual relationships. For instance, one widely held (and inaccurate) view of lesbian couples is that one member of the couple must be a "butch" and the other a "femme," imitating male–female relationships (Weitz, 1989).

Stereotyping lesbians and gay men is linked with antihomosexual prejudice. For example, Janet Swim and her colleagues showed that heterosexual women were less willing to self-identify as feminists when doing so would ally them with a lesbian in front of others. The heterosexual women were apparently trying to avoid "stigma by association" (Swim, Ferguson, & Hyers, 1999). Research on university campuses in the United States shows that at least two thirds of lesbian and gay students report that they have been verbally insulted, almost all have overheard derogatory antilesbian/antigay comments on campus, and many report that they have been threatened with physical violence (Herek, 1993). Perhaps because the masculine role is more highly valued by society and gay males are seen to be deviating from that role, such prejudice is often more obvious in relation to gay men than to lesbians (Herek, 1988; Morin & Garfinkle, 1978).

Gender and Disability

Although the general stereotype of persons with disabilities involves victimization, helplessness, dependence, social isolation, and suffering, this stereotype seems to be moderated by the gender of the person with the disability (Danek, 1992; Hanna & Rogovsky, 1991, 1992). For women, who are already stereotyped as more passive and dependent than men, the disability stereotype can reinforce the image of dependence (Fine, 1991; Fine & Asch, 1981). Indeed, newly disabled women are far more likely than their male counterparts to be advised by their physicians to retire from paid employment (S. Russell, 1985) and less likely than their male counterparts to find a job post-disability (Fine, 1991; S. A. Fulton & Sabornie, 1994). For men, the dependence on others that many disabilities enforce is perceived as a threat to their masculine image.

Physical attractiveness is another area in which gender and disability stereotypes interact. We have already noted that physical attractiveness is more central to femininity than to masculinity; it is also apparent that a woman who is visibly disabled, even if not disfigured in any way, falls short of the cultural ideal of beauty. Here, for example, is the reaction of a former executive of the Miss Universe contest to the notion of a paraplegic woman as a contestant: "Her participation in a beauty contest would be like having a blind man compete in a shooting match" (Matthews, 1985, p. 49). However, 1987 saw the first entry of a wheelchair-bound woman, Maria Serrao, in a major American beauty contest ("Paralyzed Woman," 1987). In 1994, a deaf woman, Heather Whitestone, won the Miss America pageant.

The stereotypic expectations about femininity that many women find oppressive may be experienced as more complex by disabled women. For example, the automatic expectation that a woman will have children may be greeted with resentment by a woman who has no physical barriers to such a choice, but a woman with a disability that interferes with this choice may resent the automatic expectation that she will *not* have children (Waxman, 1994). Similarly, although many women object strongly to the casual sexual harassment they encounter on the street, some disabled women may object just as strongly to the assumption that they are not "harassable" (Fine, 1991).

Like the elderly, persons with disabilities are often stereotyped as asexual (Rousso, 1986). However, even the slowly growing public awareness that disability does not imply a lack of sexual needs or interest has been channeled by gender stereotypes that say sex is more important to men than to women. Much more has been studied and written on the subject of sexuality among disabled men than among disabled women. When the stereotypes about women's "weaker" sexual needs are combined with stereotypes about disability, the results can be ludicrous. Michelle Fine (1991) tells the story of a newly disabled woman who, when she asked her physician whether her disability would preclude a satisfying sex life, was "reassured" that her vagina would be tight enough to satisfy any man!

Statistics indicate that the popular presumption that disabled women are asexual does not protect them from sexual assault. In fact, disabled women may be more likely than other women to be sexually assaulted (Furey, 1994). Children of both sexes are at high risk for sexual abuse if they are disabled, because it is often harder for them to get away from an abuser or to communicate to others about what is happening. During both childhood and adulthood, females with disabilities are more likely than their nondisabled counterparts to experience physical abuse as well. In one small-scale study, 67% of disabled women, as compared to 34% of nondisabled women, reported that they had been physically abused or battered as children (Doucette, 1986).

Gender stereotypes are pervasive, interacting with other stereotypes to shape social perceptions of persons of various races, ages, abilities, and appearances. Gender stereotyping both grows out of and reinforces the social relations between women and men and, as seen in the following section, does so in ways that are both complex and subtle.

THE PROCESS OF STEREOTYPING

Despite the pervasiveness of gender stereotyping, almost everyone can, if given a good reason to do so, summon up example after example of people, personalities, and actions that do not fit the stereotypes. Yet even in the face of counterexamples, the stereotypes persist. A good example is the notion that the "typical" North American family consists of a woman staying at home with the children and a man going out to engage in paid employment to support the family. In fact, less than half the families on the continent now fit this traditional model, but mothers who stay in the labor market are still regarded as anomalies by many people.

Why do stereotypes persist to such an extent despite lack of support and even countervailing evidence? To answer this question, it is necessary to look beyond the content of specific stereotypes to the process of stereotyping itself. In recent years, psychologists have focused on two approaches in attempts to understand and describe how stereotyping works: information processing and self-fulfilling prophecy.

Stereotypes and Information Processing

Psychologists now think of stereotypes not simply as sets of beliefs about specific groups of people but as knowledge structures that guide the way individuals process information: what they notice, what they remember, what kinds of information they seek out, and how they explain and make sense of what they see (D. L. Hamilton, 1979). These knowledge structures, often called *schemas,* act as self-perpetuating channels or filters of information, guiding the individual to pay attention to information that fits the schema or stereotype and to ignore or explain away things that don't fit. Such schemas are useful in that they allow for more efficient handling of the vast amount of information to which most of us are exposed, but, inevitably, they produce and perpetuate blind spots. Thus, for example, research participants' searching for information to explain an automobile accident of which they are given a vague description can apparently be guided by their schemas for young and elderly men, respectively. Participants told that the driver of the car was an elderly man tended to ask for information about the man's health and eyesight, whereas those told the driver was a young man requested information about whether he was speeding or drinking (Carver & de la Garza, 1984). This example illustrates how stereotypes can perpetuate themselves by orienting the individual toward information that confirms the stereotype and away from information that is irrelevant or disconfirming.

Women and men whose behavior is at odds with prevailing gender stereotypes are often startled by the apparent inventiveness observers use in linking this behavior to "normal" roles for their sex. For instance, one woman was bemused to discover that the men at the gym where she was working out with weights in an effort to develop her strength and fitness were convinced that what she was really trying to develop was her bust. And a man who had chosen to stay home with his young daughter while his wife worked outside the home was dismayed one day at the playground to overhear two mothers of other children speculating that the reason he was caring for his daughter was that his wife was dead. Such apparently creative explanations are probably the result of stereotype-guided information processing that makes it difficult or impossible for the observer, without a conscious effort, to use incoming information in ways that are not in accord with preexisting gender stereotypes. Behavior that appears to disconfirm the stereotype, if it is noticed at all, is attributed to external forces (as in the assumption that the man would not be caring for his daughter if his wife were alive) or to internal motives that can be subsumed under the stereotype (as in the assumption that the woman in the gym was striving for sexiness rather than strength). Thus, stereotypes guide the individual to interpret information in ways that keep stereotypes intact—even in the face of contradictory evidence.

But not all the evidence *is* contradictory. In fact, social psychologists have begun to show that the cognitive aspects of stereotyping are helped along considerably by a social–behavioral phenomenon known as the self-fulfilling prophecy. In many cases, people sense others' expectations of them and, in the interest of smooth interactions, act in such a way as to fulfill those expectations.

Self-Presentation and Self-Fulfilling Prophecy

It has been noted that male–female differences are more likely to be observed in interactive situations than in less social, individualistic ones (Deaux, 1977; Maccoby, 1990). The explanation for this finding may reside partly in people's sensitivity to the expectations of others. For example, Darley and Fazio (1980) described the way social interaction might result in behavior that confirms the expectations of the participants: The perceiver holds a particular expectation for the target person's behavior and acts in accordance with that expectation, the target person interprets the perceiver's actions and responds accordingly, and the perceiver uses the target's response to confirm or reevaluate the original expectation. If the target's action is very discrepant from the original perception, the perceiver may attribute it to situational constraints or may even end the interaction to avoid taking in information that is counter to expectations.

Thus, the implicit pressure on the target to play out the expected role is very strong; failure to do so may result in "bungled" or strained interaction. Moreover, if there is a motivation to be liked or approved of by the other participant, there are even stronger reasons to conform to that person's expectations. Women present themselves in a more or less stereotypically feminine manner depending on how they think a male job interviewer or potential date with whom they are interacting views women (von Baeyer, Sherk, & Zanna, 1981; Zanna & Pack, 1975). Similarly, Fried and Major (1980) found that males adjusted the way they presented themselves according to what they believed an attractive female partner would prefer.

Other aspects of the situation may also affect the likelihood of a self-fulfilling prophecy: the strength of the social desirability cues provided by the situation in which the interaction takes place, whether the situation is public or private, the target person's concern with looking good or with being true to her- or himself, the strength and certainty of the perceiver's expectation, and the power of the perceiver over the target (Deaux & Major, 1987).

A good demonstration of the way people adopt gender-role behaviors in response to the implied expectations of others was provided in laboratory research by Berna Skrypnek and Mark Snyder (1982). They asked individual male research participants to divide a series of tasks between themselves and a partner. The partners were located in separate rooms and communicated only by means of a signal system. In each case, the hidden partner was a woman, but some of the men were led to believe that their partner was male. The men who thought that their partner was female divided the tasks in a more gender-stereotyped way than those who thought the partner was male. Moreover, when the female partners, unaware of what the men had been told about them, were subsequently given the opportunity to choose tasks, they themselves chose more feminine-stereotyped tasks when paired with a man who had been expecting a female partner. All of this happened without the participants ever seeing or talking to each other.

A factor that may play a large part in the expectation-confirmation sequences for gender roles is physical appearance (Deaux, 1984). A person's appearance is a powerful influence on the initial impressions and expectations that others form of her or him. Thus, a person who looks the part of the masculine stereotype—tall, strong, sturdy, broad-shouldered—may, before having done or said anything, be the object of a set of perceiver expectations for masculine role behavior and may find him- or herself falling into step with them. Indeed, big, strong-looking men and petite, fragile-looking women may have more trouble than anyone else in trying to break out of the confines of gender-role expectations.

HOW GENDER STEREOTYPES AND PREJUDICE AFFECT US

Women university students report experiencing nearly twice as many sexist events (directed against themselves or against women in general) as do their male counterparts (Swim, Cohen, & Hyers, 1998). These experiences are most likely to involve sexist comments about gender roles and stereotypes, such as remarks about women's lack of ability in particular areas, women's supposedly characteristic traits such as passivity, or assertions that women should restrict themselves to certain arenas (e.g., that they should stay at home or should not go into politics). Also well-represented among reported sexist events are unwanted and objectifying sexual comments, such as comments about women's bodies and behaviors such as unwanted touching. Women also find themselves the targets of a significant amount of street harassment and demeaning labels.

Do women notice and react to these sexist events? Do they feel angry and make judgments about the perpetrators, or do they simply shrug off the experience? It appears that women are not complacent about such events, even if they do not respond publicly to them. Janet Swim and Lauri Hyers (1999) brought participants to their lab to work with others on a task that required group discussion and decision making. During the discussion, male confederates of the researchers made several scripted comments that were sexist. The researchers monitored the female participants' public response to these comments, administered a measure of self-esteem, and also asked the women to review a tape of the session later and record their feelings. Whether or not the women made a public response to the remarks, most women found the sexist remarks objectionable, viewed the person making the remark as prejudiced, and felt anger toward him. In addition, women who held traditional gender-role attitudes showed lower self-esteem after hearing sexist remarks than after hearing similar remarks that were not sexist.

As for responding publicly, women were cautious. Although most women (81%) in a simulated version of the study (in which they imagined themselves in the situation rather than actually being exposed to the situation) said that they would confront the person making sexist remarks, in the actual study only 45% did so, as seen in Table 1.3. Women who were the only members of their gender in the group and who held a committed, activist stance toward resisting sexism were most likely to confront the speaker. When confronting the speaker, women were most likely to use less risky, more polite strategies such as questioning the response (e.g., "What did you just say?!") than direct comments (e.g., "You can't pick someone for that reason") or exclamations (e.g., "I can't believe you said that!").

The results of this research suggest that women's caution about responding publicly to sexist events may not be justified. Most of the women found the comments objectionable, and it is likely that anyone who spoke up to object would not be viewed as impolite and would be supported by other women in the group. Confrontation serves the potentially valuable purpose of raising awareness that certain kinds of behavior are not acceptable. As the researchers point out, a person who sees that others do not tolerate sexist behavior may well become less tolerant of that behavior too—and perhaps more likely to confront it themselves.

Confrontation takes a lot of energy, however, and research shows that members of groups who are targets of stereotypes and prejudice often prefer simply to avoid situations where they think they will be exposed to such attitudes. Thus, women may choose to avoid taking classes from a professor who holds the reputation of being sexist or may steer away from career or academic paths, such as engineering, in which women form a small minority. Women who are "solos" (the only women in the group) are more likely than non-solos to want to change groups or to change the gender com-

Table 1.3 The difference between what women actually do and what they think they would do in response to a sexist remark by a male group member: Comparison between actual and anticipated public responses

Response	Percentage who actually gave the response (Study 1) (N = 44)	Percentage who anticipated definitely giving a response (Study 2) (N = 109)
No response		
1. Ignore the comment [a]	55	1
2. Wait to see what others do	55	4
Confrontational responses		
3. Question the response	25	47
4. Task-related response	20	22
5. Comment on inappropriateness	16	48
6. Sarcasm or humor	16	37
7. Surprise exclamation	16	40
8. Grumbling	2	10
9. Hit or punch	0	8
Gave at least one confrontational response	45	81

[a] Whether the lack of responses was a result of ignoring the comment and waiting to see what others would do was not differentiated in Study 1.

Source: From Swim & Hyers (1999), p. 82.

position of the group unless they have high confidence in their performance ability. If they do have high confidence, it seems to help them deal with the expectation of being stereotyped—perhaps by anticipating that they will perform well enough to disconfirm the stereotype (L. L. Cohen & Swim, 1995).

What effect does it have on a person to be in a situation where he or she has to perform well—but where stereotypes about the group suggest that the person will perform poorly? Chances are that the person's performance will suffer. In a series of studies researchers have shown that **stereotype threat,** an individual's awareness that he or she may be judged by or may self-fulfill negative stereotypes about her or his gender or ethnic group, can have a dramatic negative effect on performance. In one study, women and men who had demonstrated high math ability were brought to the lab to complete a difficult math test. In one condition, participants were told that the test was one on which gender differences in performance usually appeared. In a second condition, the test was described as not producing gender differences. When the test was described as likely to produce gender differences—that is, when stereotype threat was high—the women performed substantially worse than the men did. However, when participants had been led to expect *no* gender differences, women performed at the same level as men. This occurred even though both conditions used the same math test (Spencer, Steele, & Quinn, 1999). Even White men, who generally do not contend with a stereotype that they cannot do math, can be made vulnerable to stereotype threat by putting them in a situation where they are made aware of the stereotype that Asian students are better at math than White students are. A group of White college men were brought to the lab and randomly assigned to conditions in which they either were or were not exposed to a packet of materials about the high math performance of Asian students and told that the study was an effort to understand why Asians tend to outperform other students on tests of math ability. When later given a math test, men who had been exposed to the stereotype (stereotype-threatened men) performed significantly worse than men who had not been exposed to the stereotype threat (Aronson, et al., 1999).

Clearly, stereotypes have real consequences with respect to performance. Researchers have argued that they also have consequences for life choices. It is painful to be in a perpetual battle with negative stereotypes, to be faced continuously with evaluative threat as one attempts to perform well. Under such conditions, people show a tendency to disengage or "disidentify" with the domain in which the stereotype occurs—to move away from that domain as a basis for identity or self-esteem (Major, Spencer, Schmader, Wolfe, & Crocker, 1998; Steele, 1997). Women may stop taking math classes and decide that math is unimportant or boring, thus removing themselves from arenas where they can be judged on their math performance. In doing so, they may inadvertently reinforce the stereotype.

GENDER STEREOTYPES AND THE RESEARCH PROCESS

Researchers who study gender have not been immune to the effects of stereotypes. In an early article on "the fantasy life of the male psychologist," Naomi Weisstein (1971) sounded a stinging challenge for scholars interested in discovering the truth about human behavior to examine their own discipline for sexism. In a few pungent pages, she produced example after glaring example of cases in which researchers had accepted without question the notion that observed male–female differences in behavior were the inevitable result of natural, inborn differences in inclination or temperament. She railed against what she saw as the general failure of psychologists to consider the social context as an important contributor to gender differences and against the tendency to consider "natural" or "normal" any behavior that fit easily into gender stereotypes. Her analysis points to a conclusion with which all students of behavior should still be concerned: It is all too easy to be uncritical of research questions, findings, and interpretations that fit one's own preconceptions.

The history of psychology shows that it has indeed been far too easy to frame research questions and to interpret findings in ways that are consistent with gender stereotypes. For instance, at one period a vast amount of research energy was expended to study the possible existence of a "maternal instinct" in women, whereas the possibility of a "paternal instinct" in men was ignored. Countless studies of achievement motivation were carried out on boys and men before anyone thought of seriously studying it in women. But perhaps the most clear-cut example of the biasing effects of gender stereotypes on the research process can be found in the history of psychology's attempts to measure femininity and masculinity.

Psychology and the Measurement of Masculinity and Femininity: A Comedy of Errors

The field of psychology, along with the larger culture, has held historically to the implicit assumption that adherence to gender stereotypes is normal and desirable: that women should be feminine and men masculine. This assumption has shaped psychological conceptions of masculinity–femininity (M–F) and attempts to measure it. In particular, it has, until recently, trapped psychologists in the idea that masculinity and femininity must be thought of as opposing poles of a single dimension.

The notion that such apparently intangible concepts as masculinity and femininity could be measured first became prominent through the work of Lewis Terman and his one-time student and colleague, Catherine Cox Miles. Convinced that the "real" mental differences between the sexes were in nonintellectual mental traits, they created the 456-item Attitude Interest Analysis Survey (AIAS; Terman & Miles, 1936) to measure the differences. This test and its authors' attempts to validate it are described at length by Miriam Lewin (1984), and the following discussion owes much to her account.

The AIAS, like most of the tests that followed it, was based not on coherent theories about the "essence" of masculinity or femininity but on statistically typical sex differences in the way respondents answered particular questions. Large numbers of items were given to a sample of junior high and high school students. Items on which girls and boys tended, on average, to answer differently were included in the test; those that showed no sex differences were dropped. In its final form, the test consisted of items for which the typical male and female were expected to choose different response alternatives. People taking the test received Femininity (F) points for all answers corresponding to the typical female choice and Masculinity (M) points for all answers corresponding to the typical male choice. To obtain the total M–F score, the F score was subtracted from the M score.

It is interesting to note the kinds of answers that produced high femininity and masculinity scores, respectively, using this method. On the information subtest, Femininity points were achieved through ignorance, such as indicating that Goliath was killed by Cain or that the earth turns once on its axis every 12 hours. Masculinity points were gained by giving the correct answers. On the emotional and ethical attitudes subtest, femininity was associated with greater anger at seeing others treated unfairly; masculinity was connected with anger at "being disturbed when you want to work." On forced-choice items, boys indicated they preferred to "command others" and to do "uninteresting work with a large income," whereas girls preferred to "persuade others" and do "interesting work with a small income"—so Masculinity points were assigned to the former and Femininity points to the latter. Femininity points were also achieved by indicating a dislike for "people with loud voices," "argumentative people," and "bald-headed men" or a liking for "very forgiving people," "washing dishes," and "being alone." Masculinity points were given for reporting a dislike of "tall women," "mannish women," "thin women," or "women cleverer than you." In retrospect, it is quite clear that the items included in the test, based as they were on gender differences in the self-reports of American junior high and high school students, simply reflected the gender stereotypes of a particular group in a particular time and place. What self-respecting junior high school girl of that era, knowing full well how ladies were supposed to behave, would admit, for example, that she liked to "command others"? What young boy could face his peers after an admission that he liked women cleverer than himself? The meanings assigned to femininity and masculinity using this test, then, are not at all universal but reflect a particularly American (White? middle-class? urban?) pre–World War II set of biases. Had a similar test been developed using a sample of rural Mexican adolescents or of elderly Chinese office workers, the items associated with masculinity and femininity might have been quite different.

Terman and Miles found masculinity–femininity ratings to be less reliable (that is, less stable from one administration of the test to another) than those of almost any other personality trait. Moreover, they were unable to show that their test scores correlated with any other criteria of masculinity and femininity. For example, in keeping with the then prevalent assumption that feminine women were weak and masculine men were strong, the researchers correlated masculinity–femininity scores on the AIAS with the self-rated health ("robust" to "frail") of 533 adults. Alas, the robust men scored as slightly less masculine than the others, and the frail women were not conclusively more feminine. Other research was equally discouraging. The idea that a highly masculine husband and a highly feminine wife should make the happiest couple was tested and found wanting. Ratings of a person's attractiveness to or interest in the other sex showed no relationship with M–F scores. The researchers were undaunted, however, because they believed basing the test on observed sex differences in their original sample had ensured it was a valid test of masculinity and femininity. Their confidence in the test was not shaken even by the discovery that both women and men were very good at faking their scores to make themselves look masculine or feminine when instructed to do so.

Terman and Miles were not the only psychologists to become mired in imprecision while trying to define and measure M–F. Constantinople (1973), reviewing the literature on M–F measurement, searched in vain for a definition of the two terms that went beyond the idea of "whatever distinguishes males from females." Lewin (1984) describes the series of erroneous assumptions that underlies the AIAS and most subsequent M–F tests up to the 1970s. Among these are the notion that M–F is a static trait that does not change from an early age (hence the use of schoolchildren as a criterion group for developing the test), the idea that homosexual men and feminine women will give equivalent responses (the femininity dimension of the M–F scale of the well-known MMPI personality test was "validated" on 13 gay men!), and the belief that the gender norms of mid-20th-century America are universal and fixed rather than linked to changing social, economic, and political conditions.

Researchers currently developing or working with measures of femininity and masculinity are less likely to make these assumptions. In fact, they tend to view such tests not so much as measures of fixed personality traits but as indicators of gender-relevant aspects of a person's self-concept or of the degree to which a person's self-image conforms to gender-role stereotypes (Lewin, 1984). Their approach has changed in another way: They have abandoned the assumption that femininity and masculinity are at opposing ends of the same continuum and have accepted the possibility of androgyny.

Androgyny

Earlier, I noted the tradition of considering the sexes as opposites—of conceptualizing masculinity and femininity as extreme poles of the same dimension. Researchers developing measures of femininity and masculinity adopted this assumption without questioning it and designed tests to accommodate it. By definition, then, a low masculinity score automatically meant high femininity, and vice versa. But there is another tradition in human thinking about sex and gender: the idea that femininity and masculinity are two complementary halves of a single whole, each one needed to complete the other. According to this tradition, not only do women and men need each other, but each individual can achieve wholeness only by developing both the feminine and the masculine aspects of her- or himself. This notion is a basic aspect of the ancient Chinese philosophy of Taoism, where the male and female principles, yin and yang, are thought to be the archetypal poles of nature. The two poles are creatively interdependent, each one giving rise to the other. To achieve wholeness and peace, the individual must completely transcend the duality and opposition of the two principles and perceive their underlying unity (Bazin & Freeman, 1974).

Many myths of the origin of the sexes contain elements of this tradition—for example, the biblical account of the creation of Eve from Adam's rib, the Hindu myth of the separation of the Supreme Self into male and female, and Plato's story of Zeus's decision to cut all beings in two. Much mythology and literature contains themes of striving to reunite the two halves—male and female—into a being or state of androgyny (see C. Heilbrun, 1973, for an overview of this literature). **Androgyny** (deriving from the union of the Greek terms "andro" for man and "gyne" for woman) refers to the psychological merging of the masculine and feminine principles. An androgynous person, by this definition, is one who has reconciled femininity and masculinity within her- or himself, one who has both feminine and masculine qualities.

An examination of the procedures used to score traditional M–F tests is sufficient to show that if there is such a thing as an androgynous person these tests could not identify that person. An androgynous individual would have substantial feminine *and* masculine qualities and so should score high on both masculinity and femininity on an M–F test. But the design of these tests makes such a score impossible: One cannot score high on femininity without scoring low on masculinity, and vice versa. An androgynous person would end up looking like a zero on an M–F test—as someone who was neither like men nor like women—instead of looking like someone who was like both men and women.

Psychologist Sandra Bem was the first to design a test that would allow an individual to score as androgynous. The Bem Sex Role Inventory (BSRI; Bem, 1974) treats femininity and masculinity as two separate, independent dimensions. A respondent can score high on both, low on both, or high on one and low on the other. This change was significant, not just for conceptual reasons but because masculinity and femininity are such highly charged concepts. On the BSRI, a male who admits to some feminine qualities need not fear for his masculinity score, for instance, and people of both sexes who show a mixture of "feminine" and "masculine" traits are classified as androgynous, not maladjusted or deviant.

Besides its treatment of femininity and masculinity as two separate dimensions, the BSRI also differs from traditional M–F tests in another way. Items for the masculinity and femininity scales were developed not by using the old approach of picking the items on which males and females answered differently but by picking the items that a pool of male and female respondents rated as most desirable "for an American man or woman." Twenty items rated as highly desirable for men were selected for the masculinity scale, and 20 items rated highly desirable for women formed the femininity scale. Another 20 neutral items were chosen for the social desirability scale. People taking the test are asked to indicate on a 7-point scale how well each of the adjectives describes them. Based on their responses, they can be classified in one of four ways: Masculine (high on masculinity, low on femininity), Feminine (high on femininity, low on masculinity), Androgynous (high on both femininity and masculinity), or Undifferentiated (low on both femininity and masculinity). Using the test with samples of California college students, Bem found that about one third of the subjects scored as "sex-typed" (Feminine females and Masculine males), one third scored as Androgynous, and fewer than 10% scored as "cross-sex-typed" (Masculine females and Feminine males). Other researchers have also developed scales that allow for the measurement of psychological androgyny, such as the Personal Attributes Questionnaire (Spence et al., 1974) and the PRF Andro scale (Berzins, Welling, & Wetter, 1975). Like the original Terman and Miles (1936) scale, all of these scales reflect the particular biases of the samples (usually middle-class American college students) on which they were developed.

Abandoning the notion that femininity and masculinity were two ends of a bipolar continuum and incorporating the idea of androgyny into psychological tests of gender have been important steps, but they have not solved the problems inherent in trying to measure masculinity and femininity. Several issues in designing the tests remain unresolved: the assumption that femininity and masculinity are unidimensional constructs rather than constellations of several dimensions, the difficulty of scaling the test items so that each one is "worth" the same amount of masculinity or femininity, and the problem of sex specificity—the possibility that a given item may count more heavily toward self-perceived femininity or masculinity for one sex than for the other (Colwill & Lips, 1978).

Underlying all these problems is one major theme: Psychologists are still not sure what they are trying to measure. A major limitation of the notion of androgyny is that it is based on the combination of masculinity and femininity, and it forces attention to these concepts and to the stereotypes on which they are based. In a way, then, it tends to "reproduce precisely the gender polarization that it seeks to undercut" (Bem, 1993, p. 125). Masculinity and femininity are still defined only as the two sets of qualities that distinguish males from females, and since these distinctions vary a great deal across time and place, trying to devise standard criteria with which to assess them appears to be a hopeless task. People's perceptions of masculinity and femininity appear to be far more complex than implied by the collection of items on these scales. When ordinary people are asked to describe what femininity or masculinity means to them, their answers bear little resemblance to the items on the most widely used psychological tests (Lips, 1986a; Myers & Gonda, 1982). Psychologists are left with a dilemma: On one hand, masculinity and femininity are such slippery concepts that it seems fruitless to waste any more time trying to measure them; on the other hand, it is clear that they are experienced by people as important concepts against which to measure themselves and others. Popular conceptions of femininity and masculinity are complex and multidimensional and probably cannot be represented adequately by single scores on a personality test.

Disarming the Stereotypes: Approaches to Empowerment

Approaches to gender in psychology over the last 25 years have often rested on the desire to free people from the constraints of stereotypes based on biological sex. The freedom to be or behave in a particular way without worrying about whether or not one is being "appropriately masculine" or "feminine enough" allows individuals to seek out their own strengths, to use their energy where it will do the most good. Making gender stereotypes less rigid and inclusive of fewer aspects of behavior should be empowering for both women and men—increasing their sense of effectiveness and self-actualization and reducing the number of situations in which individuals experience stereotype threat. The process should also unleash new sources of human energy for societies, adding to a collective sense of power and accomplishment. Finally, by removing the justification for segregation of society's institutions and occupations by sex, dismantling gender stereotypes may ultimately help to reduce the power imbalance between women and men and foster an era of greater equality.

Are the approaches to gender in psychology really having this empowering effect? The answer is controversial, and the reader must judge this for her- or himself at the end of this book. Many people have argued that the concept of psychological androgyny, although initially liberating, became simply another prescription against which people must measure themselves. Now people can feel inadequate not only because they are not masculine enough or feminine enough but also because they are not androgynous enough. Even more serious, because androgyny is built on the concepts of femininity and masculinity, it continues to impart a sense that these are real entities rather than cultural constructions, and it can never transcend them. Androgyny pushed back the limitations imposed by a bipolar conception of masculinity–femininity, but it contains its own built-in limitations.

Sandra Bem (1993) has more recently argued that as children are enculturated with the notion of a gender-polarized world they are absorbing cultural messages not only about difference but about power. It is no simple matter to dismantle gender stereotypes when those stereotypes help to define the way power and status are arranged in a society. Her analysis suggests, however, that the connection between gender stereotypes and power is exactly the reason that disarming those stereotypes is empowering—especially for women.

SUMMARY

Labeling an individual as female or male has a powerful impact on others' perceptions of and reactions to that individual. Stereotypically, we expect different behaviors, personal qualities, and physical appearance from women and men. When we categorize people by sex (their biological femaleness or maleness), we tend to assume that we have also categorized them according to the set of cultural expectations for femininity and masculinity, although on many dimensions there is no necessary relationship between biological sex and cultural expectations for women and men.

Our conceptions of femininity and masculinity are framed in the language of opposites. Men are thought to be task-oriented and independent; women to be relationship-oriented and affiliative. Such gender stereotypes are more than just a random collection of groundless beliefs about women and men. Rather, they represent cultural constructions of femininity and masculinity, sometimes based tenuously on physical differences, that serve as underpinnings for the social relations between women and men as groups and as individuals. However, human beings have often failed, and still do, to recognize the extent to which gender stereotypes are products of the social context in which they exist, how resistant they are to disconfirmation, and how easily they can act as self-fulfilling prophecies. We react negatively to individuals who violate the stereotypes, as if they were acting in an "unnatural" way when, in fact, they are simply violating cultural norms. Individuals who, in defiance of cultural expectations, move into domains that are thought to be the province of the other gender can find themselves suffering from the performance decrements and disengagement that accompany stereotype threat.

The history of attempts by psychologists to measure femininity and masculinity reveals all too clearly that psychology as a discipline has not been exempt from gender stereotyping or from the mistaken belief that observed differences between the sexes automatically represent the natural state of affairs.

Psychologists have used the concept of androgyny in an effort to deal with issues of masculinity and femininity without invoking the stereotypic notion of "opposite sexes." These attempts have been only partially successful, but they have provided a framework for new thinking about sex and gender.

This book revolves around three central questions: What do we know and not know about gender similarities and differences? Where does that knowledge come from? How is that knowledge itself shaped and limited by cultural perceptions of femininity and masculinity? Cultural perceptions of femininity and masculinity have been the main focus of this chapter. What should be clear at this point is just how strongly our expectations about women and men are shaped by our culture—and how significantly those expectations affect what we observe about gender similarities and differences. We will explore this theme further in the next chapter as we examine the ways scientific theories about sex and gender have gained and lost favor in conjunction with popular attitudes about women and men.

KEY TERMS

sex stereotypes
sex
gender
instrumentality
expressiveness
prototypical traits

components of gender
    stereotypes
prejudice
sexism
hostile sexism
benevolent sexism

modern sexism
neosexism
stereotype threat
androgyny

FOR ADDITIONAL READING

Bell-Scott, Patricia. (1994). *Life notes: Personal writings by contemporary Black women.* New York: Norton. A collection of very personal perspectives on girlhood, femininity, work, love, and self-definition.

Cruikshank, Julie, in collaboration with Angela Sidney, Kitty Smith, and Annie Ned. (1991). *Life lived like a story: Life stories of three Yukon Native elders.* Lincoln: University of Nebraska Press. Three Native women born at the turn of the century in the southern Yukon Territory tell their stories in their own words.

Espín, Oliva M. (1997). *Latina realities: Essays on healing, migration and sexuality.* Boulder, CO: Westview Press. A noted psychologist explores the links between experience, theory, and method in psychology as she writes about issues in the lives of Latinas.

Gilmore, David G. (1990). *Manhood in the making: Cultural concepts of masculinity.* New Haven, CT: Yale University Press. A cross-cultural examination of what it means to "be a man" in societies around the world.

hooks, bell. (1989). *Talking back: Thinking feminist, thinking Black.* Boston: South End Press. A writer discusses, in a personal and powerful way, the experience and meaning of being Black and female in a culture that privileges those who are White and male.

King, Florence. (1985). *Confessions of a failed Southern lady.* New York: St. Martin's Press. The autobiographical account of a young woman's conflicts with Southern notions of femininity.

Mairs, Nancy. (1996). *Waist-high in the world: A life among the nondisabled.* Boston: Beacon Press. A woman eloquently writes about her own life, including the paradoxes and difficulties that accompany disability.

CHAPTER 2

Theoretical Perspectives on Sex & Gender

During the latter part of the 19th century, the idea flourished that educating women in the same way as men was dangerous and damaging. The danger supposedly arose from the energy needs of women's reproductive processes: menstruation and preparation for childbearing. Physicians theorized that the womb exercised a dominating influence over a woman's personality and ability, almost as if the "Almighty, in creating the female sex, had taken the uterus and built a woman around it" (physician quoted in Smith-Rosenberg & Rosenberg, 1976, p. 56). Women who, during puberty, used up too much precious energy on the brain function required for advanced education would enfeeble their bodies, ruining their health and crippling their capacity to bear children. These dire warnings, sounded most prominently by Dr. Edward Clarke (1873), were based on a theory of thermodynamics: All physical systems, including the human body, followed the principle of conservation of energy, so that force expended in one function would be unavailable to any other. Men, whose passage into puberty supposedly did not place such a heavy strain on their bodies, could safely turn their energies to demanding intellectual tasks without endangering their physical well-being.

Accepting two theoretical assumptions—the domination of female personality by the uterus and the principle of conservation of energy—had a profound impact on popular and scientific thinking about the differences between women and men. In the history of the study of sex and gender, the role played by theory has been substantial. But what exactly is a theory? Basically, a **theory** is a set of ideas about how and why things happen. In the realm of science, where the field of psychology is situated, the role of a theory is to guide research: to generate hypotheses (propositions) that can be tested against observed reality. For example, if one subscribed to the theory that women's personality was dominated by the uterus, one should be able to think of some testable hypotheses—things that should occur if the theory were true and should not occur if it were false—and then test them. Such testing might involve comparing women who had borne children with those who had not or comparing groups of same-age women who had or had not undergone hysterectomies.

It is easy to see how the acceptance of a particular theory can have a major impact on the kind of research that gets done: what questions are asked, what issues are investigated or ignored, what findings are considered important or trivial. It is also easy to see that a theory that did not lend itself to being checked against reality in some way might linger in people's imagination for a long time without being either proven or disproved and laid to rest, particularly if it had some popular appeal. A requirement for a good and useful theory, then, is that it can be tested.

The history of the study of sex and gender provides many examples of a problem that always besets the scientific process: Theories that fit well with the accepted assumptions at a particular time and place tend to receive a lot of attention and generate research, whereas those that seem to be at odds with accepted notions are frequently ignored. Indeed, we scientists are such creatures of our culture that our theories often incorporate as presuppositions untested aspects of the "conventional wisdom" of our time and place. For example, the basic cultural notion that men are intellectually superior to women was frequently accepted as a given by psychologists, who then set out to construct theories to explain *why* this was so. In the words of the eminent psychologist William James (1890), "It is astonishing what havoc is wrought in psychology by admitting at the outset apparently innocent suppositions that nevertheless contain a flaw" (p. 224).

Before anyone had ever heard of psychology, theories about gender were being offered by the early philosophers. Within these early theories lies an idea that influenced psychologists for years afterward— woman as incomplete man.

The idea of equality between the sexes can be found in the early writings of the Greek philosopher Plato, who described women and men as having the same nature and worth and deserving the same education and legal treatment. This idea fades out in his later writings, however, in which female weakness and inferiority are used as justification for assigning different social roles to men and women (Dickason, 1976). Later, in the writings of Aristotle, the idea of feminine inferiority and "incompleteness" was developed in detail. Aristotle claimed that the female state was an "ordinary" deformity and that a woman was, in some respects, a defective man (Whitbeck, 1976). Female inferiority lay in the fact that women supposedly had less "soul heat" than men, and so could not process their menstrual blood to what he deemed the "final stage," semen. Women's inability to produce semen meant that they could contribute nothing but formative material to the embryo in the process of conception and that they made no genetic contribution to its distinctive character.

The Aristotelian notion that women were inferior because of a shortage of intrinsic heat received a later expression in the work of Juan Huarte, a 16th-century Spanish writer expounding on individual intellectual differences. He argued that the testicles were responsible for maintaining the "heat and dryness" characteristic of the male principle. Since "dryness of spirit" was necessary for intelligence, and since the testicles maintained this quality, obviously men, who had testicles, were more intelligent than women, who did not (S.A. Shields, 1975).

Theories that viewed women as lesser beings than men—because of their inability to produce enough heat to process body fluids into semen—did not view women as *opposites* to men. Women and men were thought to be similar, but differently developed. In fact, proponents of these theories often argued that women and men had similar bodies: There were many early medical references, for instance, to the male uterus, to female testicles, and to the "fact" that the female reproductive organs were the same as the male's—only "inside out," with the scrotum equivalent to the uterus, the penis to the cervix and vagina (Laqueur, 1990). Thomas Laqueur quotes a bit of popular verse from the early 19th century:

. . . though they of different sexes be,
Yet on the whole they are the same as we,
For those that have the strictest searchers been,
Find women are but men turned outside in. (p. 4)

The second-century anatomist Galen used the simile of the eyes of a mole to describe female genitalia. As he explained it, the eyes of the mole appear the same as those of other animals, except that they do not open and thus do not allow the animal to see. The mole's eyes remain closed, as if the animal were still in the uterus. Similarly, the female's genitalia remain unopened and undeveloped after birth, as if still in the womb, whereas the male's project outward and develop fully (Laqueur, 1990).

The "woman as defective man" motif affected theories of gender inside and outside the field of psychology for centuries, appearing in the writings of men from Thomas Aquinas to Sigmund Freud. The strength of the idea is not surprising, given that these theorists, encountering women mainly in subordinate positions, developed their theories to explain and justify what seemed to them a natural and inevitable situation. However, by the 19th century, the hierarchical approach to male–female differences had been supplanted to some extent by the "opposites" approach, an approach that treated the two sexes as irreconcilably different. Echoes of both approaches can be found in psychological theories of gender.

Six general types of theories have emerged in the field of psychology to explain the differences and similarities between human males and females. Psychoanalytic/identification theories focus on personality development. Social structural theories concern social structures and culture, concentrating on how intergroup relations between women and men are linked to gender roles and stereotypes. Sociobiology attempts to explain gender issues with reference to the evolution of the human species. All three of these theoretical approaches put a heavy emphasis on the origins of gender, focusing on *why* the sexes may differ. The next three approaches—social learning, cognitive development, and social interaction process theories—focus more heavily on *how* gender differences occur, stressing the processes through which males and females may be led to adopt different or similar ways of behaving.

PSYCHOANALYTIC/IDENTIFICATION THEORIES

Sigmund Freud

Sigmund Freud, an Austrian physician whose work spanned the late 19th and early 20th centuries, was the father of **psychoanalytic theory,** perhaps the first theory of human personality to assign a central role to sexuality. His writings and the controversies they have generated fill volumes and have had a profound impact on ideas about male–female differences. Reaction to his work on gender has ranged from assertions that he has done more than anyone else to set back the cause of women to praise for his brilliant analysis of a patriarchal society.

Freud's theory was predicated on the idea that the human mind, like an iceberg that floats with only a small tip showing above the surface of the water, is only partially available to our awareness. The part of the mind available to awareness, referred to as the region of **consciousness,** contains the thoughts and feelings people know they have. The much larger part, the **unconscious,** contains the unacceptable urges, passions, ideas, and feelings that people cannot acknowledge. The contents of the unconscious can be explored only indirectly through dreams, free association, symptoms, mistakes (now sometimes called "Freudian slips"), or other "leaks" of the unconscious into conscious awareness. The unconscious was the cornerstone of Freudian theory, for he felt that the motives hidden in the unconscious are often the driving force behind conscious thoughts and deeds. The notion of the unconscious is also what makes this theory difficult to verify or disprove, however, because, by definition, the contents of the unconscious cannot be investigated with traditional objective methods for assessing people's thoughts and feelings.

Freud proposed that the personality is composed of three structures—id, ego, and superego—and that a person's behavior is produced by the interaction among these systems (Freud, 1924/1960). In his theory, the **id,** consisting of the individual's biological heritage, including sexual and aggressive instincts, provides a reservoir of psychic energy that powers the other two systems. A nonrational system, it operates strictly on the pleasure principle: Uncomfortable tension must be discharged and needs must be satisfied. The **ego** is a rational system that works on the reality principle: Discharge of tension or satisfaction of needs should be prevented until an appropriate situation is found. This second system handles transactions between an individual's subjective needs and the objective world of reality, helping to keep the individual out of trouble and ensure survival. Finally, the **superego** acts as the moral aspect of the personality, striving for perfection rather than pleasure and persuading the ego to substitute moralistic goals for realistic ones. The superego, also nonrational, was described by Freud as the internal representative of society's values and ideals as taught to the child by parents and enforced by rewards and punishments. The three systems should be balanced in an individual's personality, and domination of the personality by one of them can cause problems. A very strong id, combined with a weak ego and superego, creates a person who is impulsive, hedonistic, and unfettered by the demands of conscience; an overdeveloped superego produces one who is inhibited from most forms of self-expression by the crippling fear of imperfection.

Personality development occurs in a series of five psychosexual stages. In each stage, strong pleasurable feelings, attributed by Freud to the satisfaction of sexual instincts, are associated with particular body zones. In the **oral stage,** during the first year of life, pleasure is centered in the mouth and sucking. During the second year, the child passes through the **anal stage,** in which pleasure is linked to defecation. Next comes the **phallic stage,** in which erotic pleasure is obtained from the penis for boys and the clitoris for girls. This is followed by the **latency phase,** in which erotic impulses are repressed until just before puberty. Puberty ushers in the **genital stage,** that of mature sexuality.

According to Freud, it is during the phallic stage, which lasts from about age 3 to age 6, that the development of boys and girls diverges. This divergence, and consequent formation of appropriate masculine or feminine identification, is precipitated by the development and resolution of the **Oedipus complex,** a system of feelings named by Freud for the mythical Greek character who unwittingly killed his own father and married his own mother.

Boys at this stage develop an intense attachment for the mother and a desire to possess her sexually. The boy begins to see his father as a rival—a competitor for the mother's affections—and he wishes to replace him. Unable to acknowledge his strong negative feelings toward his father, the boy unconsciously projects the feelings onto the father, thus coming to believe that his father sees *him* as a rival. He then worries about what his father may do to him, and the fear that begins to haunt him is the fear of castration. Why castration? This is the phallic stage, the stage at which the penis is the source of a great deal of pleasure and pride for the little boy. It is a time when he has discovered masturbation and perhaps has been threatened by his parents that if he doesn't stop, they will "cut it off." Most important, according to Freud, it is a time when the boy discovers with chagrin that not everybody has a penis. His first glimpse of a naked girl or woman leaves him shocked and perturbed because it gives reality to his parents' threats and his own fears: Some people have apparently already been castrated! So intense does his fear become that he is literally forced to resolve the Oedipus complex to allay his fear. He achieves this end by identifying with his father (accepting his father as a model and incorporating many features of his father's personality into his own) and crushing his desire for his mother. Freud believed boys emerged from the Oedipus complex with either a contempt for or fear of women, based on the danger associated with attraction to the mother.

For a girl, the road to feminine identification begins, according to Freud, when she first notices that boys have something she does not: a penis. The realization produces what Freud labeled **penis envy:**

> She has seen it and knows she is without it and wants to have it. . . . The hope of someday obtaining a penis in spite of everything and so of becoming like a man may persist to an incredibly late age and may become a motive for the strangest and otherwise unaccountable actions. Or again, a process may set in which might be described as a "denial" . . . a girl may refuse to accept the fact of being castrated, may harden herself in the conviction that she *does* possess a penis and may subsequently be compelled to behave as though she were a man. (Freud, 1925/1974, pp. 31–32)

Seeing herself to be lacking such an important organ, the girl develops a sense of inferiority and contempt for her own sex. Gradually, her penis envy becomes a more general attitude of jealousy. She blames her mother, her original love object, for her lack of a penis and starts to withdraw her affection from her. She tries to suppress the tendency to masturbate because her clitoris is so inferior to the boy's penis. Her penis envy eventually leads her to enter the female version of the Oedipus complex, called the **Electra complex,** after the mythical Greek personage who urged her brother to slay their mother, who had murdered their father. "She gives up her wish for a penis and puts in place of it a wish for a child: and *with this purpose in view* she takes her father as a love object. Her mother becomes the object of her jealousy" (Freud, 1925/1974, p. 34). Gradually, she realizes that she can never possess her father. By facing this frustration, she accepts the link between pain and pleasure that is inherent in the female role and becomes masochistic. Grudgingly, she reestablishes her feminine identification with her mother and concentrates on becoming an attractive love object so that she will be adored by some other man. Sexual attractiveness becomes her primary source of self-esteem and identity.

Females, unlike males, do not have a powerful fear motivation to resolve the Electra complex. For them, after all, the worst has already happened: They have been castrated. Freud felt that, in their case, the complex was slowly abandoned or repressed, rather than smashed, as it was for boys. For boys, the necessity to destroy the Oedipus complex results in the formation of a strong superego. For girls, the more gradual abandonment of the Electra complex makes strong superego development less necessary.

Thus, the different courses followed by boys and girls in forming and resolving the Oedipus/Electra complex have far-reaching consequences in Freudian theory for the development of psychological gender differences. Among males, the result of resolution is masculine identification, contempt for or fear of women, and a strong superego. Among females, the upshot of the complex is feminine identification, a sense of inferiority, contempt for other women, a tendency toward jealousy, a rejection of clitoral sexuality, masochism, a wish for a child, an obsession with sexual attractiveness, and a weaker superego.

Two of Freud's conclusions in particular have had negative consequences for women. The first is his idea that the rejection of clitoral sexuality was a normal part of female development. Freud believed the suppression of sexual activity focused on the clitoris was necessary for the emergence of true feminine (vaginal) sexuality. In psychoanalytic theory, the clitoral orgasm was considered immature and not truly satisfying; a "real woman" found satisfaction only in vaginal orgasms achieved during intercourse. This element of Freudian doctrine is puzzling in light of the complete lack of evidence that erotic sensitivity was transferred from the clitoris to the vagina during women's maturation. Nineteenth-century medical books made it abundantly clear that the clitoris had far more nerve endings than the vagina did, and Freud, as a doctor, could hardly have been unaware of this. So powerful was his theory's hold on the popular imagination, however, that scientists "forgot" what had been well known to doctors and to ordinary women and men for centuries—that the female orgasm is almost entirely clitoral (Laqueur, 1990). When researchers in the second half of the 20th century "discovered" what 17th-century women would have thought to be common knowledge—that the clitoris has as many nerve endings as the penis and that all female orgasms originate there (see Chapter 7)—many women who had been suffering guilt and inadequacy over their inability to have "proper" vaginal orgasms suddenly realized they'd been duped. Resentment still simmers against Freudian-based psychiatry for its complicity in orienting women toward denial rather than trust of their own experience of sexuality.

The second Freudian concept that has been used against women is penis envy. Because the pressure to resolve the Oedipus complex is weak in women, Freud suggested that no resolution may be achieved. In this event, the adult woman will be a neurotic victim of penis envy. She may try to be masculine, become resentful and jealous of men, and reject the feminine fulfillment of pregnancy—all the while completely unaware that it is her unconscious wish for a penis that is making her so cranky. If women take offense at this aspect of the theory, it is little wonder, for it implies that any woman who is not satisfied with her socially defined feminine role is neurotic and psychosexually immature. Freud himself was not above using the penis envy concept as a weapon against female psychoanalysts who broke ranks and criticized his theory: "We shall not be very surprised if a woman analyst who has not been sufficiently convinced of her own desire for a penis also fails to assign an adequate importance to that factor in her patients" (quoted in Garrison, 1981).

Because Freudian theory acknowledged the importance and pervasiveness of sexual feelings and desires—experiences that were largely denied or minimized in the Victorian era in which he worked—it opened the door for consideration of some hitherto undiscussed sexual behaviors. In one such case, incest, the door was opened slightly, then hastily closed. In another, homosexuality, some light was allowed to shine on a subject that had been shrouded in disapproval.

Many of Freud's women patients told him that they had been seduced by their fathers. At first, Freud believed these accounts and attributed the women's neurotic symptoms to repressed horror over the incest. Later, however, he began to feel uneasy about the large number of his female patients who claimed to have been sexually molested by their fathers and male relatives. Refusing to accept the possibility that daughters were sexually victimized with such high frequency, he asserted in his public writings that the women's accounts (and their symptoms) were based on fantasies rather than real occurrences. In fact, he came to describe the fantasy of being seduced by the father as the expression of the Oedipus complex in women.

Unbelievable though it may have seemed to Freud, evidence suggests that most of his women patients were telling the truth. The occurrences of sexual abuse were, in many cases, confirmed by the abuser or other reliable witnesses (Sulloway, 1979). In the present day, surveys have placed the occurrence of father–daughter incest at 1.3% to 4.5% and the occurrence of sexual abuse of girls in general at 6% to 62% (Finkelhor, 1986; D. E. H. Russell, 1983a). Moreover, documentation of the widespread character of sexual abuse of girls is not new and was apparently available to Freud and known to him through medical colleagues in Paris. Some of his unpublished letters seem to suggest that, long after he had publicly discounted his patients' seduction stories, he continued to believe that at least some of the stories were true (Masson, 1984). The damage done by Freud's public refusal to believe his female patients is incalculable. Victims of incest who seek help still encounter disbelief or the charge that the incident was an outcome of their own unconscious incestuous wishes (Rush, 1980; Sheffield, 1995).

Freud's legacy with respect to homosexuality was more positive. He argued that neither masculinity and femininity nor heterosexuality and homosexuality were polar opposites; rather, every individual displayed a mixture of these qualities. As he wrote to a woman concerned about her son's homosexuality:

> Homosexuality is assuredly no advantage, but it is nothing to be ashamed of, no vice, no degradation; it cannot be classified as an illness; we consider it to be a variation of the sexual function. . . . Many highly respectable individuals of ancient and modern times have been homosexuals, several of the greatest men among them. . . . It is a great injustice to persecute homosexuality as a crime—and a cruelty too. . . .
>
> What analysis can do for your son runs in a different line. If he is unhappy, neurotic, torn by conflicts, inhibited in his social life, analysis may bring him harmony, peace of mind, full efficiency, whether he remains homosexual or gets changed. (Freud, 1961, pp. 419–420)

Freud's theory opened new possibilities for debate in the whole area of sexuality and gender—and a debate is exactly what happened.

Challenging Freud's Phallocentrism

Almost from the first, some critics felt that in looking at psychosexual development from the male point of view Freud had created a theory that overemphasized the role played by the penis and anxiety over losing or not having it in the development of both sexes. An early proponent of this viewpoint was Karen Horney, a member of Freud's circle who had a reputation as one of the foremost training analysts in Europe. She questioned the idea that women look on their bodies as inferior, and she argued that masculine narcissism is the only basis for the assumption that half the human race is automatically discontented with the sex assigned to it. Although accepting the possibility of penis envy in girls and castration anxiety in boys, she noted that males are also envious of females:

> From the biological point of view, woman has in motherhood, or in the capacity for motherhood, a quite indisputable and by no means negligible superiority. This is most clearly reflected in the unconscious of the male psyche in the boy's intense envy of motherhood. We are familiar with this envy as such, but it has hardly received due consideration as a dynamic factor. When one begins, as I did, to analyze men only after fairly long experience of analyzing women, one receives a most surprising impression of the intensity of this envy of pregnancy, childbirth, and motherhood, as well as of the breasts and the act of suckling. (Horney, 1926/1973, p. 10)

Horney also believed rejection of the female role in girls is mainly caused not by envy of the penis but by an unconscious fear of vaginal injury through penetration, aroused by guilt over masturbation. Thus, she proposed that a girl's psychosexual development centers on her own anatomy rather than that of the male. Furthermore, she argued, rejection of the feminine role is partially a response to a society that views women as inadequate and inferior and gives them few opportunities outside the home. Thus, she became one of the first psychoanalysts to draw attention to the possibilities for interaction between cultural and inner dynamic forces in shaping the personality.

Although both she and her views were rejected in orthodox Freudian circles, her work had considerable impact, and she herself became respected and renowned despite the controversy she created (Garrison, 1981).

Whereas Freudian theory can be labeled **phallocentric**—centered on the male penis—the perspective taken by Horney and a group of other psychoanalysts has been labeled **gynocentric**—centered on the female womb (Stockard & Johnson, 1979). This latter approach emphasizes the importance for personality development of both boys' and girls' pre-Oedipal relationship with the mother and links male dominance of women to that early mother–child tie. The bases proposed for the link are unconscious fear and envy of the mother and the necessity for boys but not girls to switch their identification from the mother to the father. Meredith Kimball (1995) notes that this theoretical approach did not arise in a vacuum. It emerged in a particular historical context, one in which **maternal feminisms** were popular among women in Europe. Individuals and organizations who espoused maternal-feminist ideas were strongly supportive of women's rights, but they did not argue that women and men were similar. Rather, they emphasized the differences between women and men and the importance of motherhood for women and for society.

Horney suggested that the strength of men's desire to achieve and create is an overcompensation for their unconscious sense of inferiority in the creative process of reproduction. Furthermore, she proposed, the masculine tendency to depreciate women is also an outcome of this unconscious envy, rather than of the recognition that the female lacks a penis. On this point she was echoed by Melanie Klein (1932/1960), who asserted that boys' pride in and emphasis on the penis compensate for feelings of anxiety, envy, and inferiority regarding the mother.

Horney's critique of Freud reclaimed the primacy of women's own body, rather than envy of the male body, in women's psychological development. Rather than challenge the Freudian notions of instinctual sexual drives or of female–male differences based on anatomy, she simply exposed the masculine bias in the way Freud had used these notions to describe female psychology (Kimball, 1995). In Horney's early writing on female development, she worked within the psychoanalytic framework to undermine its male-centered bias, using anatomical differences and sexual drives as her conceptual tools. In her later work, Horney rejected the notion that human behavior springs from instinctual drives (sex, aggression) and developed instead the notion that behavior is a product of experience in its cultural context (Westkott, 1986). She postulated that human beings are guided by needs for safety (inner security) and satisfaction and that a child's social environment determines whether these needs can be met easily or whether the child must develop a neurotic "solution" (such as dependency) to the anxiety and hostility that arise from an insecure environment.

According to Horney's (1939) theory, the environment presents two potential dangers to the young child: **devaluation** (parents' lack of respect for the child as unique, worthwhile) and **sexualization** (a sexual approach to the child, an emotional "hothouse" atmosphere). She argued that the clinging to one parent and jealousy toward the other that characterized what Freud had called the Oedipus complex was a child's anxious response to the abuse of parental power: devaluing or sexualizing treatment of the child (Westkott, 1986).

It is clear from Horney's writings that she felt the cultural pattern of preference for sons over daughters made girls more vulnerable than boys to devaluation and the development of a sense of inferiority. She noted as well the pervasive cultural tendency for families to treat girls as if their sexuality was the most important aspect of their identity. Thus, although theoretically applicable to both boys and girls, in a society that valued males over females the experiences of devaluation and sexualization were more likely to characterize the childhood of girls than of boys. Girls might, then, be more likely than boys to develop neurotic personalities characterized by the submissiveness and self-directed hostility that arise in response to parental devaluation. However, this gender difference is based not in anything biological but in a culture that values one sex more than the other.

Feminism and Psychoanalytic Theory

During the last three decades, much theorizing has been done about the aspect of development virtually ignored by Freud and highlighted in Horney's early writings—the early bond between mother and child. Writing in the gynocentric tradition of Karen Horney, Melanie Klein, and other pioneering analysts, Dorothy Dinnerstein (1976) argued that society allows men to hold the power outside the mother–child relationship precisely because the power held by the mother over the infant is so awesome. The relationship produces in both men and women, Dinnerstein says, a fear of female power and authority. In the process of growing up, the individual flees from the power of the mother and finds it easier to accept male than female authority. Men end up with a particular fear of becoming overly dependent on women, whereas women carry with them throughout their lives a sense of inadequacy because they can never live up to the magically powerful mother image they experienced as infants. The result is a society that accepts and encourages male dominance.

Sociologist Nancy Chodorow (1978), taking a similar perspective about the overwhelming effect of the mother–child relationship, has argued that exclusively female parenting produces men and women with very different emotional needs. Women, having been parented by an adult with whom they could identify, try unsuccessfully to reexperience this sense of unity in their sexual relationships with men.

> But families organized around women's mothering and male dominance create
> incompatibilities in women's and men's relational needs. In particular, relationships
> to men are unlikely to provide for women satisfaction of the relational needs that
> their mothering by women and the social organization of gender have produced.
> The less men participate in the domestic sphere, and especially in parenting, the
> more this will be the case. (p. 199)

Furthermore, Chodorow (1989) notes, family arrangements in which women do the primary caregiving produce different problems for males and females. Contrary to Freud, whose analysis of the Oedipal trauma emphasized the difficulties faced by girls in forming a positive gender identity, Chodorow argues that it is boys who face the most problems in initially forming their identity as males. Because of the early, close attachment between mother and child,

> [u]nderlying, or built into, core male gender identity is an early, non-verbal, uncon-
> scious, almost somatic sense of primary oneness with the mother, an underlying
> sense of femaleness that continually, usually unnoticeably, but sometimes insistently,
> challenges and undermines the sense of maleness. (p. 109)

Because boys initially identify with the mother, forming a masculine identity is a negative process that involves separation and denial. Males must form their gender identity by defining themselves as "*not* women." For girls, such drastic separation is not necessary. However, girls develop difficulties with identity later; these center on the problems of identifying with "a negatively valued gender category, and an ambivalently experienced maternal figure, whose mothering and femininity, often conflictual for the mother herself, are accessible, but devalued" (pp. 110–111).

Why is feminine identity negatively valued? Chodorow (1989) explains that men devalue it in their flight from it. Moreover, because men have more power than women, they have been able to "define maleness as that which is basically human, and to define women as not-men" (p. 111).

Chodorow notes, however, that human family arrangements are not invariant, but change in response to the economic organization of society. The arrangement that emphasizes women's mothering and male dominance is not an inevitable aspect of human social organization.

The attention paid to the mother–child relationship in the gynocentric branch of psychoanalytic theory makes it quite different from orthodox Freudian theory, in which the father–child relationship is the crucial one. An interesting implication that both Dinnerstein and Chodorow have drawn from their theoretical work is that society would be better off with a family system in which parenting was more equally shared between women and men. Such sharing of roles would presumably reduce the internalization of a perception of mothers as "all-powerful," paving the way for more egalitarian and intimate relationships between adult women and men. However, this implication may be too simplistic. As Ellyn Kaschak (1992) notes, only a small minority of families in North America now fit the model of a dual-parent family in which the mother is the main caregiver and the father is absent for most of the day. Most mothers work outside the home and are away from their children for a good part of the time. Many children are being raised by single parents or by slightly older siblings. Yet there is no convincing evidence that children not raised in the kind of nuclear family described by Chodorow and Dinnerstein differ from other children in terms of gender roles, relational orientation, or resentment of female power. Kaschak argues that the general social context—the collection of messages about gender that surround the child in the culture—weighs more heavily than particular family arrangements in the meanings children learn to associate with gender.

Male Gender-Role Identity

Chodorow's description of the difficulties associated with masculine identity echoes the ideas of other theorists who have been specifically concerned with the male role. The idea that gender-role acquisition was based on early identification with the appropriate parent led some theorists on a quest for the explanation of "masculinity problems." In contrast to Freud, who felt that girls encountered the most difficulties on the road to proper gender identification, these later theorists argued that boys faced greater obstacles. Joseph Pleck (1981) describes the historical context that led to a special concern with masculinity: the disqualification of large numbers of American males as mentally or physically unfit for the draft in World Wars I and II, the incidence of emotional breakdowns among men in battle, the erosion of the male breadwinner role through the Great Depression and women's wartime entry into the labor force, and such examples of "hypermasculinity" as wartime aggression and the rise of juvenile delinquency.

In trying to explain such "failures" of masculinity, theorists looked again to notions of identification and focused on the same critical issue identified by Chodorow: Boys, like girls, initially identify with the mother. Thus, these theorists reasoned, males have more difficulty than females in forming the appropriate gender-role identity, and overcoming their initial feminine identification is a central problem in males' psychological development.

Why should identification with the appropriate gender role be especially difficult for boys? First, the boy must *switch* identifications from his mother to his father, something the girl does not have to do. Second, the father is usually so much less available than the mother or other female caregiver as a model that the boy may have trouble knowing precisely what being masculine entails.

The potential difficulties inherent in the failure to form "proper" masculine identification were thought to be twofold: Men might be "sissified" or feminized, or they might become hypermasculine in overcompensation for their unconscious feminine identification. In the first category lay fears that boys who did not form a proper masculine identification would become homosexual—fears based on the then current stereotype that male homosexuality was equivalent, in personality terms, to femininity. In the second category lay fears of male violence deriving from men's needs to disengage from inner feminine identification. The greater the underlying feeling of weakness, supposedly, the more a man would act out aggressively to prove masculinity.

The theory had some interesting political implications. It appeared to justify the view of male homosexuality as a failure in psychological development and so provided ammunition for attempts to "cure" it and to suppress it as an open lifestyle. The theory was also used extensively to explain the problems faced by Black American men. Both Thomas Pettigrew (1964) and Daniel Patrick Moynihan (1967), in volumes that received widespread attention, attributed many of Black males' difficulties in U.S. society to their frustrated masculinity caused by father-absent, mother-dominated homes. Against the background of the Vietnam War, Moynihan recommended military service as a way for Black youths to develop a sense of masculinity in "a world away from women, a world run by strong men of unquestioned authority" (p. 42). The recommendation, expedient in the context of a war that needed manpower, reflects a biased view that male dominance is "natural," as well as an alarming willingness to sacrifice young Black men on the altar of masculinity.

The rush to blame the problems of young Black men only on father-absence, and indeed the general concern that boys need a male, heterosexual parent in the home to form a proper masculine gender-role identity, now appears to have been misguided. Evidence does not support the idea that boys need a heterosexual male parent to establish a masculine identity (Pleck, 1995). Researchers now believe a wide variety of family structures can support good child development, as long as those structures include at least one responsible caretaking adult (of any sex) who has a consistent, positive emotional connection to the child (Silverstein & Auerbach, 1999). In fact, these researchers argue that the problems sometimes experienced by boys in single-mother households have little to do with father-absence and everything to do with the way societies treat women and men:

> We speculate that the larger cultural context of male dominance and negative attitudes toward women may interfere with the ability of many single mothers to establish an authoritative parenting style with male children. Within patriarchal culture, boys know that when they become adult men, they will be dominant to every woman, including their mother. This cultural context, unmediated by a male presence, may undermine a single mother's authority with her sons. (p. 403)

Developments in research and changes in public attitudes have created some new perspectives on male gender-role identity. Some theorists now argue that the difficulties males face with respect to masculinity have more to do with role expectations than with identity conflicts. Pleck (1981, 1995), in his **gender-role strain** paradigm for understanding the social construction of masculinity, argues that the very behavior *expected* of males (for example, aggression, emotional constriction) can be dysfunctional, causing problems for males even when they conform to their masculine role. Furthermore, he notes, gender roles are contradictory and inconsistent, so it is difficult not to violate them (witness the simultaneous demands on modern men to be both sensitive and tough). He notes that gender-role strain may be especially important for men, because violating gender roles often has more severe consequences for males than for females. In North America, men are under increasing pressure to participate in child care and domestic work, yet men who do so are sometimes judged to be unmasculine. Men are encouraged to overcome their reluctance to take on "feminine" jobs, yet men who are nurses and secretaries may be the brunt of jokes. Some men may feel caught in a societal double bind in which they are being urged to abandon the old masculine roles yet punished when they try to do so.

Pleck's analysis alerts us to the difference between masculine identity and masculine role. One of the most important outcomes of the debates over the difficulties associated with masculinity has been just that: an increased awareness of the distinctions among gender identity, gender role, and sexual orientation.

Gender Identity, Gender Role, and Sexual Orientation: Distinct Issues

The "identification" theories just described make few explicit distinctions among gender identity, gender role, and sexual orientation. All three are considered aspects of identification with the same-sex parent. Researchers now acknowledge, however, that the three issues are conceptually separate and, in fact, not necessarily correlated. **Gender identity** is defined as the individual's private experience of the self as female or male—a powerful aspect of the self-concept that is formed early in childhood and, in most adults, is extremely resistant to change. Only a tiny percentage of people form a gender identity that is incongruent with their biological sex when no physiological abnormalities are present. **Gender role** refers to the set of behaviors socially defined as appropriate for one's sex. It is now quite clear that an individual can refuse to conform to society's gender-role prescriptions without experiencing any conflict about underlying gender identity. For example, a man can reject the masculine stereotype of aggressiveness and toughness without experiencing any serious doubts about whether he is actually male. **Sexual orientation** refers to an individual's preference for sexual partners of the same or other sex. A person with a heterosexual orientation is attracted to partners of the other sex; one with a homosexual orientation is attracted to partners of the same sex. Despite the early theorists' equation of male homosexuality with femininity, sexual orientation does not necessarily correlate with either gender identity or gender role. For example, a woman who is sexually attracted to other women usually has no conflict or uncertainty about whether she is indeed female, and she may or may not adhere to aspects of the traditional feminine gender role (see Chapter 7 for an extended discussion of sexual orientation). Theories of gender developed subsequent to the psychoanalytic/identification theories tend to draw clearer lines between gender identity and gender roles than the psychoanalytic approach does, and sexual orientation is often treated as a separate issue.

The debate over the merits of the psychoanalytic/identification approach to gender contains the seeds of another, quite different type of viewpoint, one that emphasizes social structure and culture as important determinants of the way females and males develop. As some of Freud's critics noted, the observations he made about parent–child relationships and sexuality were embedded in a particular culture that emphasized male dominance and had a particular, rigid set of ideas about male and female sexuality. Horney's ideas, too, were developed in the context of a society that had strong norms about female–male relationships, a society in which a cult of domesticity for women flourished and men and women were expected to occupy different, complementary spheres. Likewise, the more recent theories of Chodorow and Dinnerstein have not escaped the influence of their cultural context. As Nancy Chodorow (1989) commented after interviewing a number of the women who were pioneers in the psychoanalytic movement in the 1930s,

> I began to realize how much my perceptual and analytic categories had been shaped by my coming of age in the women's movement and my immersion in the recent literature of gender theory. Only with this recognition, that the salience and meaning of gender were products of one's time and place, could I come to understand gender within the fabric of my interviewees' lives. (p. 217)

What if the cultural context that is treated as background in psychoanalytic theory were moved to the foreground? The next theoretical approach, instead of focusing on anatomy and early parent–child relationships, concentrates the search for an understanding of gender on the culture in which these things exist.

SOCIAL STRUCTURE/CULTURAL THEORIES OF GENDER

Psychologists have often focused on identification theories as explanations for the origins and maintenance of gender roles, but the **social structure theories** have long been popular among sociologists and anthropologists. Such an approach stresses not the mechanisms through which children develop gender identity or acquire gender roles but the overarching social arrangements that define and support gender. In other words, instead of focusing on how boys acquire the notion that it is especially important for them to be tough and competent, and how girls learn that it is especially important for them to be pretty and nice, it focuses on *why* society supports their learning of this message and, in its search for answers, emphasizes the different social positions of women and men. Two themes have been the focus for much of this discussion: power and status and the division of labor.

Power and Status

Many theorists now argue that most of the differences between feminine and masculine gender roles come about because of the greater power and status accorded to males than to females in most societies. In most societies, a gender hierarchy exists such that men hold most of the more powerful, high-status positions. For instance, in the United States and Canada, women are drastically underrepresented at the top levels of business and politics and in highly paid, high-status positions generally, whereas they are overrepresented in the lower paid, lower status service occupations (Costello, Miles, & Stone, 1998; Statistics Canada, 1995). According to social structure theory, men develop more dominant (i.e., controlling, assertive, directive) behaviors as an accommodation to more powerful roles, and women develop more subordinate (i.e., compliant, less aggressive, more cooperative and conciliatory) behaviors as a way of accommodating to available roles with less power and status (Eagly & Wood, 1999). The work of Dorothy Dinnerstein and Nancy Chodorow, discussed earlier, exemplifies one branch of the power and status approach to understanding gender. Researchers in a number of areas have demonstrated that "typical" gender differences hold only or most strongly when the sexes are in the common male dominant–female subordinate relationship and that much so-called feminine behavior is actually powerless behavior (Lips, 1991). These findings lead to the hypothesis that if women and men were accorded equal status in society many of the differences in behavior we attribute to gender would disappear. Although this idea will come up at many points in later chapters, let's look briefly now at some examples of how power and status differences can be confused with or can affect gender differences.

NONVERBAL COMMUNICATION   Nancy Henley (1973, 1977; Henley & Freeman, 1995) has argued persuasively that the differences in nonverbal communication between women and men parallel those between less powerful and more powerful people. For example, people tend to "touch downward" in a status hierarchy: It is considered more appropriate for a higher status person to touch a lower status person than vice versa. Similarly, men are more likely to touch women than vice versa (Henley, 1973; Major, Schmidlen, & Williams, 1990). Also, both women and subordinates are characterized by controlled, circumspect nonverbal behavior; men and people in authority are characterized by expansive behavior. Weitz (1976) showed that the nonverbal behaviors of women in interaction with men were significantly related to the males' scores on dominance and affiliation measures. Nonverbally, women were more submissive with dominant male partners and more dominant with submissive male partners. Men showed no evidence of making such adjustments, nor did women when interacting with other women. Weitz suggests that women are specifically attuned to men's nonverbal behavior because women are so frequently subordinate in status to men.

The idea that "masculine" and "feminine" nonverbal behaviors are reflections of status differences suggests that similar nonverbal asymmetries might be found between other groups (racial, ethnic, cultural) that differ in status. This possibility is discussed by Henley and LaFrance (1984), who predict that any group that is seen as inferior to another will tend, in relation to that other group, to be more submissive, more readable, and more sensitive to others' nonverbal behavior, as well as more accommodating and adaptive to those nonverbal behaviors. This idea is reinforced by findings that nonverbal sensitivity is linked to authority rather than gender (Snodgrass, 1985, 1992).

WOMEN IN ORGANIZATIONS   Rosabeth Moss Kanter's (1975, 1976) pioneering research on women in the workplace began as an attempt to discover the gender differences that would explain the stereotype that women make poorer leaders than men. Her conclusion was that people in token or dead-end positions, whether women or men, showed poor leadership and success skills. They were rigid and hostile toward outsiders and powerful superiors, and they had more concern with socializing than with career advancement. It was the nature of the position, rather than the gender of the person occupying the position, that was linked to these behaviors. The problem was that many more women than men were stuck in such positions.

> I could find nothing about women in my own research, and that of others, that was not equally true of men in some situations. For example, some women do have low job aspirations, but so do men who are in positions of blocked opportunity. Some women managers are too interfering and coercive, but so are men who have limited power and responsibility in their organizations. Some women in professional careers behave in stereotyped ways and tend to regard others of their sex with disdain, but so do men who are tokens—the only member of their group at work. (1976, p. 56)

Thus, Kanter concluded, many of the apparent gender differences in leadership and organizational behavior have no necessary relationship with gender. Instead, they could be traced to the social structure: women's more precarious positions in organizations and their lack of power relative to men.

Researchers who have followed up on Kanter's work have discovered that the effects she noted in the way token female leaders were perceived by others—high visibility, contrast with other workers, and the rigid limiting of roles—do not happen to just anyone who holds a token position. Rather, these effects are more likely to happen to women who hold token positions in occupations deemed gender-inappropriate for them (Yoder, 1991, 1994). Apparently, the organizational environment cannot be isolated from the more general social context of discrimination against women. Thus, merely increasing the number of women so that women are no longer token representatives of their sex will not remove gender discrimination in the workplace. In fact, Yoder (1991) argues, as women increase in numbers, they are more likely to be perceived as a threat and treated in ways designed to hold them back: sexual harassment, salary inequities, and limited opportunities for advancement. Such a reaction would be a direct response to the possibility of a change in women's power relative to men.

"RAPE-PRONE" VERSUS "RAPE-FREE" SOCIETIES   Gender differences in rape and sexual assault are also linked to power differences. One gender difference to which people often point as an example of the inevitability of a "war" between the sexes is sexual aggressiveness. In its ultimate form, rape, sexual aggressiveness does differentiate the sexes: Men rape; women, by and large, do not. Yet even this difference is attenuated or magnified by the power relations between women and men in a given society. After studying 186 societies, Sanday (1981b) concluded that those in which rape was prevalent were characterized by interpersonal violence, male dominance, and separation of the sexes, whereas those in which rape was a relatively rare occurrence were societies in which male and female qualities were equally valued.

The Division of Labor

The nonverbal communication and the organizational behavior examples just discussed suggest that one important aspect of the status differences between the sexes is that they do different kinds of work: Women are the secretaries, men are the executives; women are the lab technicians, men are the scientists; men are the hunters and warriors, women stay home with the children. Anthropologists have been embroiled for years in controversies over whether the sexual division of labor is a cause or a consequence of the status differences between women and men; most likely, the process is a kind of vicious circle. It should be noted, however, that the way work is divided between women and men in our own society practically guarantees that women will have less control over economic resources than men do. Men's greater control over economic resources, achieved through better jobs with higher salaries and through more continuous participation in the paid labor force, creates the expectation that women (and children) will depend on men for support. Under this set of expectations, which is communicated to children long before they understand the economic realities on which it is based, it is little wonder that girls and boys, women and men, tend to make choices that emphasize different aspects of their skills, aspirations, and preferences. These choices lead males and females into different types of work, and the cycle repeats itself. This is one way in which the division of labor by sex and the parallel male–female difference in control over resources contribute to gender differences in behavior.

There is another way in which the division of labor may contribute to gender differences in behavior: "Women and men seek to accommodate sex-typical roles by acquiring the specific skills and resources linked to successful role performance and by adapting their social behavior to role requirements" (Eagly & Wood, 1999, pp. 412–413). Women and men know what they are expected to do, so they try to learn the skills they need to do it properly, to fit in with social expectations. According to **social role theory** (Eagly, 1987), women and men are expected to have the qualities that fit them for the tasks they normally carry out. For example, in North America women normally do much of the childcare, nursing, and social work and are expected to be nurturing and compassionate. Men normally fill most of the roles involving military service, political office, and executive positions and are expected to be tough and decisive. Thus, the qualities that are required to perform tasks typically assigned to women or men become stereotypic of women and men. In a circular fashion, the gender stereotypes make it easier for women and men to prepare for, be selected for, and perform roles that are gender-stereotypic.

Social structure theories do not assume that gender roles are completely arbitrary, depending only on the whims of particular societies. Rather, they assume that societies shape gender roles in response to factors such as men's greater size and strength, women's reproductive activities, and the activities necessary for social and economic stability in a particular culture (Eagly & Wood, 1999). Some of these factors (e.g., the fact that women are the ones who bear and breastfeed children) are common across societies and so should help to shape gender roles in similar ways in different cultures. This, according to social structural theorists, is why certain kinds of female–male differences in behavior are more common than others. For example, it is more common to find societies in which women do more of the work of child care than men do than the reverse.

Not all social scientists emphasize culture as the driving force behind the construction of gender, however. Some theorists argue that the why of female–male differences can be found in biology.

EVOLUTIONARY THEORIES OF GENDER

One set of theories about differences between women and men has stressed the possible genetic bases for behavioral differences between the sexes. According to this approach, the power differences between the sexes are not the result of learning and culture but the natural and inevitable outcome of our genetic heritage. **Evolutionary theories** were popular in North America around the turn of the century, and they have gained visibility again.

Functionalism

The functionalist school of psychology was concerned with how an organism's behavior and consciousness were functional for its survival (Shields, 1975). Men and women, it was thought, had different and complementary functions for the survival of the human race and had probably evolved somewhat differently to fulfill these functions. Psychologists using this theoretical approach came up with generalizations about sex differences in temperament that had implications for a wide range of behaviors. Perhaps the best known of these generalizations is the notion of a "maternal instinct" in women. Many functionalists held that women had evolved with an inborn emotional tendency toward nurturance—a tendency that could be triggered by contact with a helpless infant. Because the biological tasks of pregnancy, childbirth, and lactation are fulfilled by women, these theorists reasoned that the presence of a maternal instinct in women but not in men made evolutionary sense. The behavioral differences thought to result from the differential presence of such an instinct, however, went far beyond those directed specifically toward infants. Herbert Spencer (1891, cited in Shields, 1975), for example, felt that women devote most of their energy to preparation for pregnancy and lactation, with the result that they have little energy left over to develop other qualities. His ideas, along with those of Clarke (1873), were used to justify the exclusion of women from higher education, as discussed at the beginning of this chapter. Edward L. Thorndike (1914, cited in Shields, 1975), an eminent American psychologist, contended that a number of instincts were relevant to the female reproductive role. He described, for example, a nursing instinct manifested in a strong tendency to nurture others. This instinct, he suggested, is the source of women's general moral superiority to men. He also felt that women have an instinctive tendency to submit to mastery by men. Thus, Thorndike conceived of women as naturally both more nurturant and more submissive than men—a viewpoint that has gathered little empirical support but that lingers on in many people's assumptions about male–female differences.

Sociobiology

In recent decades, we have seen the emergence of sweeping claims about male–female differences by proponents of human sociobiology. **Sociobiology** rests on the notion that, in the interests of the survival of their own particular genes, women and men have evolved different strategies of sexual selection and reproduction. Men, who can produce millions of sperm with relatively little investment of energy, have evolved with an innate tendency to devote energy to short-term mating, fertilizing as many women as possible and maximizing the chances that their own genes will survive. Women, for whom re-production (both the production of eggs and the gestation of embryos) involves a greater and more time-consuming commitment, have evolved with a tendency to be sex-ually selective, choosing only the best mates and trying to trick them into monogamy. Proponents of this evolutionary approach have argued that a variety of sex differences in behavioral dispositions have evolved because of these differing sexual strategies of women and men (Buss, 1995). For instance, because men have competed with men for sexual access to women, men have evolved to favor violence and competition. Because women have had to emphasize long-term mating, they have evolved to seek out men who are particularly successful and able to provide resources for their children.

As biologist Ruth Hubbard (1990) notes, the assumption of greater investment by females in producing eggs and gestating embryos than by males in producing sperm is difficult to verify. How does one quantify the amount of energy involved in the production of a lifetime of seminal fluid and sperm, for instance? Moreover, there is no evidence to support the idea that stronger and more powerful men have more children than weaker ones do. Researchers do indeed find differences between human females and males in their sexual behavior: Males hold more permissive attitudes to-ward casual sex than females do, and males tend to have more partners than females do (Oliver & Hyde, 1993). These findings are consistent with sociobiological theo-ries, but they are also consistent with the predictions of other theories (such as social learning theory, to be discussed next) that emphasize learning attitudes and roles from cultural models and the media. Yet evolutionary approaches to social behavior claim that underneath our cultural trappings lie genetically based human universals: sexual aggressivity among men, a sexual division of labor that assigns child care to women, and an innate desire for sexual variety among men but not women. Moreover, the pro-ponents of this theory argue that the genetic basis of these social patterns makes them more or less inescapable, not for individuals but for humans as a species.

It is perhaps precisely because sociobiology offers such a direct challenge to views about the malleability of human possibilities that it has received so much press. In its earliest incarnations, the theory rested largely on inferences from nonhuman evidence, but its apparent scientific respectability made it a useful source of ammunition for pro-ponents of the status quo and a red flag to people concerned with equality between the sexes. The theory implies that such human social behaviors as war, rape, and racism have been "built in" through our evolution and that it is impossible to make funda-mental changes in the relations between the sexes. Although an ideal, objective scien-

tific process would dictate a dispassionate and careful search for supporting and countervailing evidence before a theory was catapulted into the realm of public debate,
such an ideal process has not been achieved here, nor historically in other areas of the
scientific treatment of the woman–man issue.

Traditionally, the field of sociobiology has been concerned with the social behaviors and characteristics of animals. Researchers in this field have uncovered fascinating
facts about the diversity and complexity of the social lives of different species and have
searched for links between social behavior and biology. In 1975, E. O. Wilson, an expert in the behavior of insects, wrote a controversial book in which he proposed the
thesis that *all* social behavior (including human social behavior) has a biological basis.
Wilson's version of sociobiology is based on the premise that human behaviors and
many aspects of human social organization have evolved, like such physical characteristics as the thumb or the capacity to digest certain foods, through a process of adaptation through natural selection.

The claims of Wilsonian sociobiology are couched in the language of Darwin's
(1871/1967) theory of evolution—a theory developed to explain the way the physical
characteristics of animals changed over successive generations to favor those that were
most conducive to species survival. This theory postulates that a physical characteristic is
adaptive if it contributes to the *maximum fitness* of the species, where "maximum fitness"
means being able to reach sexual maturity and leave healthy descendants. Thus, for example, if a certain skin or fur coloration enables a particular type of animal to avoid being eaten by predators and thus to reach sexual maturity and to reproduce, the genes for
that particular coloration are more likely to be passed on to the next generation than are
the genes for alternative colorations. Over successive generations, then, the protective
color will become increasingly common in that species, a process known as adaptation
through natural selection. By similar logic, if a male animal of a certain species is more
likely to have surviving offspring by mating with as many females as possible, and if a female animal is more likely to have surviving offspring by being sexually selective and mating with only the best available male, then those propensities toward male promiscuity
and female selectivity will be passed on at higher rates than male selectivity and female
promiscuity, and they will eventually become increasingly common in that species.

Although behavior always reflects some inherent limits in physical capacity imposed by the genes (e.g., humans cannot fly), the idea that such complex human behaviors as competitiveness, the selection of sexual partners, or altruism are genetically
encoded aspects of the human "biogram" (Wilson's shorthand for "biological program") that have evolved through Darwinian natural selection is a still dubious ex-
trapolation of the theory. In fact, Darwin himself was skeptical about the usefulness of
sexual selection processes for explaining behavior in modern human societies, arguing
that modern humans were more guided by foresight and reason than by an instinctive
pull toward genetic fitness in mate selection. He noted that, under conditions of civ-
ilization, men were attracted to women by their mental charms, wealth, and social position (Eagly & Wood, 1999). However, Darwin's successors have swept aside such
doubts and argued strongly for the applicability of evolutionary theory to human social behavior and, in particular, to human sex differences.

In an attempt to demonstrate that human mating preferences are consistent with
the predictions of evolutionary theory, Donald Buss and his colleagues (Buss, 1989;
Buss et al., 1990) conducted a large-scale study across 37 cultures in which respondents

were asked to specify the characteristics they desired in a mate. Evolutionary theory predicts that men would be more likely than women to specify youth and attractiveness in a mate, and women would be more likely to specify that their mate should be older and have significant resources. These predictions were upheld across cultures, leading evolutionary psychologists to point to such universality as evidence for powerful "built-in" sex differences that have evolved over time and become an innate part of human nature. This interpretation has been challenged, however. Recently, Alice Eagly and Wendy Wood (1999) argued that male–female differences in mate selection criteria stem from the division of labor by sex. In their view, a social structural approach predicts that in societies where the roles and status of women and men are relatively equal there would be fewer differences between the sexes in the criteria they chose as important for selecting a mate than in societies where the roles and status of women and men were very different. In more egalitarian societies, both women and men would place less emphasis on selecting mates whose qualities matched a sexual division of labor because there would be less expectation of such a rigid division. A man does not select a woman only on the basis of her reproductive capacity if he expects her to have two children and then return to the workforce. A woman does not select a man only on the basis of his ability to be a good provider if she expects to have her own career.

Eagly and Wood were able to test their prediction by reanalyzing the data from Buss's 37-culture study. When all the cultures were considered as a group, they found that men showed a reliable tendency to value *physical attractiveness* and *good cooking and housekeeping skills* in a potential mate more than women did. They also found that women placed more importance than men did on *good earning capacity* in a mate. As well, women showed a preference for older men, and men showed a preference for younger women across all 37 cultures. However, the most interesting findings with respect to their predictions occurred when they rated the sample of 37 cultures according to the level of gender equality, using indices of Gender Empowerment and Gender-Related Development available from the United Nations: As the gender equality in societies increased, the tendency to pick mates on the basis of a gendered division of labor decreased. Thus, in more egalitarian cultures, the tendency for women to select men on the basis of their earning capacity and for men to select women on the basis of their domestic skills was weaker than in cultures where there were large power and status differences between women and men. These findings are compatible with a social structural explanation of female–male differences and suggest that the apparent universality of certain mate selection preferences (and with it, the notion that such preferences are biologically built in to our species through evolution) can be challenged. Eagly and Wood (1999) call for future research that is "systematically designed to represent cultures with differing forms of social organization and levels of gender equality" (p. 420).

Other scientific arguments (e.g., Bleier, 1984; Fausto-Sterling, 1992) against human sociobiology tend to emphasize three themes: (1) the lack of evidence that any of the social behaviors in question are linked to any specific gene or configuration of genes; (2) the use of the circular logic that if a behavior is maintained across generations it must be genetic, and because it is genetic, it will inevitably continue to be maintained; and (3) the selective inclusion or omission of evidence based on animal behavior to bolster arguments for the genetic basis of human behavior.

Addressing the second point, the use of circular logic, Anne Fausto-Sterling (1992) suggests that the apparent universality of a behavior is, in fact, no guarantee that it is genetic rather than learned. Her counterexamples include the story of a troop of Japanese macaques who came to feast on grain that had been spread on a sandy beach. Researchers observing the monkeys noted that at first they slowly picked out the food from the sand, grain by grain. Eventually, however, one young female monkey picked up a handful of sand and grain, carried it to the water, and threw it in. The sand sank and the food floated, enabling her to scoop it off the water. This new, efficient method of separating the sand from the grain was quickly learned by other members of the troop and continues to be passed on to succeeding generations. Yet, as Fausto-Sterling notes, an outside observer, unaware of the history of the behavior, might guess from its apparent universality that it was genetically based.

Indeed, many researchers have now concluded that a wide variety of behaviors in primates are culturally (rather than genetically) transmitted. A recent article by several top field researchers lists 39 different behavior patterns, including types of tool usage, grooming, and courtship behaviors, that are present in some chimpanzee groups but absent in other genetically identical (and often geographically nearby) groups. Furthermore, these experts note that there is tremendous variation in these behaviors even within chimpanzee communities—another argument that the behaviors are culturally transmitted (Whiten et al., 1999). These findings illustrate that it may be unwise to assume that variations in social behavior, even among our primate cousins, are necessarily due to evolutionary pressures.

Writing on the dangers of ignoring unwelcome animal data, Ruth Bleier (1984) lists a number of examples that run counter to the Wilsonian thesis that males are "programmed" for promiscuity and females are instinctively more domestic: the South American male rhea bird, which builds a nest and then tends about 50 eggs that are laid in it by several females; the female jacana bird, which lays eggs in the nests of several male birds, leaving each male to incubate the eggs and care for the young; the seabird pairs that take turns sitting on the nest while the partner goes out to sea in search of food; the emperor penguin father, which incubates the egg in a fold of skin over his feet. Further examples of the variety of behavior among animal species are provided by Sarah Hrdy (1981), whose extensive descriptions of relations between the sexes among different groups of primates illustrate that a pattern of male–female differences involving male promiscuity and female sexual selectivity, male dominance and competitiveness and female subordination is neither "natural" nor universal among these, our closest animal relatives.

In summary, the sociobiological notion that gender differences in behavior stem from different genetically based strategies evolved by females and males to maximize their reproductive fitness, while intriguing, has not been proven. If a genetic basis should be established for some of the behaviors in question, to date scientists have no way of knowing whether their persistence is the result of random genetic events or (as sociobiologists argue) of adaptations for fitness maximization (Fausto-Sterling, 1992). This is not to say that there is no possible merit in an evolutionary approach to understanding human behavior; in fact, many researchers (e.g., Eals & Silverman, 1994) are amassing data to explore various possibilities of genetic components to human behavior. In many respects, however, the theory defies proof, and claims for or against the evolutionary basis of female–male differences are more re-flective of the claimant's preference for a particular explanation than of any conclu-sive evidence for that explanation.

The three theoretical approaches discussed to this point have all focused on the reasons for gender differences. Psychoanalytic/identification theories locate the ori-gins of the differences in anatomy and examine the early development of parent–child relationships. Social structure/cultural theories pinpoint culturally based power and status differences between females and males as the reason for gender differences in behavior. Evolutionary theories point to the genes as the cause for male–female dif-ferences. Let's turn now to three theoretical approaches that focus on the "how" rather than the "why" of gender differences and similarities: social learning, cognitive developmental, and social interaction process theories.

SOCIAL LEARNING THEORY

Social learning theory (Bandura, 1977) suggests that the child develops both gen-der identity and gender role through a learning process that involves modeling, imi-tation, and reinforcement. The theory rests on the assumption that boys learn to be masculine and girls to be feminine because gender-role-appropriate behavior is re-warded and gender-role-inappropriate behavior is punished or ignored. Children learn which behaviors are gender-role appropriate by observing and imitating adult and peer models, as well as through trial and error in their own behavior. Social learning the-ory suggests that a child is most likely to imitate a model who is readily available and perceived as powerful, nurturant, and similar to the self (Mischel, 1970). According to this viewpoint, parental models, particularly the same-sex parent, are the most ef-fective in influencing the child's behavior. The theory suggests that parents and other socializing agents map out gender roles for the child, and then the child is differen-tially reinforced for following the appropriate one. Children begin to be aware of the two gender roles as early as the first year of life (M. Lewis & Weinraub, 1979; Poulin-Dubois, Serbin, Kenyon, & Derbyshire, 1994), and as early as age 3, children imitate same-sex models more than other-sex models (Bussey & Bandura, 1984).

As the child is repeatedly reminded that he is a boy or she is a girl and differen-tially reinforced for doing boy-things or girl-things, it gradually becomes rewarding for him to think of himself as a boy and for her to think of herself as a girl. Thus, through observation, imitation, and reinforcement, the formation of an appropriate gender role precedes and lays the groundwork for establishing gender identity.

David Lynn (1966) developed a theory of gender role and identity development that in some ways forms a bridge between the psychoanalytic and social learning ap-proaches. Although Lynn's theory uses the psychoanalytic concept of identification to refer to an individual's internalization of the characteristics of a person or role, it also emphasizes the learning of behavior through observation, imitation, and reinforcement—the basic concepts of social learning theory.

Lynn's theory makes some of the same predictions about gender differences as Freud's does, although for different reasons. Both theories, for example, suggest that the male will follow the rules of his role more rigidly than the female will follow hers. Both also predict that males and females will both tend to devalue femininity. However, whereas Freud saw these results as a virtually inevitable aspect of human nature, Lynn's theory suggests that they are a direct result of the childrearing practices and social structure of our society. In this respect, his work anticipates the ideas of Dinnerstein (1976) and Chodorow (1978), described earlier in this chapter.

Lynn suggests, as did Freud, that the first typical human identification of both female and male infants is with the mother and that the male must shift from this early identification if masculine role identification is to be achieved. In contrast to Freud, however, Lynn emphasized the role of the cultural situation in this process. Because fathers generally spend many fewer hours than mothers and other female caregivers do with children, boys do not have as clear a model for masculinity as girls do for femininity. Thus, Lynn (1966) argues, "the father, as a model for the boy, is analogous to a map showing the major outline but lacking most details, whereas the mother, as a model for the girl, might be thought of as a detailed map" (p. 466).

According to Lynn, the boy attempting to be masculine is helped along not so much by modeling his father, who is often unavailable, but by following the stereotyped prescriptions of the masculine role spelled out by his mother and teachers. These socializing agents reward typical masculine behavior and punish behavioral indications of femininity. Gradually, the boy learns to identify not with his father but with the stereotyped masculine role. The girl, however, maintains an identification with her mother. In support of this notion, Lynn (1979) cites studies finding greater mother–daughter than father–son similarity.

Lynn postulates that the necessity for the boy to learn the masculine role in the relative absence of male models and through early and vague demands backed by punishment creates anxiety about gender-role behavior. Such anxiety causes the boy to adhere very rigidly to the rules of his role—a situation reminiscent of Freud's idea that males develop stronger superegos than females do. In fact, boys do seem more concerned than girls with playing the "right" gender role: Boys, for example, are more likely than girls to attend to same-sex models, to imitate same-sex models, and to reject behaviors and objects associated with the other sex (Bussey & Bandura, 1984; Bussey & Perry, 1982; Downs, 1983).

Because boys are so often punished for acting "girl-like," Lynn suggests, they develop a dislike of and contempt for females and femininity. Girls, who are not punished so early or so severely for "boyish" behavior, do not develop a similar degree of hostility toward males and masculinity. Thus, the male contempt for women, which Freud explained as a natural result of women's "inferior" anatomy, Lynn sees as stemming from our culture's process of male socialization. Similarly, Lynn, like Karen Horney, explains any tendency for women to feel inferior as due to cultural prejudice against them rather than to their sense of dismay over not possessing a penis.

People who have witnessed the extreme upset sometimes occasioned in parents by a young son's "feminine" behavior may well find Lynn's explanation of male gender anxiety appealing. One distraught mother approached her psychology professor panic-stricken because she had found her 3-year-old son playing with her cosmetics. Having discovered this little boy with lipstick on his face, she was terrified that he would "grow up to be a homosexual." One can only imagine the degree of anxiety and confusion that must have been engendered in this little boy by that encounter with his mother, so out of proportion to the seriousness of his "misbehavior" was the intensity of her reaction. Whatever the reason, boys are subject to more intense gender socialization pressure from parents than girls are (Lytton & Romney, 1991; Maccoby & Jacklin, 1974; C.L. Martin, 1990), and they also exert this type of pressure on one another. Even among toddlers, boys are more likely than girls to be scolded by their same-sex peers for participating in other-sex activities (Fagot, 1985).

Social learning theory may appear, at first glance, to treat the child as a relatively passive learner, but the socialization process is much more complex and interactive than such a view implies. Children's influence on their parents' behavior may be just as strong as the reverse (Maccoby, 1992). For instance, an initially small difference between a female and male infant in response to comforting may gradually be magnified because it produces, through differential reinforcement of the parents for comforting behavior, differences in the degree of comforting the parents will provide the two infants. The different levels of comforting behavior directed toward the two infants will then cause greater differences between them, which will in turn cause the parents to treat the two even more differently, and so on. Some theorists have suggested that many aspects of gender roles may be learned through reciprocal role learning: learning one gender role through interacting with a person (e.g., a parent) playing the complementary one (Lamb, Owen, & Chase-Lansdale, 1979). The process works through subtle reinforcement: "Interaction proceeds most smoothly (i.e., positive reinforcement occurs) when the behavior of the daughter meshes smoothly with the masculine behavior of the father. This is most likely to occur when she behaves in a feminine manner" (p. 94).

On the whole, there is a great deal of evidence that social learning plays a part in learning gender roles. For example, knowledge about gender stereotypes increases and becomes more complex with age from preschool to college (Leahy & Shirk, 1984; C. L. Martin, 1993; C. L. Martin, Wood, & Little, 1990), and the trend toward same-sex modeling increases during the same period (Bussey & Bandura, 1984). Children whose mothers model nontraditional (for women) activities in the home are less likely than other children to show preferences for gender-typed activities, whereas children whose fathers adhere to traditional gender roles display more knowledge of what activities and occupations are generally associated with each gender (Serbin, Powlishta, & Gulko, 1993). It is clear, however, that social learning is, by itself, insufficient to explain the development of gender roles and gender identity. In the first place, direct reinforcement does not play as strong a part as one might think. For example, parents do not treat their male and female children differently enough to account for gender-role differences (Lytton & Romney, 1991; Maccoby & Jacklin, 1974), and young children are apparently impervious to reinforcement from certain sources, with boys responding more to male peers and females responding more to teachers and female peers (Fagot, 1985). In the second place, the importance of imitation in learning gender roles is not as clear-cut as the theory predicts. Children do not always select same-sex models to imitate (Maccoby & Jacklin, 1974; Raskin & Israel, 1981), and the imitation process may be more complex than simply choosing a single model in a given situation. Research by D. G. Perry and Bussey (1979) indicates that children may observe the different frequencies with which males and females, in general, perform certain behaviors in given situations and may then use these observations to construct abstract models of female-appropriate and male-appropriate behavior. Once a child has constructed these abstract models, he or she is more likely to imitate a particular same-sex person if that person usually behaves in ways that fit the child's model for sex-appropriate behavior. Thus, a girl might not imitate the behavior of a mother whom she sees as an atypical female, and a boy might imitate his father only when the father behaves in ways the boy sees as representative of males in general.

The modification of social learning theory presented by D. G. Perry and Bussey (1979) incorporates a view of the child as an active participant in the socialization process and implies that cognitive abilities are important in this process. A similar view has been elaborated by Albert Bandura (1986), who reconceptualized social learning theory as **social cognitive theory.** This theory suggests that, although children may initially learn gender roles through external rewards and punishments, as they mature they begin to regulate their own actions through internal rewards and punishments. Research shows that children learn at a very young age to discriminate between conduct that is appropriate for girls and conduct that is appropriate for boys and then begin to evaluate and regulate their own behavior based on this knowledge (Bussey & Bandura, 1992). For example, 4-year-old boys anticipated that they would feel good about themselves if they played with a truck and bad about themselves if they played with a doll. These anticipated feelings apparently guided their behavior when they were presented with these toys. Boys presented with "feminine" toys used a variety of strategies to avoid playing with them: objected to the experimenter that they did not like dolls, tried to have the dolls removed from the room, or used the beaters in a cooking set as guns or drills. One 7-year-old boy who was induced to change diapers on a baby doll for the filming of a videotape later commented, "It's the most awful thing I have ever done" (p. 1247).

The external approval and disapproval children use to shape their personal internal standards of behavior do not come just from parents or other specific, important adults but from peers. According to one recent theory of **group socialization** (J. R. Harris, 1995), peers are the mediators and interpreters of cultural views of gender. This theory postulates that children become socialized primarily by identifying with their peer group and taking on that group's norms for attitudes and behavior. According to this theory, cultural knowledge and behavior are transmitted not directly from parents to their children but from the parents' peer group and other cultural sources to the children's peer group. The peer groups filter cultural transmissions. For example, children quickly learn what behaviors from their home context are acceptable to their peer group. They do not transfer behavior learned at home to the peer group unless it is shared and approved by most of the other children. If children come from atypical homes, they censor their home-learned behavior, and it tends not to get transferred to the group.

Each of these later approaches to the social learning process emphasizes cognition and the meanings that the child learns to attach to gender-linked behavior. The theoretical approach described next emphasizes cognition as the main issue in the development of gender-consistent behavior.

COGNITIVE DEVELOPMENTAL THEORY

Cognitive developmental theory (Kohlberg, 1966; Kohlberg & Ullian, 1974) proposes that gender, like other concepts, cannot be learned until a child reaches a particular stage of intellectual development. Between the ages of 3 and 5, a child acquires **gender constancy**—an understanding that a person's gender is fixed and cannot be altered by a change in hairstyle, dress, or name. Before that age, according to Kohlberg, although a child may have learned that people can be categorized as either male or female, she or he may sometimes make errors in classifying the self or others and think that arbitrary changes in classification can occur (e.g., a little girl may say, "When I used to be a boy . . .". Slaby and Frey (1975) describe the process of gender identity formation as having three stages: (1) an awareness that two sexes exist (attained around age 3), followed by (2) an understanding that gender does not change over time (stability), followed in turn by (3) an awareness that gender remains unchanged across situations and behaviors (constancy). The idea that children do not understand the permanence of gender categories until achieving a certain stage of cognitive development is rooted in Jean Piaget's (1954) theory that children's cognitive development occurs in stages. Piaget states that children do not have an understanding of physical constancy (e.g., constancy of mass or volume) before approximately ages 4 to 7.

According to the cognitive developmental approach, once the child has categorized herself or himself with some certainty as female or male, she or he will use this self-categorization as an organizing focus for attaching value to behaviors. The child will attach higher value to gender-appropriate behaviors and will find the performance of gender-appropriate behaviors more reinforcing than gender-inappropriate behaviors. In other words, gender-appropriate behaviors acquire a meaning that makes them self-reinforcing for the child, whereas gender-inappropriate behaviors acquire negative connotations and are avoided. The little girl embraces "feminine" values; the little boy adopts "masculine" ones. At this stage, the child may identify with the same-sex parent, using the parent as one of many guides for establishing correct behavior for her or his gender category. Other models, such as peers, television, and stories, will also be used, and rewards and punishment meted out to the child will be used by the child as additional cues to appropriate behavior.

Cognitive developmental theory portrays the child as actively searching for cues as to how to behave competently and correctly, rather than as being passively shaped by environmental forces. In the process of seeking out the correct way to behave, the child passes through a stage of great rigidity with respect to gender roles. Children ages 6 to 7 often have oversimplified, inflexible views of the two gender roles and adhere tenaciously to gender stereotypes. At this age, for example, a child may refuse to believe that women can be physicians or carpenters, even if the child's own mother holds one of these positions. It is as if the child at this stage is trying to solidify a sense of gender identity by renouncing any form of ambiguity. At a later age, secure in a gender identity, the child becomes less uncomfortable about occasional deviations from the "appropriate" gender role and less rigid about gender stereotypes.

Cognitive developmental theory receives support from a variety of studies that find that children, especially boys, value their own sex more highly (Bussey & Perry, 1982; Etaugh, Levine, & Mennella, 1984; C.L. Martin, 1989; Powlishta, 1990). Also supportive of the theory is an accumulation of evidence that children increase their accuracy at gender differentiation and labeling from ages 2 to 5 (Coker, 1984; Etaugh & Duits, 1990; Kuhn, Nash, & Brucken, 1978; Reis & Wright, 1982). Moreover, between the ages of 3 and 8, children show a progression in their views of gender stereotypes that is related to other measures of cognitive flexibility (Coker, 1984; Leahy & Shirk, 1984); this same progression has also been found in other cultures (Munroe, Shimmin, & Munroe, 1984).

Some research findings are inconsistent with cognitive developmental theory, however. Particularly contentious is the issue of *when* gender identity is established. As discussed in Chapter 5, Money and Ehrhardt's (1972) work suggests that some important aspects of gender identity are formed by the age of 2, and changing a child's assigned sex after that age proves difficult. Moreover, C.L. Martin and Halverson (1983) have shown that the age at which gender constancy is demonstrated depends on the type of test used; children responding to a real, as opposed to a pretend, situation show signs of gender constancy as young as age 3.

Cognitive developmental theory indicates that the adoption of gender roles occurs as a result of identifying with a gender category, but much gender-typing occurs *before* the age of gender constancy (Downs, 1983; Maccoby & Jacklin, 1974; C. L. Martin & Little, 1990). Preferences for gender-stereotyped toys and behaviors have been found among children who have not yet developed gender constancy (Bussey & Bandura, 1984, 1992; O'Keefe & Hyde, 1983). It has been suggested that social learning theory and cognitive developmental theory may account for two different aspects of the formation of gender role and gender identity: Early sex-typing may stem from differential reinforcement and observational learning, as social learning theory proposes, whereas the sex-typing that occurs after the child has achieved gender constancy may be due to deliberate same-sex modeling, in accordance with cognitive developmental theory (Basow, 1986). Another suggestion, based on a comprehensive study of children ages 5 to 12, is that cognitive development and social learning are associated with different aspects of the process of adopting gender roles (Serbin et al., 1993). According to this research, cognitive development is most strongly associated with *cognitive* aspects of gender-typing such as knowledge of stereotypes and flexibility in applying them; social learning is most strongly linked to *affective* aspects of gender-typing such as preferences for gender-appropriate activities, occupations, and peers.

THEORIES INTEGRATING SOCIAL LEARNING AND COGNITIVE DEVELOPMENT APPROACHES

Although some support exists for the premises of both social learning and cognitive developmental theories, neither one seems capable of explaining fully the development and maintenance of gender roles and gender identity. New theoretical approaches that incorporate new research findings and integrate and extend these two classic theories are required. Several such approaches have been proposed, including gender schema theory (Bem, 1981, 1985; C.L. Martin & Halverson, 1981); sex roles as rules theory (Constantinople, 1979); and gender roles as developmental pathways (J. Archer, 1984). Of these, gender schema theory has had the most impact to date.

Gender Schema Theory

A **schema** is a cognitive structure (a network of associations or set of interrelated ideas) that guides and organizes the way an individual processes and makes sense of information. An individual person holds a variety of schemas, each one helping to structure information into categories that are important to him or her. A person might (or might not) have a schema with respect to age, to ethnicity, to gender, to particular occupations, and to proper versus rude behavior. These schemas are used in evaluating and assimilating new information. Information that is relevant to a person and fits a schema held by that person is attended to and processed quickly, whereas information that does not relate to an existing schema is ignored. Thus, a person who is **gender-schematic** (one with a strong gender schema) would spontaneously sort people, characteristics, and behaviors into masculine and feminine categories, regardless of their differences on other dimensions unrelated to gender. He or she would, for example, be more likely to remember things relevant to gender than things relevant to nationality and to make faster, easier, and more confident decisions about the applicability to the self or others of gender-related than nationality-related traits. An individual who is **gender-aschematic** (one with a very weak gender schema) would be unlikely to categorize ideas, behaviors, and characteristics according to gender. It has been argued that when interacting with and forming initial impressions of others, people activate their gender schemas more quickly than schemas based on less easily observable attributes. The easy activation of such schemas can both stem from and reinforce gender stereotypes (Deaux & Major, 1987).

People who hold themselves to rigid standards of femininity and masculinity may be strongly gender-schematic. As Bem (1985) suggests, highly masculine or feminine individuals may differ from others "not in their *ability* to organize information on the basis of gender but in their *threshold* for doing so spontaneously" (p. 197). Bem's own research and that of others (Signorella, Bigler, & Liben, 1993) provides some support for this idea. However, research shows that a person need not adhere to gender stereotypes to be gender-schematic. For example, a woman who does not describe herself in stereotypically feminine ways may still process information readily in terms of gender, perhaps because she is interested in gender for academic or political reasons (Freedman & Lips, 1996).

Two cultural conditions explain the widespread reliance on gender schema for organizing information. First, social ideology and customs construct a large number of associations between gender and other qualities, behaviors, concepts, and categories (e.g., there is a long list of behaviors considered feminine or masculine). Second, society assigns great functional importance to gender distinction, using gender as a basis for many norms, taboos, group membership, and institutional arrangements (Bem, 1985). Thus, "gender has come to have cognitive primacy over many other social categories because the culture has made it so" (p. 212). Children are taught not only a large network of sex-related associations that can form the basis for a gender schema but also the message that "the dichotomy between male and female has intensive and extensive relevance to virtually every domain of human experience" (p. 212).

Furthermore, every association that makes up the network of associations that we call a gender schema need not be taught directly to a child. Instead, children may construct distinctions based on dimensions of meaning that emerge as part of their experience. Beverly Fagot and Mary Leinbach (1993) speculate that a young child's abstract generalizations about women and men "may have their roots in the infant's different sensory experience of men and women—their shape and texture, the sounds they make, their movement patterns" (p. 220). They note research demonstrating that 4-year-old children

> assign bears, fire, and something rough to boys and men, while butterflies, hearts, and flowers are for women and girls. We strongly doubt that such notions are taught directly. True, children may observe women, more often than men, with or wearing

flowers, but do they see men in the company of bears or women with butterflies? It is at least plausible that these youngsters have begun to associate qualities such as strength or dangerousness with males, and gentler qualities with females, whether or not they can name the attributes involved. (p. 220)

Bem (1981, 1985) suggests that people differ in the degree to which they use the gender schema to process information about themselves and others, and she argues that strongly gender-typed individuals are those who have a strong tendency toward gender-schematic processing. **Gender schema theory** states that individual differences in reliance on the gender schema stem from differences in the degree to which the gender dichotomy is emphasized during socialization. Research support for this aspect of the theory is not yet available; however, Bem (1985) has speculated on her theory's implications for parents trying to raise gender-aschematic children in a gender-schematic society. She suggests first that parents teach children about sex differences in a way that emphasizes the biological aspects and deemphasizes the cultural correlates of maleness and femaleness, thus providing the child with a much narrower and more precise network of associations on which to construct a gender schema. She argues that children should be taught that genitalia are the definitive attributes for distinguishing females from males and that other attributes such as dress, occupation, or behavior are irrelevant. Second, she suggests that parents provide alternative schemas for their children to use in interpreting the wider culture's large set of sex-related associations. In particular, she proposes that children be provided with an "individual differences schema" (a great deal more variability exists between individual members of a group than between most groups), a "cultural relativism schema" (different people believe different things), and, finally, when children are able to understand it, a "sexism schema" (an understanding of the history and process of sex discrimination). All of these alternative schemas should help the child to organize information about the cultural correlates of maleness and femaleness without incorporating them into a gender schema.

Bem (1985) provides an example of an outcome of her first suggestion:

The liberation that comes from having an unambiguous genital definition of sex and the imprisonment that comes from not having such a definition are nicely illustrated by the story of what happened to our son Jeremy, then age four, the day he decided to wear barrettes to nursery school. Several times that day, another little boy told Jeremy that he, Jeremy, must be a girl because "only girls wear barrettes." After trying to explain to this child that "wearing barrettes doesn't matter" and that "being a boy means having a penis and testicles," Jeremy finally pulled down his pants as a way of making his point more convincingly. The other child was not impressed. He simply said, "Everybody has a penis; only girls wear barrettes." (p. 216)

Gender schema theory is provocative, but it needs, and will inspire, more research. It builds on both cognitive developmental and social learning theories in that it portrays the child as both actively constructing gender categories and responding to environmental cues, and it provides an interesting perspective on how the sociocultural context influences the acquisition of gender roles.

Sex Roles as Rules

Anne Constantinople (1979) proposed a model of gender-role acquisition that bears some similarity to gender schema theory. The **sex roles as rules theory** presents the acquisition of gender roles as similar to the process of pattern recognition in vision and speech. The capacity to generate gender-role categories grows out of an interaction between the child's built-in ability to generalize, discriminate, and form categories of all kinds and the specific sex-related associations that pervade the environment. Like Bem, Constantinople suggests that children learn the distinctive features of the masculine and feminine categories through observation and direct teaching. The first step toward acquiring these categories is learning the labels associated with gender: *boy, girl, mommy, daddy, man, woman.* Words as distinctive features for gender are joined later by clothing, hairstyles, toys, and other cues that are differentially associated with boys and girls. Positive and negative reinforcement serve to focus the child's attention on relevant stimuli and to associate gender-related behaviors with positive or negative feelings. The child then combines these distinctive features into cognitive categories (or schemas), which are then used to evaluate new information and experience. The entire process is motivated both by the child's need for structure in his or her environment and by the child's desire to gain rewards and avoid pain.

Constantinople takes her model one step further and addresses the question of *how* the child combines information to form schemas concerning gender. In line with cognitive theories of pattern recognition, she suggests that gender-related schemas are developed through two types of information processing: *data-driven processing,* in which categories are formed through stimulus generalization and discrimination as the child encounters new information, and *concept-driven processing,* in which incoming information processing is guided by an already-formed expectancy. She suggests that the child's earliest attempts at handling gender-relevant information are data-driven, with the child making sense of new information by organizing it into categories. Once these categories have begun to take shape, however, the child can use them as expectations in concept-driven processing of information. These expectations or categories are revised when they lead to wrong predictions and are expanded and refined as the child becomes capable of handling more complex concepts and is exposed to a broader social environment. Constantinople suggests that the major consolidation of gender-role categories occurs at the point cited by Kohlberg (1966) as the acquisition of stable gender identity.

Constantinople closes her discussion of gender-role acquisition with an intriguing question: If children were reared without any distinctive features for gender, except for the anatomical and physiological differences between the sexes, would these cues alone be sufficient for the child to develop a gender category? And, if so, would that category then be used to search for regularities in behavior and attitudes paralleling the anatomical differences? A direct test of these questions is virtually impossible, but cross-cultural research, and perhaps some systematic investigation of some of the childrearing strategies proposed by Bem (1985), may provide clues to the answer.

Gender Roles as Developmental Pathways

John Archer (1984) proposes a model of **gender roles as developmental pathways.** He suggests feminine and masculine roles, rather than being two variations produced by the same process (imitation and reinforcement), may be separate developmental pathways. In other words, the *process* of acquiring gender roles, not just the *content* of these roles, may differ for males and females. His discussion concentrates on four related dimensions of gender-role acquisition, which, he argues, may be fundamentally different for the two sexes: (1) rigidity or flexibility (the extent to which cross-gender-typed behavior is permitted), (2) simplicity or complexity (how elaborate the content of the gender role is), (3) internal consistency or inconsistency of the role requirements, and (4) the degree of continuity or discontinuity in role development. Archer assembles evidence to suggest that, in childhood, the masculine role is more rigid, complex, and inconsistent than the female role. Boys show gender-typed behavior earlier than girls and are more specifically discouraged from cross-gender activities (rigidity); more masculine than feminine stereotypic traits are known by both boys and girls (complexity); and boys are more likely than girls to receive conflicting messages about what behavior is acceptable, such as the formal disapproval but informal approval of aggression (inconsistency). He also reviews evidence to show that gender-role development involves different discontinuities at different ages in males and females. For example, at adolescence the female begins to follow a more rigid set of rules than the more flexible ones of childhood. Her role becomes narrower and more inflexible, whereas the masculine role simultaneously becomes more flexible and varied (Nolen-Hoesema & Girgus, 1994). In another example, the birth of their first child to young couples is related to an increase in cross-gender behavior for the men and an increase in gender-typed behavior for the women, representing a shift *away* from the masculine role for men and a shift *toward* the feminine role for women (Nash & Feldman, 1981).

Archer's theory alerts us to the possibility, suggested by much of the current literature on gender socialization, that females and males may not travel along completely parallel tracks in the development of their gender roles. Furthermore, his approach illustrates the usefulness of a life-span approach to gender-role development. Further research is needed to investigate his suggestions.

SOCIAL INTERACTION PROCESS THEORIES

Both social learning and cognitive developmental theories are "process" theories that focus on the mechanisms through which gender roles are acquired. They also tend to emphasize learning behavior during childhood as a basis for lifelong gender roles. But is childhood learning the whole story when it comes to behaving "like a woman" or "like a man" in later life? Does a woman act feminine mainly because she was rewarded in childhood for doing girl-things and she internalized feminine values? Or does the process continue beyond early learning of gender roles to encompass her choices and her interactions with others throughout her life? Some theoretical models of gender-related behavior have highlighted the processes that maintain continuity in behavior once it is learned and that elicit such behavior in particular social contexts.

Continuities in Interactional Styles

Will an ill-tempered child grow up to be a grouchy adult? What determines whether a dependent child matures into a dependent adult? Does the gender of the child make a difference? Two aspects of the way an individual interacts with the social environment provide keys to answering these questions: cumulative continuity and interactional continuity (Caspi, Bem, & Elder, 1989).

Cumulative continuity is the process through which an individual, beginning in childhood, selects and creates environments that fit her or his preferred forms of behavior—and these selected environments, in turn, reinforce and sustain that behavior. A shy child, for example, may select environments where little social contact is required. Such environments will not push the child in the direction of becoming more gregarious; rather, they will sustain the child's shyness. The older the child gets, and the more independent from parentally chosen environments, the more influential is this tendency to select environments that feel comfortable and that reinforce already-existing behavior patterns (Scarr, 1988). This process is truly cumulative in that, over time, the choices have a snowball effect, reinforcing more and more strongly the original behavioral preferences.

Interactional continuity refers to the two-way transactions between the person and the social environment. The person's behavior elicits reactions from others, and those reactions promote continuity in the original behavior through reinforcement, confirmation of expectations, and confirmation of the person's self-concept. For example, an aggressive child expects others to be hostile and so behaves in ways that trigger hostile reactions in others—confirming the child's expectations and making aggressive behavior still more likely in the future.

If small initial temperamental differences exist between females and males, continuity theory suggests that such differences might well be solidified and even magnified over the life course as individuals choose compatible environments and elicit reactions from others. Some researchers have suggested that male and female infants differ on such dimensions as activity level and amount of crying. It is difficult to be certain that such differences exist at birth, however, because reactions to females and males differ from the first moments of the infant's encounter with the world. Continuity theory implies, however, that differences that exist for *any* reason can be maintained and amplified through interactional and cumulative continuity.

A particularly interesting aspect of this analysis for understanding gender-related behavior is that the outcomes of these continuity-oriented processes depend on the degree to which the individual's preferred behavior fits the social expectations for females and males. For example, one study of individuals who reached adulthood during the 1940s shows that boys who were shy grew up to be men who were described as aloof, lacking social poise, and showing a reluctance to act. These men, compared to other men, were delayed in marrying, becoming fathers, and establishing stable careers—acting out, in general, a reluctance to enter new and unfamiliar social settings and role transitions (Caspi et al., 1989). An examination of the life course of the shy men shows the snowball effect of early shyness: They tended to delay entering a stable career, which in turn lowered their overall achievement, which in turn decreased their occupational stability. The researchers suggest that these men's shyness slowed them down precisely because it did not fit with the role requirements for American men: taking the initiative during courtship and being assertive at work.

In contrast to males, shy girls did not grow up to be adults who delayed marriage and parenthood. Although their shy interactional style seemed to endure, the descriptions of them were less negatively tinged than those of the shy men. The shy women were described as quietly independent, intellectual, and inner-directed. It appears that shyness in females, being more expected than in males, elicits more positive reactions from others, and thus does not inhibit females' social relationships in the same way it inhibits men's. Similarly, shyness did not affect the timing of marriage and parenthood for women because they did not have to take the initiative in courtship. Shyness did seem to affect women's working life, however. Shy women were much more likely than other women to have no employment history or to have left employment as soon as they were married or had a child. Shyness was obviously more compatible with the traditional expectations for females than with those for males. The importance of social context and of role expectations, even in the expression and life consequences of early personality dispositions, is clear here. Early shyness meant different things for the lives of the women than for the lives of the men. Had these individuals grown up in a time and place where shyness was acceptable for men and not for women, the results would have been very different.

An Interactive Model of Gender-Related Behavior

The models of gender differences that we have considered so far focus on how people acquire gender roles. They begin with childhood and show how various forces encourage some behavior and discourage others, eventually solidifying a repertoire of behaviors that fit expectations for the person's gender. The interactive model proposed by Kay Deaux and Brenda Major (1987) does not look at long-term causes of gender-related behavior. Rather, it zeros in on aspects of the immediate social situation that promote or inhibit behavior that is congruent with femininity or masculinity. In other words, its focus is on the *display* of gender-related behaviors rather than on their *acquisition*.

The **interactive model of gender-related behavior** is built on the proposition that an individual's gender-related behaviors in a given social interaction are influenced by what others expect, what the individual believes about herself or himself, and situational cues. The processes involved in this influence are expectation confirmation (both "seeing" only what one expects to see and self-fulfilling prophecy) and the individual's strategies to both confirm her or his self-view and present an acceptable image to others.

In the abstract, the model works as follows: Two people, a perceiver and a target, approach an interaction, each with a set of beliefs *about the target*. The perceiver's beliefs about the target are based on the gender category (female or male) of the target as well as on personal experience with that individual. Beliefs related to the gender category of the target can be activated, or made especially salient, by certain occurrences or environmental conditions. These beliefs influence the perceiver's actions toward the target. The target enters the situation with a set of beliefs about the self, particular aspects of which may be emphasized by the situation or by recent occurrences. The target interprets the actions of the perceiver, weighs possible alternatives, then takes actions that may either confirm or disconfirm the expectations of the perceiver. The course of the entire interaction is affected by certain modifying conditions: the social desirability of the behavior the perceiver expects from the target, the certainty with which that expectation is held and communicated, and the relative balance between the target's concerns with sustaining her or his self-concept and presenting a positive image.

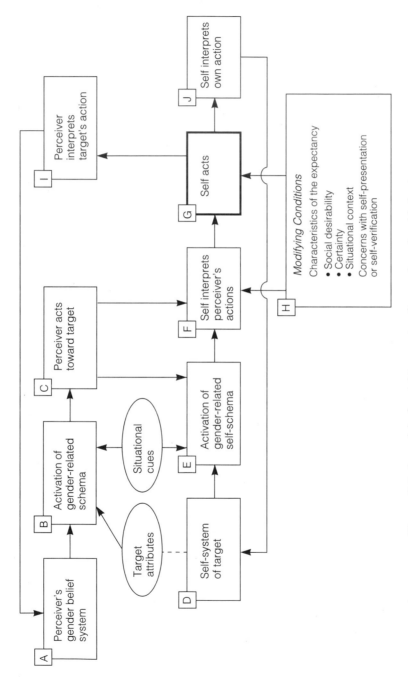

Figure 2.1 A model of social interaction for gender-related behavior (From "Putting Gender Into Context: An Interactive Model of Gender-Related Behavior" by K. Deaux and B. Major, 1987, *Psychological Review, 94 (3)*, p. 372).

An example of how the model predicts when the behavior of women and men will tend to be similar and when it will tend to differ is provided in Figure 2.1. In this example, the perceiver is Manager X, who supervises two entry-level managers, Joan and John. The situation is a performance appraisal exercise involving leadership of a small group.

> We begin by summarizing an interaction sequence that should maximize the likelihood that sex differences in leadership style will emerge. Manager X firmly believes that men and women have quite different characteristics, particularly in the area of leadership style (Box A). These beliefs are not only chronically accessible for Manager X but have been recently activated by an incident at work that highlighted differences between women and men (Box B). These beliefs prompt Manager X to convey quite different messages to Joan and John as to what is expected in the exercise (Box C). For example, Manager X hints to John that the group session is an opportunity for him to show his ability to take charge, but Manager X emphasizes the cooperative aspects of the group situation when talking to Joan.
>
> To continue our maximal sex differences example, assume that Joan and John have quite different histories of leadership experience and quite different self-images as to their leadership abilities and preferred styles (Box D). Furthermore, the group context, because of past associations, activates different issues for the two managers, differences that are accentuated by the expectancy the manager has conveyed (Box E). Not surprisingly, John interprets the situation as an opportunity to show how well he can take charge, whereas Joan interprets the situation as an opportunity to show her cooperative talents (Box F). Joan and John then act quite differently in the group setting (Box G). This observable sex difference in behavior then feeds back to confirm the initial beliefs of Manager X (Box I) as well as the initial self-assessments of John and Joan (Box J). (p. 372)

Deaux and Major note that the same basic scenario would produce few male–female differences if Manager X did not view male and female leadership styles differently, Joan and John had equivalent beliefs about their own leadership styles and abilities, and nothing happened to trigger gender-related expectations in either party. Furthermore, they point out, the situation would become more complicated if the manager's expectations were inconsistent with those of Joan and John—for instance, if Manager X believed that women and men manage very differently, but Joan and John had very similar self-concepts and behavioral tendencies. In such cases, the modifying conditions in Box H must be considered. For instance, Joan and John would be more likely to behave differently, despite their similarity in self-concepts and behavioral dispositions, if the manager had a great deal of power and conveyed the expectations very clearly and if their concern with presenting themselves in a positive light was stronger than their concern with behaving in a way consistent with their self-concepts.

The models discussed earlier in the chapter postulate explanations for the stability of and differences in the behavior of women and men. The one presented by Deaux and Major provides a possible explanation for the flexibility and variability of gender-related behavior: why, even if they have learned well how to be "feminine," women do not always act that way, and why, when the conditions are arranged a certain way, even the most predictably "macho" man will be unassertive and compliant. Both types of models are necessary for an understanding of gender-related behavior.

PERSPECTIVES ON DIFFERENCE

This book, and much of the psychological research on gender, centers on three basic questions: What do we know about the similarities and differences between women and men? Where does that knowledge come from? How is that knowledge shaped and limited by cultural perceptions of femininity and masculinity? Each of the theories discussed in this chapter provides a framework for investigating gender similarities and differences, and each of the frameworks shapes and limits what we notice. The theories address the issue of how and why female and male human beings might come to be different. Some of the theories, such as Freudian psychoanalytic theory and evolutionary theories, take female–male difference as a given and attempt to explain why it is inevitable. Others, such as social learning and social interaction process theories, emphasize the flexibility of cultural processes that produce differences and show how different social environments might produce alternative patterns of male–female difference.

But should we be focusing so strongly on differences? Or should we accept that gender differences, however produced, are minor and search instead for the similarities between women and men? Perspectives on gender differences have shifted dramatically over the centuries between a hierarchical one that looks at women and men as essentially similar though differently developed and one that looks on the sexes as opposites. Missing, of course, is a perspective that views women and men as very similar and *equally* well developed.

Both the hierarchical and the opposites views of gender differences have been used as "explanations" for female inferiority, and a generation of feminist-oriented psychologists has, beginning in the 1970s, rejected this emphasis on female–male difference and focused instead on demonstrating that men and women are similar in their abilities, in their traits, and in their reactions to many situations. However, in recent years tension has developed between this approach and another that reemphasizes the study of differences—this time from the viewpoint that the qualities distinguishing women from men are positive ones, not sources of inferiority. The latter approach emphasizes the differences in females' and males' experiences and women's role in reproduction. Rachel Hare-Mustin and Jeanne Maracek (1990) offer the labels *alpha bias* and *beta bias* for these two approaches. **Alpha bias** is a tendency toward exaggerating differences. **Beta bias** is an inclination to ignore or minimize differences. They note that each approach is problematic. Alpha bias can support the boundaries between females and males and the marginalization of women. It can also be used to uphold the status quo by arguing that the social environment has been constructed to accommodate gender differences rather than create or perpetuate status inequalities. Beta bias "draws attention away from . . . differences in power and resources between women and men" (p. 44) and ignores special needs of women and men.

Which is the best approach? Neither. Both. If we focus on similarities at the expense of differences, we risk failing to understand the ways women and men experience the world differently. If we focus on differences at the expense of similarities, we risk perpetuating the notions of inferiority that a "male as norm" tradition has foisted on women. The tension between the two approaches may be necessary. Kimball (1995) argues that we should practice "double visions," refusing to choose either the emphasis on similarities or the emphasis on differences as more true than the other. If we deliberately engage the tension between the two approaches when we compare people across genders (and other categories that are socially constructed), we will be more aware of the complexities of our social world. Moreover, as Elizabeth Percival (1991) notes, that tension may help us to be conscious of both the similarities and the differences among women and among men of different races, classes, ages, and sexual orientations. For example, just as women and men share many qualities and experiences that cut across gender lines but also are likely to have differing experiences, so women of different races, or men of different races, are also likely to share many qualities and experiences that cut across racial lines but also to have differing experiences. Although the pull to choose between emphasizing similarities or emphasizing differences is compelling, ignoring either approach is the most dangerous choice of all.

SUMMARY

Six general types of theories address the origins, development, and maintenance of behavioral and personality differences and similarities between human males and females. Psychoanalytic/identification theories emphasize individual personality development, ascribing particular importance to early parent–child relationships. Another set of theories focuses on social structure and culture, emphasizing the role of social arrangements on the maintenance of gender roles and stereotypes. Power and status differences between women and men and the division of labor by sex have been pinpointed within this theoretical context as important factors in maintaining gender differences in behavior. A third set of theories proposes an evolutionary framework to explain differences between human females and males, arguing that observed differences between the sexes have a genetic basis and have arisen through adaptation. The social learning and cognitive developmental approaches place strong emphasis on the processes governing the development of gender identity and gender roles. Both theories focus on the role of the wider social environment and the child's understanding of it in developing gender identity, roles, attitudes, and stereotypes. Social learning theory emphasizes observation, imitation, and reinforcement and conceptualizes the child as someone who acts in ways most likely to result in social reinforcement. Cognitive developmental theory stresses the child's active attempt to understand social rules and to be socially competent. More recent approaches—gender schema theory, sex roles as rules theory, and the theory of gender roles as developmental pathways—integrate some of the principles of both social learning and cognitive development. The social interaction process approach continues to focus on process but extends to an explanation of behavior over the life course. Within this approach, Deaux and Major's (1987) interaction process model focuses not on distant or long-term factors but on the specific conditions of particular social interactions that promote gender-differentiated or gender-similar behavior. Their model helps us to understand why gender-related behavior is flexible and variable and why, in the face of fairly consistent socialization pressures to be different, women and men still frequently behave similarly.

No theory discussed in this chapter has emerged as adequate to explain all aspects of gender, although some, based on the evidence, seem to be more adequate than others. All are useful, however, in that their presence gives rise to questions that can be investigated and to ideas that can be debated. They provide, at least, a place to begin the analysis.

Much of the research described in the remainder of this book is based on these theories; the careful reader will find both support and contradiction for the various theoretical approaches. She or he will also find instances in which the adoption of a different theory would have led the researcher to frame questions differently and to measure different things. The message is that in research, as in the rest of life, the answers one gets depend partly on the questions one asks—so it behooves the student of the psychology of gender to understand where the questions come from! Of course, the answers a researcher gets also depend on *how* the questions are asked, a subject to which we turn in the next chapter.

KEY TERMS

theory
psychoanalytic theory
consciousness
unconscious
id
ego
superego
oral stage
anal stage
phallic stage
latency phase
genital stage
Oedipus complex
penis envy
Electra complex
phallocentric
gynocentric

maternal feminisms
devaluation
sexualization
gender-role strain
gender identity
gender role
sexual orientation
social structure theories
social role theory
evolutionary theories
sociobiology
social learning theory
social cognitive theory
group socialization theory
cognitive developmental
    theory
gender constancy

schema
gender-schematic
gender-aschematic
gender schema theory
sex roles as rules theory
gender roles as
    developmental
    pathways
cumulative continuity
interactional continuity
interactive model of
    gender-related
    behavior
alpha bias
beta bias

FOR ADDITIONAL READING

Chodorow, Nancy. (1989). *Feminism and psychoanalytic theory.* New Haven, CT: Yale University Press. The author looks at the mother–child bond from a perspective that is both feminist and psychoanalytic.

Eagly, Alice, & Wood, Wendy. (1999). The origins of sex differences in human behavior: Evolved dispositions versus social roles. *American Psychologist, 54*(6), 408–423. The authors provide a concise overview of both evolutionary and social structural theories of gender, as well as some evidence that is consistent with a social structural interpretation of gender differences in behavior.

Hare-Mustin, Rachel, & Maracek, Jeanne. (Eds.). (1990). *Making a difference: Psychology and the construction of gender.* New Haven, CT: Yale University Press. In a collection of essays, a group of psychologists explore how the field of psychology has participated in the construction of socially accepted ideas about gender.

Kaschak, Ellyn. (1992). *Engendered lives: A new psychology of women's experience.* New York: Basic Books. The author takes a critical look at theories of female and male development, particularly psychoanalytic theories, and offers a new feminist theoretical perspective.

Kimball, Meredith M. (1995). *Feminist visions of gender similarities and differences.* New York: Haworth Press. This book encompasses a wide-ranging examination of the implications of emphasizing differences or similarities between women and men, including some fascinating historical perspectives.

Westkott, Marcia. (1986). *The feminist legacy of Karen Horney.* New Haven, CT: Yale University Press. The author explores Horney's insights, as well as some aspects of her life, and places them in relation to contemporary feminist theory.

CHAPTER 3

Researching Sex & Gender

Exploring the Whys & Hows

At the turn of the century, Helen Thompson, a graduate student at the University of Chicago, embarked on an ambitious thesis project. She wanted to "obtain a complete and systematic statement of the psychological likenesses and differences of the sexes by the experimental method" (Thompson [Woolley], 1903). Having reviewed the literature on sex differences in mental abilities, she was appalled by the inconsistencies and contradictions she found and believed that only a careful experimental investigation could produce the evidence needed to resolve the disputes about male–female psychological differences.

Thompson used 50 Chicago undergraduates, half of them male and half female, of the same age and background. She tested a variety of their motor skills and sensory abilities: auditory and visual reaction times, ability to hit a target, rapidity of finger movement, pain threshold, ability to discriminate heat and cold. It was the first time anyone had systematically compared men and women on a wide variety of abilities measured in a controlled, laboratory setting.

Thompson found a striking *lack of evidence* for sex differences in mental abilities. Although men and women performed differently on some tests, the results did not conform to popular beliefs about the nature of sex differences. Women were not, for example, uniformly more sensitive than men; men did not show consistently higher motor performance than women. On the whole, it was the similarities rather than the differences between the sexes that were most impressive. These similarities could be readily seen when Thompson graphed her data. The distribution curve of scores on any particular test for the women in her sample overlapped almost completely with the distribution curve of the same scores for the men. This research provided the first empirical basis for questioning the popular assumption, shared and promulgated by many scientists, that women's and men's different mental abilities fitted them for different social roles.

In the late 1950s, psychologist Evelyn Hooker (1957) administered clinical projective tests to groups of heterosexual and homosexual males. Contrary to the stereotypic beliefs of the day, she found that homosexual men were not more maladjusted than their heterosexual counterparts. Expert clinical judges could not distinguish between the test protocols of nonclinical homosexual and heterosexual men, nor were there any differences in adjustment ratings between the two groups. This research laid the groundwork for a change in the psychiatric labeling of homosexuality as an illness.

Helen Thompson's approach to the question of female–male differences in ability and Evelyn Hooker's investigation of the differences between men with homosexual and heterosexual orientations are classic illustrations of scientific psychology: the attempt to test ideas about human behavior against observable reality. Psychologists, like other scientists, are trained to be skeptical—to withhold their acceptance of theories or ideas until provided with evidence that the theories are correct. Although we enjoy spinning an elegant theory, we are taught that theory construction is only the first step in the scientific process; theories should be tested to see how well they fit the facts as we know them.

Much effort (and much of this chapter) is devoted to finding the right research methods: ways of testing theories against real-world data. Even with the most careful methods, however, research is an imperfect process, unable to capture "pure" truth. Even when theories *seem* to fit the facts, we must still be cautious, asking ourselves three questions: (1) How well have we been able to measure reality? (e.g., if we do not notice a change in a person's attitude, does that mean no change has occurred or that our way of assessing change is not sensitive enough?); (2) How may we have altered, or even produced, the "facts" by studying them? (e.g., if a middle-class researcher finds working-class men to be hostile, is that hostility characteristic of working-class men or merely an attitude that is elicited by the presence of the researcher?); (3) How are our own backgrounds and biases influencing what we notice and do not notice and how we "construct" reality? (e.g., in 17th-century Europe, the prevailing medical opinion was that a woman could not become pregnant through intercourse unless she experienced an orgasm, and counterexamples to this belief were simply not noticed by doctors or were explained away). The necessity of pondering such questions does not mean the research enterprise is useless, only that it exists in a constant tension between the search for unequivocal proof and the awareness that total certainty is simply not possible.

This tension is exemplified in the social sciences by two differing approaches to knowledge, labeled logical positivism and social constructionism. **Logical positivism** assumes that reality is independent of the knower and can be discerned "objectively" under the proper conditions. According to this approach, if scientific evidence is gathered rigorously, under the right conditions, a researcher can arrive at pure, unbiased truth. **Social constructionism** holds that it is impossible to discover pure truth, because there is no such thing. Rather, all of our so-called facts are really only educated guesses. Researchers hold expectations and implicit beliefs that affect the way they search for knowledge. Those expectations and beliefs, which are not only individual but are also shaped by social, cultural, and historical consensus, color their perceptions of the reality they observe. Researchers do not discover independently existing facts through objective observation; rather, they construct knowledge that is influenced by the social context of their inquiry. "What is produced by such knowledge-seeking . . . is not a free-standing and revealed truth, but a best guess, based on selective vision, using limited tools, shaped by the contextual forces surrounding the search. It is not Truth; it is a historically and contextually situated understanding, a social construction" (Bohan, 1992, p. 8).

Even if we favor a cautious, social constructionist approach to knowledge, we need not turn away from scientific research. Rather, we must remain conscious of the ways in which the research process and its results are shaped and limited by social context. Most of this chapter deals with the methods and issues that must be addressed by anyone trying to do good research on sex and gender—even though we are well aware that no amount of rigor in the research process will produce the pure truth about sex and gender.

Given the limitations of research, what constitutes acceptable evidence in favor of or against a theory? In the realm of sex and gender, this question has been crucial. As seen in the preceding chapters, the ease with which particular theories about sex and gender are accepted depends to a large extent on how well they fit with popular notions held about women and men by the culture. A theory that seems to challenge these notions will be subjected to more intense scrutiny and to higher standards of evidence than will one that seems to fit in with and justify them. And even research evidence that is conceded to be ironclad can be conveniently forgotten or overlooked when it goes against favored assumptions. Thus it is that Leta Hollingworth (1914) was moved in frustration to accuse her male colleagues in psychology of adopting a double standard of scientific proof, refusing to subject their assumptions about male–female differences to the same careful criticism they devoted to other assumptions. Her exasperation is, from our current vantage point, quite understandable. Her own adviser, Edward Thorndike, held fast, in the absence of data, to the notion of a "maternal instinct" in women long after he had abandoned other instincts as too vague and mentalistic. You will learn in this chapter that the problem noted by Hollingworth has not disappeared. The impact of biases about sex and gender on the design, conduct, interpretation, and acceptance of research continues to be felt.

ASKING QUESTIONS ABOUT FEMALE–MALE DIFFERENCES: WHAT EVIDENCE TO GATHER

Research on sex and gender tends to focus on two basic questions: (1) *What* differences exist between women and men? and (2) *Why* do these differences exist? Attempts to answer the first question bring the researcher face to face with a host of issues common to all attempts to compare naturally formed groups of people (e.g., racial groups, tall vs. short people). Attempts to answer the second question place the researcher on the shifting sands of the "nature versus nurture" debate. Also, researchers' ability to answer the *why* question is limited by their degree of success in answering the *what* question. It makes little sense to pursue an explanation for a gender difference that has not been established with any degree of certainty.

Methods for Comparing the Sexes: What Differences and Similarities Exist?

A researcher who wants to collect evidence bearing on differences or similarities between males and females can use any of several approaches. She or he may, for instance, study a few individuals in depth, using a case history or narrative approach. This allows the researcher to gather a lot of information and to delve deeply into complex issues that may be difficult to measure in large samples or with less attention to particular individuals. The **case history method,** sometimes used in clinical research, involves gathering many details about one or several individuals, usually through interviews. The information gathered is then used to support, develop, or refine a particular explanation of behavior. Freud, Horney, and other psychoanalysts relied on the case history approach to construct their theories, and it has frequently been argued that their own biases colored their interpretations of particular cases. The case history provides a richness of detail that can suggest ways of understanding very complex processes. However, the method offers little protection against the influence of researcher bias—a real disadvantage in the realm of sex and gender research where biases are often strong and unacknowledged.

The **narrative approach,** which also involves gathering a lot of information from a single individual, is designed *not* to privilege the biases of the researcher but to provide the research participant with the opportunity to react to the meanings and interpretations the researcher gives to the participant's life story. The participant's interpretations of her or his own experiences are reported and given at least equal weight with the interpretations gleaned by the researcher. For example, Rosario Ceballo (1999), who interviewed an African American social worker named Mary in depth about her life, describes how Mary's own interpretation of her life differed from that of Ceballo's:

> In the second round of interview, I asked Mary if she had always been a determined and strong-willed woman, a question obviously based on my own overall assessment of her identity. To my surprise, Mary replied:
>
> No, I don't think I'm that way. . . . When I think of strong-willed, I think of people who go out there and tackle it and get the job done and come what might, and fight all the battles, and overcome all the struggles, and knock anybody down that gets in your way, and that's not me. (p. 316)

Ceballo used Mary's comments to shape her own understanding of the issues she was studying, thus illustrating a key aspect of narrative research: the inclusion of the research participant as someone who guides and shapes the research.

The **phenomenological method,** another qualitative approach, is oriented toward understanding behavior from the perspective of the person being studied. Like the case history and narrative methods, it is based on in-depth, subjective information collected in interviews. This method, however, demands that the researcher be free of theoretical preconceptions before proceeding to construct a theory based on the information provided by the individuals being studied (e.g., see Daniluk, 1993). In addition, the analysis is supposed to be precise enough, based on specific words and phrases in interview transcripts, that two independent researchers trained in the phenomenological method will reach the same interpretation when analyzing a particular interview. This ideal may sometimes be difficult to achieve, and the approach shares a problem with the case history method: When only a small number of people are studied, they may not be representative of the population to whom the researcher wishes to generalize.

Some approaches to phenomenological methodology (e.g., Andrew, 1985, 1986) can incorporate experimental variations without compromising the qualitative approach. Such methods allow for inclusion of the investigator's standpoint as a variable to be studied as part of the research process. In addition, these methods allow the possibility of involving subjects as true participants—as conscious, intentional collaborators with the researcher—who, for instance, systematically respond to a particular research situation, provide reflections about their own responses, and respond to externally derived presentations of their responses (e.g., to a videotape or an observer's account). This type of research makes possible the study of processes such as increasing self-awareness, which can elude other methods. Also, it emphasizes the idea that the research enterprise cannot be separated from the persons or behaviors it examines. All of these factors are increasingly recognized as important to the development of a nonsexist psychology, as will be evident from later sections of this chapter.

A new, fairly influential method in the social sciences is **discourse analysis,** the analysis of the language in various texts, such as interview responses, discussions, and essays. In discourse analysis, words and phrases are not taken at face value, and language is not treated as simply a way of communicating information. Rather, the researcher tries to "deconstruct" or interpret ways of talking and writing. For example, New Zealand researchers Nicola Gavey and Kathryn McPhillips (1999) used discourse analysis to explore the reasons young women who had made a rational decision to insist on condom use in heterosexual intercourse actually failed to do so when confronted with a real situation. In interviewing these women, Gavey and McPhillips found that they talked about their heterosexual encounters in a certain way: a way that framed the encounter as a romance, in which the man took the initiative and the woman was relatively passive. Through this way of talking and thinking about heterosexual intimacy, argued the researchers, the young women constructed expectations for themselves that they found difficult or impossible to violate without threatening their own sexual identity.

Evidence may also be collected through **naturalistic observation.** For example, a researcher interested in comparing girls and boys on aggression might spend hours watching nursery school children at play, keeping track of the number and type of aggressive behaviors displayed by boys and girls. This method also has its share of problems. For one thing, it may be difficult to know how much the setting or the sample is responsible for the patterns observed. If boys are more aggressive than girls, how much is this difference a function of the particular nursery school environment or the particular group of children who attend that school? The pattern would have to be observed in a number of settings before it could be accepted as reliable.

The problem of researcher bias also comes up in naturalistic observation. Several studies have now shown, for example, that behavior by a child is rated differently by observers, depending on whether they think the child is female or male (Condry & Condry, 1976; Condry & Ross, 1985; Gurwitz & Dodge, 1975). Condry and Condry (1976), showed participants a videotape of an infant responding to emotionally arousing stimuli. They found that participants who thought the child was a boy rated an ambiguous negative reaction to one of the stimuli as anger, whereas those who thought the child was a girl rated the same response as fear. Such findings cast doubt on the ability of researchers to be unaffected by their own gender stereotypes when carrying out observational research.

Survey methods of data collection use a standardized questionnaire or interview to collect information from a large number of people. This type of investigation, if based on a large representative sample of respondents, may allow a researcher to make some general statements about female–male differences in responding to certain types of questions. However, interpretation is still difficult; questionnaire and interview responses may be heavily influenced by respondents' desires to look good or to please the researcher, and by memory biases. Thus, for example, on a survey asking subjects to rate the relative importance in their lives of marriage and career, a male–female difference in responding may not reflect an actual difference in the importance assigned by women and men to these two things. Rather, or in addition, it may reflect women's knowledge that they are expected to place more value on marriage and men's knowledge that they are expected to place more value on career. Finally, a limitation of survey research is that the results it produces are **correlational.** In other words, the method is capable of showing that two things are related to each other, or go together, but cannot show that either one caused the other. Thus, in the preceding example, the finding that females were more likely than males to rate marriage more important than career would simply mean that, for the sample studied, being female was associated with a greater likelihood of making that response. The researcher could not assume that being biologically female or male *caused* the difference in responding. Sex might be related to some other, unmeasured variable that was the real cause of the difference. For instance, maybe the underlying reason for differences in the perceived importance of career is whether one's same-sex parent has had a satisfying career, and men's fathers may be more likely than women's mothers to have done so.

The most controlled way to test the tenets of a theory is an **experiment.** In this methodology, the researcher directly manipulates (that is, sets at different levels) one variable, called the **independent variable,** while measuring its effects on another variable, the **dependent variable.** The researcher must control all other factors that might influence the dependent variable, so that the experimental conditions differ only in the level of the independent variable. This entails assigning research participants to experimental conditions randomly, so there are no systematic differences at the outset in the kinds of people assigned to each condition. It also entails manipulating the independent variable and measuring the dependent variables under identical circumstances for each level of the independent variable. If all these conditions are met, it should be possible to draw conclusions about a cause-and-effect relationship between the independent and dependent variables—to conclude that changes in the level of the independent variable *caused* changes in the dependent variable. If a researcher wanted to test the hypothesis that women who exercise during pregnancy experience fewer physical complaints than do women who do not exercise, she or he might screen a group of women for health risks early in pregnancy, then randomly assign each of them to either an exercise group or a control group. The two groups would have to be handled identically except for the amount of exercise. For instance, both would receive the same amount of attention, would be under the same constraints to report to the researcher, and would be given similar expectations about the impact on their pregnancy of participation in the project. Various dependent variables, such as symptom reports and physiological measures, would be assessed, and the two groups would be compared on their scores. If the two groups differed significantly, it would be possible to conclude that the amount of exercise had caused the difference. Lest this procedure sound too straightforward, it should be noted here that it is often extremely difficult or impractical to control all the necessary variables. In addition, researchers using the experimental method sometimes assume they are controlling for all of the important variables when, in fact, crucial variables have inadvertently been ignored. Although the experimental method provides the most potential for controlled examination of the effects of particular variables, the researcher must be mindful of the possibility that in any given study such control may be more illusory than real.

The astute reader will have noticed that the discussion of the potential to assess cause and effect using the experimental method did not feature sex as an independent variable. This is because, even using the experimental method, it is not possible to prove that biological sex differences are the cause of differences in dependent variables. Why? First, it is impossible to manipulate sex—to randomly assign people to be females or males. Second, it is a hopeless task to disentangle biological sex from the many other variables (e.g., training, expectations) associated with it. Thus, two of the conditions for inferring cause and effect through the experimental method are not met: manipulation of the independent variable and control of extraneous variables. All data on sex differences, no matter what research method is used, are correlational data, and in that sense it is more accurate to speak of "sex-related" differences than of sex differences.

The Social Psychology of the Psychological Experiment

Many years ago, Saul Rosenweig (1933), in a pioneering paper on the social psychology of the psychological experiment, mentioned sex as a "personal quality" of the experimenter that could introduce "errors of personality influence" into the laboratory. In other words, whether the experimenter was female or male might make a difference to experimental results simply because people react differently to men and women. Rosenweig suggested the sex of the researcher was one of those extraneous variables that should be controlled when not being deliberately used as an independent variable.

Rosenweig's point was largely lost on his contemporaries, but in recent years experimenter gender has become not only an accepted factor to be considered in research design but also an independent variable of interest in its own right. **Sex-of-experimenter effects,** although still sometimes overlooked, have been found in virtually every area of psychological research, from computer-related behavior (S. W. Williams, Ogletree, Woodburn, & Raffeld, 1993) and cognitive task performance (Jemelka & Downs, 1991) to sensation-seeking (Littig & Branch, 1993). There are many complex effects. Some indications are that female experimenters tend to *discon-*

firm their hypotheses, whereas male experimenters *confirm* theirs (Rosenthal, Persinger, Mulry, Vikan-Kline, & Grothe, 1964). It has also been suggested that male and female researchers each tend to design research in ways that favor the portrayal of their own gender (Eagly & Carli, 1981).

The social psychology of the psychological experiment is rife with other aspects that can interact with gender, causing artifactual findings. It has been found, for instance, that female participants are more likely than males to comply with the demand characteristics of an experimental situation (Rosenthal, 1966). Thus, reported male–female difference in a laboratory study about nurturance may really reflect the fact that women are more likely than men to respond to the demand characteristics of the experiment: to act nurturant, as they think the experimenter wants them to.

Research on human behavior is, by its very nature, a social endeavor taking place in a particular social context. As such, it would be unrealistic to expect the interactions between researcher and participant to be uncontaminated by the gender stereotypes and gender-related habits predominant in the surrounding culture. Psychologists studying female–male similarities and differences have gradually acknowledged this problem and taken measures to deal with it: by using male and female experimenters and participants, by minimizing demand characteristics, and by being aware of potential artifacts that would make gender differences appear to exist when they are not really present. Such precautions can move the interpretation of research in the direction of greater accuracy, but they cannot eliminate the difficulties completely. The problems stem not only from the personal biases of individual researchers and research participants but also from widely accepted societal values and attitudes that may be all but invisible to most members of society. Researchers must strive to be conscious of the limitations of all research methods (Peplau & Conrad, 1989).

Finally, it is worth noting that many research methods, by definition, look at a limited, and to some extent isolated, piece of behavior. They focus on an aspect of behavior that has had its context stripped away, often emphasizing control and precision at the expense of depth and breadth of understanding. In our quest for the detachment that is an ideal of scientific research, we may miss the connections linking experience and behavior to social and material conditions (Morawski, 1994). The limitations of traditional forms of experimental and survey research have increasingly frustrated feminist researchers, provoking the rise in popularity of methods such as narrative research, phenomelogical approaches, and discourse analysis.

Differences and Distributions

Whenever a researcher collects quantitative data with a view to comparing two or more groups of individuals, whether the method used is a survey, an experiment, or naturalistic observation, he or she is faced with the problem of interpreting that data—deciding whether or not it reflects a real difference between the groups. Suppose, for example, a researcher asked a sample of girls and a sample of boys to complete a jigsaw puzzle and measured the time it took each child to complete the task. How would the researcher use the data to determine whether girls and boys differ in their ability to complete such a puzzle quickly?

One fairly simple option for comparing the girls' and boys' performance would be to compare the average times taken by children in each group to complete the puzzle.

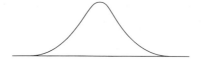

Figure 3.1 The normal curve.

Figure 3.2 Distribution of puzzle solution times, graphed separately for females and males, showing overlap between the distributions.

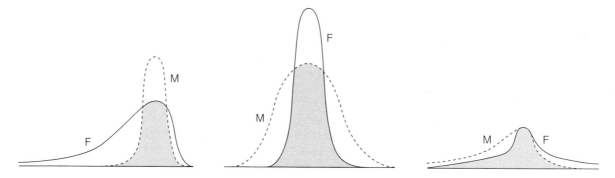

Figure 3.3 Examples of different ways in which males and females could achieve identical averages in puzzle solution times.

If the boys took an average of 5 minutes and the girls an average of 4½ minutes, it would be tempting to conclude that girls were faster than boys at this kind of task. Such a conclusion would be premature, however, until the researcher had taken into account two important issues: the distributions of the boys' and girls' time scores and the statistical significance of the difference in mean scores.

If the researcher drew a graph showing the number of children with each particular time score, as shown in Figure 3.1, the **distribution** of scores would probably look like a "normal" or bell-shaped curve. The highest part of the curve shows the scores most often attained and represents the average score for the group. Children whose scores fall to the right of the highest point have performed above average, and those whose scores fall to the left have performed below average. If boys' and girls' scores were graphed separately, as shown in Figure 3.2, the researcher could learn a great deal about how to interpret the 30-second average time difference between the two groups by examining the degree and pattern of overlap between the two distributions. In fact, even if no difference in average scores had been observed between the two groups, it would have been useful to examine the distributions. As seen in Figure 3.3, the two groups could have achieved identical averages in very different ways, and a difference between samples in their amount of variability can be just as interesting as a difference in their means. Thus, it is good practice for researchers to report on distribution overlap and variability as well as average differences when giving the results of studies that compare females and males.

In many cases, reporting or trying to interpret mean differences between groups without paying attention to the distribution of scores is misleading and encourages unwarranted stereotyping. For instance, a commonly accepted generalization based on a comparison of group average scores is that women are slower than men at mental rotation tasks (see Chapter 6). Researchers who have examined the distributions of the mental rotation scores, however, note that the average woman is not slower at this task than the average man. Rather, there appears to be a subgroup of women who are slower than the average man *or* the average woman (Favreau, 1993). Olga Favreau (1993) provides an excellent example of the difference in understanding to which focusing on averages or distributions can lead: When considering the perception of color, we could, based on averages, make the statement that women perceive color better than men do. However, more accurate information is provided by the statement that more men than women are color-blind.

When interpreting data, the researcher must also deal with the possibility that a particular finding can occur by accident. The 30-second average difference between the male and female samples in this study may be nothing more than a fluke. Maybe this sample of girls is especially quick for some reason or the boys are a slower than usual bunch. Scientists use statistical tests that take into account sample size and variability to calculate the probability that a particular result could occur by chance alone. By convention, if the probability of the result occurring by chance alone is less than 5% the finding is accepted as **statistically significant.** Even with this information, however, some caution is in order. Not all statistically significant differences are socially significant or even meaningful. As Petersen and Wittig (1979) note, since the calculation of statistical significance is based partly on sample size, extremely large samples may reveal statistically significant results that are essentially meaningless. In a sample of 100,000 males and 100,000 females, an IQ difference of 0.02 point would be statistically significant despite the fact that the difference is too small to be reliably measured by an IQ test in the first place and too tiny to have any practical implications.

Knowledge as Self-Reflexive

It is important to remember that no matter what methods social scientists use to discover whether or not particular gender differences exist, their findings tend to have a transformative effect on the very situation under study. When researchers publish a finding such as "in dual-career couples wives spend a lot more time doing housework than husbands do," the very dissemination of that information may eventually change the situation. Individual women, finding out that their situation is not unique, may become angry enough to insist that their partners take on more of the domestic duties. Individual men, seeing the documentation of the unequal distribution of household tasks, may change their own behavior out of a sense of fairness. Other men and women may respond differently, seeing the findings as confirmation that they are in step with the majority and becoming more committed to an uneven distribution of household labor. In either case, the knowledge gained by researchers who study human behavior is not independent of that behavior. It has an impact on it. By finding and reporting a gender difference, researchers can contribute to the magnitude and perceived importance of that difference.

By now it should be clear that attempts to establish the existence of particular differences or similarities between the sexes are complicated by a number of factors. The issues become even more complex when researchers confront the next question: *Why* do differences exist?

WHY GENDER DIFFERENCES EXIST: NATURE, NURTURE, AND THE INTERACTIONIST POSITION

Is human behavior determined more by environment or heredity? This question has obsessed the field of psychology for decades, and no introductory psychology student escapes exposure to it. In the realm of sex and gender, the question becomes: Are female–male differences part of our human inheritance, or do we learn to be feminine and masculine by interacting with the environment in which we find ourselves?

There are dangers in the past acceptance of either an extreme "nature" or an extreme "nurture" view. A one-sided emphasis on heredity can mean that a researcher will not look for socioenvironmental explanations for behavior that she or he observes. A rigid emphasis on environment, however, may blind a researcher to biological underpinnings of behavior, thus blocking the solution to certain problems. It is now clear that both approaches are too simplistic to explain the development of particular human behaviors. For example, postulating a genetic reason for a behavioral gender difference just because no other obvious explanation has been found contributes nothing to the solution of the mystery. As geneticists and medical researchers have now demonstrated, even knowing that a person carries a specific well-understood disease-linked genetic defect (e.g., for sickle-cell anemia) does not allow for accurate prediction of the course of the disease—what symptoms will develop and with what severity and timing (Fausto-Sterling, 1992). The course of the disease is influenced not only by the genetic defect but also by the individual's environment. In the case of behavior, which is likely to be even more susceptible than physical symptoms to environmental influence, the postulation of an undiscovered genetic basis contributes little to our understanding.

Many scientists have argued that it is meaningless to consider either heredity or environment in the absence of the other or to treat their relationship as a simple additive one: Both are always important. Anne Anastasi (1958b) contends that the question to which researchers should address themselves is not *how much* of an individual's behavior is determined by heredity and environment, respectively, but *how*—in what ways—genetics and environment work together to produce behavioral outcomes. This question implies that the presence of particular genetic or environmental components merely increases or decreases the probability of specified behavioral results; neither one may, in any fundamental sense, be considered more or less important. Both heredity and environment are always fully present and fully interacting with each other.

Even biologists are far from enamored of simple biological determinism. Anne Fausto-Sterling (1992) argues for

> a more complex analysis in which an individual's capacities emerge from a web of interactions between the biological being and the social environment. Within this web, connecting threads move in both directions. Biology may in some manner condition behavior, but behavior in turn can alter one's physiology. (p. 8)

A clear example of such a reciprocal relationship between behavior and physiology is provided by Miriam Lowe (1983) in her analysis of male–female differences in strength and physical performance. She notes that the assumption that men are strong and women are weak has powerful consequences for the way men and women both view their bodies and try to shape them according to different standards of health and beauty. Even in infancy, parents exercise boys more than girls, and, as children develop, girls are channeled into more sedentary kinds of play than boys are, a pattern that continues into adulthood. Studies show, however, that when women break out of the "weak" stereotype their bodies can change dramatically: When women and men begin training with weights, women increase their strength faster than men do, and the physical performance of American women athletes differs from that of their nonathletic female counterparts much more than men athletes' performance differs from that of nonathletic men (Bishop, Cureton, Conerly, & Collins, 1989; O'Hagan, Sale, MacDougall, & Garner, 1995). When women become more active physically, not only their strength but also other physical attributes change. Percentage of body fat decreases, and bones become stronger and more dense. All of these findings lend support to the idea that social stereotypes can influence physical attributes by influencing behavior—an example of the interactionist position that how an individual turns out is a function of the joint effects of heredity and environment.

Further examples of heredity–environment interaction illustrate just how complex the relationship between nature and nurture can be. A growing body of research indicates that the physical structure of the adult brain is established through the interaction of the maturing child with its environment. As an infant matures, nerve cells in the developing brain compete to form connections with other cells. Nerve cells that do not form such connections do not survive, and only pathways between cells that are used (through stimulation from the environment) become established. Thus, the child's environment has a direct physical effect on brain development (Greenough, Black, & Wallace, 1987; Nowakowski, 1987). Some studies show that the prenatal environment can affect body type and appetite in adulthood. Maternal starvation during early pregnancy may affect the part of the brain, the hypothalamus, that regulates appetite. Children born to such starved mothers are more likely than others to experience obesity due to overeating (Ravelli, Stein, & Susser, 1976). Other research shows that infants' development of motor skills, once thought to follow a genetically programmed timetable, seems to be speeded up by direct teaching and practice in certain cultures—a result thought to be due to the strengthening of the neuronal pathways in the brain that govern these behaviors (Super, 1976). Both examples illustrate that the environment can, by influencing brain development, interact with biology in such intimate ways that the two are inseparable.

Biologist Ruth Hubbard (1990) coined the term **transformationism** to describe the way biology and environment work together, with neither being more fundamental than the other to an organism's development. She argues, in concert with other scientists, that neither biology nor environment can be said to "determine" reactions to the other. Rather, at every level of development, the combination of biological and environmental factors transforms the organism so that it responds differently to other concurrent or subsequent biological or environmental influences:

> If a society puts half its children in dresses and skirts but warns them not to move in ways that reveal their underpants, while putting the other half in jeans and overalls and encouraging them to climb trees and play ball and other outdoor games; if later, during adolescence, the half that has worn trousers is exhorted to "eat like a growing boy," while the half in skirts is warned to watch its weight and not get fat; if the half in jeans trots around in sneakers or boots, while the half in skirts totters about on spike heels, then these two groups of people will be biologically as well as socially different. Their muscles will be different, as will their reflexes, posture, arms, legs and feet, hand–eye coordination, spatial perception, and so on. . . . There is no way to sort out the biological and social components that produce these differences, therefore no way to sort nature from nurture. (pp. 115–116)

Cross-Cultural Research

In the quest to understand just how heredity and environment work together to influence such things as ability, behavior, personality, and appearance, researchers have often turned to cross-cultural comparisons. Examining other cultures helps to jolt us out of the assumption that the social and behavioral patterns of our own culture are somehow completely "natural" or that they represent the only normal kind of human organization. (However, as seen in the following section, bias can also interfere with the way researchers from one culture see and interpret another, blinding them to certain crucial differences.) In the realm of sex and gender, the pioneer of cross-cultural research was anthropologist Margaret Mead (1935), whose research in New Guinea demonstrated that cultures could and did differ dramatically in their notions of masculinity and femininity. Mead noted that most human societies used the conspicuous categories of age and sex to structure expectations about people, "whether it be the convention of one Philippine tribe that no man can keep a secret, the Manus assumption that only men enjoy playing with babies, the Toda prescription of almost all domestic work as too sacred for women, or the Arapesh insistence that women's heads are stronger than men's" (p. xi). However, these sex-related assumptions did not follow the same pattern across all societies. Her book contrasted the Arapesh, a tribe in which both women and men were expected to be gentle, responsible, and nurturant, with the Mundugumor, in which men and women both were individualistic, ruthless, aggressive, and nonnurturant, and the Tchambuli, a group wherein the women were raised to be dominant, impersonal, and in charge and the men were less responsible and emotionally dependent. She concluded:

> If those temperamental attitudes which we have traditionally regarded as feminine— such as passivity, responsiveness, and a willingness to cherish children—can so easily be set up as the masculine pattern in one tribe, and in another be outlawed for the

majority of women as well as for the majority of men, we no longer have any basis for regarding such aspects of behavior as sex-linked. (pp. 279–280)

Mead's was the first, but not the last, word on cross-cultural differences in patterns of gender roles, and anthropologists continue to debate her specific conclusions as well as the universality of such aspects of gender role as higher male than female status. Her work, and that of her successors, alerts us to a wide variety of human behaviors that can vary as a result of different combinations of heredity and environment.

Animal Research

Research with nonhuman animals is another strategy that has been used to try to understand how biology and environment interact to produce certain behavioral outcomes. Because it is easier to control both the genetics (through breeding) and the environment of individual animals in a laboratory situation than it ever is to control such factors for humans, laboratory research with animals can investigate questions that are difficult or impossible to approach with humans. For example, it would be out of the question to inject pregnant humans with cross-sex hormones to observe effects on the behavior of their offspring, but such research can be done with animals. Similarly, we cannot isolate human infants at birth to observe the effects of a lack of socialization on sex-differentiated behaviors, but such a technique is sometimes used with animals. This type of research helps to generate ideas about what may be happening in human development to produce sex-related differences in behavior. However, there are many differences between humans and even our closest animal relatives, the primates, and it is dangerous to make direct generalizations from animal research to human behavior. We do not, for instance, know what cues are used by lower animals to differentiate between males and females and what steps they take to socialize their young and their peers into sex-appropriate behavior (Fedigan, 1982). It may be, for instance, that smell is a very important component in an animal's ability to differentiate between its male and female peers. If so, attempts to study the impact of sex hormones per se on animal behavior may be doomed to failure. Sex hormone treatments may disturb the "sex smell" sufficiently that animals that have received sex hormone treatments will be treated very differently by their peers than are those who have not received hormone injections. Thus, the impact of the sex hormones on behavior would be confounded with the impact of differential treatment. Even with animals, then, the separation of biological from environmental influences on behavior is not a simple matter. In addition, the use of animals as research subjects does not free researchers from ethical concerns. Rather, it raises a new series of ethical issues. For all of these reasons, animal research does not provide any easy answers in the nature–nurture debate.

Whether studying human beings or other animals, researchers must be mindful of the interaction between nature and nurture, between heredity and environment. The meaningful question is, as Anastasi (1958b) argued, not Which one? or How much? but How?—in what ways do our genetic heritages interact with the worlds in which we live to produce the complex packages we know as females and males?

BIASES AND PITFALLS:
PROBLEMS ENCOUNTERED IN THE STUDY
OF SEX AND GENDER

Although the idealistic view of science is that it is an objective search for truth conducted by unbiased researchers, the reality of the scientific endeavor seldom approaches the ideal. The research process cannot be completely objective or separate from the social context in which it occurs. The existence of a "value-free science" is now commonly recognized as a myth. A scientist cannot avoid being influenced by the assumptions and agendas, hidden or articulated, of the surrounding culture, and even researchers in fields such as chemistry and physics, which might seem at first glance to be immune to cultural influence, may overlook observations that seem incongruent with accepted theory. Objectivity may be an even more remote possibility in the social sciences, where the processes under study are directly and personally significant to the researcher. The study of sex and gender, which touches on an issue that is basic to self-perception and social relationships, is virtually impossible to approach in a completely unbiased way.

Studies of the values researchers hold with respect to knowledge and the research process show that differences on these dimensions can be large. For example, Mary Ricketts's (1989) study of the theoretical orientations and values of North American feminist psychologists showed that members of this group tended to place more emphasis on external or social determinants of human behavior than on internal or biological determinants. Feminist psychologists also emphasized subjectivism (an interest in persons' experience and a belief that people construct their reality) over objectivism (an interest in persons' behavior and the belief that reality constructs the person). Within the sample of feminist psychologists, differences were found between heterosexual and lesbian feminists, with the latter group favoring a more subjectivist focus and a more externally oriented search for causes. By contrast, an earlier study (Krasner & Houts, 1984) indicated that senior psychologists, founders of the behavior modification movement, preferred a more objectivist orientation than did a comparison group of nonbehaviorist psychologists.

Researchers may also differ in their orientation toward the potential uses of their research findings. An often-voiced tenet of feminist research is that research findings should be communicated back to the community of participants from whom they were obtained (G. M. Russell & Bohan, 1999). This principle probably affects what aspects of the research receive most attention from the researchers and are communicated most quickly. For example, responses to open-ended questions may provide material for more interesting and dramatic feedback to the community of participants than quantitative findings in some cases. Glenda Russell and Janice Bohan (1999) describe one way in which the words of gay and lesbian and heterosexual respondents to their questionnaire about reactions to the passage of Colorado Amendment 2 (an amendment to the state's constitution that removed legal recourse for lesbians and gays who encountered discrimination based on sexual orientation) were shared with the community of participants:

> The words and experiences of participants in the A2 study became an oratorio
> commissioned and performed by Harmony, Denver's LGB chorus—first in Denver
> and then at an international festival of LGB choruses. The experiences of heterosexual

allies heard in the second study were brought together in a documentary video produced by a local PBS affiliate and subsequently aired across the country. The experiences of research participants were reflected back to them and to the community as a whole in song and on film—individual and collective voices made available to the public through psychological research. (pp. 409–410)

Although all researchers are bound to be influenced by personal and cultural values, anyone committed to finding things out through the process of research must *try* to be aware of her or his biases, to acknowledge them, and to eliminate the blind spots they engender. The following section, which draws on several thorough examinations of sexism in research (Eichler, 1983; Favreau, 1977; McHugh, Koeske, & Frieze, 1986; Stark-Adamec & Kimball, 1984), details some of the aspects of the research process in which bias can be expressed. Armed with the knowledge of potential pitfalls, a researcher attempting to do nonsexist science has at least a fighting chance. However, most of the problems stem from biases that are not merely personal but cultural in nature. Researchers must look not only to their own blind spots but to those of the entire scientific enterprise in which they work.

Choosing a Research Topic

Laboring under the inevitable constraints of time, energy, and motivation, a scientist can do only so much research during her or his career. How does she or he choose what questions to study and what to set aside? The decision is based not on the researcher's interest alone but also on what topics are considered important by the researcher's employers, professional colleagues, and funding agencies. All of these factors are susceptible to bias. A researcher will not think to study the underlying causes of sexual harassment, for instance, if he or she is oblivious to its prevalence or is a participant in cultural assumptions that such behavior is merely an inevitable manifestation of sexual attraction between men and women who work together. Or, she or he may wish to study it but may find that employers and colleagues dismiss it as a frivolous topic and that funding agencies are unwilling to provide support. In recent years, there has been a veritable explosion of research in psychology on topics relevant to sex and gender and to women's experience, as universities, professional associations, and granting agencies have bowed to pressure to legitimize such topics. Nevertheless, some researchers report that their work on gender or on women is not taken seriously as legitimate psychology.

Formulating the Research Question

The way a particular research question is articulated may have built-in biases that keep the investigator from finding results that cast doubt on his or her assumptions. If the investigator has not considered the possibility that males' and females' experience of a particular situation (e.g., feelings after acting aggressively against another person) may differ, the hypothesis she or he formulates may reflect this lack of awareness of gender as an important variable. The reverse is also true: Researchers may perpetuate sexist biases by using different concepts to describe the same activities for women and men, as when the term *maternal deprivation* is used in conjunction with the children of employed mothers, but the parallel term, *paternal deprivation,* is never used when discussing children of employed fathers (Eichler & Lapointe, 1985). Someone who frames a hypothesis about the impact of maternal deprivation on preschool children will not interpret anything he or she observes as being due to *paternal* deprivation, even though the children being studied may actually be more "deprived" of their father's than of their mother's presence.

Within the field of the psychology of gender, a prevailing bias that has shaped many research questions has been the tendency to focus on personality and individual differences rather than on social conditions that differ for males and females. For example, researchers studying women's achievement have tended to search for personality differences between women and men that would explain why women appear to achieve less than men: women's lack of achievement motivation, fear of success, or the "mommy track." Such a focus perpetuates the status quo (i.e, stereotyping women as not achievement-oriented and discriminating against them for positions that require a strong focus on achievement) by encouraging a tendency to blame women for their lack of achievement (Kahn & Yoder, 1989). An approach emphasizing social forces rather than personality characteristics might focus instead on the "glass ceiling" that many women report encountering in their attempts to move up to higher levels in their organizations. Clearly, researchers taking these two approaches would find very different reasons for women's lack of achievement relative to men.

Research Design

I have already noted some potential pitfalls in design that can emerge from the social psychological aspects of the research process itself. A researcher must always specify, and counterbalance when appropriate, the sex of the experimenters and the participants. Further, she or he must be sure that the research context is similar for male and female participants so that gender differences do not emerge as artifacts of the research situation. For instance, in a laboratory setting, if gender differences in conformity are found in response to persuasive statements made by a male confederate, confident conclusions about gender differences in conformity cannot be drawn because male and female subjects are operating under different social conditions. Males are being pressured by a same-sex peer, but females are being pressured by an other-sex peer. Similarly, a researcher attempting to compare the on-the-job behavior of female and male secretaries could not safely draw conclusions about sex-related or gender differences because the females would be occupying a traditional role in which women form the majority whereas the males would be holding a job considered unusual and surprising for their sex. Female and male secretaries, then, would be working under different kinds of constraints and social pressures. To compare their behavior without taking these differences into consideration would be to invite inaccurate conclusions.

Another important aspect of research design is the choice of participants or respondents. Who should be studied, and with whom should they be compared? A major point here is that the people to be studied should be representative of those about whom the researcher wishes to draw conclusions. Obvious though this point may seem, it has been common practice for researchers to study only one sex (usually males) while drawing conclusions about people in general. An interesting case in point is a frequently cited effect in social psychology: the way that watching oneself on videotape affects one's judgments about the causes of one's own behavior. Research on men led to the conclusion that the videotape experience caused people to feel more like external observers of their own behavior rather than like actors—people engaged in the behavior (Storms, 1973). Although this conclusion is often presented as one that holds for people in general, some efforts to replicate it with female participants have failed (D. S. Martin & Huang, 1984; Scott & Webster, 1984).

Another problem in subject selection occurs when researchers study people who are having difficulties with a normal process (e.g., menopause or the menstrual cycle), and the researchers then generalize their conclusions to all people who are experiencing that process. Thus, information gathered about a female patient may be generalized unthinkingly to females in general, and information about male homosexual patients may be wrongly assumed to characterize gay men (Stark-Adamec & Kimball, 1984). This type of overgeneralization is most likely to occur when the observations gleaned from the patients conform to stereotypes about the larger group.

One further issue must be considered in the choice of research samples: Does the choice of one sample rather than another reflect biased assumptions? If a researcher chooses to study mother–child interaction instead of parent–child interaction, is this because he or she implicitly assumes that the mother is the only parent whose interaction with the child really has any important impact? If a researcher asks only women but not men about their experience of role conflict between paid employment and family responsibilities, does this choice reflect a belief that only women experience such conflict? Although such sample choices often reflect practical considerations as much or more than biased assumptions, they may act to reinforce stereotypes that could be challenged (e.g., that women but not men are stressed by trying to maintain dual roles).

To put information about a particular group into perspective, it is necessary to make comparisons with other groups. Where no comparisons are made, information about the group being studied may be too easily assimilated into an existing stereotype. For instance, within a climate of opinion that says pregnancy is a time of emotional instability, the finding that 24% of a sample of pregnant women agreed with the statement "I sometimes feel as if I am going to have a nervous breakdown" might easily be taken as supporting that opinion—unless, as was the case in the study in question, it was balanced by the finding that the comparison group (female college students) showed an agreement rate of 57% with the same item (Barclay & Barclay, 1976). When the symptoms reported by pregnant women are compared with those reported by their husbands, nonpregnant women, and husbands of nonpregnant women, the myth that pregnancy is a time of emotional instability receives little support (Lips, 1982a; 1985a).

Not only must researchers use comparison or contrast groups, they must choose such groups and examine the assumptions governing their choices with care. For example, when comparing males and females, it may not always be appropriate to equate the two groups for age because the order of some activities across the life span differs for women and men (McHugh et al., 1986). Moreover, when discussing the results of cross-gender comparisons, a researcher trying to avoid sexism will avoid describing male behavior as the norm and female behavior as deviation from that norm (Stark-Adamec & Kimball, 1984).

A crucial part of the research design is the choice of dependent variables or measures. If a study is concerned with marital satisfaction, for instance, how will that satisfaction be defined and measured? Will both members of the couple be asked to rate their happiness on a scale from 1 to 10? Will they be watched to see how many arguments they have? Will mood ratings be taken? Will their neighbors be asked? Obviously, the measure of marital happiness chosen can affect the results of the study.

In comparing females and males on any variable, care must be taken that the measure used to chart that variable is truly equivalent for the two groups. This procedure has not always been followed. For instance, early research on achievement motivation used a test that featured all-male illustrations as cues to elicit achievement stories (McClelland, Atkinson, Clark, & Lowell, 1953). Such a choice no doubt reflected an assumption that achievement was more important in the lives of men than women, and it made the results of the research difficult to interpret. If women and men behaved differently, was it because they differed in their basic approaches to achievement, or simply because the test that measured achievement had a different effect on women and men? Another example of bias built into dependent measures comes from the history of conformity research (Weyant, 1979). Early studies tended to support the notion that women were more likely than men to conform to group judgments. However, when researchers are careful to use topics that are equally familiar to women and men, the gender differences in conformity weaken or disappear (Karabenick, 1983). Early investigators who ignored the familiarity issue were inadvertently using measures of conformity that were not equivalent for their female and male respondents; thus, in retrospect, their findings of apparent gender differences are not surprising.

Research Design and Cultural Diversity

Questions concerning the selection of samples and of comparison groups, the kinds of measures to use, and the appropriate comparisons to make become even more complex when we acknowledge that gender interacts with ethnicity, race, class, and other variables. Most psychological research on gender has focused on middle-class White women and men. Moreover, it is all too often the case that "studies of gender differences and socialization based solely on European American women and men are regarded as revealing generalizable facts about gender per se—facts about people; but similar studies based solely on African American women and men are regarded as revealing nongeneralizable facts about African Americans alone" (Landrine, Klonoff, & Brown-Collins, 1995, p. 57).

Although feminist psychologists are increasingly conscious of the diversity among women, most research still omits the perspectives of poor women (Reid, 1993) and women of color (Landrine, Klonoff, & Brown-Collins, 1995). This happens either because members of these groups are simply not included in studies (perhaps because of the effort required to include them) or because when they are included their responses are interpreted from a White middle-class cultural perspective.

Hope Landrine and her colleagues (Landrine, Klonoff, & Brown-Collins, 1995) argue that it is critically important to design research that allows for an awareness of the differing ways members of various groups may be interpreting the same questions, words, or behaviors:

> Do African American and European American women who raise their voices in an experiment engage in "the same" behavior? If so, what behavior is it—how do we label and interpret it—as anger or as enthusiasm? Are Japanese American, Chinese American, African American and European American women who sit quietly and do

not voice an opinion in a situation engaging in "the same" behavior? If so, what should the researcher call that behavior? Were they conforming to the Japanese norm of *enryo* or to the Chinese norm of *jang;* were they being passive and nonassertive or simply nonchalant and "chilled"? How does the researcher decide what has been "observed," and what do we do if the label used to tally and report on participants' behavior does not match the label that research participants choose? (p. 60)

Landrine and her colleagues suggest that researchers collect information about how participants are interpreting the questions and the research situation to avoid stereotyping various cultural groups. In a simple demonstration of their point, they carried out research in which White women and women of color were asked to rate themselves on various adjectives, and then were asked to indicate the meaning of the adjective. They found that White women and women of color did not differ on their self-ratings on the adjectives; however, they did differ quite significantly on the meanings they chose to explain those adjectives. A failure to be sensitive to such possible differences of meaning in designing research could strongly distort the interpretation of findings.

Data Analysis and Interpretation

LOOKING FOR DIFFERENCES   Research on sex and gender is strongly oriented toward examining the differences between groups. As discussed in Chapter 2, this orientation is known as an alpha bias. Differences between males and females are used as springboards for understanding the way gender works. The problem with such a strong orientation toward differences, however, is that it leads researchers to look for evidence of differences and to ignore similarities. In analyzing data, researchers may focus on testing the difference between the mean scores of males and females while overlooking the pattern of overlap between them or the shapes of the score distributions. In reporting results, they may stress the areas in which differences were observed and give only passing mention, or no mention, to areas in which the two groups appeared to be similar. This orientation toward differences is frequently encouraged by the publication policies of scholarly journals: A finding of "no difference" is often considered uninformative and rejected for publication (Favreau, 1977). Thus, there are strong pressures in the direction of finding and reporting gender differences. The reader of the psychological literature must be mindful of the possibility that for many studies that report male–female differences comparable studies in which no differences were found may be gathering dust in file cabinets.

INTERPRETING DIFFERENCES   Once differences are found and reported, the possibility that bias may influence the research process persists. In fact, some would argue that the largest scope for the expression of bias lies in the *interpretation* of findings. A prime pitfall here is making generalizations that are too broad: drawing conclusions about human beings from the study of other animals, about all human beings from the study of one sex, or about adult gender differences from the study of children. Many other problems are less easily recognized, however, including the differential evaluation of the behaviors of males and females, the use of androcentric (male-centered) norms to evaluate female behavior, ethnocentric (focused on one's own cultural group) assumptions to explain behaviors observed among members of other cultures, the viewing of human behavior "through the lens of heterosexual experience" (L. S. Brown, 1989, p. 447), the use of anthropomorphic (human-focused) language to describe animal behavior, and the automatic assumption that observed gender differences have biological causes.

LABELS   Similar behavior by male and female participants may be labeled and evaluated differently by researchers—a situation that often originates in and perpetuates social stereotypes of the two sexes. The sexually active behavior of a female adolescent may be labeled "promiscuous," whereas that of a male adolescent is called "experimental" (Eichler & Lapointe, 1985). Where the two sexes show differences on a particular trait or skill, sexist biases may be reflected and perpetuated by the way the qualities in question are labeled. For example, some psychologists have demonstrated gender differences in the ability to recognize a pattern or shape embedded or hidden in a larger field and in the ability to focus on the overall field. The first of these abilities, long thought to be more common in males, has been labeled "field independence," and the second, often cited as more common in females, has been called "field dependence." As Dale Spender (1980) notes, these labels tend to make the female-linked ability sound negative—women are "dependent" on the context, but men can transcend it. If the concepts had been labeled "context blindness" and "context awareness," however, the male-linked ability would have a negative connotation, and the female-linked one would sound more positive. Ideally, of course, the characteristics associated with either sex should not be arbitrarily devalued through the labeling process.

ANDROCENTRIC NORMS   In the interpretation of findings of gender differences, there is a tendency to use **androcentric norms**—to apply male behavior as the norm against which to measure females. Although less blatant now than when Freud based all of feminine psychology on the female's lack of a penis, this habit still underlies much of the discussion of gender differences observed by researchers. If women are found to be less ready than men to do "whatever it takes" to succeed in a career, a researcher may discuss the finding in terms of women's relative lack of ambition. If men are found to be less ready than women to do "whatever it takes" to have time to spend with their children, it is less likely that researchers will discuss the finding in terms of men's relative lack of caring and responsibility. In fact, even the very terms used to describe a number of desirable qualities and behaviors may be defined in ways that make masculine behavior normative: *achievement* is success outside the home, not within it; *responsibility* is taking charge of others, not taking care of them; *bravery* is facing battle, not facing childbirth.

ETHNOCENTRISM   Whether as social scientists or casual observers, we often impose our own biases about male–female relations when interpreting data from other cultures. This is called **ethnocentrism.** Some feminist anthropologists argue that there has been a tendency to see evidence of male domination where little exists, to ignore evidence of parity between women and men in many hunter–gatherer societies (D. Bell, 1983; Leacock, 1983), and to interpret observed behavior in ways that fit preconceived cultural notions about the two sexes. An example of the latter tendency has been the common assumption among anthropologists that in societies where menstruating women are secluded this seclusion is a restriction imposed by men on women and is experienced by women as an exclusion. More careful research now suggests that, at least in some societies, women see their menstrual seclusion as a positive time—a holiday from their normal duties (P. G. Allen, 1986). Studying the customs of other cultures should open our eyes to new possibilities for female–male relationships, but only if the data collected are not unquestioningly interpreted to fit our own cultural preconceptions.

HETEROSEXISM   Persons whose sexual orientation is heterosexual greatly outnumber those whose orientation is homosexual. Yet those with a homosexual orientation—lesbians and gay men—form a significant minority. However, **heterosexism** often relegates their experiences to invisibility by psychologists studying gender. Researchers may mean only heterosexual couples when they speak of "couples," only two-heterosexual-parent families when they speak of "families" (L. S. Brown, 1989). Heterosexual relationships are often used as the norm against which lesbian or gay male relationships are evaluated. Yet the study of both same-gender and mixed-gender relationships is a source of clues about what works in intimate relationships in general, and examining the experience of lesbians and gay men is likely to help researchers get a clearer view of the construction of gender by providing a different perspective. But such insights can be gained only if researchers do not automatically assume that the standard for a functional intimate relationship is the heterosexual couple.

ANTHROPOMORPHISM   Although research with other animals can provide some clues about human behavior, we have already noted the dangers in careless generalizing from animals to humans. **Anthropomorphism** is often perpetuated by the use of anthropomorphic language (language that refers to human traits or behaviors) to describe animal data. This practice is common in some sociobiological writing, and it can make the researcher's understanding of an animal's motivation and behavior appear more complete than is actually the case. A widely cited example of this practice is Barash's (1979) use of the term *rape* to describe what appears to be a male's forcing of sexual advances on an unwilling female among a variety of species, including mallard ducks and even plants! Although the use of the word *rape* in such contexts may have an attention-getting function for the scientist, it does little to clarify what is indeed going on. How, for instance, does the researcher establish that a female flower or a female duck is "unwilling"? More seriously, how does this trivialization of the notion of rape, and the implication that because it happens in nonhuman species it is a biological rather than social phenomenon, affect the view of rape among humans?

Another example of anthropomorphic, biased language used to describe animal behavior is the use of the word *harem* to describe primate groups comprising a single male and many females (Bleier, 1984). In human terms, a harem refers to a group of women who are virtually owned by a powerful male and who are economically and sexually dependent on him. The word carries these same connotations when used with primates, but careful observation shows this to be inaccurate in many cases. For many primate species, the solitary male member of the group holds a peripheral rather than central position and is tolerated by the females mainly for his sexual function (Fedigan, 1982; Lancaster, 1975). Once again, the use of a term that has particular meanings in the human context creates confusion when applied to animal behavior and lends unwarranted support to the notion that a particular social arrangement among humans has a biological basis.

RELIANCE ON BIOLOGICAL EXPLANATIONS TO FILL GAPS   A distressing tendency among researchers of sex and gender is to postulate biological bases for observed gender differences whenever other explanations are not obvious. Such hasty falling back on biological explanations to fill gaps in our understanding, even when the biological mechanisms that might be involved are not apparent, is something like attributing our observations to magic—"We don't know how it happens, so it must be magic (or hormones)." Exactly this type of reasoning has sometimes emerged in the interpretation of gender differences in mathematics achievement. After their careful research on a large sample of mathematically talented children had shown that the girls in these samples performed somewhat less well than the boys, Camilla Benbow and Julian Stanley (1980) concluded that the performance differences were due to superior male math ability, a superiority based at least partly in biology. Benbow later suggested that exposure in the womb to high levels of the male hormone testosterone, rather than gender differences in upbringing, were the key to males' better performance (Benbow, 1988). Her suggestion is based on her finding that extremely mathematically gifted youngsters are much more likely than their less gifted counterparts to be left-handed and on research that indicates a possible connection between left-handedness and prenatal exposure to testosterone. The issue of gender differences in mathematics achievement will be discussed at length in Chapter 6, but for now it serves as a good example of the tendency to attribute gender differences to biology. The apparent assumption behind Benbow's conclusion is that researchers know all there is to know about social–environmental influences on the behavior in question and have exhausted these possibilities before finally putting their faith in biology. There are two potential problems with this assumption. In the first place, although some socialization explanations have been tested by Benbow herself and other researchers, psychologists are still a long way from a complete understanding of all the subtle mechanisms of social–environmental influence. It is extremely unlikely, in most cases, that all such possibilities have been ruled out. In the second place, as discussed earlier in the chapter, biology and environment work so closely together that it is virtually impossible to rule out one or the other altogether in the explanation of behavior. Although in this example, as in other cases, researchers may eventually understand the ways that biology interacts with environment to influence the gender–mathematics relationship, it is probably premature to attribute the differences with any certainty to hormonal influences.

Of course, there is little doubt that heredity plays a role in the distribution of some abilities and personality traits. Researchers have demonstrated, for instance, that the correlation between intelligence levels of identical twins (who share the same genes) is stronger than that between fraternal twins and other siblings (Bouchard, Lykken, McGue, Segal, & Tellegen, 1990), and that, within normal-functioning families, mothers' IQ levels are better predictors of their children's IQ levels than are parenting styles and certain other environmental variables (Scarr, 1991). Yet the implications of such findings for gender (or for other group differences such as race, class, or ethnicity) are far from clear. There is no solid evidence that particular abilities, such as mathematical ability, are more likely to be passed on genetically from parents to sons than to daughters (or vice versa). Also, even having the same level of ability is no guarantee that children from different groups will make the same choices or achieve similar levels of success. As discussed in the next chapter, for instance, longitudinal studies of high-IQ girls and boys have shown that gender rather than IQ has been the best predictor of what such "gifted" children accomplish in adult life. The differences in the opportunities and pressures presented to females and males by their environments ensure that similar ability levels do not predict the same outcomes for the two groups.

One additional problem with overreliance on biological explanations is faulty evolutionary theorizing. Researchers may be too quick to conclude that observed gender differences exist because they are adaptive for survival. As discussed in Chapter 2, it is difficult to prove that particular gender differences in humans offer evolutionary advantages. It is probably safe to assume that if there is a genetic basis for a particular difference it is at least not maladaptive enough to have been selected out (Stark-Adamec & Kimball, 1984). However, it is important to consider all the possible reasons for an apparently stable difference, including environmental and social learning factors.

A strategy sometimes used to support an evolutionary interpretation of observed behavior is what Ruth Bleier (1984) calls "validation by prediction." Proponents of this approach use evolutionary theory to "predict" an already established fact; then, having demonstrated the validity of the theory by the correctness of the prediction, they freely apply the theory to interpret other observations. The problem with this approach, as Bleier demonstrates, is that given any set of premises a variety of logical predictions may follow. Starting from the sociobiological premise that women have a great biological investment in each pregnancy by virtue of their need to ensure the survival of their genes, for example, Bleier draws the following predictions, all of which, she notes, are at variance with the observed facts: a low incidence of postpartum depression in women because depression interferes with optimum infant care; a high incidence of postpartum depression in fathers due to deprivation of the spouse's attention; and a low incidence of depression among women in general because most of them are following their biological urge to produce children. All of these predictions follow logically from the sociobiological premise, but none are correct.

POPULARIZATION OF FINDINGS   If the interpretation of data by researchers can be influenced by bias, the popularization of these interpretations tends to magnify the bias by oversimplifying the conclusions. In the example of gender differences in mathematics achievement discussed in the preceding section, media coverage has made the attribution of gender differences to biology sound even more conclusive than the researchers probably intended. "Do Males Have a Math Gene?" asked a *Newsweek* headline (D. A. Williams & King, 1980); with more assurance, a Canadian paper headlined an article "Male Hormones Key to Math, Study Says" ("Male Hormones," 1986).

The biases that emerge in media coverage of scientific results are partly due to the media's habit of distilling simple statements from complex facts. However, they often also reflect the biases of the writer or publication that provides the coverage. An obvious example is the headline given by *Playboy* magazine to an article on sociobiology: "Do Men Need to Cheat on Their Women? A New Science Says Yes" (S. Morris, 1978).

Although scientists cannot always be held responsible for the ways their work may be distorted or oversimplified in the popularization process, they should at least exercise care when making statements that might be taken to imply that there is scientific evidence justifying sex discrimination. Just as important, the consumer of the popular press should be sensitive to the presence of bias in the media reporting of research results. Readers should be mindful of the possibility that only the most sensational-sounding findings are likely to be reported and that coverage may reflect editorial bias, the distillation of the most dramatic conclusions from a more complex set of findings, and the stripping away of hedges and qualifications provided by the scientist.

SCIENCE, ANDROCENTRISM, AND MISOGYNY

There is much to suggest that science has served as a source of justifications for the status quo with respect to women and men, that its theories have been shaped by **misogyny** (hatred of women) and have been instrumental in promoting and maintaining male dominance over women, and that it has been for most of history a male-centered institution (Bleier, 1984; E. F. Keller, 1985; Morawski, 1994). Science has influenced women's lives without allowing women a voice in the process. Its findings have often ignored or distorted women's experience. The science of psychology specifically has been accused of furnishing support for stereotypic beliefs about women and men—beliefs that, in turn, supported patriarchal ideology and political, legal, and economic inequalities between the sexes (Morawski, 1994). Could it be that seeking out and eradicating specific sources of bias, as described in the preceding section, is merely a hopelessly superficial approach to a much larger problem—the problem that science as an institution is so shaped by masculine values and dominated by men that the bulk of it can never have anything but an **androcentric** orientation?

Many feminist scientists would feel constrained to answer a qualified no to this question; after all, if one is to continue to do scientific research, one cannot accept total pessimism about the endeavor (Peplau & Conrad, 1989). Yet there is a growing realization that science as an institution will not be easily overhauled by egalitarian or feminist concerns, that the whole scientific enterprise—its accepted way of doing things, its values, its areas of focus—has been shaped by generations of mostly masculine input, and that its rewards are still reserved mainly for men.

Values

Science is popularly held to be "value-free," but an examination of scientific institutions and processes shows this assumption to be false. Science revolves around values of objectivity, prediction, and control. Several writers have highlighted the separation and control-oriented themes in the scientific endeavor: The ultimate object is the conquest of and control over nature (E. F. Keller, 1985). "Man" is considered to be separate from and destined to dominate the natural world. Interestingly, the term *man* rather than *humanity* is probably the more accurate term in this context, both because nature is characterized as feminine (e.g., Mother Nature) and because women have historically been excluded from participation in science. Even in the social sciences, where the main focus of study is not some aspect of nature distinct from the human species but human behavior itself, women have often been treated as somehow separate from the mainstream of human activity, deviants from the male norm. From Aristotle's notion of "woman as defective man," through the Freudian explanation of most of feminine behavior as a reaction to the lack of a penis, to the current insistence that "work" means paid employment and that "productivity" excludes unpaid household labor, social science has revealed a consistent proclivity to use men as the norm and to define women as "different."

Participants

Science has traditionally been a male activity and it continues to be, despite recent increases in women's participation. In 1995 in the United States, women, who constituted a majority of undergraduate students, earned only 15.6% of the undergraduate degrees in engineering, 34.8% in the physical sciences, 46.8% in mathematics, and 28.4% in computer science. Female underrepresentation becomes more severe at the graduate level. For instance, women earned only 22.1% of the doctorates in mathematics and 11.9% of those in engineering in 1995 (U.S. Bureau of the Census, 1998). African American and Hispanic women, showing the double disadvantage of being both female and members of racial minorities, are underrepresented relative to African American and Hispanic men, who are already underrepresented relative to European American men. Among the recipients of Ph.D.'s in engineering in 1995, for example, the ratio of European American men to European American women was 5.52 to 1, the ratio of African American men to African American women was 3.73 to 1, and the ratio of Hispanic men to Hispanic women was 6 to 1. In absolute numbers, only 15 African American women and 11 Hispanic women, as compared with 320 European American women, were awarded doctorates in engineering in 1995 (National Science Foundation, 1998). Women make up about 9.6% of the engineering workforce, 30.4% of employed mathematical and computer scientists, and 31% of employed natural scientists (U.S. Bureau of the Census, 1998).

Women are moving into the social sciences in larger numbers. Thirty-four percent of psychology faculty at U.S. universities, but only 13% of the chairs of graduate departments of psychology, are women (Denmark, 1998). Seventy-three percent of recently graduated U.S. psychology majors are women (National Science Foundation, 1998). Yet training for research and access to research facilities and positions requires an advanced degree. In 1995 women earned only 36.3% of the doctoral degrees awarded in all science and engineering fields in the United States (National Science Foundation, 1998). Yet even these figures are the result of increases in women's participation in the sciences over the past three decades. Figure 3.4 illustrates the changes in the percentage of doctoral degrees in various scientific fields that were granted to women between 1971 and 1995.

Relatively few women have risen to prominence or have become influential policymakers within the realm of science, although, in a break from this tradition, the current director of the National Science Foundation is Dr. Rita Colwell, a distinguished microbiologist. Of the approximately 500 Nobel prizes that have been awarded to scientists, only 11 have been to women (and 2 of these were to the *same* woman, Marie Curie). Figure 3.5 shows the percentage of men and women who have been awarded this prestigious prize in scientific fields.

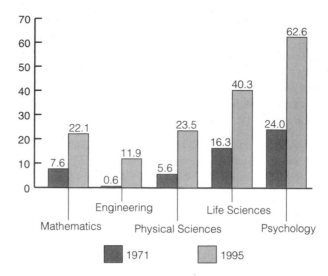

Figure 3.4 Percentage of doctorates awarded to women in scientific fields in 1971 and 1995. (Data from U.S. Bureau of the Census, 1998)

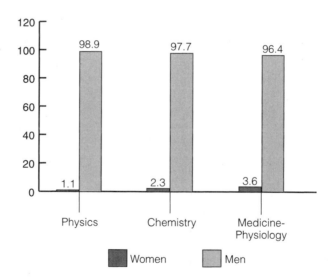

Figure 3.5 Percentage of women and men receiving Nobel prizes in science since the inception of the prize. (Lips, 1999)

Women form a very small minority of the membership of the National Academy of Sciences. They make up only 10.7% of Academy members in the field of psychology—a field in which there are many women—and only just over 1% of Academy members in the field of physics (National Academy of Sciences, 1999). Women's minority status was underscored for years by the Academy's traditional practice of awarding a membership scroll inscribed with the message that this particular woman is being honored for "his" accomplishments and that "he" is now entitled to membership in the Academy (Gornick, 1990).

The image of the research scientist continues to be a masculine one, albeit not always a particularly complimentary one (Boylan, Hill, Wallace, & Wheeler, 1992). Observers have noted that the stereotypic media portrayal of a scientist is of a neurotic man in a lab coat, often too obsessed with his experiments to be interested in the outside world (Fausto-Sterling & English, 1986), a man who is all intellect and no feelings, cold and asexual (Keller, 1985). Such an image reflects the meshing of stereotypes about gender with stereotypes about science. Science is for rational, intellectual men, not for irrational, emotional women. Small wonder that women have difficulty seeing themselves as scientists.

Psychology as a field has come some distance from the era in which such eminent research psychologists as Helen Thompson Woolley and Leta Hollingworth faced extraordinary difficulty in obtaining professional positions simply because they were women. But women with doctoral degrees in psychology are still less likely to hold tenured faculty positions than their male colleagues are (Gehlmann, Wicherski, & Kohout, 1995). In addition, some of this field's apparent progress in accommodating women is due to the so-called hard and soft divisions within psychology. The "hard–soft" distinction is here, as in other arenas, a code that is often interpreted as "masculine–feminine." Women are more likely to end up in the "soft" areas of psychology, such as developmental and clinical, whereas men are more likely to be in the "hard" areas of cognitive and perceptual processes (American Psychological Association, 1994; Ostertag & McNamara, 1991). This hard–soft distinction is basically meaningless; the intellectual effort and rigor required to understand and do good research are no less demanding in the soft than in the hard areas. The function served by the distinction is to perpetuate an implicit bias in favor of the importance of the hard branches of science and to serve as a subtle reminder that such branches are masculine (Keller, 1985).

The claim is sometimes made that if there were more women in science, science itself would be different, perhaps fundamentally so (Keller, 1985). As long as the women in a particular scientific field remain a small minority, however, the likelihood is that it is they rather than science that will be changed by their participation. Women entering the fields of science and technology have been compared to immigrants in a new country; after working so hard to gain admission and establish themselves, it is unlikely that they will be severely critical of their new milieu (U. M. Franklin, 1985). But if women enter a field in large numbers, they can have a noticeable impact on the discipline. In psychology, where relatively large numbers of women have entered the field, the effect of women's increasing participation has been dramatic on at least one dimension: the topics addressed by psychological research. Major psychological journals now carry significantly more articles dealing with gender and with issues specifically related to women. Entire journals concerned with such topics have been established. Guidelines for the conduct of nonsexist research have been published by both the American and the Canadian Psychological Associations (McHugh et al., 1986; Stark-Adamec & Kimball, 1984), and conscious efforts are made to include women on editorial boards. Yet problems remain. There is still a tendency to "ghettoize" research on women and on gender, as if such topics could be split off into a subdiscipline, and debates rage about the appropriateness of taking a feminist approach—one explicitly oriented to understanding and improving the situation of women—to the study of human behavior. Women and men trying to do nonsexist psychological research or practice, or to work from an explicitly feminist perspective, must still confront the question of how to help develop a psychology that has shed its old androcentric bias.

A TRANSFORMATIONAL PSYCHOLOGY OF GENDER?

Michele Wittig (1985) and others (Bohan, 1992; Morawski, 1994) have argued that the field of psychology as a whole needs to shift perspectives away from the old notion that behavior and our understanding of it can be separated from each other and from the social context in which they occur. Rather, psychologists must acknowledge that their research methods, their theories, and even judgments about the validity of their theories are influenced by their historical, personal, social, and cultural milieu. Such an acknowledgment inevitably brings those engaged in the research enterprise face to face with the tension that characterizes all attempts by psychologists to gather information about human behavior: the tension between trying to be sensitive to the effects of the social context and trying to transcend them. In studying the psychology of gender, researchers must continually be aware that their own notions of gender, what aspects of it should be studied, and how it should be studied are all influenced by their personal values and social milieu. That awareness should not paralyze them in their attempts to understand the psychology of gender; rather, it should force them to use research methods that include an examination of the context of behavior, that allow the complexity of multiple causes for behavior to emerge, that allow for the possibility that the very attempt to study a behavior may change it.

If researchers of the psychology of gender reject the idea that they are separate from the process they are trying to study, Wittig (1985) argues, they can resolve some of the dilemmas facing the psychology of gender. For example, she suggests that a careful study of "what is" need not imply the change-neutral, purely intellectual exercise associated with traditional ideas about an objective, detached science. A psychology of gender can be change-oriented and emancipatory without becoming trapped in ideology: "Constructing what could be requires knowledge of what is . . . propositions in the psychology of gender are both an attempt to understand the functioning of gender in the world as it is and an articulation of what could be" (p. 804). Careful scholarship need not preclude advocacy; rather, advocacy can contribute to scholarship by influencing the content of theory and the choices of topics and methods of study while scholarship acts as a check on the claims made by advocacy. Wittig argues that a "transformational psychology of gender" is oriented not only toward change in the world beyond the field of psychology but also toward a transformation of the discipline itself from within—into a nonsexist psychology. Such a psychology is not yet a reality, but the self-critical processes necessary to the transformation are being vigorously undertaken.

SUMMARY

We are concerned in this book with the questions of what is known about gender similarities and differences, where that knowledge comes from, and how the knowledge is shaped by culture. This chapter has focused heavily on the second question: Where does our knowledge of gender come from? What we have seen is that no pure and un-contaminated sources of such knowledge exist.

There are a variety of research methods for gathering information about sex- and gender-related aspects of human behavior, yet no one method is adequate to the task. Narrative, phenomenological, discourse analytic, observational, survey, and experimental methods can all shed some light on the links among sex, gender, and behavior, but none of them allow the researcher to conclude with certainty that biological sex differences cause behavioral differences. Because biological sex cannot be manipulated, and because it is always confounded with a variety of social–environmental variables, sex difference research is always correlational. Therefore, it is more accurate to speak of sex-related differences than of sex differences. Moreover, it is becoming clear that biological and environmental factors ("nature" and "nurture") have such closely linked, reciprocal roles in human development that it is usually meaningless to try to isolate either biology or the environment as the sole cause of an observed female–male difference.

Problems of bias abound in the research on sex and gender. Cultural stereotypes about masculinity and femininity influence the research at many levels and stages, from the choice of the research topic to the research instruments to the behavior of the experimenter to the language and concepts used in the interpretation of findings. There is a pervasive tendency to look for differences rather than similarities between females and males, not only because of stereotyped preconceptions by the researchers but also because findings of differences are more likely to be published than findings of similarities.

The entire enterprise of scientific research, as currently constructed, reflects an androcentric approach. It has been developed in a culture dominated by masculine values, and most of the participants in the scientific enterprise have been men. A transformation is under way, however, fueled by feminist concerns and by the entry of increasing numbers of women into the scientific professions. This change is beginning to be felt in the field of psychology, where increasing attention is being paid to research on gender and on topics of special concern to women, and where many traditional assumptions about the research process are being critiqued. Although we do not yet have a psychology free of sexism, we are more conscious of the potential pitfalls in researching sex and gender. We are moving away from a psychology that unwittingly helped to perpetuate masculine and feminine stereotypes and the power imbalances between women and men.

KEY TERMS

logical positivism	survey methods	statistically significant
social constructionism	correlational methods	transformationism
case history method	experiment	androcentric norms
narrative approach	independent variable	ethnocentrism
phenomenological method	dependent variable	heterosexism
discourse analysis	sex-of-experimenter effects	anthropomorphism
naturalistic observation	distribution	misogyny
		androcentric

FOR ADDITIONAL READING

Crawford, M. C., & Kimmel, E. B. (Eds.) (1999). *Psychology of Women Quarterly: Special Issues: Innovations in Feminist Research. 23*(1 & 2). These two issues contain a number of intriguing examples of innovative research methods along with commentary on each example.

Edwards, Carol, & Whiting, Beatrice. (1987). *Children of different worlds.* Cambridge, MA: Harvard University Press. The authors describe the variations in gender roles across many cultures.

Hubbard, Ruth. (1990). *The politics of women's biology.* New Brunswick, NJ: Rutgers University Press. A professor of biology examines the ways that the assumptions made by researchers have shaped the scientific investigations and findings about human nature, sexuality, and female–male differences.

Morawski, Jill G. (1994). *Practicing feminisms, reconstructing psychology: Notes on a liminal science.* Ann Arbor: University of Michigan Press. The author surveys the development of feminist psychology and explores the feminist challenges to such concepts as objectivity and validity.

Tavris, Carol. (1992). *The mismeasure of woman.* New York: Simon & Schuster. The author illustrates the pitfalls inherent in traditional social science assumptions that treat male behavior as a standard against which female behavior should be measured.

CHAPTER 4

Worlds Apart?

Gender Differences in Social Behavior & Experience

In May 1995, when Alison Hargreaves becomes the second person to complete a solo ascent of Mount Everest without supplementary oxygen, and three months later, when she falls to her death after reaching the summit of K2, many press reports focus more on her status as a "mother of two" than on her elite climbing accomplishments. On March 14, 1990, Susan Butcher storms into Nome, Alaska, recording her fourth victory in five years in the 1158-mile Iditarod Trail Dog Sled Race. As in previous years, people make much of the fact that she is female; her victory is somehow more surprising because of her sex. Similarly, when Manon Rheaume begins to play hockey for Tampa in 1992, more attention is paid to the fact that she is the first *woman* to play professional hockey than to her record. And when a young professional puts career ambitions on hold to care for a new baby or follow a spouse to a new job in a distant city, it causes considerably more comment if that young professional is a man than if she is a woman.

Expectations for women and men are still so different in some domains that observers are surprised, even shocked, when an individual woman or man "crosses the line" to behave in a way that is thought normative for the other group. Women and men are, in fact, often described as "opposite sexes." How different are we really? A look around North America quickly shows that, in terms of how we spend our time, women and men are very different indeed: Women do most of the housework, men play most of the football, women do most of the typing, men run most of the corporations, women do most of the child care, men commit most of the violent crimes. Small wonder if the casual observer were to conclude that human males and females differ dramatically in abilities, motivation, and temperament.

As illustrated in the preceding chapters, however, an observed gender difference in behavior can often be shown to result from a complex interaction between characteristics of the individuals involved and characteristics of the social environment. The observation that men commit more violent crimes than women cannot automatically be interpreted as proof that males are always and under all conditions more aggressive than females. The fact that women do most of the child care does not itself prove that women are generally more nurturing than men. This chapter surveys the research evidence for the existence of gender differences in several areas of social behavior: aggression, influenceability, dominance, nurturance, empathy, and altruism. These particular behavioral areas are chosen partly because they are all aspects of the qualities stereotypically assigned to women and men in our society. Men are supposedly more aggressive, dominant, and independent of influence than women are; women are believed to be more nurturing, empathetic, and altruistic than men are. Perhaps because each of these qualities is stereotypically either feminine or masculine, they have been the focus of a good deal of research aimed at exploring gender differences. Large gender differences sometimes exist in the probabilities that people will perform particular behaviors, but sweeping statements about general differences, such as "Women are more altruistic than men," are usually difficult to justify.

Gender differences appear in some contexts but not others, leading to the suspicion that many behavioral differences between women and men, girls and boys, are not "built in" or "set," either by biology or early learning. Instead, they are a product of—or at least amplified by—circumstance. The idea that gender differences in behavior stem from qualities that are resident in, or possessed by, women and men is sometimes labeled **essentialism** in feminist theory. This approach can be contrasted with social constructionism, first described in Chapter 3, which is the idea that gender is something that is not composed of traits possessed by individuals but rather something that occurs in interactions among persons. That is, there is a social agreement that certain behaviors are appropriate for women and men (or girls and boys) in certain situations. The difference between the two approaches is illustrated by Janice Bohan (1997):

> By way of analogy, consider the difference between describing an individual as friendly and describing a conversation as friendly. In the former case, "friendly" is constructed as a trait of the person, an "essential" component to her or his personality. In the latter, "friendly" describes the nature of the interaction occurring between or among people. Friendly here has a particular meaning that is agreed upon by the participants, that is compatible with its meaning to their social reference groups, and that is reaffirmed by the process of engaging in this interaction. Although the essentialist view of gender sees it as analogous to the friendly person, the constructionist sees gender as analogous to the friendly conversation. (p. 33)

Theorists disagree over whether the essentialist or the social constructionist approach is most useful or correct. It is important to keep in mind, however, that much of the psychological research on gender is grounded in essentialist assumptions.

"HEAVY-DUTY" STRATEGIES FOR COMPARING THE SEXES: LONGITUDINAL STUDIES AND META-ANALYSIS

When trying to uncover evidence that can be used to evaluate claims of very general male–female differences in behavior, researchers have two techniques that both add to and incorporate the arsenal of methods described in Chapter 3. The first, the **longitudinal study,** involves following the same research participants over an extended period of time, usually years, and obtaining data from them repeatedly during that time. Such a strategy allows the researcher to find out the age at which particular gender differences first appear and to assess their stability over time. This information is important; apparent gender differences may arise because one sex is developmentally ahead of the other during a particular age range or because one sex runs into a unique set of cultural constraints at a certain age. Longitudinal research can also identify variables that predict later differences in behavior *within* gender groups; such variables may turn out to be much better predictors of later behavior than gender itself. The second approach was adopted in the 1990s by investigators studying gender differences. **Meta-analysis** involves using statistical methods to combine the findings of a large number of different studies of the same behavior to evaluate the overall pattern of findings. This approach allows the researcher to begin to make sense of a collection of contradictory findings.

Longitudinal Studies

Perhaps the most famous longitudinal study in psychology was Lewis Terman's (1925) "gifted children" research. Beginning in 1922, Terman selected over 1000 preschool and elementary schoolchildren and 300 high school students, all of whom had intelligence test scores of 140 or more. For more than half a century, Terman, and after his death other psychologists, maintained contact with these people and monitored their achievements (H. S. Friedman et al., 1995; Oden, 1968; Terman & Oden, 1947, 1959). It was a gigantic undertaking, and one that provided a wealth of information about the extent to which high tested intelligence in schoolchildren predicts achievement in a variety of domains across the life span. Interestingly, although the project was not conceived with the idea of examining gender differences, its findings in this area have been very telling. High IQ was a much better predictor of achievement for males than for females. Very bright boys were likely to go on to chalk up accomplishments in the arts, science, literature, business, or public affairs as adults. Very bright girls were considerably less likely to do so. More than two thirds of the girls with IQs of 170 or more became housewives or office workers in adulthood. Follow-up studies show that many of them devoted their lives to supporting their husbands' careers or to child-rearing (Tomlinson-Keasey, 1990). Many of the questionnaire responses of these high-IQ women in later life reflect a sense of failure or lack of confidence in their abilities:

You might be interested to know that if I ever had a good mind, it has been lost in the shuffle. I seem to have stagnated and I am aware that I'm not using any capacity that I have to the fullest; however, don't give up hope, maybe I'll make you proud yet.

As I grow older, I am more and more surprised at the thought that I was ever considered a gifted child. I realize that I am slightly more intelligent than the average, but only slightly.

I have not used my gifts and regret this very much. Also I believe IQs change and mine dropped considerably. I'm no longer very competent in any area. My children all turned out well but not due to me, rather to a strict father who allowed no nonsense. (pp. 229–230)

Being male or female, then, was a far better predictor of recognized achievement in adulthood than intelligence was. Furthermore, opportunities for achievement in adulthood (opportunities that were disproportionately available to men) helped to maintain a high IQ. Those women who were able to transcend gender-role expectations in their educational and occupational pursuits, however, maintained intellectual levels similar to those of the men. Occupation, not gender, accounted best for IQ changes over the life span (Bayley & Oden, 1955). Interestingly, when this study is described in textbooks, the issue of gender is rarely raised and the predictability of achievement from IQ is discussed as if it held for all subjects. The study does not explain the gender difference, but it serves a crucial function by demonstrating two points: (1) The gender difference in adult achievement is clearly not due to an earlier difference in intelligence; (2) Gender is eclipsed by occupation as an explanatory variable for adult changes in IQ.

Jeanne Block (1973) used data from the longitudinal archives of the Institute for Human Development to examine the relationship between family background and sex-typing. Among those who were highly socialized (that is, whose personality test scores indicated they had internalized social standards), she was able to demonstrate that adults who scored as highly appropriately sex-typed on the California Personality Inventory had grown up in family contexts of clear and conventional gender roles. Those who scored as low-sex-appropriate came from families in which parents had offered more complex role models. In addition, her data suggested that for men high socialization was associated with androgyny—a mixture of such "feminine" traits as nurturance and warmth with traditionally "masculine" qualities. In contrast, for women, high socialization seemed to be linked with a reinforcement of the most conservative aspects of the traditional feminine role: passivity and dependence.

The Terman and Block studies were designed to link variables measured during childhood with other variables measured in adulthood. A longitudinal study that took a more fine-grained approach is the Stanford Longitudinal Study (e.g., Maccoby, Snow, & Jacklin, 1984; J. A. Martin, Maccoby, & Jacklin, 1981; M. E. Snow, Jacklin, & Maccoby, 1981). This study has followed three cohorts of children from birth through the preschool years, gathering data at frequent intervals on a long list of child behaviors and aspects of parent–child interaction. The researchers began by collecting information about hormone levels at birth for each child, then went on to measure such things as tactile sensitivity, muscle strength, sociability, timidity, and parental responsiveness. Among the most interesting findings is that for many variables birth order seems to account for as much or more variability as sex does (e.g., M. E. Snow et al., 1981). Also intriguing are findings that offer support for earlier indications (e.g.,

Baumrind, 1979; Block, 1973) that similar socialization practices may have different effects for girls and boys. The Stanford researchers examined the relationship between the mother's responsiveness to a child at 9 months of age and the child's willingness, 9 months later, to interrupt the mother's conversation with another adult (J. A. Martin et al., 1981). They found that mothers' nonintrusiveness (their tendency to avoid interrupting the child when she or he was playing successfully alone) had different correlates for girls and boys. Boys whose mothers had been nonintrusive at 9 months tended to play independently at 18 months; girls whose mothers had been nonintrusive were more likely than other girls to seek proximity and attention from their mothers when observed 9 months later. The reason for the difference is unclear; it is likely that parenting style interacts with other variables—environmental, biological, or both—to produce different outcomes for the two sexes. What *is* clear is that careful studies of the same individuals over time are necessary to understand whether, how, and why males and females develop differently.

One final reason for doing longitudinal research is to examine the historical aspects of gender differences. Anastasi (1981) suggests that researchers replicate their studies on subjects who have been socialized under the different cultural conditions created by different historical periods (e.g., compare 30-year-olds tested in 1950 with 30-year-olds tested in 1980). Such comparisons would allow for an examination of the impact of cultural change on gender differences. Ideally, she argues, research comparing males and females would follow a **cross-sequential method:** incorporating cross-sectional comparisons of different age groups tested at one time period, longitudinal comparisons of the same individuals tested repeatedly over time, and time-lag comparisons of same-age samples at different time periods.

The usefulness of incorporating information about history and culture into longitudinal research has been clearly demonstrated by researchers who have compared respondents who reached a particular age at different historical periods. For example, Abigail Stewart and Joan Ostrove (1998) examined data obtained from two groups of women at the age of 24. Women in the first group were 24 in 1967; those in the second group were 24 in 1978. In the first group, nearly two thirds of the women were married, and 16% were mothers at the age of 24. In the second group, whose members reached the age of 24 eleven years later, only 13% were married, and none were mothers at that age. Thus, the experience of early adulthood was clearly different for these two cohorts of college-educated American women—and a longitudinal study that followed only one of these cohorts would have risked making inappropriate generalizations related to women's life course.

Unfortunately, the resources required to conduct long-term research projects are hard to find, and too few large-scale longitudinal studies have been done. This chapter's discussion of the relationship between gender and social behavior relies largely on short-term and cross-sectional research.

Meta-Analysis

Efforts to draw conclusions about the existence of gender differences in a particular behavior have always involved collating the results of many studies of that behavior. Thus, if someone wanted to determine whether there were gender differences in nurturance, for example, he or she would gather all the studies that examined nurturing behavior in males and females and would look at the overall pattern of results. Suppose 70% of the studies showed that females behaved in a more nurturant way than males, 10% showed males to be more nurturant, and the remaining 20% showed no gender differences. Faced with this pattern, the researcher might well conclude that gender differences in nurturance were fairly well established and that females were, in general, more nurturant than males. A number of painstaking literature reviews of this type have been carried out, perhaps the most frequently cited of which is Eleanor Emmons Maccoby and Carol Nagy Jacklin's *The Psychology of Sex Differences* (1974). Maccoby and Jacklin, in a mammoth undertaking, reviewed the psychological literature relating gender to a large number of behavioral domains. They concluded that there were only four areas in which female–male differences were well established: aggression, spatial ability, verbal ability, and quantitative ability. They reserved judgment about a number of others.

Psychologists now recognize that this approach has some serious limitations. Although the studies included in a review may vary greatly in quality and on dimensions such as the variability in the sample and the size of the difference found, all are simply tabulated together and given equal weight. The now popular technique of meta-analysis allows for a more sophisticated appraisal of the overall picture that is created when a large number of studies are examined. Using this technique, all four "well-established" gender differences cited by Maccoby and Jacklin have been challenged or qualified (see this chapter for results of a meta-analysis of aggression studies and Chapter 6 for information on meta-analyses of studies in the three ability areas).

Meta-analysis begins with a concerted attempt by the researcher to gather a well-defined, complete set of studies of the behavior in question. She or he must be careful to find and include well-done but unpublished studies, such as theses and studies that went unpublished because they found no gender differences. Then, using the means and standard deviations for males and females reported in each article, the researcher calculates the **effect size** (the amount of variation in the results that is attributable to gender) for each study. There are two commonly used measures of effect size: (1) the proportion of variation in the mixed (male + female) population that can be accounted for by gender differences, and (2) the distance, in standard deviation units, between the means for males and females. Once the researcher has determined the effect size for each study in the collection, she or he can calculate the average effect size across all the studies to draw conclusions about the robustness and importance of the gender difference in question. The effect sizes may also be compared across studies that used different kinds of dependent variables, different ages of subjects, male versus female experimenters, and other variations that could possibly influence the size of the gender difference obtained. Other types of meta-analysis combine probability levels for effects found in the studies sampled; still others use techniques to pool the data for the various studies. The effect-size analysis has, however, been the most popular among investigators of gender differences.

The following example of meta-analysis provides a good illustration of the kind of information the technique can yield. Warren Eaton and Leslie Enns (1986) gathered 127 studies of male–female differences in human motor activity level (defined as the individual's customary level of energy expenditure through movement). Although there has been a widespread belief that males have a higher motor activity level than females, reviewers of the literature, including Maccoby and Jacklin (1974), have found the results too mixed to be conclusive. If females and males do differ in activity level, the difference might have some interesting implications. For example, more active infants receive more attention from their caretakers. If males are generally more active, they may be eliciting different kinds of caretaker behavior than females. Such a difference in caretaker behavior might be the basis for other behavioral differences between female and male infants. Thus, Eaton and Enns attempted to use meta-analysis to determine whether and to what extent a gender difference in human motor activity level exists.

When Eaton and Enns calculated the effect size for the gender differences reported in the 127 studies, they found that the average difference between the male and female mean activity level scores was just under one half of a standard deviation. Furthermore, the proportion of total population variance in activity level that could be accounted for by gender was about 5%. That means 95% of the variability in activity level could be attributed either to variation *within* gender groups or to experimental error (random fluctuations, measurement error).

The finding that only 5% of the variance in the activity level of mixed-sex populations could be explained by gender differences appears, at first glance, to argue that male–female differences in activity level are too small to be important. However, many of the group differences or experimental effects reported in psychological research are of this magnitude (Eagly & Wood, 1991). Moreover, as Eaton and Enns note, small differences in means can translate into large differences in the proportions of males and females at the extremes of a given behavior. (As noted in Chapter 3, however, the implications of a difference in means depend on the shapes of the distributions of scores for the two groups. If the distributions of scores for males and females are both normal and have similar variances, differences in means will translate into differences at the extremes; otherwise, they may not.) The presence of different proportions of females and males at the extremes of activity level may cause the females and males to be differentially included in diagnostic categories such as "hyperactive." Eaton and Enns argue that despite the small number of people of either sex whose activity level reaches an extreme threshold, the difference in the proportions of males and females who show especially high activity levels will tend to be readily noted and remembered by observers, who will use the information to define or reinforce their gender stereotypes. Thus, a teacher who has, over several years of working with children, encountered four boys and one girl who could be characterized as "hyperactive" may find it easy to subscribe to the belief that boys are more active than girls, even though, among the hundreds of normally active other children the teacher has taught, no striking gender differences in activity level appear. In this way, a gender difference that is noticeable only at the extremes of a behavioral distribution can form the basis for a much broader gender stereotype.

Meta-analysis is so far the most useful tool researchers have found for aggregating the results of many studies of a particular male–female difference. It can provide information about the average strength of the relationship between gender and a particular behavior and tell the researcher what other variables, such as age or situational effects, may be mediating that relationship. Yet caution is in order: The results of a meta-analysis are only as good as its sample of studies. If a complete sample of studies is not included, or if the studies included have inaccurate results due to bias or sloppy data collection, the meta-analysis is worth little. Also, if the sample of studies used is overrepresentative of biased situations (e.g., if most of the experimenters in the sample are male, or if most of the measures used are biased in favor of females), the results of the meta-analysis will reflect a similar bias (Eagly & Carli, 1981). Finally, when researchers determine an average effect size for gender, they face the same problem in interpretation that anyone faces in knowing what an average score means (Favreau, 1993). Is the effect the result of a few males or females who differ strongly from the other gender group? Is it the result of a general difference between most females and most males? The statistics currently used to describe effect size do not answer these questions.

GENDER DIFFERENCES IN SOCIAL BEHAVIOR: A SAMPLING OF CURRENT FINDINGS

Having explored the techniques available for determining the presence of gender differences, let's turn to an examination of what these techniques have found in the realm of social behavior. For each of several kinds of social behavior, we examine the evidence for the reliable presence and magnitude of female–male differences. Where differences are found to exist, evidence concerning the reasons for these differences is reviewed. Similar examinations of evidence for gender differences and similarities in other domains, such as intellectual abilities, achievement, communication, intimacy, sexuality, and morality, will be presented in later chapters.

Aggression

In many societies, including our own, male aggression is tolerated and expected more than female aggression. Instances of serious male aggression against other men and against women are tragically common. In Columbine High School in Littleton, Colorado, in the latest of many similar incidents, two young men open fire on teachers and fellow students, killing and wounding many. In Washington, D.C., three young men beat and kill a 65-year-old man whose car collides with theirs—apparently merely because he is inebriated and verbally belligerent ("Driver, 65," 1991). In Kenya, a group of young men at a church boarding school attack the women's dormitory, beating and raping all the women they can lay their hands on. Seventy-one women have been raped and 19 young women are dead at the end of the rampage, which the head of the school characterizes as "a joke turned nasty" ("School Rapes," 1991). It is difficult to imagine these situations with women as the aggressors. Is that because males really are more aggressive than females, or do they simply commit more "spectacular" acts of aggression? Do males have stronger aggressive drives than females do, or have they simply not been taught as carefully as females that they must control those drives?

Maccoby and Jacklin (1974) concluded from their extensive review that greater male than female aggressiveness was a well-established finding. The difference occurred for both physical and verbal aggression and was found across a variety of cultures. It appeared between ages 2 and 3 and continued through the college years, after which there was little information available. A decade later, Janet Hyde (1984b) used meta-analysis to evaluate the size of the gender difference and to examine developmental aspects of it. She found that gender differences were not large, even though they were well established. Gender accounted for an average of 5% of the variance in aggression found in the combined-sex populations of the 75 studies in her sample, with the male mean being about one half a standard deviation higher than that of the females. Thus, within-gender variation in aggression appears to be considerably larger than between-gender variation. The size of the gender difference tended to be larger for younger than for older people: for children under the age of 6, gender accounted for 7% of the variance in aggression, whereas for college students, gender accounted for only 1%. The interpretability of the latter finding is made difficult, however, by the fact that aggression was generally measured differently for preschool children and college students. For preschoolers, physical or verbal aggressive behaviors were often measured, whereas for college students, aggression tended to be measured by willingness to administer an electric shock to another individual. Hyde also found that gender differences tended to be larger in naturalistic, correlational studies than in experimental studies, and in earlier (1966–1973) than later (1978–1981) studies. The smaller differences in later studies may be due to changes in gender socialization patterns, changes in perceptions by experimenters or other observers, or an increased likelihood of publication of "no difference" findings after Maccoby and Jacklin's (1974) review.

Hyde (1984b) also noted that larger gender differences were found when aggression was measured by direct observation, projective methods, or peer reports than when measured by self-reports, parent, or teacher reports. Such a finding may point to observer bias in noticing and reporting aggression. Observers, influenced by gender stereotypes, might be more likely to notice aggressive behavior in males than females. One study suggests, however, that observer bias may be working in the reverse direction, toward the minimization of observed male aggression and the exaggeration of observed female aggression. John Condry and David Ross (1985) showed college students a videotape of two children playing roughly in the snow. The children's actual gender was disguised by their snowsuits, and the researchers varied the gender labels for each child. Observers who thought they were watching a boy acting aggressively against another boy rated the behavior as significantly less aggressive than those who thought they were watching a boy acting aggressively against a girl or a girl acting aggressively against either a boy or a girl. Apparently, the observers tended to discount the aggressiveness of an interaction when two boys were engaged in it and to inflate the aggressiveness of the same interaction when it involved a girl. The authors argue that such an observer bias would work to minimize observed gender differences in aggression, and they speculate that the existing literature may therefore underestimate the magnitude of male–female differences. It is difficult, then, to be sure of the magnitude of gender differences in aggression. Nevertheless, it appears that where such differences are found it is more likely to be males than females who are engaging in aggressive behavior.

Another meta-analysis of female–male differences in aggression suggests that such differences are largest in situations where expectations for women and men differ most strongly (Eagly & Steffen, 1986). The researchers asked college students to imagine the aggressive behavior detailed in each of the studies included in the meta-analysis and to rate the harmful consequences of the act, the anxiety or guilt they themselves would feel in performing it, how much danger they would face in performing the act, and the likelihood that the average man or woman would perform the act. The results showed that not only were women more likely than men to rate the aggressive acts as harmful, potentially guilt-inducing, and likely to be dangerous to the performer, but also that the raters believed the average man was more likely than the average woman to perform these aggressive acts. Significantly, the size of the gender-differentiated beliefs and norms among these college students was positively related to the size of the behavioral gender difference in aggression found in the studies. For studies of aggression using behaviors where expectations and norms for women and men were most different according to the raters, the greatest female–male differences in aggressive behavior were found.

The consensus among reviewers is that male–female differences in aggression are largest and most consistent for physical aggression (Hyde, 1984b; Maccoby & Jacklin, 1974). One possible qualification to this conclusion is that much of the apparent difference may stem from extremely aggressive behavior by a few boys. Such a finding was reported by J. Archer and Westeman (1981); it may have gone unnoticed in other studies. Indeed, Eleanor Maccoby (1998), having spent most of her career observing children's behavior, notes that "most boys are *not* aggressive, in the sense of possessing a consistent personality disposition that involves frequent fighting and getting into trouble with adults and peers through fighting" (p. 36). Rather, she says, boys' rough play often seems to indicate high spirits rather than aggression.

Maccoby points out that we are used to thinking of boys' aggressiveness as a personality trait, but it may be more accurate to think of it as a product of particular situations: "a characteristic of male–male play—better seen as a property of male dyads or groups than of individuals" (p. 37). She arrives at this conclusion after observing that boys are not equally aggressive under all conditions but are especially likely to aggress when interacting with other boys. Boys, she says, almost always choose other boys as targets for their aggression, and they are less likely to respond aggressively when *girls* direct aggressive or assertive actions against them than when boys do.

Maccoby's observations recall the distinction between the essentialist and social constructionist modes of thinking about gender, discussed earlier in the chapter. Aggression, she is arguing, is not necessarily an essential trait more likely to be possessed by individual males than by individual females. Rather, shared particular situations permit and encourage more aggressive behaviors among males than among females or between males and females. A key situational factor in whether a boy will behave aggressively appears to be the gender of the other people in the situation. As Maccoby says, "the gendered aspect of an individual's behavior is brought into play by the gender of others" (p. 9).

Should the research findings on gender differences in aggression be interpreted to mean that women tend to behave nonaggressively? Probably not. As Jacquelyn White and Robin Kowalski (1994) note, there is ample evidence of aggressive behavior by women, and it is likely that women have as much potential as men do to be aggressive—under the right conditions. However, women face more social restrictions in their expression of aggression than men do; thus, men's aggression may be more public and physical, whereas women's may be more private and indirect. Early studies showed that girls and boys were equally aggressive when offered equal rewards for aggressive behaviors (Bandura, 1973). Equal rewards are rarely present, however, given the differing norms for behavior learned by girls and boys. Boys approve of and expect more rewards and fewer punishments for aggression than girls do (Huesmann, Guerra, Zelli, & Miller, 1992; Perry, Perry, & Weiss, 1989). Thus, unless especially angered or provoked, females may be more inhibited than males about *expressing* aggression (Frodi, Macaulay, & Thome, 1977).

Also, there is evidence that women have more anxiety about aggressive feelings than men do and that they feel more anxious after being aggressive than men do (Frodi et al., 1977). Women are more likely than men to make self-critical statements about their own aggression to avoid disapproval (A. Campbell & Muncer, 1987). In situations where aggression anxiety is reduced, either through strong justification for the aggression or confidence that aggression will be an effective strategy, women's likelihood of aggression may rise. For instance, Jack Hokanson and his colleagues (Hokanson & Edelman, 1966; Hokanson, Willers, & Koropsak, 1968) found that males' physiological arousal decreased dramatically after they were allowed to give electric shocks to someone who had insulted them. Females showed no such "relief response" following aggression; in fact, their arousal decreased following a friendly response toward their insulter. However, the researchers were able to teach the relief response for aggression to the female subjects simply by changing their reinforcement history: rewarding aggressive responses with nonshock trials and shocking subjects if they made a friendly response.

Do females and males follow similar paths toward becoming violent? Relatively little is known about possible gender differences in the factors that predispose individuals toward aggressive behavior. However, there are indications that physical or sexual abuse in childhood is more strongly related to later violent behavior among girls than boys. Also, women who engage in antisocial violence are more likely than their male counterparts to have relatives who are socially deviant. These findings provide hints at possible differences in the ways that men and women become aggressive and in the kinds of interventions that might be effective (Loeber & Stouthamer-Loeber, 1998).

There are some serious limitations to the psychological literature on gender differences in aggression. Most of the studies have been carried out on populations that are the most easily accessible to researchers: preschool and schoolchildren and college students. There are practically no laboratory studies of adults older than college age. Moreover, the measures of aggression used in controlled studies have, of necessity, been artificial and limited. When real life is considered, the pattern of greater male than female involvement in aggression appears more clear-cut. Men commit far more of the violent crimes than women do, and men are also more frequently victims of such crimes (U.S. Department of Justice, Federal Bureau of Investigation, 1997). Also, far more wives than husbands are driven from their homes or live in fear because of a violently abusive spouse (U.S. Department of Justice, Office of Justice Programs, 1995). When these statistics are considered, it appears that, whatever the size of the average gender difference in aggressive behavior, men are much more likely than women to engage in very physically violent behavior.

Women are certainly capable of violence toward family members. A national survey found no difference between women and men in their rates of physical child abuse (Wauchope & Straus, 1990). Indeed, the majority of studies of perpetrators of physical child abuse have focused on women (Margolin, 1992). However, this focus may stem from the perception that women's violence is more surprising, and thus more interesting to study, than men's, which may provide a misleading picture. Leslie Margolin (1992) notes that males commit more of the severe abuse than females. She also points out that, given the disparity between women and men in the amount of time they spend caring for children, the finding that men commit half the physical abuse suggests, in fact, that men are much more likely than women to physically abuse children in their care.

Possible social psychological reasons for gender differences in aggression include the direct teaching of more aggressive behaviors to boys than girls, the rewarding of males more than females for aggressive behavior, the rewarding of girls more than boys for inhibiting aggressive behavior, and the presence of more male than female aggressive models. All of these factors may help to create social conditions in which male aggression, particularly male–male aggression, is more accepted than female aggression.

There is evidence that males are more rewarded by their peers than females are for aggressive behavior (Fagot & Hagan, 1985) and that aggression in females meets with disapproval, even in children. An interesting example of the social disapproval of female aggression is the negative reaction to women boxers (J. Archer & Lloyd, 1985). Aggressive models for males are provided in abundance in sports and in the popular media; physical aggression by females is much less frequently portrayed. Moreover, when aggression by women is portrayed in the media, as in the movie *Thelma and Louise,* it seems to be met with far more public outrage than portrayals of equivalent behavior by males. Taken together, the different socialization pressures for boys and girls could well lead to greater readiness by males to behave aggressively in many situations and to a stronger inhibition by females against aggression.

It should already be clear that gender differences in aggression do not reflect a straightforward personality difference between women and men. Rather, these differences reflect a more complicated interplay between social expectations, predispositions, and particular circumstances. One more issue to consider in understanding gender differences in aggressive behavior is power. In a context of social power in which males are more likely than females to learn that it is acceptable and that they have a *right* to get their way through aggression, males are more likely than females to engage in aggression. Power and status differences between females and males in their social environment are likely to support gender differences in aggression. To the extent that males are bigger, stronger, and better trained in aggressive techniques than females are, aggression is more likely to be an effective strategy for them. Furthermore, in situations where women are economically dependent on men—situations that are frequent in societies where men are given preferred access to resources such as education, employment, and income—men may find aggression a less risky strategy than women do and so employ it more. Male aggression that is specifically directed against women is greater in cultures in which women have little economic or political power or authority (Sanday, 1981a). These power-related issues are discussed further in Chapters 11 and 12.

Some of the biological factors postulated as causes for the gender difference in aggression include the influence of the Y chromosome, the prenatal influence of male hormones *in utero* on the developing brain of the fetus, and the level of male hormones circulating in the mature individual's bloodstream. All of these factors will be examined in the following chapter in the discussion of sexual differentiation. It is possible but unproven that one or more of these biological factors contributes to a predisposition for males to behave more aggressively than females, perhaps by building in a sensitivity to certain kinds of stimuli or by making certain aggression-related responses more rewarding. However, the existence of such a predisposition would not lead inevitably to male–female differences in aggressive behavior; biological and social influences on behavior work in combination. Cross-cultural studies show that societies differ in the degree to which they encourage male aggression, and gender-related differences in aggression reflect these cultural norms (e.g., Block, 1973; Mead, 1935). Societies in which there is a great deal of emphasis on warfare, aggressiveness, and bravery tend to foster conditions in which women become property to be conquered or prizes to be won by male warriors. In contrast, in certain forager societies aggression and violence of all kinds are frowned upon. In such societies, gender differences in aggression appear to be minimal (O'Kelly & Carney, 1986). The expression of aggressive tendencies occurs through the individuals' interaction with their social and cultural environment.

Influenceability

There is little evidence to support the stereotype that women are generally more easily influenced, or more compliant, than men (Eagly & Wood, 1985; Maccoby & Jacklin, 1974). When gender differences are found, they are usually in the direction of greater female conformity (e.g., Collin, Di Sano, & Malik, 1994); however, a meta-analysis of social influence studies by Eagly and Carli (1981) indicates that the size of the difference is quite small, with male and female means about one quarter of a standard deviation apart. Furthermore, their analysis indicates that findings of gender differences tend to be associated with particular situational variables. The difference is larger in laboratory studies when subjects are confronted with group pressure and in studies where subjects know they are under observation. Male researchers are more likely to find gender differences in influenceability than female researchers are. Also, the small amount of evidence that is available suggests race or ethnicity may be an important variable. In the United States, African American females tend to be less easily influenced than their African American male or European American female counterparts (K. A. Adams, 1980, 1983).

Both sexes show less conformity when dealing with a topic or task that is familiar or gender-appropriate (Karabenick, 1983; Sistrunk & McDavid, 1971). But even though gender-biased topics may contribute artificially to findings of gender differences in particular studies, there is no evidence that the research in this area has an overall masculine content bias (Eagly & Carli, 1981). Thus, the general finding of modestly greater female than male influenceability in certain situations cannot be attributed solely to this bias.

One reason for the finding that females are slightly more influenceable than males under some circumstances may lie in gender roles. Research by Eagly, Wood, and Fishbaugh (1981) shows that at least some of the observed differences may occur not because women conform more but because men conform less when they are subjected to group pressure. It has usually been assumed that women more often than men change their opinions to coincide with those of a group in the interest of group harmony. However, these researchers showed that women's opinions tended to remain unchanged when confronted with a group. Rather, it was the men's opinions that changed—in the direction of greater nonconformity. Eagly and her colleagues suggest that the sometimes observed gender difference in who can be influenced may stem not from greater female compliance but from male concern with not *appearing* influenceable. Males may tend to think of nonconformity or independence as "masculine" and tailor their behavior in that direction. Congruent with this explanation is the finding that conformity appears to vary with gender-typing.

"Masculine" and "androgynous" individuals of both sexes tend to conform less than "feminine" individuals (Bem, 1975; Brehony & Geller, 1981).

Another explanation for gender differences in conformity in certain kinds of situations may be the status differences between women and men (Eagly, 1983; Eagly & Wood, 1982). Men are automatically ascribed higher status than women under many circumstances; they also tend to hold higher-status positions (Lockheed, 1985; Lockheed & Hall, 1976). With higher status come expectations for greater influence, and these expectations may become self-fulfilling prophecies. Men are expected to exert more influence because of their higher status; thus, they act in influencing ways, whereas women, who are not expected to exert as much influence, act in conforming ways. The result is a status difference disguised as a gender difference.

Important to the evaluation of this body of research (and other research on gender) is Alice Eagly and Linda Carli's (1981) finding that greater female influenceability is significantly more likely to be found by male researchers. The finding cannot easily be explained as an effect of higher status male experimenters or influencing agents: group pressure studies commonly use same-sex groups, and many conformity studies do not identify the influencing agent by sex. Rather, Eagly and Carli suggest that bias related to the gender of the researcher may enter the design in a number of ways. Researchers may choose topics that favor the interests and expertise of their own gender, or they may unwittingly design settings and procedures that make subjects of their own gender more comfortable and self-confident and therefore less easily influenced. To find out about the generality of the tendency for male researchers to report more gender differences, Eagly and Carli compared their findings to those in a sample of studies collected by Hall (1978) on interpreting nonverbal communication. Where gender differences are found in the accuracy of interpreting nonverbal communication, they tend to favor females; however, the male researchers in Hall's sample were *less* likely than female researchers to find such gender differences. Eagly and Carli suggest, then, that there is no overall tendency for male researchers to find more gender differences; rather, both male and female researchers introduce bias in ways that make the portrayal of their own gender more favorable. If their suggestion is correct, the fact that the majority of researchers in psychology has been and continues to be male has serious implications for the view of women that has been generated by research.

Dominance

Dominance encompasses a wide range of behaviors that have to do with imposing one's will on others and controlling and influencing others' behavior. In our culture, males are stereotypically viewed as more dominant than females, and there is some truth to that stereotype, at least in certain situations. However, as was the case with aggression and conformity, it is difficult to disentangle the effects of gender on dominance behavior from the effects of status.

Studies of African American, European American, and Hispanic undergraduate students show a stronger orientation toward social dominance among men than women across all three groups (Sidanius, Pratto, & Rabinowitz, 1994), and males score higher than females on personality measures of dominance (Feingold, 1994a). In mixed-sex groups or pairs, men tend to dominate the conversation, talking more than women, interrupting or ignoring women, and failing to pick up conversational topics raised by women (Eakins & Eakins, 1978; Krupnick, 1985; Lockheed & Hall, 1976; Spender, 1980; Zimmerman & West, 1975). Women speak more tentatively than men do when they are in mixed-sex pairs, and this strategy has a mixed payoff. Women who speak tentatively are more influential with men but less influential with women in such groups (Carli, 1990). Nonverbally, men signal dominance in these mixed-sex situations by gesturing expansively, touching women, and controlling physical space. Women are more likely to be circumspect and tense in their posture, to avoid touching, and to take up little space (Henley, 1977).

In initially leaderless groups of women and men, men are more likely than women to emerge as leaders, particularly if the groups are short-term or working on tasks that do not require much social interaction. However, women are slightly more likely than men to become social leaders (Eagly & Karau, 1991). When college women and men whose dominance has been measured with a personality test are placed in same-gender pairs, the high-dominant individual assumes leadership most of the time. However, in female–male pairs, the male partner is more likely to assume leadership, regardless of dominance score (Carbonell, 1984; Megargee, 1969; Nyquist & Spence, 1986). In male–female pairs where the woman is high-dominant and the man is low-dominant, the highest percentage of female leaders selected in any study is 50% (Fleischer & Chertkoff, 1986). Where the man is high-dominant and the woman is low-dominant, the percentage of male leaders selected has averaged between 85% and 90%. When women and men are interacting together, then, men often act in more dominant ways than women do. This pattern appears to provide another example of Maccoby's (1998) contention that, to a large extent, gendered behavior is prompted by the gender of others in the interaction.

In same-sex groups, men show no more tendency to try to dominate the conversation than women do (Kimble, Yoshikawa, & Zehr, 1981). However, there may be some differences in dominance behavior between all-female and all-male groups. Aries (1976) found that all-male groups established a more stable dominance order over time and showed more instances of one member addressing the group as a whole than did all-female groups. Paikoff and Savin-Williams (1983) found that among adolescents female groups tended to be less structured, more cohesive, and show less evidence of linear dominance hierarchies than male groups. There is some evidence, then, that men may be more concerned than women with dominance, even in same-sex groups.

Some researchers have argued that gender differences in dominance are linked to gender differences in aggression and may have a biological basis. However, aside from the problem that a biological basis for gender differences in aggression has not yet been established, many forms of dominance in human society do not involve aggression. Successful dominance in some situations may even involve an inhibition of aggression. It is more likely that status and role expectations govern dominance behavior. There is some evidence, for instance, that the more competence a person is seen as having in a particular situation, either by others or by her- or himself, the more leadership she or he will be able to assume. Postulating that men take on group leadership roles because, having automatic higher status than women, they get more respect and deference from the group from the beginning, Lockheed and Hall (1976) devised a way to reduce the impact of these initial status differences. They provided females with task experience, to build task-specific expectations of competence before putting them into mixed-sex groups to work on the task. This strategy had a marked impact. In mixed-sex groups, males were 4 to 7 times more likely than females to emerge as leaders *unless* the females in the group had been given the opportunity to develop competence on the task ahead of time, in which case female ranking improved fairly dramatically. In groups where the female participants had been given, through experience, task-specific expectations of competence, females were more active than in other groups and a female was ranked either first or second in leadership-related behaviors in all groups.

Another example of the impact of perceived competence on dominance can be found in the relationship between leadership and the gender stereotyping of the group task. One study (Wentworth & Anderson, 1984) found that male undergraduates were more likely than their female counterparts to emerge as leaders when the group was working on a "masculine" (how to invest $10,000) or neutral (how to spend $10,000 on entertainment items) task; however, females took the leadership role for the "feminine" task (how a young woman should spend $10,000 on her wedding).

How does perceived competence or status translate into leadership or the ability to dominate a group? Apparently, group members behave quite differently toward those whom they view as having high or low status. Butler and Geis (1990), for instance, found that male leaders received more smiles and fewer frowns than female leaders when making equivalent contributions to group discussions. In fact, the more a female leader talked, the more unfavorable were the facial expressions directed toward her by other members of the group—male and female alike. The researchers attribute the differing reactions to perceptions by group members that females were violating role and status expectations by taking on leadership. Given the differing nonverbal reactions to female and male leadership attempts, it is likely that males find it easier than females to dominate or lead a group, but this may have little to do with gender differences in predisposition toward dominance.

The complexity of the relationship among status, social expectations, and dominance behavior is illustrated by research on how gender and race interact in helping to determine dominance behavior. Race, like sex, is considered by researchers to be a status characteristic—a characteristic that automatically influences the status ascribed to a person. Although an individual's overall status is thought to be made up of a combination of all the status characteristics relevant to the person judging it, it seems to be more complex than a simple average (Adams, 1983). American research indicates that being Black is associated with a lower status than being White, just as being female is associated with a lower status than being male. African American women, then, might be expected to have the lowest perceived status of the four possible sex–race combinations. In line with predictions about status and dominance behavior, African American women would be expected to be less dominant than anyone else. This prediction is not supported, however. Black women have been found to be more likely than White women to assume leadership positions in all-female groups (Fenelon & Megargee, 1971), and a study of influence in dyads showed that Black females were better than Black males and White females at resisting challenges to their preferences (Adams, 1980). Black males sustained fewer challenges from White than from Black partners. More recent research on conversations within mixed-gender, same-race groups suggests that African American women work more assertively at conversational control in mixed gender groups than European American women do (Filardo, 1996). In European American groups, a significantly higher percentage of the women's than of the men's utterances were interrupted and never completed—but this was not true in the African American groups. In the African American groups, the men had a high percentage of speech that expressed commands, dominance, or a lack of consideration for the viewpoint of others (e.g., "That's stupid," or "*This* way!"), but the women in these groups still managed to say what they wanted to say. Thus, African American women's tendency to complete what they wanted to say was apparently based on their own assertive and active behavior rather than on any particular accommodating behavior on the part of African American men.

Clearly, it is too simple to think of status as something that is unchanging across social contexts. The status accorded to gender, race, or other attributes may vary according to the norms of the situation and the status characteristics of the person with whom the individual is interacting (Adams, 1983). On the whole, the interaction between gender and race in dominance situations suggests that gender differences in dominance may be largely socially produced and vulnerable to situational change. This research also illustrates the dangers of trying to understand gender differences by studying only members of a particular racial or cultural group.

The limitations of a narrow cultural perspective on gender differences are further highlighted by cross-cultural research on dominance. Leadership and dominance are behaviors that are often encouraged in American society, but cultures such as the Arapesh (Mead, 1935) and the Mbuti (Sanday, 1981a) favor equality and discourage leadership and dominance hierarchies. In such groups, there tends to be more equality of power and less role differentiation between women and men. Among the Mbuti, for example, diversity of opinion may be expressed through discussion, and participation in such discussions is evenly divided between males and females of all adult age levels. However, prolonged disagreement is labeled "noise" and is discouraged because it is considered offensive to the forest.

In still other societies, certain aspects of leadership and status are or have been assigned to women. For example, the constitution of the Iroquois, the North American Indian confederacy of six nations that was formed in the mid–15th century, declared that women were the progenitors of the Nation, that descent of the people would run in the female line, and that the women would own the land and the soil (Sanday, 1981a). This principle acknowledged significant power for the women. For example, women of the Seneca, one of the six nations, controlled all cultivated tribal land, had the final say over the distribution of surplus food, and exercised strong influence, through their councils, over tribal decisions with respect to warfare and peace negotiations (Jensen, 1990). Other North American Indian groups, such as the Hopi and the Navajo, also have strong traditions of female power (Katz, 1977; O'Kelly & Carney, 1986). Part of the process of the colonization of Native Americans by invading Europeans was the undermining of this female power. Native Americans were increasingly pressured by missionaries and government officials to adopt the European values and practices of female subordination (Jensen, 1990). Research on gender differences in dominance might have produced quite different results in certain Native American and European American groups at this time.

Nurturance

Women score higher than men do on personality measures of nurturance (Feingold, 1994a). Women are so often seen in nurturing roles, not only as mothers caring for small children but as nurses, child-care workers, and social workers, that it is easy to accept a stereotype of women as the more nurturant sex. This stereotype permeates the writings of professionals about women and about motherhood (Ruddick, 1989), and in North America it is applied to European American middle-class women (Rich, 1976), poor women (Belle, 1984), Latina women (Mirande & Enriquez, 1979), and African American women (McCray, 1980). In fact, as seen in earlier chapters, the idea that women had a maternal instinct, a built-in tendency to care for small children, was popular in psychology for a time. It is now understood, however, that greater female than male participation in nurturant activities cannot by itself be taken as an indication that women are "naturally" more nurturant than men; rather, the participation rates may reflect social pressure and the nature of the choices available to women and men.

Nurturance involves caring for and promoting the welfare of others. Many activities fall under this definition, from comforting a sick child to soothing the ruffled feathers of a tired, grumpy spouse to mending a leaky roof so that one's family will be warm and dry. There is no evidence of a gender difference in nurturance that holds across all such activities. Even for responses to babies, where, stereotypically, one might expect the most clear-cut gender difference to favor women, the research reveals a cloudy picture. The sexes do not differ in their physiological responses (heart rate, blood pressure, skin conductance) to an infant's cry, although females are more likely to report that the crying bothers them (Frodi & Lamb, 1978). Men can be as good as women at feeding infants and at correctly identifying the meaning of a baby's cry. College males and females have been found to be equally good at discriminating among different kinds of baby cries (Parke, 1981), and fathers are as good as mothers at using infants' cues to guide their own caregiving behavior (Parke & Sawin, 1976). In the hospital, just after their babies' birth, and later at home, fathers observed by Parke and Sawin were as likely as mothers to hold, rock, talk to, and smile at their babies; during bottle feeding, babies took just as much milk from their fathers as from their mothers. However, some studies show that boys are less responsive than girls to an unfamiliar infant in a waiting-room situation (Feldman, Nash, & Cutrona, 1977) and that new mothers paid more attention than other adults to a baby who was not their own (Feldman & Nash, 1978). In the latter case, however, more than a simple gender difference was observed: The new mothers were more responsive not only than men but also than women who did not have children and women who were pregnant.

Expectations in the area of nurturance differ for women and men. There is evidence that children perceive their mothers as more nurturing than their fathers (Carunungan-Robles, 1986; Hopkins & Klein, 1993). This perception may be based partially on the different ways mothers and fathers express their care and support. Furthermore, the feminine stereotype of emotional expressiveness and nurturance seems to make it easier for women than for men both to provide and to obtain social support from close relations (Barbee, Cunningham, Winstead, Derlega, et al., 1993).

There seems little doubt that gender differences in nurturant behavior, where they are found, can be traced to social context, stereotyping, and social pressure. Cross-cultural research shows that girls and boys differ more in nurturance in those societies where girls are directly socialized more toward nurturance than boys are. In cultures where these differential socialization pressures are minimal—where, for instance, both girls and boys are expected to help with infant care—gender differences in nurturance are minimal as well (Whiting & Edwards, 1973). In our culture, differences in reactions to infants are more likely to show up in self-reports or in situations where participants know they are being observed and evaluated than in other situations (Berman, 1976, 1980). Also, it is masculine sex-typing, rather than being male, that seems to interfere with nurturant behavior. In one study, androgynous men were as responsive to a baby and to a kitten as women were, but masculine men were less responsive (Bem, Martyna, & Watson, 1976).

Although evidence for the impact of gender expectations on nurturant behavior is strong, researchers have not ruled out the possibility that biology plays a role, through prenatal hormones, in the development of some gender differences in nurturance. This research will be discussed in Chapter 5. Once again, whatever potential differences may be provided for by biological factors would have to develop through the individual's interaction with her or his social and physical environment. Despite some interesting changes that have begun to take place in that environment, it is still less supportive of male than female nurturance.

Empathy

Empathy, the quality of being sensitive and responsive to the feelings of others, is often cited as a feminine characteristic. Women are said to have "woman's intuition," to be good at listening to people's problems, and to be more easily swayed than men by emotional appeals. This stereotype has been echoed in decades of social and psychological theory about women, from Freud's notion of women's weak superego to Parsons and Bales's instrumental–expressive distinction between male and female roles (Eisenberg & Lennon, 1983). When the evidence is examined, however, this particular stereotype does not hold up very well.

A meta-analysis of empathy research showed that where gender differences in empathy exist they tend to favor females (Eisenberg & Lennon, 1983). However, such differences were found inconsistently and seemed to depend on the method used to measure empathy. When the measure used was self-report—subjects' responses to questionnaire items such as "I tend to get emotionally involved with a friend's problems"—females scored much higher than males on empathy. Every study in the sample showed a statistically significant difference, and the mean empathy score of the females was, on average, almost a full standard deviation above that of the males. For other measures, however, the gender difference was considerably less clear-cut. When subjects were asked to respond to emotional situations simulated in the lab or on videotape, most studies found no gender difference in reports of sympathy or concern or of feeling the same emotion as the story's protagonist. Measures of physiological response to another person's emotional distress also yielded no evidence of greater female than male sensitivity to others' feelings. When children's reactions to others' distress were observed unobtrusively, gender differences were not found. However, when children were explicitly questioned about their reactions, girls showed more nonverbal signs of empathy than boys did.

On the whole, the reviewers noted, the gender difference in empathy was most evident in studies where it was most obvious that empathy was being measured. Largest differences were found in studies using self-report or explicit questioning; no differences were found using physiological measures or unobtrusive observation. More recent findings of greater female than male empathy are similarly based on self-reports (e.g., Lang-Takac & Osterwell, 1992; Trobst, Collins, & Embree, 1994). Eisenberg and Lennon (1983) suggest that the appearance of gender differences in empathy is largely influenced by the demand characteristics of the research situation—that is, the cues to the participant about how to behave. Why should demand characteristics produce a gender difference instead of across-the-board increases in empathy responding? Females and males are quite likely to differ in how empathetic they would like to appear to others. Because empathy is a stereotypically feminine trait, it is not surprising that when they know empathy is being measured, as in the case of the self-report studies, females produce more empathy responses than males do.

Further support for the influence of gender stereotypes on the gender difference in empathy can be found in research linking empathy to gender-typing. Self-reports of empathy are correlated positively with self-ratings of femininity and negatively with self-rated masculinity (Foushee, Davis, & Archer, 1979), and people who are gender-typed as masculine show fewer empathetic behaviors than androgynous or feminine individuals when listening to someone describing personal problems (Bem et al., 1976).

One measure of empathy for which there is a fairly consistent finding of higher levels for females is sensitivity to nonverbal cues. Females seem to be moderately better than males at all ages at interpreting the meaning of auditory cues (such as tone of voice), and among adults, women are better than men at decoding visual cues such as facial expression, particularly when the nonverbal message is intentional (Eisenberg & Lennon, 1983; Hall, 1978, 1984; Rosenthal & DePaulo, 1979). Some investigators feel that women learn to refrain from "eavesdropping" on nonverbal cues that the sender cannot control. This pattern appears to strengthen from childhood to adulthood—a clue that it may be shaped through social learning.

Empathy for others' feelings in general, and sensitivity to nonverbal emotional cues in particular, probably relate to situational factors such as status and role. Rosenthal and his colleagues (Rosenthal, Archer, DiMatteo, Kowumaki, & Rogers, 1974) found that men who were training for or working in occupations that required nurturance or sensitivity were as good as women at decoding nonverbally expressed emotions. Whether this finding can be attributed to the effects of practice or to the self-selection of unusually sensitive men for such occupations is difficult to know. Women's greater sensitivity may be due to their lower status in many situations. People with subordinate status generally have to develop more sensitivity to others' feelings than high-status people do, as a matter of survival (Snodgrass, 1985). Lipman-Blumen (1984) has argued that "woman's intuition" is a skill developed by women to help them to predict and thus control or at least cope with the moods and behaviors of the more powerful men with whom they must interact. Of interest in this regard are findings of greater nonverbal sensitivity among Blacks than Whites in the United States.

Altruism

Consistent with the stereotype that females are more nurturant and empathetic is the notion that they have a stronger tendency than men to do things for others, to be helpful to people in need. This assumed gender difference has been widely studied, but results have proved inconsistent. Girls clearly have more of a reputation for altruistic behavior than boys do (Zarbatany, Hartmann, Gelfand, & Vinciguerra, 1985). However, when actual helping behavior is measured, females do not consistently come out ahead. In fact, differences are found more often in the direction of greater male than greater female helpfulness (Eagly & Crowley, 1986; Piliavin & Unger, 1985).

Researchers trying to make sense of apparently contradictory findings in this area have focused on the situational variables that distinguish settings in which males tend to be more helpful from those in which females do (Eagly & Crowley, 1986). In general, they have found that men are more likely than women to help when some kind of active intervention is required, such as when a victim has apparently collapsed on the subway. The presence of an audience also accentuates the tendency for men, more than women, to be helpful to strangers (Wollman, Griggs, & Stouder, 1990), probably because an audience is a reminder of the norm that men are supposed to be chivalrous. The kind of activity required of the helper also makes a difference: Each sex, but especially males, is more likely to help when the activity required is gender-role appropriate. There is also evidence that characteristics of the person who needs help can be important. Some research has found that males are more likely to help females and females to help males, at least in nonthreatening situations (Bickman, 1974). Another investigation suggests that this pattern is magnified by how dependent the potential recipient appears to be (Wolfson, 1981). The latter pattern may hold only in relatively nonthreatening laboratory-type situations, however. In real-world situations, such as hitchhiking or stopping a stranger on the street at night, women may receive more help from both sexes, both because women are presumed to be frailer and more dependent than men and because both males and females may feel more suspicious and threatened when approached by a male than a female for help.

In summary, gender differences in helping behavior seem to be largely determined by situational factors. There is no overall tendency for either females or males to be more helpful to others.

WHAT HAPPENED TO THE DIFFERENCES?

Gender differences in various aspects of social behavior generally range in size from small to moderate and are often sensitive to situational factors. Criteria for labeling a difference "small" or "large" can be controversial (Eagly, 1995; Hyde & Ashby Plant, 1995), and differences that seem inconsequential at first blush may have important consequences (Rosenthal, 1990). Yet the gender differences in social behavior and personality discussed in this chapter seem minor when contrasted with some of the virtually nonoverlapping behaviors of women and men we observe in daily life. If gender differences in the lab are not striking and dramatic, how is it that women and men end up leading such different lives? How is it that most bank managers are men and most tellers are women? That most single parents are women? That most of the world's nations have never had a female head of state? That so many more men than women play hockey and football? We are faced with the task of reconciling research findings of frequently unremarkable behavioral differences between the sexes with our observations that in daily life women and men often seem to differ dramatically in their concerns, their accomplishments, and the way they spend their time.

Several things can work to maximize the apparent disparity between the findings of carefully controlled research in laboratory or classroom situations and casual observations in everyday life. Psychologists have designed their research to determine whether, all things being equal, females and males will differ in the way they respond to certain situations. They have tried, although not always with success, to ensure that conditions in their studies are equivalent for males and females. But outside the laboratory, all things are seldom equal for males and females. Men and women face different expectations, different pressures, and different constraints. Psychological research has demonstrated that, for instance, women *can* be as aggressive as men and men *can* be as nurturant as women, but it does not follow that, given current social conditions, they *will* be. One reason for the apparent discrepancy between some of the research findings and everyday life is the difference between potential and actual behavior. Psychologists have often tried to control or minimize the impact of social context on the behavior they are studying. To the extent that they succeed in doing this, they may see gender differences that are smaller than those we observe in everyday life. In everyday life, however, two aspects of the social context are often confounded with being female or male: role expectations and status.

Role Expectations

We have seen that some of the largest gender differences appear in situations where people know they are being observed and that self-reported behaviors often differ more than unobtrusively observed behaviors for women and men. According to a gender-role perspective, female–male differences in social behavior occur partly because people are responding to social norms about how women and men should behave and partly because, by playing their expected roles, women and men tend to develop different attitudes and skills. This perspective is articulated in social roles theory (Eagly, 1987), discussed in Chapter 2.

Clearly, gender-related behavior is influenced by people's ideas about how others want and expect them to behave. Aggression and dominance are prescribed behaviors for the masculine role; compliance, nurturance, and empathy for the feminine role. Role expectations extend beyond the general concepts of masculinity and femininity, however, to the more specific roles occupied with differential frequency by women and men: secretary, company president, wife, husband, mother, father, scientist, cab driver, and so on. Company presidents, more often than secretaries, are put in situations where they are expected to be dominant. The fact that most company presidents are men is both a result of and a perpetuation of the expectation that men are more dominant than women. Men are more likely than women to be promoted to this position because they are seen as having the capacity to be appropriately dominant; once in the position, a man confronts many situations where dominance is expected, so his behavior becomes more dominant. Thus, the demands of the roles in which people are more or less likely to find themselves because of their gender act to reinforce gender-related behavior and gender stereotypes. When women and men are in similar occupational roles, however, as in studies of female and male managers, they respond to similar role pressures and their behavior tends to be similar (Eagly & Johnson, 1990).

It is noteworthy that most of the studies comparing females and males on social behavior have been done with children or college students—people who, although certainly subject to gender-role expectations, have not yet become heavily involved in the occupational or parental roles that reinforce these gender expectations.

Status

It is all but impossible for researchers to disentangle gender and status. In most situations, males are ascribed higher status than females, so when behavioral differences between the sexes are observed, it is difficult to know whether to attribute them to gender or status. As noted earlier in this chapter, high-status people may find it easier and more appropriate than low-status people to act aggressively and dominantly; low-status people are more likely than high-status people to find themselves in situations where conformity and sensitivity are required.

In confronting this problem, researchers have often been at great pains to be aware of the effect of status in research on gender, to measure it and to control for it, if possible. The latter is not always easy. For instance, in trying to construct stimuli in which a male and a female are each portrayed in role-appropriate but equally high status jobs, researchers have been stymied by the impossibility of finding a really high status job that is typically considered female-appropriate. To make the issue even more complicated, the status ascribed to gender may be inconsistent with the status achieved in a particular occupation. A woman who holds a high-status position such as physician is likely to be pegged as a nurse by people who do not know her. Similarly, male nurses are often mistakenly taken as physicians. Such situations of status inconsistency add to the difficulty of investigating the relationship between gender and status.

To the extent that status differences between males and females are successfully controlled in research, the researcher may observe few gender differences. For example, the use of a speaking style that is filled with intensifiers, hedges, hesitations, and questioning intonations—often considered a "feminine" speaking style—is linked much more strongly to social power and status than to gender. Both females and males, when in low-status positions, are more likely than high-status individuals to use this speaking style (Erickson, Lund, Johnson, & O'Barr, 1978). Similarly, when researchers manipulate the amount of power or expertise held by partners in mixed-sex interactions, persons high in power—whether they are women or men—display high visual dominance (Dovidio, Ellyson, Keating, Heltman, & Brown, 1988). When power and expertise are *not* manipulated by the researcher, however, gender-related expectations about status apparently take over. Men display high visual dominance (looking at the other person more when speaking than when listening), and women show low visual dominance (looking more when listening than when speaking).

Because researchers generally try to control for status when comparing females and males, even though they are not usually completely successful, they probably observe smaller gender differences in the laboratory than others see in the outside world. A research participant coming into a psychologist's lab is removed from her or his normal social context, with all its expectations. The researcher is careful to treat female and male subjects exactly the same way, to have them respond to identical stimuli. In the outside world, however, there are many dimensions on which males and females are probably *not* treated the same way. For example, a study of influence might expose males and females to a series of identical challenges to their opinions, to see whether one gender is more persuasible than the other. Using this method, the researcher may find minimal gender differences in persuasibility. Outside the lab, however, it is unlikely that people use exactly the same tactics to challenge the opinions of women and men. Instead, the status and role expectations associated with femininity and masculinity will produce, in many situations, different approaches to influencing women and men and more noticeable gender differences in susceptibility to influence.

Choosing Behaviors to Study

Researchers find it most practical to study behaviors that can be defined clearly and measured precisely. This predilection usually leads them to focus on isolated behaviors rather than on complex processes or the expression of a behavioral disposition across a wide range of situations. For example, researchers studying nurturance may focus on parental reactions to a new infant during the first few weeks after birth. They may define nurturance as the amount of time the parent spends holding, touching, smiling at, or talking to the baby during the hours of observation. Yet nurturance is potentially a much broader concept. It could be thought of as including awareness of the infant's needs, the amount of one's attention focused on the child even when not interacting with him or her, the proportion of one's daily decisions and choices that are made with the child in mind, and so on. The latter aspects of nurturance would be much harder to measure than holding, touching, and smiling. If they could be measured, perhaps conclusions about gender differences in nurturance would be very different. It is important to remember that researchers' conclusions about sweeping categories of behavior such as nurturance and aggression are based on analyzing isolated, easily measurable behaviors. This focus on easily measurable behaviors may be another factor responsible for the difference between research findings of small gender differences and casual observation of apparently larger differences on certain dimensions.

The Observer Bias Problem— Exaggeration of Small Differences

A final important reason for the apparent discrepancy between research findings and casual observation is the bias built into casual observation. As discussed in earlier chapters, people are strongly influenced in what they notice and remember by their stereotypes and schemas. Observations that fit into preexisting cognitive categories tend to be more easily incorporated than those that do not. Thus, if a person is a believer in the general stereotype that women are more altruistic than men, he or she will tend to notice and remember instances of women being helpful as confirmation of the stereotype, while discounting instances of selfish behavior by women and unselfish behavior by men as exceptions to the general rule.

As noted in the discussion of meta-analysis, the frequency of extreme levels of behavior can make a strong impression on people. If the sexes are seen to differ in the frequency with which they engage in extreme levels of a particular behavior, this observation can contribute dramatically to gender stereotypes. Taking aggression as an example, it is likely that most of us have heard of many more instances of extreme violence perpetrated by men than by women, and thus it is easy for us to believe that men are much more aggressive than women. At most levels of aggression, however, the gender difference is probably much less dramatic; the behavior of a relatively small number of very violent individuals has a disproportionate impact on our beliefs about women and men in general.

In weighing the results of research against one's own observations, then, neither the research nor one's own observations should be taken entirely at face value. Apparent gender differences often reflect differences in situational role expectations and status. When researchers successfully control for these factors, they find smaller gender differences. Such findings say much about what the social world might be like if differential role and status expectations about women and men were abolished; they say less about the social world as it is. Moreover, the control and precise measurement required to carry out research often preclude the study of aspects of behavior that are less tangible or not as easily observed, in favor of the obvious and easily quantifiable. Many of the more complex and subtle aspects of behavioral gender differences may thus be overlooked by research, although they may be apprehended in a qualitative way by observers. It is dangerous to rely too heavily on one's casual observations, however, since they too are heavily prone to bias.

SUMMARY

What do we know about the differences and similarities between women and men? The research provides us with limited answers. Despite the popular habit of referring to women and men as "opposite sexes," psychological research finds little evidence for such dramatic distinctions in many areas of social behavior. Men are found to be more often aggressive and dominant than women, but women are aggressive and dominant too under certain circumstances. Women show a small but reliable tendency to be more easily influenced than men; this difference appears in some situations but not others. Women self-report more nurturance and empathy than men do; no across-the-board differences in behavior are found, but the range of behaviors studied has been small. Gender differences in altruism seem to depend on the circumstances.

Much of our research-based knowledge about gender similarities and differences comes from studies that focus on behavior in the absence of its social context. Yet for all the social behaviors discussed here, status and role expectations seem to be important mediators of gender differences. The influence of role expectations is seen in the tendency for larger gender differences to appear when research participants are reporting their own feelings or are aware of being observed. The influence of status is seen in the tendency to find smaller gender differences under conditions in which an effort has been made to equalize the status of male and female participants. It is reasonable to expect, then, that the overall picture of gender differences in behavior will be different across cultural and historical situations in which role and status expectations for males and females vary. Currently, North America seems to be experiencing a period when gender roles are overlapping and merging more than they have in the past, a phenomenon that may be reflected in findings of smaller behavioral gender differences as the years go by.

The literature on gender differences in social behavior has many limitations. Behavior tends to be studied apart from its social context to achieve careful control of variables confounded with gender; thus, results are sometimes uninformative about the processes through which the social environment supports or discourages gender differences in behavior. Behaviors that are chosen for study tend to be ones that are most easily measured; thus, many subtle, complex aspects of the relationship between gender and behavior may be lost. Despite its limitations, however, research on gender and social behavior provides an important corrective to the biases of the casual observer.

The newfound popularity of meta-analytic methods for examining patterns of gender differences has contributed a great deal to knowledge about the relationship between gender and particular behaviors. This approach has shown that even though a gender difference may be found reliably its size may be quite small. More longitudinal and cross-sequential research is needed, however, to build understanding of the developmental and historical aspects of gender differences and of within-gender variables that predict behavior.

KEY TERMS

essentialism
longitudinal study

meta-analysis
cross-sequential method

effect size

FOR ADDITIONAL READING

Bem, Sandra L. (1993). *The lenses of gender: Transforming the debate on sexual inequality.* New Haven, CT: Yale University Press. The author illustrates the numerous ways culture defines gender, suggesting that many differences between women and men are "obvious" only because we are looking through cultural lenses.

Elshtain, Jean Bethke. (1987). *Women and war.* New York: Basic Books. Drawing on the historical records of wars and of peace movements, the author challenges the stereotypes of men as eager warriors and women as peacemakers and helps the reader think in new ways about gender and aggression.

Fausto-Sterling, Anne. (1992). *Myths of gender.* New York: Basic Books. The author, a biologist, examines the myths that surround some of the gender-related differences discussed in this and other chapters.

Maccoby, Eleanor. (1998). *The two sexes: Growing up apart, coming together.* Cambridge, MA: Harvard University Press. A distinguished researcher summarizes findings on gender differences. She argues that a key factor in individuals' gendered behavior is the gender of others with whom they are interacting.

McCaughey, Martha. (1997). *Real knockouts: The physical feminism of women's self-defense.* New York: New York University Press. The author, who started out as a self-confessed "frightened feminist" describes a participant-observation study of the women's self-defense movement. Her book challenges stereotypes that say women must be victims of violence and that they cannot enjoy being aggressive.

CHAPTER 5

Biology & Environment

The Process of Becoming Female or Male

At the 1985 World University Games in Kobe, Japan, a young Spanish track and field athlete was quietly summoned by officials and ordered to withdraw from a scheduled race. Heartsick and shaken, Maria Patino faked an injury during warmup and did not run because the officials had warned that the alternative was to make public a devastating discovery: She had "failed" the sex test. According to the results of the buccal smear, a test of the sex chromosome pattern in cells scraped from inside her cheek, Patino was not a normal female. Instead, her chromosome pattern was that of a male. The discovery made her an unwilling member of a small sorority: About a dozen women have been banned from Olympic competition for not being sufficiently female (Carlson, 1991).

Patino had never for an instant doubted her own femaleness. Months of subsequent medical examinations revealed that hers was a case of androgen insensitivity: a male chromosomal pattern that had not resulted in the development of a male body because of complete and permanent inability to respond to testosterone. She has no uterus, but she has female genitals, female body proportions, female secondary sex characteristics, and normal sexual response.

Femininity testing was introduced by the International Amateur Athletic Federation (IAAF) in the late 1960s after reports that men had been masquerading as women in female sports. Maria Patino became the first woman to publicly challenge her disqualification. During her struggle for reinstatement, she lost her scholarship and her access to her coach. Her records and titles were stricken from the books. Her boyfriend and many of her friends abandoned her. Finally, three years later, acknowledging that her body did not, in fact, give her any unfair advantage with respect to other female athletes, the International Olympic Committee officially requalified her. Furthermore, her case helped to convince the IAAF that the system of testing should be changed.

If Maria Patino's story sounds complicated, consider this story. Several years ago a research team, working first in the Dominican Republic and then in New Guinea, reported on an unusual phenomenon. A small number of children who had been raised as girls developed male secondary sex characteristics at puberty. Their voices deepened, they grew beards, and they developed adult-size penises and scrotums. Almost all of these "girls" made successful transitions to being male, married, and fathered children (Imperato-McGinley, Guerrero, Gautier, & Peterson, 1974; Imperato-McGinley, Miller, et al., 1991; Imperato-McGinley, Peterson, Gautier, & Sturla, 1979).

What is going on here? Surely, despite all the cautious talk about overlapping distributions of behavior for women and men, cannot one safely hold to the belief that, at least in biological terms, the categories "female" and "male" are discrete, nonoverlapping, and unambiguously separate? It turns out, in fact, that things are not so simple. The preceding examples are only two of a number of cases in which sex—biological maleness or femaleness—has turned out to be a fuzzier category than it first appeared. There are several biological indicators of sex: chromosomes, sex glands or gonads, hormones, internal reproductive organs, and genitalia. All of these indicators are usually congruent, all male or all female, but occasionally they are not. To make matters more complex, there are also questions about the sexual differentiation of the brain and about the relationship between all these variables and behavior.

This chapter begins with an examination of the normal process of biological differentiation into female or male. This is followed by a discussion of what happens when something goes awry with this process, producing an individual with mixed indicators of biological sex. The relationship between biological sex and various aspects of gender has been the subject of a great deal of curiosity and controversy, and the study of the gender-related behavior of individuals whose indicators of biological sex are mixed has been regarded as a unique source of clues to this relationship. In this context, this chapter will focus first on studies of gender-role behavior and then on gender identity, asking what it is that governs a person's sense of maleness or femaleness. To further explore the question of gender identity, there follows a discussion of gender dysphoria and transgenderism, the sense of dissatisfaction with, and rebellion against, one's given sex or sexual identity. The impact of sexual differentiation on sexual orientation is discussed briefly, and the chapter concludes with an examination of attempts to link aggressive behavior with male hormone levels in normal individuals.

THE BIOLOGICAL PROCESS OF SEXUAL DIFFERENTIATION

Sexual differentiation is a complex process, and one that differs considerably across species. Among reptiles such as crocodiles and turtles, eggs are laid with the potential to hatch into either females or males. The temperature in their environment determines their sex: A colder temperature produces more males and a warmer one results in more females (Angier, 1999). Among many species of tropical fish, it is common for individuals to change sex during their development. All members of the sand tile species are born female—and then a few of them change into males in adulthood as required for sexual reproduction. In a rarer pattern, all clown fish are born male, and they all change into females upon reaching later adulthood (Rabin, 1998). At any rate, there is no species that has no females. There are a few species that breed asexually, through self-replication, and these species have no males. It has been argued that females are the "ancestral" sex among animals, with males evolving later in response to pressures for sexual reproduction (Crews, 1993).

The process of human sexual differentiation is accomplished in several steps. First, the individual's sex is genetically determined at conception. Then, as the embryo develops, the "indifferent gonad" develops into male or female sex glands. In turn, these glands begin to secrete the appropriate male or female sex hormones, which circulate throughout the bloodstream and are responsible for the sexual differentiation of other bodily organs: the internal reproductive tract, the external genitalia, and, to a disputed extent, areas of the brain. At each step of this process, the basic tendency is for development to proceed in the direction of producing a female unless this pattern is disrupted by the presence of the Y chromosome or male hormones.

Genetic Determination of Sex

Every normal human cell contains 46 chromosomes, arranged in 23 pairs. One chromosome of each pair is contributed by the mother of the individual and one by the father. Twenty-two of the chromosome pairs carry genes that determine hereditary characteristics of the person. The 23rd pair, called the **sex chromosomes,** differs for women and men. If the individual is female, the sex chromosomes are represented as XX; if male, the pair is designated XY. The two types of sex chromosomes are illustrated in Figure 5.1. Only males carry a Y chromosome, which is very small and contains little genetic material. However, it does apparently carry a gene that acts as a "switch" for maleness (Braun, reported in Angier, 1990). Thus, a person's genetic sex is determined by his or her father. If the sperm cell that happens to fertilize the egg at conception carries an X chromosome, the individual will be female; if it carries a Y chromosome, the individual will be male. This system has the interesting result that sons inherit more characteristics from their mother than daughters do: the genetic material carried on the son's X chromosome, always contributed by the mother, is active in every cell of his body. However, for the daughter, who has two X chromosomes, one contributed by each parent, each cell "decides" (apparently randomly) whether to keep the genes on the maternal or paternal X chromosome active—the other X chromosome is inactivated. Thus, in some cells of the daughter's body, the genes on the X

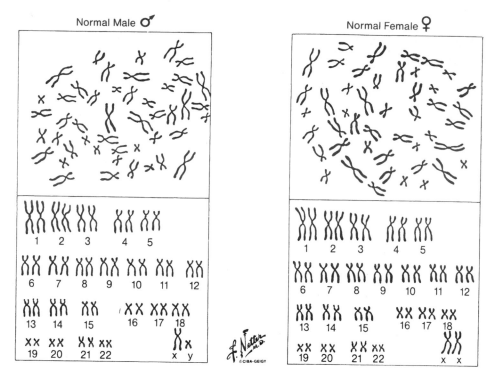

Figure 5.1 The 23 pairs of chromosomes in the normal male and normal female person. The sex chromosomes are the 23rd pair.

chromosome contributed by her mother are active, and in other cells of her body, the genes on the X chromosome contributed by the father are active. She becomes a "mosaic" of the traits carried on her two parents' X chromosomes (Angier, 1999).

For the first 5 weeks, the anatomical development of XX and XY embryos seems to be identical. Each develops a "neutral" gonad or sex gland and begins to form two sets of internal reproductive structures: female **Müllerian ducts** *and* male **Wolffian ducts.** Until the 6th week of development, then, all embryos have the potential to develop in either a male or female direction. Whatever genes are involved up until this point must be present in both sexes.

SEX-LINKED CHARACTERISTICS   When the genes for a particular trait are carried partially or totally on one of the sex chromosomes, the trait is said to be **sex-linked.** Almost all of the relatively few traits currently identified as sex-linked are associated with genes carried on the X chromosome, and these traits are typically pathological. The presence of such X-linked genes accounts for the greater male than female susceptibility to certain genetic disorders. For instance, the gene for hemophilia is sex-linked and recessive. A father carrying this gene cannot transmit it to his son because he contributes only a Y chromosome to his son, and the gene is carried on the X chromosome. He can, however, transmit the gene to his daughter, to whom he contributes an X chromosome. His daughter, however, will not express any symptoms of hemophilia unless she has also inherited a hemophilia gene on the X chromosome contributed by her mother. If, as is normally the case, the genetic material on the X chromosome from at least one of the parents is programmed for the development of a healthy blood-clotting mechanism, the daughter will not develop hemophilia. Because the trait of hemophilia is recessive, it will be masked by the presence of a normal blood-clotting gene on the other X chromosome. The daughter continues to carry the gene, of course, and may transmit it to her sons or daughters. If she does transmit to her son, the hemophilia will be expressed, because the son has no other X chromosome (only a Y chromosome) carrying a normal dominant gene that would mask the recessive trait. Scientists have now developed the technology for identifying the sex of 3-day-old embryos, with the objective of helping prospective parents who want to conceive a female to avoid passing on serious genetic diseases to males ("Scientists Identify Sex," 1990).

SEX-LIMITED CHARACTERISTICS   Some traits are **sex-limited** rather than sex-linked. These traits are carried on genes that are not on either of the sex chromosomes but are, nonetheless, generally manifest in only one sex. In this case, the trait requires the presence of male or female sex hormones to appear. Baldness, for example, is a trait that is carried genetically but that requires the presence of a certain level of male sex hormones to be expressed.

ABNORMALITIES   Occasionally, through errors in cell division, an individual is conceived who has some chromosomal abnormality—extra or missing chromosomes. Such abnormalities are sometimes present in the sex chromosomes. For example, an individual may be born with a single X chromosome (XO), an extra X chromosome (XXX), an extra Y chromosome (XYY), or with patterns such as XXY (Klinefelter's syndrome) or even XXXY. In these rare instances, unless there is at least one Y chromosome present, the body type will tend to develop as female unless some subsequent factor interferes. The basic pattern of mammalian development is female, and every fertilized egg will tend to develop into a female unless the pattern of development is altered by the presence of a Y chromosome, which stimulates testosterone production, or the addition of testosterone from another source (Sloane, 1993). It is thought that an individual with only a single Y chromosome cannot survive, and no person with this chromosome pattern has ever been found (Money & Ehrhardt, 1972). Various behavioral, personality, and intellectual difficulties have been ascribed to the presence of chromosomal anomalies, but the rarity of the conditions and the fact that in some cases they are noticed only when the individual gets into trouble or seeks help for a problem makes the evidence difficult to evaluate.

Some attempts have been made to demonstrate that particular abilities or behavioral tendencies are linked to the sex chromosomes. For example, there has been speculation that aggression might be partially linked to the Y chromosome. Some studies show that XYY males (men with an extra Y chromosome) were found in higher rates in prisons and institutions for the criminally insane. However, careful examination of the findings indicates that these men are no more likely, indeed less likely, to commit *violent* crimes than normal males are (Price & Whatmore, 1967a, 1967b), so there is no basis for the belief in a link between aggression and the extra Y chromosome. Investigators now attribute the overrepresentation of XYY males in institutions to their generally lower intelligence—a characteristic associated with excess genetic material provided by the presence of extra Y *or* extra X chromosomes (Witkin et al., 1976).

Gonadal Development

The influence of chromosomes on sexual differentiation appears to be most important during the 6th week of development, when the indifferent gonad begins the process of either male or female organization. At this point, if a Y chromosome is present, it promotes the synthesis of a protein called the H-Y antigen, which, among other things, helps the gonad to differentiate into an embryonic testis—the male sex gland. If no Y chromosome is present, the gonadal tissue begins, in later weeks, to differentiate into an ovary, the second step in female development. Once again, the basic pattern of development is female, unless that pattern is changed by the presence of a Y chromosome. Whether there is a specific "ovarian initiator" such as a genetic signal that acts, in concert with the absence of the Y chromosome, to trigger this next phase of female development is uncertain; however, some scientists are trying to discern the presence of such a signal (Angier, 1999).

Hormones

Once the gonads are formed, they begin to secrete the sex hormones. The rest of the process of sexual differentiation is directed by these hormones, chemical substances secreted into the bloodstream and carried to every cell of the body.

In the developing male embryo, the testis synthesizes testosterone, part of a group of chemically similar male hormones called androgens. Testosterone influences the male reproductive tract, the Wolffian duct system, to begin developing. At the same time, the testis secretes a hormone called the Müllerian Inhibiting Substance (MIS), which causes the female duct system to degenerate and disappear (Yahr, 1988).

In the developing female embryo, the ovary begins to secrete the hormones estrogen and progesterone. The male duct system degenerates, and the female system develops to form the internal organs of the female reproductive system. Exactly what controls this process in females is not known. Scientists have traditionally believed it is the absence of testosterone rather than the presence of estrogens that accounts for female differentiation at this stage, but recently more attention has been focused on the role of the ovarian hormones (Collaer & Hines, 1995; Fausto-Sterling, 1992). Some scientists have argued that there must be, in females, a "wolffian inhibiting factor" (comparable to the MIS in males) that causes the wolffian duct system to self-destruct; however, such a substance has not been found (Angier, 1999).

Although the androgens are often called male hormones and the estrogens and progesterone are called female hormones, individuals of both sexes synthesize these hormones. All three hormones can be produced in the ovaries, testes, or adrenal glands. Researchers who assayed the concentrations of two androgens, two estrogens, and progesterone from the umbilical cord blood of infants at birth found that the concentration of only one of these hormones, testosterone, differed for female and male infants. The level of the estrogens and progesterone actually varied more according to birth order than sex: firstborns of both sexes had higher levels of all three than later-borns did (Maccoby, Doering, Jacklin, & Kraemer, 1979).

At puberty, the sex hormones are responsible for the development of secondary sex characteristics such as breast development for females and beard growth and muscular development for males. It is the phenomenon of muscle growth in response to testosterone that motivates athletes—both male and female—to take steroids (which are similar to this hormone in structure and action) despite their negative side effects. In fact, the complexities of taking steroids are very little understood; they sometimes seem to have unexpected effects—and different effects on women and men. For instance, baseball hero Mark McGwire was criticized for his use of the steroid androstenedione, a substance that is produced naturally in the body and used to make testosterone. However, a recent study found that men who took supplemental androstenedione did not get any advantage in strength over a control group of men and that the steroid had no apparent effect on testosterone levels in their blood. What the steroid-takers did get was an increase in blood levels of the female hormone estrogen and a significant decline in levels of the "good" cholesterol that helps to prevent heart disease. Interestingly, it is reported that women who took androstenedione did experience an increase in blood levels of testosterone (B. G. Coleman, 1999).

The extent to which hormonal influence extends beyond the anatomical differentiation of the sexes and into the realm of behavior is an issue that has generated much research and controversy. It will be addressed in detail later in the chapter.

Internal Reproductive Tract

In males, the androgens secreted by the embryonic testis organize the internal ducts into the male reproductive tract: vas deferens, epididymis, seminal vesicles, urethra, and prostate. Meanwhile, the MIS causes the still-present female ducts to atrophy. In females, the male ducts atrophy, while a female reproductive tract—Fallopian tubes, uterus, and vagina—develops from the female ducts.

External Genitalia

The external genitals of the male and female differentiate from the same basic structure, as shown in Figure 5.2. Until the 8th week of fetal life, the external genital appearance of both sexes is identical, and the genitals can differentiate in either direction. In males, under the influence of testosterone, the genital tubercle develops into a penis and the labioscrotal swelling becomes a scrotum. In females, by the 12th week, the genital tubercle has turned into a clitoris, and the labioscrotal swelling has become the labia. Female development at this stage has been attributed to the absence of testosterone, but the possible role of the estrogens or progesterone in the development of the genitals has not been explored.

Brain

"How Female Is Your Brain?" asks the headline of a *Washington Post* article (Moir & Jessel, 1991). The 10-item test includes queries about how well you can remember a song you've recently heard, how likely it is that you would detect a clandestine affair between two of your friends, and how likely you would be to try to back your car into a tight parking space. Can the answers to such questions really tell us anything about the femaleness of our brains? According to the questionnaire authors, the answer is yes—female and male brains are better at different things because of the way they are organized and that organization is the direct result of the early process of sexual

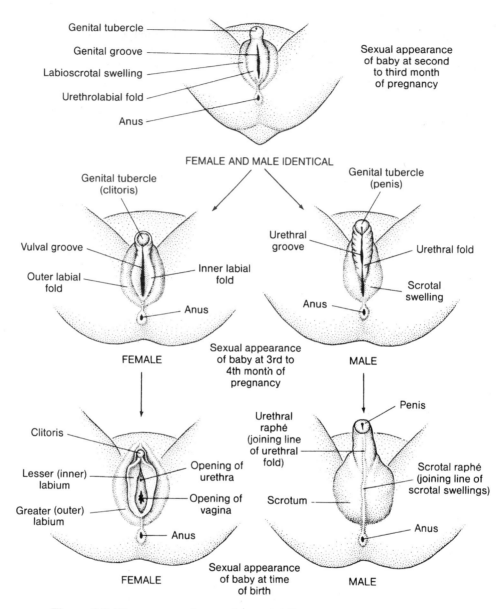

Figure 5.2 Three stages of external genital differentiation in the human fetus. (From *Man and woman, boy and girl* by John Money and Anke A. Ehrhardt, Baltimore: The Johns Hopkins University Press, 1972, p. 44. © 1972 by the Johns Hopkins University Press. All rights reserved. Reprinted by permission of the publisher.)

differentiation: "What gives us a male or a female brain is the degree to which our embryonic brains are exposed to male hormone. The die is cast *in utero;* after that, the luggage of our bodies, and society's expectations of us, merely supplement this biological fact of life" (p. K3).

Is it really true that hormone levels *in utero* somehow fix the brain in a male or female organization, in the same way they determine the development of the genitals as male or female? Genital differences between females and males are obvious; brain differences are far less so. In light of the transactional perspective on the biology–environment relationship discussed in Chapter 3, the notion that everything that comes after a critical exposure to hormones before birth is merely "supplemental" to an essential biological fact is absurdly simplistic. However, that is not to say that prenatal hormone levels make no contribution to the brain organization of the developing fetus. Animal studies indicate that, in some species, sex hormone levels present at a critical prenatal or postnatal period *do* influence the development of the brain. In rats, exposure to testosterone at a critical period just after birth results in a subsequent sensitivity of the brain to male hormones and an insensitivity to female ones (Levine, 1966). This differential sensitivity is demonstrated in the response of the mature animal to hormone injections. For example, if testosterone is injected into a newborn female rat, the rat's normal female sexual receptivity behavior seems to be permanently lost. In adulthood, she fails to show the usual female response even when given large replacement injections of female hormones. Moreover, she tends to show extremes of *male* sexual behavior, including the motions associated with ejaculation, when injected with testosterone.

Research on rats also indicates that early hormonal exposure affects the hypothalamus, the part of the brain that controls the pattern of release of gonadotropins by the pituitary gland (Levine, 1966). The gonadotropins, in turn, control the secretion of the sex hormones by the gonads. The presence of testosterone during a critical period causes a noncyclic pattern of hormone release to develop, whereas the absence of testosterone causes the development of the characteristically female pattern of cyclic release of hormones and the occurrence of ovulation at regular, fairly predictable intervals.

The findings for animals led to speculation that the human brain too may be affected by sex hormone levels at critical periods. However, the relevance of the animal literature to humans is limited in this area, because human behavior is, in general, more subject to learning and the social environment and less governed by hormones than is that of animals lower on the phylogenetic scale (Collaer & Hines, 1995). We can conclude little about human hormone–brain–behavior relationships from such relationships in animals. Thus far, the impact of prenatal and early postnatal hormone levels on the developing human brain remains an area of research and controversy. It has not been demonstrated that early exposure to androgens is the critical factor in establishing the pattern of hormone release in humans. In fact, if adult male primates are, via transplant, given ovaries, they can ovulate and have menstrual cycles (Norman & Spies, 1986).

Despite the difficulty of generalizing from other animals to humans, it has been suggested that the presence of testosterone at critical periods of the human sexual differentiation process might "masculinize" or "defeminize" the central nervous system, perhaps influencing brain structure and organizing it so that the individual is predisposed or prepared to learn specifically masculine patterns of behavior. If testosterone, or one of the hormones into which it metabolizes, affects the nervous system, how might this occur? The hormone could perhaps affect the activity of genes within nerve cells or act on the outer membrane of the cells, thus having an impact on the growth of cells, their electrical activity, or their biochemistry. A variety of complex effects are possible, but there is little certainty about what is actually happening in humans and what the critical periods may be for particular effects.

Researchers have reported some apparent structural differences in the brains of human females and males. For example, there appears to be a sex difference in one part, now labeled the sexually dimorphic nucleus, of the preoptic area of the hypothalamus that becomes noticeable after age 2 to 4 (Breathnach, 1990; Swaab & Hofman, 1988). The implications of this and other reported structural differences are not yet clear, however.

DO PHYSICAL SEX DIFFERENCES
HAVE IMPLICATIONS FOR BEHAVIOR?

Animal Studies

If there is any truth to the notion that the presence of testosterone at a critical differentiation period "masculinizes" the central nervous system so that the individual is predisposed to learn certain particularly masculine behaviors, then an animal that is injected with testosterone during the critical period should later show more "masculine" behaviors than one that was not. Some animal studies using this method have provided support for a link between critical-period testosterone administration or removal and nonsexual behaviors such as rough-and-tumble play and threat.

A group of researchers (Goy, 1968, 1970; Phoenix, Goy, & Resko, 1968) found that young female rhesus monkeys whose mothers had been injected with testosterone during pregnancy showed more play initiation, rough-and-tumble play, threats, and chasing behavior than normal females did. These findings suggest that hormones may indeed, through action on the developing brain, influence behavior. However, the extent of the testosterone effect is difficult to assess, for two reasons. First, behavioral differences are ascertained through direct observation of the animals by investigators who cannot but be aware of each animal's condition. Although this procedure probably has no serious effect on the measurement of gross and dramatic behavior differences, it may possibly have a biasing effect on the interpretation of more subtle behaviors. Second, animals castrated or treated with testosterone during early development may well differ in appearance, and even in smell, from their normal same-sex peers. Goy's androgenized female monkeys, for example, although genetically female, had a scrotum and a penis. It is possible that their difference in appearance affected their treatment by their cohorts—accounting, perhaps, for at least some of their deviation from expected female behavior.

Animal research also makes it clear that environmental variables can influence the physiological processes that produce sex differences in the brain and behavior, and such influences do not have to occur prenatally. For instance, among rodents a group of neurons called the spinal nucleus of the bulbocavernosus (SNB), which helps to control erection and ejaculation, grows and shrinks in males according to the season. It shrinks in the winter, which is not a good time to have young, and swells in the summer. However, when male hamsters that have been in winter-like conditions are placed in a cage with a receptive female hamster, their SNB increases in size, testes enlarge, and hormone levels rise. Thus, the nervous system responds to the environment and to experience (Breedlove, as cited in Azar, 1998).

Human Studies

Humans depend greatly on the learning process in the development of behavior patterns. Our behavior is largely mediated by cognitive factors: our thoughts about the meanings of objects and actions. Also, human social organization is complex. These factors make physiological influences on human behavior difficult to isolate and interpret. The presence of strong social–environmental pressures toward behavioral gender differences is always a confounding factor in the assessment of physiological effects. Also, for ethical reasons, researchers cannot experiment with the hormone balance in human fetuses. Attempts to address the question of the behavioral implications of physical sexual differentiation in humans have thus been, of necessity, limited and not entirely conclusive.

Three major hypotheses, based on the early evidence, guided research on the behavioral impact of biological sex differences for many years (S. W. Baker, 1980):

1. *Gender-role behavior* is influenced, in some respects, by the prenatal hormonal environment.

2. *Gender identity* is determined not by chromosomes or hormonal influence but by rearing. Furthermore, there is a critical period, between 18 and 24 months of age, after which it is very difficult or impossible to reassign a child successfully to the other gender.

3. *Sexual orientation* is determined more by rearing than by chromosomal, gonadal, or hormonal factors.

These hypotheses have been modified somewhat over the years, with researchers now tending to lump all three dimensions—gendered behavior, gender identity, and sexual orientation—together under the heading of behavioral sex differences (i.e., behavior for which there is a disparity between the average female and the average male, although there may be a large overlap for the two sexes) (Collaer & Hines, 1995). Researchers have sought evidence that prenatal levels of androgens, estrogens, and progestins affect the probability that an individual will demonstrate behaviors that are closer to the norm for one sex or the other. The most popular model guiding this search is the idea that prenatal androgens tend to masculinize or defeminize behavior (i.e., make it more likely that the individual's behavior will be more like that of the average male and less like that of the average female). However, there are also suggestions that prenatal estrogens may masculinize or defeminize behavior, or that they may have a feminizing or demasculinizing effect (Collaer & Hines, 1995). Whatever impact prenatal hormones may have on behavior, it is not certain that this impact occurs through an organizing action of hormones on the brain (C. L. Moore, 1985). In reading about this research, it is important to notice that the findings represent *correlations* between various kinds of exposure to hormones in the womb and various patterns of later behavior—and that they tell us virtually nothing about how those effects may have come about.

Most data on the effects of prenatal hormones on human development and behavior have come from the study of people whose sexual differentiation was disrupted *in utero* by hormonal imbalance. Such individuals, known as **intersexed** individuals (sometimes also labeled pseudohermaphrodites in the medical literature), form between 1% and 4% of the population but have been extensively studied over the past three decades. The hormonal imbalance can be the result of drugs administered to the pregnant mother, stress experienced by her, or a glandular malfunction of genetic origin. As a result of the prenatal hormonal disruption, the individual is born with the sexual anatomy incompletely differentiated. For instance, an intersexed baby may be born with ambiguous external genitalia or with genitalia incongruous with internal reproductive structures. By studying the behavioral and personality concomitants of various forms of intersexuality, investigators have hoped to discover the connection between specific aspects of physiological sex and behavior.

What happens to an infant whose sex at birth is ambiguous? In our society, an individual's sex is not allowed to remain ambiguous. It is thought crucial to assign the child a male or female identity as quickly as possible—even if that assignment is fairly arbitrary—and to provide treatment (drugs or surgery) that will help the child's body fit the assigned identity. To help make the assignment of identity as definite as possible, doctors routinely tell parents that an infant whose sex appears indeterminate is "really" male or female and simply needs treatment to bring all bodily features in line with the "correct" sex (Kessler, 1990). However, the determination of sex assignment is not based on discovering the child's "true" sex (because the child possesses a mixture of sexual characteristics and is thus truly intersexual). Rather, it is based on an assessment of how well, given the physical characteristics present at birth and the possibilities for treatment, the child will be able to function as a female or male in later life. Such an assessment is necessarily based on sociocultural assumptions surrounding gender. For instance, in the late 19th century, women's ability to bear children was viewed as their essential characteristic. In that period, the presence or absence of ovaries was often the determining factor in assigning gender to intersexed individuals. Current thinking, perhaps because of the emphasis on sexuality in our culture, appears to favor the importance of external genital anatomy over internal reproductive organs. An infant with a normal-appearing penis would likely be reared as a male, even if normal female internal reproductive structures were present (Kessler, 1990), because the alternative of surgically removing the penis is disturbing to physicians and parents.

We have little information, then, about what would happen to intersexed children if they were left to grow up in our society with ambiguous sex assignment. Most of the research discussed in the following sections deals with individuals who did receive some form of treatment or intervention because of their ambiguous sex. However, it is instructive to consider the strong cultural bias that is implied in such procedures. Culture and medical practice work very hard to maintain clear distinctions between the sexes and to make sure that everyone can fit into a two-sexed society, despite longstanding scientific knowledge that a significant number of individuals simply do not fit this binary distinction. What would happen if scientific knowledge were directed at helping intersexed individuals live happily and healthily as intersexuals—and helping the wider society to acknowledge and accept their presence?

Gender-Role Behavior

ELEVATED PRENATAL ANDROGENS   Studies of intersexed individuals have covered a wide range of disorders, and the interested reader is referred to reviews by S. W. Baker (1980), Collaer and Hines (1995), Ehrhardt (1985), and Hines (1982), and to an important summary work by two pioneers in the field, John Money and

Anke Ehrhardt (1972). Their most frequently cited set of studies deals with the effects of a specific hormonal problem: the **adrenogenital syndrome (AGS).** This syndrome, which is genetically transmitted, causes the adrenal glands of the fetus to malfunction, resulting in a release of excess androgens from the prenatal period onward, thus setting the stage for a variety of masculinizing effects. Girls with AGS are born with masculinized genitalia, but the internal reproductive organs are female. If the syndrome is diagnosed at birth, these girls receive surgery to feminize their genitals and are placed on lifelong cortisone therapy to compensate for the continuing adrenal malfunction. These individuals, then, are in some respects comparable to the genetically female animals who were experimentally exposed to androgens during the early critical period of central nervous system differentiation. Boys with AGS are born with a normal masculine appearance. However, they too must be treated with cortisone, or the extra output of androgen will cause their puberty to occur years early.

If the presence of significant amounts of androgens during a prenatal critical period causes the brain and central nervous system to differentiate in a masculine direction, children with AGS might be expected to show evidence of this effect. Two early studies examined children born with this syndrome for signs of masculinization of behavior and personality. In both cases, the sample is small and covers an age range of young children to middle adolescence, so the reliability of the findings is difficult to assess. Nonetheless, the results of the two studies are quite consistent, and they provide us with some clues about possible effects of prenatal androgenization on humans.

The first study (Ehrhardt & Money, 1967, described in Money & Ehrhardt, 1972) compared 25 fetally androgenized girls (15 with AGS and 10 who had been androgenized by progesterone taken by their mothers during pregnancy) with a control group of 25 normal girls, matched on the basis of age, IQ, socioeconomic background, and race. Data were collected by interviewing each girl and her mother, using a standard format. On the basis of the interviews, several significant differences were found between the two groups. The fetally androgenized girls were more likely to regard themselves as tomboys, tended to have a higher preference for athletic activity and for joining boys in energetic play, preferred practical rather than pretty clothes, showed less interest in dolls, and showed relatively more interest in a career and less in marriage than the control girls did. No differences were found on several other dimensions such as aggression, sexual orientation, enjoyment of personal adornment such as jewelry and perfume, and observable amount of sexual play or interest. These interesting findings cannot be accepted uncritically, however. Data were collected by interview, and the interviewers apparently were not blind to the diagnostic category (androgenized vs. nonandrogenized) of the girls they were questioning. Thus, the possibility of unintentional researcher bias cannot be excluded. Furthermore, no observational data were collected, so the conclusions rest heavily on self-report. Some critics have also noted that many variables are confounded with exposure to excess prenatal androgens in the AGS children. The social environments of the two groups may have been different. The families of the androgenized girls may have been affected by the birth of an "abnormal" child, and the girls may have received special treatment because of parental guilt over their condition or expectation of a tendency toward masculinity. Also, these children must take regular doses of cortisone to counteract the effects of the excess androgens. In adults, cortisone treatment can cause mood elevation and hyperactivity; thus, there may be reason to suspect that the differences between AGS children and controls were caused by the cortisone rather than the prenatal androgen exposure (Fausto-Sterling, 1992). Finally, the girls themselves, who were aware of their condition, may have felt they had more excuse than their counterparts to behave in a masculine way.

A second study (Ehrhardt & Baker, 1974) was designed to take some of these criticisms into account. In this investigation, 17 females and 10 males with AGS were compared with their unaffected same-sex siblings and parents. Thus, the possibility of general family differences between androgenized and control children was removed. Also, the inclusion of males in the study allowed for a broader examination of early androgen effects. Data were still collected through interviews, however, with interviewers aware of the diagnostic category of the children. This study found several differences between androgenized girls and their unaffected sisters and mothers. The androgenized girls were more often described by themselves and their families as having a high level of intense physical energy expenditure and showing a preference for boys over girls as playmates. Girls with AGS were less likely to show an interest in dolls or infants or to daydream or role-play about marriage or motherhood than were their sisters or their mothers during childhood. No differences between the groups were found on career interest. Significantly more of the AGS girls identified themselves as having been tomboys during all of their childhood, preferred functional clothing over clothing considered attractive for girls at that time, and showed low interest in jewelry, makeup, and hairstyles. Despite these differences from their sisters and mothers, however, the androgenized girls were clearly identified in the female role and were not unhappy with being girls. Their behavior was not considered abnormal by themselves or their families, but followed a pattern of tomboyism that is quite acceptable for girls in this culture. Interestingly, a follow-up of this sample of girls when their mean age was 16 showed that about half of them had become much more interested in their appearance, in grooming, and in dressing attractively (Ehrhardt & Baker, 1976).

For the males in this study, only one difference was found. Boys with AGS were more often reported as showing a long-term high level of energy expenditure in sports and rough outdoor activities than their brothers were.

In this study, the investigators intensively interviewed parents to determine whether they had any ambivalence or anxiety about their AGS offspring's sexuality—anxiety that might be manifested in differential treatment. They were able to uncover none. Similarly, their interviews with the girls themselves revealed no significant, persistent concern with being "born different." The accuracy of these findings is difficult to ascertain because of the possibility of interviewer bias and evaluation apprehension on the part of the subjects.

On the whole, the studies show results that are reasonably consistent: Girls in the AGS groups more often than control girls were described as showing behavior such as high energy expenditure, tomboyism, preference for functional over attractive clothing, and low interest in and rehearsal for marriage and motherhood roles. Because these are behaviors on which groups of normal boys and girls are thought to differ, on the average, the tentative conclusion has been drawn that prenatal androgenization, through action on the developing brain, masculinizes behavior. "Masculinizes" may not, however, be the most appropriate word. As A. G. Kaplan (1980) notes, the behavior of the AGS girls seems more androgynous—a combination of femininity and masculinity—than masculine. More problematic than the terminology used, though, is the confounding of the effects of prenatal androgenization with a number of other variables: cortisone treatment, knowledge of being different, and parental attitudes and behavior. The virtual impossibility of separating out the hormonal effects from these confounding variables means that conclusions about the impact of prenatal androgenization on behavior must be tentative.

Further studies of AGS children have tried to remove some of the confounding variables. For example, some researchers have found that there appears to be little relationship between the degree of genital virilization (the extent to which the girl's genitals look male) and the degree of male-typical play—suggesting that the latter is not simply the result of looking or feeling "different" or of the amount of medical attention required (Berenbaum & Hines, 1992). Though none of the studies can rule out all possible confounding variables, some reviewers argue that we can discern a pattern by looking at the findings of a large number of studies (Collaer & Hines, 1995). In general, these reviewers report that the most consistent finding for AGS girls is a higher probability of male-typical "rough" play. These girls also tend to self-report more aggressive tendencies; however, there is no evidence that they behave more aggressively than other girls. The extent to which these differences may persist into adulthood is also not clear. For example, one study followed into adulthood 12 girls who had been exposed prenatally to masculinizing hormones. The researchers found that none of the girls maintained an active participation in sports, despite a high level of interest and participation during high school (Money & Mathews, 1982).

What if the correlation between high levels of prenatal androgens and high levels of physically active play behavior in childhood does reflect a process whereby variations in hormone levels before birth predispose an individual to physically active play? Researchers who accept this explanation argue that it does not mean that behavior is mechanically predetermined by hormones:

> A predisposition possibly related to prenatal androgens simply means a greater likelihood of developing a certain behavior pattern. Whether and how the behavior will be expressed depends on the socialization process after birth. Girls who have a predisposition to physically active play behavior may frequently join boys rather than girls in active outdoor play. They are also more likely to be called tomboys. However, this will occur only if they grow up in a family and a large social context that permits and encourages this type of behavior for girls. If, on the other hand, the environment imposes a greater degree of sex stereotyping and explicitly discourages physically active play behavior in girls, the original predisposition may not be expressed at all or may lead to maladjustment and unhappiness. (Ehrhardt, 1985, pp. 45–46)

ANDROGEN INSENSITIVITY   Some individuals who are genetically male have a genetically transmitted disorder that makes their cells partially or completely unable to respond to their high prenatal levels of androgens. This is called **androgen insensitivity syndrome (AIS).** They may be born with female or ambiguous external genitalia—labia, clitoris, and a short vaginal opening. However, they do not have internal female reproductive organs such as fallopian tubes and a uterus. They are usually reared as females, because there is nothing obviously masculine about their appearance, and sometimes their condition is not diagnosed until they fail to menstruate during adolescence.

At maturity, these women look feminine in body shape, with generous-sized breasts, thick hair, and clear, attractive skin. Studies of such individuals indicate that their gender-role behaviors are consistent with their sex of rearing (Masica, Money, & Ehrhardt, 1971; Money & Ogunro, 1974). When reared as females, these individuals, though genetically male, reportedly show no sign of the "masculinized" behavior patterns reported for the AGS girls. In fact, they do not think of themselves as males at all, but as females. The case of Maria Patino, described in the opening paragraphs of this chapter, is that of an individual who is androgen-insensitive.

Women with androgen insensitivity provide an interesting counterpoint to some myths about testosterone: the notion, for example, that testosterone is the key element of libido, that without testosterone there can be no sex drive. Women with AIS, who cannot respond to testosterone, should therefore have no sex drive. However, these women report that they certainly *do* have sexual feelings, erotic fantasies, and orgasms (Angier, 1999). The notion that testosterone is the hormone of aggression is also brought into question by this group of women—women who should be mild-mannered and passive according to this belief but who can be as aggressive as anyone else. As one AIS woman is quoted as saying: "I'm just like my mother, an aggressive, obnoxious human being. . . . I'm the daughter my mother created. I'm the woman I was meant to be" (as quoted in Angier, 1999, p. 35).

ELEVATED PRENATAL PROGESTERONE   If prenatal exposure to androgens might possibly "masculinize" behavior, what about prenatal exposure to female hormones? Some research on individuals whose mothers were treated with progesterone during pregnancy hints that such exposure could have a "feminizing" effect on behavior. One double-blind study of 20 male teenagers who had been exposed prenatally to progesterone reported that these males were less assertive and aggressive and had decreased athletic coordination, fewer "masculine" interests, and less heterosexual experience than controls did (Yalom, Green, & Fisk, 1973). A second study found that progesterone-exposed males had less interest in dating and marriage than those in a matched control group did. Progesterone-exposed females had less interest in tomboyish behavior and more interest in their appearance than controls did (Zussman, Zussman, & Dalton, 1975). In this research as well, there are possible confoundings of hormonal exposure with other variables. Mothers taking progesterone during pregnancy were usually doing so because of diabetes or some other risk factor; thus, the hormone-exposed boys were probably also products of more stressful pregnancies than the controls were.

In all the research cited here, the most basic difficulty in determining physiological influences on human gender-role behavior is that there are simply no clear, agreed-upon criteria concerning which behaviors are male and which are female. In most areas, there is an enormous degree of overlap between the behavior of the two sexes. We cannot say for people, as we can for rats, for instance, that male sexual behavior always follows a certain pattern—beginning with mounting the female! Indeed, the range of male sexual behavior patterns that we would call both "masculine" and "normal" is wide enough that a change brought about by hormones would have to be very dramatic to capture our attention. Similarly, the tomboyish behavior of the AGS females in the foregoing studies would almost certainly have gone unnoticed had it not been specifically sought, because it falls well within the range of normal female behavior in this culture. In fact, the majority of girls and women report themselves to have been tomboys at some time during childhood (Hyde, Rosenberg, & Behrman, 1974; Morgan, 1998).

If sex hormones, through their influence on the fetal brain or some other mechanism, do produce the substrata for gender-role behavioral differences, these substrata merely provide basic predispositions that interact with environmental forces. Such interactions can produce a variety of behavioral outcomes. For instance, as noted by Ehrhardt (1985), though it is plausible that higher androgen levels affect the brain, predisposing boys to exhibit more physically active play, the socialization process widens this gap through a complex interaction of many factors. Being reinforced for physically active play, as boys more often are than girls, may encourage competition in active sports, which may in turn foster a competitive orientation, assertiveness, leadership skills, and dominance. The sex hormone difference may affect a specific, limited aspect of behavior, such as the threshold for expression of physically energetic play; however, this difference may be amplified and made more important by a variety of other factors.

Gender Identity

Gender identity is the individual's private experience of his or her gender: the concept of the self as male or female. This is such a powerful and important part of a person's self-image that in most adults it is virtually impossible to change it. (If you don't believe this, try for a moment to think of yourself as still "you" but as the other sex.) Are we born with a gender identity, or does it develop after birth?

Money and Ehrhardt (1972) describe a case in which a 7-month-old boy was the victim of a surgical accident that destroyed his penis. The boy had been normal in every respect, but the loss of the penis resulted in a decision by his parents to reassign his sex as female and to rear him as a girl. At the age of 17 months, the child's name, clothing, and hairstyle were changed to fit feminine norms, and surgery to feminize the genitals was undertaken shortly thereafter. Because the child had an identical twin brother, it became possible to compare the way two children with exactly the same genetic and prenatal background developed when one was reared as a boy and the other reassigned and reared as a girl.

According to Money and Ehrhardt, the child who was reassigned as a girl quickly developed typical feminine interests and behavior, whereas the other child maintained his masculine patterns. Moreover, they said, the girl clearly thought of herself as a girl, whereas the boy's self-concept was unambiguously masculine. Thus, they reported, the gender identity of each child was apparently shaped by the sex of assignment and rearing more than by genetic or other physiological determinants.

Recent developments have shed doubt on this conclusion. A follow-up of the sex-reassigned individual, now an adult, revealed that he had reclaimed a masculine gender identity during his teens and that he remembered always feeling uncomfortable and "not right" as a girl—even though he had no idea about the accident and the drastic solution (Colapino, 1997; Diamond & Sigmundson, 1997). In her mid-teens, almost immediately after being told what had happened, the individual adopted a male name and demanded male hormone treatments and surgery to change herself back into a male. He had his breasts surgically removed and a rudimentary penis constructed just prior to his 16th birthday. At age 21, he underwent surgery for the construction of improved male-looking genitalia. At the age of 25, he married and is now living an apparently well-adjusted life as a man.

A number of other studies have compared the gender identities of intersexed individuals who had the same physiological indicators of sex; some were assigned and reared as females, others as males. In most cases, core gender identity developed consistent with the sex of assignment and rearing, as long as the assignment was made between the child's 18th and 24th month of life and the parents communicated no ambiguity or doubt about the child's sex. The AGS girls discussed in the preceding section all formed female gender identities. In cases of AGS where genetically female individuals were reared as males, however, they formed a male gender identity (Money & Daley, 1977). Similarly, among the subjects with a history of androgen insensitivity, almost all formed a gender identity concordant with their sex of rearing. In the same vein, the males with a history of prenatal exposure to progesterone had no difficulty maintaining a male gender identity. On the whole, the evidence suggests that people form their gender identities according to whether, from an early age, they are labeled and treated as males or females. There is no clear, consistent evidence that early exposure to sex hormones influences the development of core gender identity (Collaer & Hines, 1995). However, the outcome of the famous twin case, as well as scattered findings that girls and women who have been exposed to excessive androgens prenatally may sometimes be less content with female gender identity (see Collaer & Hines for a review) suggest that perhaps hormonal influences should not be completely ruled out. As in other areas of female–male differences, core gender identity must be a product of a continuing interplay between genetic potential and environment.

Once formed, how resistant to change is a person's gender identity? There is some controversy around this question. Early research showed fairly consistently that gender identity was "set" very early in life and thereafter could not usually be altered successfully. Some of the most dramatic findings in this respect were reported by Hampson and Hampson (1961), who studied 31 AGS females. In these patients, the syndrome had not been treated at birth, and they continued to be exposed to excess androgens postnatally. Thus, they had grown from childhood with masculine-appearing genitalia and had a tendency to develop male secondary sex characteristics at puberty. They had been raised as girls, however, by parents who had been told their daughters were genetically female. Despite the problems these girls must have had in coping with their paradoxical appearance, however, all but 5 of them established an unambivalently female gender identity. This identity did not change even when male secondary sex characteristics began to develop at puberty.

The study of a population of intersexed males in the Dominican Republic, cited at the beginning of this chapter, has challenged the conclusion that gender identity, once formed, is virtually irreversible in later life (Imperato-McGinley, Guerrero, et al., 1974; Imperato-McGinley, Peterson, et al., 1979). Julianne Imperato-McGinley and her coworkers identified a group of intersexed males whose condition was caused by a genetically transmitted enzyme defect that interfered with the body's ability to use testosterone for sexual differentiation. This syndrome, 5-alpha-reductase deficiency, occurs in approximately 1 per 90 males in one isolated area of the Dominican Republic. These genetic males were born with ambiguous genitalia—a clitoris-like phallus and an incompletely developed scrotum—and many of them had been reared as girls. Of 18 males who had been reared as females and for whom adequate interview data were collected, 17 had changed to a male gender identity at adolescence. These individuals recalled feeling different from other girls as they approached adolescence, usually because of physical differences. Their change in gender identity occurred gradually, paralleling to some extent the development of male secondary sex characteristics. Most of these males also successfully adopted the male gender role and developed sexual relationships with women.

The findings of the Imperato-McGinley team were startling because they appeared to fly in the face of the notion that gender identity was set in the 2nd to 3rd year of life. A closer look at the research reveals, however, that the individuals studied by these researchers probably had not consolidated a female gender identity during childhood because they had not been unambiguously reared as females. In the first place, these children cannot have been regarded by their parents as proper girls because they did not possess a vagina and were thus incapable of intercourse and childbearing. In their village societies, where the feminine role was strongly focused around marriage and bearing and rearing children, these "girls" would have great difficulty finding a satisfactory niche. In the second place, the genetic disorder affecting these children was apparently common enough in this small society to have acquired a name. Affected children were labeled *guevote* (penis at 12) or *machihembra* (first woman, then man). Such labels reflect an expectation that gender will change, and this expectation may have been incorporated into the developing child's sense of gender identity. It is unlikely, then, that the individuals met the criterion of unambiguous rearing as girls that would have been necessary for them to form a solid female gender identity in early childhood.

The controversy surrounding the Imperato-McGinley findings arose not just because of the unusual reports of individuals changing gender identity at adolescence but also because of the interpretation the authors gave for this change. They argued that the change to a male gender identity reflected biological predispositions based on prenatal androgen influences on the brain. In other words, these individuals had "masculinized" brains because of their exposure to male hormones *in utero* and, when their social environment allowed it, their brains were "activated" by the upsurge of testosterone at puberty into a readiness to adopt a male gender identity. Thus, these researchers used their findings to argue that gender identity is biologically determined.

Appearance and behavior are susceptible to hormonal influence, but identity seems more likely to be socially constructed—though it might well be affected by appearance and behavior and by the masculine or feminine labels applied to them. As discussed in earlier chapters, the very categories "female" and "male" are social constructions, agreed-upon classifications with characteristics assigned, to some extent, by social consensus. It is known, for example, that some groups, such as the Mandaya of the Philippines, have languages that do not use gender distinctions and use occupation or status rather than gender as ways of classifying people or activities (Yengoyan, 1982). It is difficult to believe, then, that brain organization directly predisposes an individual to adopt one or the other of these socially constructed gender identities. Yet the findings of this study are challenging and provocative. They suggest that gender identity may be more fluid than once thought, evolving and becoming reintegrated as the individual develops. They raise more questions about the conceivable role of prenatal or postnatal hormones in affecting the brain's possible "predisposition" toward maleness or femaleness (S. W. Baker, 1980). However, the environmental and biological factors leading up to the observed shift in gender identity are so confounded with each other that there are no grounds for accepting the findings as proof that gender identity is biologically determined. Furthermore, studies of children in the United States who are affected by the same enzyme defect indicate that, in this cultural context, the children reared as females maintain their female gender identity, even after the development of male characteristics at puberty (R. T. Rubin, Reinisch, & Haskett, 1981). Clearly, there is much that is yet to be discovered about the process of gender identity formation, but the evidence is weighted heavily against the notion that gender identity is determined in any automatic way by hormones.

Gender Dysphoria and Transgenderism

A small but significant number of persons find it difficult or impossible to reconcile themselves to the sexual or gender identity they have been assigned. These individuals are deeply dissatisfied and unhappy with their assigned label of "female" or "male." This dissatisfaction is sometimes labeled **gender dysphoria.** Part of the feeling is summed up by Kate Bornstein (1994):

> I know I'm not a man—about that much I'm very clear, and I've come to the conclusion that I'm probably not a woman either, at least not according to a lot of people's rules on that sort of thing. The trouble is, we're living in a world that insists we be one or the other—a world that doesn't bother to tell us exactly what one or the other is. (p. 8).

In a similar vein, Holly Boswell (1997) says, "I have [n]ever understood what it is to be a man or a woman. . . . I seem to be neither, or maybe both, yet ultimately only myself" (p. 54).

This sense of discomfort with gender identity has led a number of people to question gender categories in general. Why must there be only two genders? Who makes the "rules" about what women and men should be like? There now exists an active **transgendered community** made up of people who, in various ways, are transgressing gender boundaries. This group includes pre- and post-operative **transsexuals** (people who have had or want to have surgery to change their bodies to match those of the other sex), **transvestites** (also called cross-dressers, who enjoy dressing in the clothing of the other sex), as well as individuals sometimes called **transgenders** (people who live all or part of the time in the identity of the other sex but have no intention of having surgery to change their bodies).

Transgender activists argue that the binary system of gender is a social construction: something that is agreed to by society because it is convenient, not based on "natural" distinctions. They argue for the freedom to transcend this binary system:

> I started out thinking that a theory of gender would bridge the long-standing gap between the two major genders, male and female. I'm no longer trying to do that. Some people think I want a world without gender, something bland and colorless: that's so far from how I live! I love playing with genders, and I love watching other people play with all the shades and flavors that gender can come in. I just want to

question what we've been holding on to for such an awfully long time. I want to question the existence of gender, and I want to enter that question firmly into the fabric of this culture. (K. Bornstein, 1994, p. 58)

So the word "transgender" describes much more than crossing between the poles of masculinity and femininity. It more aptly refers to the transgressing of gender norms, or being freely gendered, or transcending gender altogether in order to become more fully human. Transgender has to do with reinventing and realizing oneself more fully outside of the current system of gender. (H. Boswell, 1997, p. 54)

Much of the time, the transgender community is fairly invisible. To society at large, the most obvious reminder that gender is not a simple "two sizes fit all" matter has come from highly publicized stories of a few transsexuals.

TRANSSEXUALISM   Over the last three decades, several individuals in the public eye have made headlines by undergoing surgical procedures to change their sex assignment. James Morris, a well-known writer and reporter, chose to become Jan Morris and told the story of the transition from male to female in a best-seller called *Conundrum* (1974). Renee Richards, playing on the female professional tennis circuit, created doubts and protests because she had previously been a man playing on the male circuit. What mysterious process, many people asked, would cause an adult with an outwardly settled, stable life to want to change his or her sex?

A transsexual is a person—male or female—who firmly believes he or she was born with the body of the wrong sex. This conviction dates from early childhood, usually as far back as the person can remember. It is usually not amenable to change through life experiences, rewards for "normal" behavior, or therapy (R. Green, 1974). The transsexual may well believe that he or she can be helped only by changing, in terms of both identity and body, to the other gender and sex—because modern Western culture does not easily allow an individual to claim a gender or sexual identity other than female or male. If a person is deeply unhappy with his/her given gender/sex, the only way out seems to be to switch to the other gender/sex.

Transsexualism is an extreme form of gender dysphoria. It is a rare experience, estimated to occur once among every 20,000 to 30,000 genetic males and once among every 50,000 to 100,000 genetic females (American Psychiatric Association, 1994; Gooren, 1990). To all appearances, a transsexual has acquired the *wrong* gender identity, and, once acquired, this identity seems to be virtually unchangeable. Such individuals may lead lives that are outwardly congruent with their anatomical sex, but their conviction that their body is wrong for them is often strong enough to cause them to seek surgery to change it. Thus, a male-to-female transsexual may achieve a body congruent with a feminine self-image by taking regular doses of estrogen to acquire female secondary sex characteristics and having a vagina surgically constructed from the penile tissue. A female-to-male transsexual may take male hormone treatments and have surgery to construct a makeshift penis. Of course, in neither case is chromosomal sex changed; the individual remains genetically male or female despite surgically and hormonally wrought changes in appearance.

A transsexual who is seeking surgery must convince doctors that she or he is reasonably emotionally stable. Then, before any surgery is performed, the transsexual is required to spend a significant period living the life of the other gender, adopting the appearance and mannerisms associated with that gender. The rationale for this requirement is to ensure that the individual will be comfortable in the new identity. Some critics have suggested, however, that by promising the surgery only to those people who can successfully live as members of the other gender doctors are acting as agents of social control, promoting gender-stereotypic behavior by their clients (Raymond, 1979). In any case, the individual is not generally encouraged to become comfortable with a transsexual identity but rather to choose to be either male or female—and to "play that part" for the world at large. Kate Bornstein (1994) recalls:

> I was told by several counselors and a number of transgendered peers that I would need to invent a past for myself as a little girl, that I'd have to make up incidents of my girl childhood; that I'd have to say things like "When I was a little girl. . . ." I never was a little girl; I'd lied all my life trying to be the boy, the man that I'd known myself *not* to be. Here I was, taking a giant step toward personal integrity by entering therapy with the truth and self-acknowledgment that I was a transsexual, and I was told, "Don't *tell* anyone you're transsexual." (p. 62)

During the 1- to 2-year trial period, preoperative transsexuals receive hormones to begin changing their bodies. A male is treated with estrogen to stimulate breast development, smoother skin, and reduced muscularity. A female takes testosterone to suppress menstruation and cause the growth of facial and body hair. After the trial period, if surgery is judged appropriate, a male-to-female transsexual has the penis and testicles removed and external female genitals constructed. The female-to-male transsexual has the breasts removed, and a penis is constructed from abdominal skin. Depending on the surgical method used, this penis may be semierect and may or may not be sexually sensitive.

There is much controversy over the benefits of sex-reassignment surgery. Some studies of postoperative transsexuals have found high levels of satisfaction with the surgery and the new life (Blanchard, Steiner, & Clemmensen, 1985; Pauly, 1968). Critics have charged, however, that such an outcome is comparable to the satisfaction neurotics feel when allowed to carry out their obsessive behavior or that addicts feel when allowed access to their drug; it does not justify such drastic surgery. Defenders of the treatment argue that, within a medical framework, no other methods have been found effective for reducing the distress transsexuals experience (Blanchard et al., 1985). One interesting outcome of sex reassignment may be a change in economic status. Blanchard (1985) found evidence that taking on the male role was correlated with superior economic status for females, whereas reorientation in a female direction was associated with inferior economic status for males. Being male, no matter how it is achieved, is apparently associated with a higher income.

The origin of the transsexual's conviction of not fitting his or her assigned sex or of the transgendered person's discomfort with gender boundaries remains a mystery. As Holly Boswell (1997) muses, "So, is transgender simply a result of being more honest with oneself and resistant to socialization, or is it chromosomally or hormonally induced, or better described as spirit taking precedence over form? All I know is that I could no longer live any other way, and have since found many others who share this experience" (p. 54). Suggestions that such feelings may have a physiological basis have received no support, because these individuals appear to be normally sexually differentiated and not intersexual in any sense. Bardwick (1971) proposed that the prenatal sexual differentiation of the brain in transsexuals may have proceeded in an incongruent direction, causing their gender identity to differ from their anatomical sex. This explanation has never been supported, however, and it seems inadequate, given that transsexuals have generally been found not to differ physiologically from the rest of the population (R. Green, 1974) and that intersexuals usually form a gender identity congruent with their sex of assignment and rearing.

Consistent patterns of socialization and rearing associated with transsexualism have also been hard to identify. R. Green (1974) reports that the parents of some of his transsexual patients appear to have wanted a child of the other sex and may have communicated this to the child at a young age, but this pattern is not always found. Although psychoanalytic theory might propose that the transsexual identified with the wrong parent at the Oedipal stage, there is little evidence to support or reject this notion. Social learning theory, which might suggest that the transsexual's difficulty was caused by rewards for performing the behaviors of the other sex, does not easily explain why the transsexual often lives a successful life consistent with his or her anatomical sex while remaining firmly convinced that his or her gender identity is different. The cognitive developmental approach might interpret transsexualism as due to a child's initial faulty learning of the male–female concept or a mistaken gender categorization of the self at a critical period. It does not, however, suggest what forces might bring about such faulty learning.

Some writers have speculated that transsexualism is an outcome of the social definition and construction of gender roles. Janice Raymond (1979), for example, notes that male-to-female transsexuals frequently adopt an exaggerated version of feminine role behavior, becoming more stereotypically feminine than most women. This tendency may be based an extremely rigid view of masculine and feminine gender roles. Perhaps, Raymond suggests, if each sex were allowed greater latitude in terms of what behavior was considered appropriate for their gender role, individuals would not feel the need to change their bodies to match their behavioral preferences. There is, in fact, some evidence that in societies that allow for gender-role categories other than the usual male and female individuals can sometimes live outside the limits of strict masculinity or femininity without feeling dissatisfied with their bodies. For example, Unni Wikan (1977) describes a "third gender" in the Arab state of Oman, the *xanith*. The *xanith* are biologically men, but they do not adopt the traditional male role. They work as homosexual prostitutes and as skilled domestic servants. They have male names, adopt dress and hairstyles that are distinct from those of both men and women, and can, with impunity, violate the restrictions of purdah, the cultural system of female seclusion. Thus, they may speak with women on the street and see a woman's unveiled face. In addition, Wikan reports, the *xanith* are not irrevocably stuck in their role; they can adopt the male role simply by getting married and proving themselves able to perform heterosexual intercourse. Perhaps the existence of this third gender-role option undercuts the development in some men of an urgent sense that their bodies are wrong and must be changed.

The unanswered questions surrounding transsexualism illustrate the extent of our ignorance about how gender identity develops. Although on one hand individuals with ambiguous sexual differentiation often hold firmly to the gender identity consonant with their assigned sex despite contradictory signals from their body, on the other hand transsexuals refuse the gender to which they were assigned, even though it matches their body.

Sexual Orientation

Sexual orientation, the degree of erotic and affectional responsiveness to the other sex (heterosexuality) or to one's own sex (homosexuality), is a third aspect of behavior in which the sexes differ, on average. The available data on intersexual patients suggests that the sex of rearing is one decisive variable in establishing this orientation. Studies of AGS females in adolescence found that most of these prenatally androgenized girls developed a heterosexual orientation (Ehrhardt & Baker, 1976; Money & Schwartz, 1977), although a somewhat larger proportion of them than might be expected expressed a homosexual or bisexual preference (Money, Schwartz, & Lewis, 1984). Similarly, androgen-insensitive genetically male individuals reared as females generally were found to display a heterosexual orientation; many went on to marry men and adopt babies (Masica, et al., 1971).

Some researchers have argued that there is a genetic component to male homosexuality, citing the finding that brothers of gay males are 4 to 5 times more likely than those of heterosexual males to be homosexual or bisexual and that identical twins usually show the same sexual orientation (Pillard & Weinrich, 1986). One study showed that 48% of identical twin sisters of lesbian women also were lesbians, compared with only 16% of fraternal twins and 6% of genetically unrelated adopted sisters (Bailey, Pillard, Neale, & Agyei, 1993). A similar pattern was found for gay men (Pillard & Bailey, 1991). However, the cases in which identical twins show different sexual orientations indicate that if there is a genetic predisposition it works in concert with other factors.

Although no conclusive evidence exists that prenatal hormones contribute to the determination of sexual orientation, some scattered evidence points to at least a possible link between the two (Collaer & Hines, 1995). A "gestational neurohormonal" theory of human sexual orientation has been proposed, based on an overview of both animal and human research (Ellis & Ames, 1987). The theory suggests that, in all mammals, sexual orientation is primarily guided by the degree to which the nervous system is exposed to testosterone, estradiol, and other sex hormones while the organization of the brain and central nervous system is taking place (that is, prenatally, for humans). Based primarily on animal research, the theory is nonetheless consistent with certain observations about sexual orientation in humans—for example, the difficulty of altering a person's sexual orientation, the greater prevalence of homosexuality among males than females (based on the notion that sexual differentiation tends in a female direction at each stage unless some masculinizing process occurs), and the still insufficiently documented findings of differences between heterosexual and homosexual men in their bodies' responses to injections of estradiol (Gladue, Green, & Hellman, 1984). It is possible that prenatal hormones can have some effect on predispositions toward heterosexual or homosexual orientations, but the evidence is still far from conclusive, especially given the findings that so many individuals with known prenatal exposure to hormonal abnormalities establish an orientation that is heterosexual for their sex of rearing. However, hormones may play an indirect role through their effects on body build or gender-role behavior (Meyer-Bahlburg, 1980).

The findings of a recent study have been used to suggest that male homosexuality is correlated with specific aspects of brain organization. Using brain tissue from autopsies of 41 individuals (19 men identified as homosexual, 16 men identified as heterosexual, and 6 women identified as heterosexual), Simon LeVay (1991) found that one node of the hypothalamus was, on the average, significantly smaller (similar to the average size for the women) in the homosexual than in the heterosexual men. The sample is small, and the correct interpretation of the correlational findings is impossible to determine with certainty, especially since the members of the three groups died from different causes. The brain difference, if found to be reliable, could be an effect rather than a cause of sexual orientation, or it could be an anatomical feature that happens to be correlated with homosexuality but does not contribute to it. Despite the headlines that greeted these findings—"Brain May Dictate Sexuality: Differences Found in Critical Region" (Suplee, 1991)—researchers are a long way from identifying the precise ways biological factors may contribute to male homosexuality.

As for female homosexuality, its determinants seem even more complex. Some women report that their lesbian orientation is an aspect of themselves that is beyond their control—something they were born with or that dates back to their early memories. Others describe lesbian identity as a choice, often made later in life after considerable heterosexual experience (Golden, 1987). For the latter group, sexual orientation seems to be experienced as more fluid than popular notions of homosexuality–heterosexuality have described. These findings, which are relatively recent despite decades of research on sexual orientation, remind us that researchers' assumptions often preclude the investigation of certain questions. It has taken psychologists a long time to examine the variations in lesbian experience instead of treating lesbianism as a unidimensional, single-cause phenomenon. The newer findings bring us face to face with the notion that people may not always be so easily classified as homosexual, heterosexual, or bisexual. They suggest, as well, the necessity to consider a social constructionist view of sexual identity along with the traditional essentialist view that sexual orientation is a quality or characteristic of an individual. Finally, they remind us of the gaps that remain in scientists' understanding of sexual orientation.

The difficulties in determining the biological correlates of behavioral "feminization" and "masculinization" suggest that it is too simplistic to think of general feminizing or masculinizing effects of gonadal hormones. Collaer and Hines (1995) speculate that "a comprehensive theoretical model of sexual differentiation will require expanding the concepts of a separate dimension of masculinization and feminization to posit a separate dimension for each sexually differentiated characteristic." Each behavioral characteristic that shows gender differences, they argue, is "regulated by different neural circuitry and might be expected to have somewhat different critical periods and hormone sensitivities" (p. 90). A newer, more complex model of the influence of prenatal hormones on sexual differentiation would be required to explain findings that, for example, high prenatal testosterone is sometimes associated with no change in some female-stereotypical behaviors, an increase in others, and a reduction in still others. Such a model does not yet exist.

VARIATIONS IN NORMAL DEVELOPMENT

All males are not hormonally identical, and neither are all females. In fact, there is considerable variation within each sex as to the relative proportions of male and female hormones present in the body at any given developmental stage. This variation is most obvious at puberty, when the release of larger amounts of the appropriate sex hormones in the male or female body results in a more dramatic development of secondary sex characteristics. If hormones influence behavior in any way, then, they may contribute as much to individual differences as to sex differences. As Ehrhardt and Baker (1974) conclude in their report on AGS children:

> If prenatal hormone levels contribute to sex differences in behavior, the effects in human beings are subtle and can in no way be taken as a basis for prescribing social roles. In fact, we rather like to make an argument from the opposite point of view. If it can be documented that prenatal hormone levels are among the factors that account for the wide range of temperamental differences and role aspirations within the female, and possibly also within the male, sex, a great variety of adult roles should be available and can be adequately fulfilled by both women and men, and they should be equally acceptable and respectable for either sex. (p. 50)

Researchers trying to uncover relationships between neonatal hormone levels and characteristics of normal children have found that within-sex differences in hormone levels are sometimes as important as sex differences in predicting what children will be like. Jacklin, Maccoby, and Doering (1983) assessed timidity in 6- to 18-month-old children for whom sex hormone levels in umbilical cord blood had been measured at birth. They found marginal male–female differences in timidity, with girls more timid than boys. However, among the boys, neonatal sex hormone levels were significantly related to across-age timidity scores. The higher their levels of progesterone and testosterone had been at birth, the lower their timidity was. Conversely, boys' neonatal estrogen levels were positively related to later timidity. No relationship between hormone levels and timidity was observed for girls. Other work by these researchers showed that, among children in the first 3 years of life, simple sex differences in muscular strength were overshadowed by more complex hormonal effects (Jacklin, Maccoby, Doering, & King, 1984). Although there was a small tendency for boys to have higher average strength scores than girls, strength in both girls and boys was negatively related to levels of androstenedione (a male hormone) measured at birth. In addition, neonatal progesterone levels related differently to strength for boys and girls. Girls with high umbilical cord progesterone showed low strength, whereas boys with high progesterone showed high strength. Researchers do not yet know enough about the prenatal and postnatal action of hormones on the nervous system and the rest of the body to explain these findings, but they seem to bear out Ehrhardt and Baker's (1974) claim that hormones may contribute as much to individual differences as to group differences between females and males.

A note of caution is in order here. The results just cited are correlational; thus, it cannot be stated with any degree of certainty that neonatal hormone levels *caused* differences in timidity or muscular strength. Moreover, it is not even certain that neonatal hormone levels are related to later hormone levels because hormones were measured only once, at birth. In general, a number of factors aside from sexual differentiation can affect the levels of sex hormones circulating in a person's body. Emotional stress can cause drops in both male and female hormone levels (Archer, 1979; Kreuz, Rose, & Jennings, 1972; R. M. Rose, 1969); sexual activity can increase testosterone secretion, as can winning in competition (Gladue, Boechler, & McCaul, 1989); and social isolation, defeat, and unavoidable punishment can decrease testosterone secretion (Ellis, 1982). If there is a causal relationship between hormones and behavior, then, there is no reason to suppose it is a one-way street.

Aggression

One behavior that researchers have thought might be linked to variations in sex hormone levels is aggression. Controlled experiments with animals and research on humans who have been exposed prenatally to excess androgens suggest a link between prenatal androgen levels and rough-and-tumble play. As noted earlier, Goy (1970) found that female rhesus monkeys whose mothers had been injected with male hormones during pregnancy engaged in more rough-and-tumble play and chasing and threatening behaviors than their female age-mates did. Similarly, human females who were accidentally exposed to excess androgens *in utero* may engage in more rough-and-tumble play than other girls (Money & Ehrhardt, 1972), although it is not clear that this difference can be attributed to prenatal hormones. However, even an unambiguous connection between male hormones and rough-and-tumble play would not suffice as proof that aggression is linked to prenatal androgen exposure. Most psychologists define aggression as behavior with intent to injure. Although the AGS children, both girls and boys, were described as more energetic and likely to engage in rough-and-tumble play than their normal counterparts, they were *not* reported to be more aggressive against other children or to initiate or engage in more fights. Across a number of studies of children prenatally exposed to excess androgens, the reporting of an effect on rough-and-tumble play is quite a bit more consistent than the finding of an effect on aggression (Collaer & Hines, 1995; Hines, 1982). Indeed, research indicates a clear distinction between rough and-tumble play and aggression (DiPietro, 1981). Children have little trouble distinguishing between playful mock fighting, which requires a great deal of cooperation, and real aggression, although rough-and-tumble play can lead to aggression through accidental injury or through increased sensitivity to threatening stimuli. If there is a connection between prenatal hormones and aggression, then, it cannot simply be assumed on the basis of a correlation between hormones and rough-and-tumble play.

One study examined the relationship between prenatal hormone exposure and a measure of aggressive orientation (Reinisch, 1981). Boys and girls whose mothers had been treated with various forms of progesterone during pregnancy were compared with their siblings on a test that asked them to choose one of four solutions to each of six common conflict situations. The choices involved physical aggression, verbal aggression, withdrawal, and nonaggressive coping. Boys whose mothers had taken progesterone during pregnancy were twice as likely as their brothers to choose the physical aggression response; girls whose mothers had taken the hormones chose physical aggression 1.5 times more often than their sisters did. These findings are difficult to interpret, but such difficulties are themselves instructive: They show why hasty conclusions can be perilous in this area of research. In the first place, aggressive orientation was linked with exposure to progesterone, a female hormone, but the supposition has always been that it is *male* hormones that are related to aggression. As it turns out, the type of synthetic progesterone taken by the mothers of some of these children was a chemical that had androgen-like effects. However, the progesterone taken by some of the other mothers in the sample seems to behave as a female hormone and has been studied by other researchers for its potential feminizing influence. Thus, it is not clear that all of the children in this study had been exposed prenatally to masculinizing hormones. In the second place, the average daily dose of progesterone taken by the mothers during pregnancy was a small one, between one third and one tenth the amount being naturally produced by the mother. The mothers' blood hormone levels were not measured, so it is not certain that the treatment significantly raised the already high level of progesterone in the mothers' bloodstream. Given these difficulties, it is far from certain that the differences in aggression-related responding between the two groups of children can be attributed to the fact that one group was exposed to extra progesterone prenatally. Fausto-Sterling (1992) suggests an equally plausible explanation: that the mothers who were treated with progesterone during pregnancy were having more difficult than average pregnancies. As noted earlier in the chapter, women who receive hormone treatments are usually suffering from specific complications or risks during pregnancy and thus may be experiencing more than the usual stress of pregnancy. Perhaps it is the stress itself, rather than the hormone treatments, that causes the children of such pregnancies to differ from the children of less stressful pregnancies. The data do not allow us to choose between the two explanations. The evidence for an organizational effect of prenatal exposure to masculinizing hormones on predisposition to later aggression is equivocal.

Taking a different approach to the androgen–aggression connection, some researchers have examined the possible activational effect of testosterone: the relationship between testosterone levels in the blood of adult men and their aggression levels. The assumption that testosterone levels and aggression are related has been so strong until recently that violent male criminals were sometimes castrated as a way to reduce their aggressive tendencies. Currently, treatment with synthetic female hormones has replaced surgery for this purpose, but follow-up studies indicate that neither method is necessarily effective at reducing violence (Angier, 1999; Whitehead, 1981).

Studies of normal men, in which both aggression and testosterone levels in the blood have been measured, show mixed results. Some studies yield little evidence of a correlation between circulating testosterone levels and aggression (Doering, Brodie, Kraemer, Becker, & Hamburg, 1974; Meyer-Bahlburg, Boon, Sharma, & Edwards, 1974; Moyer, 1974), although some studies of male prisoners indicate a positive relationship between testosterone levels and history of arrests or aggressive behavior in prison (Kreuz & Rose, 1972) and history of violent crimes (Dabbs, Frady, Carr, & Besch, 1987). One study showed hockey players' testosterone levels were strongly correlated with response to threat when faced with an aggressive situation in a game or practice (Scamarella & Brown, 1978). Another found that men producing high levels of testosterone were less likely to marry, more likely to divorce, and more likely to leave marriages because of troubled relationships, extramarital affairs, and throwing things at or hitting their spouses (Booth & Dabbs, 1993). Positive correlations between testosterone levels and dispositional aggressive tendencies have been found for college-age men (Christiansen & Knussman, 1987) and younger adolescents (Susman et al., 1987).

Any link that may exist between circulating testosterone and aggression appears to hold more strongly for men than for women. Testosterone levels are higher among trial lawyers than among tax lawyers—if they are male, but not if they are female (Dabbs et al., 1998). Female prison inmates who have high testosterone levels display more domineering and intimidating behavior than their low-testosterone counterparts do. But this correlation is muddied by the fact that those with the higher testosterone were also younger and thus perhaps stronger and with less sense of vulnerability (Dabbs & Hargrove, 1997).

A study of nearly 4500 U.S. military veterans found that testosterone levels were correlated with a variety of antisocial behaviors: delinquency, drug use, alcohol abuse, and military AWOL (Dabbs & Morris, 1990). The relationship between testosterone and these behaviors was considerably weaker in high-socioeconomic-status than in low-socioeconomic-status groups, however, indicating that social class moderates the relationship between hormones and behavior. Furthermore, the size of the effect is small; it becomes noticeable mainly at extreme levels of testosterone. Another series of studies, using small samples of men in different occupations, found that actors tended to have higher testosterone levels than ministers (Dabbs, de La Rue, & Williams, 1990). The latter finding proves nothing about aggression per se, but the authors suggest that the two types of occupations are differentiated by the amount of dominance and antisocial tendencies they require. However, the small sample sizes and such inconsistencies as the fact that football players did not differ significantly from physicians or professors in their testosterone levels cast some doubt on this interpretation.

Some studies show that men's levels of testosterone can change in response to victory or defeat in male–male competition. Testosterone levels were found to stay elevated longer among winners than losers of a tennis match, but no such pattern differentiated winners and losers of a lottery (A. Mazur & Lamb, 1980). Among wrestlers, testosterone levels declined more quickly among losers than among winners (Elias, 1981). Winners of a competition involving computer-driven reaction-time tasks showed higher postcompetition testosterone levels and a slower decline of those levels than losers did (Gladue et al., 1989). And male winners of chess competitions showed higher testosterone levels than their losing counterparts did (Mazur, Booth, & Dabbs, 1992). These findings are not directly relevant to aggression; however, they suggest the possibility of a link between testosterone and the experience of dominance. Here, though, there is no implication that high testosterone levels cause dominant behavior; rather, it is the experience of prevailing in competition that appears to cause changes in hormone levels.

Clearly, the search for a simple, one-way cause-and-effect model of testosterone's influence on aggression is misguided. Individual differences in baseline levels of testosterone are sometimes correlated with differences in behavior, but the level of testosterone in a single individual's bloodstream can also vary dramatically, sometimes changing over the course of minutes, in response to social stimuli. The research on circulating testosterone implicates it as both a cause *and* an effect of social behavior (Dabbs, 1992). Furthermore, testosterone is only one of many hormones in the human body, which may vary simultaneously and interact with one another in ways as yet unknown. Thus, a narrow focus on the link between one hormone and one behavior such as aggression may be unwarranted.

SUMMARY

The biological categories "female" and "male," often thought of as completely discrete, have been shown to have some potential for overlap. Physiological differentiation of the sexes begins at conception with the genetic determination of sex and continues through several stages of fetal development: the differentiation of the gonads, their secretion of sex hormones, and the resulting differentiation of the internal reproductive organs and the external genitalia. In addition, some researchers believe the sex hormones also have an impact on the developing brain, differentiating it in some respects for males and females. The extent, mechanism, timing, and implications of sexual differentiation of the human brain remain controversial.

Under normal circumstances, the differentiation proceeds in the same direction at every stage, producing an individual who is unambiguously either female or male at birth. However, on rare occasions the process is disrupted and the individual differentiates as male at some stages and as female at others. Such individuals, called intersexuals, are a source of valuable information about the relationship between the physiological and psychological aspects of sex and gender.

Many questions have been raised about the biological bases of sex dimorphic behavior—behavior on which groups of females and males tend to differ. Research using intersexed individuals has focused on three types of behavior: gender-role behavior, gender identity, and sexual orientation. At present, the evidence linking sexual orientation to irregularities in the sexual differentiation process is suggestive but inconclusive. For gender identity, most of the research suggests that children usually adopt an identity that is congruent with their sex of assignment and rearing, regardless of biological abnormalities that may tend to contradict it. For the latter pattern to hold, researchers believe sex assignment must be done before the 3rd year of life, and the individual must be reared unambiguously according to the gender to which she or he was assigned. There is more for scientists to learn about gender identity, though, as illustrated by the outcome of the famous identical twin study, the Imperato-McGinley findings of gender identity shifts in adolescence among one group of male intersexuals, and by some individuals' experience of gender dysphoria and transsexualism. For gender-role behavior, some evidence suggests a connection between prenatal exposure to androgens and such "masculine" behaviors as rough-and-tumble play. However, early hormonal exposure is usually confounded with other variables, such as continuing cortisone treatments, the awareness of having been born different, and perhaps parental anxiety, and the evidence remains equivocal.

Even among normal individuals, both male and female hormones are synthesized by both sexes, and there are wide individual variations in the levels of circulating sex hormones. These variations affect the development of secondary sex characteristics at puberty, and so may affect gender-related behavior indirectly by helping to create a more or less stereotypically masculine or feminine body build and appearance. Studies on muscle strength and timidity in young children suggest that within-sex individual differences in hormone levels at birth may be as important as sex in predicting these qualities. Attempts have been made to relate within-sex differences in male hormone levels to aggression; however, the evidence on this point remains weak. Scientists still have much to learn about biological influences on human behavior in general and on human sex and gender in particular. Nothing that has been uncovered so far, however, points to chromosomes, hormones, or anatomy as direct unilateral determining factors in gender-role behavior, gender identity, or sexual orientation.

KEY TERMS

sex chromosomes	intersexed	gender dysphoria
Müllerian ducts	adrenogenital syndrome	transgendered community
Wolffian ducts	(AGS)	transsexuals
sex-linked traits	androgen insensitivity	transvestites
sex-limited traits	syndrome (AIS)	transgenders

FOR ADDITIONAL READING

Angier, Natalie. (1999). *Woman: An intimate geography*. Boston: Houghton Mifflin. In witty and entertaining prose, this science writer discusses the research on all aspects of female biology, including the X chromosome, androgen insensitivity syndrome, estrogen, ovaries, hysterectomies, and more. As Gloria Steinem said, "Anyone living in or near a female body should read this book."

Bornstein, Kate. (1994). *Gender outlaw: On men, women, and the rest of us*. New York: Vintage Books. This book combines the personal story and theoretical/political musings of a transgender activist who is also a male-to-female transsexual.

Fausto-Sterling, Anne. (1993). The five sexes: Why male and female are not enough. *The Sciences 22*(2). A biologist discusses five broad sexual categories: females, males, herms, ferms, and merms.

Garber, Marjorie. (1991). *Vested interests: Cross-dressing and cultural anxiety*. New York: Routledge. This is a wide ranging study of transvestism that questions why men sometimes dress as women and vice versa.

Kessler, Suzanne. (1998). *Lessons from the intersexed*. Rutgers, NJ: Rutgers University Press. A researcher writes about how her study of intersexed individuals leads to the necessity to question traditional notions of gender.

Morris, Jan. (1974). *Conundrum*. New York: Harcourt Brace Jovanovich. A transsexual journalist who lived a successful life as a man until middle adulthood tells the story of her early life and her transition to a feminine body and gender role.

CHAPTER 6

Perceptual & Cognitive Abilities

Gender Similarities & Differences

In 1903, James McKeen Cattell, an influential professor of psychology at Columbia University, published a study of 1000 eminent persons. In title and content it was, in fact, a study of eminent *men;* only 32 women were included in Cattell's list. Cattell himself made no apologies for the dearth of female representation in his catalogue of eminence, noting that it was well known that women were much less likely than men to depart from average levels of ability (Cattell, 1903).

Cattell's argument was completely in step with his times. Only a few years earlier, the renowned Francis Galton, after testing 9337 persons in his Anthropometric Laboratory in England, had declared that women were inferior to men in all their capacities (Boring, 1929). And in 1879 Gustave Le Bon, one of the founders of social psychology, had noted that "all psychologists who have studied the intelligence of women. . . recognize today that they represent the most inferior forms of human evolution and that they are closer to children and savages than to an adult, civilized male" (as quoted in Gould, 1981, p. 104). Indeed, many of the research efforts of the new discipline of psychology in the early part of the 20th century were devoted to demonstrating the assumed biological inferiority of women (Shields, 1975) and non-Caucasian racial groups (Guthrie, 1976).

Many psychologists and educators of Cattell's generation held firmly to the belief that men, as a group, were more variable than women—that men were more likely than women to be found at the high and low extremes of intelligence. Men were more likely than women to be geniuses; they were also more likely than women to be mentally subnormal. Women were most likely to be of average intelligence.

The belief in greater male variability was congenial to those who were interested in maintaining the status quo between the sexes. In the first place, the greater variability claimed for the male sex was considered a positive quality—a progressive force in the evolution of the human species. Greater variability was one more plank in the platform of male superiority, as was the idea that the greater male variability meant most geniuses would be male. It was an idea that provided ammunition to those who wished to exclude women from graduate and professional schools and to channel educated women into low-paying, low-status jobs.

The idea that males varied more in intelligence than females was probably accepted as a truism by many early-20th-century observers. Most areas where eminence could be achieved were clearly dominated by men; males also tended to outnumber females in institutions for the mentally retarded. The notion that these male–female differences might be explained by causes other than sex differences in the distribution of intelligence received little consideration. In the end, it was a female psychologist, Leta Hollingworth, who most successfully cast doubt on the greater-male-variability hypothesis (Silverman, 1989).

Hollingworth knew from bitter personal experience that the road to eminence for a woman had as much to do with social custom and prejudice as with her degree of intelligence. Her graduate education in psychology occurred in a climate in which graduate scholarships were not open to women, most faculty members had never worked professionally with women or taught female students, the chairman of her department was an active campaigner against higher education for women, and the dean of her faculty stated publicly that few women were capable of truly advanced, original work (R. Rosenberg, 1982). Her own major adviser, Edward L. Thorndike, a believer in the variability hypothesis, argued that "in particular, if men differ in intelligence and energy by wider degrees than do women, eminence in and leadership of the world's affairs of whatever sort will inevitably belong oftener to men. They will oftener deserve it" (Thorndike, 1910, p. 35). It was while working at her first job, as a tester at New York City's Clearing House for Mental Defectives, that Hollingworth began to focus her attention on the variability hypothesis. Although most of the retarded children referred to her for testing were boys, a situation predicted by the variability hypothesis, she noted that the disproportionate number of males was due primarily to the large number of boys under the age of 16. Her observations led her to believe boys of below-average intelligence were likely to come to the attention of the law at a much earlier age than their female counterparts were. Boys were less restricted and so were more likely to get into trouble; moreover, the undemanding social expectations for girls—that they be passive and dependent—made it less likely that low intelligence would be noticed. In adulthood, a low-intelligence female sometimes found a niche as a housewife, domestic worker, or prostitute and came to a mental institution only when illness or the death of the man on whom she was depending intervened. A low-intelligence male had fewer options and was likely to end up in a mental institution much sooner (Hollingworth, 1922). Social factors rather than differences in the variability of intelligence, then, could explain the preponderance of males in institutions for the mentally retarded.

Hollingworth believed the apparent underrepresentation of women at the top end of the distribution of intelligence could also be explained by social factors. After reviewing measurements made on 20,000 infants at birth, she concluded that there was no difference in variability between females and males. She went on to chastise psychologists for failing to consider the impact of domestic and childrearing tasks—"a field where eminence is impossible"—on women's capacity to achieve the distinction associated with genius (Hollingworth & Montague, 1914). Only when the latter explanation had been ruled out, she argued, should psychologists consider differences in intelligence or variability as an explanation for sex differences in the attainment of eminence.

After Hollingworth's articles on sex differences in mental traits appeared in the prestigious *Psychological Bulletin* (Hollingworth, 1916, 1918), the greater-male-variability hypothesis was discredited. Arguments have continued to rage, however, about whether the sexes differ in intellectual abilities or in cognitive style, that is, in the way we think and approach problems. Even the discredited variability hypothesis has not been allowed to die entirely, despite a lack of supporting data (e.g., see Lehrke, 1972). This chapter reviews the recent findings on gender and intellectual abilities. Because intellectual abilities can be measured only through performance on various tests, the discussion will also encompass some of the many nonintellectual affective factors that can influence performance on such tests.

GENDER DIFFERENCES IN INTELLECTUAL PERFORMANCE

Many of the popular stereotypes of women and men are based on the assumption that the two sexes approach the task of thinking in very different ways. It is widely held, for instance, that men are logical and women are intuitive, that it is a rare woman who has a "head for figures," and that men are more quickly frustrated and bored than women when performing simple repetitive tasks. Is there any basis to the idea that males are better suited to the task of calculating formulas or that females are better at spelling and typing? Researchers in this area have found a few gender differences in performance, but they tend to be smaller than the stereotypes would lead us to expect.

General Intelligence

There are no differences between male and female performance on tests of general intelligence (Collaer & Hines, 1995; Maccoby & Jacklin, 1974). This finding is not surprising: Early versions of the Stanford-Binet intelligence test showed a slight tendency for women to score higher than men, but items that contributed to this difference were subsequently eliminated. Later IQ tests were constructed by including various subscales, on some of which females tended to score better and on some of which males tended to score better, thus effectively eliminating gender differences in overall scores. In addition, there is little evidence linking intelligence to specific biological indicators of sex, such as the X or Y chromosomes (Wittig, 1979) or prenatal hormones (Hines, 1982). One interesting finding is that gender-role nonconformity is positively related to IQ for both sexes (Maccoby, 1966).

Sensation, Perception, and Motor Skills

From the age of 4 onward, females tend to outscore males on tests of perceptual speed and accuracy (Antill & Cunningham, 1982; Fairweather, 1976; Feingold, 1988). Boys over the age of about 9 show faster reaction times than their female counterparts. However, in situations where semantic or symbolic information must be processed to choose a response, females react faster than males, and the female advantage increases as the amount of information to be processed increases (Fairweather & Hutt, 1972).

In childhood and adulthood, females show more sensitivity to touch in the fingers and hands than males do (Weinstein & Sersen, 1961), as well as more sensitivity to pressure on various parts of the body (Gandelman, 1983). In the realm of manual dexterity, findings are mixed (J. R. Thomas & French, 1985). On a pegboard task, females usually outperform males; however, this finding appears to be due to females' smaller finger size rather than dexterity (Peters, Servos, & Day, 1990). The only other fine motor task for which female–male differences are consistently found is finger tapping, which men perform better (Dodril, 1979). Motor tests of gross strength and speed favor males, who are generally larger and stronger (J. R. Thomas & French, 1985).

Studies on auditory threshold indicate that females have better high-frequency hearing than men do (Gandelman, 1983; McGuinness, 1972). Evidence also suggests that females react more strongly than males to sound intensity. Females are more intolerant than males of loud sounds; by about the level of 85 decibels, females may hear a sound as twice as loud as males do (McGuinness, 1972). Females also seem to be more sensitive than males to changes in sound intensity (Zaner, Levee, & Gunta, 1968). In the visual mode, men seem to be more sensitive than women to intensity changes; in dark conditions, however, women adapt more rapidly than men to lower light levels and show more sensitivity at these levels (McGuinness, 1976, 1985).

In auditory search tasks, when males and females are asked to tell, by listening to a list of words, where a particular sound or letter occurs in each word, males perform much more poorly than females (McGuinness & Courtney, 1983). These researchers conclude that males have more trouble than females in forming a visual image of a word while operating in an auditory, or listening, mode. They suggest that this difficulty may be a factor underlying some gender differences in linguistic performance.

There is some evidence that male and female infants differ in the kinds of visual stimuli to which they pay most attention. Girls show greater interest in and greater ability to discriminate among faces than boys do (M. Lewis, 1969); boys have been found to show stronger attentional responses to blinking lights, geometric patterns, and novel objects (Cornell & Strauss, 1973; Kagan & Lewis, 1965; McCall & Kagan, 1970). In an interesting experiment with adults, Diane McGuinness and John Symonds (1977) presented pairs of photographs to subjects stereoscopically (that is, one photograph is presented to one eye while the other photograph is simultaneously presented to the other eye). In this situation, the two stimuli compete to be "seen," and the person sees either one of them at a time or an image that combines them in some way. Each pair of photographs contained one picture of an object and one picture of a person. Male subjects reported seeing objects more than people, but females reported the reverse. This phenomenon was tested again, this time using a simple measure of time spent looking at each of two pictures (Jobson & Watson, 1984). These researchers found a gender difference in the attention paid to objects versus persons, but only for younger subjects. For subjects older than 35, there was no gender difference: Both females and males spent more time looking at pictures of persons.

The implications of male–female differences in perception and attention are uncertain. Some of them, such as females' greater perceptual speed and accuracy and their greater tactile sensitivity in the fingers and hands, have been used to argue for women's "suitability" for clerical work, such as typing. They could just as logically be used to argue that women would make better neurosurgeons than men. The fact that such an argument is seldom seen is a reminder of how easily the "neutral" findings of science can be used to justify the status quo. It has been suggested that male–female differences in sensory processing may underlie gender differences in cognitive performance; however, in most cases, no connection has yet been established.

Learning and Memory

A review of the literature by Maccoby and Jacklin (1974) indicated no gender differences in learning and memory. The stereotype that females are better at rote learning and males are better at learning complex tasks receives no support. Some research shows that women may process information more rapidly than men do (McGuinness & Pribram, 1979). Most studies show no female–male differences on tests of memory (e.g., Joseph, McKay, & Joseph, 1982; Savage & Gouvier, 1992). However, others have found a female advantage on tests of verbal memory (Trahan & Quintana, 1990). Some apparent gender differences in the recall of visual material have been attributed to gender differences in verbal fluency: Females may simply be better than males at describing what they remember, rather than at remembering itself (McGuinness & McLaughlin, 1982). Where gender differences in learning or memory are found, they can usually be traced to gender differences in familiarity with or interest in the topic at hand (Herrmann, Crawford, & Holdsworth, 1992). These authors found that women were better than men at memorizing a shopping list, but men performed better than women when asked to memorize directions to a particular place. In another study, words that had been previously classified as "masculine" were better recalled by males, and "feminine" words were better recalled by females (A. Brown, Larsen, Rankin, & Ballard, 1980).

The tendency to learn and remember gender-related information better than non-gender-related information seems to be strongest among individuals who are highly gender-typed (Cann & Garnett, 1984; Hepburn, 1985). This finding is perhaps best explained by gender schema theory—the notion that individuals who are gender-typed have learned to perceive and process information in terms of gender categories (Bem, 1985).

Verbal Performance

For years, it was consistently reported in the psychological literature that females outperform males on verbal tasks (Anastasi, 1937/1958a; Hyde, 1981; Maccoby & Jacklin, 1974; McGuinness & Pribram, 1979; Tyler, 1947/1965). Although the gender difference in verbal performance appeared consistent, its size was very small. A meta-analysis by Hyde (1981) showed that gender accounted for an average of only 1% of the variance in verbal performance scores, leaving the other 99% of variation in verbal performance to be explained by other factors.

Research comparing test performances of samples of children and adolescents between 1947 and 1983 shows that gender differences in verbal performance, as well as in other cognitive skill areas, have declined drastically over the years—at least among adolescents (Feingold, 1988). A meta-analysis using 165 studies found no gender differences in verbal performance, either across all types of verbal tests or within specific tests such as vocabulary, reading comprehension, and essay writing (Hyde & Linn, 1988). However, these reviewers did find small gender differences favoring females in anagrams and general/mixed verbal abilities, a small difference favoring males in analogies, and a moderate difference favoring females in speech production. It appears that there are consistent gender differences on some types of verbal performance, but many types of verbal tasks show no differences.

Researchers continue to report gender differences in some aspects of verbal performance. For example, Hines (1990) reports a large female advantage of more than one standard deviation on tests of associational fluency (generating synonyms). Some differences in the frequencies of particular verbal difficulties are striking: Boys are 3 to 4 times more likely than girls to be stutterers (Skinner & Shelton, 1985) and 5 to 10 times more likely than girls to be dyslexic (Vandenberg, 1987).

Gender differences in aspects of verbal performance such as reading, spelling, and grammar are reported most consistently among children; girls perform better than boys in many samples (Feingold, 1993). However, studies of adolescents also show some differences in verbal performance. A study of high school students in Japan and the United States showed that in both countries girls averaged significantly higher than boys on word fluency (Mann, Sasanuma, Sakuma, & Masaki, 1990). A study of cognitive performance among Chinese high school students showed girls performing at higher levels than boys on word knowledge (Huang, 1993). However, males have scored higher than females on the verbal portion of the Scholastic Assessment Test (SAT) since the early 1970s. This may be because low-ability males do not take the test and because SAT-Verbal is weighted heavily with analogies—the only verbal test on which males tend to outscore females (Halpern, 1992).

Quantitative Performance

Meta-analyses done more than a decade ago showed a tendency for males to outperform females on mathematical tests; however, only between 1% and 5%, of the variance in mathematics performance could be explained by gender (Hyde, 1981; Rossi, 1983). Meta-analyses that include more recent studies indicate that the gender gap in average level of mathematics performance is slowly decreasing (L. Friedman, 1989; Hyde, Fennema, & Lamon, 1990; Nowell & Hedges, 1998) and is often negligible. Figure 6.1 shows two overlapping distributions that approximate the size of the gender difference in mathematics performance, averaging over the more than 100 samples (representing almost 4 million subjects) used in the Hyde, Fennema, and Lamon meta-analysis.

In this meta-analysis, gender differences in mathematics performance were found to be greater for White Americans than for African, Hispanic, or Asian Americans, or for Canadian or Australian samples. A similar pattern of larger gender differences in

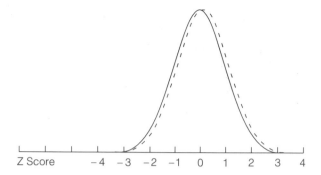

Figure 6.1 Two normal distributions that are 0.15 standard deviations apart (i.e., $d = 0.15$. This is the approximate magnitude of the gender differences in mathematics performance, averaging over all samples).

samples of White American students than in samples of minority students emerged in the L. Friedman (1989) meta-analysis. Cross-cultural studies often do not show the same pattern of males outperforming females in mathematics that is found in the United States (Feingold, 1994b; Huang, 1993; Skaalvik & Rankin, 1994).

The majority of studies show no gender differences in performance on general mathematics achievement tests until early adolescence—a finding that holds across a variety of cultures (Lummis & Stevenson, 1990). Girls show a slight advantage in arithmetic computation in elementary and middle school (Feingold, 1993). Some studies find that boys do better than girls on one particular type of quantitative performance, mathematical problem solving, as early as the first grade (Lummis & Stevenson, 1990). In the latter study, first-grade males outperformed females in problem solving by equivalent amounts across samples in three countries: the United States, Japan, and Taiwan. Although Japanese girls achieved higher average scores on problem solving than American boys did, the gap in problem-solving performance between Japanese boys and Japanese girls was as great as that between American boys and American girls. This difference occurred despite girls' and boys' apparently equivalent adeptness at computation and understanding the mathematical operations needed to solve the problems.

Gender differences favoring males in mathematical problem solving appear most reliably in high school and are maintained or increased in college. The estimated size of the gender difference is such that about 43% of high school females and 57% of high school males will score above the average score for the whole high school sample (Hyde, Fennema, & Lamon, 1990). Problem solving, then, appears to be the only area of mathematics achievement in which the gender difference may be a cause for concern. As Hyde and her colleagues note, problem-solving skill is critical for success in such fields as engineering and physics.

On the whole, gender differences seem to be smallest, and may favor females, when the samples studied are from the general population. The differences are larger with more selective samples and appear largest for samples of highly precocious persons (Hyde, Fennema, & Lamon, 1990). There are some indications that gender and social class interact with respect to mathematics achievement test results. Smaller gender differences in performance are found in samples from lower than from higher socioeconomic groups (Fischbein, 1990).

Despite the finding that by high school males tend to outperform females on standardized tests of mathematical problem solving, girls often obtain higher grades in mathematics than boys do (Kimball, 1989). This anomalous finding is shrugged off by researchers convinced of male quantitative superiority as being due to girls' better behavior in school (Benbow & Stanley, 1982). It may, however, reflect differences between the two types of testing situations such that boys are advantaged in the standardized testing situation and girls are advantaged in the classroom testing situation. Such differences could involve issues such as test anxiety (Crocker, Schmitt, & Tang, 1988) or content of items included on the tests.

Some researchers have linked performance in mathematics and science to visual–spatial ability, and correlational studies show a strong relationship between spatial abilities and mathematical reasoning (Linn & Petersen, 1985). However, as discussed in the next section, the kinds of spatial tasks that show the strongest gender differences do not correspond to the processes required for good mathematical performance, and spatial ability does not appear to moderate the development of mathematical ability (Lubinsky & Humphreys, 1990). The correlations that do exist may reflect the shared degree of general or analytic ability required for the two types of tasks. Research with children in the sixth through eighth grades indicates that children who differ in visual–spatial skill do not differ in their ability to solve mathematical problems (Fennema & Tartre, 1985). However, poor spatial performance seems to be linked more strongly to poor mathematical performance for girls than for boys (Ethington & Wolfle, 1984; Fennema & Tartre, 1985). There are no obvious explanations for this correlational finding.

Considerable interest in the possibility of gender differences in mathematical ability was aroused by the work of Benbow and Stanley (1980, 1982, 1983; Benbow, 1988). These researchers examined scores on the SAT-M (a standardized test of mathematical reasoning) for about 50,000 seventh- and eighth-grade children identified by the Johns Hopkins National Talent Search. To be included in the sample, a child had to score in the top 3% nationally on a standardized achievement test. Among these high-ability children, Benbow and Stanley found a mean difference in performance of 30 points favoring boys. Although this difference is statistically significant, it represents only about three-eighths of the size of the combined standard deviations for males and females in the sample. Benbow and Stanley's most striking finding, however, was the ratio of boys to girls among the highest scorers. In the upper reaches of the distribution, the higher score, the greater the ratio of males to females who attained it. Among children who scored above 500, the ratio of boys to girls was 2.1 to 1; among those scoring above 600, the ratio of boys to girls was 4.1 to 1; among those scoring over 700, boys outnumbered girls 13 to 1 (Benbow & Stanley, 1983).

Although the research carried out by Benbow and Stanley has provided a wealth of useful information about gifted children, it is easy to make too much of these dramatic-sounding results. In the first place, they are based on a comparison of two sample groups (high-performing females and males) that do not necessarily represent a common population (Nesselroade & Thompson, 1995). Any comparison of naturally existing groups, such as high-ability females and males, is plagued with potential selection problems. In this case, a variety of other variables may be confounded with gender. In other words, the "high-ability population" from which the children in this study were picked may actually be different in a variety of ways for girls and boys. For example, perhaps, for various reasons unrelated to ability, more boys than girls participated in the Talent Search. In the second place, they are based on a sample of girls and boys who are much more mathematically talented than average. Furthermore, these children, as voluntary participants in the Talent Search, were to some extent self-selected for motivation and interest. As noted earlier, gender differences in mathematics performance are found to be greatest in the most select samples. Benbow and Stanley's research provides no information about gender differences in mathematical performance among average males and females. In the third place, their focus on male–female ratios among extremely high scorers makes gender differences in mathematics performance appear more important than they are (J. D. Rossi, 1983). For example, in their sample, which already represents only the top 3% of intellectually talented children, only about 7 of every 1000 boys and 5 of every 10,000 girls score over 700. At this rarefied level, so few individuals are actually affected that even a large difference in the proportions of males and females has little practical significance. Benbow (1988) reports that follow-up data on the mathematically gifted children in her sample show that, of the 47% who went to graduate school, 42% of the men and 22% of the women chose scientific or mathematical fields—statistics that show, by implication, that the majority of even this highly gifted sample did *not* take up science or mathematics as a career. In the fourth place, the gender differences occur specifically on the SAT-M, a test that seems, perhaps because of its content or administration, to produce larger gender differences in performance than other tests (Hyde, Fennema, & Lamon, 1990), although in the general student population the gender difference in SAT-M scores has decreased steadily since 1981 (Friedman, 1989). Finally, some critics have noted that there was a great deal of variability in males' performance at the top levels; in fact, variability among the males was consistently greater than among the females (Becker & Hedges, 1988). For example, in one year, 19% of the boys outperformed the highest-scoring girl in the sample, but in another year, the highest-scoring girl did better than all but 0.1% of the boys (Tobias, 1982). Thus, the significance of gender differences in mathematical performance remains a matter of debate.

Visual–Spatial Performance

Visual–spatial abilities are those that enable us to visually perceive and locate objects and their interrelationships. This broad class of abilities includes, among other things, the capacity to mentally rearrange and rotate objects or figures and to pick out or "disembed" a simple figure or shape from its background.

Gender differences in visual–spatial performance favoring males have been reported more consistently than any other cognitive differences (D. Cohen & Wilkie, 1979; Connor & Serbin, 1985; Halpern, 1992; Maccoby & Jacklin, 1974; Willis & Schaie, 1988). Hyde (1981) reported that across all the studies she reviewed gender accounted for less than 5% of the variability on visual–spatial tests. More recent reviews suggest that gender accounts for substantially more of the variance in some types of visual–spatial performance than in others (Linn & Petersen, 1985; Voyer, Voyer, & Bryden, 1995). There are some indications that gender differences are decreasing (Feingold, 1988; Rosenthal & Rubin, 1982; Voyer et al., 1995) and that, like the gender differences in mathematical performance, they appear largest in the highly select samples (Becker & Hedges, 1984). Gender differences often involve speed of responding rather than accuracy (Blough & Slavin, 1987).

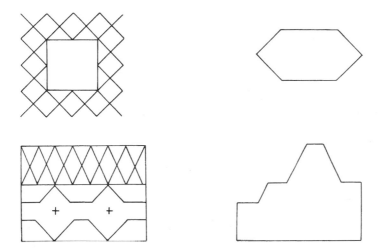

Figure 6.2 Examples of drawings used in the embedded figures test.

Critics of the research in this area argue that visual–spatial ability has not been defined precisely or separated from spatial abilities in general and that different measures of visual–spatial ability actually assess different abilities (Caplan, MacPherson, & Tobin, 1985; Linn & Petersen, 1985; Voyer et al., 1995). Marcia Linn and Anne Petersen concluded that at least three different types of spatial ability are represented in the literature on gender differences: spatial visualization, spatial perception, and mental rotation. **Spatial visualization,** most often measured using the embedded figures test (see Figure 6.2 for an example), involves complicated, multistep mental manipulations of spatial information. Participants may be asked to "disembed" a simple figure from a complex background or to imagine how a piece of paper would look when folded a certain way. This type of task, which seems to require analytic ability, shows no reliable gender differences at any point in the life span, according to Linn and Petersen's meta-analysis. The second type of ability, **spatial perception,** involves determining spatial relationships with respect to one's own body orientation, in spite of distracting information. It is often measured by the rod-and-frame test, in which a subject must adjust a tilted rod inside a tilted frame to true vertical, in the absence of visual context clues. This ability is a spatial, but not necessarily a visual, one. Good performance requires the use of kinesthetic cues (cues relating to body motion, position, and gravity). Linn and Petersen found that beginning at age 8 males show a small advantage over females on this type of task, and the size of the gender difference is larger (two thirds of a standard deviation) for samples in which participants were older than 18. The third type of spatial ability, **mental rotation** of figures, is the only one for which Linn and Petersen concluded that strong gender differences exist. Performance in this category is measured by showing the person a picture or object and asking questions about it that require the visualization of that picture or object from another angle. Scores are based on speed rather than accuracy of rotation (accuracy tends to be very high). Gender differences favoring males were detected across all ages on this type of task, although the size of the effect varied from one quarter of a standard deviation to an entire standard deviation, according to the specific test used. The reason for better male performance on this type of task is not yet clear. It may reflect the acquisition or use of different cognitive strategies for finding a solution that could, in turn, be related to differences in males' and females' experiences with this type of task.

A more recent replication and extension of Linn and Petersen's analysis provides support for their finding that the gender differences in mental rotation are the most robust (Voyer et al., 1995). These researchers also note that some tests are more likely than others to show gender differences and that the administration procedures used can affect the magnitude of the female–male difference obtained. They conclude on the basis of a meta-analysis of 286 comparisons of female and male performance that gender differences are clearly established in some areas of spatial abilities.

A fourth type of spatial ability, **spatiotemporal ability,** involves judgments about moving visual displays, such as predicting when a moving object will reach a particular spot. Some researchers have found that females are less accurate than males in such judgments (Halpern, 1992). However, it is as yet difficult to draw conclusions about gender differences in this type of performance, because recent research has shown that prior experience affects performance on this type of task, and feedback improves the performance of both women and men (Law, Pellegrino, & Hunt, 1993). It is possible, therefore, that men and boys perform better on this type of task simply because they have more experience with similar tasks.

What are the implications of gender differences in certain visual–spatial abilities? Are they important to scholastic success or career choice? The implications are uncertain, but it may be tempting to attribute more importance to them than they deserve. For example, Paula Caplan and her colleagues (1985) note the frequency with which anecdotal examples of female inferiority in spatial ability are cited (e.g., the shortage of female chess masters), in contrast to equally valid examples of female spatial competence:

> the buying of furniture with a view toward how it can be rotated and fitted within a particular space; learning to type without watching the keyboard . . . and the designing and using of clothing patterns that must be turned, flipped, and inverted, and then worked on while the user visualizes how they will look when re-turned, reinverted and reflipped. (p. 789)

An implication of the erroneous stereotype that there are large and important differences between the sexes in visual–spatial ability is that such differences account for the shortage of women in professions that require this ability, such as architecture and engineering. However, this is demonstrably not the case. Hyde (1981), making the initial assumption that a person would have to be in the top 5% of the range of spatial abilities to be qualified for a profession such as engineering, calculated that if spatial ability were the only determining factor the ratio of males to females in such professions would be 2 to 1. In actual fact, the proportion of women in the engineering fields has been less than 10% for many years, and women in the United States have only recently begun to earn as many as 15% of undergraduate engineering degrees. Gender differences in spatial ability could potentially explain only a small part of this male dominance in the engineering profession. This conclusion is reinforced by a recent computer simulation study, in which researchers created a virtual organization in which promotion through eight levels of seniority was based *solely* on ability. They then plugged in equal numbers of imaginary female and male entry-level employees, along with the assumption that the women had less ability than the men by either 1%

or 5%. When there was assumed to be a 1% difference in ability levels, women ended up with 35% of the top-level jobs, and when the women's ability deficit was assumed to be 5%, they received 29% of the top jobs (Martel, Lane, & Emrich, 1996). In most scientific and technical organizations, women do not hold anything like such high percentages of the top jobs—suggesting that many other factors besides ability differences come into play in keeping women out of such positions.

EXPLAINING THE DIFFERENCES

Despite the relatively small size and limited nature of the observed gender differences in performance on some cognitive tasks, psychologists have invested a great deal of energy in trying to explain these differences. The result is an often bewildering array of possible explanations for the existence of differences that may or may not be important. Most of the differences are too small to worry about, but some, such as the difference in mathematical problem solving, may have practical implications for education. Understanding the cause of gender differences in performance could provide clues to educational strategies that would minimize those differences (Halpern, 1997).

Biological Explanations

Many researchers have sought biological explanations for female–male performance differences. A demonstration that performance differences are partially based in biology is often mistakenly interpreted as a sign that they are inevitable and immutable. As seen in earlier chapters, however, biology and environment interact so closely that a biologically based predisposition in the direction of a particular behavior or ability is usually only one of many determining factors in the development of gender differences.

GENETICS   Most attempts to link genes with cognitive gender differences have focused on visual–spatial performance. The suggestion has been made that some aspect of visual–spatial ability may be X-linked (Bock & Kolakowski, 1973; Stafford, 1961). However, the research evidence does not consistently support that hypothesis (Linn & Petersen, 1985). Because it is so difficult to separate the effects of an individual's environment from those of his or her genetic endowment, attempts to link a specific ability to genetic factors face many difficulties (Wittig, 1979). For example, greater similarity between mother–son than father–son performance levels—sometimes taken as a clue that an ability is carried genetically on the X chromosome—could be due to an environmental factor: fathers' lesser contact than mothers' with their sons. Because sex is a stimulus variable, which serves as a cue to other people in the environment about how the individual should be treated, conclusions about the impact of genetic as well as other biological aspects of sex must always acknowledge the impact of the social psychological context.

HORMONES   There are at least two ways hormones can potentially influence ability and performance: The actual level of hormones circulating in the bloodstream might somehow have a direct effect, or there might be an indirect effect of prenatal hormones through their action on the developing brain. In this section, we examine research that deals with the first possibility: an impact of circulating hormones. The next section, on brain lateralization, includes a discussion of the second possibility.

One of the problems with trying to relate hormone levels to cognitive task performance has been the difficulty in measuring hormone levels. Some researchers have tried to get around the problem by inferring hormone status from hormonally influenced physical characteristics such as muscle versus fat distribution, body shape, penis or breast size, and pubic hair distribution. Presumably, more masculine physical characteristics indicate high levels of androgens, and more feminine ones indicate higher levels of female hormones. A. C. Petersen (1976) measured spatial visualization, which requires perceptual restructuring, and fluent production, a rapid accurate production of names, for male and female adolescents. At ages 16 and 18, males who were less sex stereotypic in physical appearance (and thus, presumably, had lower levels of male hormones) were better at spatial visualization than at fluent production; males who had more extremely masculine physical characteristics (and thus higher levels of male hormones) were better at fluent production than spatial visualization. For the females, good performance on the spatial visualization task was also related to less sex-stereotypic physical characteristics, but fluent production was completely unrelated to physical appearance. Other researchers have also found that women with high testosterone levels obtain higher spatial scores, but men with high testosterone levels score lower on some spatial tests (Gouchie & Kimura, 1991; Shute, Pellegrino, Hubert, & Reynolds, 1983).

How do these findings relate to gender differences? The finding of within-sex correlations between inferred hormone levels and spatial visualization performance is not indicative of a simple relationship between circulating hormone levels and sex-related differences in cognitive performance. In the first place, it is not the case that high levels of male hormones relate to good performance on spatial tasks and high levels of female hormones relate to good performance on verbal tasks, as the pattern of observed gender differences in cognitive performance might lead us to expect. In the second place, we have already seen that the sexes do not differ reliably in spatial visualization performance. Thus, this line of research has so far produced no conclusive evidence that gender differences in cognitive performance can be explained by a simple, linear relationship between sex hormones and cognitive abilities. In fact, men with lower levels of testosterone actually perform better on spatial tasks than their counterparts with higher levels of testosterone do; for women, the relationship between testosterone levels and spatial performance is the reverse—a pattern of findings that may suggest that, for spatial ability at least, there is an optimal androgen/estrogen balance that is slightly below that of the average man and above that of the average woman (Kimura, 1987).

Some researchers interested in the relationship between circulating hormone levels and cognitive performance have studied women's performance at various phases of the menstrual cycle, when levels of circulating estrogen are high or low (Kimura & Hampson, 1994). Findings are that women perform somewhat better on verbal articulation tasks (e.g., saying "A box of mixed biscuits in a biscuit mixer" five times in a row as quickly as possible) and fine-motor-skill tasks at times in their cycle when estrogen levels are high rather than when they are low, and somewhat better on certain spatial tasks, such as the rod-and-frame task, at times when estrogen levels are low rather than when they are high (Hampson, 1990a, 1990b). However, the differences related to menstrual-cycle phase were small in comparison to individual differences among the women. Fluctuating hormone levels in men, such as the drop in testosterone between morning and evening, might also show some small relationship to cognitive performance, but so far these relationships have not been examined. Researchers studying men have, however, found a negative relationship between levels of FSH (follicle-stimulating hormone) and tests of some forms of visual–spatial functioning (Gordon & Lee, 1986). This line of research, then, provides some suggestive evidence for a link between circulating hormone levels and cognitive–perceptual performance, but the effects are small and may be of little practical significance. Menstrual and other hormonal cycles will be discussed in more detail in Chapter 8.

BRAIN ORGANIZATION   The notion that sex-related cognitive differences are caused by sex differences in brain organization has received a good deal of press in the last decade. "Women's Intuition Linked to Thicker Nerves in Brain," proclaimed a newspaper headline ("Women's Intuition," 1986); "Male Brain, Female Brain: The Hidden Difference," announced *Psychology Today* (Kimura, 1985).

The idea that male and female brains are different has a long history. At one time, the explanation for women's "obvious" intellectual inferiority was their smaller brains—an idea that was quickly dropped when it was demonstrated that, relative to body weight, women's brains were proportionally larger than men's (Shields, 1975). The current focus, however, is not on brain size but on the organization of functions within the brain.

Although the human body appears relatively symmetrical—the left side looking more or less like a mirror image of the right—we are not symmetrical in terms of our competence at different activities. A person is better at writing with one hand than with the other, kicks a football better with one foot than the other, prefers one ear over the other when listening closely. The majority of people are right-handed; handedness may or may not be consistent with foot or ear preferences. The tendency for individuals to be better at certain activities using one side of their body than the other has been taken as evidence for the way functions are organized in the brain.

The outermost part of the human brain, the **cerebral cortex,** is divided into left and right halves, or hemispheres, connected by a mass of nerve fibers called the **corpus callosum** (see Figure 6.3). Each hemisphere of the brain's cerebral cortex governs the activities of the opposite side of the body (that is, the left side of the brain controls the right hand, the right ear, the right leg, and the right visual field). Scientists also believe, to some extent, that the two hemispheres of the brain are the locations for different abilities. In normal right-handed people, the capacities for language and for analytical, mathematical, and sequential information processing tend to be located in the left hemisphere. The right hemisphere is the site for more holistic and nonverbal information-processing skills, musical ability, and certain types of spatial skills. These generalizations do not hold for left-handed individuals; nor is it the case that the locations of various abilities are simply reversed for left-handers (Springer & Deutsch, 1998).

Because verbal and certain spatial skills seem to be located on different sides of the brain, researchers have found it tempting to speculate that female superiority on verbal tasks and male superiority on some spatial tasks might be related to sex differences in the development of the left and right hemispheres. Could it be that females have a

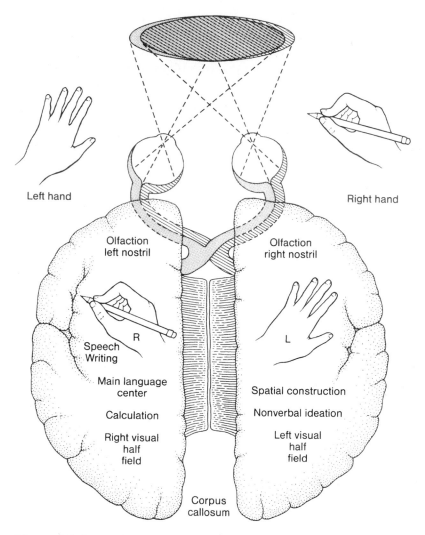

Figure 6.3 Sensory inputs to and functions of the two brain hemispheres for the normal right-handed person.

better-developed left hemisphere (to explain the female advantage—albeit a rapidly disappearing one—in verbal skills) and males have a better-developed right hemisphere (to explain the male advantage in some spatial skills)? At first blush, the explanation sounds seductively simple. But wait. In addition to verbal skills, the left hemisphere also seems to be the location for analytic and sequential skills, in which the sexes do not differ. If earlier or stronger left-hemisphere development explains female superiority on verbal tasks, might it not also be reasonable to expect that the same process would guarantee female superiority in mathematical performance? If brain organization does relate to gender differences in cognitive performance, the relationship must be more complex than each sex simply being better developed on different sides of the brain.

The focus of research has been on possible sex differences in the degree to which particular functions are localized in one side of the brain—that is, the degree of hemispheric **lateralization** or specialization. Levy (1972) proposed that greater hemispheric lateralization for spatial ability enhances performance for that ability and that male superiority on spatial tasks was due to greater lateralization of spatial skills among men than among women. Her proposal laid the groundwork for a dizzying flurry of research in which males and females were compared for their lateralization of verbal and spatial abilities.

Three sorts of evidence have been used to gauge lateralization in women and men: clinical studies of brain-damaged patients, behavioral tests of normal individuals, and studies of brain activity and anatomy. Many of these studies have been reviewed by Merrill Hiscock and colleagues (Hiscock, Inch, Jacek, Hiscock-Kalil, & Kalil, 1994; Hiscock, Israelian, Inch, Jacek, & Hiscock-Kalil, 1995) and by Springer and Deutsch (1998). In general, clinical studies of brain-damaged individuals have found that for men damage to the left hemisphere is associated with more impairment of verbal than nonverbal performance, whereas damage to the right side of the brain is associated with greater impairment of nonverbal than verbal performance. For women, however, verbal and nonverbal performance do not seem to be differentially affected by the side of the damage, suggesting that verbal and nonverbal abilities are distributed across both hemispheres. Several studies have failed to confirm this pattern, however, finding no differences between males and females in the effects of damage to the left or right hemispheres (Bornstein, 1984; Herring & Reitan, 1984; Snow & Sheese, 1985). Moreover, the earlier work has been criticized on a number of grounds, including the lack of similarity to the general population of the samples used and the confounding of sex with other variables. Research with brain-damaged patients by Doreen Kimura and her colleagues now indicates that no single rule about sex differences in brain organization holds across all aspects of thinking (Kimura, 1985, 1987, 1993). They are finding that for producing speech and making hand movements that contribute to motor skill, women's brains seem to be more focally organized than men's (that is, these abilities seem to be localized in a more restricted area of the brain for women than for men). Basic speech function appears to be more dependent on the anterior (front) than the posterior (back) region of the brain for women and more equally distributed between the two regions for men. However, for tasks such as defining words, the sex difference appears to go in the opposite direction: Women's brains are organized more diffusely than men's. Finally, for a variety of other verbal tests, there is no obvious sex difference in brain organization. Clinical research, then, does not support the simple view that men's brains are more lateralized, in general, than women's brains. According to Kimura (1987), her research with brain-damaged persons demonstrates differences in brain organization between human females and males. She notes, however, that there are wide individual variations within each sex, that sex is only one of several individual-difference variables that are correlated with brain organization, and that "the population differences in abilities that we see between men and women do not have a high predictive value for individuals. As a means of screening for admission to occupations or life activities, genital sex is a very poor instrument" (p. 146).

Behavioral tests with normal participants use tasks in which two different stimuli are presented simultaneously to the different sides of the brain, with participants tested later to determine which inputs are best recalled. Perhaps the most common of such tests is the dichotic listening test, in which different lists of numbers or spoken syllables are simultaneously presented through earphones to the participant's left and right ears. If the participant later shows a tendency to remember the stimuli presented to one ear better than those presented to the other, the result is taken as evidence that the person's verbal abilities are more strongly lateralized in the brain hemisphere corresponding to that ear. If males are more strongly lateralized than females for verbal abilities, we would expect men to show a greater right-ear (left-hemisphere) advantage than women on this test. Of 14 such studies cited by McGlone (1980), 9 showed no relationship between sex of participants and right-ear advantage, 4 found a stronger right-ear advantage in men, and 1 found a right-ear advantage in women. Studies in which information is presented to the right and left visual fields and studies in which the response required is nonverbal rather than verbal also show a mixed pattern of results, although when male–female differences *are* found they are more likely to be in the direction of greater lateralization for men than for women. After an exhaustive review of auditory and visual laterality studies, Hiscock and colleagues (Hiscock et al., 1994; Hiscock et al., 1995) came to the conclusion that female–male differences in lateralization are small, with sex accounting for only 1% to 2% of differences in lateralization. The sexes do seem to differ reliably in manual asymmetry—the degree to which one hand is dominant—but in this case it is the women who show more "handedness," and thus, presumably, greater lateralization (L. J. Harris, 1992). On the whole, then, the results of behavioral studies, like those of the clinical studies discussed earlier, do not provide overwhelming support for the idea that men's brains are more lateralized than women's.

Studies of brain anatomy have reported some evidence of small differences between male and female brains, which have been interpreted as implying more lateralization for males than females (de Lacoste-Utamsing & Holloway, 1982; Wada, Clark & Hamm, 1975). In particular, researchers have focused on the corpus callosum, the "bridge" between the left and right hemispheres. If that bridge is more developed in one sex than the other, would that mean transmission between the two hemispheres is more efficient for that sex? Some research on brains examined at autopsy shows that the corpus callosum is larger, at least in the posterior of the brain, in women than in men (Kimura, 1987). Two studies of the brains of living human beings, using magnetic resonance imaging, contribute to the controversy by providing contradictory results. In one of these studies, no male–female difference in the size or surface area of the corpus callosum was found. However, a striking difference in the *shape* was observed. The posterior region of the corpus callosum (the splenium) was more bulbous-shaped in females and more tubular-shaped in males (L. S. Allen, Richey, Chai, & Gorski, 1991). This difference was not evident in children younger than age 16. Another study did not find sex differences in the posterior region (Byne, Bleier, & Houston, 1988). According to the latter group of researchers, the most striking finding was the large variation in the size and shape of the corpus callosum, irrespective of gender or age. Clearly, research in this area is not yet at the stage when it can be cited with confidence to prove or disprove the hypothesis of greater male than female lateralization. To further complicate the issue, researchers are increasingly convinced that sex differences in brain anatomy may vary across the life span, indicating that whatever sex differences in brain organization exist may be dynamic rather than static, present at some periods of life but not at others (Kimura, 1985).

On the whole, then, there is no overwhelming evidence that males are more lateralized in general than females. However, at least for some particular abilities, the brains of the two sexes may differ in their organization. Suspending all doubts for a moment and accepting the hypothesis as true, we would still be left with two basic questions: Does brain organization really make a difference to cognitive performance, and, if so, how?

Many of the theories about the relationship between brain organization and performance focus specifically on lateralization. We have already seen, however, that whatever sex differences in lateralization may exist are more likely to be specific to particular types of abilities, such as speech production or vocabulary, than to encompass broad categories such as "verbal abilities" or "spatial abilities." Yet most of the research designed to explore the relationship between brain organization and performance in women and men has been aimed at showing a relationship between gross measures of lateralization (that is, is one sex more lateralized than the other?) and broad categories of abilities. The studies are ingenious, but they cannot provide completely useful answers because they are focusing on the wrong questions.

For example, Melissa Hines and Carl Shipley (1984) tested the hypothesis that prenatal hormone levels affect the degree of brain lateralization, which, in turn, affects cognitive abilities. The idea that prenatal hormone levels may indirectly affect cognitive abilities by influencing the developing brain is a popular one that has received support from animal research and forms the basis for some theories about male–female differences in cognitive abilities among humans (e.g., Kimura, 1987; Nyborg, 1983). The research by Hines and Shipley provides one of the few direct tests with humans of these proposed prenatal hormone–brain organization–cognitive performance links. They compared women who had been exposed prenatally to DES, a synthetic estrogen, to their nonexposed sisters, hypothesizing that the DES-exposed women would show greater hemispheric lateralization and a more masculine pattern of cognitive performance (that is, better visual spatial performance and poorer verbal performance) than their sisters. (Although DES is an estrogen, it is now thought by researchers to have a masculinizing effect because it is now known that testosterone converts to estrogen.) They found, in fact, that the DES-exposed women did seem to be more lateralized, at least as measured by their performance on a dichotic listening task. It is possible that prenatal hormone levels affected brain lateralization. However, they found *no* relationship between lateralization and cognitive performance. The DES women did not differ from their sisters on verbal or visual–spatial measures. Although this one study does not rule out the possibility that lateralization is related to cognitive abilities, it certainly indicates that the relationship is too weak or too complex to be measured in a small sample of women. Indeed, the potential complexity of lateralization–ability relationships is illustrated by findings that the degree of lateralization can show *opposite* relationships with spatial performance in the two sexes: Greater left–right differences in electrical brain activity are sometimes associated with higher spatial scores for males and lower spatial scores for females (Hoyenga & Hoyenga, 1993). Thus, there is as yet no clear evidence of how lateralization differences are linked to specific cognitive abilities.

It is worthy of note at this point that sex differences in brain asymmetry, if they exist, could be the result of environmental as well as genetic or hormonal factors. For example, some studies suggest that children's lateralization of verbal skills is affected by the quality and quantity of their exposure to language (Borowy & Goebel, 1976; Geffner & Hochberg, 1971). Thus, if the sexes do differ in brain lateralization, the difference could be, at least in part, a function of such environmental factors as the amount of talking parents do to their male and female infants.

One further line of research attempting to tie brain lateralization to cognitive functioning involves the rate of physical maturation. Deborah Waber (1977) attempted to show a relationship among verbal and spatial performance, degree of hemispheric specialization, and rate of physical growth at adolescence. Girls and boys age 10 to 16 were classified by a medical examination as early or late physical maturers and were tested for verbal performance, spatial performance, and lateralization of speech perception. The results were striking because they indicated that the relationship between sex and spatial performance was overshadowed by the relationship between maturation rate and spatial performance. Late-maturing adolescents, male or female, performed better on tests of spatial ability than early-maturing adolescents did. No significant relationship between verbal performance and rate of maturation was found. However, the older an individual subject was at the onset of puberty, the better was his or her performance on spatial relative to verbal tests. These data fit with the general observation that boys, on the average, physically mature later than girls and also tend to do better than girls on some spatial tasks. Some subsequent research supports the link between late maturation and spatial performance (e.g., Sanders & Soares, 1986), but such a link is not always found (e.g., Waber, Mann, Merola, & Moylan, 1985).

How does hemispheric specialization fit into these results? Waber found, among the older children only, that the late maturers showed greater hemispheric specialization for speech perception than early maturers of the same age and sex did. She postulated that maturation rate had physiological correlates, probably having to do with hormone levels, that were present from an early age and that influenced the development of the organization of brain functions. She suggested that late maturers show more hemispheric specialization of abilities than early maturers do and that this difference in specialization mediates the effect of maturation rate on spatial ability. Her data do provide partial support for this suggestion, as does some later research (Vrbancic & Mosley, 1988; Waber, Bauermeister, Cohen, Ferber, & Wolff, 1981), but some other researchers have failed to find support for it (Bryden & Vrbancic, 1988; Petersen, 1976). At this point it is not certain that maturation rate relates to spatial ability or that, if it does, the relationship occurs through the impact of maturation rate on hemispheric specialization.

In fact, an interesting alternative explanation for a relationship between maturation rate and spatial performance was suggested and tested by Nora Newcombe and Mary Bandura (1983). They noted that timing of puberty is known to be associated with personality differences. For one thing, there appears to be more cross-sex typing or androgyny among late maturers of both sexes than among early maturers. Early-maturing girls date earlier and develop more conventional feminine interests than their late-maturing counterparts; similarly, late-maturing boys are found by some researchers to be lower in masculine orientation and aggression than their early-maturing peers. Newcombe and Bandura suggest that these differences in gender-role-related interests and orientation between early and late maturers may help to shape the relationship between maturation rate and spatial performance, perhaps by affecting participation in particular activities. In their study of sixth-grade girls, they found that later maturation was positively related to good spatial performance *and* to stereotypically masculine personality traits and interests. However, they found no relationship between maturation rate and lateralization, between lateralization and spatial performance, or between gender-role orientation and spatial performance. Thus, the study provides no definitive answer to the question of what mechanism might be responsible for the observed link between spatial performance and the timing of puberty, but it tends to undercut the notion that maturation rate affects spatial ability through differences in hemispheric lateralization. A subsequent longitudinal study showed that personality characteristics at age 11 were predictive of spatial ability at age 16 (Newcombe, 1987).

Before leaving the topic of brain organization, a final comment is in order. Understanding the organization and functioning of the human brain is still far from complete. Furthermore, the emphasis on lateralization as the most crucial feature of brain organization is rapidly diminishing (Efron, 1990). The network of connections in individual human brains may be so unique as to make the individuality "of fingerprints or facial features gross and simple by comparison" (Sperry, 1982, p. 1223). Divisions of the brain other than left–right (e.g., up–down, front–back) might yet prove to be important; moreover, scientists are still trying to understand the way the brain functions as a coherent whole (Sperry, 1982). One commentator compares our current understanding of the brain with that which might be achieved by someone totally unfamiliar with cars if he experimented by removing parts of the car:

> He removes different parts of the car, observing that the removal of a wheel makes the ride bumpy, draining the brake fluid makes it difficult to stop, and removal of the battery or engine prevents forward motion altogether . . . he thus localizes some functions . . . [but] . . . uncovers little information about their mechanisms. (Fausto-Sterling, 1992, p. 48)

Fausto-Sterling may be too harsh in her evaluation of the current state of neuropsychology. Nevertheless, given the contradictory evidence and the large gaps in our knowledge about the brain, we should be extremely cautious about jumping to conclusions about a simple relationship between hemispheric lateralization and gender differences in cognitive performance.

We probably should also be cautious about the practical significance of some of the findings relating hormones or brain organization to performance. Scientists have, for example, found some evidence for relationships among handedness, testosterone, allergies, myopia (nearsightedness), and mathematical performance (Benbow, 1986; 1988; Geschwind & Behan, 1982). Interesting theories have been developed to explain these correlations (e.g., Geschwind & Galaburda, 1985). They are fascinating because they suggest connections among such diverse findings as the higher frequency of left-handedness and speech disorders in males, females' greater resistance to viral and bacterial diseases, and the greater female susceptibility to autoimmune disorders such as lupus, arthritis, and allergies. The theories may have little practical significance for the issue of gender-related differences or similarities in particular abilities, however. And how useful is it to confirm such interrelationships? If we could say for certain that left-handed myopic males with a lot of allergies make the best mathematicians, would we give up on everyone else? And, as McGuinness (1988) asks, how would such a finding help us to understand the majority of mathematically talented people, who simply do not fit such a category?

Social/Affective Explanations

Anyone who has ever taken a test knows there is more to success or failure than intellectual competence. There are matters of long-term training and immediate preparation, mood, fatigue, confidence, and motivation—all of which may, in turn, be influenced by the expectations of others, the cultural or institutional climate, and immediate situational factors.

When the cognitive performance of females and males is compared, it is necessary to examine how the kinds of emotional and social factors just listed might systematically differ for the two sexes and thus help to explain differences in their performance on certain kinds of tasks. We will look briefly at the possible roles of direct training, gender-role socialization with respect to the development of particular skills, and gender-related differences in self-confidence and motivation as causes of some of the observed gender differences in cognitive performance.

TRAINING AND EXPERIENCE   Even in cases where the level of a particular ability is partially determined by physiological factors, the ability is usually susceptible to training. For example, some of us may have more potential than others to become great athletes, but all of us can improve our athletic skills to some extent through instruction and practice. It is quite clear, likewise, that spatial, verbal, and mathematical skills can all be increased through training.

Evidence now shows that both sexes show a positive relationship between experience and practice on visual–spatial tasks; the more a person has participated in visual–spatial activities, the better she or he is likely to score on tests of visual–spatial ability (Baenninger & Newcombe, 1989; Connor & Serbin, 1985; Newcombe, Bandura, & Taylor, 1983). Traditionally, masculine toys and activities involve more visual–spatial skills than feminine ones do, and it may be that the male–female differences in performance on visual–spatial tasks mainly reflect differences in their spatial experience. One study found that 37% of the male–female differences in elementary schoolchildren's block design (a spatial test) scores could be accounted for by the difference in the availability of "masculine" toys in their home environment (Serbin, Zelkowitz, Doyle, Gold, & Wheaton, 1990). However, these correlational findings may imply only that people who are good at spatial activities seek them out. A stronger argument for the effect of experience on performance comes from experimental studies of training in spatial skills. A meta-analysis of such studies shows that both females and males benefit, apparently equally, from direct training (Baenninger & Newcombe, 1989).

It appears that the gender difference in mathematics performance can also be partially explained by the fact that females simply take fewer math courses than males (Benbow & Stanley, 1982; Fox, 1981). When the number of courses taken is held constant, gender differences in mathematics achievement are greatly reduced, although not always eliminated (De Wolf, 1981; Ethington & Wolfle, 1984; Fennema & Sherman, 1977; Kimball, 1989).

Researchers have noted, however, that even when males and females take the same courses in mathematics, they do not necessarily receive the same training. In the first place, mathematically gifted males are more likely than gifted females to engage in extracurricular study and activities related to mathematics (Kimball, 1989) and are more likely to receive parental encouragement for mathematics achievement (Fox, 1981;

Yee & Eccles, 1988). In fact, a study of the parents of the mathematically gifted children in the Johns Hopkins National Talent Search found that parents of the boys were considerably more likely than those of the girls even to be aware that their child was mathematically talented (Tobias, 1982). In the second place, even within the same mathematics class, boys and girls may not be getting the same education. In high school mathematics classes, boys are consistently spoken to and called on more and receive more social interaction, individual instruction, feedback, and encouragement (Eccles, 1989; Leder, 1990; Stallings, 1985). Researchers have also shown that when working in small groups in mathematics classes girls receive less information from their peers than boys do (Webb & Kenderski, 1985; Wilkinson, Lindow, & Chiang, 1985).

Further evidence for the importance of training and practice on mathematics achievement comes from findings showing that the international gap in math achievement between the United States and China and Japan is far greater than the average male–female gap observed within countries. Researchers who tested kindergarten, first, and fifth-grade children in these three countries found no differences in reading or general intelligence, but they did find increasing international differences in mathematics performance with increasing age. (No significant male–female differences in mathematics performance were found for any of the grade levels.) American first-graders were surpassed by those in China and Japan by an average of 10% on a standard math test. By the fifth grade, the top American class scored, on average, below the lowest Japanese class and the second-lowest Chinese class. Of the 100 highest-scoring fifth-graders, only one was American (Stevenson, Lee, & Stigler, 1986). Rather than looking for biological explanations, as they might have done had they been reporting gender differences, these researchers sought social explanations for these vast international differences. What they discovered is that Chinese and Japanese students receive more formal school training in mathematics than their American counterparts: They spend 240 days a year in school compared to the Americans' 180. Also, Japanese and Chinese parents gave their children more help with math homework than U.S. parents gave theirs. The basis for the difference in parental actions can be found in their beliefs about the reasons for academic success: American parents attributed success more often to ability, Chinese and Japanese parents attributed it to effort.

For verbal skills as well, evidence points to the impact of specific training. Starting in infancy, females are vocalized to more often than males, which may, in turn, lead to increased vocalization by female infants (Bee, Mitchell, Barnard, Eyres, & Hammond, 1984; Maccoby & Jacklin, 1974). Regardless of the reason for the original difference, the two processes probably act in an ever-strengthening feedback loop to increase females' experience and practice with speech production skills at an early age. This pattern does not seem to hold across cultures, however. In Greece, where there is strong cultural preference for male over female infants, mothers speak more affectionately to male than female infants, and home-reared male infants seem to be more vocally responsive and interactive with their mothers than females do—a finding researchers have speculatively linked to other studies showing that Greek males tend to outperform females in cognitive tasks, even verbal ones (Roe, Drivas, Karagellis, & Roe, 1985). Even in North America, some research shows that by the time children are toddlers mothers' speech to boys and girls differs significantly on dimensions thought to stimulate cognitive development. Mothers' communication to their sons included more questions, more numbers, more verbal teaching, and more action verbs than their communication to their daughters did (Weitzman, Birns, & Friend, 1985). It is becoming increasingly clear that early parent–child interactions have an impact on the child's cognitive development and that these interactions may differ in many subtle ways for girls and boys. Much more research is needed to understand just how this process works.

GENDER-ROLE SOCIALIZATION   In North America, female and male gender roles fit neatly into the observed pattern of performance differences between women and men. Even among children and adolescents, mathematics and technical and mechanical pursuits based on spatial ability are thought to be masculine domains, whereas verbal and artistic skills are considered feminine (S. L. Boswell, 1985). A study of elementary school students in Taiwan, Japan, and the United States found that as early as first grade children and their mothers in all three countries believed boys were better at mathematics and girls were better at reading (Lummis & Stevenson, 1990).

From preschool onward, children set very gender-stereotypic occupational goals (Archer, 1984; Franken, 1983). These findings are not surprising given that the activities and toys encouraged for boys and girls are so different. For example, boys are given more mechanical toys such as models and tools; not only do such toys encourage the development of spatial ability, their definition as "boys' toys" encourages the attitude that this type of ability is a masculine one. It has also been found that fathers and mothers tend to encourage gender stereotypic play and choice of toys with their sons and daughters—a pattern that is bound to result in girls' having fewer opportunities than boys to engage in play that involves mechanical and spatial skills (Caldera, Huston, & O'Brien, 1989).

The fact that children learn to label various tasks as masculine or feminine is clearly relevant to their performance on these tasks. Many studies support the contention that children perform better, work longer and harder, and evaluate the appeal of the same task as greater when it is labeled as appropriate to their own gender than when it is labeled as appropriate to the other gender (Davies, 1989/90; Hargreaves, Bates, & Foot, 1985), although some researchers have found the effect of gender-typed labeling to be stronger for boys than girls. For both sexes, mathematics achievement in elementary and junior high school is positively correlated with the belief that mathematics is gender-role appropriate (Paulsen & Johnson, 1983). The impact of gender labeling of tasks can be seen even more clearly when cultures are compared. In cultures that label reading a masculine-appropriate skill, for example, males' performance on reading and vocabulary tests equals or exceeds that of females (Finn, 1980).

The gender appropriateness of particular academic subjects may be conveyed through the gender of the teacher. Because, beginning in junior high school, more mathematics teachers are male and more English teachers are female, the notion that math is for boys and English is for girls may be reinforced. Certainly, by the time students reach the college level, courses in mathematics, the physical sciences, and engineering are far more likely to be taught by male than by female professors and to be dominated by male students. Female students often report that they feel excluded and out of place in such courses (Seymour, 1995).

The impact of gender labeling of academic subjects has potentially serious implications beyond immediate academic performance because it can affect children's course choices and thus, eventually, their career paths. For example, a belief that mathematics is a male domain has been found to relate to females' lower self-confidence in learning math (J. A. Sherman, 1982) and avoidance of mathematics courses in high school (J. A. Sherman & Fennema, 1977). The avoidance of mathematics courses in high school closes a number of college study options for women, thus helping to perpetuate male–female segregation into different careers. Actually, males are more likely than females to stereotype mathematics as a male domain (Hyde, Fennema, Ryan, Frost, & Hopp, 1990). It is likely that, especially during adolescence, females are sensitive to these male stereotypes and may avoid mathematics and technical subjects in response to them (Lips & Temple, 1990).

Not only the labeling of specific tasks and skills as masculine or feminine but also the overall flexibility of gender-role socialization may affect cognitive performance. For example, research uncovered larger gender differences in spatial visualization among the Temne tribe in Sierra Leone than among the Canadian Inuit, for whom no gender differences are found (Berry, 1966). Among the Temne, females are more strictly controlled than males, whereas the Inuit encourage independence and autonomy for both sexes.

SELF-CONFIDENCE   Some of the effects of gender-role socialization on cognitive performance may have their impact through gender differences in self-confidence. Simply labeling a task "for girls" or "for boys" raises the expectations of the "appropriate" group for success on that task. Males are more likely to expect to do well on masculine tasks and intellectual areas (Crandall, 1969; Deaux & Emswiller, 1974). Females are more confident of success on feminine-typed tests, such as verbal ones, and less confident on masculine-typed tests, such as spatial ones (Lenney, 1977). In high school and college, males have more self-confidence than females do in their mathematical, scientific, and technical abilities (J. R. Campbell, 1991; Hyde, Fennema, Ryan, et al., 1990; Seymour, 1995). Mathematics self-efficacy expectations (beliefs about one's ability to perform a given task) are consistently and significantly stronger for college males than for college females (Betz & Hackett, 1983). Even when girls are doing well in mathematics, they do not feel competent, perhaps because they are so often surrounded, in academic settings, with people who do not think females can do well in mathematics and technical areas. Male students tend to believe females are not talented in mathematics and science (Seymour, 1995), and teachers have generally lower expectations of female than male students in these fields (Fennema, Peterson, Carpenter, & Lubinski, 1990; Seymour, 1995). In fact, when teachers are asked to nominate their most successful math students, they tend to choose males disproportionately and inaccurately—overestimating how well male students will perform (Fennema et al., 1990; Walkerdine, 1989) and underestimating how well females will perform (Kissane, 1986). All of these factors may contribute to girls' and women's experience of stereotype threat (Steele, 1997), a tendency to perform poorly in situations where individuals fear they will be judged by or are at risk of confirming a negative stereotype about their gender (discussed at length in Chapter 1).

Parents seem to expect more from their children in gender-stereotypic areas. Thus, for instance, parents expect higher achievement from sons than from daughters in mathematics and credit sons with more talent than daughters for successful mathematics performance (Yee & Eccles, 1988). Particularly in the realm of mathematics achievement, research shows that parents' differential expectations for their sons and daughters are communicated to their children at a young age (Entwisle & Baker, 1983). After tracking 1100 children semester by semester over the first three grades, these researchers noted that, despite the fact that the boys' arithmetic marks or general aptitude did not exceed girls' in first grade, boys developed higher expectations for their performance in mathematics than girls did. These higher expectations do not seem to be based on past performance or teachers' evaluations but rather on parents' expectations for their children's performance. Other research also shows that parents' beliefs about their children's math aptitude are better predictors of the children's attitudes toward math than measures of past performance are (Parsons, Adler, & Kaczala, 1982).

There are many indications that gender-role socialization predisposes females and males to different levels of general self-confidence. Girls receive strong messages that they are "incapable" of doing certain things, such as mathematics, and boys' gender-related prohibitions are based on the notion that they should not do certain things, such as play with dolls, rather than on the notion that they *cannot* do them. Jeanne Block (1984) has argued that the end result of the differing patterns of socialization for females and males in our culture is that males tend to develop "'wings'—which permit leaving the nest, exploring far reaches, and flying alone" (p. 137), whereas females tend to develop "'roots'—roots that anchor, stabilize, and support growth" (p. 138). Boys, she concludes, are encouraged to explore, to be independent, to try difficult things. At the same time, girls are "oversocialized"—closely supervised at home and given fewer chances to master the environment or to figure out how things work, to make decisions, or to take risks. Small wonder, then, if girls and boys differ in their confidence at tackling the new, abstract, and sometimes difficult material that is presented in mathematics courses.

MOTIVATION   A potentially useful framework for understanding gender differences in achievement choices is the expectancy/value model developed by Jacquelynn Eccles and her colleagues (Eccles, 1985; Eccles [Parsons] et al., 1983). The model proposes that the decision to pursue achievement in a particular area is most directly linked to expectation for success and to the importance or value an individual attaches to achievement in that area. We have already seen that male and female expectations for success may differ for mathematical, verbal, and spatial tasks. Do the sexes also differ in the value they attach to success in these areas?

There is some evidence from studies of achievement in mathematics and science that males and females do differ in the way they attach values to various achievement activities. As early as the seventh grade, boys see mathematics as more useful than girls do (Fennema & Sherman, 1977; Sherman & Fennema, 1977), and in college, women have difficulty imagining themselves in science careers (Lips & Asquith, 1995). One study of fifth- and sixth-graders found that girls were relatively unaware of the relevance of mathematics to careers other than strictly scientific ones. A program that emphasized the applications of mathematics to art and social problems had a positive impact on these girls: They felt better about school, reported liking mathematics more, and even showed some increased interest in scientific careers (L. H. Fox, 1976).

Among high school students, the value males attach to mathematics achievement is strongly related to their performance history: The better they have done in the past, the more highly they value mathematics achievement (Eccles, 1985).

For females, the value placed on mathematics achievement is much more independent of their past performance. College women's enrollment in mathematics and science courses is strongly predicted by their reported enjoyment of learning science and mathematics and by positive experiences in such courses (Lips, 1996c). Eccles (1987) suggests that gender roles influence achievement patterns mainly through their effect on the value that females and males attach to different achievement options.

Other research supports the idea that task value is an important determinant of achievement behavior and that males and females differ in the factors that influence these values. One study of mathematics and science participation among female college students found that the reason given most often for avoidance of math and science was a lack of interest in and enjoyment of these academic subjects (that is, low intrinsic value)—a reason that was cited far more often than perceived difficulty or lack of career relevance (Lips, 1984). Female students may not enjoy their classes in mathematical and scientific fields because they feel their approaches to learning and problem solving are not welcomed or valued in these classes. For example, Turkle and Papert (1990) examined the reactions of first-year Harvard University students as they negotiated their first computer programming course. The students were instructed to adopt a formal approach to programming that required breaking the problem into parts. This approach felt alien to many students, particularly the women. They were discouraged from adopting a more holistic approach, however, even though that would have been equally effective. Consequently, they became alienated from their work and did not enjoy the class.

In a study of computer-related attitudes among college students, women's intentions to major in computer science were related more strongly to interest in and enjoyment of computers than to a more pragmatic desire to find a high-paying, advancement-oriented job, but the reverse pattern was true for men (Lips & Temple, 1990). Research shows, as well, that one reason for college males' greater tendency to choose courses and career goals in mathematics and science is their concern with status and success. College men and women see science careers as equally difficult and demanding, but men seem to see that demandingness as a more positive feature than women do (Lips, 1992). Thus, females and males, at least in high school and college, may be motivated by different factors in their pursuit of achievement in mathematical, scientific, and technical fields. The precise origin of these differences, how they affect performance, whether they extend to other areas, and how early they begin to appear are all matters that await further investigation.

In general, it seems that all four of the social/affective factors discussed in this section—training, gender-role socialization, self-confidence, and motivation—work in interlocking ways to help produce small performance differences between males and females in certain verbal, mathematical, and visual–spatial tasks. Girls and boys are taught, implicitly and explicitly, that mathematical and visual–spatial tasks are masculine and that verbal tasks are feminine. In concert with this differential labeling goes differential training, starting with parental vocalization to infants and toddlers and continuing with gender-typed toys and activities and different amounts of teaching in school. The labeling also produces gender differences, both in self-confidence on these tasks and in the value attached to achievement in these areas, which, in turn, relate to decisions about trying to achieve and to performance itself.

Social–environmental factors clearly overshadow ability differences between women and men in determining achievement in various fields. One way to get a feel for this is to examine the distribution of prestigious awards such as the Nobel prizes in science and literature. Males have dominated these awards in the areas of science, in which women have won just over 2% of the total number of prizes in physics, chemistry, and physiology and medicine since the awards began in 1901—a male-to-female ratio greater than 43 to 1. Some might argue that this distribution reflects male superiority in quantitative and spatial abilities, but these ability differences are far less dramatic than the ratio of male to female prize winners. However, in literature—a field based on verbal abilities, which are not claimed to be superior in men—women have won fewer than 17% of the Nobel prizes awarded over the century—a ratio greater than 9.5 to 1 in favor of men (Lips, 1999). Men's domination of both sets of awards is so striking that it is impossible to attribute it only to gender differences in cognitive abilities—particularly in the case of literature, where there is no indication at all of superior male ability.

SUMMARY

Despite the field of psychology's long history of searching for intellectual differences between the sexes, such differences have, for the most part, proved relatively small and elusive. There is some evidence for male–female differences in sensation and perception: Females outscore males on tests of perceptual speed and accuracy, show more sensitivity to touch in their fingers and hands, and are more sensitive than males to changes in sound intensity. Under lighted conditions, males seem to be more sensitive than females to changes in the intensity of visual stimuli. Male and female infants have been found to differ in the kinds of stimuli to which they pay the most attention, with females showing stronger responsiveness to faces and males responding more to blinking lights and other novel objects.

Most of the recent research attention has, however, concentrated on cognitive rather than perceptual performance differences. Traditionally, males and females have been thought to differ in their performance on verbal, quantitative, and visual–spatial tasks. Generally speaking, research now shows a tendency for females to outscore males on tasks that require certain verbal skills, and small differences favoring males on mathematical problem-solving tasks and tasks requiring spatial perception. A somewhat larger difference favoring males is found for visual–spatial tasks that require rapid mental rotation of pictures or objects. For these broad areas of cognitive performance—verbal, quantitative, and visual–spatial—the presence and magnitude of a gender difference depends on the specific aspect of performance being tested and the specific population being studied. Given the current state of the research, it is no longer appropriate to make general statements about one gender outperforming the other in one of these three broad areas. As for the specific differences that have been observed, none are nearly large enough to explain the disproportionate number of males, as compared to females, in the scientific and technical professions.

Psychologists have spent a great deal of energy trying to explain the observed small gender differences in certain aspects of verbal, mathematical, and visual–spatial performance. A number of biological mechanisms have been postulated as causal factors: genetic linkage of particular abilities to the X chromosome, direct action of circulating sex hormones, sensitizing effects of prenatal hormones on the developing brain, and the degree of lateralization of specific functions in the left and right hemispheres of the brain. At present, evidence for the X-linkage explanation is very weak, new evidence is emerging in support of some aspects of the circulating-hormones hypothesis, and, under the glare of a great deal of research attention, the hypothesis linking cognitive performance differences to greater lateralization of functions in the male than female brain has begun to look overly simplistic. Some evidence suggests, however, that particular abilities may be organized differently—some more diffusely and some more focally—in female and male brains.

Several social/affective factors appear to play interlocking roles in helping to produce gender differences in cognitive performance. Some verbal tasks are gender-typed as feminine, whereas mathematical and certain visual–spatial tasks are labeled masculine. As a consequence of this labeling, boys and girls receive different amounts of direct training and parental encouragement for achievement in these areas. The labeling, training, and parental support all influence children's self-confidence and the value they attach to success on particular tasks, which, in turn, influence performance. These social/affective factors, in interaction with whatever biological predispositions toward gender differences exist, help to increase gender differences in performance. Yet despite all these pressures in the direction of differences, the result is only a small to moderate gender gap on a few cognitive tests. For tasks in all three cognitive areas, the gap is most noticeable at the top extreme of the performance distribution, and appears to be decreasing very gradually. Sizeable gender differences continue to be observed in curricular and career choices; however, it appears that these differences have little to do with cognitive abilities and a lot to do with gender-related expectations and cultural barriers to participation.

None of the research discussed in this chapter provides any justification whatsoever for sex discrimination in education, employment, the law, or any of our social institutions, or for the segregation of jobs according to gender. The finding that gender differences in abilities are so few in number and so small in size indicates clearly that individual differences rather than gender differences are the ones to be kept in mind when deciding what educational programs are best suited to various people, what roles each spouse should play in a marital relationship, or who is the best person for a particular type of job. As a favorite women's movement slogan puts it: "The best man for the job is often a woman," and we might add, "The best woman for the job is often a man."

KEY TERMS

spatial visualization	spatiotemporal ability	lateralization
spatial perception	cerebral cortex	
mental rotation	corpus callosum	

FOR ADDITIONAL READING

Halpern, Diane F. (1997). Sex differences in intelligence: Implications for education. *American Psychologist, 52,* 1091–1102. The author thoroughly reviews the complex findings on cognitive gender differences, making it clear why it is dangerous to try to sum up this area with sweeping generalizations.

Hollingworth, Harry L. (1990). *Leta Stetter Hollingworth: A biography*. Bolton, MA: Anker. The woman whose research first challenged the variability hypothesis was considered a "scientific pillar" of the women's movement. Here, her life and work are described in respectful detail by her husband.

Keller, Evelyn Fox. (1983). *A feeling for the organism: The life and work of Barbara McClintock*. San Francisco: W. H. Freeman. The author describes the work of one of the few women scientists to have won a Nobel Prize and raises questions about whether women and men approach science differently.

CHAPTER 7

Sexual Lives & Orientations

Women need a reason to have sex," muses Billy Crystal's character, Mitch, in the movie *City Slickers,* "men just need a place." This comment reflects something of the popular opinion about gender differences in a realm where such differences may seem especially relevant: sexuality.

Two of the best-known sexual stereotypes, particularly in the context of heterosexuality, are the reluctant, uninterested female and the male who is always ready. Such beliefs in fundamental male–female differences in sexual response, drive, and desires have served as a justification for practices and institutions as diverse as prostitution, stag parties, "men's magazines," romance novels, men-only clubs, and the custom of veiling women from head to toe in certain cultures. Basic to the gender stereotypes about sexuality has been the notion that men have a much stronger sex drive than women do. Conveniently paired with this belief has been the idea that there are, however, two kinds of women: the promiscuous, seductive ones who tempt men away from their more important pursuits and who fill the roles of prostitutes and performers in pornographic films, and the virtuous ones who are restrained and selective in their sexual behavior. Although such stereotypes have begun to fade in some quarters, there are many indications that people expect women and men to differ in their approach to sexuality.

How do these expectations relate to the research findings about male and female sexuality? This chapter presents some answers by reviewing the findings on the physiology of sexual response for women and men, the types and frequency of sexual behavior by the two sexes, and sexual attitudes. Also discussed will be issues surrounding sexual orientation, the social construction of heterosexuality, homosexuality, and bisexuality, and the experiences of these identities. Finally, we will turn our attention to the uncomfortable intersection between cultural notions of sexuality and power. Some important and disturbing issues involve the use of sexuality in the service of dominance and aggression: pornography, rape, and incest. Rape and incest are acts of aggression, but because they are often construed by participants as sexual, they are discussed in this chapter. The first step, however, is an examination of a constellation of beliefs that for centuries has promoted differing sexual values for women and men: the double standard.

THE DOUBLE STANDARD

The **double standard** means just that: two different standards of sexual behavior, one for women and one for men. It is based on the assumption that males have a greater desire and need for sexual activity than females do. This supposed difference in males' and females' need for sex makes it seem appropriate, in a heterosexual context, for men to be the sexual aggressors and pursuers and for women to be the sexual gatekeepers, making sure things don't get out of hand. Believers in the double standard do not hold a man responsible for pushing an unwilling woman to engage in sexual activity; rather, they maintain it is the woman's responsibility to set limits. *He* supposedly cannot help himself; *she,* with her supposedly weaker sex drive, can.

This set of assumptions carries enormous implications for the sexual behavior and experience of women and men and for the power relationship between them. First of all, it trivializes women's sexual feelings, refusing to allow for the possibility that female sexual desire is important in its own right. Second, it trivializes men's capacity for self-control, suggesting that men are helpless before their sexual impulses. It means that women more than men risk ruined reputations by becoming known as sexually active, that men more than women risk ruined reputations by becoming known as sexually inactive, and that women who have been sexually assaulted, harassed, or raped are often blamed for their own victimization. Fallout from the double standard may include men's failure to learn that there are ways of controlling their sexual responses, women's failure to learn about their own capacity for sexual pleasure, and a reluctance of sexual partners to communicate with each other about their feelings.

Despite its long history, the double standard is not rooted in fact. Women and men are very similar in the physiology of sexual response, and women have an enormous capacity for sexual pleasure. It may be, in fact, that the gender differences we observe in sexual behavior are a result of the different ways social disapproval is dished out to women and men because of the double standard, and of women's awareness that if sexual activity results in pregnancy, their lives will be the ones most dramatically affected.

THE PHYSIOLOGY OF SEXUAL RESPONSE

Until the 1960s most people's knowledge about the body's response to sexual arousal was limited to their own (and what they could tell about their partners') experience. Because sexuality was considered an extremely private matter, the idea that researchers could actually observe and measure in the laboratory the bodily reactions of people engaged in sexual activity was unthinkable. However, in 1966, the pioneers of this type of research, William Masters and Virginia Johnson, published data on 382 women and 312 men whom they had observed in thousands of cycles of sexual arousal and orgasm (Masters & Johnson, 1966).

Sexual Response: Four Phases

One thing Masters and Johnson did not find was a fundamental difference between women and men in their patterns of sexual arousal and orgasm. For both sexes, the physical response to sexual stimulation were described as four phases: excitement, plateau, orgasm, and resolution. The two basic physiological processes involved in these phases are **vasocongestion** (the accumulation of blood in the blood vessels of a particular region) and **myotonia** (muscle contraction). The four phases envisioned by Masters and Johnson, described in the following sections, are diagrammed for females and males in Figures 7.1 and 7.2.

EXCITEMENT   The initial **excitement phase** can be triggered by any of a variety of sexually arousing stimuli. Vasocongestion of the genital organs begins to occur. In males, this increased blood flow to the genitals causes the penis to become erect, a reaction that tends to occur within a few seconds of the stimulation. In females, the increased blood flow causes fluids to seep through the membranes of the vaginal walls, producing lubrication. This lubrication, which signals the beginning of arousal, begins within 30 seconds after the arousing stimuli. The glans of the clitoris also swell as a result of vasocongestion. In both sexes, the nipples may harden and become erect as a result of contraction in muscle fibers.

During the excitement phase, the labia swell and the upper two thirds of the vagina expands. In males, the scrotum is pulled closer to the body and the testes begin to be elevated. In both males and females, there is an increase in heart rate and blood pressure. Although this phase is governed by the same physiological processes for males and females—vasocongestion and myotonia—the different anatomies of the two sexes dictate different physical and social consequences. The erect penis cannot be ignored as easily as the moist vagina.

PLATEAU   If sexual stimulation continues with sufficient intensity, a peak level of vasocongestion is reached in the **plateau phase.** Rate of breathing, pulse rate, and blood pressure increase further. The male's penis becomes fully erect and the testes swell and are further elevated. In females, the clitoris retracts, the labia deepen in color, and the tissues surrounding the outer third of the vagina swell to form the "orgasmic platform"—a change that has the effect of narrowing the opening to the vagina. As stimulation continues, both vasocongestion and myotonia continue to build toward the tension required for orgasm. If stimulation is withdrawn before orgasm, the person

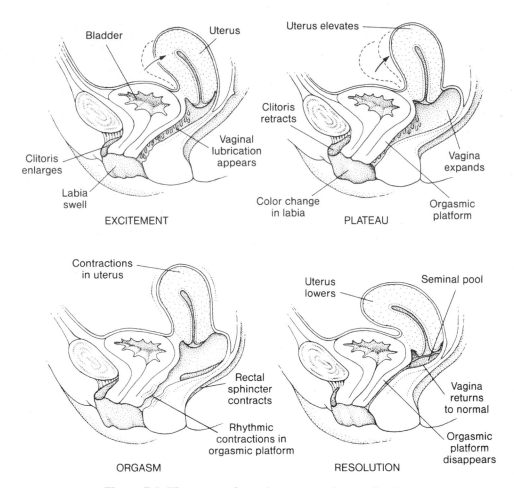

Figure 7.1 The stages of sexual response in human females.

enters directly into the resolution phase. However, without the discharge of tension that occurs in orgasm, the resolution phase progresses slowly and can be quite uncomfortable. Men call this condition "blue balls"; women do not seem to have an equivalent phrase, despite the fact that, as will be discussed later in the chapter, not reaching orgasm is a more common experience for them than for men.

ORGASM   In both sexes, when arousal reaches a critical point, it triggers **orgasm,** a series of involuntary rhythmic contractions of the pelvic organs. For males, the first part of orgasm involves the contraction of the vas, seminal vesicles, and prostate to force the semen into position in a bulb at the base of the urethra. Once this has happened, ejaculation is inevitable. Next, the bulb and the penis begin rhythmic contractions, causing the ejaculation of the semen.

For females, orgasm is a series of contractions of the orgasmic platform and the uterus. Surrounding muscles may also contract. In both sexes, pulse rate, blood pressure, and breathing increase sharply, and muscles throughout the body, such as legs,

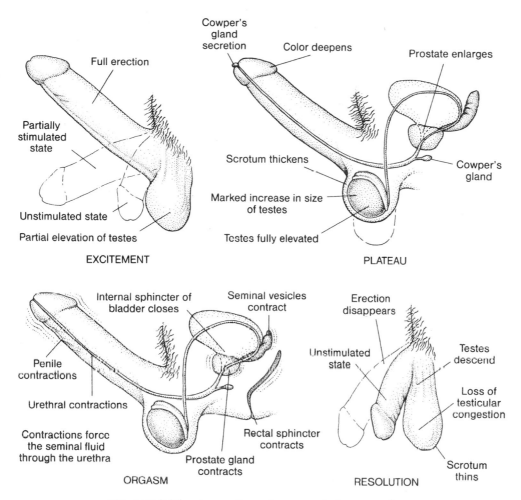

Figure 7.2 The stages of sexual response in human males.

thighs, and back, may contract. The whole process lasts only a few seconds. Some research has raised the possibility that some women also ejaculate during orgasm (Perry & Whipple, 1981). These researchers discovered a fluid that is chemically similar to seminal fluid spurting from the urethra during orgasm in a few women. Female ejaculation has been speculatively linked to an area called the **G-spot** (in honor of a physician named Grafenburg, who first raised the possibility that this area was an especially sensitive one), located on the top side of the vagina. The whole notion of female ejaculation is still very controversial, however. The G-spot cannot be located for all women, and even among those for whom it can be, there is not always evidence of ejaculation. In some studies, chemical analysis of the fluid ejaculated by women found it to be similar to urine rather than to male semen (Alzate & Hoch, 1986; Goldberg et al., 1983). However, questions about ejaculation aside, some sex researchers continue to be intrigued by the possibility that, at least for some women, stimulation of the anterior wall of the vagina is an important aspect of sexual arousal (McCormick, 1994).

Whether or not the sexual partners experience simultaneous orgasm, or whether there is even a partner, orgasm is the same physiological process. For females, however, there is greater individual variation in duration and intensity of orgasm than there is for males. Also, for women, orgasm achieved through masturbation appears to be more intense than orgasm from intercourse, probably because a woman has better control over the type and intensity of stimulation during masturbation. Women seem to attach much importance to the interpersonal aspect of sexuality, however, and masturbation has not threatened to replace intercourse.

People would not go to so much trouble to have orgasms if they were simply a set of muscular contractions. The sensations of orgasm are very intense and pleasurable, and the release of sexual tension leaves the individual feeling satisfied and relaxed. These feelings are much the same for women and men. In one study, male and female college students gave written descriptions of what an orgasm felt like. A panel of experts (doctors and psychologists) who read the descriptions could not reliably distinguish between those that had been written by women and those that had been written by men (Vance & Wagner, 1976).

RESOLUTION   Following orgasm, the body enters the **resolution phase.** The processes that led up to orgasm—vasocongestion and myotonia—are reversed. Muscular tension is relaxed, and blood is released from the engorged blood vessels. In women, the clitoris shrinks to its normal size, the orgasmic platform relaxes, and the vagina and uterus return to normal. In men, the erection of the penis is lost and the scrotum and testes return to normal. In both sexes, pulse rate, breathing, and blood pressure gradually return to unaroused levels.

Resolution usually takes 15 to 30 minutes after orgasm. However, when orgasm has not occurred, it can take up to an hour. Among women who frequently experience sexual arousal without orgasm, the buildup of vasocongestion without discharge by orgasm can produce a great deal of discomfort.

One notable sex difference in response occurs in the resolution phase: Men experience a **refractory period,** lasting from a few minutes to 24 hours, during which they typically cannot be restimulated to erection and orgasm. No such refractory period occurs for women, making it possible for them to experience multiple orgasms.

LIMITATIONS OF MASTERS AND JOHNSON'S RESEARCH   The four phases of sexual response Masters and Johnson described are commonly spoken of as "the human sexual response cycle." The physiological responses they identify are undoubtedly characteristic of many instances of sexual arousal, but there are many reasons to doubt their vision of this cycle as universal. A number of biases in the way participants were selected for this research have been noted (Tiefer, 1995). First, to be accepted as a research participant, a person had to have a history of achieving orgasm through masturbation and sexual intercourse. Thus, anyone who did not masturbate or who did not regularly have orgasms was excluded from the study. Second, the researchers deliberately sought a sample of participants who were above average in intelligence, education, and socioeconomic status. Third, volunteers for the study were characterized by a strong interest in effective sexual performance and a willingness to have that performance observed and analyzed, probably making them different from the general population. All of these selection biases make it difficult to be sure that the sexual responses observed by Masters and Johnson are characteristic of human beings in general rather than of a particular population. Of particular concern, according to Leonore Tiefer, is the probability that the women who participated were less representative of women in general than the male participants were of men in general. Why? Because, as we will see later in this chapter, women are less likely to masturbate and are less consistent in experiencing orgasm—both requirements for inclusion in the study—than men are.

There are other problems as well. Participants who did not experience orgasm in the laboratory were reassured and coached to help "improve" their future performance. Participants were clearly exposed to a strong message that only certain sexual responses were adequate and that effective sexual stimulation was stimulation that led to those responses. In general, the research seems oriented toward confirming a particular model of human sexual response rather than exploring the potential diversity of such response.

Critics have also assailed the assumptions implicit in the Masters and Johnson model, particularly the reduction of sexual activity to physiological responses and the omission of sexual desire, attraction, and emotions. Tiefer (1995) argues that the seemingly gender-neutral model actually favors a male approach to sexuality by focusing on the physical aspects of sexuality and leaving out the emotional and intimacy aspects that women are trained to value. The Masters and Johnson model, she notes, "assumes that men and women have and want the same kind of sexuality since physiological research suggests that in some ways, and under selected test conditions, we are built the same. Yet our social realities dictate that we are not all the same sexually—not in our socially shaped wishes, in our sexual self-development, or in our interpersonal sexual meanings" (p. 56).

Sexual Response: Issues

THE MYTH OF THE VAGINAL ORGASM   One of the most popular misconceptions about orgasm, arising from Freudian theory, was that females can experience two distinct kinds of orgasm: one kind resulting from clitoral stimulation and a different (better) kind resulting from stimulation of the vagina by the penis during intercourse. As mentioned in Chapter 2, Freud believed that part of the psychological maturation process for women involved abandoning the attainment of orgasm through clitoral stimulation and shifting to a preference for orgasm attained through heterosexual intercourse. Indeed, his theory characterized the clitoral orgasm as "infantile," and many women seeking to avoid this label spent hours (and fortunes!) in psychiatrists' offices trying to figure out what unconscious fixation was blocking them from reaching orgasm with their partners without clitoral stimulation.

Masters and Johnson's research undercut the distinction between the clitoral and vaginal orgasm by showing that there is no physiological difference between orgasms that occur during intercourse and those that occur as a result of manual or oral stimulation of the clitoris. In fact, almost all orgasms involve stimulation of the clitoris. The vagina is a relatively insensitive organ—a useful feature given that one of its main functions is to serve as the route through which childbirth occurs. It is, however, sensitive to pressure, and it is this sensitivity that makes insertion of the penis pleasurable (Barbach, 1976). The clitoris, which grows from the same fetal structure as the penis (see Chapter 5), is an exquisitely sensitive organ—so sensitive, in fact, that direct contact can be painful. Vaginal intercourse can indirectly stimulate the clitoris by pulling on the inner labia, which in turn causes the clitoral hood to move back and forth against the clitoris. Thus, clitoral stimulation is usually what triggers orgasm, and the distinction between the clitoral and vaginal orgasm does not make sense.

MULTIPLE ORGASM   In the sample studied by Masters and Johnson, women did not enter a refractory period after orgasm, and many women were capable of having a series of orgasms within a short period of time. During the resolution phase, if a woman is stimulated again she can often be aroused, return to the excitement or plateau phase, and have another orgasm. Much less stimulation is required for these subsequent orgasms although they can be just as intense as the first, and the cycle can be repeated several times. Masters and Johnson found that, using masturbation, some women could have 5 to 20 orgasms—up to 50 using a vibrator.

Not all women experience multiple orgasms, and even those who do can often feel satisfied with just one. It should also be noted that some men may be capable of multiple orgasms, although data supporting this are scant (Robbins & Jensen, 1977; Zilbergeld, 1978).

SEXUAL DYSFUNCTION   Difficulties with sexual functioning, such as the inability to get an erection in men and the inability to have an orgasm in women or men, are common problems that cause a great deal of anxiety to the individuals experiencing them. Besides the obvious fact that they interfere with sexual pleasure, there are other reasons these problems are sources of so much distress: People feel they cannot discuss them with others, and the cultural labels attached to the problems (e.g., "impotence" and "frigidity") are very negative ones. Masters and Johnson's research dispelled a lot of the secrecy surrounding sexual dysfunction and fostered a behavioral approach to treatment (Masters & Johnson, 1970).

The sexes are not so different with respect to sexual dysfunction. Both males and females can experience difficulty with arousal and orgasm, painful intercourse, and low sexual desire. However, there are differences in the frequencies with which these problems occur for women and men. Women are considerably more likely than men to report difficulty achieving orgasm. Men are much more likely than women to have a problem with their orgasm happening too quickly (premature ejaculation).

It is estimated that about 50% of men experience occasional difficulty in getting an erection (H. S. Kaplan, 1974). Such difficulties can affect men at any age. In recent years, there has been an apparent increase in social acceptability of admitting this problem, fueled by the availability of the new drug Viagra and the huge advertising campaign that has accompanied it.

Early sex surveys found that about 30% of women reported never or only occasionally having orgasms during intercourse (Kinsey, Pomeroy, Martin, & Gebhard, 1953; Terman, 1951), but later surveys show only about 10% to 15% of women saying they seldom or never have orgasm (Hunt, 1974). The latter study also uncovered some evidence for orgasm inconsistency in men, particularly under the age of 25. Perhaps, then, the gender difference in orgasm consistency is diminishing. Although the number of women who reach orgasm *some* of the time may be increasing, there is still a discrepancy between women and men. A recent survey in the United States found that 75% of men report *always* reaching orgasm during sexual activity, but only 29% of the women do (Michael, Gagnon, Laumann, & Kolata, 1994). The discrepancy between the early and later surveys may partly reflect a difference in the populations sampled. One of the difficulties with sex surveys is that the people who choose to respond to them may not be representative of the "average" population. Alfred Kinsey's research took place at a time when sexuality was a taboo topic. Thus, not only may he have had trouble obtaining honest responses, but his respondents, by agreeing to discuss their sexual habits with him, showed themselves to be a rather daring segment of North American society in the late 1940s. Morton Hunt tried hard to obtain an unbiased sample of the U.S. population but did not succeed completely. We do know that the Kinsey and Hunt samples are not fully comparable in terms of the age, race, marital status, and socioeconomic status of the respondents. Another possible problem with the comparability of the two surveys is that it may have been more acceptable in the 1940s for women to admit to difficulties with orgasm. Now, in the age of the multiple orgasm for women, it may simply be harder for women to admit orgasm inconsistency, even on an anonymous questionnaire.

The finding that women report more difficulty with orgasm than men do may be largely a function of ineffective stimulation of the woman. Women can masturbate to orgasm about as quickly as men can; it is during intercourse that they tend to experience difficulty or slowness in responding.

SEXUAL DESIRE   In 1978, and again in 1982, researchers conducted studies in which college students were approached by attractive members of the other sex and asked one of the following questions: "Would you go out tonight?" "Will you come over to my apartment?" or "Would you go to bed with me?" (R. Clark & Hatfield, 1989). Not surprising to those of us familiar with sexual norms for women and men, men were more willing than women to accede to sexual invitations from potential partners. The great majority of men were willing to have a sexual encounter with the woman who approached them; however, not one woman agreed to such an encounter with a man.

Do these findings mean that women are less interested in sex than men are? Not necessarily. The double standard of expectations for females and males affects the way female-to-male and male-to-female propositions are interpreted. The women might have been worried about what the attractive man would think of them if they agreed to have sex with him so casually. The men who were propositioned would have few such worries. Beyond the double standard, another consideration might well have inhibited women from accepting the man's invitation: fear. As discussed in a later section, women have good reason to fear sexual violence, and women may well be cautious about making themselves vulnerable.

Despite the competing possible explanations of the double standard and the fear of sexual violence, a traditional stereotype has held that women simply have less desire for intercourse than men. Kinsey and his colleagues noted that wives wanted intercourse less often than their husbands did. However, according to the Hunt survey, fewer than 5% of the wives wanted intercourse less often than their husbands did, and in a survey conducted by *Redbook,* one third of the wives reported a wish for more frequent intercourse (Levin & Levin, 1975). It is difficult to infer a trend here because the samples may be very different. The more recent findings do indicate, however, that many women are interested in intercourse, and that interest is not limited to married adults. A *Seventeen* magazine survey of a national sample of single females and males between the ages of 14 and 21 found that, of those who were sexually active, 99% of the males and 91% of the females reported that they enjoyed intercourse (Pesmen, 1991).

Perhaps, in the attempt to study sexual desire, it is inappropriate to focus on the desire for intercourse. We have already seen that intercourse may not be the most satisfying form of sexual activity for women. If middle-class wives prefer, as one study found, to read a book rather than engage in sexual activity with their husbands (Mancini & Orthner, 1978), that preference may reflect not a lack of sexual desire but a lack of sexual satisfaction through intercourse.

When it comes to sexual activity, women and men may differ not so much in the frequency with which they desire the activity but in the kinds of activities they desire. Research with college students and newly married couples shows that women desire more activities in sex that demonstrate love and intimacy, whereas men want more activities that are sexually arousing (Hatfield, Sprecher, Pillemer, & Greenberger, 1988). Another study focused on sexual urges and fantasies outside of heterosexual activity (Jones & Barlow, 1990). Male and female undergraduate students self-monitored their sexual fantasies (internally generated sexual thoughts), urges (externally provoked sexual thoughts), and masturbatory fantasies for 7 consecutive days. Women and men did not differ in the frequency of their sexual fantasies. However, men reported more urges and masturbatory fantasies than women did.

Despite stereotypes that women experience less physical sexual desire than men do, there is evidence that women do indeed "embody" their feelings of sexual desire; they do not simply desire a disembodied emotional experience of sexual connection. Researchers who interviewed adolescent women about their experiences of sexual desire found that the women associated sexuality with strong feelings of physical pleasure and with self-knowledge:

> Both sexual desire and sexual pleasure are known to them as profoundly physical experiences—as feelings that they perceive in their own bodies. They are able to describe these experiences in specific terms, reflecting their clear acquaintance with these feelings: Zoe called it a "tingling or shivering," Eugenia explained that it is "a burn, a throbbing down there, in between my legs . . . sometimes I get wet . . . it was just like my body wanted to just be like touched and explored." (Tolman & Szalacha, 1999, p. 29)

These researchers noted, however, that experiences of sexual violation or living in a social context in which sexual violence was prevalent appeared to dampen young women's emphasis on pleasure and increase their emphasis on vulnerability in connection with sexuality. Girls who had not had to negotiate much sexual violence in their personal lives, relationships, or social landscapes spoke "about having feeling bodies and about knowing that their bodies and sexuality can be a source of physical, emotional, and relational pleasure and even strength" (p. 30). However, girls who had experienced sexual violation personally or close to them in their social environment spoke of their sexual feelings with a sense of dissociation and disconnection from their bodies. For example, one young women from this group said, "It's all in my head, I think about it, but my body has nothing to do with it. You know, sure my body feels desire if someone touches me or feels pleasure, but pretty much it's in what you're thinking about" (p. 31).

Some writers have suggested that women's sexual desire may fluctuate with the menstrual cycle. A peak in desire may occur at the ovulation phase for some women and at the menstrual or postmenstrual phase for others (A. R. Gold & Adams, 1981; Kinsey et al., 1953). Although such correspondence between the menstrual cycle and sexual desire may be experienced by individual women, there is, as yet, no evidence that women as a group show any regular pattern of cyclic fluctuation in sex drive (Morrell, Dixen, Carter, & Davidson, 1984).

SEXUAL ACTIVITY

Information about the type and extent of people's sexual activity generally comes from self-reports elicited through surveys (e.g., A. P. Bell, Weinberg, & Hammersmith, 1981; Hite, 1976, 1981; Kinsey, Pomeroy, & Martin, 1948; Kinsey et al., 1953; Michael et al., 1994; Pesmen, 1991). Although such surveys have proven invaluable in providing knowledge about sexual activity, there are reasons to be skeptical about the degree to which the survey results reflect the sexual behavior of the general population. Volunteer participants in sex research tend to be more experienced and less inhibited in their sex lives than most people (Kaats & Davis, 1971; Maslow & Sakoda, 1952), so they are not an unbiased sample of the population. Making the sample still more biased may be the deliberate exclusion of particular groups. For example, the Kinsey report did not include Black respondents, and Hunt, in an effort to make his sample comparable with Kinsey's, dropped Black respondents when comparing his results with the Kinsey report. A recent representative survey of 3432 adults was limited to respondents over the age of 18 (Michael et al., 1994). In addition, the reliance on self-reports of sexual practices has some potential pitfalls. Respondents may distort reality by tending to exaggerate or minimize their sexual activity, they may be unable to remember accurately events that are long past, and they may have difficulty estimating frequencies and time spent in certain activities. Given these drawbacks, it might be more appropriate to take the data provided by these surveys as rough approximations of the experience of the general population than as completely accurate representations of it.

Heterosexual Intercourse

Kinsey's data, collected in the 1940s, indicated that 33% of women and 71% of men had had premarital sexual intercourse by the age of 25. The Hunt report indicated that by the 1970s, the comparable percentages were 67% for women and 97% for men. Other surveys show a similar increase in premarital sexual activity among adolescents and young adults, with a larger increase evident for women than for men and a trend toward first intercourse occurring at earlier ages. A survey by Zelnick and Kantner (1980) showed that 69% of females and 77% of males reported having premarital intercourse by the age of 19. The *Seventeen* magazine survey (Pesmen, 1991) indicated that 51% of both single males and single females in the 14-to-21 age range had had sexual intercourse and 71% of young women age 18 to 19 were sexually active. By 1994, one survey found that 59% of teenagers had engaged in sexual intercourse by the age of 17 and 82% by the age of 19 (Ingrassia, 1994). A survey by Gladue (1990) indicates that 73% of women had had intercourse by the age of 19, 68% by the age of 18, 50% by the age of 17, 29% by the age of 16, and 13% by the age of 15. African American women are more likely than Hispanic or European American women to report engaging in sexual intercourse in early adolescence (Michael et al., 1994). There is little evidence, however, that the average young adult has a great deal of variety in sexual partners before marriage. Surveys taken in the early 1970s suggested, for example, that more than half the women who engaged in premarital intercourse had only one partner, often their fiancé (Hunt, 1974; Kantner & Zelnick, 1972), and that married men had typically had about six premarital partners. The average number of premarital partners may have increased for women (Zelnick & Kantner, 1977); however, the majority of young single women report that they prefer to date one person exclusively (Pesmen, 1991). Also, a large number of female teenagers report having tried sex once and then put it "on hold" (L. B. Rubin, 1991).

Men are more likely than women to have a large number of sexual partners in their lifetime. For example, one survey found that 28% of men and 42% of women had had 10 or fewer sexual partners, and 21% of men and 19% of women had had between 31 and 60 partners (Janus & Janus, 1993). Could these respondents be overreporting their number of partners? A recent representative survey of American adults found that 26% of Americans reported having had only 1 sexual partner, and only 9% said they had had 21 or more (Laumann, Michael, Gagnon, & Michaels, 1994).

Sexual activity is affected by a variety of factors. Currently, the AIDS epidemic, as well as the prevalence of other sexually transmitted diseases, may be a factor in people's decisions with respect to whether or not, and with whom, to be sexually active. These issues are discussed in later sections.

First intercourse is often greeted with different reactions by females and males, at least among the adolescents studied by Sorenson (1973). Males were more likely to report feeling positive: excited, joyful, and mature. Females were more likely to say they felt negative emotions: guilt, sorrow, and disappointment. Disappointment may be a common reaction for women. One sample of college women, rating their experience of first intercourse on a 1 to 7 scale (1 = didn't experience pleasure at all, 7 = strongly experienced pleasure), gave it an average rating of only 3.9 (Weis, 1983). About 90% of men and 70% of women reported in a recent survey that they wanted to have intercourse the first time they did it (Michael et al., 1994). The reasons for doing so differed for the two genders: Nearly half the women, but only a quarter of the men, said they had intercourse out of affection for their partner. More than half the men, but only a quarter of the women, cited curiosity as their main motivation.

Among married couples, there is a great deal of variability in the frequency of coitus. According to the most recent surveys, the average couple in their mid-20s has intercourse between two and three times a week, with the frequency declining gradually over the years (Michael et al., 1994). Women report slightly less satisfaction with marital sex than men do, but both women and men express relatively high levels of satisfaction. On surveys, men are more likely than women to say they have engaged in extramarital sex, with about half the men and one quarter of the women engaging in it at least once. The incidence of extramarital sex for women seems to have increased since the 1960s (A. P. Thompson, 1983), but, in general, the affairs do not seem to be casual ones. Many of the women who have had extramarital sex have done so with only one partner (Blumstein & Schwartz, 1983). A recent large-scale survey indicates that more than 80% of women and 65% to 85% of men of all ages report having no extramarital affairs (Laumann et al., 1994).

Most surveys report a higher incidence of heterosexual activity for men than for women. A greater proportion of men than women say they are sexually active, and men report having had more partners than women do. This finding is difficult to explain. Each act of heterosexual intercourse involves one man and one woman: Where are the women with whom the male respondents in these surveys claim to be having intercourse? Diane Phillis and Mark Gromko (1985) list three possible explanations for the men's reported higher number of partners: (1) overreporting by men or underreporting by women of sexual activity; (2) the existence of a minority of women who have many partners; and (3) males and females in the surveys, or their partners, are drawn from different populations. Phillis and Gromko's own study of students at a Midwestern university revealed no evidence for the existence of a small group of women having intercourse with a large number of men: 6% of sexually active women and 9% of sexually active men reported having had 12 or more partners. Furthermore, there was no evidence that the men were finding a disproportionately larger number of partners away from the campus than the women were. Phillis and Gromko finally concluded that the differences in the proportions of males and females reporting sexual activity could be explained by the unequal sex ratio at the university (57% women and 43% men). Their reasoning went like this: Suppose that, on an island populated by 300 women and 100 men 80% of the men are heterosexually active. If each sexually active male has 1 female partner, then 80 men are paired with 80 women. In terms of proportions, though, a researcher could report that 80% of the men but only 27% of the women report heterosexual activity. When Phillis and Gromko corrected for the unequal proportions of males and females in their own sample, the gender difference in reported heterosexual activity disappeared. They tried to test the generalizability of this finding to the Kinsey, Hunt, and other sex surveys but were unable to find the information on sex ratios needed to do so. Nonetheless, their findings suggest that the commonly accepted finding of greater male than female heterosexual activity may be more illusory than real, at least in some populations.

Homosexual Activity

The Kinsey surveys indicated that 37% of men and 13% of women had at least one homosexual experience leading to orgasm during adulthood (Kinsey et al., 1948, 1953). However, only 4% of males and 2% of females reported that they were exclusively homosexual. Hunt's (1974) data reveal a somewhat similar frequency of homosexual experience: 20% to 25% for men, 10% for married women, and 20% for unmarried women. The numbers are lower in more recent surveys. The large University of Chicago survey found that only 4% of women reported having had sex with another woman after the age of 18, and fewer than 2% had had sex with another woman in the past year (Laumann et al., 1994). In the same survey, 9% of men said they had engaged in sex with another male since puberty, just over 5% had had sex with a man since turning 18, and only

2% had had sex with a man in the past year. Surveys in Canada, France, Britain, Norway, and Denmark have all found homosexual behavior in 1% to 3% of men and a slightly lower percentage in women (Muir, 1993).

Some of the reported gender differences in homosexual behavior seem to parallel those reported for heterosexual activity. Males report more sexual activity with more partners than females do, and females are more likely to want and to be involved in long-term, emotionally close relationships (Bell & Weinberg, 1978; Hunt, 1974; Meredith, 1984; Peplau, 1981). Women in our culture are socialized more strongly than men are to value close relationships, so this finding is not surprising. However, a large proportion of both lesbians and gay men live with a partner in a committed relationship (Cabaj, 1988).

Within same-gender relationships, the amount of sexual activity varies widely, just as it does in mixed-gender relationships. This variation can be seen in the conflicting results obtained by researchers studying lesbian sexuality. One review of the literature led to the conclusion that lesbian women and heterosexual women are similar in the frequency with which they have sex (Peplau & Amaro, 1982); by contrast, however, a large-scale survey indicates that lesbian couples have sex much less frequently than any other type of couple (Blumstein & Schwartz, 1983). Some research shows that the frequency of genital sex often declines dramatically between lesbians in long-term, committed relationships (McCormick, 1994; Nichols, 1990).

Like heterosexual activity, homosexual activity is responsive to the norms of the surrounding culture. For example, studies of the history of lesbian relationships show that, under some conditions, lesbian couples of the 1940s and 1950s adopted the sexual roles of "stone butch" and "femme" (M. D. Davis & Kennedy, 1990; E. Newton, 1984). The butch was the sexual initiator or doer, and the femme was the more passive partner. Although, at first glance, these roles may seem to echo traditional male–female heterosexual roles, they were actually quite different. The ideal of the "stone butch" was to be untouchable: to gain sexual pleasure from giving pleasure, and not to allow her partner to reciprocate. The active, butch partner's fulfillment came from satisfying her partner. The femme, being more passive, was able to acknowledge and focus on her own sexual responses, to demand and receive sexual pleasure. These roles were socially constructed as ways of expressing lesbian cultural identity and female–female sexual love, and they were enforced by the norms of the lesbian community of the times (M. D. Davis & Kennedy, 1990). Currently, the emphasis on these roles has greatly diminished, as lesbian communities have found other ways to express their distinct identity:

> In the late sixties in Buffalo, with the development of the political activities of gay liberation, explicitly political organizations and tactics replaced butch-fem roles in leading the resistance to gay oppression. Because butch-fem roles were no longer the primary means for organizing the community's stance toward the straight world, the community no longer needed to enforce role-appropriate behavior. (M. D. Davis & Kennedy, 1990, p. 397)

Masturbation

Both the Kinsey and Hunt surveys indicated a large gender difference in the proportion of respondents who reported having masturbated to orgasm. Almost all males but only about two thirds of females reported having masturbated. Furthermore, males reported having begun masturbating at an earlier age than females. Current data support these findings (J. K. Davidson & Moore, 1994; Leitenberg, Detzer, & Srebnik, 1993; Oliver & Hyde, 1993). Although part of the gender difference may be attributable to males' greater willingness than females' to report masturbation, it is interesting to note that females *do* report more of some kinds of sexual activity in recent surveys than they did in earlier ones, suggesting that they now feel freer to admit sexual activity than they did in Kinsey's day. However, the percentage of women reporting that they masturbate has remained relatively constant.

Some experts feel that there is a connection between the finding that a large proportion of women do not masturbate and the finding that many women have difficulty reaching orgasm. Women who have not masturbated may be unaware of the kind of stimulation that gives them the most pleasure and may not learn to be comfortable with their own body and sexual responses. Kinsey's data did, in fact, suggest that women who masturbate to orgasm before marriage are more likely to experience orgasm during sex with their husbands (Kinsey et al., 1953). At least one writer has argued that sex, like any other skill, must be learned and practiced; learning about one's own body through masturbation can build a sense of independence and pleasure (Dodson, 1974).

Contraception

Despite the emphasis on sexuality in our culture, there is a curious reluctance to connect sexuality with pregnancy. Media depictions of sexual encounters have increased in number and explicitness in the last two decades (Brown, Childers, & Waszak, 1990). However, these depictions virtually ignore the reproductive potential of sexual intercourse: Rarely does the heroine of a romance novel stop to demand condom use before she allows herself to be seduced by the hero, and even the most sensitive of movie heroes aren't seen to use contraception themselves or to inquire of their sex partners whether they are using birth control before jumping into bed. Yet, in reality, the possibility of pregnancy cannot but affect heterosexual relationships, and, given that women are the ones who get pregnant, the effect is bound to be different for women and men. Women are more likely than men to report that fear of pregnancy interferes with the free expression of their sexuality (Pesmen, 1991).

One of the sources of the fear of pregnancy has traditionally been the disgrace associated with unwed motherhood. That stigma has lessened somewhat. A report by Rutgers University's National Marriage Project in the summer of 1999 revealed that the percentage of teenage girls who say having a baby out of wedlock can be a "worthwhile lifestyle" has risen from 33% to 53% over the past two decades (Popenow & Whitehead, 1999). In the United States, more than 1.2 million babies were born to unmarried mothers in 1997—30% of them to women in their teens (National Center for Health Statistics, 1999a). In the United States, the percentage of first births that were to unmarried women was higher than 40% from 1990 to 1994, in contrast to just over 8% in the period from 1930 to 1934 (Bachu, 1999). In many other industrialized countries, the percentage of births to unmarried mothers is similarly high: 31% in Britain, 30% in France, 23% in Canada, and 43% in Norway (United Nations, 1995a). Births to unmarried mothers made up 32.5% of births to White women, 76.9% of births to Black women, and 40.1% of births to Hispanic women in the United States during the period from 1990 to 1994 (Bachu, 1999).

The fear of pregnancy, while still real enough, is less salient to present-day North American women than it was to women in the first half of this century. The provision of birth control information to women was technically illegal in the United States until 1918, when the law was changed as a result of the energetic efforts of Margaret Sanger and her colleagues in the National Birth Control League. Sanger, who started her career as a nurse, was moved to tears and anger by her repeated exposure to the plight of poor women who were worn out from a continuous series of pregnancies that they could not prevent and who were dying in childbirth or from self-induced abortions. These women begged her for the facts about how to prevent pregnancy; however, even her nurse's training had not included that information. A turning point came for Sanger after a woman whose life she had helped save in the aftermath of an abortion pleaded with the doctor to tell her how she could avoid becoming pregnant again. The doctor laughed and told the woman to get her husband to sleep on the roof. Three months later, the woman died from another abortion, and Sanger left her nursing career behind to devote herself full time to making birth control available to women. During the struggle, she was publicly reviled, jailed, and frequently subjected to frustration and humiliation. In the end, however, she and the organization she founded prevailed: It became legal for doctors to give contraceptive information to women, and a network of birth control clinics was eventually established (Sanger, 1938). In Canada, too, the birth control movement, under the guidance of women such as Mary Elizabeth Hawkins and Dr. Elizabeth Bagshaw, had a positive impact on the availability of contraception for women—although as late as the mid-1930s an Ottawa social worker was charged with criminal activity for distributing family planning information (Van Preagh, 1982).

Despite the current availability of effective methods of birth control, not all sexually active adolescents use them consistently. One American survey showed that only about 75% of sexually active single males and females age 14 to 21 said they used contraception "absolutely all of the time" or "nearly all of the time" (Pesmen, 1991). However, teenage women's reported use of contraception at first intercourse rose from 48% in the early 1980s to 78% in 1995 (Alan Guttmacher Institute, 1999). In some developing countries, the rates of contraceptive use may be far lower. For example, one study of Guatemalan teenagers found that only 10% of sexually active teens were using contraception (Berganza, Peyre, & Aguilar, 1989).

After years of alarming rises, recent years have seen a decrease in teenage pregnancies. From 1991 to 1997, teen birth rates declined by 16% (National Center for Health Statistics, 1999b). Nonetheless, there are almost 1 million adolescent pregnancies each year in the United States. Almost 1 in every 9 girls between the ages of 15 and 19 gets pregnant, and 40% of these pregnancies occur in women who are 17 years old or younger (Alan Guttmacher Institute, 1999). Nearly 4 in 10 teen pregnancies, excluding miscarriages, end in abortion; teens account for 20% of legal abortions in the United States. Teen pregnancy is more common in some racial/ethnic groups than others: Among 15- to 19-year-old-women, there were 39.3 births per 1000 women among European Americans, 99.3 births per 1000 women among African Americans, and 106.7 births per 1000 women among Hispanic Americans (Coley & Chase-Lansdale, 1998).

The United States has the highest teen birth rate in the developed world: 52.3 births per 1000 teenagers (Havemann, 1999). By comparison, the rate is 29 per 1000 in Britain, 11 per 1000 in Germany, and 4 per 1000 in Japan. American teenagers do not show different patterns of sexual activity than teens in these other countries; however, they seem to use contraception less consistently. The causes may lie partly in a lack of information about or easy access to birth control techniques; other Western countries have for years made contraceptives and birth control information more easily accessible to adolescents. Studies of Black and Hispanic inner-city teenagers show, for instance, that these young people are often aware of contraceptive methods but do not know how to go about getting them and know little about how effective they are (Herz & Reis, 1987; Smith, Chacko, & Bermudez, 1989). However, attitudes toward sexual activity, some of them based on our old friend the double standard, also seem to contribute to the problem. The gender-role norms that say women do not take the initiative in sex may make it especially difficult for a young woman to prepare actively for the possibility of intercourse (Hynie & Lydon, 1995).

The attitude that women should be the gatekeepers of sexuality means the responsibility for preventing pregnancy is usually placed squarely on their shoulders, making men less likely to take responsibility for contraception. But what happens when a man *does* take such responsibility? In one study, college students were shown a videotape of the development of a first sexual encounter between a young man and young woman (Bryan, Aiken, & West, 1999). In three different versions of the video, the man either did not say or do anything about using contraception, verbally proposed using a condom, or nonverbally introduced the condom into the encounter. Students viewing the video were asked to rate the man on several characteristics. The researchers found that when the man proposed using a condom, he was viewed as nicer and more mature but less romantic and exciting than when he did not suggest condom use. Women seemed more favorably impressed when the condom was introduced verbally rather than nonverbally. Interestingly, men who viewed the videos estimated that suggesting condom use diminished the chance that sexual intercourse would take place—but the women made no such prediction. It appears that young women are quite willing to share the responsibility for condom use with their sexual partners.

If adolescents do become pregnant, the consequences can be serious for both the female and the male involved. Women who become mothers and men who become fathers during their teenage years are less likely than their counterparts to graduate from high school, and teenaged mothers trying to juggle the development of their own identities with the conflicting demands of parenthood may experience distress and depression (Coley & Chase-Lansdale, 1998). Adolescent males involved in a pregnancy show more psychological distress as young adults than do their counterparts whose girlfriend did not become pregnant. This is true whether the pregnancy ends in abortion, in the assumption of fathering responsibility, or in the abdication of parenting responsibilities to the girlfriend (Buchanan & Robbins, 1990).

Throughout the adult years of fertility, women are far more likely than men to take the responsibility for preventing pregnancy. When college students submit anonymous written questions about sexuality, the women ask twice as many questions about contraception and pregnancy as the men do (Valois & Waring, 1991). The most frequently used methods of birth control among American women are those that do not require male cooperation: sterilization and the birth control pill. Considerably less common are the diaphragm, vaginal spermicides, and the intrauterine device (IUD).

Injectable and implant contraceptives are used by a combined total of about 3% of women. The use of methods that depend on male cooperation—vasectomy (male sterilization), condom, withdrawal, and rhythm—is reported by a combined total of only 22.3% of women (National Center for Health Statistics, 1999a).

Experts now urge sexually active persons to use condoms, not just for the prevention of pregnancy but for protection from sexually transmitted diseases such as herpes and HIV. This new emphasis on the importance of condoms, in combination with the greater visibility of condom advertising, has apparently led to an upsurge in their use in some populations. One nonrandom survey indicates that 72% of teenage girls and 79% of teenage boys who have had sexual intercourse have used condoms, compared to 48% and 61% in a comparable 1986 survey (Pesmen, 1991). Among teenagers at least, condoms are a popular method of contraception, relied upon by 38% of those women who regularly use contraception. This method is slightly exceeded in popularity by the birth control pill (44%), and a significant number of young women regularly use these two methods in combination (Alan Guttmacher Institute, 1999). Among noncollege adults, condom use is rather low. About 13% of women report using condoms for contraception. One third of the population uses condoms consistently (Geringer, Marks, Allen, & Armstrong, 1993), and among those with two or more partners, less than 50% use condoms (Michael et al., 1994; Pepe, Sanders, & Symons, 1993).

Sexually Transmitted Diseases

Americans were stunned in November 1991, when basketball superstar Magic Johnson called a news conference to announce that he was retiring from the game because he had become infected with the **human immunodeficiency virus (HIV)** that causes **acquired immunodeficiency syndrome (AIDS)**. In that news conference, Johnson urged young people to heed his message that "safe sex is the way to go." Johnson's high profile and popularity brought new attention to bear on the issues of safe sex and AIDS—attention that may cause at least some people to take more seriously the risks associated with sexually transmitted diseases.

A host of potentially serious diseases is transmitted through sexual contact: HIV, herpes, chlamydia, syphilis, and gonorrhea. Three million American teenagers contract a sexually transmitted disease every year (Alan Guttmacher Institute, 1999), and about two thirds of all sexually transmitted diseases occur in individuals under the age of 25 (Hatcher, Trussell, Stewart, Stewart, et al., 1994). It is estimated that in a single act of unprotected sex with an infected partner, a teenage woman has a 1% risk of contracting HIV, a 30% risk of acquiring genital herpes, and a 50% chance of contracting gonorrhea (Alan Guttmacher Institute, 1999). Yet fear of such diseases apparently does little to deter many adolescents from becoming sexually active. In addition, knowing that the risk of contracting AIDS and other diseases can be reduced significantly by using condoms does not necessarily mean that condoms will be used. One study found that 90% of teenage girls questioned knew that unprotected sex put them at risk for contracting AIDS, but fewer than 40% had used condoms the last time they had intercourse (Fishbein, 1988). However, other research suggests that knowledge and anxiety about AIDS are related to such changes as decreased frequency of sexual activity and increased condom use among urban high school students (Zimet,

Bunch, Anglin, Lazebnik, et al., 1992). Findings from the Youth Risk Behavior Survey, conducted by the U. S. Department of Health and Human Services, suggest that sexually risky behavior by adolescents is decreasing somewhat. Results from the survey show that, from 1991 to 1997, the prevalence of sexual experience (defined, for purposes of the survey, as having ever had sexual intercourse) declined among male high school students by 15% (from 57.4% to 48.8%), and the prevalence of multiple sex partners declined by 25%. Neither behavior decreased significantly among female high school students. Among sexually active students, condom use increased by 23% over the same time period. However, in 1997 only 62.5% of male students and 50.8% of female students reported that they used condoms the last time they had sexual intercourse (U.S. Department of Health and Human Services, 1998).

The source of the most serious concern about sexually transmitted disease has been the discovery of and publicity given to AIDS. AIDS is caused by HIV, a slow-acting retrovirus. An individual who tests positive for the presence in the blood of antibodies to this virus (that is, an individual who is HIV-positive) does not necessarily have AIDS. However, current thinking in the scientific community is that 40% of persons with HIV will develop AIDS within 5 to 10 years. The virus attacks the immune system, the body's natural system for fighting off disease, allowing other diseases, such as rare cancers and infections, to go unchecked. Although there are some long-term survivors of the disease and increasingly effective treatments have been developed in recent years, most victims have a short life expectancy.

As far as researchers can tell, the disease is transmitted through bodily fluids—blood, semen, or the milk of nursing mothers—often by carriers who have no symptoms themselves (Ho et al., 1984). The virus is known to be passed from person to person through sexual contact, blood transfusions, the use of contaminated hypodermic needles (e.g., among intravenous drug users), and from an infected mother to the fetus in her womb or to her nursing child through breast milk. During heterosexual contact, the disease is up to 17 times more likely to be passed from a man to a woman than vice versa (Padian, Shiboski, & Jewell, 1991). In North America and Latin America, the most common focal points of infection are men who have unprotected sex with other men and drug injectors who share needles, although heterosexual transmission is on the rise. In sub-Saharan African and South Asian countries, infection with the virus is common among men who have sex with women. Worldwide, heterosexual intercourse is the most common mode of transmission of HIV (World Health Organization, 1998). This and other evidence has made it clear that the risk factor for AIDS is not sexual orientation but frequency of sexual contact or exposure to contaminated blood.

The World Health Organization estimates that at the end of 1998, 33.4 million people were living with HIV/AIDS—over 41% of them women and 3.6% of them children—and that 13.9 million people have died of AIDS since the beginning of the epidemic (World Health Organization, 1998). In North America, the incidence of AIDS increased rapidly after the first cases were reported in 1981. In 1985, the incidence among men in the United States was 81 per million; by 1992 it had increased to 304 per million. Among women during the same time period, the incidence increased from 6.7 to 53.3 per million (Franceschi, Dal Maso, La Vecchia, Negri, & Serraino, 1994). In 1998, the incidence among men was 341 per million; among women it was 96 per million (Centers for Disease Control and Prevention, 1998b). Women, particularly young women, are the fastest-growing category of people with AIDS, and many women whose only risk behavior is having sex with their husbands become infected because their husbands contract the virus through other sexual contacts or through drug injection (World Health Organization, 1998). In the United States, young African American women appear to be at particular risk. In one study of 16- to 21-year-olds, young African American women had the highest infection rates of any group (Centers for Disease Control and Prevention, 1998a). In this study, there were dramatically higher rates of infection among women 16 to 18 years of age than among men in the same age group, suggesting that young women are likely to be infected by men older than themselves.

For women, the disease is complicated by its relationship to reproduction. Without intervention, an HIV-infected pregnant woman has a 15% to 30% chance of having an infected baby. Transmission of the virus from an infected pregnant mother to her fetus accounts for 92% of all AIDS cases reported in children, and HIV infection was the seventh leading cause of death in the United States among children ages 1 to 4 in the early 1990s (S. F. Davis et al., 1995). Recent developments in drug treatments for and monitoring of pregnant women have led to a dramatic drop in AIDS cases among children in the United States, leading to the hope that perinatal transmission of HIV could be eliminated in this country (Centers for Disease Control and Prevention, 1998b). However, around the world nearly 600,000 children were infected with HIV during 1997; many countries do not have the resources to test pregnant women for HIV or to provide the drugs and alternatives to breast milk necessary to prevent mother–child transmission.

The incidence of AIDS cases varies dramatically among racial/ethnic groups in the United States. In 1998, the rates were highest among African Americans: the rate of AIDS cases per 100,000 population was more than 7 times higher among African American than European American men, more than 20 times higher among African American than European American women, and more than 16 times higher among African American than European American children (Centers for Disease Control and Prevention, 1998b). Because many poor African American women lack access to adequate health care, they tend to be sicker by the time they are diagnosed, and they die 5 times more quickly than White males with AIDS do (H. Dalton, 1989).

To reduce the risk of AIDS, it is critical that all sexually active individuals practice safer sex: decrease the number of sexual partners, learn more about the backgrounds of their partners, and use latex condoms with spermicide. These cautions apply equally to heterosexual and homosexual activity, yet the warnings have had a larger impact in gay populations than among heterosexuals. Some years ago, as the magnitude of the problem became clear, there was a shift away from casual sex in gay communities (Lyons, 1983). Condom use has increased, and more gay men than heterosexual men now use condoms (Treffke, Tiggemann, & Ross, 1992).

Life-Span Issues

Sexuality changes across the life span, and the patterns of change seem to be different for females and males. For one thing, women often find themselves much more able to enjoy sexual activity in middle age than they did when they were younger. Women are more likely than men to report increases from young adulthood to old age in measures such as frequency of orgasm, subjective pleasure in sexual activity, and satisfaction with sex life (Adams & Turner, 1985). Kinsey's survey indicated that women had orgasms more consistently at age 40 than they did as young adults, and the University of Chicago survey of American adults found that more women in their 50s reported that they "usually" had orgasm during sex with their partners than women in the earlier decades of life did (Michael et al., 1994). Men are more likely to enjoy sexual activity from adolescence onward. One analysis (H. S. Kaplan & Sager, 1971) suggests that teenage males in our culture have an intense genitally focused sexuality. With the passing years, male sexual desire becomes somewhat less urgent, so that by age 30 a man is satisfied with less frequent orgasms. The adult man expands his sexuality from a narrow focus on genital pleasure to include the broader sensual and emotional aspects of sexuality. In women, there is an early appreciation of the sensual and emotional aspects of sexuality, but the genital response is often limited and inconsistent in adolescence and young adulthood. Often it is only in later adulthood that women develop a capacity for intense genital pleasure.

It is important to note that the pattern just described is not necessarily "natural." In different cultures, the male and female patterns of sexuality can vary widely from this one. Thus, our socialization and expectations in the area of sexuality are highly likely to affect our experience of it. For example, researchers described the sexual practices in two contrasting societies: a small Irish community on the island of Inis Beag (Messenger, 1971) and a South Pacific island called Mangaia (D. S. Marshall, 1971). On Inis Beag, where there was an attitude of secrecy and fear about sex, premarital sex was all but unknown, intercourse was something that happened infrequently and quickly, and many people could not imagine that female orgasm existed. On Mangaia, by contrast, both boys and girls received sexual instruction from adults, were encouraged to have sexual experience with several partners before marriage, and all the women apparently learned at a young age to have orgasms. These two cases are not isolated instances of variation in human sexual customs and expectations. Anthropologists have uncovered a wide variety of rules governing sexuality in different cultures. For example, among the Truk of the Caroline Islands in the western Pacific Ocean, a man may sleep with the wives of any of his wife's brothers and a woman may sleep with her sisters' husbands; also, men, but not women, can demand a divorce on grounds of adultery. In many foraging societies, there is little or no sexual double standard, and virginity is not an important issue. Among the Hagen of New Guinea, conversely, virginity is highly prized in brides, and wives are supposed to be chaste. However, sex is thought to be unclean and dangerous for both men and women, and hence the value placed on abstinence is almost as great for males as it is for females (O'Kelly & Carney, 1986). Clearly, sexuality can vary dramatically with cultural context.

The influence of culture on sexuality is particularly striking in the way our society regards sexuality and aging. Elderly people are often considered asexual (Kay & Neelley, 1982), so that, as people age, they commonly fear the loss of sexual interest and ability. Also, sexuality among the aged is sometimes thought of with disgust or amusement in our youth-oriented culture—the same behavior that might be taken as evidence of "virility" at 25 is called "lechery" at 65. North America is not the only part of the world where such myths flourish. Japanese researchers, for instance, have found that a decline in sexual activity among the elderly is partly attributable to cultural expectations (Mamiya, 1984).

The myths about aging and sex affect women and men somewhat differently, both because of gender roles and because of the difference in male and female life spans. The performance-oriented male sexual role is threatened when erections start to occur more slowly, and the female sexual role as an attractive object is threatened when her appearance no longer conforms to the youthful stereotype that is synonymous with beauty in our culture. Physiological changes that occur with age can slow down sexual response: Men may have slower erections with more need for direct genital stimulation, women may lose fatty tissue around the vagina, making intercourse uncomfortable without added lubrication. However, good health and regular sexual activity can promote men's and women's sexual functioning into their 70s and 80s if they do not fall victim to the myth that "old" means "sexless." A particular difficulty for women in heterosexual relationships, however, is that they are extremely likely to outlive their mates. Because there is a shortage of men in the over-65 age group, and because women in our culture tend not to seek out younger partners, widowhood often implies forced celibacy for women whose orientation is exclusively heterosexual. In fact, while only one third of men in their 70s report that they are not having partnered sex, 70% of women in this age group report that they did not have sex with a partner over the past year (Michael et al., 1994).

SEXUAL MOTIVES, VALUES, AND ATTITUDES

Motives

Females and males, at least during the college years, respond differently to the question "What are your motives for having sexual intercourse?" Women tend to stress love and commitment to their partner (e.g., "emotional feelings that were shared"), whereas men emphasize physical needs and pleasure (e.g., "need it," "to gratify myself") (Carroll, Volk, & Hyde, 1985). Twice as many male as female teenagers say they would have sex with a date simply because they were sexually attracted (Pesmen, 1991). Given the changes that are hypothesized to occur over the life cycle in female and male sexuality, we would not necessarily expect to find the same pattern of differences for adults in their 30s or older.

One researcher examined the correlates of sexual experience for women and men in an attempt to test the hypothesis that sexual experience serves a compensatory function by bolstering self-esteem and self-confidence (M. D. Newcomb, 1984). His research found that for men but not for women sexual experience was correlated with assertiveness, education, self-esteem, and a self-perception of invulnerability. This finding could be interpreted to mean that sexual experience enhances self-esteem and self-confidence for men—or it could simply mean that highly self-confident men are better at attracting sexual partners. In any case, the fact that no relationship was found between self-esteem variables and sexual experience for women does suggest a difference in the reasons women and men have for engaging in sexual activity.

Values

There is a stereotype that women and men value different things in heterosexual relationships. For instance, the accepted wisdom says that women place a higher value on love, intimacy, and togetherness, whereas men tend to emphasize the importance of the physical relationship and sexual variety. Evidence on these points is mixed. Clark and Hatfield (1981, as cited in Hatfield, 1983), for example, found some support for the notion that men are more interested than women in sexual variety. They interviewed casual dating and newlywed couples about their desire for variety in sexual experience and found that men tended to wish their sex lives were more exciting while women were more likely to be satisfied with the way things were. The idea that love is more important to women than to men in sexual relationships is supported by some findings but not by others. One study found that 45% of college females but only 8% of college males answered "Always" to the question "For you, is emotional involvement a prerequisite for participating in sexual intercourse?" (Carroll et al., 1985). These researchers estimated that 29% of the variability in attitudes toward casual premarital sex could be explained by gender, suggesting that gender differences are quite a bit larger on this dimension than they are on measures of aggression or cognitive performance (discussed in earlier chapters). Research also shows that women in heterosexual couples feel more passionate and companionate love for their partners than men do, at least until old age (Hatfield, 1983). However, researchers have also found that men tend to be more romantic than women: They are more likely to fall in love quickly, view the relationship in romantic terms, and suffer terribly when the relationship ends (Hill, Rubin, & Peplau, 1976; Rubin, Peplau, & Hill, 1981).

One study (Cochran & Peplau, 1985) examined the importance college students assigned to three kinds of values in heterosexual relationships: attachment (having a close and secure love relationship), autonomy (the freedom to have separate interests apart from a primary relationship), and equality (both partners having equal say in decisions within the relationship). Despite the stereotype that women are more oriented toward intimacy and men toward independence, these researchers found that women and men did not differ in the value they placed on attachment. Women and men were equally concerned with having a secure, committed, sexually exclusive relationship. Also in violation of the stereotype, women placed significantly more value on autonomy and independence than men did. Finally, women attached more importance to equality than men did.

On the whole, there is evidence for both differences and similarities in the value orientations of women and men in sexual relationships. Because most of the research has been conducted with middle-class college students, however, it is impossible to draw general conclusions from these data about the impact of gender on values in sexual relationships.

Attitudes

Attitudes toward sexual activity have changed quite dramatically over the last several decades. In general, Americans, particularly those under the age of 30, have become more permissive of sexual activity, especially premarital sex. A Harris poll taken in the early 1980s showed that 79% of men and 70% of women ages 18 to 29 approved of sexual intercourse for regularly dating couples (Fink, 1983). A later survey of Americans ages 14 to 21 showed that 28% of the females and 16% of the males said they did not intend to have sex before marriage (Pesmen, 1991). These percentages are in sharp contrast to surveys taken in 1937 and 1959, in which 56% and 54% of respondents, respectively, disapproved of premarital intercourse (Hunt, 1974).

According to North American studies, women are generally found to be less permissive than men about sexual behavior. They have much more negative attitudes than men do about casual premarital sex, and women are moderately less approving than men are of premarital sex in a committed relationship. Women are also moderately more likely to feel anxious or guilty about sex and to endorse the double standard. But gender differences have a tendency to narrow with age and also seem to be diminishing over time (Oliver & Hyde, 1993).

Astin's (1985) nationwide representative survey of college freshmen revealed that nearly two thirds of the men but less than one third of the women approved of sexual intercourse between "people who like each other." In a more recent survey of American adolescents, there was more permissiveness. However, females continued to appear somewhat more conservative than males: Only 6% of the females and 21% of the males agreed that it was okay to have sex with someone simply because it's fun (Pesmen, 1991). Among college students in another study, males scored higher than females on every item of a scale measuring sexual permissiveness (Hendrick, Hendrick, Slapion-Foote, & Foote, 1985). The differences were not extreme, however, and the researchers characterized the males as "moderately permissive" and the females as "moderately conservative."

Sexual attitudes involve more than permissiveness, and the latter study, which compared males and females on a spectrum of sexual attitudes, found gender differences on several dimensions. Females tended to score higher than males on sexual responsibility, an orientation that included concern with pregnancy and other consequences of sexual activity for a relationship. Women also scored higher than men on sexual conventionality, a scale concerned with the acceptability of such sexual practices as masturbation, using "sex toys," and using "dirty" words. There was also some tendency for women to give stronger endorsement than men to items measuring sexual communion, an attitude that sex involves close communication and can be "the ultimate in human interaction." Men gave stronger endorsement than women to items assessing sexual instrumentality—a self-centered, physical orientation to sex. However, the latter two differences did not appear when the individual item scores were summed to form scales.

In summary, although there is evidence that the sexual attitudes of women and men are becoming more similar, differences still exist. Researchers are not sure whether the trend toward convergence of male and female sexual attitudes will continue or whether there will be a shift toward more conservatism, reflecting political trends. A major determining factor in the trend will be the media portrayal of sexuality. There is little doubt that our sexual attitudes are shaped by the way sexual relationships are depicted in movies, television, music videos, magazines, and books. If these media continue to emphasize a double standard of sexual behavior, an absence of sexual responsibility for males, and a greater concern among females than males for the relationship context of sexuality, then these attitudinal gender differences are likely to persist.

EXPLAINING THE GENDER DIFFERENCES IN SEXUALITY

Where differences between males and females in sexual behavior exist, they seem to be in the direction of more sexual activity for males, although there seem to be no gender differences in the intensity of sexual response. Men are also more likely than women to be sexually coercive. Several theories have been applied in an effort to explain these differences.

Physiology and Anatomy

Some animal research links testosterone to sexual behavior, and there has been some speculation that in humans men's higher levels of sexual activity are due to their having higher levels of testosterone than women do. The logic of this argument is not overwhelming. It is quite possible, for instance, that women's bodies are more sensitive to testosterone than men's are (Sherfey, 1966; Sherwin, 1988). Some research does link androgen secretion to sexual arousability in humans (Knussman, Christiansen, & Couwenbergs, 1986; Sherwin, 1988), but social factors and past experience apparently outweigh the hormonal effects (Barfield, 1976).

The male–female difference in sexual anatomy has also been postulated as a source of gender differences in sexual behavior. As noted earlier in the chapter, males can easily see their sexual organs and their arousal has obvious, visible signs. Females, however, can visually examine their own genitals only by using a mirror, and their arousal response is not as obvious and unmistakable as the male's erection. This difference may lead males to discover masturbation earlier and to feel more comfortable with their sexual anatomy and responses than females do. This explanation may provide part of the reason for the gender differences in masturbation and other sexual activity.

Sociobiology

The sociobiological approach to behavior (see Chapter 2) postulates that much of our social behavior has evolved as strategies to ensure reproductive success—to produce as many healthy offspring as possible. Sociobiologists see reproduction as the main function of sex and the differences in male and female sexual behavior as stemming from the different conditions that favor reproductive success for the two sexes (e.g., Buss, 1994; Symons, 1979). According to sociobiology, because males can produce millions of sperm, the best way for them to ensure that their genes will be reproduced is to impregnate as many women as possible; hence, the tendency to greater promiscuity among males. Because females can produce only one egg per month, their best reproductive strategy is to be very selective about whom they mate with, choosing someone who is healthy and likely to sire healthy children, and perhaps who will provide safety and security for those children. Sociobiologists even extend their theory to coercive sexuality, arguing that rape is simply a way for men to maximize their reproductive fitness by mating with as many partners as possible (Barash, 1979).

The limited approach taken by sociobiology ignores all the nonreproductive aspects and functions of sexuality. The logic becomes particularly strained when attempting to explain homosexuality and other sexual behaviors that are irrelevant to the production of offspring (see Futuyma & Risch, 1984, for a review and critique of the sociobiological approach to homosexuality). The theory also ignores recent data on female sexuality that show women to be sexually responsive to erotica and to be capable of intense, prolonged sexual pleasure. Although evolution may be one of several influences that has shaped gender differences in sexuality, the explanations of these differences offered by sociobiologists are still speculative. Many of the differences they cite in support of the theory, such as the finding that men are more permissive toward casual sex, can be as easily explained by gender differences in sexual socialization or in women's fear of sexual violence. Convincing evidence for a sociobiological explanation of this difference would involve demonstrating both that the behavior in question has a genetic basis and that it is adaptive for reproductive fitness.

Sociocultural Influences

The double standard has long dictated that women restrict and are restricted in their sexuality more than men are. This difference in what males and females are implicitly given permission to do may well influence the sexual expression and experiences of both. Women, more often watched and warned about sexuality than men are and encouraged to play a "gatekeeper" role, may learn to inhibit their sexual responses. Once in a committed sexual relationship, when they have no reason for inhibition, they may find they have learned the lesson too well: They find it difficult to let go. Men, who are allowed more leeway in terms of masturbation, exposure to erotica, and heterosexual activity and who may even learn to view sex as a way to "prove" their masculinity, may learn early on to treat sex as a goal-oriented activity—the goal being to produce an orgasm or to "score." This narrow focus may cause them to miss out on some of the pleasure of sexual experience. The "sexual scripts" that lead women to associate being "good" with avoiding sex and lead men to associate sex not with intimacy but with achievement and conquest, tend to limit the sexuality of both women and men. They are also the source of a good deal of grief, especially in adolescence and young adulthood, as the two genders find themselves working at cross purposes in their attempts to develop satisfying sexual relationships. As noted in our discussion of sexual attitudes, there has been some relaxation of the double standard in recent years—a change that may explain why males and females have become more similar in their sexual behavior.

The double standard itself is based on the notion that male sexual needs are stronger, and therefore more important, than female sexual needs. This notion is one more reflection of the greater power and status accorded to men than women in our culture. Perhaps we have not come so far from the time when Freudian theory could describe the whole process of psychosexual development as revolving around male anatomy. Despite the vast increase in technical knowledge about sex since Freud's day, some of the assumptions remain unchanged. Sex is still often defined in terms of the penis (Rotkin, 1972). "Real" sex involves male ejaculation into the female vagina. The terms *foreplay* and *afterplay* underline this point. Anything that occurs before or after intercourse is somewhat beside the point, even if it includes female orgasm. Children are still sometimes taught that the female sexual organ is the vagina, when in fact the clitoris is the center for female sexual gratification. Men are still made to feel inadequate if they cannot bring a woman to orgasm during intercourse, despite the research showing that the thrusting of the penis in the vagina is not a particularly effective way to stimulate a woman to orgasm. When the aim of sexual activity is reproduction, intercourse is, of course, necessary. However, when the aim is sexual pleasure and intimacy, intercourse is not necessary, as many gay and lesbian couples will attest. It is quite likely that both women and men would be happier in their sexual relationships if sexual intercourse were defined as just one of the possible expressions of sexuality rather than as the most important one. A redefined sexuality that places as much emphasis on the clitoris as the penis and that removes the performance-in-intercourse orientation for males may help to make sex not one more expression of the status difference between women and men but rather a source of pleasure, self-esteem, and empowerment for both.

SEXUAL ORIENTATION

In May 1991, Heidi Leiter, a 17-year-old high school senior, broke new ground at her high school prom: The date she brought was a woman. The pair became the first openly lesbian couple to attend a high school prom in their region (B. A. Masters, 1991). Reaction of Heidi's classmates was generally unenthusiastic, and her choices apparently isolated her from other students. However, the fact that she was able to be open about her sexual orientation at all is one indication of change in public attitudes about homosexuality.

In recent years, the movement for lesbian and gay rights has had a dramatic influence on public awareness of differences in sexual orientation. Gays, lesbians, and bisexuals, long a virtually invisible minority, are shedding negative labels, refusing to accept stigmatization, and fighting for an end to discrimination against them. Despite some new openness, however, many people hold mistaken beliefs about sexual orientation: what it means, how many people fall into the various categories, how the different orientations come about.

Heterosexuality, Homosexuality, and Bisexuality

Sexual orientation refers to a person's preference for sexual partners of the same or other sex. **Heterosexual** is the label used for a person who prefers partners of the other sex, **homosexual** is the label applied to a person who prefers partners of the same sex, and **bisexual** is the term used to describe a person who can be attracted to partners of either sex. The terms **gay** and **straight** are often used to refer to homosexually oriented and heterosexually oriented persons and their communities, respectively, and women who are sexually and affectionally attracted to other women (i.e., whose sexual orientation is homosexual) are called **lesbians,** after the island of Lesbos. In ancient Greece, Lesbos was the home of the poet Sappho, famous for her love poetry to women.

It is difficult to say how many people practice heterosexuality, homosexuality, or bisexuality because these orientations seem to be points on a continuum rather than completely discrete categories. The data do seem to indicate, however, that more males than females have homosexual experiences and that males are more likely than females to practice exclusively homosexual lifestyles (Hunt, 1974; Kinsey et al., 1948, 1953; Michael et al., 1994). A study that investigated sexual orientation in one sample of adults, based on reported percentage of sexual fantasies and sexual experiences with women and men, found that one third of both females and males reported at least occasionally fantasizing about sexual encounters with same-sex partners. In addition, one third of the males also reported having at least one intimate sexual experience with another man; only 10% of females reported an intimate homosexual experience (Ellis, Burke, & Ames, 1987).

As discussed earlier in the chapter, people can have homosexual experiences without labeling themselves as homosexual, and many people who think of themselves as gay still relate sexually to other-sex partners. Kinsey's conceptualization of heterosexuality–homosexuality as a continuum with many points in between was an important breakthrough in understanding sexual orientation. More recently, Storms (1980) offered a new model of sexual orientation based on two independent dimensions—homoeroticism and heteroeroticism—instead of a single continuum. In this model, a person who is high only in heteroeroticism (sexual attraction and arousal to members of the other gender) tends to be involved only in heterosexual sexual relationships; a person high only in homoeroticism (sexual attraction and arousal to members of his or her own gender) tends to be involved only in homosexual sexual relationships; and a person high in both tends to be involved in both. This scheme allows us to think of homoeroticism and heteroeroticism as different dimensions rather than opposites: being high on one does not automatically mean being low on the other.

A major difficulty with research into the frequency of different sexual orientations, the reasons for the differences, and the characteristics of different sexual orientation groups is the lack of agreed-upon conceptual and operational definitions of sexual orientation. One survey of 228 research articles found that only 28 of them provided a conceptual definition of sexual orientation. These definitions varied from study to study, including or excluding such elements as physical sexual activity; affectional attachment; erotic fantasies; arousal; self-identification as bisexual, heterosexual, or homosexual; and awareness of attraction to one sex (Shively, Jones, & De Cecco, 1983/84). There is confusion even among researchers, then, about the exact meaning of sexual orientation. Indeed, some researchers have called for an abandonment of such categorical labels as heterosexual, bisexual, and homosexual, arguing that vast individual differences within each category make the distinctions artificial (Paul, 1985). Others have called upon researchers to stop imposing identities and labels on people and to focus instead on articulating a descriptive language of relationships (De Cecco & Shively, 1983/84).

It is possible that researchers' struggle to come to grips with the meaning of sexual orientation will eventually lead to a major reevaluation of our understanding of sexual desire and sexual relationships. One source of movement in this direction is the attempt to reevaluate sexual orientation from a social constructionist perspective. Janice Bohan (1996) notes that psychology has approached sexual orientation from "the essentialist assumption that sexual orientation is a primary, nuclear quality of self with which each individual must come to terms" as opposed to "a socially constructed meaning imposed on experiences that could equally well accommodate myriad other meanings" (p. 9). In other words, if, as a culture, we had learned to put different interpretations and labels on the experiences associated with sexual attraction, we might think very differently about sexual orientation. However, collectively we have learned a particular set of conceptual categories and terms about sexual orientation: "the culture we live in constructs sexual orientation as a core, nuclear, essential defining attribute of identity, which can be defined by membership in one of two (or at best three) categories. Hence, individuals living in this culture . . . experience their own and others' sexual orientation in these terms" (p. 9). So, in our culture, if a person feels attraction to members of her or his own sex, she or he is likely to accept, or at least consider strongly, a lesbian or gay identity—because that is what such feelings are interpreted to mean.

As Bohan (1996) points out, most research on sexual orientation has been carried out in an essentialist framework, treating sexual orientation as a core quality of an individual, the cause and correlates of which can be discovered. Using this approach, scientists have been only moderately successful; they do not agree on what causes people to develop different sexual orientations. There is a fair amount of negative evidence—that is, studies failing to find relationships between various factors and particular sexual orientations. As discussed in Chapter 5, for example, there is suggestive, but still insufficient, evidence for a biological basis for homosexuality. Evidence for various environmental causes is just as weak. One very comprehensive study of homosexuality found no evidence that homosexuality could be traced to disturbed parental relationships, being labeled by others as a homosexual, unpleasant early heterosexual experiences, or being seduced at a young age by an older person of one's own sex (A. P. Bell et al., 1981). A study that set out to investigate the idea that women's traumatic sexual experiences with men might be a significant factor in the development of a lesbian identity found no support for this notion (Brannock & Chapman, 1990). The only significant difference found between lesbians and heterosexual women was that heterosexual women reported more categories of traumatic heterosexual experiences than lesbians did.

Why has it been so difficult to uncover the antecedents of sexual orientation? Perhaps because researchers have allowed their assumptions about sexuality to narrow their approach to the question. First, despite increasing evidence that there are many kinds of homosexual and bisexual preferences, just as there are many kinds of heterosexual preferences, researchers have tended to treat each category as discrete rather than fuzzy and to look for a single cause to explain each sexual orientation. Probably there are many different causes and combinations of causes that lead to many different shades of sexual orientation and experience. Second, researchers have often been guided by theories that suggest sexual orientation is always "set" very early in life. In fact, many individual case histories suggest that sexual identity and orientation can evolve and change across the life span; for example, many bisexual women do not have their first sexual experience with another woman until middle age (Blumstein & Schwartz, 1976), many women make the transition from heterosexuality to a lesbian identity in adulthood (Kitzinger & Wilkinson, 1995), and some lesbian women also adopt a heterosexual identity in later life (Bart, 1993). Finally, researchers have operated under the assumption that heterosexuality is the natural state, and they have spent their energy trying to explain the occurrence of the "deviant" orientations of homosexuality and bisexuality. Only recently have researchers begun to study the underpinnings of heterosexual identity instead of taking it for granted as something that unfolds "naturally" (Eliason, 1995; Freedman & Lips, 1993). An alternative approach might be more fruitful. For example, what if bisexuality were considered as the natural state? Then the important questions would concern not what errors in development and upbringing lead to homosexuality but rather what leads people to reject half the population as potential sex partners in order to become exclusively heterosexual or exclusively homosexual. Or what if no particular object choice, but only the existence of sexual desire, were considered natural? Then research would focus on the combinations of factors leading to different possible foci of that sexual desire.

Attitudes Toward Homosexuality

Homosexuality is still considered a stigma in our culture, so much so that Lehne (1976) coined the term *homophobia* to describe the widespread irrational fear and intolerance of homosexuality. Gay men and lesbians risk discrimination in employment and housing, and "coming out" as gay can precipitate the loss of support of friends and family.

Discrimination on the basis of sexual orientation, not prohibited by the Civil Rights Act of 1964, is legal in most workplaces in the United States, although some states, cities, and counties have adopted antidiscrimination ordinances. In Virginia, a law banning gay bars was overturned only in 1991 (J. F. Harris, 1991), and in some states laws still exist that allow law officers to enter a private home to arrest consenting adults performing homosexual acts. Thousands of service persons have been dismissed from the U.S. military over the past decade because of their homosexuality. Often these have been people whose military records were outstanding, as in the case of Col. Margarethe Cammermeyer, a 30-year veteran with meritorious service in Vietnam and a Bronze Star, who admitted to being a lesbian during an interview in which she was being considered for the position of chief nurse of the National Guard. The epitaph of one discharged air force veteran, Leonard Matlovich, points to the irony in the way he was treated: "When I was in the military, they gave me a medal for killing two men and a discharge for loving one" (Duke, 1991).

One apologist for the military's position on homosexuality, Col. Michael McAleer, is quoted as saying that it is the military's sworn duty to defend the beliefs of Americans—and that part of what Americans believe is that homosexuality is against Christian ideals (Duke, 1991). Many people do indeed hold negative attitudes about homosexuality. Only 17% of females and 14% of males in a survey of American adolescents said they had "no problem" with the idea of homosexuality (Pesmen, 1991). Research on university campuses in the United States indicates that at least two thirds of lesbian and gay students report that they have been verbally insulted, one quarter have been threatened with physical violence because of their orientation, and nearly all have overheard derogatory comments about gays and lesbians (Herek, 1993).

Homosexuality is more negatively sanctioned in males than in females, particularly by men (Whitley & Kite, 1995), perhaps because, as members of the higher status sex, males can be less easily forgiven for deviating from their assigned role than females can. Homosexuality also receives more disapproval from male than female college students, but there are no gender differences in attitudes in general adult samples. The bias against homosexuality is apparent in the evaluation of lesbian and gay love relationships. In one study, heterosexual undergraduates presented with identical information about a hypothetical couple described that couple as "less in love" and "less satisfied with their relationship" when the couple was portrayed as gay or lesbian than when it was portrayed as heterosexual (Testa, Kinder, & Ironson, 1987).

These negative attitudes have made it difficult to study lesbian and gay populations. The gay and lesbian population is difficult for researchers to identify, a situation that may result in the use of biased samples to draw conclusions about these groups. In addition, these attitudes have a direct impact on the feelings of gays and lesbians, making it difficult, for instance, for researchers to unravel the correlates of identifying oneself as gay or lesbian or of incorporating same-gender sexual relationships from being labeled deviant or of being a victim or potential victim of discrimination. These concerns were especially pronounced when Evelyn Hooker, the first psychologist to study a sample of normal gay men at a time when homosexuality was triply stigmatized as "a sin, a crime, and a disease," began her work in 1953. It was the McCarthy era, and the consequences of being labeled homosexual could be disastrous. Thus, Hooker (1993) gave the highest priority to developing a sense of confidentiality and trust:

The first absolute condition was secrecy and confidentiality. By great good fortune, our home was a very spacious estate of an acre of ground with a garden study separate from the house. It was there that the research was conducted. Once a person opened the garden gate, he was invisible to the neighbors. Without this superb place in which to conduct the research, I would never have attempted it. (pp. 450–451)

The words of Joseph Beam, a gay African American writer who died of AIDS at the age of 33, capture some of the feeling of isolation that can accompany the acceptance of this identity:

In the winter of '79, in grad school, in the hinterlands of Iowa, I thought I was the first black gay man to have ever lived. . . . I lived a guarded existence: I watched how I crossed my legs, held my cigarettes, the brightness of the colors I wore. I was sure that some effeminate action would alert the world to my homosexuality. . . . Several years passed before I realized that my burden of shame could be a source of strength. (as quoted in Trescott, 1991, p. C5)

A contributor to negative attitudes toward gay men has been the emergence of and publicity given to AIDS. In North America, AIDS appeared first and most noticeably among gay and bisexual men; some evangelists originally pointed to it as a "plague" or a judgment on these groups for their sexual behavior. The atmosphere of fear surrounding the disease has intensified homophobic attitudes, leading, in some cases, to the treatment of all gay men as if the slightest contact with them were potentially deadly. There is no justification for such treatment; the virus that causes AIDS is not transmitted through casual contact but through the exchange of blood or semen.

SEXUALITY AND POWER: EROTICA, PORNOGRAPHY, AND COERCIVE SEXUALITY

Part of the stereotype that men have a stronger sex drive than women is a belief that men are more frequently and more easily sexually aroused by erotic material. The consequences of this belief for women's and men's feelings about their own sexuality and for the sexual power relationship between the sexes are enormous. Most material that is meant to be sexually arousing is produced for a male audience. Perhaps because it is explicitly geared to men rather than to both sexes, this material tends to present a view of women that is simultaneously idealized (in terms of physical beauty) and belittling (women are portrayed as passive objects of sexual desire, as bodies rather than people). Not surprisingly, women have never been encouraged to view this type of material; its very presence sometimes renders a store, a pub, or an entire section of a city virtually off-limits for women. One impact of the presence of large amounts of male-oriented erotic material, then, is to make real live women feel unwelcome and out of place in the areas where images and fantasies of sexuality are sold. Such a situation is highly unlikely to foster in women a sense of empowerment and joy in their own sexuality. To make matters even more difficult, there is an increasing trend toward the portrayal of brutalization and degradation of women in sexually oriented materials, a development that makes such materials even less palatable to women and that reinforces the myths of male sexual dominance and female sexual powerlessness and passivity. The development of an entire industry dedicated to producing and marketing sexually arousing materials specifically for a male audience obviously makes at least good economic sense: The pornography industry makes millions of dollars per year in sales to men. But does it make sense on any other dimension? Are women really not interested in erotic materials? What impact does the consumption of existing erotica and pornography have on men? And how does pornography fit into the larger problem of coercive sexuality?

Responses to Erotica

The women in the early Kinsey surveys reported less responsiveness than the men to most types of erotic materials. However, more recent studies suggest that women and men are not very different in their arousal response to erotic stories, pictures, and films. In general, it appears that women can be as physically aroused as men by the typically available X-rated films and videos (Griffitt, 1987), and women and men can masturbate to orgasm equally quickly when viewing these materials (Fisher, Pollack, & Malatesta, 1986). Yet women are less likely than men to seek these materials out. This fits with the commonly reported finding that women engage in sexual fantasy less than men do (Leitenberg & Henning, 1995). However, the latter authors also speculate that most commercial pornography is aimed at, and fits better with, the sexual fantasies of men than those of women:

> If one examines the typical X-rated movie, one immediately sees naked bodies engaged in sexual activity without much story line, gradual buildup, affection, emotional ties, and so forth. The fantasy being portrayed is primarily the male fantasy of multiple female sexual partners ever ready for sexual activity of any kind without any chance of the man being rejected. On the other hand, the primary fantasy of the typical romance novel is a woman who inflames the passion and lifelong love of a desirable man under difficult circumstances. The strong, dominant man is overcome by feelings of love and sweeps the heroine away. (p. 484)

There is an obvious problem with relying on self-reports to assess sexual responsiveness to erotic material: People may not want to admit they are sexually aroused. Thus, researchers in this area often try to obtain physiological measures of sexual arousal as well as self-reports. For men, such a physiological measure can be obtained using a device called a penile strain gauge—a flexible loop that fits around the base of the penis and measures vasocongestion. For women, arousal is also measured through vasocongestion, using a photoplethysmograph—a tampon-like acrylic cylinder that fits inside the entrance to the vagina. A groundbreaking study by Julia Heiman (1977) used these devices to show that what subjects report about sexual arousal in response to erotica does not always reflect what their bodies are experiencing. Heiman had male and female participants listen to one of four kinds of audiotapes: erotic (explicit descriptions of heterosexual sex), romantic (a couple expressing affection and tenderness but not engaging in sex), erotic-romantic (containing both explicitly sexual and romantic elements), and control (neutral conversation). Each set of tapes also contained variations in the stories according to who initiated the activity (female-initiated vs. male-initiated) and whose physical responses were the focus of the description (male-centered vs. female-centered). In general, she found few differences between males and females in their physiological and self-reported arousal by the tapes: Both men and women showed the most responsiveness, both physiologically and in their self-reports, to the tapes containing explicit sex, both the erotic and erotic-romantic tapes. Neither sex tended to respond to the romantic or control tapes. Also, for both males and females, the female-initiated, female-centered tape was the most arousing. One difference did emerge, however. Although both women and men showed a high correlation between physiological and self-reported measures of arousal, women were significantly more likely than men to "miss" their physiological arousal. When men were physically aroused, they never failed to notice and report it. About half the women, conversely, did not rate themselves as aroused when physiological measures indicated that they were. As noted earlier in the chapter, it is harder to ignore an erect penis than a moist vagina; it appears that women can sometimes be unaware of the early stages of their own physical arousal.

The gender difference in awareness of arousal may have as much to do with differences in sexual attitudes as with anatomy. Perhaps the prevalence of the double standard causes some women to internalize their "gatekeeper" role so strongly that they inhibit acknowledgment of sexual arousal. Support for this notion comes from a study by Morokoff (1985), who found that women high in the tendency to feel guilty about sex reported less arousal but showed higher physiological arousal while watching erotic videotapes than did women who were low in sex guilt. The tendency to regard sex as "forbidden," then, may be associated with both a refusal to acknowledge sexual arousal and a tendency to respond with strong physiological arousal to the erotic stimuli.

Impact of Erotica and Pornography on Behavior

There are several areas in which it might be reasonable to expect an impact as a result of viewing or listening to sexually arousing material. There might be an effect on the level of sexual interest, the performance of particular sexual acts, the perception of one's sexual partner, or satisfaction with one's sexual relationships. There is little evidence that exposure to erotica has any long-term effects on sexual interest or behavior, but there are indications that it can affect the sexual interest and behavior of both sexes in the short term. For instance, one study of male exposure to sexually explicit slides found that in the week following there was no increase in sexual activity although there was a significant increase in masturbation on the day of exposure (M. Brown, Amoroso, & Ware, 1976).

Exposure to erotic material may affect a man's evaluation of his mate. Men, but not women, who saw a series of nude photographs from *Playboy, Penthouse,* and *Playgirl* magazines later rated their mates as less sexually attractive than did their counterparts, who were exposed instead to pictures of abstract art (Gutierres, Kenrick, & Goldberg, 1983). Research also shows that even nonviolent pornography may reduce male sensitivity to female victims of sexual assault by making women appear sexually promiscuous—in other words, by suggesting that women are "asking" to be raped (Zillman & Weaver, 1989). However, other researchers have failed to find any link between exposure to nonviolent pornography and attitudes toward women or rape (Padgett, Brislin-Slutz, & Neal, 1989). Research does not appear to have addressed the question of how exposure to erotica and pornography affects women's and men's own self-perceptions and body image. One might, for example, predict that exposure to the photographs of apparently flawlessly beautiful women in magazines such as *Playboy* could shake a normal-looking woman's self-confidence in her own attractiveness.

Because so much of the sexually arousing material that is produced for men tends to portray women more as objects than as human beings, it is not surprising that there has been a trend toward increasing portrayals of violence against women in such material. When explicit violence is added to sexually arousing material, the issues of impact become even more complex. There is concern that a viewer who learns to associate sexual arousal with depictions of rape scenes, for example, may be tempted to try rape in real life. Moreover, in pornography, a woman who is raped, humiliated, or brutalized is usually shown to resist initially, but eventually to become sexually aroused by the way she is treated. Exposure to this type of fantasy may encourage men to behave in sexually coercive ways in the mistaken belief that the experience will not ultimately be a bad one for the woman. Research now indicates that exposure to sexually violent pornography can increase men's acceptance of interpersonal violence against women and of rape myths such as "Every woman secretly wants to be raped" (Demaré, Briere, & Lips, 1988; Malamuth & Check, 1981). Repeated exposure to violent pornography also results in decreased sensitivity to female victims of violence in nonsexual contexts (Linz, Donnerstein, & Penrod, 1984). Furthermore, laboratory studies in which males are exposed to aggressive or nonaggressive pornography and then given the opportunity to behave aggressively against another person by delivering electric shocks show that exposure to aggressive, but not nonaggressive, pornography increases the aggressive behavior of male participants against females but not against males (Donnerstein, 1980, 1983; Malamuth, 1984). Exposure to aggressive pornography is strongly related to arousability to rape scenes, acceptance of rape myths, and self-reported likelihood of committing rape (Briere, Corne, Runta, & Malamuth, 1984). Finally, a survey of college males indicates that self-reported use of sexually violent, but not nonviolent, pornography plays a significant role in predicting self-reported likelihood of using sexual force or rape against women and of self-reported use of actual sexual coercion or force (Demaré et al., 1988; Demaré, Lips, & Briere, 1993).

In summary, although exposure to pornography does not seem to have a major, lasting impact on sexual behavior, there is evidence that violent pornography can have an impact on men's aggressive behavior against women, as well as on their attitudes toward violence against women and toward female victims. However, the correlational research is equally suggestive of the possibility that men who are predisposed to sexual violence and who already hold disparaging attitudes toward women are more likely than other men to use violent pornography. The sexual socialization of males provides the market for such material, and the material reinforces the way many men have been taught to view women. Little research has addressed the impact of exposure to violent pornography on women, probably because men are the main consumers of pornography. However, since violent pornography is now a fairly visible feature of the media environment, it may well be having an impact even on those who are not its intended audience. Individual women often report that they feel humiliated and angry when forced to stand next to a rack of pornographic magazines at the checkout counter of their local store; such feelings are compounded when women have their children with them. Women speak of feeling violated and hurt when confronted with the violent antiwoman images in pornography, particularly when they discover that their male partners are consumers of such images. And one South African study shows that viewing images of sexual violence—or other violence—against women can cause women to feel disempowered (Reid & Finchilescu, 1995). There seems little doubt that exposure to pornography affects women's feelings about themselves and their attitudes toward men, although these relationships have not been extensively researched.

Coercive Sexuality

Relating sexually to another person implies exposing oneself to that person, at least physically and often emotionally. That exposure gives the partners some power over each other. In addition, knowing that one is desirable and desired sexually can confer a sense of power and secure self-esteem. Thus, sexuality almost always involves issues of vulnerability and power. Perhaps it should not be surprising, then, to find that power and dominance can sometimes overwhelm the relationship aspects, even the physical pleasure aspects, of sexuality—that sex can become an expression of dominance rather than of love or lust. There is a very noticeable gender difference here: Sexual coercion or violence is much more likely to be used by men than women. In a social context that tends to accept and encourage male dominance in so many situations, such a gender difference is almost inevitable.

RAPE   Forcing sexual relations on someone against that person's choice is a common crime of sexual violence. In fact, most people would argue that there is nothing sexual about this violent act—so what is it doing in a chapter on sexuality? **Rape** is discussed here because so many people, perhaps particularly men, include rape in their understanding of sexuality, and something that starts out construed by the participants as a sexual encounter can become a violent one instead. Interviews with a random sample of San Francisco women led researchers to conclude that a woman faces a 26% chance of being raped during her lifetime (D. E. H. Russell & Howell, 1983). One reviewer found that most estimates of the prevalence of rape or sexual assault among adult women range from 14% to 25% (Koss, 1993). Although this figure is much higher than police reports of rape, it is widely acknowledged that rape is one of the most underreported crimes (Koss, Heise, & Russo, 1994). According to the results of the federally funded National Women's Study, 683,000 American women were raped in 1990, and 12.1 million American women have been raped at least once ("Estimate of Rape Victims," 1992). The Bureau of Justice Statistics showed that in 1998 women were the targets of 333,000 rapes or sexual assaults (U.S. Department of Justice, 1999). More than half of rapes or sexual assaults are committed by friends or acquaintances of the victim, and more than one quarter are committed by someone with whom the woman had an intimate relationship (U.S. Department of Justice, 1995). Half the women who reported they had been raped during 1992 were younger than 18 years old, and 16% were younger than 12 (U.S. Department of Justice, 1994a). Statistics on forcible rapes actually reported to law enforcement agencies (which do not include the many cases in which the rape was not reported or force was not used) show that more than 96,000 such crimes occurred in the United States in 1997 (U.S. Department of Justice, 1999). One study found that 14% of a sample of women who had ever been married had been raped by a husband or ex-husband (D. E. H. Russell, 1983b); another study found marital rape to be a common correlate of wife-battering (Frieze, 1983).

Men have less reason to fear rape than women, unless they are in prison, where the rape of men by other men is common (Lockwood, 1980). However, there are rare instances in which men are raped by women (Sarrel & Masters, 1982). Although the latter occurrence might seem physically impossible, it is not; penile erection is not under strict conscious control and may occur in response to such emotions as anger or fear.

College students have been found to estimate that 45% of men would commit rape if they could be sure they would not be caught and that 32% of women would enjoy being raped if no one would know about it. When these same students were asked to project their own reactions, 51% of the men reported at least some likelihood that they would commit rape if they would not be caught, but only 2% of the women reported any likelihood at all that they would enjoy being raped (Malamuth, Haber, & Feshbach, 1980). The average number of college males indicating some possibility that they would rape a woman under certain conditions has been estimated to be about 35% (Malamuth, 1981), although in different samples it can be as high as close to 60% (Briere & Malamuth, 1983) or as low as 17% (Demaré et al., 1988). The self-reported likelihood of rape is correlated with acceptance of rape myths, fantasies about forced sex, and sexual arousal in response to rape depictions.

There is some evidence that men may be reluctant to recognize their own sexual aggression. In one survey, 54% of women said they had been sexually victimized or coerced in some way, but only 25% of men said that they had engaged in any sexual aggression (Koss, Gidycz, & Wisniewski, 1987). The large discrepancy suggests that men do not recognize, or acknowledge, their behavior as sexually coercive. And who is most likely to be sexually coercive? One model suggests that the men who are most likely to be sexually coercive against women are those who engage in a lot of casual, impersonal sex and who are high in hostility toward and desire to dominate women (Malamuth, 1996).

Attitudes about the acceptability of force in sexual interactions have an early start. When Zellman and Goodchilds (1983) questioned a broad spectrum of Los Angeles teenagers, they found that only 21% of them replied that, under each of nine specific conditions, it was definitely not all right for "a guy to hold a girl down and force her to have sexual intercourse." Force was viewed as most acceptable in cases where the girl had led the boy on or gotten him sexually excited, or when the couple had been dating for a long time. Both male and female teenagers were reluctant to define forced sex as rape, particularly when the couple involved was portrayed as dating steadily, and they tended to assign some of the blame for forced sex to the female. These findings reflect the presence of the traditional double standard in teenagers' attitudes, particularly in the stereotype that it is the girl's responsibility to control sexual behavior. Against such a background, it is perhaps not surprising that a significant number of college males say there is some possibility that they would commit rape.

College students' self-reported attitudes about rape may stem in part from the prevalence of rape on college campuses. As many as 27.5% of college women in the United States and 23.3% of college women in Canada have experienced rape or attempted rape (Koss, et al., 1994). The danger of rape on campuses has become even more serious in recent years with the availability of "date rape" drugs, such as Rohypnol, which can be slipped into a drink, quickly rendering a woman unconscious and unable to resist. Few women report their experiences of rape or sexual assault, perhaps because campus administrations have traditionally treated rape as a prank that got out of hand rather than as a crime. However, the consequences of academic institutions' silence in the face of rape are very negative for female students: Victims may drop out of classes or even leave school, and a ripple effect through the female student population may diminish confidence levels and assertiveness (Hirsch, 1990). The words of one young college graduate, several years after being gang-raped at a fraternity party during her junior year, provide some sense of the pervasive, lasting effects of such an experience: "I'm a lot more hesitant about things, more cautious. I'm much more comfortable with things I'm used to. I think I'm probably more scared. Like, I'm much more comfortable just being home" (as quoted in Hirsch, 1990, p. 56).

WHY IS SEXUAL ASSAULT SO COMMON?   The finding that many ordinary men say there is some likelihood they would commit rape lends support to the argument, often made by feminists (e.g., Brownmiller, 1975; D. E. H. Russell, 1984), that a tendency toward sexual aggression against women is part of the traditional masculine gender role. Males are socialized to be dominant and aggressive, and there are many messages, including those contained in violent pornography, that it is appropriate to express these tendencies in a sexual context. Clearly, rape is not simply a result of a sexually frustrated male's need for an outlet: Self-reported adequacy and importance of his sex life are not related to a man's self-reported likelihood of rape (Briere & Malamuth, 1983). The high incidence of gang rape (a rape committed by more than one assailant) also points to the conclusion that rape is a way of proving masculinity and dominance, rather than achieving sexual release. The feminine gender role may also contribute to rape, in that females are socialized to be passive, weak, and fearful—prime qualities for the construction of vulnerable victims. In fact, research on the avoidance of rape shows that women whose socialization does not reflect the traditional feminine image are more successful at avoiding attempted rape (Bart, 1980). Bart found that background differences involving women's autonomy, competence, and self-reliance were related to the ability to avoid rape—for example, size and weight, never being married, regular sports involvement, knowledge of first aid and self-defense, and assertiveness training. Moreover, in the actual attempted rape situation, women who used the most strategies to avoid rape were the most successful; the likelihood of being raped increased when the woman relied on only one strategy to avoid it. These data suggest that women should be prepared to use many methods of avoiding rape and that reliance on such "feminine" modes of influence as pleading and reasoning with the rapist is ineffective.

A set of social norms, based on the double standard, that suggest only "virtuous" women deserve full protection from sexual assault also contributes to the prevalence of rape. In certain Latin American countries—Costa Rica, Ecuador, and Guatemala—the law does not recognize forced sexual intercourse as rape unless the woman is chaste and honest (Heise, Pitanguy, & Germain, 1993), and in the courts of Pakistan, the testimony of women who are determined to be of "easy virtue" is heavily discounted (Koss et al., 1994). The rape of a prostitute is thought by some to be a contradiction in terms. One Australian judge, for instance, noted during sentencing of a man who had raped a prostitute at knifepoint that rape was less traumatizing for prostitutes than for other women because prostitutes were involved in sex as a business (Magazanik, 1991).

A man's rape of his wife has also been thought, until recently, to be a contradiction in terms. The thinking was that marriage gave a man full sexual access to his wife, so there could be no such thing as rape in the marriage relationship. The wife's willingness to engage in sex on any particular occasion was not relevant. In 1977, Oregon became the first U.S. state to make marital rape illegal, and since then all other states have followed suit (Neft & Levine, 1997). Until 1983, Canadian law said that a man who raped his wife, even if the couple were separated, could be charged with assault only if there were injuries; that has now changed (Duffy & Momirov, 1997). In 1990, France ruled that rape could exist within marriage ("Rapist Husband," 1991); Britain has made this change more recently.

INCEST   Incest, defined as sexual relations between relatives, is often coercive and exploitative, because in many cases it involves an older powerful relative forcing sex on a younger, inexperienced one. Studies show that female children tend to be sexually victimized by adult males more often than male children are victimized by males or females. Between 4% and 12% of all women surveyed report a childhood sexual encounter with an adult male relative, and for 1 woman in 100 that adult male relative is her father (Herman, 1981). In a 1991 study in three states—Alabama, North Dakota, and South Carolina—20% of female rape victims under the age of 12 had been raped by their fathers, and 46% had been raped by other family members (U.S. Department of Justice, 1994a). Fewer men report having been sexually victimized by an adult during childhood; among those who do, the adult is far more likely to have been male than female. It appears that men are far more likely than women to try to take sexual liberties with children. This may be because men tend to hold more power in the family situation than women do, giving them a sense that they have a right to impose their will on other family members and making it unlikely that others will interfere. It may also be due partly to our culture's sexual socialization of men and women. Men are conditioned to be attracted to sexual partners who are young, delicate, and naive—the qualities of children—whereas women do not learn to associate these characteristics with sexual desirability.

SUMMARY

Research on gender and sexuality has occurred in the context of a double standard of behavior for women and men. Men have been thought to have the stronger sex drive, and thus they have implicitly been given more permission to engage in sexual activity. However, research indicates that, physiologically, there are strong similarities between males and females in their response to sexual stimulation. The main difference is that females are capable of multiple orgasms whereas most males are not. Women, however, are more likely than men to report difficulty in achieving orgasm, at least during intercourse. Both sexes can masturbate to orgasm quickly and easily; however, women are considerably less likely than men to masturbate. Women who do masturbate are less likely to have trouble reaching orgasm during sexual activity with a partner.

Frequency of premarital intercourse has increased over the years, especially among women, leading to a reduction in the gap between men and women in the extent of such activity. Men still tend to have more sexual partners before marriage than women do and are more likely than women to feel positive about their first experience of intercourse. Men are more likely than women to report engaging in extramarital sex. Among heterosexuals, the possibility of pregnancy has a greater effect on female than on male sexuality: Women are more likely than men to report that fear of pregnancy interferes with the free expression of their sexuality, and women are more likely than men to take responsibility for birth control.

The AIDS epidemic appears to be having some impact on sexual attitudes and behavior. Sexually active teenagers of both sexes worry about contracting the disease although they often fail to use condoms, which reduce the risk. Gay males have become significantly more cautious in their sexual behavior.

No single explanation seems to account for gender differences in sexual behavior. Differences in anatomy may provide some of the basis for the differences in the way males and females explore their feelings and are socialized, by both parents and peers, with respect to sexuality. Different cultural standards of sexual behavior for women and men contribute to the development of different value orientations, attitudes, and behavior. The cultural tendency to define sexuality in terms of male anatomy and needs leads to coercive sexual behavior by males and often to frustration and dissatisfaction for both females and males in heterosexual relationships. Yet, despite all this, a reasonable number of people achieve happy, satisfying heterosexual relationships. Apparently males and females are not so different that their shared humanity and concern for relationships cannot transcend the difficulties wrought by anatomy, gender-role socialization, and the cultural ideology of male dominance—at least some of the time!

Men are more likely than women to report engaging in homosexual activity and to define themselves as exclusively homosexual. Homosexuality is more negatively sanctioned in men than women in our culture, and men also express more disapproval of homosexuality than women do. The AIDS epidemic has stimulated increased levels of discrimination against gay men, worsening an already difficult situation. On the positive side, individuals in gay and lesbian relationships do not have to accommodate the gender-role expectations that have such a powerful impact on heterosexual relationships.

Some gender differences exist in the motives, attitudes, and values surrounding sexuality. In general, sex seems to be more closely linked to emotional and affectional ties for women than for men in our culture. However, within sexual relationships defined as love relationships, men are as concerned as women are (some research suggests even more concerned) with attachment. In general, women hold less sexually permissive attitudes than men do, and show some tendency to be more conventional and responsible in their approach to sexual activity.

Both men and women can be easily aroused by erotic material or fantasies. However, most commercially produced erotic material is aimed at heterosexual males. Much of that material depicts sexual violence against women as sexually arousing. Research shows a link between men's consumption of such sexually violent material and tendencies to accept violence against women, to actually behave aggressively against women in laboratory situations, to report some likelihood of raping a woman if given a clear opportunity, and to report having achieved intercourse with a woman through coercion or physical force. The availability of violent pornography is only one source of the message to males in our culture that the use of aggression and power in a sexual context is often permitted and approved. The high incidence of rape and incest seems to result not from uncontrollable male sexual desire but from masculine socialization toward sexual dominance and an ideology that allows males to feel they have a right to impose their will on females. Females' frequent lack of success in combating these assaults stems partly from the feminine gender-role socialization toward passivity and powerlessness. Rape has much more to do with power than with sexuality. The high prevalence of this crime is a strong signal that social power differences are built into gender differences. If we imagine a society in which rape is an extremely rare occurrence, we are probably imagining one in which women and men hold equal status.

KEY TERMS

double standard
vasocongestion
myotonia
excitement phase
plateau phase
orgasm
G-spot
resolution phase

refractory period
human immunodeficiency
    virus (HIV)
acquired
    immunodeficiency
    syndrome (AIDS)
heterosexual
homosexual

bisexual
gay
straight
lesbians
rape

FOR ADDITIONAL READING

Bohan, Janis S. (1996). *Psychology and sexual orientation: Coming to terms.* New York: Routledge. The author discusses the meaning of sexual orientation and the diversity of experiences connected with lesbian, gay, and bisexual identity development, partnering, parenting, and community. She includes a thoughtful examination of the various psychological theories about sexual orientation and of the debate between essentialist and constructionist approaches to understanding these issues.

Herdt, Gilbert. (1997). *Same sex, different cultures.* Boulder, CO: Westview Press. A cultural anthropologist explores gay and lesbian lives in the context of a variety of cultures. The book challenges many cultural myths about sexual orientation.

Laqueur, Thomas. (1990). *Making sex: Body and gender from the Greeks to Freud.* Cambridge, MA: Harvard University Press. A social historian looks at the ways scientific thinking about sex has mirrored social attitudes and morality.

McCormick, Naomi B. (1994). *Sexual salvation: Affirming women's sexual rights and pleasures.* Westport, CT: Praeger. An expert in the psychology of sexuality writes about the sexuality of all women: women of all sexual orientations, women of color, women with disabilities and chronic illnesses. She includes chapters on women sex trade workers, pornography, and woman-affirming modes of sexual fulfillment.

Sang, Barbara, Warshow, Joyce, & Smith, Adrienne. (Eds.). (1991). *Lesbians at midlife: The creative transition.* San Francisco: Spinsters Book Company. This anthology by and about lesbians from ages 40 to 60 includes personal perspectives on topics such as mother–daughter relationships, menopause, body image, couple relationships in transition, and being single at midlife.

Scully, Diana. (1990). *Understanding sexual violence: A study of convicted rapists.* Boston: Unwin Hyman. A sociologist interviews men convicted of and incarcerated for rape.

Tiefer, Leonore. (1995). *Sex is not a natural act and other essays.* Boulder, CO: Westview Press. The author, a feminist sexologist, writes critically, incisively, and with a great deal of wit about the naturalistic assumptions of the biomedical model of sexuality.

Wyatt, Gail. (1997). *Stolen women: Reclaiming our sexuality, taking back our lives.* New York: Wiley. The author is renowned for her studies of African American women's sexual attitudes and behaviors. She writes in a compelling way about how the history of slavery and exploitation has influenced African American women's sexuality, often leaving them "captives to stereotypes."

CHAPTER 8

Hormonal &
Reproductive
Connections

*I*n England, during the past two decades, several women have been given reduced sentences or probation for murder because they committed the crimes during the week before the onset of their menstrual cycle—and each used the defense that she suffered from severe premenstrual syndrome (PMS; Sommer, 1984). PMS was cited as a source of diminished responsibility, making the women prone to uncontrollable acts of violence during the premenstrual period. A Virginia physician, arrested for driving under the influence of alcohol, successfully used PMS as her defense ("PMS Defense," 1991).

There are numerous other anecdotes of women's hormonal or reproductive physiology being labeled a source of instability. Several years ago, a Canadian judge disallowed the evidence given by a woman in her 50s because, he said, women at that stage of life (presumably referring to menopause) were known to imagine things. And once, during an interview about my research on the psychology of pregnancy, a reporter greeted my finding that most pregnant women did not report unusual emotional difficulties with open astonishment and disbelief: "Everyone knows," she sputtered, "that women go a little crazy for 9 months when they're pregnant"! "Everyone knows," indeed, that the hormonal changes involved in female reproductive processes—menstruation, pregnancy, childbirth, postpartum adjustment, breastfeeding, menopause—render women less emotionally stable than men. But is "everyone" correct? Are the physiological processes involved in reproduction really debilitating to women?

And what about men? Researchers have suggested, for instance, that high testosterone is related to antisocial behavior (Dabbs, 1992), but they have focused on one-time measurements of testosterone rather than an examination of changing levels. Could men's moods be affected by hormonal cycles? Is there such a thing as "male menopause"? Are there cycles besides the menstrual cycle that might be linked to emotions or behavior in both women and men? To answer these questions, it is necessary to move beyond the stereotypes to the research.

One aspect of physiological sexual differentiation is the development of an approximately month-long cycle of sex hormone release in women and not in men (see Chapter 5). The most obvious consequences of this difference are female menstruation and the fact that a man's potential to impregnate a woman is apparently not limited by any cyclic variations, whereas a woman can become pregnant only during a particular part of her monthly cycle. The implications of this difference between the sexes, however, have been carried far beyond the area of fertility. For centuries, the existence of the menstrual cycle has been used to characterize women as unstable and therefore unfit for certain responsible social and economic positions. This is, of course, in contrast to men, whose physiological state has been thought to be relatively constant. (As will be noted later in the chapter, however, male hormone levels are *not* particularly constant.) In fact, women's reproductive anatomy and physiology have long been considered a source of danger to both physical and emotional health. At the turn of the century, some educators took strong stands against coeducation in adolescence on the basis that daily association with boys would interfere with the "normalization" of a girl's menstrual period; the suggestion was also made that if girls were forced to exercise their brains at puberty they would use up the blood needed later for menstruation (see Shields, 1975). In fact, for well into the 20th century, doctors viewed women as more or less always potentially sick by virtue of the mere possession of a uterus and ovaries; menstruation, pregnancy, and menopause were seen as physical diseases and intellectual handicaps (Ehrenreich & English, 1979). In addition, even dry scientific texts have tended to wax lyrical when discussing menstruation, sometimes describing it as a sign that a woman's body *wants* to have children! For example, Ganong's 1977 *Review of Medical Physiology* unabashedly noted that "Menstruation is the uterus crying for the lack of a baby" (as quoted in Laqueur, 1990). The echoes of these beliefs still haunt our culture's approach to women and to reproduction.

THE MENSTRUAL CYCLE

In women, the cyclic pattern of sex hormone levels is maintained through a negative feedback system involving the hypothalamus, the pituitary gland, and the ovaries. The ovaries, which produce the sex hormones estrogen and progesterone, are regulated by the pituitary gland, which in turn is regulated by the hypothalamus, which responds to the levels of estrogen and progesterone produced by the ovaries. The **menstrual cycle,** which lasts 28 days on the average but may vary a great deal among individuals and even within the same individual, happens in four phases:

1. In the **follicular phase,** the pituitary secretes follicle-stimulating hormone (FSH), stimulating a follicle in one of the ovaries to secrete estrogen and to bring an egg to maturity.

2. In **ovulation,** the follicle ruptures to release the mature egg. At this point, the estrogen level is high—a condition that stimulates the hypothalamus to produce LH-releaser, which in turn causes the pituitary to produce LH (luteinizing hormone). The high estrogen level also inhibits production of FSH. In the uterus, the high levels of estrogen stimulate the lining to thicken and form glands that will secrete substances to nourish the embryo if conception occurs.

3. In the **luteal phase,** the LH stimulates the follicle to turn into a glandular mass of cells called the corpus luteum, which in turn manufactures progesterone. As the progesterone levels rise, they stimulate the glands of the endometrium, or uterine lining, to secrete nourishing substances. They also inhibit the pituitary's production of LH, eventually causing the corpus luteum to degenerate and the levels of both progesterone and estrogen to drop sharply after 10 to 12 days. However, if the egg has been fertilized and implanted in the womb, the hormone levels will not drop and the next phase will not occur.

4. The final phase, **menstruation,** involves shedding the inner uterine lining, the endometrium, which flows out through the cervix and the vagina. Levels of progesterone and estrogen are low, and FSH levels are beginning to rise again in preparation for the beginning of another cycle.

Although menstruation is technically the end of the cycle, the first day of menstruation is counted as day 1 of the cycle because it is the easiest to identify. The changes in the levels of ovarian and pituitary hormone levels across the cycle are shown in Figure 8.1.

Given the dramatic shifts in the levels of estrogen and progesterone over the 28-day cycle, we should not be surprised by the suggestion that the cycle variation affects moods, feelings, performance, and behavior. In fact, many women do report symptoms such as periodic shifts in mood that seem to correlate with their menstrual cycle. Some women report that they become depressed and irritable just before or during their menstrual period. Others report physical symptoms such as cramps or headaches at this time of the month. There is a lack of universal agreement on what symptoms occur when, but because a significant number of women report *some* symptoms that seem to vary with the phase of their menstrual cycle, it seems worthwhile to pursue the issue of what might cause such symptoms. It must be remembered that the fact that certain symptoms may correlate (that is, occur together) with certain phases of the menstrual cycle does not necessarily imply that they are *caused* by the hormonal changes that characterize that part of the cycle. It is very difficult, in fact, to ascertain whether these reported symptoms are due to physiological changes in the woman's body or to her learned expectations of menstrual effects. Research (e.g., Schacter & Singer, 1962; Walster, 1974) indicates that people actually tend to label their moods according to their expectations about how they should feel in certain situations.

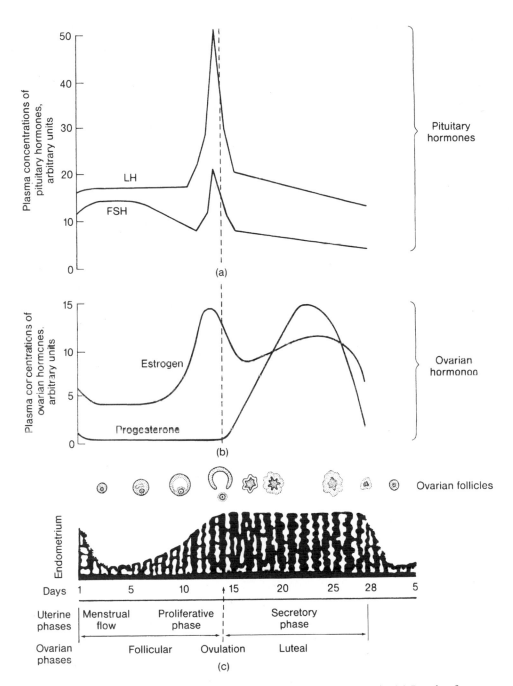

Figure 8.1 Changes in hormone levels across the menstrual cycle. (a) Levels of hormones produced by the pituitary. (b) Hormones produced by the ovaries. (c) Changes in follicles in the ovary and the endometrium of the uterus.

Expectations about the menstrual cycle vary widely across times and places. Great powers, danger, and impurity have all been attributed to menstruating women. According to first-century Roman historian Pliny, the touch of a menstruating woman would cause new wine to turn sour, razors to become blunt, and boiled linen to turn black. In some societies, a menstruating woman is viewed as polluting anything she contacts, and sometimes, as among the Arapesh of New Guinea, women are secluded in menstrual huts during their periods to protect others from their dangerous powers. In other cultures, there are positive—albeit less powerful—images for menstruation. According to Japanese tradition, a girl's first menstruation is "the year of the cleavage of the melon." One Indian phrase for menstruation is the "flower growing in the house of the god of love" (Delaney, Lupton, & Toth, 1987).

Emotional, Behavioral, Sensory, and Cognitive Correlates of the Menstrual Cycle

MOOD   For decades, psychologists have referred to a **premenstrual syndrome** of high tension, depression, irritability, and assorted physical symptoms that is said to occur during the days immediately preceding the onset of menstruation (K. Dalton, 1964; R.T. Frank, 1931). Some research has found that women report more anxiety, hostility, or depression during the premenstrual and menstrual phases than at other times (e.g., Golub, 1976; Hamilton, Gallant, & Lloyd, 1989; Paige, 1971). However, other studies have found no relationship between mood and the menstrual cycle (e.g., Laessle, Tuschl, Schweiger, & Pirke, 1990; Mansfield, Hood, & Henderson, 1989), and some have reported findings contradictory to those expected (e.g., McFarlane, Martin, & Williams, 1988; Parlee, 1982). Some support for a hormonal cause for mood fluctuations comes from the finding that women taking oral contraceptives (and thus not experiencing normal cyclic variations in hormone levels) tend not to report cyclic mood changes (Paige, 1971; Rossi & Rossi, 1977). However, there is another possible explanation for the absence of mood fluctuations in women taking oral contraceptives: Oral contraceptives reduce the monthly menstrual flow and make it more predictable—and negative moods may be due to anticipated flow and the bother that goes with it rather than to hormone levels (Paige, 1971; Parlee, 1982).

When women are asked to keep daily records of their moods and symptoms over several months, the results generally indicate a great deal of variability in individual women's patterns, with individual records showing very little evidence of rhythm. However, when the records of many individual women are combined, some studies show regular cyclic changes in such things as fatigue, abdominal pain, breast tenderness, appetite, headaches, and irritability (Laessle et al., 1990; Parlee, 1973). However, different studies tend to show cyclic changes in different patterns, and these inconsistencies remain unexplained. Accurate estimates of the proportion of women who experience mood fluctuations across the menstrual cycle are unavailable; different studies provide substantially different numbers. One reviewer estimates that 50% to 75% of women show some mood fluctuation, but at least 25% show none at all (Hyde, 1986). Moreover, despite the menstrual cycle, the variability in women's moods does not seem to differ appreciably from the variability of men's moods, as shown by a study in which husbands and wives charted their daily moods for 2 months (Dan, 1976). Finally, the influence of the menstrual cycle on mood seems to pale in comparison to that of other variables. Studies show, for instance, that environmental and social variables account for more variability in mood than cycle phase does (Good & Smith, 1980; Mansfield et al., 1989).

Frequently, reports of current symptoms do not match retrospective reports (based on memory) from the same women (McFarlane & Williams, 1990, 1994). The situation looks even more complex when researchers include men in their samples, and when they broaden their focus to include the possibilities of other cycles, such as lunar and day-of-week. Jessica McFarlane and Tannis Williams (1994) followed 60 women and 10 men for 12 to 18 weeks, obtaining daily mood data. Mood ratings were later matched against information about menstrual cycles, lunar cycles, and days of the week. They found that two thirds of both the women and the men showed cycles in their moods. Thus, it might be viewed as "normal" for a person to have a regular pattern of emotional ups and downs. However, these mood cycles were very different for each individual, and few of them matched such expected patterns as premenstrual blues or weekend highs. The data showed that more of the women had a negative mood phase at some other point in their menstrual cycle than premenstrually and that 55% had no mood changes that correlated with the menstrual cycle.

Even in cases where a relationship between the menstrual cycle and mood has been demonstrated, interpretation is difficult. Most people assume that hormonal changes associated with the cycle cause the mood change. However, the direction of causality in some cases may be precisely the reverse, as it has long been known that psychological stress can delay menstruation or cause it to begin ahead of schedule (Parlee, 1973). Another problem is that the focus of investigation has often been on negative symptoms, the assumption being that women experience more negative moods than "normal" during the premenstrual and menstrual phases. However, when researchers look for positive changes in the premenstrual phase, they can find those as well. In one study, 66 women out of a sample of 100 reported at least one positive change associated with premenstruation. In all, seven different positive changes were reported: increased sexual interest, tendency to clean or tidy, increased sexual enjoyment, tendency to get things done, more attractive breasts, more energy, and more creative ideas (D.E. Stewart, 1989). One group of researchers developed the "Menstrual Joy Questionnaire," which asked respondents about their experience of high spirits, increased sexual desire, vibrant activity, revolutionary zeal, intense concentration, and feelings of affection, self-confidence, euphoria, creativity, and power during their menstrual cycle (Delaney, et al., 1987). When another group of researchers later administered the questionnaire to female college students, they found that it seemed to "prime" the respondents to include more positive responses in later, broader measures of attitudes toward menstruation (Chrisler, Johnston, Champagne, & Preston, 1994). Clearly, the questions asked by researchers shape what we "know" about menstruation.

Others have looked for positive symptoms at midcycle. Perhaps women feel "normal" most of the time, except for feeling especially positive at midcycle, a pattern that would be impossible to detect using only negative symptom measures. Barbara Sommer (1975) had participants complete daily checklists of positive and negative moods for 4½ weeks. When the results were analyzed, the only statistically significant finding was an increase in positive affect at midcycle. It is interesting to speculate on the changes in attitudes toward the menstrual cycle that might take place if women began to think of the midcycle as a high point rather than focusing on the premenstrual and menstrual phases as low points.

BEHAVIOR, PERFORMANCE, AND COGNITION   Some investigators have looked for correlations between phases of the menstrual cycle and the occurrence of specific behaviors. Cyclic changes have been reported in behaviors such as volunteering to be a participant in a study (Doty & Silverthorne, 1975), consumption of sweet food (Bowen & Grunberg, 1990), deciding to seek psychological services (Surrey, Scott, & Phillips, 1975), alcohol consumption (Dumas, Calliet, Tumblin, & King, 1984), and maternal response to a child's illness (Tuck, 1975). Mary Parlee (1973) notes that investigators have tended to report that abnormal behaviors are most likely to occur in women during the premenstrual or menstrual phase of their cycle. The alleged link between these behaviors, which include commission of violent crimes, loss of control of an aircraft, suicide, and admission to hospital with acute psychiatric illness, might seem at first glance to imply that women are a menace to themselves and others for a few days every month. However, as Parlee's careful critique shows, such a general conclusion is unwarranted. Some of the reports are based on extremely small samples of women, and many have used methods such as retrospective reports of cycle phase, the accuracy of which is highly suspect. Moreover, she cautions, correlational data from special groups of women (e.g., female criminals) should not be used to make general statements about all women or about other special groups of women (e.g., female artists). Even supposing that women disposed to commit violent crime are more likely to commit it premenstrually, we cannot assume that women with strong inhibitions about violent behavior will be significantly more likely to commit violent acts at a particular point in the menstrual cycle. One group of reviewers concludes that among women who are potential committers of pathological acts, the period surrounding the beginning of menstruation is a likely time for such acts to occur (Friedman, Hurt, Arnoff, & Clarkin, 1980). However, others have concluded that there is no acceptable evidence linking the menstrual cycle to criminal behavior and that the lack of scientific knowledge is so glaring that evidence about menstruation and crime should not be admissible in criminal trials (Harry & Balcer, 1987).

Popular opinion holds that women perform tasks more poorly during the premenstrual phase of the cycle. When the heroine of the popular movie *Clueless* offered the excuse that she was "surfing the crimson tide" for her inability to attend class and complete the required assignments, she was using a time-honored strategy. Female high school and college students have long used (and abused) the stereotype that menstruation impairs performance. Most objective measures do not show any general impairment in cognitive tasks, work and academic performance, or perceptual–motor performance associated with the menstrual cycle (Sommer, 1973, 1983, 1992). Studies using standard cognitive tests, academic examinations, reaction-time measures, quantity and quality of factory production, typing, and keypunching all fail to show menstrual cycle–related changes in performance. However, studies do show that women *believe* their performance is lower during the premenstrual and menstrual phases.

Female college students say they believe their academic performance is impaired by premenstrual symptoms. However, their performance, when measured objectively by tests and examination scores, does not show cyclic variation (Richardson, 1989). Another study examined the performance of female professional typists throughout the menstrual cycle (Black & Koulis-Chitwood, 1990). This study found no evidence for any variation in typing performance (errors or speed) as a function of the cycle. A study of hand steadiness, conducted by military researchers to assess individual differences in the skills necessary to perform such tasks as holding and firing a handgun, did show that women with normal menstrual cycles showed a drop in hand steadiness during the premenstrual phase. On the whole, however, normally cycling women showed more steadiness than a comparison group of men did (Hudgens, Fatkin, Billingsley, & Mazurczak, 1988).

As noted in Chapter 6, one research lab has found evidence for cyclic changes in the performance of selected cognitive tasks (Kimura & Hampson, 1994). These researchers have found that women perform somewhat better on verbal articulation and fine motor-skill tasks at times during the cycle when estrogen levels are high (midcycle) and are better at certain visual–spatial tasks at times when estrogen levels are low. However, the differences related to menstrual-cycle phase were small in comparison to differences among women. These findings suggest that, if there *is* a small effect of menstrual cycle phase on cognitive performance, it is more complicated than a general increase in performance at midcycle and a decrease in the premenstrual phase.

Researchers in sports medicine have tried to determine whether there are links between the menstrual cycle and performance of female athletes. The results are mixed. One recent study of female athletes found no difference between the early follicular phase (the phase between menstruation and ovulation) and the midluteal phase (the phase between ovulation and menstruation) on variables such as muscle strength, anaerobic performance, aerobic endurance performance, maximum heart rate, and body composition (Lebrun, McKenzie, Prior, & Taunton, 1995). They did, however, find a slight tendency for aerobic capacity to decrease during the luteal phase. Although the magnitude of the effect varied a great deal among participants, it was large enough in some individuals to make it worthy of consideration. Another group of researchers demonstrated with a small sample of women that adapting a weight-training regimen to the phases of the menstrual cycle may be beneficial for building muscle strength. They compared a training routine in which women trained every 3rd day throughout their cycle (regular training) with one in which they trained every 2nd day during the follicular phase and about once a week during the luteal phase (menstrual–cycle-triggered training). The differences in resulting muscle strength were noteworthy: All participants showed better gains in muscle strength using the routine that was adapted to the menstrual cycle (Reis, Frick, & Schmidtbleicher, 1995). Why? The researchers postulate that the high levels of estradiol during the follicular phase have an anabolic (muscle-building) effect, which works in synergy with the training.

SENSATION AND PERCEPTION   A number of studies have examined sensory responsiveness across the menstrual cycle. Visual, auditory, olfactory, taste, and touch sensitivity have all been studied in relation to the cycle, along with skin conductance and brain wave activity. Some studies have found changes in sensitivity to such stimuli as tactile vibrations and auditory thresholds. Others have examined heart rate and blood pressure reactivity to stressors, some finding a correlation between reactivity and cycle phase (Tersman, Collins, & Eneroth, 1991) and others finding no such correlation (Weidner & Helmig, 1990).

Much of the research is reviewed by Parlee (1983) and Sommer (1983). There is a great deal of variation in the findings: Some studies report cyclic fluctuations in sensitivity, but others do not. The studies that do report variation, particularly for visual and olfactory thresholds, tend to find increased sensitivity or responsiveness in the middle of the cycle and reduced sensitivity around menstruation. Pain thresholds seem to be lower in the premenstrual phase. However, conclusions are hampered by a number of problems: (1) Much of the research was designed to uncover the reasons for cognitive impairment associated with the menstrual cycle—impairment for which there seems to be little evidence. (2) Many of the findings have never been replicated. (3) In many studies, measures are not taken often enough during the cycle to provide an accurate and complete picture of the pattern of fluctuations in sensitivity. (4) There is a wide variation in the way cycle phases are defined. Menstrual-cycle effects on sensory processes are probably very small, and it may be too early to try to explain them given the large discrepancies that exist in the findings. However, it is important for researchers to be aware of the possibility that changes in the action of the central nervous system may accompany the cyclic changes of the menstrual (or, indeed, any other) cycle.

Special Difficulties: PMS and Dysmenorrhea

PMS   In recent years, most women's magazines have devoted considerable space to the topic of the premenstrual syndrome (PMS). The articles tend to be negative in tone, emphasize negative aspects of the menstrual cycle, and support the stereotype of women as maladjusted by virtue of their normal reproductive processes (Chrisler & Levy, 1990).

Treatment groups for PMS have sprung up at women's health clinics around the continent, and the shelves of health food stores display a variety of products supposedly geared to the relief of this syndrome. The advertisements for such products are calculated to heighten women's anxiety about the possible debilitating side effects of menstruation, and their widespread visibility encourages the assumption that the majority of women suffer from severe menstrual problems. Clearly, popular interest in PMS is high.

The publicity and interest surrounding PMS are fascinating, given that it is a poorly defined cluster of severe premenstrual symptoms that appears in a very small proportion of the female population. The number and type of symptoms said to characterize PMS varies from study to study. However, there seems to be agreement that the syndrome can include emotional problems (e.g., tension, anxiety, depression, irritability, and hostility), physical problems (e.g., abdominal bloating, swelling, breast tenderness, headache, and backache), and behavioral problems (e.g., avoidance of social contact, change in work habits, increased tendency to pick fights, and crying spells) (Abplanalp, 1983). As all of these are common symptoms that may be experienced in varying degrees of severity by almost anyone at any time of the month, some caution is indicated in labeling women as sufferers of PMS. In general, PMS should involve, on a regular basis, a significant increase in moderate to severe physical *and* psychological symptoms during the premenstrual phase, with marked relief associated with onset of menstruation. When stringent criteria are used to define PMS, it is difficult to find enough women from a large unselected sample to study it; severe, disabling premenstrual symptoms are reported by relatively few women (Abplanalp, 1983). The label "PMS" seems to be easily applied by women to their own symptoms, perhaps because of the publicity surrounding the term. However, when women who label themselves as PMS sufferers are compared to other women on daily prospective symptom reports, researchers find few or no differences between the two groups (McFarlane & Williams, 1994).

Despite the difficulties in diagnosing PMS, a formal psychiatric diagnosis, **premenstrual dysphoric disorder (PMDD),** has been included in an appendix (as a disorder requiring further study) of the latest revision of the American Psychiatric Association's catalog of psychiatric disorders, the DSM-IV. Many believe much more research is needed before such a diagnostic category could be used with confidence, and it is dangerous to women to assume that the physical symptoms some women experience premenstrually are signs of mental illness (Caplan, 1993; Hamilton & Gallant, 1990).

Various treatments for PMS have been heralded by the press. So far, there is no good evidence that any of them work. Most of the studies allow for the contamination of treatment effects with the effects of expectations because women who are given the treatment are told they are getting something that will cure their problem. A high proportion of women with PMS report benefiting from treatment, no matter what is used; in other words, they show a placebo effect—an effect apparently caused by the *expectation* that the treatment will help rather than by the treatment itself (Elsner, Buster, Schindler, Nessim, & Abraham, 1980). When double-blind, controlled studies are conducted (that is, studies in which neither the researcher nor the participant knows until the study is over which women have been given the treatment drug and which have been given an ineffective placebo), none of the treatments turn out to be any more effective than the placebo. This conclusion holds even for progesterone therapy, the most widely acclaimed treatment for PMS, now shown to be ineffective (Freeman, Rickels, Sondheimer, & Polansky, 1990; Robinson & Garfinkel, 1990). Research shows that the most effective management of PMS involves simple stress control and sensible levels of diet and exercise (Robinson & Garfinkel, 1990).

Various interests have been quick to cash in on the popularity of PMS. A good way to sell a lot of vitamins, for example, is to help convince a lot of women that their problems are due to PMS and that PMS can be relieved by a certain new vitamin formula. This strategy has been widely used, despite the lack of evidence either that there is a high incidence of PMS or that any particular treatment is effective. Perhaps one of the reasons so many women have been quick to accept the media-backed notion that PMS is a widespread disease is that the syndrome provides a "valid" label for menstrual-related discomfort and represents one of the first times that menstrual complaints have been taken seriously by doctors. However, the level of discomfort experienced by most women is not severe or disabling enough to qualify as PMS, and it is dangerous to women to foster the idea that large numbers of them experience the normal fluctuations of the menstrual cycle as a disease. There is no reason to return to the era when women's "raging hormonal influences" were thought to disqualify them from important jobs, for example. This is not to say that the severe premenstrual problems experienced by a few women are not real or important, but PMS should be acknowledged for what the evidence shows it to be—a rare disorder, and one that is as yet poorly understood.

DYSMENORRHEA   Dysmenorrhea, or painful menstruation, is the most common menstrual problem, reported by 31% to 92% of women (Friederich, 1983; Wildman & White, 1986). The frequency and severity of discomfort vary widely among women, and even in the same woman over time. Under normal conditions, the cause of the problem is now thought to be the release of **prostaglandins** (hormonelike substances) from the lining of the uterus (Budoff, 1980). These chemicals cause excessive contractions in the uterine muscles, decreased blood flow, and increased sensitivity to pain, all of which contribute to menstrual cramps. Women reporting severe menstrual pain have been found to have unusually high levels of prostaglandins. Various prescription antiprostaglandin drugs are used to treat menstrual pain, and studies show that about 80% of women are helped by these drugs (Friederich, 1983). Aspirin, which is a mild antiprostaglandin, is also effective for some women. In addition, strategies to increase blood flow and release congestion are helpful. Thus, physical exercise may be a good idea, and many women report that orgasm, whether achieved through masturbation or sex with a partner, works very well to relieve menstrual cramps.

Social and Cultural Influences on the Menstrual Experience

According to historical and anthropological evidence, menstruation has never been merely a physiological event. The menstruating woman has often been regarded as a participant in a strange and dangerous process, as someone who is unclean, or as someone who is especially powerful. In many cultures, she was secluded during her period and forbidden to prepare food or to have any contact with men. She could be punished with death if found concealing the fact that she was menstruating (see Weideger, 1977, and Delaney et al., 1987, for accounts of the rituals surrounding menstruation). Even today in our culture, menstruation is sometimes referred to as "the curse," some religions regard menstruating women as unclean, and some people hold a taboo against sexual relations during the menstrual period. Some have argued that cultural reactions to menstruation reflect attitudes toward women. Gloria Steinem (1983), for instance, fantasizes that if men could menstruate cyclic fluctuations would be viewed as an advantage rather than a liability. At any rate, as many observers have noted, societal concerns about the possible debilitating effects of menstruation seem to have resurfaced with every new push for gender equality.

It would be surprising if the cultural meanings attached to menstruation did not have an influence on how women experience it. Indeed, it is probable that the biological influences of the menstrual cycle on women's experience are magnified many times by the cultural influences. Research on cultural attitudes toward menstruation, and the impact of these attitudes on women's experience, are examined in the following sections.

MENARCHE   The first onset of menstruation is called **menarche,** and it represents an important developmental milestone in women's lives. One study of 137 women ages 18 to 45 found that every one of them remembered their first menstruation and most could describe the associated events in detail (Golub & Catalano, 1983). Yet such is the air of embarrassment surrounding menstruation in our culture that menarche usually occurs not only without fanfare but often in relative secrecy. In addition, research on menarche has, until recently, been in short supply (Golub, 1983). Studies of premenarcheal girls and their male classmates indicate that a substantial proportion of them have negative beliefs about menstruation—for example, that it is accompanied by physical discomfort, increased emotionality, and disruption of activities (Brooks-Gunn & Ruble, 1980). One study of 9- to 12-year-old girls found that most of them equated menstruation with growing up and being normal, but almost a third of them believed menstruation to be embarrassing, a nuisance, or disgusting, and many of them believed menstruating women should not swim or be active in sports (L. R. Williams, 1983). Eighty-five percent of these girls thought that a girl should not talk about menstruation to boys; 40% thought she should not discuss it even with her father. It appears, then, that negative attitudes toward and expectations about menstruation have been part of the anticipation of menarche for many girls. The advertisements for tampons and sanitary napkins may well contribute to these negative attitudes. Such advertisements tend to suggest that their product will help get the menstruating woman through a difficult and embarrassing time, that its use will make the woman able to carry on "almost as if she were her normal self." Not surprisingly, at the time of menarche, mixed feelings, such as fear and excitement, are commonly reported (A. E. Petersen, 1983), and a substantial number of women recall it as a negative event (Golub & Catalano, 1983). There is some evidence that early-maturing girls have special difficulties adjusting to menstruation, perhaps because it thrusts them into a new stage not yet encountered by their peers (A. E. Petersen, 1983).

Some researchers have wondered whether the social events and emotional experiences surrounding menarche may set the stage for how a woman will experience menstruation in subsequent years. One group has suggested that to overcome some of the negative meanings associated with menarche a positive new tradition or ritual should be developed (Logan, Calder, & Cohen 1980, as cited in Golub, 1983). These researchers wrote five brief stories describing possible responses to a girl's first period. They gave the stories to girls between the ages of 8 and 17, mothers of girls in this age range, and women psychologists. The mothers and daughters chose "Congratulations, our little girl is growing up" as the best response to being told about the beginning of menstruation, and the psychologists preferred "Something special has happened." What symbolic gesture might be appropriate? Mothers favored a special toast to the girl from both parents or a meal in her honor. However, the girls themselves, shying away from a situation in which they would be the center of attention, thought that the best gesture would be a hug or kiss and a gift to mark the occasion. It is difficult to be sure what effect such a positive celebration of menarche would have on women's later menstrual experience, but it should certainly help to counteract the negative expectations and attitudes with which many girls approach menstruation.

ATTITUDES, EXPECTATIONS, AND THEIR IMPACT ON MENSTRUAL SYMPTOMS   About two decades ago, a survey of 1034 Americans, a representative sample over the age of 14, indicated that a significant minority of people associated menstruation with some degree of impairment: 35% believed menstruation affects a woman's ability to think, 26% believed women cannot function as well at work when menstruating, and 30% believed women need to restrict their physical activities during menstruation ("The Tampax Report," 1981). Eighty-seven percent of the respondents agreed that women are more emotional when menstruating, although when asked about their or their partner's most recent menstrual period, 42% and 58% respectively, reported no mood or personality changes either menstrually or premenstrually. There is little evidence that attitudes have changed since that survey. Even among well-educated women, knowledge of the menstrual cycle is often incorrect and negatively biased (Koff, Rierdan, & Stubbs, 1990).

Widespread cultural stereotypes exist about menstruation (E. Martin, 1987), and they are often found to be most negative among younger women (Brooks-Gunn &

Ruble, 1983; Stoltzman, 1986). Parlee (1974) asked women and men to complete a symptom questionnaire according to their beliefs about what women in general experience at various cycle phases. Both men and women gave responses that showed fluctuations of symptoms across the menstrual cycle—fluctuations similar to the self-reports of menstrual symptoms found in other samples. Koeske and Koeske (1975) used a questionnaire to measure participants' reactions to a written excerpt from a hypothetical student's interview with a college counselor. They examined the effect of information about the student's menstrual cycle phase, mood, and environment on the participants' formation of attributions about the student. Results showed that participants displayed a clear-cut attributional pattern in which they linked the negative moods of depression and irritability to the occurrence of the premenstrual phase of the student's cycle. It appears that our culture provides an emotional label of "premenstrual tension" to any negative moods that may occur at this point in a woman's cycle. The researchers note that this attribution pattern presents a number of dangers. It obscures the very wide individual variation among women in menstrual and premenstrual symptoms. It uses women's biology to explain negative, but not positive, moods, and it may result in the exaggeration of the likelihood or recall of negative moods. If a woman accepts this attribution for her own emotions, it might even reduce the likelihood of her taking action to alter an upsetting external situation. She might believe premenstrual tension, not the external situation, was the source of the upset.

Do women accept the stereotypic beliefs about menstruation with respect to their own experience, or only for "women in general"? In one study (Brooks, Ruble, & Clarke, 1977), college women were asked to respond to a symptom questionnaire *as if* they were premenstrual or at midcycle. Their responses indicated that they expected to experience more severe symptoms in the premenstrual than in the intermenstrual phase, a result that parallels the stereotypic expectations for women in general found in previous studies.

If cultural expectations about menstrual symptoms are so prevalent, might they not influence the self-reports or even the actual experience of menstrual symptoms? Probably. When women are told that the menstrual cycle is the focus of a daily symptom-reporting study, they report significantly more negative psychological and physical symptoms at premenstrual and menstrual cycle phases than do women who are given a different rationale for the study (Aubuchon & Calhoun, 1985).

In one study, women completed daily questionnaires in which they reported their physical and emotional symptoms. Later, some of these women were asked to recall the ratings they had made on a day when they were menstruating; others recalled a day when they were not menstruating. Finally, the women completed a questionnaire about how they thought they were "typically" affected by menstruation. The women who thought that menstruation was typically associated with distress tended to remember their menstrual days as distressing—more distressing, in fact, than they had reported at the time. The more a woman believed in the phenomenon of menstrual distress, the more exaggerated were her recollections of her negative menstrual symptoms (McFarland, Ross, & DeCourville, 1989).

When obtaining symptom reports from women, how do researchers know how much of the symptomatology is caused by the biological changes associated with the menstrual cycle and how much is caused by expectations and stereotypic beliefs? Diane Ruble (1977) used a creative approach to separate the effects of expectations from the effects of biology. She told 44 undergraduate students that new scientific techniques made it possible to predict the expected date of menstruation. Then, after using this bogus technique on each woman (hooking her up to an EEG machine), she informed her, according to the group to which the student had been randomly assigned, that (1) her period was due in 1 or 2 days (premenstrual group); or (2) her period was not expected for 7 to 10 days (intermenstrual group); or (3) no information was available about cycle phase (control group). Thus, these women were given supposedly accurate information about their cycle phase, but the information each was given was, in reality, randomly determined and independent of her actual cycle phase. After being given this information, each woman went to a second room, where another experimenter, unaware of the group to which the woman had been assigned, asked her to rate her experience of a set of supposedly menstruation-related symptoms. All of the women were really in the 21st or 22nd day of their cycles, and their testing had been scheduled on the basis of a menstrual history taken earlier. However, regardless of their actual cycle phase, women who believed they were premenstrual reported more premenstrual symptoms than did those who believed they were intermenstrual. These findings suggest that expectations can and do influence women's self-reports of menstruation-related symptoms and indicate caution in the interpretation of such studies.

How are expectations about menstrual symptoms formed and maintained? By administering a questionnaire to a large sample of Protestant, Catholic, and Jewish women, Karen Paige (1973) explored two issues: (1) the possibility that women use menstruation to explain bodily discomfort and psychological distress that actually have origins in other events, and (2) the possibility that different religious or cultural groups may promote attitudes conducive to different levels of menstrual symptoms. Her findings demonstrate that learned social attitudes play a significant role in determining women's reactions to the menstrual cycle. They indicate, first, that women *learn* to attribute various forms of physical discomfort to menstruation and, second, that groups of women with similar menstrual cycles but different subcultural religious backgrounds differ in the way social factors relate to their reports of menstrual distress.

Paige found, first of all, that women who reported many menstrual distress symptoms were also significantly more likely than other women to report higher psychological stress, greater use of drugs, and more illnesses in general. It appears that for some women menstruation merely represents a specific, socially acceptable explanation for symptoms that actually occur all month long and that, at midcycle, would be attributed to external causes such as overwork, family disputes, or other stressors. Second, although there were no overall differences among religious groups in quantity of menstrual symptoms reported, she found that the three groups differed in the ways various social factors were related to symptom reporting.

For Paige's Jewish subjects, the only dimension that seemed to relate strongly to complaints of menstrual distress was menstrual social behavior. Those women who found sex during menstruation unenjoyable or embarrassing or who tended to follow certain prescribed social rituals connected with menstruation were the women most likely to report menstrual problems. Among Catholics, the factors that related most strongly to reported menstrual distress were sexual experience and family/motherhood orientation. Catholic women with more sexual experience were less likely to report menstrual symptoms. Also, among Catholics, the women who indicated most strongly that a woman's place was in the home and who listed no personal career ambitions were those most likely to report menstrual problems. For the Protestant group, no especially strong relationship between reported menstrual distress and any of the social factors was demonstrated.

The relationships that Paige found cannot be used to prove that certain social factors cause menstrual distress or vice versa. But there is no reason to believe the women in different religious groups differed in their menstrual cycle patterns, so her demonstration of intergroup differences in the correlates of menstrual discomfort provides suggestive support for the idea that social and cultural factors have an impact on women's reactions to menstruation. As Paige notes in her article, this should not be particularly surprising because we are quite aware that cultures label and control other basic biological functions. For example, eating is obviously a response to a basic biological need controlled by physiological processes. Yet, as Paige reminds us, our culture has a tremendous influence on what, when, where, how, and with whom we eat.

Although there is reason to believe hormonal changes during the menstrual cycle may affect mood and behavior, the research indicates that sociocultural factors play a major role, perhaps the most significant role, in determining these effects. There are still many unanswered questions, however. For instance, we know little about the specific reasons for the wide individual variations among women (or even in the same woman over time) in the level of menstrual and premenstrual symptoms. Issues such as diet, stress, and fatigue may well be important, but they remain to be investigated. Also, it is clear that most women must continue to perform their jobs in the workplace or home despite any menstrual symptoms they may experience. It would be interesting and practical to study the strategies used by the women who cope most successfully with recurring menstrual symptoms.

HORMONES AND THE MALE EXPERIENCE

Male Puberty

The onset of puberty occurs about 2 years later for boys than for girls. In both sexes, the physical changes of adolescence are triggered when the hypothalamus increases secretions that cause the pituitary gland to release gonadotropins in large amounts. **Gonadotropins,** hormones that stimulate the gonads to activity, are chemically the same in males as in females, but their presence produces different results in the two sexes because the gonads they act upon are different. In males, they stimulate the testes to increase testosterone production; in females, they cause the ovaries to produce estrogen.

Under the influence of increased hormone levels, both sexes experience a growth spurt and develop secondary sex characteristics. Internal reproductive organs also undergo further development. In girls, this development has a dramatic manifestation in menarche. In boys, the penis and testes increase in size, as do the prostate gland and seminal vesicles. When the prostate and seminal vesicles begin functioning under the influence of increasing testosterone levels, ejaculation becomes possible. **Spermarche,** or the first ejaculation, usually occurs about a year after the growth spurt has begun, often at age 13 or 14, but the timing can vary widely among individuals. Early ejaculations may or may not contain viable sperm, as the timing of sperm production also varies. Sperm production is necessary for fertility.

Just as girls may be shocked and upset by menstruation when they are unprepared, boys may be frightened by their first experience of ejaculation. Although boys are typically used to masturbating before puberty, and have experienced orgasms, they are often taken by surprise the first time masturbation leads to ejaculation. As one man, looking back on his first ejaculation during masturbation, commented to a researcher, "[I] couldn't believe it when something shot out of my penis" (Crooks & Bauer, 1987, p. 460). A major worry, he went on to say, was that God was punishing him for his sinful behavior.

One study shows that boys are often unprepared for their first experience of ejaculation but that the lack of preparation is not necessarily associated with a negative reaction to the event (Gaddis & Brooks-Gunn, 1985). Only 3 of 13 adolescent boys interviewed had had ejaculation explained to them, in all cases by an adult male; most had obtained their information from reading. Furthermore, only 4 had discussed their first ejaculation after the experience. The majority of the boys reported that they had experienced strong positive feelings at spermarche. No one was upset or strongly ashamed; however, 1 was very embarrassed, and 2 were very frightened. It appears that first ejaculation is less likely to be discussed than first menstruation is, and that, for a minority of boys, this lack of discussion can contribute to negative reactions to the event.

Male Cycles

If the menstrual cycle is associated with some changes in mood and behavior for a certain proportion of women, one possible implication is that women are, on the average, more variable in mood and behavior than men are. This suggestion is based, of course, on the assumption that men are not subject to any cycles of their own. Investigation of this assumption dates back to Leta Hollingworth (1914), who painstakingly followed 6 women and 2 men with daily tests of cognitive performance over 4 months. She found no female–male differences in performance variability or patterns of performance change. More recently, Alice Dan (1976) followed 24 married couples for 2 months, using tests of mood and problem-solving performance. She also found no differences in variability between women and men.

If the menstrual cycle contributes to variability in women, and women on the whole are not more variable than men, men must have their own sources of variability. It is of interest, then, to look briefly at the issue of male cycles, an issue that has been virtually ignored by researchers. Is it possible that men experience physiological cycles that create as much variability and vulnerability as the female menstrual cycle does but that these cycles have been ignored by the culture and hence not magnified in their effects by social expectations? Indeed, it is. Researchers studying biological rhythms in males have identified monthly cycles of efficiency and irritability (J. C. Hoffman, 1982).

Cycles are a universal aspect of life. Both men and women experience daily rhythms on physiological dimensions such as body temperature, blood sugar levels, and sleeping/waking. Such cycles can affect alertness, mood, and performance (Monk, Moline, Fookson, & Peetz, 1989). There may also be seasonal cycles. One Italian study of suicide records over 12 years identified different seasonal variation cycles in suicide for women and men (Micciolo, Zimmerman-Tansella, Williams, & Tansella, 1989). Estelle Ramey (1972) reviewed limited evidence that men show cyclic mood variations ranging in periodicity from 4 to 9 weeks. These studies show that there may be a great deal of variability among individual men in the cyclic patterns of their moods and physical symptoms, just as there are large individual differences among women. McFarlane and Williams (1994), who found evidence for mood cycles among both women and men, also found that there was a great deal of individual variability in both sexes. Furthermore, the mood cycles did not necessarily conform to the menstrual cycle for women or to such obvious social markers as weekends for either men or women. Thus, the female menstrual cycle may be only one of a number of human biological cycles that have a potential impact on mood or behavior.

Ramey (1972) cites one study, carried out in Denmark, in which fluctuations of testosterone levels in male urine were followed for 16 years. Reportedly, a 30-day rhythmic cycle of hormone levels was found. Another study cited by Ramey involved male managers and workers in a factory. The investigator in this case measured not hormones but mood and found an emotional cycle of 4 to 6 weeks in which low periods were characterized by apathy, indifference, and overreactions to minor problems and high periods by feelings of well-being, energy, lower body weight, and a decreased need for sleep. A study by Doering, Brodie, Kraemer, Becker, and Hamburg (1974) measured both hormonal fluctuations and moods in 20 men for 2 months and found evidence supporting a link between the two. They reported a significant positive correlation between levels of self-reported depression and concentration of plasma testosterone in the blood. Their data, however, showed only weak evidence for rhythmic changes in testosterone levels.

We have seen that women's responses to the biological changes of the menstrual cycle are subject to sociocultural influences. It is logical to suppose, as well, that men's mood fluctuations are sensitive to social forces. One demonstration of this phenomenon is reported by Rossi and Rossi (1977), who found that the "social time" of the 7-day week may be as important as the "body time" of the menstrual cycle. These researchers had 67 female and 15 male college students complete daily mood-adjective checklists for 40 days. Many of the women showed menstrual cycle–related variations in mood, but the day-of-the-week effect was more pronounced for males, making overall mood variability the same for both sexes. A similar study of couples ages 25 to 45 found that, even for women, day of the week accounted for more mood variability than menstrual cycle phase did: For females and males, negative moods and arousal levels decreased on weekends (Mansfield, Hood, & Henderson, 1989). A third study also shows more fluctuation in women's moods over the days of the week than over the menstrual cycle (McFarlane, et al., 1988). It appears that "social time" creates important cycles for both women and men.

Another possible source of variability in males is the influence of their female partners' menstrual cycles (Dan, 1979). Such an effect could have both social and biological components. In one study, after 90 days of daily mood reporting, the only significant effect associated with the menstrual cycle was that *men's* arousal scores were higher during their wives' menstrual phase than during their follicular phase (Mansfield et al., 1989).

Much more research remains to be done before male hormonal cycles are understood. Other cycles do not have the clear marker of menstruation to help researchers determine cycle phase, making the discovery of fluctuations more difficult. The lack of an obvious marker also makes it difficult for the individual man to be aware of any regular fluctuations he may be experiencing in mood or performance. It is interesting, however, to speculate on the possible impact on men of knowing or not knowing about their own cycles. It may be that men, lacking a knowledge of their own cycles, are more disadvantaged by them than women are by the menstrual cycle. When a man experiences a "low" time, he may be unaware of any cycle-based reason for it and so may wrongly attribute difficulties to his own incompetence, dislike of his work, or unreasonable coworkers. However, knowledge of an upcoming "low point" in his emotional cycle might, through a self-fulfilling negative expectation, cause a man to be more depressed or to perform more poorly during this time than he would have if he had not been given this information about his cycle (as suggested for women in Ruble's 1977 research). As researchers begin to attend to the issue of male cycles, we begin to see that the menstrual cycle in women is not unique among human cycles in the magnitude of its effects. We are also beginning to understand how effects on female and male mood and performance are produced by awareness of and learned expectations about cyclic physiological changes.

PREGNANCY AND CHILDBIRTH

Physical and Emotional Aspects of Pregnancy

When a woman becomes pregnant, her normal monthly hormonal cycle is interrupted, and she experiences a state in which both estrogen and progesterone levels are more or less constantly high. Hormonally, pregnancy is most similar to the phase of the menstrual cycle that occurs just after ovulation and that has been characterized by some researchers as one of generally positive moods. In our culture, it is not unusual to hear pregnant women described as happy, content, fulfilled, and glowing. Could it be that a sense of well-being associated with pregnancy is produced by high hormone levels?

Conversely, there is much to suggest that pregnancy, far from being viewed as a time of particularly positive feelings, is seen by many as a disability. Medical research on pregnancy often seems based on the notion that the pregnant woman is to some extent disabled and tends to focus on negative symptoms. So pervasive is this focus that it is difficult to find a pregnant woman described as healthy or normal in the medical literature. As Rothman (1982) notes, healthy pregnant women are classified simply as "low risk." Social scientists, too, have been influenced by the notion of pregnancy as a time of special difficulty and vulnerability for women. Psychological research on pregnancy has until recently been dominated by the psychoanalytic idea that pregnancy brings up a host of unconscious conflicts about femininity, sexuality, and the woman's relationship to her own mother (see, for example, Bibring, 1959; Deutsch, 1945). Thus, there has been a tendency, in both medical and psychological research, to focus on the problems of pregnancy, and only recently have researchers begun to examine the normative aspects of the experience.

PHYSICAL SYMPTOMS OF PREGNANCY   Research on the pregnancy experience of normal women indicates that a group of physical symptoms is commonly reported during pregnancy, but the variation among women is tremendous (Lips, 1982a, 1985b). Perhaps the symptom most commonly linked to pregnancy in the popular consciousness is morning sickness—a tendency toward nausea and vomiting shortly after rising. It has been difficult to get an accurate estimate of the proportion of women who suffer from morning sickness during their pregnancies. To complicate the issue, women who have been pregnant several times often report that each pregnancy was different with respect to this symptom. The lack of frequency data has not, however, inhibited physicians and researchers from theorizing that the symptom has a psychological basis. It has been suggested that women who experience nausea or related difficulties during pregnancy are denying their femininity (Deutsch, 1945), are unconsciously rejecting or expressing their ambivalence toward their unborn child (Chertok, 1969), or are just generally neurotic (Pajntar, 1972). These explanations accompany a stereotype that *most* pregnant women suffer from morning sickness, and they seem to reflect a view of women that is uncomplimentary, to say the least. It is a view that sees women teetering precariously on the brink of neuroticism, requiring only the normal changes of pregnancy to push them over. A review of the research on pregnancy nausea provides little support for any of these explanations; researchers still do not know why some women experience these symptoms and some do not (Macy, 1986).

My own research on a sample of 108 normal, healthy middle-class women revealed that 24% of them reported moderate to high levels of nausea and vomiting when questioned between the 3rd and 5th months of pregnancy. That this rate of nausea is linked to pregnancy can be seen by the rate at which it was reported by three comparison groups: 3% for expectant fathers, 5% for nonpregnant women, and 3% for husbands of nonpregnant women. Thus, a substantial minority of pregnant women do report this particular symptom, but it appears, nevertheless, that the majority do not.

Responses to a 55-item list of symptoms showed that pregnant women could be distinguished from comparison groups by a small cluster of physical symptoms (Lips, 1982a, 1985a). In the first half of pregnancy, this cluster included nausea and vomiting, a desire to take naps and stay in bed, dizziness or fainting, and a definite lack of bursts of energy and activity. In the 6th to 8th months of pregnancy, it included feelings of heaviness and excessive weight gain. In the 9th month, it included feelings of awkwardness, discomfort, heaviness, swelling, general aches and pains, and backache. However, although more pregnant women than other people reported these symptoms on the average, many pregnant women did not.

EMOTIONAL SYMPTOMS OF PREGNANCY   Our cultural "script" for pregnancy includes a variety of emotional dimensions. We allow pregnant women to act a little unreasonable and are tolerant of emotional outbursts and strange requests. Conversely, as noted earlier, there is an expectation that the pregnant woman will "glow." The self-reports of pregnant women provide little support for these generalizations. Pregnant women do not differ from other women in the tendency to describe themselves as beautiful, attractive, and radiant—the "glow" factor—and a group of adjectives describing negative emotionality (irritability, mood swings, tension, depression, anxiety, and upset) failed to distinguish pregnant women from comparison groups at any stage of pregnancy (Lips, 1985b). Some studies have, however, found higher rates of depression among pregnant than nonpregnant women (Lips, 1985b) and increased rates of depression as pregnancy progresses (Gjerdingen, Froberg, & Kochevar, 1991). In addition, pregnancy does not seem to be associated with increased psychological well-being for most people. According to one study, fewer than 15% of women and 10% of men report increased psychological well-being during pregnancy (Condon, 1987).

It is theoretically possible that hormone levels may tend to predispose the pregnant woman toward positive moods, at least during some stages of pregnancy. However, if this tendency exists, the mixed evidence about the types of emotions actually experienced by pregnant women suggests that it can be overwhelmed by other factors. These factors might include the fatigue and other physical discomforts sometimes associated with pregnancy, changes in body image, anxiety about new responsibilities, or resentment of an unwanted pregnancy (Lips, 1982c). Even the positive moods associated with pregnancy are undoubtedly not totally explainable by hormone levels. Pleasure and excitement about having a child could certainly produce a positive mood shift during pregnancy. Furthermore, in a culture that still emphasizes childbearing as the route to fulfillment for women, women are actually socialized to "glow" when pregnant, and pregnant women sometimes comment that they feel guilty or inadequate if they display negative emotions.

Social and Cultural Influences on the Pregnancy Experience

Besides being a biological state, pregnancy is also part of a social role. Pregnancy apparently is a social stimulus, eliciting particular responses from people with whom the pregnant woman interacts. Two researchers did an experiment in which a woman made up to look pregnant rode a busy elevator in a high-rise building (Taylor & Langer, 1977). She stood in one back corner of the elevator and another woman, carrying a parcel so that she would take up as much space as the "pregnant" woman, stood in the other back corner. The reactions of people, particularly men, boarding the elevator were striking: They studiously avoided crowding the "pregnant" woman, sometimes almost trampling on the other woman in the process. Moreover, they did a lot of staring at the "pregnant" woman—a reaction people often display to someone with an obvious physical handicap or stigma. It is no wonder that pregnant women sometimes feel self-conscious about their appearance or notice that people seem to be treating them differently. They are reacting to a real change in their social environment.

Other research indicates that people think of pregnant women as emotional, irritable, and suffering from various physical symptoms. In one study, college students were given a description of a day in the life of a young woman and were asked to rate her mood as well as various factors on their importance in determining the woman's mood (Lips, 1980). In half the descriptions, the woman was said to be 5 months pregnant, and in the other half, no mention of pregnancy was made. The students generally rated the woman's mood as more positive when she was described as pregnant. However, when trying to give reasons for the woman's mood, they used pregnancy more often as an explanation for negative than for positive moods. Moreover, pregnancy was, almost without exception, described as a source of stress by students who mentioned it spontaneously. Clearly, these students, most of whom had never been pregnant, had learned the social stereotypes about pregnancy. They are not alone. Recently, I asked another group of college students to complete a symptom checklist "as if they were a woman who was 5 months pregnant." In general, their answers indicated that they thought pregnancy was characterized by a variety of physical symptoms, notably nausea, feeling overweight, and fatigue. For pregnancy, as for menstruation, there is apparently a well-known set of cultural expectations.

In trying to determine the links among physiological changes, expectations, and emotions, it cannot always be assumed that causality works in a particular direction, from physiological to emotional change. A case in which emotional changes apparently have physiological consequences is **pseudocyesis,** or pseudopregnancy. The physical symptoms that characterize pseudocyesis are similar to those associated with pregnancy: menstrual disturbance, abdominal enlargement, swelling and tenderness of the breasts, softening of the cervix, enlargement of the uterus, nausea and vomiting, and weight gain. Pseudocyesis patients have even reported that they can feel fetal movements. The symptoms of pseudocyesis, although not common, are not extremely rare, appear most frequently in women who are sterile, and can appear occasionally even in men. Key causal factors are thought to be a fear of, or wish for, pregnancy (Barglow & Brown, 1972; Whelan & Stewart, 1990).

Another instance in which emotions appear to lead to the physiological reactions of pregnancy rather than vice versa is the **couvade syndrome** (Trethowan, 1972), in which expectant fathers suffer from physical symptoms during their wives' pregnancy or labor. These symptoms are sometimes, but not always, similar to those experienced by the pregnant woman: nausea and vomiting, alterations of appetite, abdominal pain, swelling, and spurious labor pains. In one study, expectant fathers were found to have significantly more backaches, colds, and headaches than a comparison group of men. In addition, the expectant fathers showed unintentional weight gain, particularly during the third trimester (Clinton, 1987). There is speculation that the symptoms are caused by the man's high anxiety about his wife's pregnancy. Trethowan, who suggests that the expectant father is not usually aware of the connection between his symptoms and his wife's pregnancy, estimates that 1 out of every 4 or 5 expectant fathers experience this syndrome. However, other research shows that the syndrome is much less common than this (Lips, 1982b).

The couvade syndrome takes its name from a set of customs in various cultures that anthropologists have named **couvade** (from the French verb *couver*—to brood or hatch). Couvade rituals are expressions of father involvement in the birth process. One form that such rituals may take is that of the father-to-be, simultaneously with his wife's confinement, taking to his bed, simulating labor and delivery, and receiving attention comparable to that received by the laboring mother. The practice may be carried out to protect the mother and infant by decoying evil spirits away from them during the vulnerable time of childbirth, to help the woman in her efforts, or to announce in a powerful nonverbal way that a particular man is the father of the child. The couvade syndrome when observed in our industrialized society is not part of such a ritual, yet it may, in a sense, reflect some of these same motives.

The existence of pseudocyesis and the couvade syndrome, despite their relative rarity, underlines the complexity of the interaction that can occur between hormones and social and emotional factors in the production of physical symptoms. The finding that nonpregnant women, and even men, sometimes experience symptoms that simulate those of pregnancy lends weight to the notion that our culture teaches us how a pregnant woman is supposed to feel and act. If most members of the culture acquire this information through a process of social learning, those who eventually find themselves pregnant may develop the symptoms they (and others) have learned to expect. It is difficult to determine the extent to which expectations or hormones are responsible for this development.

PREGNANCY AND THE NEW REPRODUCTIVE TECHNOLOGIES
New technologies such as artificial insemination, in vitro fertilization, fetal monitoring, ultrasound, embryo transplants, and surrogate motherhood have expanded some people's choices in the area of childbearing and have implications for the psychology of childbearing. The psychological, not to mention political, implications of some of these technologies have not been adequately explored. For instance, little is known about what a surrogate mother—a woman who agrees, or contracts, to carry a pregnancy to term and then to turn the baby over to someone else—can expect to experience and what factors might shape that experience.

One issue that has been studied to some extent is the effect on expectant parents of knowing the sex of the fetus. Yet the findings here are mixed. For instance, one study found that parents' reactions to their infants were unaffected by knowledge of fetal sex before birth (Sweeney & Bradbard, 1988), whereas another found that parents who knew the sex of the fetus scored lower on attachment to the fetus than did parents who did not know the sex (Wu & Eichmann, 1988).

Knowledge of fetal sex can and has been used by some parents to select the sex of their children (by aborting fetuses not of the desired sex). There is a long tradition in many cultures of preference for male children, especially for male firstborns, and this preference may be reflected in the way so-called sex selection technology is used. One study of American undergraduate students found the preference for a male firstborn still in place. In this sample, of those who indicated a willingness to use sex selection, 73% preferred sons—a finding that held across race, religion, age, and income levels (Steinbacher & Gilroy, 1990).

Expectant Fatherhood

The expectant father does not experience the dramatic physiological changes of pregnancy, but he is not altogether exempt from its effects. It has now become common for the father-to-be to take an active role in pregnancy: attending childbirth preparation classes with his spouse, working with her on prenatal exercises, and being present during childbirth to provide support. This change has been relatively recent. In 1972, one survey showed that fathers were permitted in the delivery room in only 27% of American hospitals; by 1980, this number had increased to 80% (Parke, 1981).

Some expectant fathers say they feel caught in a double bind: encouraged to participate in pregnancy and birth but simultaneously excluded from the childbearing experience, with few good models to point the way to active, involved fatherhood (P. L. Jordan, 1990). They may have a number of concerns, such as queasiness, increased responsibility, uncertain paternity, and worry about losing their spouse; however, men often keep these concerns to themselves (Shapiro, 1987). Despite the adjustment they are making and the possibility of couvade symptomatology, however, expectant fathers show a lower rate of health-care seeking during their wife's pregnancy than before conception or after delivery (Quill, Lipkin, & Lamb, 1984).

Psychological theories about expectant fatherhood, like those concerning expectant motherhood, have until recently emphasized a psychoanalytic approach. His partner's pregnancy has been thought to stir up the man's underlying conflicts about his own masculinity and femininity, his relationship to his father, and his needs to be dependent and nurtured (A. Coleman & Coleman, 1971; Lacoursiere, 1972). If such feelings are experienced, some of them may be directly attributable to the social norms regarding the father's role in pregnancy and childbirth. It is not surprising to find that a man may feel anxious and dependent at a time when his partner is involved in a life-changing experience from which he is excluded. In the social climate of father participation in pregnancy and childbirth, however, expectant fatherhood is experienced positively by many men (Grossman, Eichler, & Winickoff, 1980; Lips, 1982c). In one study of middle-class couples expecting a child, the themes mentioned most frequently by the men in response to an open-ended question about how their lives had changed since the beginning of the pregnancy were a new emphasis on planning for the future, concern with finances, and an increased necessity to help with the housework (Lips, 1982c). What expectant fathers said they liked most about the pregnancy was the anticipation of the baby and their wives' happiness; what they liked least was their wives' discomfort and fatigue. A positive aspect of pregnancy, especially first pregnancy, for many modern fathers is that the shared experience draws them closer to their spouse (Lips & Morrison, 1986). Contrary to what many pregnant women think, men do not necessarily count the woman's pregnant body as a disadvantage of pregnancy. Men frequently report finding their pregnant wives attractive, and they complain about a diminished frequency of sexual activity (W. E. Miller & Friedman, 1988).

For years, research on expectant fatherhood lagged behind that on pregnancy, probably because the father's inclusion in the preparation for and experience of childbirth has been relatively recent and because the father experiences no physiological changes comparable to those of pregnancy. Research is still particularly lacking on certain issues that are unique to fathers and prospective fathers. Little is known, for example, about the psychological aspects of fatherhood achieved by proxy—through the woman's artificial insemination with another man's sperm. Still less is known about men's reactions to the loss of a potential child through women's decisions to abort a pregnancy, to give up a baby for adoption, or to refuse to acknowledge a man's paternity.

Childbirth and the Postpartum Experience

Childbirth, which used to be a female domain from which men were largely excluded, has changed dramatically in our culture during the past century. Two changes in particular stand out: (1) The process of childbirth is now largely governed by medical procedures. (2) Fathers are frequently present at the birth of their children. During the transition, women have lost considerable control over childbirth. Midwives and female relatives have been replaced by doctors and husbands, and although such changes may have positive aspects, they also have negative ones. The management of birth is now considered a medical specialty; birth is treated as a physical–mechanical process rather than a spiritual or social one. In our society, the doctor, not the woman, is said to deliver the baby. The husband may be present to support and "coach" his spouse, but the real control is in the hands of the physician. In this context, it is easy for a woman to feel powerless and vulnerable during labor and delivery—feelings that no doubt color her experience of childbirth and its aftermath. However, the woman experiencing childbirth in a modern medical context need worry considerably less than her 19th-century counterpart that she will die in childbirth, a factor that must also influence the way she approaches and experiences the birth.

The experience of labor and delivery in our North American context is a dramatic, emotional, and physically draining experience for the mother, and often for the father as well. Both women and men often report that it was a "peak" experience (Lips & Morrison, 1986), although, if difficulties or complications arise, it can be frightening and very painful. Both partners can share the experience up to a point, but only the mother's body goes through the physical trauma of childbirth. During labor, the woman experiences increasingly strong and frequent contractions of the uterus as the baby moves into and down the birth canal. These contractions, although painful, can often be made tolerable by the woman's use of special breathing techniques and by the partner's use of massage and focusing exercises. After the delivery, the woman is likely to be exhausted, but this fatigue is not the only physical change she experiences. Some researchers estimate that during labor a woman's progesterone level drops so rapidly as to represent the greatest change in concentration of this hormone she experiences in her lifetime, compressed into a few hours (Hamburg, Moos, & Yalom, 1968).

One researcher has argued that both childbirth and breastfeeding have a sexual pleasure component for women that has been ignored (Newton, 1971). Childbirth in particular, she notes, shares some physical and psychological similarities with orgasm. Breathing patterns, facial expression, uterine and abdominal contractions, clitoral engorgement, lowered inhibitions, increased physical strength, greater flexibility, and decreased sensitivity to external stimuli are similar in childbirth and orgasm; in fact, some women experience orgasm during childbirth. (This does not mean that the pain of childbirth is pleasurable for women. It is the combination of pressure and vasocongestion that may trigger orgasm.) Immediately after childbirth, as after orgasm, there is typically a sudden return of sensory acuity and feelings of joy and well-being. The possibility of a woman's experiencing sexual pleasure in childbirth is rarely mentioned, probably because our culture views any sexual connotations of this event as inappropriate.

For women, physiological and social factors conspire to make the period following the birth of a child (the postpartum period) a stressful one. Many new mothers experience some negative emotions in the days, weeks, or months after childbirth. Clinicians and researchers have labeled these negative feelings **postpartum depression,** a label that may be misleading because it is used to refer to several different types of experience. Experts now acknowledge three kinds of postpartum depression: (1) the "blues," characterized by emotionality and readiness to cry, which lasts for the first few days after delivery; (2) "neurotic" postpartum depression, characterized by depressed feelings and symptoms such as loss of appetite and insomnia, which lasts at least 2 weeks and occurs within the first few postpartum months; and (3) postpartum psychosis, a serious breakdown in the ability to cope, often including delusions and suicidal thoughts, and requiring psychiatric care. Indications from the research literature are that the blues occur in 50% to 80% of women (Harding, 1989; Hopkins, Marcues, & Campbell, 1984), whereas postpartum psychosis occurs in less than 1% (Herzog & Detre, 1976; Kaij & Nilsson, 1972). For the intermediate category of neurotic depression, frequency estimates range from 10% to 30% (Cutrona, 1982; Hopkins et al., 1984). A recent review of 59 studies placed the prevalence of this nonpsychotic postpartum depression at 13% (O'Hara & Swain, 1996).

Some researchers have theorized that the large drop in the woman's progesterone level at delivery and the dramatic drop in estrogen levels during the first postpartum week are responsible for postpartum depression. However, a causal link between the hormonal change and the emotional change has not been demonstrated (O'Hara, 1997). Studies in which hormone levels were measured during pregnancy and the postpartum period have found no consistent differences in these levels between those women who developed postpartum depression and those who did not (Cutrona, 1982). However, since some studies find that women who experience severe menstrual problems are more likely to experience postpartum depression, Cutrona speculates that there may be a small group of women whose depression is due to an unusual sensitivity to hormonal changes.

The hormonal changes associated with childbirth and the postpartum period are real enough, but culture affects the way physical changes and symptoms are interpreted. Social expectations are likely to contribute to a woman's labeling of her feelings as postpartum depression—especially since some of the physical changes associated with late pregnancy and the early postpartum period (such as sleep difficulties) often characterize depression in other circumstances (B.J. Kaplan, 1986). Furthermore, the social context can affect both a woman's experience of and labeling of symptoms.

Researchers have investigated a number of psychological and cultural–environmental correlates of postpartum depression. Their findings suggest that stressful life events, delivery-related stress, poor marital relationship, lack of social support from others, and prior history of psychiatric symptoms are all factors that may be important in predisposing a woman to postpartum depression (Cutrona, 1982; O'Hara & Swain, 1996). In addition, there are reports of postpartum depression in new fathers (McEwan, 1985; O'Hara, 1985; Richman, Raskin, & Gaines, 1991) and in adoptive mothers (Melges, 1968), suggesting that the hormonal changes occurring during labor are not necessary to precipitate these feelings. In the postpartum period, as with pregnancy and the menstrual cycle, the relationships that may exist between hormone levels on one hand and feelings and behavior on the other are complicated by the presence of many social and environmental factors.

Researchers who have examined women's accounts of their own experience of postpartum depression have found that there is a great deal of variation in women's responses to childbirth and that much of that variation seems linked to the reactions of others in their social environment. Natasha Mauthner (1999), who interviewed 40 new mothers, concluded that postpartum depression was most likely to occur when women did not have a supportive, nonjudgmental social/cultural environment in which to experience and express their feelings and needs. In a similar vein, Paula Nicolson (1999), who interviewed 25 women periodically as they progressed through pregnancy and the postpartum period, found that new mothers were bothered by the assumptions of those around them that their feelings of depression were inappropriate responses to a happy event. Women in her study noted that they were happy to be mothers but unhappy at the losses that accompany the early stages of motherhood: loss of autonomy and time to themselves, changes in appearance, sexuality, and occupational identity. Nicolson argues that "if these losses were taken seriously and the women encouraged to grieve . . . postpartum depression would be seen by the women and their partners, family and friends as a potentially healthy process towards psychological re-integration and personal growth" (p. 162).

Of course, there is more to the postpartum period than depression. Attachment to the baby develops gradually in both parents over the first several months (Leifer, 1980). This process of attachment can be influenced by a number of variables. Fathers present at the birth of their infants show more intense attachment to the baby (G. H. Peterson, Mehl, & Leiderman, 1979). Mothers who have experienced marital problems and ambivalence about the pregnancy are more likely to be depressed and to have difficulties interacting with the baby (Field et al., 1985). Conversely, despite popular concern about the psychological impact of birth technology, interventions such as caesarean section have not been shown to have an adverse effect on the mother–infant relationship (Bradley, 1983). On the whole, it is clear that both parents have the capacity to develop an intense attachment to the new baby, given the close contact necessary to do so.

Abortion

Every year, more than 1 million women in North America end their pregnancies through abortion. Researchers estimate that 49% of pregnancies among American women are unintended, that one half of these unintended pregnancies are terminated by abortion, and that 43% of women will have at least one abortion by the time they are 45 years old (Alan Guttmacher Institute, 1998). The decision to terminate a pregnancy is a difficult one for many women, often made more problematic by the raging political controversy that surrounds the issue.

Women who seek abortions come from a wide variety of backgrounds. The majority are White and non-Hispanic; almost one third are still in school, and a large number are poor and unemployed (Russo, Horn, & Schwartz, 1992.) More than half are under 25 years of age and unmarried. In 1987, 47% of all women seeking abortions in the United States were already mothers. One study found that 12% of the mothers seeking abortions had a youngest child less than 1 year old, and 25% had a child younger than 2 (Russo et al., 1992). Women usually have several reasons for choosing abortion. Commonly cited are external reasons such as the inability to afford a child, responsibilities to existing children, education and job responsibilities, social disapproval, and partner's unwillingness to have a child and internal reasons such as a lack of maturity and personal health (Russo et al., 1992).

The political controversy surrounding abortion has made it difficult for researchers to determine the psychological impact of abortion itself (Wilmoth, 1992). A long-term prospective study, recommended by the Surgeon General in 1989 (Koop, 1989), has not been funded. Women's responses to national surveys reflect an underreporting of abortions. Most studies of reactions to abortion have focused on local populations, not on national, representative samples of women. Furthermore, no studies have done long-term follow-ups of women who have had abortions to see whether, as some clinicians claim, psychological distress shows up years later. Thus, more research is needed to determine the prevalence and seriousness of negative reactions among women who have abortions.

The most careful studies that have been done suggest that abortion is not linked to severe psychological trauma; women may feel some guilt and regret, but they also feel relief and happiness after the termination of an unwanted pregnancy (Adler, 1975; Shusterman, 1976; Turell, Armsworth, & Gaa, 1990). In most cases it appears that abortion is no more likely to cause psychological problems than giving birth (Wilmoth, de Alteriis, & Bussell, 1992). However, certain factors may predispose women to experience negative consequences: being pressured into abortion

(Greenglass, 1976), lack of support from significant others (Major & Cozzarelli, 1992; Turell et al., 1990), younger age, having no other children, abortion during the second trimester of pregnancy, strong religiosity (Turell et al., 1990), and blaming the pregnancy on one's character (Major & Cozzarelli, 1992).

Regardless of the ultimate decision, confronting the choice to have or not to have an abortion can force a woman to grapple with the balance between her own needs and those of others (Gilligan, 1982). Thus, counseling during the decision period can be very important. Yet sometimes abortion counseling is inadequate to help women explore their feelings surrounding the issue, taking instead the narrow emphasis of handing out contraceptive information and warning women not to become pregnant again (McDonnell, 1984). Although this emphasis is prompted by social concern over the large number of repeat abortions, it is possible that the problem would be better addressed by helping women to work through feelings about their pregnancy and abortion.

In men, one reaction to abortion may be a sense of helplessness and loss of control. Anecdotal reports suggest that men may also feel isolated, angry at themselves and their partners, and worried about emotional and physical damage to the woman. Among men who are supportive of their partner, many focus on concern for her and hide or deny their own feelings (Wade, 1978). They may keep silent about the decision in an attempt to allow the woman to make her own choice, but some women may experience this silence as an abdication of responsibility. Many men truly do abdicate their responsibility in this situation, leaving the woman to cope on her own with whatever decision she makes.

Many aspects of the psychology of abortion are still poorly understood, perhaps because it has been difficult to separate the reasons for and impact of abortion itself from the legal and ethical controversies that surround it. However, it is an experience that affects enormous numbers of people, and a better understanding of it should be an important item on psychologists' research agenda.

Some research has examined the values, belief systems, and characteristics of the people who take active stands either against abortion or in favor of choice with respect to abortion. Sociologist Lorna Erwin studied members of Canadian groups who identify themselves as "pro-life" and "pro-family" (Rauhala, 1987). She found that religion was the single most important factor distinguishing these people from the general public in Canada. They were far more likely than the average Canadian to say that religion was important to them and to attend church more than once a week. More than 85% of them were concerned about feminism and about homosexuality as threats to the family, and a majority disapproved of the mothers of preschoolers working outside the home. Kristin Luker (1984), who studied American pro-choice and anti-abortion activists, found that more than 80% of the highly involved persons on both sides of the issue were women and that these two groups of women differed in many ways besides their views on abortion. The typical pro-choice activist had one or two children, was married to a professional man, had some professional training herself, was employed, and had a relatively high family income. Religion was not an important part of her life and she rarely attended church. By contrast, the typical anti-abortion activist had three or more children, was a high school graduate, was married to a man who ran a small business, and enjoyed a family income that was about $20,000 a year less than that of her pro-choice counterpart. Religion was very important to her, and she attended church at least weekly.

The pro-choice activists tend to believe men and women have equal rights and responsibilities, that parenthood is not a "natural" role for women but one that should be chosen freely, and that sex is for pleasure and enhancing intimacy rather than only for procreation. By contrast, the anti-abortion women tend to believe women are naturally more suited than men for filling nurturing family roles, that men are more suited for work in the public sphere outside the home, and that the main purpose of sex is procreation. Thus, the two groups of women differ sharply in their values and life choices, and Luker argues that their stances on abortion act to rationalize and justify these personal commitments. Women who have made traditional motherhood and family roles central to their lives may well feel threatened and devalued by a movement that would give women the power to restrict their involvement in such roles. Women who have defined themselves not just as mothers but also as workers outside the family circle are profoundly uncomfortable with an ideology that enshrines motherhood as the primary role for most women. Abortion is the issue over which these two groups of women have come into obvious conflict, but Luker argues that the conflict actually encompasses a struggle between two very different ways of life.

Can common ground between these two groups be discovered? Yes, according to anthropologist Faye Ginsburg, who has studied abortion activism in the United States. She describes the brief emergence during the 1980s of a group called Pro-Dialogue in North Dakota, which enabled people on both sides of the abortion debate to agree on a policy that stressed positive alternatives to abortion: effective sex education, research on safer means of contraception, improved adoption services, and economic support programs for parents. More recently, she notes, an organization called the Common Ground Network for Life and Choice has begun to provide a framework for activists from both camps to work together on issues such as teen pregnancy and the provision of resources for impoverished mothers and their children (Ginsburg, 1996). The flowering of this group demonstrates that shared values can sometimes be found between pro-choice and anti-abortion activists if they are willing to examine together the context in which childbearing takes place.

MENOPAUSE

Around age 40, a woman's ovaries begin to stop responding to stimulation by pituitary hormones to produce estrogen and progesterone. Over the next 10 to 15 years, the menstrual periods become increasingly irregular. During this time, sometimes called perimenopause, a woman may experience some changes such as very heavy menstrual flow, vaginal dryness, and sleep difficulties. Eventually, the menstrual periods stop. When a woman has had no menstrual periods for 1 year, she is said to have reached **menopause** (Voda & Eliasson, 1983). As estrogen levels fall, the woman may experience a number of physical changes. It is not known whether the drop in estrogen causes all of these changes, and there is some debate about the proportion of women who experience them. For example, in one study of 40- to 60-year-old women, those going through menopause reported no greater frequency of physical symptoms than pre- or postmenopausal women (Frey, 1981). The most common symptoms attributed to menopause are hot flashes, vaginal dryness, urinary problems, and bone thinning (osteoporosis). In North America, hot flashes are perhaps the best known of menopausal symptoms, although their cause is not well understood. During a hot flash, the blood vessels in the woman's skin dilate and her skin conductance increases—and she feels extremely hot (Freedman, 1989; Swartzman, Edelberg, & Kemmann, 1990). However, there is great cultural variation in the prevalence of this symptom. It is so uncommmon among Japanese women, for instance, that there is no specific term for it (Lock, 1993).

Women's reactions to menopause are complicated by a barrage of sometimes frightening and conflicting information from medical sources. Some physicians regard menopause as a *disease* of estrogen deficiency that must be "managed" by the medical profession until a woman's death. One medical expert draws an analogy between diabetes, a disease of insulin deficiency, and menopause, arguing that it is just as natural to give estrogen to menopausal and postmenopausal women as to give insulin to diabetics (Rauramo, 1986). This medical model of menopause focuses on debilitating physical symptoms and implies that the only way for women to prevent the inevitable downhill slide is to comply with estrogen replacement therapy (ERT).

By contrast, a nonmedical, "life transition" model of menopause implies that menopause is

> a natural development process that signals a life transition in much the same way as puberty does. Puberty may be associated with skin problems and emotional distress, but these problems are not viewed as symptoms of an underlying "clinical disorder" nor are attempts made to prevent puberty by suppressing hormone production. Similarly, according to this model, menopause may be accompanied by hot flashes and the emotional turmoil associated with identity and role issues, but these are dealt with as problems associated with a normal and expected transition rather than as indicative of a disease process. The focus is not on "deficiency" and artificially maintaining a particular hormonal state but rather on viewing menopause as an inevitable life stage associated with new challenges and freedoms. (Gannon & Ekstrom, 1993, p. 277)

The sociocultural context that is prevalent with respect to menopause may well affect a woman's attitudes toward this change in her life. Suggestive evidence for this conclusion is provided by two researchers who asked a large sample of adults to express their attitudes toward menopause in one of three contexts (Gannon & Ekstrom, 1993). One group gave their attitudes toward three medical problems, including menopause; a second group described attitudes toward three life transitions, including menopause; and a third group responded to three symbols of aging, including menopause. They found that the medical context elicited the most negative and least positive attitudes from respondents. Older respondents and those who had experienced menopause also showed more positive attitudes.

Attitudes toward menopause are important because they may mediate a woman's experience and behavior. Negative attitudes, beliefs, and expectations among premenopausal women have been found to predict reported distress at the time of menopause (Avis & McKinlay, 1991; Hunter, 1990).

The lowered levels of estrogen that begin at menopause do reduce a protective effect that younger women enjoy against heart disease (Stuenkel, 1989; Voda & Eliason, 1983) and against the thinning bones of osteoporosis (Ziegler, Scheidt-Nave, & Scharla, 1995). Each of these diseases is a serious health hazard for older women, so women are often pressured to begin ERT at menopause and continue for the rest of their lives. Yet there are risks associated with ERT: possible side effects and increased risk of endometrial and breast cancer (F. Davis, 1996). Studies show that whether women think of menopause as a medical problem bears more weight on their decision to use ERT than does their perception of risk from osteoporosis and heart disease (Logothetis, 1991) and that women are more likely to be concerned about the relief of short-term problems such as hot flashes than longer-term problems such as osteoporosis (Rothert et al., 1990).

In making decisions about ERT, women must weigh their own medical history and susceptibility to particular health problems. However, there is a set of noncontroversial recommendations to improve the odds against osteoporosis: adequate dietary intake of calcium and vitamin D, a daily program of weight-bearing exercise including a 30-minute walk, and no smoking (Nagia & Bennett, 1992). Some of these behaviors have a beneficial effect on other menopausal symptoms; for instance, women who are physically active experience fewer symptoms (Wilbur, Dan, Hedricks, & Holm, 1990).

Some women report increased depression and irritability around the time of menopause. To put these reports in perspective, consider the findings of Neugarten and Kraines (1965), who studied "menopausal" symptoms among women of different ages. They found the highest levels of symptoms in menopausal women and adolescents and the lowest level among postmenopausal women. Adolescents reported more psychological symptoms; menopausal women noted more physical ones. Thus, psychologically, adolescence may be a more difficult time for women than menopause. At any rate, there is no evidence for a general increase in depression at menopause (Lennon, 1987).

The emotional changes that some women experience around menopause may well be linked to social–environmental variables. A woman at this stage is losing her ability to bear children—an ability that our culture tends to emphasize as crucial to the feminine role. If she had children during her 20s, they are growing up and moving away and are no longer dependent on her, a change that may be experienced by her as either positive or negative. She may also be conscious of "losing her looks" as she ages and may feel that this change in appearance jeopardizes her relationship with her husband or partner. There are reasons here for a woman to reappraise her life and her priorities and possibly to become depressed if she decides that she is losing everything that is worthwhile. One study of middle-aged women indicated that depression at menopause was strongly related to the degree of role loss a woman was experiencing and linked menopausal depression to the "empty nest" (Bart, 1971). This researcher also found that in cultures where a woman is still gaining rather than losing status as she ages negative emotional reactions at menopause are rare. Other research has found that many women are, in fact, overjoyed to have an empty nest again—to be free of the responsibilities of parenthood so that they can reorganize their lives and try something new (Rubin, 1979). Another study has shown that the most marked increases in depression among postmenopausal women were associated with multiple causes of worry and stress, including adolescent children, ailing husbands, and aging parents (McKinlay, McKinlay, & Brambilla, 1987). These findings indicate once more that cultural–environmental factors can strongly modify a person's reaction to physiological changes.

"Male Menopause"

In men, there is no sudden change in hormonal level at a particular age. Rather, a man's level of testosterone and sperm production decreases very gradually from the age of about 30 onward. In their 70s and 80s, in a transition sometimes labeled **andropause,** men experience a thinning of the ejaculate, a reduction of ejaculatory pressure, and a decrease in the levels of FSH and LH. One physical change that is quite common for men over the age of 40 is enlargement of the prostate gland. This enlargement, which is thought to be related to changes in hormone levels, causes urinary problems; it can be remedied by surgery or drugs. Another change is a gradual drop in libido (Davidson, 1989).

Although the physical changes are very gradual, some men seem to experience a psychological crisis at middle age—a crisis that has sometimes been dubbed "male menopause." Research shows that men in their 40s show higher depression scores and more alcohol and drug use than other adult men; however, they do not differ from other men in anxiety, life satisfaction, or happiness (Tamir, 1982). The problems that men in this age range experience have been attributed not to their changing hormone levels but to psychosocial factors. For example, David Gutmann (1972) refers to the male midlife crisis as a "loss of the future." He claims that by about the age of 50 many achievement-oriented men begin to feel that they are not going to become any more successful or move any closer to their goals. Gutmann's interviews with men in this age group in several different cultures offer some support for this concept. His research suggests that a man may greet the realization that he cannot improve his future either with a relieved sense of letting go and a moving out of the rat race or with an inner crisis in which he struggles with the fact that he has not achieved his goals to his own satisfaction. This theme of an aspiration–achievement gap for middle-aged men is echoed by D.J. Levinson (1978).

Another explanation that is offered for a male midlife crisis is the change in family relationships that occurs at this time. Children are moving away from home, leaving their parents alone together for the first time in many years. Women, freed from their parental roles, may return to work or school, developing new interests and responsibilities and forcing a renegotiation of the couple's relationship. These changes may be experienced as threatening by the man; conversely, they may be viewed as opportunities to explore new directions.

It is clear that both women and men can experience negative emotional reactions to the important changes in role that occur at midlife. Women, however, have been taught to expect these changes and to label them as menopausal. These expectations probably contribute to the strength of the symptoms they experience and to their coping strategies. Although some midlife symptoms are related to the physical aspects of aging, it seems reasonable to suggest that both women and men may react negatively when they find themselves no longer able to fulfill some aspects of the roles that society has defined as central for them: childrearing for women and successful career achievement for men. As feminine and masculine gender roles become more flexible, perhaps midlife will be regarded increasingly by both women and men as a welcome opportunity to shift gears and try something different.

SUMMARY

Women's menstrual cycle makes it obvious that they are experiencing cyclic fluctuations of hormone levels, whereas men display no easily discernible signs that their physiology is not completely stable. However, research shows that both women and men are subject to a variety of biologically and socially induced cycles that relate to mood and behavior, and women are no more variable than men in mood and performance. There is also strong evidence that relationships between biological cycles and such correlates as symptoms, moods, or performance can be modified dramatically by factors in the person's environment. Furthermore, although women are subject to the processes of pregnancy, childbirth, and menopause that involve both large hormonal changes and culturally recognized sets of physical and emotional symptoms, men are not unaffected by the drastic life changes that go along with having a child or losing an important role. Thus, even with regard to the particular experiences of pregnancy and menopause, causality of symptoms cannot be attributed simply to hormonal changes, but must be considered a blend of biological and social factors.

In general, research on hormonal and reproductive issues seems to have been guided by the assumption that they are "women's problems" and has focused on trying to understand them by reference to hormone levels. Accordingly, research on male reactions to these events has been scanty. Much more research on both women and men is needed before the myths about "raging hormones," pregnancy, postpartum depression, and menopause can be replaced with facts.

KEY TERMS

menstrual cycle	premenstrual dysphoric	pseudocyesis
follicular phase	disorder (PMDD)	couvade syndrome
ovulation	prostaglandins	couvade
luteal phase	menarche	postpartum depression
menstruation	gonadotropins	menopause
premenstrual syndrome	spermarche	andropause
dysmenorrhea		

FOR ADDITIONAL READING

Greer, Germaine. (1992). *The change: Women, aging, and the menopause*. New York: Knopf. Citing medical, historical, anthropological, and literary sources, the author challenges accepted stereotypes of the physical and emotional effects of menopause and aging.

Lock, Margaret. (1993). *Encounters with aging: Mythologies of menopause in Japan and North America*. Berkeley: University of California Press. An anthropologist discusses the attitudes toward menopause in different cultures and presents the results of her own studies comparing samples of women from Canada, the United States, and Japan.

Rothman, Barbara K. (1982). *In labor: Women and power in the birthplace*. New York: Norton. A sociologist describes the ways the medical approach to pregnancy and childbirth affects women's experience of these processes.

Siebers, Tobin. (1999). *Among men*. Lincoln: University of Nebraska Press. This is a personal book about the meaning of masculinity, including sections on male bonding, male emotions, and sexuality. It does not address the issue of hormones directly, but does examine some of the transitions and body issues men face.

CHAPTER 9

Mental &
Physical Health

Stress, Change, & Adaptations

*O*ur culturally accepted gender roles associate femininity with weakness, delicacy, and vulnerability. Masculinity, in contrast, is associated with images of strength, toughness, and invulnerability. It is perhaps not surprising, then, that women's physical and mental health has been considered fragile in comparison to men's and that the history of professionalized health care has, at least until recently, been largely one of male doctors giving advice to female patients (Ehrenreich & English, 1979). Women's vulnerability to both physical and mental ailments was once believed to be traceable in large measure to their reproductive physiology and anatomy: The mere possession of a uterus rendered a woman susceptible to a variety of disorders. During the 19th century, doctors argued that normal feminine functions put all women at risk. As one physician put it, those women who were not "crippled on the breakers of puberty" might be "dashed to pieces on the rock of childbirth" or "ground on the ever-recurring shallows of menstruation, and . . . the final bar of menopause" (Engelmann, 1900, as quoted in Ehrenreich & English, 1979, p. 110). Furthermore, doctors asserted that in women diseases of the stomach, liver, heart, lungs, and other organs were usually no more than sympathetic reactions to disorders of the uterus. Even tuberculosis, which was attributed to environmental causes when contracted by males, was believed to be a result of menstrual malfunction when it occurred in females (Ehrenreich & English, 1979). Most famous of all female disorders, however, was **hysteria**—from the Greek word meaning uterus—a mysterious disease marked by fainting or fits and a variety of symptoms such as loss of voice or partial paralysis, with no apparent physical cause. It was considered a disease of the uterus, despite the lack of evidence that the symptoms had any organic basis whatsoever. Sigmund Freud eventually redefined hysteria as a mental rather than physical disorder; nevertheless, it was still considered a feminine disease. In retrospect, modern commentators have explained it as a result of the stifling restrictions attached to the role of the upper-class woman during the 19th and early 20th centuries.

VULNERABILITY AND STRENGTH

The idea that women are the weaker, more vulnerable sex and men are stronger and better able to withstand the rigors of life and work both stems from and provides a convenient justification for the social arrangements of the cultures in which it prevails. In fact, however, the evidence provides a rather mixed picture of male–female differences in vulnerability and strength. In brief, although some studies show that women report more minor physical symptoms and seek medical help more often than men do, men are more vulnerable than women to serious illnesses at every stage of life, and the male's life span is shorter than the female's. Women and men each report higher rates of certain mental illness symptoms. In terms of muscular strength, men generally outperform women, but the gap is not necessarily as large as the "tough man–fragile woman" stereotype would suggest.

Physical Vulnerability and Mortality

Males are more likely than females to suffer injury or death prenatally or during the birth process and to be victims of childhood diseases. Although 108 to 140 males are conceived for every 100 females, by the time of birth, the ratio of males to females has dropped to between 103 and 106 to 100 in the United States. Miscarriage, stillbirth, and death from birth-related injuries are more likely to affect males than females. Male infants are more likely than females to suffer from congenital malformations and from a wide variety of genetically linked diseases and to die during the first year of life. During the teenage years, males are more likely than females to die in accidents. The survival rate of women from such conditions as starvation, exposure, fatigue, and shock is better than that of men. In the United States, females outnumber males by the early 20s; by the age of 65 there are about 3 women for every 2 men, and among those who live to be 100, the ratio of women to men is 4 to 1. The sex differential in longevity has traditionally been smaller among African Americans and Hispanic Americans, whose life expectancy at birth is 6 to 7 years shorter than that of European Americans. This effect is likely due to low income, which tends to be correlated with race. As the life expectancy of these minority groups increases, so does the gender difference in that expectancy, thus leading to increased rates of widowhood in these groups (Go, Brustrom, Lynch, & Aldwin, 1995; Markides, 1989).

In developing countries, where poverty and malnutrition are more prevalent, sex differences in life expectancy are narrower: closer to 2 years than to the 7 years found in developed countries (Reddy, 1994). In Nepal and Bangladesh, men's life expectancy actually exceeds that of women (United Nations, 1995a). This higher female mortality has been linked to the low cultural value placed on females relative to males. Boys are given better care, including better nutrition and access to medical treatment, than girls, who are more likely to be neglected.

Although the possession of a uterus does not endanger a woman's health in the way 19th-century doctors claimed, it does present one potentially serious risk to women's health and survival: childbearing. The World Health Organization estimates that in third-world countries deaths from maternal causes (pregnancy and childbirth) are among the five major causes of death for women aged 15 to 44; in one third of the countries, these causes rank first or second in overall death rates. In the United States, complications of pregnancy and delivery account for less than 1% of the deaths of women between 15 and 49, but in developing countries, these causes may account for up to one quarter of such deaths. And within the United States, maternal death rates vary dramatically among ethnic/racial groups, probably because of differences among these groups in socioeconomic status and access to health care. Whereas for non-Hispanic White women, the maternal death rate is about 6 in every 100,000 births, the death rate for Hispanic women is 10 per 100,000 and for African American women it is a sobering 25 per 100,000 (L. Bell, 1999).

Even when it does not directly lead to the mother's death, pregnancy is a serious drain on women's health in countries where women do not have access to enough food to meet their increased caloric and nutritional requirements. Countries with the lowest life expectancy for females also tend to have the highest fertility rates (United Nations, 1991, 1995a).

Illness Rates

Men are more likely than women to die from heart disease, cancer, lung disease, pneumonia and flu, and liver disease. Women are more likely than men to die from strokes and diabetes, and they account for almost all the deaths from breast cancer. Prostate cancer, which affects only men, kills about 80% as many men as breast cancer kills women (National Center for Health Statistics, 1999a). The rates of death due to suicide and homicide are strikingly higher for men than for women (U.S. Bureau of the Census, 1998). The leading cause of death for men in the 25- to 44-year-old age group is accidents and other injuries; for women in the same age group, the leading cause of death is cancer (National Center for Health Statistics, 1999a). Men use and abuse alcohol and illegal narcotics more than women do; however, women are much more likely than men to be treated with drugs for their mental and emotional problems (Ogur, 1986; Travis, 1988).

These statistics can be somewhat misleading. An emphasis on the differences between women and men obscures the fact that, depending on a variety of conditions, both sexes can be threatened by such serious illness as heart disease and cancer. For example, although more young men than young women die of heart disease, heart disease is the leading killer of American women older than 55, and a woman's first heart attack is more likely than a man's to be fatal. In fact, women in the United States are

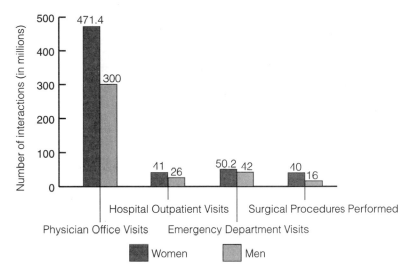

Figure 9.1 Interactions of women and men in the United States with the health care system.
Source: National Center for Health Statistics (1999) Fastats, A to Z [Online]. Available: http://www.cdc.gov/nchswww/fastats

50% more likely than men to die when they have a heart attack ("Studies Show," 1998). Women who both smoke and take oral contraceptives are at substantially increased risk for heart attacks. African American women between the ages of 35 and 74 die from heart disease 1½ times as often as their European American counterparts, partly because they are more likely to have high blood pressure (P. Long, 1991). As well, African American women have a higher fatality rate from breast cancer than do European American women. The 5-year mortality rates after diagnosis with breast cancer are 34.2% for African American women and 18.4% for European American women. When access to health care is approximately equal for the two groups of women, as in the military, the gap in mortality rates narrows. However, even among women in the military, African American women have a higher mortality rate from breast cancer (24.77%) than do European American women (18.08%) ("Black Breast-Cancer Deaths," 1998).

Across all ages, women report more physical illness symptoms than men do, take more prescribed and nonprescribed medication, and visit the doctor more often (Muller, 1990; U.S. Department of Health and Human Services, 1995). The dramatic differences between women and men in their interactions with the health care system are shown in Figure 9.1. The types of symptoms reported by women and men also differ: Women report more headaches, urinary problems, abdominal pain, and weight problems, whereas men report more ulcers, asthma, and eye problems (Kane, 1991). However, for both women and men, the most common chronic condition is sinusitis, and the most common acute condition is influenza (National Center for Health Statistics, 1999a). When the definition of mental illness is restricted to diagnoses involving mental disorganization (e.g., confusion, disorientation) or personal discomfort (e.g., anxiety, depression), women are considerably more likely than men to be diagnosed and treated for mental illness (Kane, 1991; Russo & Sobel, 1981). This finding holds across all ethnic groups but not across all types of marital status. In fact, it is only among the married population that women are more likely than men to receive psychiatric treatment. When particular categories of mental disorders and treatments are examined, the pattern of observed gender differences is mixed. Men have higher rates of treatment for alcohol and drug disorders, but women far outnumber men in depression, and the sexes are diagnosed and treated for schizophrenia with about equal frequency (Belle & Goldman, 1980). Women are far more likely than men to suffer from the eating disorders anorexia and bulimia.

Fitness and Strength

As a group, women are shorter, lighter, and less muscular than men and are regarded in our society as generally unable to perform heavy manual work. Research has demonstrated, however, that young women (college students without special training) are able to do strenuous work, expending 2369 kilocalories for 8½ hours (Wardle, 1976). This expenditure of energy is approximately equal to that required in unmechanized coal mining—usually considered one of the most demanding occupations. Thus, although women have, on average, less muscular strength than men, it would be a mistake to characterize them as weak. This conclusion is affirmed by a look at women in other cultures. For example, researchers working in a University of Nairobi laboratory found that an African woman who is accustomed to the task can easily carry on her head a load that is equal to two thirds of her body weight—and do so while expending far less energy than a male U.S. Army trooper hauling an equivalent load (Maloiy, Heglund, Prager, Cavagna, & Taylor, 1986). Women become both stronger and more muscular with training. Research on the responses of young women and men to resistance training (training with weights) makes it clear that in response to the same short-term training program women and men achieve similar increases in muscle size—and that women make greater relative gains in strength (O'Hagan et al., 1995). In addition, weight training lowers cholesterol levels in both women and men (Vergano, 1999).

Men's advantage in muscular strength has been amply demonstrated by their performance in athletic competition. In Olympic events in which both sexes participate, men consistently obtain better performance records. However, the differences between men's and women's records in track, field, and swimming events are decreasing rapidly as female athletes receive proper training. For instance, during the 12 years between 1972 and 1984, the women's record for the marathon dropped more than 23 minutes while the men's dropped only 22 seconds. The world swimming record set by Janet Evans in the 400-meter freestyle in the 1988 Olympics was 2 seconds *faster* than Mark Spitz's 1968 world record in the same event (Swardson, 1991). Florence Griffith Joyner's 1988 world-record time in the 100-meter run is faster than the Olympic gold medal times of male runners up until the 1930s. And speed skater Bonnie Blair's winning time for the 500-meter Olympic gold medal in 1994 was faster than the times of all male gold medal winners in the same event up until 1976 (Funk and Wagnalls Corporation, 1994). In events that require endurance as well as speed, such as the ultramarathon, women can outcompete men. Women hold the speed record for swimming the English Channel in both directions, and in 1995 Allison

Streeter set a new world record for the number of crossings when she swam the Channel for the 32nd time. In 1988, Paula Newby-Fraser won the women's division of the famous Ironman Triathlon—with a time that placed her ahead of all but 10 of the hundreds of male contestants. In 1988, Susan Butcher became the first person to win a third consecutive Iditarod, a grueling long-distance sled dog race. And in 1989, Ann Trason won the mixed-sex TAC/USA 24-Hour Race in New York City.

Among nonathletes, men generally are stronger than women and participate in more physical activity than women do. On average, women have lower levels of cardiovascular fitness than men do at all age levels, although in North America neither men nor women meet the standards for cardiovascular fitness set by health organizations (Adams, Johnson, Cole, Matthiasson, et al., 1990). For both sexes, fitness levels improve markedly with regular physical exercise.

Examining these three lines of evidence—vulnerability and survival rates, illness rates, and measures of fitness and strength—the reliability of the strong man–weak woman stereotype is far from clear-cut. Let us turn next to an examination of gender-related patterns in specific areas of physical and mental health and their underlying causes. Physical and mental health are discussed under separate headings, but it will soon become clear that they are strongly interrelated, each one unavoidably affecting the other.

GENDER AND PHYSICAL HEALTH

General Health and Fitness

Men have a shorter life expectancy than women, and males are more likely than females to succumb to a variety of serious diseases. Part of the explanation for these differences is genetic. Males, as seen in Chapter 5, are more likely than females to inherit a variety of sex-linked disorders. Other biological explanations have been offered for some of the gender differences. Women's relatively high estrogen levels may offer them at least temporary protection against heart disease (Hazzard, 1986); heart attacks increase for women as their estrogen decreases. Another suggestion is that women's lower metabolic rate and relatively greater percentage of body fat than men's contributes to their survival in difficult conditions. Support for the biological vulnerability explanations of gender differences in health comes from studies in which populations of males and females living very similar lifestyles are still found to differ in life expectancy. For example, a study of 40,000 American monks and nuns, all of whom were, of course, unmarried, did not smoke or drink alcohol, had similar diets, and were teachers, found that despite the similarity in lifestyle the women had a life expectancy advantage of more than 5 years by the age of 45 (as cited in Nicholson, 1984). Other research, however, has shown that there is a tendency for males and females to die at equal rates from specific diseases when their environment and lifestyle are similar. For example, among male and female long-term psychiatric patients, the death rate from heart disease is similar for the two sexes, whereas in the general population men are 4 times more likely than women to die of heart attacks (Craig & Lin, 1984).

Several writers have argued that gender roles make an important contribution to gender differences in health. One way in which this might happen is that the masculine role prompts men to behave in ways that are dangerous to health (Harrison,

1978; Waldron, 1983). Brannon (1976), for example, has argued that the stereo-typed masculine role contains four elements: the avoidance of femininity, the need to be superior to others, the need to be self-reliant and independent, and the need to be more powerful than others. The attempt to live up to such a role may cause a great deal of anxiety. The stress of not meeting his achievement aspirations, for instance, may be difficult for a man to handle, and a man trying to live up to the "self-reliant" part of the masculine role has another potential handicap: He cannot allow himself to relieve his anxiety by talking about his problems. The physical effects of stress generated by a competitive orientation may be worsened by the man's attempts to relieve that stress through drinking, smoking, or other drug use. Furthermore, the desire to appear powerful may lead a man to engage in risky behaviors, such as driving dangerously or fighting. Young men, particularly young African American men, are far more likely than young women to be the victims of homicide (U.S. Department of Justice, 1998). All of these factors, each one stemming in some way from the masculine role, contribute to the likelihood of an earlier death for men than for women (Ortmeyer, 1979). As women take on more and more of the stresses traditionally associated with the masculine role, the male–female difference in mortality may begin to decline. For example, statistics show that from 1975 to 1990, the number of women drivers killed in traffic accidents rose by about 60% while the number of men drivers killed dropped about 10%. In concert with this finding, researchers note, the arrest rate for driving under the influence of alcohol went up for women and down slightly for men (Fehr, 1992).

The feminine gender role may also contribute to gender differences in health patterns. The feminine ideals of expressiveness and intimacy may help women avoid the stress-generating patterns of competitiveness and suffering in stoical silence that are encouraged by the masculine role. In addition, the lack of necessity to show off strength or power may keep women out of risky situations. There is a potential trade-off here, of course: Men die during their risky undertakings, but women may die of boredom! In fact, boredom, the lack of a sense of purpose, and the absence of intellectually challenging work has been cited as a source of ill health for women caught in restrictive roles—from the affluent "hysterical" women of the early part of this century to the middle-class housewives experiencing the numbing malaise that Betty Friedan in *The Feminine Mystique* (1963) characterized as "the problem that has no name."

A direct and obvious contribution of the feminine role to women's lower levels of fitness has been the notion that strength is unfeminine and that athletic activity is primarily for men. In recent years, there has been an increased media focus on female athletic activity in the United States, due largely to the equality of access to athletic training and facilities in schools and colleges legislated by Title IX and to corporate sponsorship of "big-time" sports events for women. The World Cup soccer win by the U.S. women's team in 1999 led to unprecedented public awareness of women's sports. However, the attitude that muscles and sweat are not ladylike may still hold for many people. Not until the 1984 Olympics in Los Angeles was a woman's marathon considered an appropriate event; little girls are still sometimes taught to do special "girls' push-ups," to throw a softball underhand, to play certain sports less intensively than boys, and to rule out participation in other sports altogether. Females participate less regularly in physical exercise than males do, and studies show that a variety of sports activities continue to be perceived as essentially masculine. In fact, the gender gap in participation in sports and fitness activities appears to be widening. Between 1985 and 1990, participation in sports and fitness activities declined 12% among the American public—and the declines were greater among women than men (Robinson & Godbey, 1993). Young women showed greater rates of decline than older women did, despite the growing media visibility of young female athletic stars. The names of soccer stars such as Mia Hamm, Brianna Scurry, and Brandi Chastain, basketball greats such as Chamique Holdsclaw, tennis stars such as Martina Hingis and Venus Williams, track and field athletes such as Gail Devers and heptathlete Jackie Joyner-Kersee, and others such as speed skater Bonnie Blair, have become household words—at least in some households. Girls and women with disabilities are also presented with athletic role models, such as Jean Driscoll, world record holder in the wheelchair division of the Boston Marathon, or Laura Schwanger, gold medalist in the pentathlon at the 1991 World Wheelchair Games. The visibility accorded such women may gradually erode the stereotype that women are, or should be, weak and fragile; however, it has not, as yet, encouraged the majority of girls and young women to become regular participants in sports and exercise.

Yet the evidence is mounting that exercise is important to women's health. Among young women, exercise appears to be of critical importance in building the bone density needed to help stave off osteoporosis in later years (Klohn & Rogers, 1991). Regular exercise is also associated in women with a reduced risk of breast cancer (Bernstein, Henderson, Hanisch, Sullivan-Halley, & Ross, 1994), improved cardiovascular fitness and blood levels of "good" (HDL) cholesterol (Hardman & Hudson, 1994), and increased strength and lowered levels of body fat (Marks, Ward, Morris, Castellani, & Rippe, 1995). Exercise has also been found to promote increased feelings of self-efficacy in both women and men—with a more dramatic effect for women (McAuley, Courneya, & Lettunich, 1991).

A particular source of concern about physical exercise for women has been the relationship between exercise and reproduction. Some women who follow a very demanding exercise schedule experience a temporary disruption or cessation of their menstrual cycle. This is most likely to occur in women with a history of irregular menstruation, although menstrual periods tend to return when the athlete reduces the intensity of her training regimen. If a female athlete maintains her normal body weight, the menstrual cycle change may simply be a temporary way for the body to conserve energy under stress—a normal, adaptive, and transient body phenomenon (Bonen, 1994). However, if an athlete participates in very high levels of aerobic exercise and consumes an inadequate supply of calories, she may experience a rapid loss of body weight in concert with the cessation of menstruation. In this case, the missing menstrual periods may signal lowered estrogen levels and the loss of calcium from bone tissue, setting the stage for the development of early osteoporosis (Aulin, 1995). Thus, it can be extremely dangerous for female athletes to set unrealistic goals for weight loss.

Research shows that there is no reason for the average woman to avoid moderate exercise during pregnancy; such exercise helps to keep the mother healthy and seems to have no adverse effect on the fetus (Lutter, Lee, & Cushman, 1984). Until very recently, however, expectant mothers have been cautioned to "take it easy"—advice that may actually contribute to the fatigue that many women report during the second half of pregnancy.

Occupational Health and Safety

Because women and men often do different kinds of work, they are vulnerable to different kinds of job-related injuries and illnesses (Doyal, 1995). Exposure to toxic chemicals is common for women in such female-dominated occupations as lab technology, computer chip manufacturing, laundry and textile work, and cosmetology. Exposure to radiation may be a problem for dental hygienists, X-ray technicians, and some nurses. The necessity to sit or stand for long periods of time places workers such as secretaries, telephone operators, waitresses, and sales clerks at risk for circulatory diseases and back problems (Stellman, 1978). The female-dominated jobs of teaching, child care, social work, and health care all carry a high risk of infection. The male-dominated jobs in trades and construction make their occupants vulnerable to accidental injury, as do certain factory jobs. Police and military work, also male-dominated, carry risks of death and injury through accidents and violence.

Some occupational hazards, such as radiation and toxic chemicals, may be especially problematic for women of childbearing age, as they may affect a developing fetus. Thus, some companies have tried to exclude fertile women from jobs that involve this kind of dangerous exposure (Randall, 1985). The economic implications for women of such restrictions can be enormous; some women may choose sterilization in preference to losing a high-paying job. However, some analysts have argued that the focus on pregnancy risks obscures the issue that exposure to toxic chemicals or radiation is not good for anyone and that, rather than excluding fertile women from certain jobs, companies should find ways to reduce dangerous exposure for *all* workers (Stellman, 1977; Win-O'Brien, 1980). This argument gleans support from findings that not only the female reproductive system is at risk from toxins; occupational exposure of male workers to certain chemicals can damage their reproductive abilities as well. For example, exposure to lead can result in reduced sexual drive, decreased ability to produce normal sperm, and sterility in males (Gold, 1981). In 1991, the Supreme Court agreed with this argument in a ruling on the employment practices of Johnson Controls, a leading manufacturer of automobile batteries. The company had refused to employ women in departments where lead was used because lead exposure could pose a risk to a woman's fetus. No similar restriction on men's lead exposure existed, although lead exposure can cause cardiovascular problems and infertility in both sexes. The Supreme Court ruled that the company's policy was discriminatory and that concerns about fetal risk could not legally be used to keep women out of jobs they could perform satisfactorily (Dabrow & Ameci, 1991).

Both women and men who are employed outside the home report more Type A coronary-prone behavior (a behavior pattern characterized by competitiveness, impatience, and aggression) and more marital disagreement than women at home do. For both employed women and men over the age of 45, the psychosocial risk factors associated with coronary heart disease are Type A behavior and suppressed hostility. For both men and women, these behaviors may be encouraged by high-pressure jobs; however, in women they may also stem from such job-related frustrations as discrimination and juggling work and family obligations. Employment in general, though, does not make women more vulnerable to health problems. In fact, employed women report fewer illnesses and fewer days in bed than housewives do (Verbrugge & Madans, 1985; Waldron & Herold, 1984).

Socioeconomic Risk Factors

In general, the poor are more vulnerable to illness and disabilities than are upper- and middle-income groups (Doyal, 1995; Gladwell, 1990). Blue-collar workers are about 2.3 times more likely to die of heart disease than managers and professionals are; people making less than $10,000 annually report getting sick more than 4½ times as often as do those making at least $35,000. Poverty is becoming increasingly "feminized" all over the world (in the United States about 2 out of 3 adults living below the poverty line are women), and women, particularly African American women, are at higher risk than men for health problems associated with low socioeconomic status. In the United States, an African American woman is almost 3 times more likely to be poor than a European American woman is; a Hispanic woman is 2½ times more likely than a European American woman to be poor (Kemp, 1995; Shortridge, 1989). The risk of sudden death by heart attack is greater for African American women than for any other U.S. group, and, in a difference from the pattern for the European American population, hypertension is about as great a problem for African American women as for African American men (National Center for Health Statistics, 1998). Low-income women of color are more likely than other women to die from complications of pregnancies and abortions. Stress levels associated with being poor and belonging to a marginalized group are potential contributors to health problems. Ratings of stress have been found to be higher among female immigrants from Central America than among Mexican Americans or Anglo Americans (Selgado de Snyder, Cervantes, & Padilla, 1990).

Among men, African Americans are more likely than European Americans to have hypertension or to die from injuries suffered at work, and they have higher death rates from cerebrovascular diseases, cirrhosis of the liver, tuberculosis, diabetes, and homicide (National Center for Health Statistics, 1998).

Health and Illness Behaviors

There is evidence that women and men differ in some of the behaviors that are related to maintaining health, responding to symptoms of illness, and treating health problems. These differences, which frequently seem to reflect gender-role expectations, may well explain some of the differences in illness rates and life span between the sexes.

Maintaining health involves proper nutrition, rest, exercise, and cleanliness; the avoidance of self-destructive activities such as smoking, overindulgence in alcohol and other dangerous drugs, and overexposure to the sun; and preventive health care such as medical and dental checkups and self-examination for signs of cancer and other problems. Women seem to engage in such health-oriented behavior more than men do. Women are more knowledgeable about and interested in health than men are, place a higher value on health (Kristiansen, 1984), have more dental and medical checkups (U.S. Department of Health and Human Services, 1995), and engage in fewer behaviors that are a direct risk to health (Muller, 1990). Women's greater use of preventive health-care services may help to account for both their higher illness rates and their lower mortality rates; women tend to be diagnosed and treated earlier for certain diseases that cause death in men. However, despite their tendency to use health services more than men do, American women still make less than optimum use of preventive health care. Among women age 50 and over, of all education levels, the use of mammograms to screen for breast cancer doubled from 1987 to 1993. However, screening levels were as much as 35% lower among women with lower levels of education (U.S. Department of Health and Human Services, 1995). Just over 50% of women have a yearly Pap smear—a test that is critical for the early detection of cervical cancer (U.S. Bureau of the Census, 1994). African American women are slightly more likely than European American women to do monthly breast self-examinations and to have regular Pap tests and mammograms. Women may forgo medical tests because of a lack of health insurance, which, in the United States, is almost exclusively tied to full-time employment. Women's self-reported incidence of Pap smears, mammograms, and breast examinations by doctors are strongly correlated with their income levels (U.S. Bureau of the Census, 1994).

One difference in men's and women's behavior that can be linked to their different mortality rates is smoking. Years ago, in a rare and dramatic example of gender-role stereotypes exerting a genuinely protective effect on women, it was considered unladylike to smoke. Tobacco companies have done all they can to reverse this stereotype. Advertising campaigns reminding women that they've "come a long way" were designed to link smoking with women's liberation, and smoking increased among teenage girls and older women during the 1970s and 1980s. Smoking rates among high school students rose by almost a third between 1991 and 1997; recent statistics show that more than half of European American male high school students and more than 40% of European American female high school students smoke, and that smoking rates have increased by 80% among African American high school students (Schwartz, 1998). Between 1970 and 1991, deaths from lung cancer among women increased by over 200% whereas those among men increased by 57% (U.S. Bureau of the Census, 1994). Women now account for more than 40% of new cases of lung cancer and 27% of lung cancer deaths. Research shows that, in contrast to rates for American men, which are relatively steady, tobacco-related deaths among American women under age 70 have been rising dramatically since 1965 (D. Brown, 1992). Recent studies show that women who smoke are about 13 times more likely to die of lung cancer than women who do not smoke, 2.3 times more likely to die of other smoking-related cancers, and almost twice as likely to die of heart disease (National Institutes of Health, 1997).

When illness symptoms do arise, women are more likely than men to try to do something about them, by treating them or by seeking medical help. Part of the explanation for this gender difference may be that women are more attentive than men are to their internal state (Pennebaker, 1982). In addition, admitting weakness and seeking help are acceptable parts of the feminine, but not the masculine, role, making it easier for women than men to report illness (Verbrugge, 1979). Finally, women are more likely than men to be socialized to pay attention to and deal directly with symptoms of illness, because mothers have traditionally taken primary responsibility for health care in families. However, lack of information or money may keep women from seeking medical help in certain situations. For example, women delay much longer than men in seeking treatment for heart attack symptoms, possibly because, unlike men, they do not expect to be at risk for heart attacks and they may feel they cannot afford a visit to the doctor (Moser & Dracup, 1993). Also, women are less likely than men to experience a crushing chest pain when they have a heart attack. Women may have more ambiguous symptoms such as shortness of breath or pain in the neck or jaw.

Health Care

Although women use the health-care system more than men do, it frequently does not meet their needs. Medicine is still dominated by men, despite the influx of women into medical schools and the fact that women fill most of the support roles in health care. Gender stereotypes abound in what medical students are taught. Disorders specific to women are often trivialized or described as psychological in origin, whereas men's symptoms are more likely to be seen as physically than emotionally based (P. Long, 1991; Wallston, DeVellis, & Wallston, 1983). A clear illustration of this tendency was found by two researchers who examined standard medical texts for discussions of dysmenorrhea, nausea of pregnancy, pain in labor, and infant behavior disorder (Lennane & Lennane, 1973). They found that each of these problems was routinely attributed to the women's mental or emotional state, despite the lack of any evidence that these problems are psychological in origin and a great deal of evidence in the other direction. The textbooks have slowly begun to change in the last two decades; however, physicians, especially male physicians, may still tend to attribute women's symptoms to emotional causes. Studies show that female patients are more likely to have tests ordered for them by female than by male doctors (Lurie, Slater, McGovern, Ekstrum, et al., 1993; Muller, 1990).

If women do feel better about care they receive from a female physician, they are still unlikely to find one in certain specialties. For example, only 4% of all board-certified plastic surgeons in the United States are women, but the vast majority of cosmetic surgery patients are women. Women are also scarce in most surgical specialties and in tenured faculty positions in medical schools (Kuczynski, 1998; Steinhauer, 1999).

There is some evidence that doctor–patient interactions may differ for male and female patients, although the data are based on male physicians only. Researchers analyzed more than 300 taped interactions between doctors and patients, looking for patterns of seeking and offering information (Wallen, Waitzkin, & Stoeckle, 1979). Doctors spontaneously offered information equally often to men and women, but women asked more questions than men and so received more informative statements. However, when total time spent explaining rather than number of explanations was measured, there were no differences between male and female patients—a finding that suggests that men received fuller explanations without asking as many questions. There was also a tendency for the doctors to "talk down" to the female patients. It appears that women may have to work harder to extract information from doctors, at least male doctors. If so, the outcome may be to reinforce women's dependence on the medical care system. Some women may give up trying to get information and simply go along with whatever their doctor advises, thus becoming trapped in a situation where they must seek medical advice or reassurance every time they experience symptoms.

Further insights into the ways doctors treat women and men come from a study showing that male and female patients with similar symptoms were treated differently by physicians (Armitage, Schneiderman, & Bass, 1979). Male patients were given more extensive lab tests and other forms of attention—a finding that led the researchers to conclude that women were given less medical attention than men were for the same problem. The disparity may be more serious for women of color. Doctors and nurses often treat African American women with less respect than they show to European American women and are more likely to medicate or restrain them if they show uncooperative behavior (E. Martin, 1987). One recent study suggests that African American and older women are less likely than their European American and younger counterparts to receive the minimum expected treatment for a diagnosis of cancer. The disparity seems to be linked to the lack of a regular health-care provider, leading to less screening and later diagnosis—all of which are related to a lack of access to private health insurance among these groups of women (National Cancer Institute, 1999).

A women's health movement emerged in recent decades as women began to try to reduce their dependence on the medical system and assume an active role in their own health care. The focus has been on education and empowerment in the area of health, encouraging women to obtain full information, be aware of treatment consequences, exercise the option to refuse treatment when appropriate, and seek complete access to their medical records. The approach is one that puts as much knowledge and power as possible in the hands of the patient, rather than treating the patient as a passive recipient of physician recommendations. Although the movement has arisen among women because they were dissatisfied with the male-dominated medical system, such an approach could also be empowering for male patients.

The Politics of Health Research

A 1984 report by the National Institutes of Health titled *Normal Human Aging* was based entirely on data obtained from men (Horwitz, 1990). A prestigious large-scale study of the relationship between coffee consumption and heart attacks used 45,589 subjects—all of them men. A study testing the efficacy of low daily doses of aspirin against migraine headaches included 22,071 male subjects—and no females (Adler, 1990). These examples are illustrative of a general pattern in the way health research dollars have been spent in the United States. Until very recently, most research has studied the health of men.

Why the omission of women from health research? Until 1985, studies funded by NIH and other agencies routinely excluded females (even female mice or rats)—because their menstrual cycles complicated the findings. The idea that such "complications" should be studied because of their very relevance to women's health appears to have been overlooked. Not until pressure from women brought these patterns to light did official NIH and Alcohol, Drug Abuse and Mental Health Administration policy change to include females in clinical research.

Because research on women's health has been neglected for so long, the extent to which many health issues are gender-related has not been well explored. Attempts to remedy the situation include the Women's Health Equity Act passed in 1991. This act included bills to establish an NIH Office of Research on Women's Health and a women's research office in the Alcohol, Drug Abuse, and Mental Health Administration, as well as provisions to include more women as participants in publicly funded research (Freiberg, 1991b). The new NIH office is coordinating a 14-year women's health initiative, studying 15,000 women across the United States to discover ways of reducing women's rate of cardiovascular disease, cancer, and osteoporosis. This study includes a representative mix of women from various social classes and races, and new guidelines now mandate gender and other forms of equity in all government-funded health research projects. All applicants for funding must show that any gender, racial, or other bias in their research sample is necessary to answer the particular research question (U.S. National Institutes of Health, 1992).

More recently still has come a realization that the health needs of lesbians have been ignored by the research community. A study released in 1999 by the Institute of Medicine showed that "gay women's medical needs are largely a mystery to their doctors" (Herscher, 1999, p. A2). The study concluded that additional data are needed to establish whether the health risks faced by lesbians are different from those faced by heterosexual women and called for research that would address these issues.

Gender and Health Among the Elderly

Proportionately more women than men live to an advanced age, and the gap between the number of women and the number of men widens with increasing age. Between the ages of 65 and 69, there are 81 men for every 100 women; over the age of 85, there are only 39 men for every 100 women (Barer, 1994). More women than men live alone in later life; elderly women are also considerably more likely than elderly men to live in poverty (Dodge, 1995). Partly as a consequence of being alone, elderly women are more likely than men to live in nursing homes.

Elderly women and men do not differ in their self-reported health status. However, their health status does differ according to a number of other measures. Elderly women are slightly more likely than men to need eyeglasses and to have cataracts; men are more likely than women to have hearing difficulties. Older women have higher rates of injuries than older men; they also report more disabilities in work-related activities and more trouble with such daily living activities as bathing, dressing, shopping, and housework (Muller, 1990). Although women report more difficulties, they are less likely than men to receive help with such activities as preparing meals and doing housework (Dawson, Hendershot, & Fulton, 1987; Doyal, 1995).

Elderly women make more visits to doctors than elderly men do, and when they do see a doctor, they are more likely than their male counterparts to be seen for less than 10 minutes and to be prescribed drugs (U.S. Department of Health and Human Services, 1995).

Cultural gender roles as well as sex differences in longevity contribute to the different health issues that face women and men as they age. The tradition that women marry men older than themselves means that more women than men will be widowed during old age. Women's traditional assignment to low-paid or unpaid work means they have less economic security with which to face their old age—a factor that is intensified for poor women and women whose economic opportunities have been further hindered by racism. But women's traditional task of maintaining family and friendship connections can translate into more social and emotional support as they age; elderly women report more contact with their children than men do (Barer, 1994). The health issues of aging are difficult for both women and men. Women face more physical impairment and have fewer financial resources with which to compensate, but a lifetime of adhering to masculine role expectations ill-prepares men to cope with disabilities, living alone, or taking on the care of a disabled spouse.

WOMEN, MEN, AND MENTAL ILLNESS

Patterns of diagnosis and treatment for mental illness are very different for women and men. Surveys of communities to determine the incidence of mental health problems suggest that women and men have similar rates of mental illness but that there are gender differences in the prevalence of certain specific diagnoses (A. Eichler & Parron, 1987). Women are more than twice as likely as men to suffer from clinical depression (Nolen-Hoeksema, 1987, 1990). In 95% of the cases of anorexia nervosa, an eating disorder characterized by self-starvation, the patients are female (Oakes, 1984). Women are more likely than men to develop phobias and anxiety neuroses; men are more likely to suffer from personality disorders, alcohol and drug addiction, and pathological gambling. It is quite possible that feminine and masculine roles predispose women and men to express their distress in different ways and to seek help with different frequencies, thus laying the groundwork for these gender-differentiated patterns of symptoms. It is also possible that gender stereotypes affect how symptoms are responded to by others and how they are diagnosed.

Two sets of findings are often used to illustrate the impact of gender roles on patterns of mental illness. The first is that women are more likely than men to talk about and seek treatment for their symptoms (Klerman & Weissman, 1980; Muller, 1990). The feminine role makes it acceptable for women to acknowledge weakness and to seek help; the masculine role encourages men to "tough it out" when they experience problems. The extremes of both styles are problematic. The drawbacks of the masculine role can be seen in the findings that men are more likely to deal with depression by turning to drugs or alcohol (J. B. Williams & Spitzer, 1983), or by committing suicide, rather than seeking treatment. Conversely, the disadvantage of the feminine help-seeking approach is that it can encourage dependence and low self-esteem. Women learn to feel that they cannot solve their own problems and must rely on the authority of a doctor or therapist. Such dependency may reinforce the very feelings of overwhelming helplessness that produced the symptoms in the first place and contribute to a prolongation of the illness. A frequently serious outcome of depending solely on medical treatment to solve certain emotional problems is an addiction to mood-altering prescription drugs. The majority of the prescriptions for mood-altering drugs, such as tranquilizers, are written for women, and women are the major abusers of these drugs (Muller, 1990; Verbrugge, 1982a).

The second set of findings pointing to a major impact of gender roles on mental illness is that the relationship between marital status and mental illness differs dramatically for women and men. Among married people, the rate of admission to mental health facilities and scores on measures of psychological dysfunction are higher for women than for men. However, among single people, the pattern is reversed: Men show higher rates of admission and higher rates of psychological dysfunction than women do (Gove, Style, & Hughes, 1990; E. Walker, Bettes, Kain, & Harvey, 1985). Some researchers have blamed the traditional gender-role expectations associated with marriage for this difference. The married woman tends to suffer a loss of autonomy because the husband is still often considered the "head" of the family (Maracek, 1978). Moreover, if she stays at home and is not employed, or if she works part time and thus earns a low income with few benefits, she becomes dependent on her husband for money and for status. Her work as a homemaker tends to be unstructured and invisible, with few objective standards of performance and few rewards for doing well. For a man, however, marriage has traditionally meant no loss of status but a gain in social support and in having someone to "look after him" in many small domestic ways. Also, because the masculine role discourages men from talking about their anxieties with other men, a wife is sometimes the only person who can serve as a confidante in certain areas. The reverse is not true for women; the feminine role makes it quite acceptable for them to share their anxieties with other women, making them less dependent on marriage for this type of emotional relief. Indeed, some studies find that never-married childless women report more life satisfaction and less dependence on others for social support than do women who have been married (Rice, 1989). Within marriage, women are often expected to do not only the bulk of the housework, which research shows is associated with depression (Glass & Fujimoto, 1994), but also the "emotional housework" of managing social relationships, ensuring harmony between family members, and promoting the emotional well-being of others (Doyal, 1995). In return, women in many families receive little emotional support from their male partners or from other family members.

In certain ways, then, marriage may be protective for men and emotionally dangerous for women. These conclusions are complicated, however, by studies of positive well-being that suggest marriage is positively associated with reports of happiness and life satisfaction for both women and men—but more so for women (W. Wood, Rhodes, & Whelan, 1989). These authors note that women, long encouraged to pay attention to the emotional aspects of intimate relationships, may be more sensitive than men to both the emotional lows and highs associated with marriage.

Both the masculine and feminine role differences in the acceptability of seeking medical help and the gender differences in the relationship between marriage and mental health point to the impact of gender roles on the patterns of mental illness in women and men. Their influence is most obvious in certain specific diagnostic categories. We turn briefly now to an examination of four particular types of mental illness for which gender differences have been found: depression, alcoholism, eating disorders, agoraphobia, and antisocial personality.

Depression

Serious, clinical **depression** is signaled by feelings of extreme sadness and hopelessness and by a loss of interest in most activities. Women are more likely than men to experience serious depressions (Chino & Funabiki, 1984; Leon, Klerman, & Wickramaratne, 1993; Nolen-Hoeksema, 1987) and to be diagnosed and treated for depression (Nolen-Hoeksema, 1990). Married, divorced, and separated women are more likely to be depressed than their male counterparts, but single men and widowers are more likely than comparable women to experience depression (Radloff, 1980). American women are twice as likely as men to be depressed (Nolen-Hoeksema, 1990). Gender differences first become noticeable in adolescence, when girls begin to show significantly more depressive symptoms than boys do (Cicchetti & Toth, 1998).

The relationship between depression and gender may vary according to ethnicity, but the research is unclear on this point. Greater female than male rates of depression have been found among European Americans (Radloff, 1980), Native Americans (Lafromboise, Berman, & Sohi, 1994), and among Cuban Americans (Narrow, Rae, Moscicki, Locke, & Regier, 1990) and other Hispanic American groups (Russo, Amaro, & Winter, 1987), but some studies show no gender difference in depression for African Americans (Markush & Favero, 1974). However, it is difficult to evaluate differences among ethnocultural groups using instruments (such as the scales or symptom categories psychologists use to measure depression) that were designed primarily for European Americans. With respect to depression, European Americans may be more likely to express sadness and guilt, whereas African Americans may be more likely to express similar feelings through somatic symptoms, irritability, or suspiciousness (Jacobsen, 1994). Furthermore, it is difficult to compare depression across groups without taking into account a variety of other variables. For example, one study showed that what appeared to be ethnocultural group differences in depression were explained largely by the differing socioeconomic circumstances of the various groups. When socioeconomic status and substance abuse were controlled, African American, Irish American, and Dominican and Puerto Rican women showed similar scores on depression, negative affect, and somatic complaints (H. L. Johnson, Johnson, Nusbaum, Glassman, Bejarano, & Rosen, 1999).

Female–male differences in depression rates may sometimes be explainable by the presence of a few women who score very high on measures of depression (Golding, 1988). In addition, the gender effect, like the effect of ethnicity, may be an indirect reflection of other factors such as employment, low socioeconomic status, and stress. For example, one study of depression in an employment setting showed that after the effects of salary, age, education, and job classification had been taken into account no gender differences in depression remained (Maffeo, Ford, & Lavin, 1990).

Theories that have been proposed to account for the gender differences in depression include (1) the notion that the feminine role predisposes women to depression by encouraging them to feel and act helpless, (2) the idea that women face more stress than men and so are more likely really to be helpless or powerless, (3) the possibility that women are particularly sensitive to stressors that are related to the disruption of interpersonal relationships, (4) the hypothesis that the differences in depression are biologically based, and (5) a developmental model suggesting particular feminine qualities that develop in childhood interact with environmental challenges that occur in adolescence to produce a greater incidence of female depression. No general agreement among researchers has been reached about which explanation is best; it is quite likely that each of these theories captures a portion of the truth.

It has been argued that the feminine role makes women susceptible to depression by encouraging them to feel helpless and have lower expectations and by literally teaching them to respond to stress in powerless, helpless ways (Radloff, 1980; Ruble, Greulich, Pomerantz, & Gochberg, 1993). When a person discovers that the rewards or punishments in a given situation are independent of her or his actions, that person learns that she or he is helpless in that situation. The sense of helplessness, that one's actions make no difference, can generalize to new situations if experienced strongly or regularly. A generalized "learned helplessness" is related to depression; in particular, the expectation that one's responses will be ineffective may produce failure to cope and a susceptibility to depression. A great deal of evidence suggests that female socialization is more likely than male socialization to lead to the belief that one's responses are ineffectual and thus to a susceptibility to depression. Radloff (1980) notes, for example, that females are stereotypically expected to be weaker, less competent, and more in need of help than males, that the actions of boys are more likely than those of girls to have consequences of reward or punishment, that female competence is more likely than male competence to be ignored or greeted with ambivalence, and that work produced by females is less rewarded with pay, promotions, and status than similar work produced by males. One possible source of gender differences in depression, then, is that males are socialized more strongly than females to believe their responses make a difference and that they can affect their rewards or punishments by the way they act.

A second possible explanation for the preponderance of women in the depressive diagnostic category is that women lead more stressful lives than men do. If this is true, it would mean that women have more problems and changes to cope with and so objectively have more difficulty than men do being in control of their lives. Thus, an actual rather than a perceived difference in controllability of rewards and punishments would explain gender differences in depression. As seen in the section on stress later in this chapter, the evidence pertaining to gender differences in exposure to stressors is mixed. Research on whether women or men experience more stressful life events is inconclusive; however, women are more likely than men to have low status and to live under a variety of chronically stressful life conditions. Thus, it is possible that some of the gender difference in depression can be explained by gender differences in exposure to or reactions to stress. In particular, women tend to face threats of rape and other forms of sexual abuse, domestic violence, and sexual harassment at considerably higher rates than men. As one depression researcher has commented, "Simply reducing the number of women who are victimized should reduce the number of women who are depressed" (Nolen-Hoeksema, as quoted in Freiberg, 1991a, p. 39).

The stressful aspects of the feminine role seem to figure importantly in women's own explanations for their distress and depression. For example, when researchers interviewed women in Wales and Ghana about their psychosocial health, common themes emerged in the way women explained their distress. The women's accounts emphasized three key issues—money problems, relationships with men, and motherhood—and they placed their emotional problems in these contexts (Walters, Avotri, & Charles, 1999). Stress is also favored as an explanation for women's mental health problems in the Beijing Platform for Action, the document that emerged from the United Nations–sponsored International Congress on Women in Beijing. In that document, stressors that threaten women's mental health are listed as including such things as the disproportionate responsibilities on women, poverty and economic dependence, violence, negative attitudes toward women and girls, racial and other forms of discrimination, marginalization, powerlessness, and overwork (Okorodudu, 1999).

There is a third explanation for the higher rates of female depression: Women may be more sensitive than men are to disruptions in close personal relationships. It is difficult to evaluate this hypothesis. On one hand, researchers have found that women are more concerned than men about rejection and abandonment (Pidano & Tennen, 1985), and the loss of an important relationship is a more common trigger of depression for women than for men (Scarf, 1979). On the other hand, there is quite a bit of evidence, as discussed in Chapter 7, that men are more devastated than women by breakups of intimate relationships. Researchers and clinicians have long acknowledged that relationship loss is an important precursor of depression for both women and men. It remains to be seen whether women are more affected by it than men.

One proposed explanation for the female preponderance in depression is a biological one: Depression may be linked to the hormonal changes associated with women's reproductive processes. This idea stems from the long-held belief that menstruation, the postpartum period, and menopause are times when women are at significantly higher risk for depression. Could it be that the reason the gender difference in depression first makes its appearance during adolescence is that hormonal changes associated with puberty help to create the biological underpinnings for greater depression among women? However, researchers have found that information about pubertal status (whether or not a person has reached puberty) adds nothing beyond information about age in predicting levels of depression among adolescents (Angold & Rutter, 1992). Also, as seen in earlier chapters, menopause is not linked to an increase in depression, and the research linking depressed mood to the menstrual cycle and to the postpartum period has not demonstrated that the link has a hormonal basis. Thus, some researchers suggest that hormone levels or changes alone cannot account for the large differences in depression that have been observed (Klerman & Weissman, 1980).

A newer theory to explain female–male differences in depression focuses on the ways women and men respond to depressive episodes (Nolen-Hoeksema, 1987). The theory is based on findings that men and women show different patterns of responding to their own feelings of depression. In general, there is evidence that men, when depressed, tend to engage in activities to distract themselves from their feelings. Women tend to react to depression by reflecting on it and thinking about its possible causes and implications. These differing response styles are in tune with gender roles: Men are taught to be active and to ignore feelings of weakness, and women are taught to be concerned with their feelings.

Susan Nolen-Hoeksema (1987) argues that a ruminative, inactive response set for depression might amplify and prolong a depressive episode in several ways, whereas an active response set might dampen and shorten it. Reflecting on the depression might interfere with concentration on other tasks, leading to failures and an increased sense of helplessness. Conversely, becoming active in response to depression leads to more chances for controlling one's environment and obtaining positive rewards. Focusing on the depression might activate a storehouse of negative memories, which strengthen the depressed mood and reinforce negative interpretations of events. Becoming active, however, might distract an individual from the mood and negative thoughts, breaking the cycle and dampening the depression. Finally, ruminating on a depression increases the likelihood that an individual will generate depressing explanations for things that are happening, thus increasing the depression further. This theory suggests that constant attention to one's own mood may be counterproductive and that mildly depressed women might be best helped by advice that emphasizes an active response to depression and discourages thinking about it too much. The author also notes, however, that the other extreme—denying the signs of a severe depression—can be equally counterproductive. Although expectations associated with masculinity might prevent a seriously depressed man from seeking help, expectations associated with femininity might encourage a mildly depressed woman to pay too much attention to her mood and thus to become moderately or severely depressed. This theory illustrates one more way that cultural gender roles may be influencing the incidence of mental illness in women and men.

The latter perspective is reflected in the newest theory proposed to explain female–male differences in depression. This developmental approach suggests that even before adolescence girls and boys tend to differ on qualities that are risk factors for depression. These early differences then interact with the challenges posed by adolescence to produce gender differences in depression (Nolen-Hoeksema & Girgus, 1994). What are the risk factors for depression on which girls and boys might differ? One is the ruminative, self-focused response to depression described above, which appears to be greater in females even during childhood. Another is an interactive style based on cooperation and the maintenance of positive relationships rather than on dominance and competition. The more cooperative style is more characteristic of girls than boys in childhood. The tendency for girls to be less aggressive, particularly less physically aggressive, than boys may also put them more at risk than boys for responding to difficulties with depression.

But the model presented by Nolen-Hoeksema and Girgus does not suggest that being cooperative and less aggressive necessarily leads females to be more depressed. Rather, the model suggests that these qualities make girls more vulnerable to a sense of defeat and distress when they encounter the challenges that can accompany female adolescence: greater restrictions on their activities by parents, greater peer pressures to narrow their activities to fit feminine gender-role expectations, and a dramatic increase in the risk of sexual abuse and harassment. The model also suggests that the gender differences in depression that first appear in adolescence become the precursors of adult gender differences in depression. Depression in adolescence interferes with performance, thus restricting opportunities for future choices. Depression also creates negative self-concepts and interpretations of events, influencing decision making about relationships and careers that can affect an individual's life for years into adulthood. Does this complex new model capture what is really going on in the development of gender differences in depression? Much more research is needed to evaluate its usefulness.

Alcoholism

It is well documented that men are more likely than women to drink and to abuse alcohol (U.S. Department of Health and Human Services, 1988). This finding holds even though women, because they have less body mass and less of the stomach enzyme that breaks down alcohol than men do, become impaired more easily, and for longer periods of time, than men do when they drink (Graham, Wilsnack, Dawson, & Vogeltanz, 1998). Data from both the United States and Canada indicate that among problem drinkers the ratio of men to women is about 3 to 1. The groundwork for this gender difference may be laid very early; research shows that even among adolescents males report more use of all drugs (U.S. Bureau of the Census, 1994). These findings fit the gender stereotypes about drinking. When people think of a skid row alcoholic they usually think of a man; the image of a temperance advocate is inevitably female.

Two gender-role theories were proposed in the 1970s to explain the large ratio of male to female alcohol abusers: the power theory (McClelland, Davis, Kalin, & Wanner, 1972) and the dependency theory (Bacon, 1974). The *power theory* suggests that men drink as a way of enhancing their feelings of power—feelings that are much more important for the masculine than for the feminine role. In this framework, the increased energy and adrenaline levels that accompany alcohol intake are thought to produce a sensation of increased strength. Women, who are not expected to be strong and powerful, supposedly have less need than men do for alcohol as a source of power feelings. The *dependency theory* proposes, conversely, that alcohol creates feelings of security, warmth, and acceptance and allows the drinker to feel dependent. Men, who are pressured by society's stereotype of masculinity to hide their dependency needs, are thus more inclined than women are toward the relief from this pressure provided by alcohol.

A more straightforward explanation for the gender difference in alcohol abuse may be simply that women receive more negative societal responses than men do for heavy drinking. When a drug is regulated by a society, a common tradition exists that the rules of access, both formal and informal, are different for men and women, and alcohol is no exception (Gomberg, 1982). Female drunkenness is viewed with less tolerance than male drunkenness, and alcoholism is judged more negatively in women than in men. Part of the gender difference in alcohol abuse may well stem from social rules that encourage women to find expressions other than drinking for their distress. Thus, for instance, the finding that male relatives of alcoholics often become alcoholics, whereas female relatives of alcoholics show a greater tendency toward depression (Cotton, 1979), might be interpreted to mean that alcoholism and depression are gender-specific expressions of similar underlying problems.

There are some differences in the routes to alcoholism for women and men. For example, women are more likely than men to abuse alcohol at home (Corrigan & Butler, 1991). A significant proportion of women with alcohol problems have also experienced sexual abuse. A national survey revealed that women with a history of childhood sexual abuse were significantly more likely than women without a history of childhood sexual abuse to report recent alcohol use, intoxication, drinking-related problems, alcohol dependence symptoms, and lifetime use of psychoactive drugs and illegal drugs. They were also more likely to report symptoms of anxiety and depression (Wilsnack, Vogeltanz, Klassen, & Harris, 1997). Recent studies show that between one third and two thirds of women in substance-abuse treatment programs suffer from **post traumatic stress disorder (PTSD)**—a disorder that is caused by a traumatic event such as abuse, rape, or domestic violence and is characterized by symptoms such as anxiety, depression, flashbacks, nightmares, and somatic symptoms (Rabasca, 1999).

Ethnocultural factors may interact with gender in the development of alcohol dependency. For example, alcohol dependency is a serious health problem for Native Americans, and Native American women have the same rates of alcoholism as Native American men (Manson, Shore, Baron, Ackerson, & Neligh, 1992). Although researchers disagree about the reasons for the problem, there is no doubt about its consequences: a tragically high death rate among young Native American women and men and an increasing incidence of fetal alcohol syndrome among their children (Lafromboise et al., 1994).

Women often face difficulties in alcohol treatment programs that are designed for men (Duckert, 1989). African American women may face additional difficulties seeking help in predominantly European American therapeutic environments (Amaro et al., 1987).

Eating Disorders

Two eating disorders, anorexia nervosa and bulimia, have been the objects of a surge of professional and public interest over the past two decades. **Anorexia nervosa** involves self-starvation in an effort to maintain an unrealistically low body weight. It is characterized by an intense fear of becoming obese and by a disturbed body image—a tendency to "feel fat" even when severely underweight. **Bulimia,** which involves a pattern of "binge" overeating followed by self-induced "purging" through a variety of means, including dieting, vomiting, or laxatives, is also characterized by an obsession with food and with body weight. Both syndromes are far more common among women than men, with most studies indicating that females make up about 90% of cases (American Psychiatric Association, 1994). The "typical" sufferer from one of these disorders is a White, middle-class woman under the age of 25. Subgroups of young women for whom thinness is especially important, such as modeling students, athletes, and professional dancers, show a higher than average incidence of eating disorders (Brooks-Gunn, Burrow, & Warren, 1988; Szymanski & Chrisler, 1990/91).

A number of writers have suggested that sociocultural factors, particularly the current emphasis on thinness, play a part in the development of eating disorders (e.g., Boskind-White, 1985; Chernin, 1981; Wooley & Wooley, 1985). An increase in the incidence of eating disorders over the past 20 years has occurred simultaneously with a shift toward thinness in the ideal of feminine beauty and a rise in interest in diets and weight reduction. Fat people, especially fat women, are disparaged as unattractive in our culture. The more dependent a person is on physical attractiveness for self-esteem, the more vulnerable she or he is to such cultural messages. Because women tend to be identified more in terms of their appearance than men are, it is perhaps not surprising that more women than men fall victim to eating disorders. Moreover, research shows that, in contrast to males, females tend to see their bodies as heavier than the ideal figure or than the figure that would appeal to the other sex (Fallon & Rozin, 1985). Among college students, women are more likely than men to see themselves as overweight and to diet. One survey found that nearly one third of a sample of college females reported either self-induced vomiting or laxative use as a weight loss strategy (Connor-Greene, 1988). The pressures to be thin and to match some media vision of attractiveness have affected American women from all cultural groups. Eating disorders are now reported frequently among African American women (Hsu, 1987), Native American and Hispanic women (Snow & Harris, 1989), mixed-race women (Root, 1990), and Asian American women (Yi, 1989).

Recent research by Harvard medical anthropologist Anne Becker (reported in Goodman, 1999) offers suggestive support for the notion that the obsession with thinness that characterizes eating disorders is fueled by cultural notions of attractiveness. Becker studied teenage girls on the South Pacific island nation of Fiji before and after the introduction of television to the island in 1995. Before the introduction of television, big was considered beautiful in Fiji, and women often complimented each other by saying things like "You look wonderful! You've put on weight." In fact, when someone lost weight, it was a cause for concern, referred to as "going thin," and thought to be a sign of social or emotional problems. However, all that apparently began to change when the girls of this tiny country began to watch programs such as *Melrose Place, ER,* and *Beverly Hills 90210.* Thirty-eight months after the introduction of television, the number of teenaged girls at risk for eating disorders had more than doubled to 29% and the number of high school girls who vomited for weight control had quintupled to 15%. At that time, 74% of the young women in the study reported that they felt "too big or fat," and 62% said they had dieted during the previous month.

Some theorists have suggested that eating disorders are associated with rigid adherence to or anxiety about the feminine gender role—a role that includes thinness and attractiveness. In a recent test of this hypothesis, researchers administered the Feminine Gender Role Stress Scale to female inpatients at a psychiatric hospital and to female college students (Martz, Handley, & Eisler, 1995). They found that scores on the scale, which measures the tendency of respondents to appraise certain situations as highly stressful because they threaten the individual's femininity, could distinguish women with eating disorders from those with other psychiatric diagnoses and from normal college women. This research suggests that women with eating disorders have internalized the requirements of femininity more strongly than other women have and may be willing to starve themselves to comply with these requirements.

The cultural premium on thinness, then, particularly for women, may stimulate the obsession with food and weight that helps to generate the distortions of body image and appetite characteristic of eating disorders. How can we fight back against the pervasive messages to young women that they must be thin at all costs? Poet Marilou Awiakta (1993) has an idea: Instead of heeding the message to "starve your power," she recommends that young women remember that

> . . . if you was to take on weight
> you might start throwin' it around.
> No way they can handle
> a full-grown woman
> With a full-grown dream. No way. (p. 194)

Agoraphobia

Phobias are persistent, irrational fears of, and a desire to avoid, specific objects, activities, or situations, and they are more common among females than males (Brehony, 1982). **Agoraphobia,** the most common, involves a fear of being in public places from which escape might be difficult or in which help may be unavailable in case of sudden incapacitation. Sufferers from this disorder may fear situations such as busy streets, crowded stores, elevators, or public transportation; thus, they may literally be trapped in their own homes by the fear of venturing out. The symptoms may represent a passive way of avoiding stressful situations. Women are far more likely than men to be diagnosed as agoraphobic; in the United States, women account for up to 82% of cases (Clum & Knowles, 1991).

Researchers are still unsure of the reasons for the female preponderance among agoraphobics, but the most popular theories center on the different expectations for coping with fear that are built into the masculine and feminine roles. Research has shown that girls and boys are fairly similar in fearfulness until adolescence. But from adolescence onward, males admit to many fewer fears than females do (Macfarlane, Allen, & Honzik, 1974). Masculine socialization encourages boys to confront and master their fears, whereas girls are reinforced not for mastery but for expressing their fears and remaining helpless and dependent (Hoffman, 1972).

Another theory is that agoraphobia, which often begins in the mid-20s, within a few years of marriage, may be triggered when an individual experiences the conflicting demands of the feminine role to be submissive and nurturing in the home and competent, independent, and assertive in the public world (Watkins & Lee, 1997). The stress may cause some women who have been conditioned by a lifetime pattern of avoidance to become increasingly helpless and dependent—a reaction that may be reinforced by the attention and sympathetic responses of those around them. Although men may have similar reactions of fear and helplessness, they are far less likely than women are to be reinforced for them. Moreover, the men are more likely than the women in this group to be employed and to be the major economic provider for the family, so they simply cannot afford to avoid leaving the house. Thus, men who have a tendency toward agoraphobia may instead display symptoms of alcoholism or anxiety neuroses.

For agoraphobia, then, as for the other disorders discussed in this section, at least part of the explanation for the gender difference in incidence may well be found in gender-role expectations. Psychological distress is manifested in different symptoms and diagnosed differently for women and men. The differences seem to derive not from a differential vulnerability to mental illness but from the different patterns of behaviors that are reinforced for the two sexes and the different kinds of pressures built into the masculine and feminine roles.

Antisocial Personality

Antisocial personality disorder, which is characterized by a lack of ethical or moral sensitivity and the absence of guilt or anxiety about hurting others, is more frequently diagnosed among males than females by a ratio of about 3 to 1 (American Psychiatric Association, 1994). Individuals who fall into this category often have difficulty forming good interpersonal relationships and frequently show indifference to relationships. They also display a general disregard for authority and behave in impulsive and thoughtless ways toward others—including such behaviors as lying, stealing, unwarranted aggression, and physical cruelty.

The characteristics of this disorder sound like an exaggerated and distorted version of the masculine role; perhaps it is not surprising that men outnumber women with this diagnosis. Male socialization is frequently in the direction of aggression, dominance, uncommunicativeness, competitiveness, and a suppression of tender emotions. Such an orientation may provide the groundwork for the development of antisocial behavior patterns and for the personality characteristics associated with this disorder in adulthood.

The Politics of Diagnosis

We have already seen one of the implications of deciding how to diagnose and "count" mental illness. When certain categories of mental illness are excluded from the tally, women appear to suffer more from mental illness than men do. However, when these categories are included, the overall gender difference in mental illness rates tends to disappear. It is important to remember that sexist biases built into the diagnostic categories may well influence perceptions of whether women and men are psychologically healthy. If the categories are based on an idea that male behavior represents the norm or standard for health—an idea that is certainly not inconceivable in view of the historic male domination of the psychiatric profession—then women who are behaving in ways that are normal, given their socialization and the situation of women in society, may be diagnosed as mentally ill. For instance, since women learn to deal with their emotions differently than men do, they may become very enmeshed in their feelings without losing their sense of self. Thus, "many women diagnosed as borderline may actually be functioning in a normal way for a woman, even though their behavior may make male-identified therapists anxious" (L. E. Walker, 1984b, p. 15).

There is a danger that the mental health system will apply diagnostic categories in gender-stereotypic ways (M. Kaplan, 1983). Indeed, the diagnoses that are most commonly applied to members of specific subgroups of the population tend to embody the roles and stereotypes attributed to those groups (Landrine, 1987, 1989). Landrine (1987) gave stereotyped descriptions of lower-class men, single middle-class women, married middle-class women, and married upper-class men to a sample of clinical psychologists and psychiatrists. The clinicians were asked to provide diagnoses for these "cases" and were explicitly reminded that the cases might be normal. Landrine found that the stereotype of the lower-class man was labeled antisocial, the stereotype of the married middle-class woman was labeled dependent, that of the single middle-class woman was labeled histrionic/hysterical, and the stereotype of the married upper-class man was labeled prototypically normal. There were no differences in the ways male and female clinicians, or psychoanalytic and feminist therapists, labeled the cases—suggesting that all were influenced by prevailing social stereotypes.

Researchers have found a general pattern of gender bias in the way physicians diagnose psychological disturbance. Women tend to be overdiagnosed (identified as having psychological disorders they *do not* have), whereas men tend to be underdiagnosed (not identified as having disorders that they *do* have). This study found no differences between interns and practicing physicians in these patterns of gender bias, suggesting that the bias is not disappearing (Redman, Webb, Hennrikus, & Sanson-Fisher, 1991). The findings seem to underline the presence of a stereotype in which women are more easily regarded as "sick" and men as in control of their lives.

An example of the politics of diagnosis occurred in the controversy over the inclusion of several new diagnostic categories in the *Diagnostic and Statistical Manual* (DSM) of the American Psychiatric Association. Two of these categories, premenstrual dysphoric disorder (earlier called **late luteal phase dysphoric disorder**) and self-defeating personality disorder, have the effect of labeling female experiences and stereotypically feminine traits as signs of mental illness. Controversy over the inclusion of these diagnostic categories in the manual was intense; more than 6 million North Americans signed petitions and wrote letters opposing their inclusion. However, late luteal phase dysphoric disorder was assigned an official number and included in an Appendix to the fourth edition of the manual, the DSM-IV.

What if stereotypically male traits were grouped together and labeled "sick"? In an article that satirizes the labeling of gender-related behavior patterns as "disorders," Kaye-Lee Pantony and Paula Caplan (1991) highlight the bias implicit in diagnostic politics. They propose inclusion of a new diagnostic category—"delusional dominating personality disorder"—in the diagnostic manual. The "symptoms" of this disorder (first detailed by Caplan & Eichler, 1989) include, among others, the "tendency to use power, silence, withdrawal, and/or avoidance rather than negotiation in the face of interpersonal conflict or difficulty" and a "tendency to feel inordinately threatened by women who fail to disguise their intelligence" (Pantony & Caplan, 1991,

p. 121). The incidence of this disorder is, according to the authors, highest among males but occasionally present in females and tends to be pronounced among "leaders of traditional mental health professions, military personnel, executives of large corporations, and powerful political leaders of many nations" (p. 121). The "disorder" proposed by Pantony and Caplan seems absurd precisely because it characterizes as "sick" the attitudes and behaviors of powerful and successful people. Their approach underlines the point that mental health policy as it relates to gender and other social categories is not value neutral but tends to define the behavior of powerful groups as normative and that of other groups as sick.

GENDER AND MENTAL HEALTH

Good mental health is more than the absence of serious mental illness; it is often viewed as satisfaction, or as adjustment to, acceptance of, and ability to cope with one's life situation. Women, on average, report greater life satisfaction and happiness than men do—a seemingly paradoxical finding in view of women's higher rates of depression (Wood et al., 1989). It is not clear whether this gender difference represents a difference in experience, a difference in the willingness to report extreme emotional responses, or a difference in sensitivity to internal emotions. One study indicates that women respond with greater emotional intensity to stimuli than men do, suggesting that women's more intense positive emotions may help to balance their higher levels of negative feelings (Fujita, Diener, & Sandvik, 1991).

There is a catch-22 in the "adjustment" definition of mental health: The more difficult and stressful one's situation, the more problematic it is to adjust to it. Although most of us would consider it mentally healthy for a person to accept and adjust to the necessity of working for a living rather than clinging to the improbable hope of winning a lottery, we would not counsel a woman who is being beaten regularly by her husband that it is mentally healthy to "adjust" to the situation. Thus, the conception of mental health as adjustment must be tempered by a keen awareness of both the situation to which a person is being expected to adjust and whether an acceptance of that situation will ultimately be beneficial or harmful to him or her.

In the past, gender roles have figured strongly in psychologists' notions of what represented proper adjustment—and thus good mental health—for women and men. People who conformed to gender expectations, masculine men and feminine women, were considered healthier than those who did not. Indeed, "rejecting" one's femininity or masculinity was considered cause for psychotherapy. Over the years, however, three major problems with this approach have been recognized. The first is that the gender role to which women are expected to adjust is inherently less healthy, in terms of coping abilities and a sense of self-worth, than is that to which men are expected to conform. The second is that rigid adherence to one's gender role, like too much rigidity in any area, interferes with a person's capacity to cope with a variety of situations and thus can be counterproductive for mental health. The third is that society's gender roles channel women and men into situations that differ in the kinds of stress they exert and the requirements for coping they demand. An acceptance of one's gender role often means not just acceptance of a certain style of interpersonal behavior but of a certain position in the family, in the workplace, and so on.

The Double Standard of Mental Health

The influence of gender stereotypes on standards of mental health for women and men was demonstrated in a landmark study of the ideals of mental health professionals (psychologists, psychiatrists, and social workers) for healthy adult men and women (Broverman, Broverman, Clarkson, Rosenkrantz, & Vogel, 1970). These researchers found that clinicians actually held different ideals for a healthy, fully functioning adult male than for a healthy, fully functioning adult female. The ideal healthy woman was described as being more submissive, less independent and adventurous, more easily influenced, less aggressive and competitive, more easily excitable in minor crises, more easily hurt, more emotional, more vain about her appearance, less objective, and less interested in math and science than the ideal healthy man. Also, the clinicians' ideal of the healthy man was similar to that of a healthy, mature adult (gender unspecified), but their ideal of a healthy woman was quite different from both. It appeared, then, that women were caught in a double bind. If they met the mental health standards for their own gender, they automatically fell short of those for the general adult population. If they met the standards for a healthy adult, they were automatically defined as unfeminine—and thus poorly adjusted.

The double standard of mental health seems to have gone underground to some extent. Therapists no longer list very different characteristics as desirable for mentally healthy women and men (Davidson & Abramowitz, 1980; Phillips & Gilroy, 1985), but some studies find that, in practice, clinicians' judgments about their clients are influenced by gender roles (Abramowitz & Herrera, 1981; Teri, 1982). Therapists may have become sensitive to the issue of gender bias and so are less likely to respond in a biased way to a questionnaire or a hypothetical situation presented to them on paper. A meta-analysis of 30 studies of gender bias in counseling and therapy found little overall evidence for the existence of bias, and the greatest bias that was shown was found in the earlier studies (M. Smith, 1980). However, naturalistic studies, in which the therapist is confronted with a real live client instead of a hypothetical one, suggest that gender bias is alive and well (Hare-Mustin, 1983). Even some studies that involve hypothetical case vignettes presented on paper still show gender bias. For example, in one recent study, psychologists, along with university professors and students, showed a bias in favor of individualism for men but not for women (Tredinnick & Fowers, 1997).

Cultural pressure on women to adjust to the feminine role is antithetical to development of the healthy behaviors of independence and competence, just as pressure on men to adjust to the male role interferes with the healthy behaviors of expressiveness and warmth. Moreover, the association of good adjustment with gender-role conformity may mask problems for both women and men. It has been argued, for instance, that when women in our culture exhibit signs of hysteria or masochism, these signs often go unnoticed because of their similarity to the prescribed stereotype of feminine behavior (Belote, 1976). Similarly, when men in our culture exhibit the aggressiveness and disregard for others characteristic of the antisocial personality, they may be perceived as acting within the boundaries of the normal masculine role (Doyle, 1995).

Gender-Role Flexibility and Mental Health

Research over the past two decades has increasingly challenged the notion that conformity to gender stereotypes is associated with good mental health. Indeed, for both women and men, the rigidity associated with strong adherence to gender roles may interfere with coping and adaptability in a variety of situations. For example, Pleck (1981) has argued that many men overconform to the masculine role out of anxiety about possible violations. Such overconformity prevents the exploration of potentially satisfying behaviors and interests. Women too may suffer adverse consequences from conforming too closely to traditional feminine roles. One study that followed a group of women from the 1950s to the early 1980s found that, although traditionality of role was related to positive well-being and effective functioning at age 21, such traditionality was related to negative changes in psychological and physical health by age 43 (Helson & Picano, 1990).

A series of studies by Sandra Bem and her colleagues using the BSRI (discussed in Chapter 1) indicated that strong gender-typing in the direction of either masculinity or femininity was associated with restricted behavior in certain settings. For example, in a situation that required the "feminine" behavior of nurturing a small baby, they demonstrated that participants of both sexes who were classified as either feminine or androgynous performed significantly better than masculine men and women (Bem et al., 1976). In another study, Bem (1975) demonstrated that masculine and androgynous subjects of both sexes performed better than feminine subjects at a task that required the stereotypically "masculine" behavior of independence in the face of social pressure. A third study (Bem & Lenney, 1976) demonstrated that masculine men and feminine women were more likely than androgynous women or men to choose activities that were "appropriate" for their own gender and to reject out-of-role activities. After performing cross-gender activities, masculine men and feminine women also reported experiencing more discomfort and feeling worse about themselves than did androgynous subjects of either sex. These findings were taken as evidence that "appropriate" gender-typing, as measured by the BSRI, is related to behavioral inflexibility and a tendency not to adapt one's role to the requirements of unfamiliar situations—hardly a hallmark of good mental health.

Later research indicates, however, that the relationship between gender stereotypes and mental health cannot be summarized adequately by the motto that "androgyny is good; sex-typing is bad." For one thing, androgyny may be more of an advantage for women than for men in this culture (A. B. Heilbrun, 1984; Wiggins & Holzmuller, 1981). Some studies have found that people with masculine qualities—those who score either androgynous or masculine on the BSRI or other scales—show the most adaptive behavior and social effectiveness, have higher subjective well-being and self-esteem, and report lower stress (B. Long, 1989; V. Long, 1991; Lubinski, Tellegen, & Butcher, 1981; O'Heron & Orlofsky, 1990). The instrumental qualities tapped by contemporary measures of masculinity, then, are apparently very important for successful social functioning in our culture. Thus, although the research is inconclusive about whether androgyny is preferable to masculinity (at least as assessed by current tests) in terms of behavioral flexibility or other aspects of mental health, it seems safe to conclude that there is no mental health advantage to women to being "properly" sex-typed as feminine. In fact, feminine sex-typed individuals, especially women, show more depression, anxiety, and low self-esteem than do those scoring as masculine or androgynous (Burchardt & Serbin, 1982; Heiser & Gannon, 1984; Tinsley, Sullivan-Guest, & McGuire, 1984). Although rigid adherence to gender roles may interfere with behavioral flexibility for both women and men, the consequences for women, at least in a culture that is structured so that most rewards are obtainable only through the instrumental behaviors we associate with masculinity, may be more serious.

Gender Roles and Environmental Stress

It is sometimes argued that the environments in which women and men are expected to function differ in terms of stress, a difference that would help to explain women's higher rate of certain mental health problems. **Stressors** are external events or conditions that are appraised as threatening by an individual and thus are the source of upset, worry, discomfort, and general distress. Researchers examining this issue have looked at both life events and life conditions. Traditionally, they have found little evidence to suggest that women and men differ in the quantity or quality of stressful life events they experience; however, this may be because, until recently, studies have not focused on the stressful events that are particular to each gender. There is strong evidence that women are more likely than men to experience stressful long-term life conditions.

STRESSFUL LIFE EVENTS   A great deal of research shows that life events that involve change or disruption are experienced as stressful and that the onset of both physical and mental illness is often preceded by a cluster of such events: an accident, job loss, promotion, pregnancy, divorce, wage increase, family discord, and so on. Because women and men differ in both their daily lives and their patterns of mental illness, it seems reasonable to ask whether they experience different numbers of stressful life events. As it turns out, most research shows no gender differences in the number of stressful life events reported (Makosky, 1980; Mulvey & Dohrenwend, 1984). How, then, can we explain women's apparently higher rate of stress-related mental illness? Perhaps the contents of the life-events lists are biased so as to include more of the stressful events that men rather than women face. Perhaps the life changes faced by men are more likely to be positive ones, and thus less distressing, than those faced by women. Or perhaps women experience more stress than men do in response to the same life events. Each of these possibilities has received some attention from researchers.

There are good arguments for the notion that the item content of the life-change lists used in stress research may produce misleading life-change scores for women (Makosky, 1980). For example, most lists do not include items about events happening to significant others that may be stressful to oneself (e.g., spouse fired or promoted, child changed schools), yet some research has shown that women are far more likely than men to report the occurrence of such events (Dohrenwend, 1976, as cited in Makosky, 1980). Also missing from most lists are some items of particular concern to women: rape, changes in child-care arrangements, incidents of sexual harassment, and physical abuse by spouse. It is difficult to define a list of life changes that is equally appropriate to everyone; yet if group comparisons are to be made, the list must reflect fairly the changes likely to be important for each group.

Researchers have found no gender differences either in the desirability of stressful life events or in the degree to which individuals say they are able to anticipate such events. However, in one study, when participants were asked about the extent to which they could control the occurrence of stressful events, an unexpected and counterstereotypic gender difference was found: Middle-aged and late-middle-aged men reported less control over their life events than women did (Mulvey & Dohrenwend, 1984). In the same study, young men reported *more* control over life-change events than any other group. The researchers speculate that men may feel an exaggerated sense of control when young, so that the obstacles and unrealized goals they face later in life seem more problematic in contrast to their earlier expectations. Women, they suggest, are accustomed to obstacles and low status from an early age and do not experience the same sense of relative deprivation as they age.

There is some evidence that the same stressor may result in different amounts of stress for women and men. For example, when respondents were asked to imagine how much stress they would be experiencing at the present time if specific events (e.g., deaths, separations, arguments, threats to self-image, financial setbacks, general changes) had occurred 1 week ago, 1 month ago, and so on up to 3 years ago, women rated all the sets of events as more stressful than men did (Horowitz, Schaefer, & Cooney, 1974). Similarly, a study of college students found that the women reported that they found more events stressful than men did—although women and men said they used similar methods for coping with stress (Ptacek, Smith, & Zanas, 1992). Also, it has been argued that such events as separation, divorce, widowhood, and childbearing are more stressful for women than for men because women tend to experience greater financial loss, are less likely to remarry, and are more likely to have the major burden of child care (Makosky, 1980).

One type of stressful event that women are more likely to experience than men is sexist treatment. Two researchers who developed a new scale, the Schedule of Sexist Events (SSE), to measure the incidence of such treatment found that 99% of the women they sampled had experienced a sexist event at least once in their lives (Klonoff & Landrine, 1995). The most common events experienced at least once were being forced to listen to sexist or sexually degrading jokes, being sexually harassed, being called sexist names, being treated with a lack of respect because of being female, and wanting to tell someone off for being sexist. More than half the sample reported being picked on, hit, shoved, or threatened because of being a woman; 40% said they had been denied a raise or promotion because they were women, and over 19% reported they had filed a lawsuit or grievance or taken other drastic action in response to sexist discrimination. A fairly similar pattern appeared when women were asked to describe events that had occurred in the past year. White women and women of color reported experiencing the same kinds of sexist discrimination; however, women of color reported significantly more sexist discrimination, both in their lifetimes and in the past year, than White women did. When the women's scores on the SSE were examined in relation to their self-reported psychiatric and physical symptoms, the researchers found that experience of sexist discrimination was significantly linked to women's symptoms. Knowing women's SSE scores as well as their scores on more traditional measures of stressful events enabled the researchers to predict their symptoms with significantly greater accuracy than simply knowing their scores on the traditional measures (Landrine, Klonoff, Gibbs, Manning, & Lund, 1995). Thus, it appears that the traditional measures have inadequately captured at least one source of stress for women.

STRESSFUL LIFE CONDITIONS   In contrast to stressful life events, stressful life conditions are chronic environmental factors that have a long-term impact on individuals. In terms of such conditions, we have already noted that women are more likely than men to be poor; they are also more likely than men to be employed in low-status, low-paying jobs and to be heading single-parent families. They are also more likely than men to be victims of unpredictable, uncontrollable family violence. Finally, they are more likely than men to be trying to perform two concurrent full-time jobs: homemaker/mother within the home and paid employee outside the home. It is fairly easy to argue that, on the average, life conditions are more stressful for women than for men.

Particular groups of women and men may be exposed to different kinds of chronic stressors. One measure of stress for African American women (Watts-Jones, 1990) includes items that reflect the following chronic stressors: inadequate resources (e.g., unable to afford your own place, living in a neighborhood with high crime), work-related stress (e.g., working at a boring job), relationship conflict/dissatisfaction (e.g., man is possessive/jealous), role functioning (e.g., being a single parent), racism (e.g., working with prejudiced coworkers), and personal health (e.g., being overweight).

Poverty is associated with mental health problems, and the combination of poverty with responsibility for young children is devastating for women (Doyal, 1995). One study of married women living in central London showed that the rate of mood disorders was 5% for middle-class women, 25% for working-class women, and 42% for working-class women with preschool children (W. B. Brown, Bhrolchain, & Harris, 1975). Other research indicates that women who are single parents are at even greater risk for emotional problems (Pearlin & Johnson, 1977). It is unlikely that there is anything specifically "feminine" about this pattern of reactions; men living in poverty with sole responsibility for preschool children would probably get depressed too.

One reason chronic conditions such as poverty, discrimination, and fear of violence are linked to emotional problems such as depression is the lack of control over one's life that these conditions engender. It is difficult to maintain a sense of well-being and self-esteem when it is impossible, despite one's best efforts, to feed and clothe one's children properly, or to keep the household running smoothly. However, for some women, one potentially stressful life condition can add to their sense of control and self-esteem instead of detracting from it: combining having a family with outside employment.

Employment is certainly a potential source of stressors for both women and men. However, it is also a potential source of satisfaction, accomplishment, and mastery, as well as a reason for leaving the isolation of one's own home. Some analysts have argued that one reason for high mental illness rates among housewives is that they have only one role from which to derive a sense of satisfaction, whereas the typical employed man has two (Gove & Tudor, 1973). Some evidence seems to suggest that people with few roles are vulnerable to mental and physical health problems. For example, Verbrugge (1983) found that the women with the poorest health profile were those without employment, husband, or children. Others (Baruch, Barnett, & Rivers, 1983; Hong & Seltzer, 1995) found the highest overall indications of mental health among women with the most roles. Among employed African American and European American women and men, job satisfaction is positively related to life satisfaction, and occupational status is positively linked to perceived control for women of both racial groups (Crohan, Antonucci, Adelmann, & Coleman, 1989).

However, lack of outside employment is not necessarily linked to discontent for women. Some researchers have found that married, full-time homemakers with young children express more pleasure and satisfaction with their lives, and have fewer worries, than other women (Baruch et al., 1983; Veroff, Douvan, & Kulka, 1981). The ability to *choose* roles, not just the *number* of roles, seems to be crucial to mental health (Sales & Frieze, 1984). Homemakers who are dissatisfied with their role have high rates of depression, physical and mental problems, and drug use (Pearlin, 1975; Verbrugge, 1982b).

For women who have good marriages and who have adequate resources to handle child care, employment during the early childrearing period may be less stressful than staying home. The additional demands imposed by juggling two roles can be balanced by the fact that the satisfactions of one role can act as a buffer for the problems and frustrations encountered in the other (W. B. Brown et al., 1975; Stewart & Salt, 1981). Thus, just as men have traditionally been able to forget temporarily about failures and anxieties at work by coming home to families where the relationships and tasks are different, so employed mothers may be able to avoid becoming trapped in feelings of frustration and anxiety about childrearing by having the additional set of goals, rewards, and concerns that the workplace provides. In addition, outside employment reduces the isolation often experienced by new mothers. For both women and men, the quality of their experiences at work and at home, as well as the meaning they assign to their work and family roles, mediate the effect of these roles on their well-being (Lennon, 1994; Pugliesi, 1995; R. W. Simon, 1995). For men, control over their work and positive marital interactions promote a less risky, healthier lifestyle (Wickrama, Conger, & Lorenz, 1995). For women, less routinized work (Lennon, 1994), spousal support (Matsui, Ohsawa, & Onglatco, 1995), equality in decision making and companionship in marriage (Hibbard & Pope, 1993), and perceived equity in the performance of housework (Glass & Fujimoto, 1994) are associated with better mental and physical health.

In general, researchers have found that employed women, both middle-class and working-class, are in better mental and physical health than those who stay at home, at least on some dimensions (Elstad, 1996; Glass & Fujimoto, 1994; Reviere & Eberstein, 1992). Women who work outside the home report fewer symptoms and use mental health services less than do women who stay home (Wheeler, Lee, & Loe, 1983). They also report greater feelings of mastery, but not more positive feelings about life (Baruch et al., 1983). Thus, employment may be linked to only certain aspects of mental health. For example, employed women may have stronger feelings of competence and self-esteem but be no happier on the whole than other women (Sales & Frieze, 1984). Furthermore, researchers cannot yet say unequivocally that employment *causes* women to be more mentally healthy; it may be simply that healthier women choose to seek employment. Yet employed women no longer represent an elite or unusual minority; more and more women enter the workforce out of economic necessity. The fact that the positive relationship between employment and mental health has remained stable with increasing numbers of women entering the labor force suggests that employment does make a contribution to women's well-being (Sales & Frieze, 1984).

For women with unsatisfying marriages, inadequate resources to guarantee good child care in their absence, or jobs that are stultifying or unpleasant, the mental health costs of combining employment and motherhood may sometimes outweigh the benefits. Moreover, there may be an "overload" point at which the positive relationship between role involvement and mental health reverses; beyond a certain limit, it may be unhealthy to juggle too many roles at once (Glass & Fujimoto, 1994; Verbrugge, 1983). Single working mothers, for example, are often overstressed and vulnerable to illness.

In summary, women tend to have to cope with more stressful life conditions than men do, a difference that may help to explain why women are more likely than men to become depressed. Paradoxically, however, women who add to their potential stressors by combining employment with motherhood often report fewer symptoms of stress than do women who stay at home, perhaps because employment confers an additional source of self-worth and control. Heavily overloaded women, however, may be very distressed by the demands of multiple roles.

Treatment of Emotional Problems

PSYCHOTHERAPY   A common response to mental or emotional distress is to seek psychotherapy. An individual who enters therapy has often failed to find solutions to problems using other strategies and hopes that the therapist will be able to provide help, support, and guidance in dealing with painful, difficult situations. Often, these hopes are realized. Therapy has helped many people solve serious problems. However, therapy as an institution can reflect some of the same sexist biases that are found in the diagnostic arm of the mental health system. The potential consumer of therapy services is well advised to evaluate therapists with care before choosing one.

Women are much more likely than men to consult a therapist, and some writers have argued that psychotherapy as an institution, like marriage as an institution, poses some inherent dangers for women (Chesler, 1972; Greenspan, 1983; Tennov, 1975). The danger stems partly from reinforcement of the dependency and helplessness that are built into the feminine role. Therapy, like marriage, can put a woman into a dependency relationship with an authority figure. If the therapist is male, the process may further reinforce the notion that a woman needs a man to solve her problems.

A therapist may hold strongly to particular values that work against the growth and problem-solving capacity of the client. If a client is trying to transcend gender-role stereotypes, a therapist who believes implicitly in the appropriateness of these stereotypes is unlikely to provide much support. For example, a woman struggling to find the courage to leave or renegotiate a stifling marital relationship is unlikely to be helped much by a therapist who adheres strongly to the belief that the man is the natural head of the family. Likewise, a man whose relationships are failing because he is unable to express any warmth and tenderness may receive little useful advice from a therapist who believes the most important qualities for male adjustment are autonomy and independence.

Sexism may well affect the psychotherapeutic process. There have been many reported instances of therapists fostering traditional gender roles, telling sexist jokes, refusing to take violence against women seriously, and seducing their female clients (American Psychological Association, 1975). Furthermore, therapists may be simply uninformed about the psychology of women and about sexual and reproductive issues (Sherman, Koufacos, & Kenworthy, 1978). Ignorance about women's experience may be particularly serious when the client is a minority or low-income woman (Comas-Díaz & Greene, 1994). Many clinicians limit their attention to intrapsychic issues, ignoring such potential contributors to emotional distress as inadequate income, poor health, substandard housing, unsafe neighborhoods, and racial discrimination. One researcher found that only 7.7% of the European American psychologists in his sample said that socioeconomic problems were among the most common ones experienced by the African American families who were their clients, but European American social workers and African American psychologists and social workers saw such problems as widespread (Boyd, 1979). The ignorance or denial of the importance of environmental factors can lead therapists to negative stereotyping of low-income and minority women, women who are victims of violence, and other individuals exhibiting stress-related emotional problems.

It is becoming increasingly clear that gender and ethnocultural factors interact in the ways that clients and therapists perceive and interact with each other (Brown & Root, 1990; Comas-Díaz & Greene, 1994). Race and gender of client and therapist influence diagnosis and treatment (Loring & Powell, 1988). However, psychologists are only beginning to gather the information needed to provide therapy that acknowledges and respects the differences among women and men of different ethnic and cultural groups. This issue is especially problematic because the therapy profession in the United States and Canada is still predominantly European American and middle-class, making it difficult for an individual who belongs to another group to find a therapist whose ethnocultural background matches her or his own.

One area in which therapist knowledge and understanding is often crucial to the success of treatment is sexual assault. According to some surveys, anywhere from 13% to 48% of female psychiatric patients have histories of sexual assault (Dye & Roth, 1990). Women who have been sexually victimized may suffer psychological distress for years. They may develop depression, phobias, sexual dysfunction, social withdrawal, and other symptoms. Yet victims of sexual assault are often the targets of negative social attitudes: blame for the assault and social derogation. If therapists hold such negative attitudes, their reactions to female clients who have experienced sexual assault will not be helpful.

Some research shows that therapists are not very likely to endorse rape myths (e.g., "Every woman secretly wants to be raped"). Younger age and being female are associated with less acceptance of such myths; psychiatrists are more likely than other mental health professionals to accept rape myths. Therapists who hold more negative stereotypes about sexual assault victims are more likely to endorse and to employ treatment approaches that blame the victim for the assault (Dye & Roth, 1990).

Some efforts have been made to reduce bias in psychotherapy through education. Both the American and the Canadian psychological associations published guidelines for therapy with women (American Psychological Association, 1978; Canadian Psychological Association, 1980). The Canadian Psychological Association also prepared a handbook of educational materials geared to help therapists confront and deal with their own gender biases and to practice nonsexist therapy or "sex-fair" counseling (Canadian Psychological Association, 1982). Nonsexist therapy is based on the idea that women and men should be treated in similar ways and should be viewed as individuals rather than as women or men. Some excellent examples of such nonsexist therapy and counseling approaches have appeared in the psychological literature (Pyke, 1979; Rawlings & Carter, 1977). Because of the availability of such materials, it may become easier, in the long run, for people seeking therapy to find a therapist who has struggled to overcome sexist (and racist) biases.

FEMINIST THERAPY   Awareness of the potential problems in the therapeutic relationship, particularly with respect to gender roles, has given impetus to the development of feminist therapy (Butler & Wintram, 1991; Rosewater & Walker, 1985;

Worrell & Remer, 1992). There are many versions of feminist therapy, but they tend to share the following features. Feminist therapy explicitly discards traditional gender-stereotypic assumptions about behavior, and the stereotypes themselves are openly discussed rather than ignored or assumed. The female perspective is explored and valued. The therapist is aware of the impact of ethnic and cultural differences between herself and the client. Therapy incorporates instead the assumption that the differential roles and statuses prescribed for women and men are potentially harmful to both sexes, particularly women. The approach rejects the notion of the therapist as an authority figure, emphasizing instead empowerment of the client. Moreover, instead of focusing only on individual difficulties and failings, this approach encourages the client to see her or his problem in its sociopolitical context. Most important of all, the client, not the therapist, defines the changes that are desirable.

Both female and male therapists can adopt the principles of feminist therapy. However, in the current context of lower status for women, some debate has surrounded the issue of whether women should be treated by male therapists at all. Beginning with Phyllis Chesler (1971), many feminists have argued that a female therapist provides a better role model for female clients and also that women seeing female therapists are spared the opportunity to reinforce feelings of dependency on men—feelings that may be the source of problems. Also, as Lynne Rosewater (1984) notes, "Women therapists share with their women clients the experiences of being second-class citizens" (p. 271), making it easier to develop mutual understanding and respect. Thus, it may be advantageous to women to have a female therapist, given the current intergroup relations between women and men. For some of the same reasons, there may be advantages for a man in having a male therapist—someone who can empathize with the difficulty of shedding some aspects of the male gender role and who can provide a good model of the possibilities for male nurturance and self-disclosure. This is not to say, however, that a woman cannot be helped by seeing a feminist male therapist or that a female feminist therapist cannot do useful work with a male client. A significant minority of male therapists identify themselves as feminist and report using a feminist perspective in their work (Dankoski, Penn, Carlson, & Hecker, 1998). Personal as well as social contextual variables influence the success of any client–therapist relationship; individuals must seek a therapist whose style meshes successfully with their own.

HETEROSEXISM IN PSYCHOTHERAPY   The problem of finding a suitable therapist may be especially difficult for gay and lesbian individuals. Research shows that therapists, particularly males, tend to rate gay and lesbian clients as less healthy than heterosexual clients and to set different therapeutic goals for them (Garfinkle & Morin, 1978). A therapist may show such biases by devaluing same-sex relationships, by emphasizing a search for the cause of the homosexuality rather than dealing with current problems, or even by expecting the client to be able to be impervious to the widely publicized negative images of homosexuality (Riddle & Sang, 1978; Rigby & Sophie, 1990). It is difficult for a gay or lesbian client to be helped by interactions with a therapist who defines homosexuality as the problem, or who does not help the client to see her or his difficulties in a social context. Because of the negative attitudes toward homosexuality in our culture, lesbians and gay men lead more stressful, and often more isolated, lives than many heterosexual individuals—a difference that must be acknowledged in the therapeutic process. In addition, because much of the stress on individuals is created by negative social responses to behavior that is considered strange or unhealthy simply because of the sex of the person who is engaging in it, the promotion of mental health for all groups of women and men involves changing homophobic and sexist attitudes in society.

Drug Prescriptions

Psychotherapy is not the only treatment for emotional or mental distress. A common clinical response to such problems is to prescribe psychoactive (mood-altering) drugs such as antidepressants or tranquilizers. Women are proportionally far more likely than men to receive drug prescriptions for psychological problems (Cafferata & Meyers, 1990; Fidell, 1982). One study showed that psychiatrists were more likely to recommend drug treatment for a hypothetical female client than for a male client described as having the same symptoms (Schwartz & Abramowitz, 1975). Physicians' biases in this direction are reinforced by drug advertisements in psychiatric journals. Most of the clients depicted in such advertisements are women, and the messages can be extremely gender stereotypic (Prather & Fidell, 1978). Other factors such as age and race interact with gender in physicians' readiness to prescribe mood-altering drugs. Older women (Doyal, 1995) and women of color (Jacobsen, 1994) are often more likely than other women to be treated with drugs than other methods for emotional symptoms. In addition to reflecting stereotypic expectations, this propensity to overmedicate older women and women of color presents some danger. Most of the drugs being prescribed were tested on younger, European American populations, and they may have different effects on members of different groups (Jacobsen, 1994).

One negative aspect of a treatment response to mental or emotional problems that centers completely on prescription drugs may be the lack of opportunity for the person experiencing the illness to find ways of increasing a sense of effectiveness and control. Instead, the person becomes dependent on a drug to alleviate her symptoms. A study by Deanna Gammell and Janet Stoppard (1999) explored the experiences of women who had been diagnosed and treated for depression by physicians. In interviews, the women discussed how they came to be diagnosed as depressed, how they experienced their treatment, how they understood the causes of their depression, and how the diagnosis had affected their views of themselves and of their futures. These women all provided accounts of their depression that emphasized its medical, biological aspects and most of them had, in conjunction with the treatment, made changes in their lives that lessened, rather than increased, their sense of personal empowerment. The researchers concluded that "a medicalized understanding and treatment of women's depressive experiences cannot readily co-exist with personal empowerment" (p. 112) and argued that treatment strategies must be developed that combine the benefits of a medical approach with the possibility of personal empowerment.

In the realms of both psychotherapy and drug treatment, the presence of gender bias is being highlighted by concerned researchers and therapists. Yet breaking down these biases is likely to be a long process. For the present, mental health, mental illness, and the treatment of mental illness continue to be gender-defined.

SUMMARY

The "strong man–fragile woman" stereotype is far too simplistic to describe gender differences in physical and mental health. Males are more vulnerable than females to death and serious physical illness across the life span, and they have a shorter life expectancy. Females, however, report more physical and emotional symptoms and seek treatment for physical and mental illnesses more often than men. Men are muscularly stronger than women and have higher fitness levels (at least in North America), but women can outperform men in some endurance situations.

An examination of the patterns of gender differences in health and illness suggests strongly that gender roles and stereotypes make a significant contribution to these differences. Part of men's higher death rate from disease and accidents, for example, is attributed to the dangers of trying to live up to the competitive, achievement-oriented, risk-taking masculine role. Women's higher rates of depression and agoraphobia are linked to the lack of independence and control built into the feminine role.

Not only role expectations but the whole social and physical environment may well provide different stresses and be the source of different problems for women and men. Women are more likely than men to be poor and to be single parents. Marriage, which often involves a loss of status and autonomy for women but not for men and a larger gain in social support for men than for women, tends to be physically and emotionally protective for men but may be dangerous in some ways for women. Employment, which often means the addition of one full-time job to another for a woman with children, may have different health implications for women and men. Even the health-care system, strongly influenced by gender stereotypes, responds differently to women and men and sometimes labels people as unhealthy when they violate norms of femininity, masculinity, or heterosexuality. The promotion of good physical and mental health for women and men requires, in many instances, that such stereotypic thinking be confronted, questioned, and changed.

KEY TERMS

hysteria
depression
posttraumatic stress
    disorder (PTSD)
anorexia nervosa

bulimia
phobia
agoraphobia
antisocial personality
    disorder

late luteal phase dysphoric
    disorder
stressors

FOR ADDITIONAL READING

Comas-Díaz, Lillian, & Greene, Beverly. (1994). *Women of color: Integrating ethnic and gender identities in psychotherapy.* New York: Guilford. The editors have gathered a range of articles that address historical, cultural, and psychological psychotherapeutic issues for many groups of women: Native American women, African American women, Asian American women, Latinas, West Indian women, and women of the Indian subcontinent.

Nelson, Mariah Burton. (1995). *The stronger women get the more men love football: Sexism and the American culture of sports.* Avon Books. A former basketball player writes incisively and provocatively about what sports have to tell us about the relationship between women and men in American culture.

Raz, Hilda. (Ed.). (1999). *Living on the margins: Women writers on breast cancer.* New York: Persea Books. The statistics about the epidemic of breast cancer among women become terribly personal in this book. The collection of essays, poems, and articles by breast cancer survivors speaks eloquently to the experience of this disease.

CHAPTER 10

Sex & Gender & Childhood

Constructing Gender

$\mathcal{A}$ researcher tells the following story about her own experience of discovering the seriousness with which young children take gender stereotypes. While interviewing 3- to 6-year-olds about their career aspirations, she asked each of them what they would want to be when they grew up if they were members of the other sex. Their responses showed that not only did most of the children choose careers that fit the stereotypes for the other gender but also that their perceptions of the limitations imposed by gender were sometimes quite extreme. One little girl confided with a sigh that her true ambition was to fly like a bird, but she could never do it because she was not a boy! One little boy put his hands on his head, sighed deeply, and said helplessly that if he were a girl he'd have to grow up to be nothing (Beuf, 1974).

A study of the way 3- to 5-year-old children made up stories in response to such story beginnings as "Two children are playing outside one day. They discover a secret door" showed that, given the same starts, girls and boys developed very different fantasies (Libby & Aries, 1989). The girls' stories tended to involve caregiving and responding to others' needs. Their stories often contained friendly figures who offered assistance to female characters. The stories told by the boys centered more often on aggression and on attempts to master challenging situations. At this early age, these children were already reflecting gender-stereotypic expectations.

Research on a wider age range of children shows they feel that a change in their gender would cause a dramatic change in the behavior that was possible and acceptable for them (Baumgartner, 1983). The general notion one gets from reading the responses of these 3rd- to 12th-grade students is that a change from male to female would involve a restriction of activities and horizons, whereas a change in the opposite direction would involve a widening of possibilities. For instance, girls noted that as boys they would be more outspoken, noisier, rowdier, have to adhere to fewer rules, worry less about their appearance, and be closer to their fathers. Boys thought that as girls they would have to be quieter and more reserved, less active, more restricted in what they were allowed to do, worry more about their appearance, worry about safety, and do fewer things with their fathers. The boys, especially the younger ones, tended to view the possibility of becoming a girl with revulsion; girls, however, were likely to see advantages to being male.

Clearly, the impact of gender roles and rules on a child's social world begins very early, and one big part of that impact is that males learn to expect more choices and more power and control over their lives than females do. Chapters 1 and 2 discussed some of the mechanisms through which this impact occurs. Children learn quickly that gender categories are important and pervasive and develop gender schemas for processing information according to those categories. Certain activities, certain clothes, certain toys are found to be appropriate only for girls or only for boys and are duly assigned to "masculine" or "feminine" categories. The child's efforts to categorize things correctly are helped along by modeling, reinforcement, and explicit instruction. In short order, children become quite confident that "boys don't play with dolls" or "girls can't be pilots," and their social relationships reflect and strengthen these expectations.

This chapter examines some of the social forces that help children construct gender stereotypes: parental socialization, the media, and language. It also explores the ways that two of the processes involved in growing up—friendship formation and the search for achievement—affect and are affected by gender stereotypes and roles.

"GETTING THE WORD": SOURCES OF EARLY GENDER LEARNING

Parents and Children

Parents are the first source of children's gender learning, and indications are that parents both hold and communicate different expectations for males and females. Researchers who interviewed 30 first-time parents within 24 hours after childbirth found that parents of boys and girls had already begun to view their infants differently (J. Rubin, Provenzano, & Luria, 1974). Those with daughters saw their babies as softer, finer featured, and more delicate than those with sons did; those with sons saw them as firmer, stronger, better coordinated, hardier, and more alert. These differences in describing male and female infants were most marked among fathers. Objective measures of the size and health of the infants showed no differences between females and males, so it appears that parental perceptions were influenced by gender-stereotyped expectations. Such expectations probably, in fact, take hold before the child is born. One study (Sweeney & Bradbard, 1988) found that parents who saw an ultrasound picture of their fetus still in the womb and who knew its sex rated female fetuses as softer, littler, calmer, weaker, more delicate, and more beautiful than male fetuses.

The culture encourages parents in these stereotypes. In a study of the birth congratulations cards being sold in four diverse communities, one researcher found gender stereotypes embedded in the congratulatory messages (Bridges, 1993). Cards intended for the parents of baby boys had more active visual images: active babies and action-oriented toys. Cards intended for parents of baby girls contained more verbal messages of emotional expressiveness, including themes of sweetness and sharing. The baby was more often described as "little" in girl cards than in boy cards, and parental emotions were more often described as happy in boy cards.

Once parents get to know their infants, do the stereotyped perceptions and expectations give way to ones that more accurately reflect the children's individual differences? The answer to this question seems to be mixed. Strong differences in the way parents treat their daughters and sons have not been found in all studies (e.g., Bee et al., 1984; Bellinger & Gleason, 1982). Researcher Carol Jacklin has commented on the surprising lack of evidence in the Stanford Longitudinal Study for the existence of parental pressure on preschoolers to conform to gender stereotypes, providing examples such as the burly father who looked sheepish but made no protest as his hair was rolled into curlers by his young son (Jacklin, 1985). A meta-analysis on studies of parents' different socialization of girls and boys found that on most dimensions (such as amount of interaction, discipline, warmth) differences in the ways parents treat their sons and daughters appear small and nonsignificant (Lytton & Romney, 1991). Some tendency was found for parents to inflict more physical punishment on boys than on girls and to stimulate motor behavior in sons more than in daughters.

Conversely, many studies do indicate that parents treat daughters and sons differently in areas specifically related to gender expectations: giving them different toys, dressing them differently, and assigning them different tasks. One study of middle-class preschoolers' bedrooms showed that boys' rooms were filled with sports equipment, toy vehicles, military toys, and toy and live animals; girls' rooms were more likely to contain dolls and dollhouses and to be decorated with floral wallpaper and lace (Rheingold & Cook, 1975). A later study suggests that the situation changed little in 15 years (Pomerleau, Bolduc, Malcuit, & Cossette, 1990). Before the age of 2, girls' and boys' environments were found to be very different: Boys were given more sports equipment, tools, and vehicles; girls had more dolls and children's furniture. Girls were more likely to be dressed in pink or multicolored clothes and to have pink pacifiers and jewelry; boys wore blue, red, and white clothing and were given blue pacifiers. Another study of the household tasks performed by boys and girls between the ages of 2 and 17 found that the boys were mowing the lawn, shoveling snow, taking out the garbage, and doing other yard work; girls were cleaning the house, washing dishes, cooking, and babysitting for younger children (L. White & Brinkerhoff, 1981). Lytton and Romney's (1991) review showed that the dimension on which parents were most likely to treat girls and boys differently was encouragement of gender-typed activities.

There is evidence that parents play and interact with boys and girls differently. They are more likely to talk with their daughters and to roughhouse and play actively with their sons (Tauber, 1979). Parents asked to work on a jigsaw puzzle with their 6-year-olds and to teach them to remember a series of picture cards were found to use different strategies for sons and daughters. They were more performance- and task-oriented with sons, tried to teach them more general problem-solving strategies, and were both more directive and more approving and more disapproving of sons than daughters. With daughters, parents interacted in a more cooperative, concrete way, and daughters were given more feedback about their performance (Frankel & Rollins, 1983).

It is quite possible that parents have no idea of the extent to which they are treating boys and girls differently. For example, one study examined the way 11 mothers interacted with a 6-month-old infant. Five of the mothers played with an infant who was dressed in blue pants and called "Adam," and 6 later played with the *same* infant wearing a pink dress and called "Beth" (Will, Self, & Datan, 1976). These mothers were more likely to offer a doll to Beth and a toy train to Adam and to smile at and hold the baby more closely when they thought they were dealing with Beth than when they thought they had Adam. Actually, the infant was male, yet 2 of the mothers later commented that Beth was a "real girl" because she was sweet and cried so softly. Moreover, in later interviews every one of the 11 mothers said that boys and girls were alike at this age and should not be treated differently and that they would not treat their own sons and daughters differently.

It is not only in middle-class North America that parents socialize their sons and daughters differently. Cross-cultural studies indicate that it is not uncommon for parents to pay more attention to boys than girls, to interact more sociably with girls, and to emphasize more achievement and autonomy with boys. For example, in a study of Mexican families, fathers, but not mothers, were found to differ in their behavior toward daughters and sons:

> Boys were listened to and shown how to do things, which would seem to convey the message that what they have to say is important and that they are capable of mastering new skills. Girls, on the other hand, were treated especially gently, and at the same time, with a lack of full attention and an imposing of opinions and values. The gentle treatment would seem to convey the message that they are fragile and docile. . . . The inattention and imposing of opinion would seem to communicate the view that what females have to say is less valuable than what males have to say, so that females need to be told what to think and do, and can more readily be interrupted or ignored. (Bronstein, 1984, p. 1001)

Further evidence for differential socialization of boys and girls comes from an examination of childrearing data from more than 100 societies (Zern, 1984). This research confirmed that boys are more strongly pressured in the direction of self-reliance, achievement, and general independence than girls are, although both sexes receive some pressure in this direction.

Within North America, there is some evidence that parents in different social classes and racial groups do not follow identical patterns of gender-role socialization. For example, research on African American families shows that parents in this group socialize their daughters more toward economic responsibility and a commitment to employment than European American parents do (Greene, 1994a; E. J. Smith, 1982).

African American women report androgynous patterns of gender-related traits, suggesting that they were socialized to have a mixture of instrumental and expressive qualities (Binion, 1990). One reason for this less rigid pattern of gender-role socialization may be the extended kinship bonds that characterize African American families. For example, many women in African American families may be involved in the socialization of children who are not their biological children, a situation that provides the children with several alternative role models (Greene, 1994a). It is inappropriate to assume that the patterns of differing parental treatment for girls and boys that have been found in European American middle-class families hold in all respects for other racial and class groups. More careful research of the patterns followed in a variety of groups is needed. However, it does appear that children's gender is a relevant dimension to parents in every group—a dimension that helps to shape parent–child interaction.

Media

Twenty-five years ago, the average North American child spent more time in the first 15 years of life watching television than doing any other waking activity (Clark, 1972). Now, some of the time a child spends staring at a television screen may be used to interact with fantasy characters in video games—particularly if the child is male (Oldenburg, 1994). Add to this the time spent listening to the radio, watching movies and music videos, and reading, and it becomes very clear that for most children beyond infancy the media is the most potent and pervasive source of information about their social world. Gender stereotypes form a significant component of the media message.

TELEVISION   By the age of 17, the typical American adolescent has viewed some 350,000 television commercials. What messages about gender are touted along with the products in these commercials? That males are the authorities, for one thing. Approximately 90% of the narrators in commercials are male. Although differences in the portrayal of women and men have decreased over the past 20 years, women are still more likely than men to be seen in domestic settings and less likely than men to be shown as employed (Bretl & Cantor, 1988). When the realm is a domestic one, women may be portrayed as authorities. In commercials for over-the-counter drugs, women are more likely than men to be portrayed as caregivers and experts at home medical care (Craig, 1992). In the United States, one study of the portrayal of women on prime-time network television showed that, despite the arrival of such female-centered shows as "Murphy Brown" and "Designing Women," the proportion of women in prime-time shows has changed little since the 1950s (D. M. Davis, 1990). In this study, about 65% of the characters in prime time were male, and 35% were female. Differences in the ways females and males were portrayed were also evident. Males were far more likely than females to be included in action–adventure shows and to be of indeterminate marital and parental status. Females were far more likely than males to be shown in provocative dress (nightwear, underwear, swimsuits, tight clothing) and to be blonde or red-haired.

Commercials that are directed specifically at children and adolescents also convey gender-stereotypic messages. In commercials shown on Music Television (MTV), male characters outnumber females more than 2 to 1 (Signorielli, McLeod, & Healy, 1994). The female characters are more likely to have beautiful bodies, wear skimpier clothing, and be looked at by others. In televised toy advertisements, sharp distinctions between boys' toys and girls' toys continue to be portrayed (Rajecki, Dame, Creek, Barrickman, et al., 1993). All-boy ads also tend to have a practical message; all-girl ads are more emotional in tone.

Studies of the content of children's television have shown that males are overrepresented among the characters and that males and females are usually portrayed in gender-stereotypic ways (Durkin, 1985). In one early study, Sternglanz and Serbin (1974) analyzed 10 commercially produced children's programs and found striking differences in the depictions of male and female characters. Males were shown as more aggressive and constructive and were more likely than females to be portrayed as rescuing others from dangerous and distressing situations; females were depicted as submissive and inactive. In addition, males both showed more behaviors and received more rewards for their behavior, whereas the behavior of female characters often seemed devoid of consequences.

Other studies have found similar results. Long and Simon (1974), in a study of the portrayal of women in children's and family programs, concluded that not only were women numerically underrepresented in these shows, but that they were presented in a distorted way. Women were almost always portrayed in comic roles or as wives and mothers; none were shown as simultaneously married and working outside the home. The female characters were subservient and dependent on men, behaved less rationally than their male counterparts, held no positions of authority, and tended to be silly and overemotional. Moreover, most of the women in these programs fell into a single narrow image: well-groomed, under 40 years of age, attractive, and extremely concerned with their appearance.

Animated cartoons, the programs that children prefer beginning around 2 years of age, convey a message about gender that is fraught with stereotypes. In these cartoons, male characters are given more prominence, appear more often, talk more, and engage in a wider range of behaviors than female characters do (Thompson & Zerbinos, 1995). The male characters tend to be more independent, assertive, athletic, important, attractive, technical, and responsible than the female characters. The females, by contrast, are more likely to be emotional, warm, romantic, affectionate, sensitive, frail, mature, and domestic. Male characters show more ingenuity, anger, leadership, bravery, and aggression. Female characters ask for advice or protection, emphasize relationships, are helpless, serve others, and show affection. Male characters are more likely than females to express opinions, give orders, brag, interrupt, insult, threaten, and laugh at others. Furthermore, subtle and not-so-subtle sex-discriminatory behaviors are modeled for children on television. One study of male–female behavior as portrayed on the 10 programs most popular among a sample of eighth-graders found that female characters appeared less often than male characters, and the men in these programs manifested avoidance and exclusion with respect to women by distancing themselves from women more than from one another and more than the women distanced themselves from men (Lott, 1989).

An interesting aspect of the gender stereotyping presented on television involves physique. One study (Busby, 1974) found that married men tended to be portrayed as overweight with poor physiques; heroes and other single men were sleek and agile. (Married men were never portrayed as heroes!) Ironically, both married and single women were shown as trim and agile despite their apparent avoidance of all physical activities. Husbands' participation in sports activities such as baseball and bowling did not seem to ameliorate their tendency to be overweight.

Both women and men are affected by such stereotypic portrayals. After viewing TV ads that portray women as slender, attractive sex objects, women in one study judged their own body size as larger and more discrepant from their ideal size than did women who viewed nonsexist advertisements. Similarly, men who were exposed to these ads revealed more dissatisfaction with their own body size—believing their bodies were smaller than the ideal (Lavine, Sweeney, & Wagner, 1999).

There is little doubt that children notice the different ways female and male characters and feminine and masculine content are portrayed on television. When children ages 8 to 13 were asked, in one study, to rate the behavior of the characters in Saturday morning cartoons, they evaluated the characters in ways consistent with extreme gender stereotypes. Male characters were described as brave, dominant, intelligent, making decisions easily, not having to be rescued, independent, keeping out of trouble, acting as leaders, harsh, aggressive, and unconcerned about appearance. Female characters, conversely, were rated as needing to be rescued, easily excited in a crisis, having a strong need for security, and crying easily (Mayes & Valentine, 1979). But children's comprehension of gender-related messages on television is not limited to the content of those messages: It also encompasses form—the different ways feminine and masculine content is presented. Form of presentation includes visual techniques such as cuts, fades, and dissolves; auditory features such as music, sound effects, and types of speech; and variables such as action level and pacing of the presentation. Research has shown that masculine and feminine content on children's television tends to be presented with different formal features. For example, commercials designed for boys have rapid action, frequent cuts, loud music, sound effects, and many scene changes, whereas those designed for girls have background music, fades and dissolves, and female narration (Welch, Huston-Stein, Wright, & Plehal, 1979). As early as first grade, children seem to be aware of the connotations of these different forms. When presented with pseudocommercials in which the content was identical but the formal features were either "masculine" or "feminine," 6- to 12-year-old children were able to identify correctly each form as appropriate for advertising either a toy truck or a baby buggy and for advertising directed to girls or to boys (Huston, Greer, Wright, Welch, & Ross, 1984). It is possible, then, that the form of presentation of various objects and activities on television influences children's attention and interest in subtle ways, cueing them as to the gender appropriateness of particular content. If this is indeed the case, television can act as a powerful agent of gender-role socialization even in the absence of content that explicitly defines certain activities as appropriate only for girls or only for boys.

Research has made it quite clear that television viewing is related to gender-stereotypic attitudes among children and teenagers. Research shows that the more television children, teenagers, and adults watch, the more they subscribe to male–female stereotypes (Eisenstock, 1984; Eron, Huesmann, Brice, Fischer, & Mermelstein, 1983; Frueh & McGhee, 1975; McGhee & Frueh, 1980; M. Morgan, 1982; Sternglanz & Serbin, 1974; Zemach & Cohen, 1986). Does watching television actually contribute to children's gender stereotypes, or is it just that those who already hold strong stereotypes spend more time than their counterparts do in front of the television set? At least one study suggests that heavy TV viewing may help to produce an increase in gender stereotyping. Teenagers responded twice (2 years apart) to a questionnaire measuring sexism so that researcher Michael Morgan (1982) could assess whether heavy viewing was associated with an increase in sexism. What the research revealed was that those subjects who were the least sexist to begin with, high-IQ girls, seemed to be most affected by watching television. After 2 years, girls in this group who had watched a lot of television showed more sexist attitudes than they had earlier; those who were light viewers showed no increase in sexism.

Some studies have shown that television messages have a direct effect on children's attitudes. A mere 5 minutes of viewing commercials about either traditional (housewives and mothers) or nontraditional (professional businesspeople) women has been shown to affect third- and eighth-grade children's attitudes toward women (Pingree, 1978). Similarly, 5 minutes of exposure to two television Muppets labeling a toy as appropriate only for the other sex was enough to make 4- to 6-year-olds refuse to play with the toy (Cobb, Stevens-Long, & Goldstein, 1982).

In adolescence, much of the TV viewing is focused on music videos. One study of California high schoolers found that these adolescents watched music videos for an average of 2 hours per day (Sun & Lull, 1986). These videos frequently enshrine gender stereotypes, portraying women as emotional, frivolous, and passive, and men as aggressive, "cool," and adventuresome (J. D. Brown, 1985; Hansen & Hansen, 1988). Many such videos are far more blatant in their sexual stereotyping than current television programming and commercials are, often portraying women as aloof seductresses and men as angry, macho conquerors or brooding, rejected introverts. The words of the rock songs that accompany these visual presentations frequently reinforce the sexist message. A content analysis of videos shown on MTV and other television music channels showed that young White males appeared in these videos twice as often as females, that Whites appeared four times as frequently as persons of color, and that most of the videos contained both violent acts and sexual imagery (Sherman & Dominick, 1986).

The videos sometimes portray rape and other forms of sexual aggression against women. A recent analysis of the content of 40 MTV videos found that men appeared nearly twice as often as women and that men engaged in significantly more aggressive and dominant behavior. Women were portrayed significantly more often in implicitly sexual and subservient behavior, and they were more frequently the objects of implicit, explicit, and aggressive sexual advances (Sommers-Flanagan, Sommers-Flanagan, & Davis, 1993). Is there a cumulative effect of exposure to such material? Apparently yes. Frequent viewing of music videos increases the probability that the viewers will later judge women's and men's behavior in gender-stereotypic ways (Hansen & Hansen, 1988). Even listening to heavy-metal music, without the video, has been found to increase young men's gender stereotyping and negative attitudes toward women (St. Lawrence & Joyner, 1991). And violent videos have been found to foster a greater acceptance of stereotypical beliefs about rape among both male (D. L. Peterson & Pfost, 1989) and female (Barbarino, 1991) viewers.

Adolescents also watch many hours of televised sports. Here, too, they are exposed to gender stereotypes. One study analyzed the verbal commentary of televised coverage of the "Final Four" of the women's and men's National Collegiate Athletic Association basketball tournaments and the women's and men's singles and mixed doubles matches of the U.S. Open tennis tournament (Messner, Duncan, & Jensen, 1993). Commentators tended to "mark" the gender of female athletes but not male athletes (i.e., male players were simply players, but female players were female players), implicitly treating females as outsiders or special in sports and treating their accomplishments ambivalently.

Interestingly, television viewing is strongly correlated with depression among college students, and depressed women watch more hours than depressed men (Dittmar, 1994). There is no evidence at all that television *causes* college women's depression; however, given the messages that television sends out about women, watching it is unlikely to do anything to alleviate their depression.

VIDEO GAMES   For many children and adolescents, the video screen is no longer something only to stare at passively. Rather, the screen has become an interactive playing field for a variety of fantasy games. In the media realm of video games, gender stereotyping is rampant. A few years ago, 99% of video games were bought by or for boys; currently, 21% of the purchases and main users of video games are female (Oldenburg, 1994). The games are still overwhelmingly oriented toward a hypermasculine stereotype, focusing on search-and-destroy missions, kicking and fighting contests, fighter pilot fantasies, or male sports. The few that explicitly target females are either equally stereotypic (shopping games and games featuring Minnie Mouse or Barbie) or create "female warrior" characters that are simply slightly feminized versions of the male characters. A few companies are marketing games meant to be gender-inclusive rather than oriented to boys or girls; however, for now, the world of video games remains largely a bastion of gender stereotypes.

THE PRINTED WORD   Stereotyped portrayals of females and males abound in the print media. Even the comic pages of newspapers show a preponderance of male characters (Chavez, 1985). The gender stereotyping in children's books parallel those found on television. Male characters outnumber females; far more stories are boy-centered than girl-centered; and males are portrayed as adventurous, brave, competent, and clever, whereas females are depicted as incompetent, fearful, and dependent on others (usually males) to solve their problems (A. J. Davis, 1984; S. B. Peterson & Lach, 1990). Despite some improvement in recent years in the ratio of males to females portrayed, and some avoidance of obvious sexism, children's books continue, for the most part, to reflect traditional gender roles (Crabb & Bielawski, 1994; Davis, 1984; Kortenhaus & Demarest, 1993; Pursell & Stewart, 1990). However, these "traditional" gender roles are now more fictional than real. For instance, books written for children continue to show mothers working only in the home, but the majority of North American mothers in fact hold outside jobs.

Like television, books appear to influence children's behavior. For instance, nursery-school boys have been shown to work longer and harder on a task after hearing a story about achievement behavior by a male character than after hearing about the same behavior by a female character, and the reverse trend is found for nursery-school girls (McArthur & Eisen, 1976). It has also been shown that preschoolers are more likely to choose a gender-stereotypic toy after exposure to a stereotypic picture book and a nonstereotypic toy after exposure to a nonstereotypic book (Ashton, 1983).

The stereotyped picture of males and females presented to children in books and other media may well have a strong influence on the children's capacity or willingness to imagine a world that is free of such stereotypes. A disturbing finding is that children's own writing reflects the very same stereotypic thinking evident in the books written *for* them. When the creative writing of children from grades 1 to 6 attending a "young authors conference" in Michigan was examined, it was found to reflect social perceptions of gender roles (Trepanier & Romatowski, 1985). Male characters outnumbered female ones in the stories written by both girls and boys, although the girls did include more female characters in their stories than the boys did. Not only did male characters outnumber females, but more attributes—both positive ones, such as courageous and determined, and negative ones, such as mean and nasty—were ascribed to male than to female characters. Moreover, when occupational roles were considered, there were dramatic differences in the number of such roles assigned to male and female characters. Of 127 occupational roles assigned to their characters by these young authors, 111 (87%) were assigned to male characters and only 16 (13%) to female characters. The roles themselves were stereotypic. For example, a female could be a princess, cook, teacher, babysitter, or nurse; a male could be a doctor, astronaut, dentist, clown, professor, or police officer. Even at this young age, then, children seem to have "gotten the message" that females are less interesting, less important, and have narrower horizons than males.

Language

Most of an individual's relations with the social world are mediated by language, and the learning of language is one of the first and most important tasks facing a developing child. Furthermore, as discussed in Chapter 2, at least one theorist (Constantinople, 1979) has suggested that children's development of gender identity and gender role is inextricably bound up with the acquisition of language. The labels that children learn—boy, girl, man, woman, daddy, mommy—help them form the categories around which they build a fundamental understanding of gender and help guide their thinking about this concept.

A problem with the role language plays in children's learning about gender is that language contains built-in biases about gender—biases that reflect the sexism and gender stereotypes of the culture. In English at least, these biases are reflected in the way language ignores females or labels them as special cases. The masculine gender is used to refer to people in general (e.g., mankind, the nature of man, sons of God, everyone must do his part). Females are labeled in ways that indicate they are exceptions, often with the additional implication of inferiority. A male, for instance, is a "real" poet, whereas his female counterpart is a "poetess." And a female colleague and I were once referred to as "professorettes."

Does the sexism built into language affect children's learning and thinking about gender? The evidence is clear that it does. Children in kindergarten, first, third, and fifth grades give male-biased responses to story cues that contain the pronoun "he," as do college students (Fisk, 1985; Gastil, 1990; Hyde, 1984a). In Hyde's study, when the pronoun in the sentence cue "When a kid goes to school, _____ often feels excited on the first day" was "he," only 12% of the stories the students went on to create were about females, as compared to 18% when the pronoun was "they" and 42% when the pronoun was "he" or "she." Clearly, the masculine pronoun makes children think of males. Moreover, fewer than half the children, even by fifth grade, indicated an awareness that "he" could be used as a generic term referring to people in general. Perhaps even more telling is the impact of masculine, feminine, or neutral pronouns on children's evaluation of how well women or men could perform the fictional job of "wudgemaker." When the pronoun used in the job description was "he," children's ratings of how well a woman could perform the job were lowest. The ratings were intermediate when neutral pronouns were used and highest when "she" was used. It appears that the choice of pronoun influenced children's perception and gender categorization of the neutral, fictional wudgemaker job. The implications for children's gender stereotyping of occupations labeled policeman, draftsman, or chairman of the board are obvious.

Hyde concludes that most elementary schoolchildren have learned to think of males when they hear "he" in a gender-neutral context, and do not know that "he" can refer to both males and females. Because they are exposed to a constant stream of information using the masculine gender as normative, they learn to think of the typical person as male—an important step toward the cultural assumption that the male is normative and the female atypical or deviant. Such thinking is probably reinforced in many schoolrooms. In one study of teacher behavior in preschool classrooms, teachers regularly used masculine pronouns in a generic way, particularly to refer to animals and to gender-ambiguous characters (Gelb, 1989). In their instructions and storytelling sessions, these teachers used 3 times as many male as female pronouns.

Some steps have been taken toward a more gender-egalitarian language. Publishers of textbooks now frequently use guidelines to eliminate sexist writing, advising their authors to avoid the use of "he" when they really mean "he" or "she" and to use gender-neutral terms to refer to occupations. Teachers attend workshops on the use of nonsexist language. A few writers, such as Marge Piercy in her science fiction novel *Woman at the Edge of Time,* have experimented with the use of a neutral singular pronoun (Piercy used "per"). A study of speeches given by male business leaders across three decades showed that the use of gender-exclusive language had dropped sharply in the 1970s and remained low (Rubin, Greene, & Schneider, 1994). However, ironically, the tendency to use gender-biased language persists in academic circles. High school and college students receive little training in using nonsexist language (Kennedy, 1993), and college professors often show little awareness of sexist language (Stewart, Verstraate, & Fanslow, 1990). It may be many years before gender-inclusive language becomes the norm. In the meantime, children are using gender-biased language as the cornerstone of their initial concepts of sex and gender.

Language joins parental socialization and the media as a potent source of information and social pressure with respect to gender roles. As described in Chapter 2, children use the information and reinforcement provided by these and other sources to build an understanding of gender and a set of behaviors congruent with that understanding. These cognitive and behavioral aspects of gender affect virtually all areas of the child's life. The remainder of this chapter looks at how gender-role socialization in childhood and adolescence affects two major aspects of the developing individual's life: the formation of friendships and the emergence of achievement goals.

CONSTRUCTING AN IDENTITY: THE RELATIONAL AND INDIVIDUAL SELF

A developmental task faced by every person is the construction of an **identity** or sense of self. This sense of self includes the sense of belonging to particular social groups, such as the individual's gender, ethnic, racial, social class, sexual-orientation, and reli-

Table 10.1 Four Dimensions of Racial Identity

Racial Salience	The extent to which one's race is a relevant part of one's self-concept in a particular moment or situation.
Racial Centrality	The extent to which a person normatively defines himself or herself with regard to race.
Racial Regard	A person's affective and evaluative judgments of her or his own race in positive–negative terms; the extent to which a person feels positively about her or his own race.
Racial Ideology	A person's beliefs, opinions, and attitudes with respect to how she or he feels members of the race should behave.

Source: Sellers et al. (1998).

gious groups. It encompasses the qualities the person sees as part of the self, as well as the acceptance for the self of labels or identities, such as "feminist" (Freedman & Lips, 1993; Lips & Freedman, 1992). A racial identity might, for instance, be defined as "the significance and qualitative meaning that individuals attribute to their membership with the . . . racial group within their self-concepts. This definition can be broken into two questions: 'How important is race in the individual's perception of self?', and 'What does it mean to be a member of this racial group?' " (Sellers, Smith, Shelton, Rowley, & Chavous, 1998).

Identities are not static; they tend to alter in response to changes in the individual's social environment and life stage. For example, the formation of the ethnic aspect of identity takes place over time, as young people explore and make decisions about the role of ethnicity in their lives. This process may occur in several stages, beginning with a phase in which ethnicity is largely unexamined and is taken for granted, moving through a period of questioning and exploring the meaning of one's ethnicity, leading finally to a committed ethnic identity (Phinney, 1989, 1990). The exploration stage may be triggered by a significant event that awakens the person to an awareness of the implications of her or his ethnicity (Helms, 1993; Kim, 1981). Identities may also have several different dimensions. For example, one recent model of African American identity postulates four dimensions, as seen in Table 10.1. Similar dimensions might be assumed for other identities.

Gender-related expectations may play a part in the way a person responds to ethnic identity issues and vice versa. For example, in some cultures there is an assumption that women are the carriers of ethnic traditions. Also, for any individual, the relative importance of one identity, such as race, in comparison to other identities, may have important implications for the meaning that she or he ascribes to other identities. "For instance, an African American woman for whom both gender and race are important to her definition of self is more likely to incorporate gender with her conceptualization of what it means to be Black than an African American woman for whom gender is not a central part of her identity" (Sellers et al., 1998, p. 23).

Traditional theories about how a person forms an identity or sense of self have tended to emphasize separation–individuation as the basic task of human development (e.g., Erikson, 1950). To develop a clearly defined, separate sense of self, this approach stresses, the person must disconnect to some extent from relationships. Thus, for example, the child must weaken ties with the mother, must gradually become less dependent and more self-reliant, and must develop an individual set of goals and sense of purpose. Contemporary theorists argue, however, that this traditional conception of development is based largely on masculine role expectations and ignores a different and equally important aspect of identity: the development of a sense of **self-in-relation** (Calloni & Handal, 1992; Surrey, 1983, as cited in A. G. Kaplan & Surrey, 1984). The sense of oneself as a relational being, someone who is developing and growing in the ability to connect with and relate to others, is arguably as much a core aspect of identity as is the sense of oneself as a separate, independent being striving for one's own particular goals. Although theorists have noted that the self-in-relation aspect of identity may be an especially important factor in women's psychological development, it must be important to men as well. It is likely that both males and females construct identities that include both individuated and relational aspects, although gender-related expectations may lead them to place differential emphasis on the two components. The following discussion of development focuses on both relational and individual achievement issues.

FRIENDSHIP

Childhood

From the beginning, girls and boys learn different expectations about friendship. Girls receive many messages that personal relationships are an important, perhaps *the* most important, life priority. They are encouraged to develop the qualities on which relationship skills are built: empathy, nurturance, expressiveness, and sensitivity to others. They are urged to consider the needs of others when making their own decisions and plans. Boys, although not taught that relationships are unimportant, are often more strongly encouraged to be independent, self-reliant, assertive, and achievement-oriented than to give high priority to friendships. This difference in emphasis for girls and boys is probably related to the traditional expectations for females and males: that, for females, security and success ultimately reside in their ability to form and maintain relationships with others, whereas for males, they reside in individual achievements.

Beginning in early childhood, boys and girls tend to separate into same-sex play groups, and best friends are almost always of the same sex (Howes & Phillipsen, 1992; P. A. Katz & Boswell, 1984; Maccoby, 1990). This division is no doubt influenced by cultural norms that encourage girls and boys to play different games and to engage in different kinds of activities; however, segregation prevails even during gender-neutral activities. The reason for children's strong preference for same-sex play appears to be twofold. First, the rough-and-tumble play and orientation toward competition and dominance that characterize boys' interactions seem to make girls nervous. Second, girls find boys unresponsive to their influence attempts and so do not enjoy interacting with them (Maccoby, 1990).

The same-sex peer groups that develop during childhood reinforce cultural norms and play a powerful role in maintaining gender differences. Children make harsh judgments about peers who do not conform to gender-role standards (Fagot, 1984; Hartup, 1983); two of the most deprecating epithets that can be flung at one child by another are "sissy" and "tomboy." For boys in particular, the same-sex peer group seems to play an important role in reinforcing masculine gender identity and male dominance, a process that occurs largely through the derogation of girls and all things feminine.

The kinds of relationships that characterize girls' and boys' friendship groups differ in some respects, perhaps in response to gender roles that stress intimacy for females and adventurousness for males (Berndt & Hoyle, 1985; M. L. Clark & Ayers, 1991; Humphreys & Smith, 1987). Boys' groups tend to be larger, providing them with more friends but less intimacy, and giving them a "gang" with which to embark on explorations of their world. Certainly, this is the image of male childhood friendships that has been celebrated in movies and television. Girls, however, limit the size of their friendship groups and tend to have fewer, more intense friendships—relationships that provide the arena for exploring interpersonal concerns (S. M. Rose, 1995). Even in childhood, girls seem to be more comfortable than boys are with intimacy. In one study of 7- and 8-year-olds, same-sex pairs of children either sat close together and drew pictures of each other (high-intimacy condition) or sat with a screen separating them (low-intimacy condition). The girls smiled more and laughed less than boys did in the high-intimacy condition—an indication, according to the researchers, that they were more comfortable than the boys were in this situation (Foot, Chapman, & Smith, 1977). The same study found similarities for boys and girls in the effects of being with a friend. Children who watched a cartoon when paired with a friend showed more social responsiveness—laughing, smiling, talking, looking at their partner, and touching—than did those who were paired with a stranger. Clearly, there are gender similarities as well as differences in children's friendships.

The different kinds of activities encouraged for schoolage boys and girls may help to maintain the pattern of small intimate friendship groups for girls and larger "gangs" for boys. Team sports such as softball, hockey, and football form a large part of boys' recreational activities. The boys who play these sports may well learn to associate having fun with being in the company of a fairly large, diverse group of peers. Until fairly recently, only a minority of girls has been given the opportunity to engage in team sports. Researchers have yet to examine the interesting question of whether there is a relationship between friendship patterns and participation in team sports.

Another male–female difference in recreational activities is in the use of computerized video games, a pastime much more common among boys than girls. This activity, far from fostering the development of a large friendship group, promotes a one-on-one relationship of boy to machine. It is difficult to say what impact the widespread use of this form of recreation may have on boys' friendship patterns in the future. However, casual observation suggests that although boys play these games as individuals they often come and go from the game situation in groups, and their individual success with the games is a matter of status in the group.

One of the most interesting aspects of children's preference for all-boy and all-girl groups is that different styles of interaction develop in groups of boys and groups of girls. Boys' groups show more concern with dominance. Boys are more likely than girls are to interrupt one another, command and threaten, boast, refuse to comply, give information, and call other boys names. Girls, conversely, seem more interested in sustaining social relationships. They are more likely than boys to say they agree with another speaker, acknowledge points made by other speakers, and pause to allow another girl to speak (Maltz & Borker, 1983). The interaction styles characterizing boys' and girls' groups have been labeled, respectively, **constricting** and **enabling** (Hauser, Powers, Weiss-Perry, Follansbee, Rajapark, & Greene, 1987, as cited in Maccoby, 1990). Because groups of girls and boys differ in their habitual interaction styles, and because children spend so much time interacting in same-sex groups, girls and boys are socialized by their peers into different ways of relating. These different styles of interaction apparently carry over into adolescence and adulthood.

As Maccoby (1990) notes, the different ways males and females have learned to interact with others from childhood onward have implications for later, cross-sex, relationships:

> What happens . . . when individuals from these two distinctive "cultures" attempt to interact with one another? People of both sexes are faced with a relatively unfamiliar situation to which they must adapt. Young women are less likely to receive the reciprocal agreement, opportunities to talk, and so on that they have learned to expect when interacting with female partners. Men have been accustomed to counterdominance and competitive reactions to their own power assertions, and they now find themselves with partners who agree with them and otherwise offer enabling responses. It seems evident that this new partnership should be easier to adapt to for men than for women. (p. 517)

Adolescence

Adolescence is a time when friendships often become very intense, perhaps because it is a time of personal transition and uncertainty. The pattern of fewer, more intimate friendships for girls and larger, less intimate friendship groups for boys persists. Moreover, there is some evidence that relationships are more important to girls than to boys during this period. When teenagers were asked to rank-order a number of concerns according to their importance, both sexes ranked identity and sexuality at the top of the list, but girls placed interpersonal relationships third whereas boys chose autonomy as their third most important concern (Strommen, 1977). Researchers have also found that high school girls express greater concerns about their friendships than high school boys do (Schneider & Coutts, 1985). Adolescent girls are more likely than their male counterparts to share information about their emotional state with their parents and friends (Papini, Farmer, Clark, Micka, & Barnett, 1990). Male friends tend to be more similar to one another than female friends on status variables such as nominations for the neatest and nicest clothes, and female friends tend to be more similar in personality and verbal achievement (M. L. Clark & Ayers, 1991). These researchers also found that African American adolescents, both females and males, choose friends who are less similar to themselves on achievement and academic status than White adolescentss do.

Boys may be less concerned with friendship, *or* boys may simply be inhibited about admitting an interest in same-sex friendships. College males are significantly more reluctant than females to volunteer for studies listed as investigations of same-sex friendship and are even unwilling to sign up for studies of issues unrelated to friendship that require them to bring along a same-sex friend (Lewis, Winstead, & Derlega, 1989). Furthermore, teenage boys who are highly affiliative (that is, very interested in being with other people) report more negative emotional states, both when they are alone and when they are with friends, than do teenage girls who are highly affiliative (Wong & Csikszentmihalyi, 1991). This finding may reflect boys' expectations that they should be independent, coupled with the suspicion of homosexuality that our culture imposes on male–male friendships.

An early extensive study of adolescent friendships points to gender differences in the focus and quality of these relationships (Douvan & Adelson, 1966). For girls in their midteens, sensitivity to others and mutual trust are cited as important qualities in a friend. Girls in this age range describe a friend as someone who will provide emotional support during personal crises and who will not gossip behind one's back. By contrast, boys in the same age range list relatively impersonal qualities (e.g., easy to get along with, does favors) as the important ones for a friend to have. In addition, boys are more likely than girls to view the friendship group as a source of support against adult authority and to mention that a friend is someone who stands by you when you are in trouble with that authority. A popular film about male adolescent friendship, aptly titled *Stand By Me,* is built largely on this aspect of peer relationships. Four boys, feeling unloved by parents, scorned by teachers, and persecuted by older teenagers, find in their relationship not only solace but a source of humor about adult authority and the courage to challenge it. Movies about female adolescent friendships are in shorter supply. However, as women gradually begin to occupy decision-making positions in the film industry, some movies are beginning to address this theme. A recent example, *Now and Then,* portrays the adult reunion of four female childhood friends. Through flashbacks, the film tells the story of their early adventures and the ways they supported one another through the difficulties they encountered in adolescence.

It appears that friendships during childhood and adolescence tend to follow patterns that support girls and boys as they follow the paths laid down by traditional gender roles. Girls' friendships are geared to helping them explore and deal with personal relationships. Boys' friendships provide support for defiance of authority and assertion of independence. Of course, the differences in emphasis are not always so pronounced, particularly in later adolescence. Some studies of college student friendships have found more gender similarities than differences (Caldwell & Peplau, 1982; Rose, 1985).

One factor that may influence social relationships in different ways for girls and boys during adolescence is the timing of physical maturity. In general, girls reach puberty sooner than boys do. However, maturing earlier or later than one's peers has different implications for the two sexes. For a girl, early development of breasts and a more sexually mature appearance is likely to be associated with early pressures in the direction of the traditional feminine role. Parents may place new restrictions on her, and older boys may begin to pressure her for sexual behavior (Golub, 1983; Katz, 1986). The early-maturing girl may be dating at an age when her cohorts are still relying heavily on same-sex friendships to explore interpersonal issues. In fact, dating may actively interfere with a girl's same-sex friendships. To the extent that males keep the role of initiator in the heterosexual dating situation, females simply react to male invitations. Thus, a girl may find herself unable to pick the times when she can get together with a boy. Rather, her only control in the situation lies in saying yes or no to a specific invitation. Under these circumstances, girls often find themselves forced to choose between previously established plans with their girlfriends and the chance to go out with a boy they like. It is perhaps not surprising, then, that girls sometimes break plans with same-sex friends to accept a date. Some evidence shows that such early dating is disadvantageous to girls' self-esteem (Golub, 1983; Simmons, Blyth, Van Cleave, & Bush, 1979), perhaps because girls are not yet equipped emotionally to handle the sexual and affective pressures of the dating situation, or perhaps because of the loss of control over her life that waiting to be asked out can involve for a girl. Moreover, some have speculated that a girl who is physically well developed at an early age receives more reinforcement for following a traditional feminine script, making it less likely that she will explore alternatives such as a career (Katz, 1986). Early-maturing girls also tend to be dissatisfied with their weight and their appearance, causing them to focus more concern on these issues. Overall, early physical maturation appears to be linked to changes in the pattern of girls' social relationships—changes that involve increased pressure to be "feminine."

For a boy, early maturation is not likely to be associated with increased parental restrictiveness, although it may be associated with an increase in responsibilities. Also, since our culture has traditionally placed males "in charge" of the dating situation, there is less likelihood that early dating will cause problems for them. The boy who is quicker than his peers to develop the muscularity, strength, and physique of the adult is likely to be regarded with envy. If he begins to cultivate relationships with girls, it is still unlikely that he will significantly loosen his ties with his male friendship group. He may gain increased status in that group, however, and be expected to provide leadership. These pressures are in line with masculine role expectations.

In comparing the experience of the early-maturing girl and the early-maturing boy, it is clear that both involve earlier than usual stress on gender-role conformity. However, this early pressure has quite different implications for girls and boys. For girls, it means more curtailment of their activities, significant loss of control over their social relationships, and being placed in the role of sexual object before having a chance to explore their own sexual feelings. For boys, it often means less rather than more curtailment of their activities, increases in responsibility and status, and the frequently unnerving challenge of initiating (or, at least, appearing to initiate) heterosexual relationships.

Given the gender segregation of activities that occurs through childhood and adolescence, it is not surprising to find that cross-sex friendships are relatively rare. Some do appear in adolescence; however, the cultural inclination to define any female–male relationship in sexual terms makes it difficult for them to thrive.

In middle and late adolescence, there is an increased focus on sexuality, and dating becomes a prominent concern. Girls, who must attract boys, become very concerned with physical appearance and social skills. Although boys display a parallel concern with their attractiveness to girls, the development of heterosexual relationships is far from their only priority. Boys receive a great deal of reinforcement for other activities such as athletic pursuits and scholarly achievement. Nonetheless, for both females and males at this stage, peers of the other sex become quite important as sources of social approval and status. This pattern seems to hold even for those individuals who will eventually identify themselves as gay or lesbian. In fact, there is some evidence that lesbians and gay males tend to begin dating earlier than their heterosexual counterparts (Saghir & Robins, 1973). These researchers also found that about half of the gay and lesbian and the heterosexual adults they studied remembered having a romantic attachment to a member of the other sex before the age of 14. By the same age, 80% of those who eventually identified as gay or lesbian, but only 6% of the heterosexual men and 25% of the heterosexual women, had also formed same-sex romantic attachments. Most of these same-sex romantic attachments were to peers and did not involve sexual contact. In fact, the relationship between adolescent sexuality and adult sexual preference is not particularly clear-cut (Bidwell & Deisher, 1991). As the early Kinsey surveys show, although up to 10% of adolescents who engage in homosexual behavior go on to identify themselves as gay in adulthood, most do not. Regardless of their sexual orientation, then, it appears that male and female adolescents tend to form some cross-sex attachments and to experience the gender-role pressures involved in dating.

For young women and men who are moving toward affirmation of an identity as lesbian or gay, dealing with gender-role pressures in relationships is only part of the task they must face. If they embrace a lesbian or gay identity, they are embracing a self-definition that is stigmatized by the dominant culture (Herdt, 1989; H. P. Martin, 1991). One model of the formation of a gay or lesbian identity (Cass, 1979, 1984) proposes a series of six steps, beginning with the initial realization that particular thoughts, feelings, or behavior can be identified as homosexually oriented. This realization feels incongruous, given that the person and the environment have assumed the person is heterosexual. Gradually, the individual begins to come to terms with the social alienation that the new identity represents and then to establish contacts with other lesbians and gays to obtain a sense of community and a validation of this identity. The individual develops a sense of pride in the new identity, but must still confront the incongruity between strong self-acceptance and society's negative labeling of homosexuality. The incongruity produces anger; the person may become interested in confronting the dominant heterosexual culture. At this stage, she or he may become increasingly open about homosexuality. Finally, the model suggests, the person reaches a stage in which public and personal sexual identities can be synthesized. Identifying as lesbian, gay, or bisexual then becomes not an all encompassing identity but only one aspect of the self. The whole process embodies a gradual movement from denial of a self-view that is seen as negative to embracing an identity that is ultimately seen as positive.

This model, encompassing a movement from an initially negative to an eventual positive reaction to one's sexual identity, may not adequately represent the experience of every person who forms a lesbian or gay sexual identity. Research on a national sample of 2000 lesbians suggests that there are many lesbians who experience their lesbian identity as positive and comfortable from their first recognition of it (Slater & Rabin, in preparation). Clearly, there is a good deal of diversity in the ways such identities are developed.

The intersection of sexual identity with ethnic, religious, or other aspects of identity may be complicated and difficult in some cases. For instance, Espín (1987) reports that Latina lesbians sometimes feel they must make a choice to emphasize either their ethnic or their lesbian identity because lesbianism is labeled even more negatively in Latin cultures than in mainstream North American society. For lesbian women of color, the risk of alienation from their families and friends if they come out publicly as lesbian may be especially frightening, because the social support from these networks provides an important buffer against the racism they encounter in the larger society (Greene, 1994b).

It is clear that on the interpersonal dimensions of affiliation, friendship, and sexuality, the developing child and adolescent is strongly influenced by gender roles and expectations. Does gender play a role of comparable importance in the more individualistic dimension of achievement? As the following section will show, the answer is a resounding yes.

ACHIEVEMENT

From an early age, children are expected to respond to the query "What do you want to be when you grow up?" They soon learn that their gender is relevant to the answer; indeed, the influence of gender exists at every stage in the development of achievement goals and orientation. The different ways girls and boys are treated in task-oriented situations results in different levels of self-confidence, expectations for success, and feelings of self-efficacy and control for the two sexes. The kinds of expectations for their future that are portrayed for them by parents, teachers, school counselors, peers, and the media, and the kinds of interests in which they are encouraged or discouraged, help to shape the specific achievement pathways girls and boys choose to follow and the tasks they try to accomplish.

Socialization for Achievement

When psychologists discuss achievement motivation, they usually mean a person's disposition to seek success: a stable, general personality disposition to strive for success in any situation where standards of excellence are applied (McClelland et al., 1953). Many researchers have stressed the importance of the parent–child relationship in the development of the child's motivation to achieve. Interestingly enough, the conclusions about the best way to socialize a child to be achievement-oriented differ for boys and girls. For example, parental warmth (accepting, affectionate, child-centered behaviors) has more often been found to be positively related to the achievement orientation of males than to that of females (Manley, 1977). Whereas high levels of maternal warmth and affection were associated with strong achievement orientation in boys, moderate warmth and slight hostility related most strongly to girls' achievement orientation. Similarly, maternal warmth appears to relate to boys' but not girls' ego development (Richards, Gitelson, Petersen, & Hurtig, 1991). A number of explanations for the apparently paradoxical situation have been offered. Crandall, Katkovsky, and Preston (1960) suggested that girls who do not receive as much maternal affection turn to achievement as an alternate source of satisfaction. These authors also suggested that the less nurturing mother may be more involved with her own achievement and thus be providing her daughter with a female achieving role model. However, some of the research results themselves may be suspect on the grounds that behavior labeled "hostility" when directed toward girls might not be so labeled when directed toward boys (Hoffman, 1972). Finally, it must be noted that if parental warmth does relate differently to girls' and boys' achievement orientation, the existence of the relationship does not specify cause and effect. It is just possible that whereas parents who see a daughter becoming independent and achievement-oriented may withdraw a small portion of their warmth from her, a son exhibiting similar behavior may be the recipient of extra praise and approval. In other words, nurturing parents may be reinforcing accepted cultural definitions of appropriate behavior for girls and boys. There are, in fact, indications that such a pattern is sometimes present in the interactions of children with their teachers. For example, a preschool child's compliance with a teacher predicts the teacher's evaluation of the child's intellectual competence—if the child is a girl (Gold, Crombie, & Noble, 1987). Less compliant girls are evaluated as less intellectually competent; compliance does not affect teacher evaluation of boys' competence, however. It appears that female intellectual competence is most likely to be rewarded in the classroom if it is manifested in an "appropriately feminine" way.

An important factor in the socialization of achievement is the presence of models. We have already noted the scarcity of achieving female role models in the media; the presence of real live role models is also important. Where girls are provided with achieving female models, their attitude toward success and career attainment seem to be favorably affected. The literature on the effects of maternal employment indicates that in middle-class families daughters of employed women have higher educational and occupational aspirations than do daughters of women who are full-time home-makers (Betz & Fitzgerald, 1987; Etaugh, 1974; Stein & Bailey, 1973). Daughters of employed women also regard the professional competence of women more highly than do those whose mothers work in the home (Baruch, 1972), and there is a corre-spondence between mothers' and daughters' career interests and aspirations (Zucker-man, 1981). Among African American female college students, those pursuing nontraditional careers were more likely than their more traditional counterparts to have mothers who were well educated and working in nontraditional fields themselves (Burlew, 1982). One study found that as early as kindergarten and first grade girls whose mothers were working in nontraditional fields also tended to aspire to less gender-stereotypic careers (Selkow, 1984). In fact, in the same study, both girls and boys whose mothers were currently employed chose a greater number of future occu-pations and showed less gender-stereotypic vocational aspirations than did children of nonemployed mothers. Because more than half the women with young children in North America are now employed outside the home, a gradual reduction in the strength and pervasiveness of occupational stereotyping by gender may be occurring. Most college women now believe they will have careers in addition to family respon-sibilities (Baber & Monaghan, 1988; Bridges, 1987). Indeed, one recent survey by a task force of the American Psychological Association showed that adolescent girls were more concerned with their future careers and financial responsibilities than with ques-tions of marriage and children (Murray, 1998). Daughters whose parents hold less rigid gender stereotypes are more likely to feel capable of moving in this direction: These young women have a stronger sense that they control their lives, more inde-pendent coping skills, and higher achievement test scores (Hoffman & Kloska, 1995). However, many social forces still support the stereotype that men are more achieve-ment-oriented, intelligent, competent, and independent than women.

Self-Confidence, Self-Esteem, and Expectations for Success

In adolescence and early adulthood, males show higher self-esteem than females do (Dukes & Martinez, 1994; Keltikangas-Jarvinen, 1990; Richards et al., 1991). One survey of 2400 girls and 600 boys in the 4th through 10th grades suggests that the gender gap in self-esteem widens during adolescence (Freiberg, 1991a). At the ages of 8 and 9, 60% of the girls and 67% of the boys reported feeling confident and positive about themselves. Among high schoolers, however, the percentage who reported feel-ing positive about themselves had dropped to 29% for girls and 46% for boys, leaving a considerably larger gap between the two groups. When the findings were broken down by race, it became clear that many more African American girls maintained high self-esteem in high school than did their European American or Hispanic counterparts.

This fits with other findings suggesting that African American female adolescents have higher self-esteem than young Hispanic, Native American, Asian American, and European American women (Dukes & Martinez, 1994). However, with age, the African American girls showed large drops in positive feelings about their teachers and schoolwork. Hispanic girls expressed less confidence in themselves than African American girls did, and between elementary school and high school their confidence dropped further than either of the other two groups.

What is responsible for many girls' drop in self-esteem and self-confidence during the transition to adolescence, and how do African American girls manage to resist the trend? One researcher who has interviewed many girls making this transition argues that as girls move from childhood to adolescence they become aware that there is a conflict between the way they see themselves and the way others (teachers, authorities) view them. They suddenly confront a message of female inferiority, exclusion, and subordination (Gilligan, 1990). They can respond to this conflict by submerging their own feelings and accepting the view of reality conveyed by adult authorities—or by insisting on their own feelings and knowledge. Many girls follow the first strategy. However, a substantial number of African American girls, buoyed perhaps by the support of their families, choose the second. In so choosing, they may become alienated from the educational system, but their self-esteem apparently remains intact.

Socialization and the presence of gender stereotypes have an impact on the way females and males react to their own achievements. As early as the third grade, boys begin to predict more successful task outcomes for themselves than girls do, a difference that seems to last into adulthood (Crandall, 1969; Vollmer, 1984). The gender difference reflects both an overestimation of their performance by males and an underestimation of their performance by females. Some factors limit this effect. For example, there is evidence that expectations are affected by the gender-role appropriateness of the task. Davies (1989/90) found that when presented with the same tasks girls predicted better performance for themselves when the task was labeled "girls generally do better" and boys expected more success when the task was labeled "boys do better"—a finding that is similar to the impact of stereotype threat, discussed in Chapter 1. Among a sample of college students, women reported lower occupational performance expectations than men did for male-dominated occupations but higher expectations for female-dominated occupations (Bridges, 1988). However, perhaps due to the stereotyping of achievement itself as masculine, even feminine tasks are sometimes greeted with more male than female self-confidence (Lippa & Beauvais, 1983). The timing of the assessment may also affect the findings; girls expect less success than boys do early in the school year, but these differences sometimes disappear as the year progresses (Dweck, Goetz, & Strauss, 1980).

The tendency for boys to have higher achievement expectations than girls may be mainly a European American middle-class phenomenon. Much of the literature suggests that African American females have higher career aspirations and expectations than both African American males and European American females (Harris, 1993; E. J. Smith, 1982). One study of African American adolescents found that higher male than female expectations for success were chiefly evident in middle-class schools (Teahan, 1974). Moreover, when samples include a high proportion of African American and low-socioeconomic-status children, gender differences in expectations for success on specific tasks are not found (Fulkerson, Furr, & Brown, 1983). Gender differences in achievement expectations and educational attainment also do not appear among Asian American students (Brandon, 1991).

The different pattern of gender differences for European American and African American children may relate to teachers' expectations. Studies show that both African American and European American elementary school teachers hold lower expectations for African American males than females (Grant, 1984; Washington, 1982). Even when teachers are presented with hypothetical case histories in which all qualities are held constant except gender, the teachers consistently hold lower expectations for African American males than for African American females (Ross & Jackson, 1991).

In elementary school classrooms, teachers allow boys more than girls to talk and interrupt them—a practice that ensures not only that more time will be spent on boys' than girls' problems but that both groups will learn that male concerns take first priority. Apparently getting this message, girls ask fewer questions than boys (Pearson & West, 1991). African American girls escape this pattern in the earliest grades, often receiving more attention and feedback than European American girls. However, by the middle of elementary school, African American girls have apparently been socialized into the same pattern of inconspicuousness to the teacher as their European American counterparts (Irvine, 1986). Even in preschool, teachers pay more attention to boys and respond more to boys who act aggressively and to girls who act dependently (Serbin & O'Leary, 1975). Yet teachers are apparently unaware that they are treating boys and girls differently. The pattern of greater teacher attention to males carries through to college, where women experience the classroom atmosphere as less encouraging for themselves than for men because of an aggregation of small, nonconscious discriminatory actions on the part of professors. Students report that instructors know the names of more male than female students and that female students are more likely than males to be squeezed out of lab projects and demonstrations and are more hesitant to intrude on an instructor's time by asking for help (Schnellmann & Gibbons, 1984; Seymour, 1995).

The study of how gender-differentiated patterns of self-confidence in achievement situations are transmitted to children has occupied researchers for many years. One of their chief findings has been that girls and boys are treated differently in the classroom, and the differences produce relatively more feelings of control among boys and relatively more feelings of helplessness among girls (Dweck, 1975; Dweck, Davidson, Nelson, & Enna, 1978; Dweck et al., 1980; Dweck & Leggett, 1988; Elliott & Dweck, 1988).

Teachers tend to punish boys and girls for different kinds of behavior—boys for being unruly and girls for academic mistakes. However, when praise is handed out to girls, it is likely to be for good appearance or conduct, whereas for boys it is more likely to be for good academic performance. The lessons are obvious: Girls learn that the route to appreciation is by being "good," and boys learn that they are appreciated for their academic efforts. Most damaging of all, perhaps, is the way teachers encourage girls and boys to react to their own mistakes. A boy giving the wrong answer is encouraged to keep trying until he gets it right. A girl is frequently told not to worry about a mistake, and the teacher spends less time suggesting new approaches and encouraging her to keep working on a problem until it is solved. In fact, girls are more likely than boys to be simply left in the dark about the quality of their answers. Teachers often do not tell them whether their answers are excellent, need improvement, or are completely wrong (Sadker & Sadker, 1985). The differences in teacher interactions with boys and girls may communicate that teachers expect more and better thinking from boys. Thus, boys are more likely to learn to respond to an unsolved problem as a challenge, whereas girls are given the message that failure is beyond their control.

The consequences of these gender-differentiated patterns of responses by teachers may, paradoxically, be especially severe for high-achieving girls. When students who have been succeeding at problem-solving tasks are then exposed to a task on which they fail, Carol Dweck and her colleagues (summarized in Dweck, 1999) have shown that the highest-achieving girls—the A students—tend to show the most helpless response of any group, trying fewer strategies to solve the new problem and giving up more quickly. Why are high-achieving girls so vulnerable? Dweck notes that, because girls mature earlier and often cope better and perform better in elementary school than boys do, they are often praised for being good and for being smart. In receiving this praise, the girls are also receiving the message that their traits (such as "goodness" and intelligence) are discernible from their performance outcomes. A diet of early success and praise may encourage these high-achieving girls to adopt what Dweck calls an **entity approach to abilities:** the notion that each individual has a fixed amount of ability, which is revealed by her or his performance. The girl learns to think of herself as smarter than others, a self-description that becomes an important part of her identity. If high-achieving girls accept this belief that intelligence is a fixed entity, and Dweck's research shows that they do in large numbers, they will find failure devastating because failure is taken as a sign that they are "not smart" after all. They will also be reluctant to enter into achievement situations that put them at risk of failure and will concentrate on performance goals (performing well, to demonstrate their ability) rather than learning goals (learning to master something new). As Dweck notes, this motivational pattern may not be a problem for high-achieving girls in elementary school, but

> after grade school, the game changes. Now students that are challenge-seeking and persistent and can tolerate periods of confusion have the advantage. This is because the work becomes more rigorous, as new and different subjects, such as algebra and geometry, are introduced. If bright girls doubt their ability when they encounter challenging tasks, then the occasions for ability doubting and helpless responses will become more numerous. . . . [Furthermore, if] bright girls are most attracted to tasks they're sure they'll do well on (so they can keep on feeling intelligent), then they may opt for easier programs of study, avoiding advanced math and science because these may feel too risky. (p. 124)

Dweck (1999) argues that it is much more important to emphasize challenge, effort, and strategy attributions for both success and failure than to praise students for their ability. Boys are often exhorted to "try harder" in school, because they tend to be less attentive and diligent and more disruptive than girls are. Girls are perceived as working well and paying attention and are not given such feedback. Girls learn to make ability attributions for success and failure, which leaves them reluctant to try tasks on which they may fail. According to Dweck,

Our analysis implies . . . that an emphasis on challenge, effort, and strategy is absolutely essential for girls. Their successes should indeed be praised, but for the effort and the strategies that went into them. They should be taught that challenges are exciting and should be praised for taking on challenges and sticking with them. They must learn that the hallmark of intelligence is not immediate perfection, but rather the habit of embracing new tasks that stretch your skills and build your knowledge. (p. 125)

SEXUAL HARASSMENT   Sexual harassment is a common problem faced by female students, and it has a potential impact on self-confidence and achievement. In one survey of more than 1100 college students, 17% of the females and 2% of the males reported having been sexually harassed by teachers. More than one third of the incidents reported by these students had occurred in high school (McCormack, 1985). Many schools do not have an adequate system for dealing with student reports of sexual harassment, and the absence of such a system communicates to students that the problem is not considered common or serious. Yet the impact on a female student's self-confidence of being sexually harassed can be dramatic. One young high school student who had been on the honor roll, a flag corps captain, and a soloist in the school chorus found herself the target of advances from one of her teachers. He stared at her breasts, told her to wear sexier clothes, hugged her, and threatened her with social ostracism if she told anyone about his behavior. This formerly enthusiastic, confident student fell behind in her classes and dropped out of school just before graduation, and says, "I was scared of him, scared of what he might do or say, scared to be alone with him. He ruined high school for me" (T. Moore, 1996, p. 59).

The cumulative effect of the differential experiences of females and males in the educational system is a decrease in the self-confidence of female students—this despite the fact that females generally obtain higher grades than males at every academic level. It is difficult for education to have an empowering effect on girls and women as long as the subtle messages behind teacher–student interactions remain that females are valued less than males, that females are valued more for their appearance and good behavior than for their competence and intellectual skill, and that sexuality can be used as a weapon against female students.

Competition and Cooperation

Much of what is labeled "achievement" in our society is linked to competition, to winning. Gender stereotypes suggest that boys are more competitive than girls, and some research supports the stereotypes. For example, one study of preschoolers found that females preferred cooperative social values and males preferred competition even before the age of 6 (Knight & Chao, 1989). Among college students, males have been found to perform best in competitive task situations, whereas females perform better in cooperative task situations (S. A. White, 1991). A study of African American sixth- and seventh-graders found that girls reported a higher preference for cooperative learning than boys did (C. Johnson & Engelhard, 1992). Interestingly, in this study, girls' preference for competition increased as their GPA increased, whereas boys' preference for competition *decreased* as their GPA increased. These are some indications, then, of support for the notion that girls tend toward cooperation and males tend toward competition. However, there are some indications that cooperation and competition may mean different things to boys and girls, so the gender difference may not be as straightforward as it appears.

One study examined the possibility that cooperation and competition in school might be linked with somewhat different attitudes for girls and boys (Ahlgren, 1983). The results showed that during the early school years competition is a more positive construct for boys than for girls. For elementary school boys, competitive attitudes are positively related to a sense of personal worth as a student and to internal motivation, but no such relationships are observed for elementary school girls. In the same age range, however, both sexes show a positive relationship between cooperative attitudes and personal worth. By senior high school, the sexes have become similar in some respects: Both show a positive link between competition and sense of personal worth and internal motivation, and neither females nor males show any links between cooperation and negative school attitudes. Nevertheless, some differences still exist: Although boys lose all negative correlates of competition, for girls competition retains some negative associations. Also by senior high school, boys show no correlation between cooperative attitudes and a sense of personal worth, but girls still show a link between these two attitudes.

In summary, then, by senior high school, cooperation has become completely positive for both sexes, but girls link it more strongly than boys do to their sense of personal worth. Competition has also become positive for both sexes, but girls retain some negative associations with it. Thus, changes in the affective connotations of cooperation and competition follow a somewhat different pattern for girls and boys during the school years, and girls seem to end up feeling less comfortable with competition and more conscious of the importance of cooperation than boys do. In view of the strength of gender stereotypes that characterize boys as task-oriented and competitive and girls as relationship-oriented and cooperative, these findings are not surprising. Thus, girls may find themselves more uneasy than boys are in the many achievement situations in our society that stress competition at the expense of cooperation. Where cooperation is the requisite orientation for success, however, girls may have the advantage.

Person Orientation Versus Task Orientation

The common wisdom born of gender stereotypes suggests that males are task-oriented and females are person-oriented: that males tend to be intrinsically interested in the task at hand whereas females, who are more interested in relationships than in tasks, tend to focus on the social consequences of performing well or poorly. In other words, for females affiliation needs predominate over achievement needs, often interfering with females' performance. The evidence in support of such a hypothesis is weak at best. Females do score higher than males do on paper-and-pencil measures of need for affiliation (Maccoby & Jacklin, 1974; Schneider & Coutts, 1985). However, Maccoby and Jacklin's (1974) extensive review of the literature uncovered no evidence to indicate that boys were more intrinsically interested in task performance than girls were, with the exception that preschoolage boys showed more exploratory behavior than their female counterparts did. In terms of person orientation, the same review suggests that task performance of males is more likely to be affected by the presence of peers than is task performance of females, a finding that argues for more person orientation in males than in females.

Some research shows that at least during high school person orientation may interfere more with male than female academic achievement. Starting from evidence that schoolwork and academic achievement may be viewed by high school students as more female-appropriate than male-appropriate (Stockard et al., 1980) and that boys may be more susceptible than girls to peer pressure against conforming to adult standards (Andersson, 1979), Schneider and Coutts (1985) formulated the hypothesis that boys would be more likely than girls to report a negative influence of peers on their achievement behavior. Their survey of students in grades 10 and 12 supported that hypothesis: Boys reported less positive pressure from peers to get good grades and more negative peer pressure against achievement striving than girls did. Neither boys nor girls viewed high grades as very important for attaining popularity with either their own or the other sex. However, boys ranked scholastic excellence significantly lower in importance to popularity than girls did. Moreover, boys were more likely than girls to report that they wished they could work harder in school but didn't because of what their friends would think and that it was harder to study if their peers were going out. Also, among 12th-grade students, boys were more likely than girls to report that they thought they would study harder and improve their grades if members of the other sex were not present in their classes. The researchers concluded that high school boys were more susceptible than girls to peer influences that interfered with their achievement strivings.

Choosing Career Paths

Even in elementary school, children are quizzed about "what they are going to *be*"; by high school, there is considerable pressure on adolescents to choose a career path. It is a truism in vocational psychology that the choice of an occupation is the choice of a means to implement one's self-concept (Super, 1951); thus, it is not surprising that such choices reflect gender-role socialization.

One aspect of current gender roles that has implications for career paths is experience with computers. Because computers are technical, there seems to be a general assumption that boys will take to them more naturally than girls will. This assumption is reflected in both the opportunities provided for boys and girls to use computers and the behavior of the children themselves (Shashaani, 1994). In some studies, boys using computers in school outnumber girls by as much as 2 to 1; 40% of boys but only 7% of girls use computers outside the classroom, and 25% more boys than girls live in homes with computers ("Boy Still Meets Girl," 1987). Some observers have noticed that boys are more assertive than girls about getting access to scarce computer time and getting help with computer problems (Linn, 1985; Rosser, 1982), and a number of researchers have found that boys like computers more than girls do at every grade level (Badagliacco, 1990; Collis, 1985; Wilder, Mackie, & Cooper, 1985). Positive attitudes toward computers often correlate with experience (Shashaani, 1994); being European American and male makes it more likely that students will have such experience, whereas being Hispanic and female makes it less likely (Badagliacco, 1990). However, girls respond positively to educational strategies aimed at equalizing computer use (Fish, Gross, & Sanders, 1986).

In an occupational climate that is increasingly dominated by computer technology, females are destined to be relegated once again to low-level jobs if they do not obtain some basic understanding of computers and learn to master some of the skills associated with computer technology. Yet the strong social message still exists that expertise in computer technology is for males—and girls and young women are quick to pick up this message.

Social pressure against choosing occupations that are seen as gender-inappropriate is strong. Children and adolescents continue to express gender-traditional career choices (Eccles, 1994; Hammond & Dingley, 1989; Houston, 1991; Lips, 1998). Nontraditional occupational choices are seen as less appropriate than traditional choices for both women and men (Fitzgerald, 1980); in fact, there is some evidence that men have even less support than women for choosing nontraditional occupations. Perhaps this lack of support for nontraditional males is related to the fact that males hold the majority of high-salary, high-status positions. A man who chooses a nontraditional career is forgoing high rewards. Yet this pattern is likely to continue for the foreseeable future. The high rewards associated with traditionally male occupations are not a sufficient inducement for most young women to follow a nontraditional path. Even among very gifted students, female adolescents indicate career preferences for occupations paying considerably less than the occupations to which their male peers aspire (Kelly & Cobb, 1991).

What factors are related to the choice of nontraditional career aspirations? For both African American and European American college women, choosing a nontraditional career is related to holding nontraditional gender-role attitudes and having high educational aspirations. African American women display less conflict over combining professional and family roles in such careers than their European American counterparts do (Murrell, Frieze, & Frost, 1991).

Vocational counselors play a part in guiding males and females into traditional careers. One study, for example, found that practicing counselors reacted more negatively to and were less willing to work with a hypothetical male client who aspired to a "feminine" (nurse) than to a "masculine" (physician) occupation (Fitzgerald & Cherpas, 1985). However, a number of other factors also serve to orient males and females toward traditional career paths, not the least of which may be an awareness of the very real difficulties associated with breaking from the traditional route.

One interview study of 150 Canadian teenagers found a tendency for girls to make traditionally feminine occupational choices and to express less confidence than boys that they would reach their occupational goals (Baker, 1985). About three quarters of the girls planned to hold paying jobs as adults; however, they tended to see the responsibility for housework and child care as primarily theirs and to assume that paid work must fit in with these other duties. These girls showed little awareness of skilled or technical positions, of the economic penalties for part-time work, of the potential problems in finding suitable child care, or of the probability that, by age 30, they would be working for pay as a matter of economic necessity rather than choice. In another interview study (Gaskell, 1985), girls from working-class families also assumed they would have primary responsibility for domestic work and that paid work outside the home would have to take second priority. These assumptions seemed to be based on their own experience that men were unwilling to share domestic responsibilities and that women earn less money than men. Gaskell argues that these girls were probably being quite realistic and that planning in a gender-unequal labor market leads to traditional choices. Yet one national survey of high school students suggests that adolescent girls are now beginning to envision their futures not primarily in terms of getting married but in terms of being able to take care of themselves financially and find the "right" career (Murray, 1998).

Clearly, for adolescents planning their future, there is a potential conflict between career and family life. The conflict is more intense for females, who are more likely than males to anticipate having to juggle two sets of responsibilities (Eccles, 1994). Perhaps for this reason, there has long been an assumption in vocational psychology that, for females, commitment to career goals and commitment to home and family goals were opposite ends of a single continuum: the stronger the commitment to one, the weaker the commitment to the other. However, that particular piece of conventional wisdom has now been challenged. Using girls in grades 8, 10, and 12, Holms (1985) found no negative relationship between the two types of commitment; the two dimensions were independent.

There are many signs that females are aspiring in greater (though still small) numbers to traditionally masculine careers (e.g., National Science Foundation, 1998); however, the reverse trend is much weaker for males. If gender-role socialization becomes less restrictive, perhaps both boys and girls will learn to base their occupational aspirations more heavily on their individual talents and the needs of the marketplace and less on the arbitrary limitations of masculine and feminine roles.

SUMMARY

Beginning in early childhood, girls and boys learn that a different set of expectations holds for each sex. Parents are the first to communicate these expectations, but their influence is quickly built on by the media. Even the patterns of everyday language reinforce the notion that different tasks and occupations are more suitable for one gender than the other and that males represent the norm and females are the exceptions.

In developing a sense of identity, the growing child must develop both a sense of self-in-relation to others and a sense of separateness and individual purpose. Traditionally, the relationship aspect of development has been stressed for girls, and the individualistic, achievement-oriented aspect has been emphasized for boys. Although some research does support the idea that, probably as a result of gender-role socialization, relationships are more important to girls and achievement to boys, other research indicates that for both sexes concern with either of these two domains can interfere with the other. Boys sometimes allow interpersonal concerns to inhibit their achievement strivings, and girls may permit concern over achievements in the social arena (e.g., getting a date for Saturday night) to interfere with ongoing important relationships.

Girls and boys differ in their friendship patterns, with girls having fewer, more intense friendships than boys, and boys more than girls depending on their friends to back them up in conflicts with authority. They also differ in their achievement patterns. Despite a tendency to get better grades at every scholastic level, girls display less confidence than boys in their ability and seem more easily discouraged by failure. These differences may be a result of differential treatment of male and female students by teachers, who tend to pay more attention to boys than to girls, to reward boys more for good performance and girls more for good behavior, and to encourage boys more than girls to make "effort" attributions for success and failure.

Finally, as girls and boys begin to develop their occupational goals, they are influenced by gender-role expectations. Boys assume they will someday work to support a family; girls often assume that their paid work will take second priority to domestic responsibilities. Perhaps with these assumptions in mind, girls report less confidence than boys do that they will achieve their career goals. By adolescence, then, the impact of gender-role expectations has had its effect—through parental admonishments, cartoons and children's books that show males in a wide variety of occupational roles and females in very few, teacher expectations, and counselor bias—on the life goals of girls and boys. Girls and boys have been taught to expect different amounts of control over their lives, and they have been channeled in different directions; as adults, their lives will consequently differ in many respects.

KEY TERMS

identity	constricting interaction	enabling interaction style
self-in-relation	style	entity approach to ability

FOR ADDITIONAL READING

Dweck, Carol S. (1999). *Self-theories: Their role in motivation, personality, and development*. Philadelphia, PA: Psychology Press. The author describes, in an accessible and readable style, her 30 years of research on motivation and achievement in the classroom, including some interesting implications with respect to gender.

Elgin, Suzette Haden. (1984). *Native tongue*. New York: DAW. This feminist science fiction novel imagines a world in which women develop their own secret language. The narrative provides a good feel for the power of language and its importance in maintaining power relations between women and men.

Fine, Michelle. (1992). *Disruptive voices: The possibilities of feminist research*. Ann Arbor: University of Michigan Press. The author introduces some of the possibilities that can be opened up when feminist scholarship is applied to issues such as adolescent sexuality, the education process in public schools, and reactions to rape.

Gilligan, Carol, Lyons, Nona P., & Hanmer, Trudy J. (Eds.). (1990). *Making connections: The relational worlds of adolescent girls at Emma Willard School*. Cambridge, MA: Harvard University Press. This is a collection of the accounts of researchers who have listened to adolescent girls as they talked about connection and separation, their relationships, and their conflicts.

Pipher, Mary. (1994). *Reviving Ophelia: Saving the selves of adolescent girls*. New York: Grosset/Putman. A therapist who sees many adolescent girls discusses the challenges that confront them as they become increasingly sensitive to cultural messages about what they should become.

CHAPTER 11

Family & Friends

Attachment, Intimacy, & Power

In a village in the remote Himalayas, it is common practice for a woman to have several husbands—all brothers. The system ensures that most men will find wives in this land where men outnumber women 4 to 3. It also holds advantages for the women, who need not endure being left alone for long periods of time while one husband is away from home and whose children have several fathers to care for them. Because women are in short supply, they need not put up with an intolerable family situation. Divorce is easy, and every time a woman changes husbands she commands a larger bride-price, usually in recognition of her increased experience and proven fertility (Zorza, 1986).

This example is often surprising to North American observers, yet it is only one of a variety of reasonably satisfactory ways human beings have devised to structure their family and other intimate relationships. Depending on the culture, various versions of **polygyny** (one husband having several wives at the same time), **polyandry** (one wife having several husbands at the same time), or **serial monogamy** (an individual having a series of mates, one at a time) may be taken for granted as accepted practice. People may have most of their needs for intimacy met by their mates, other kin, or same-sex friends. Fathers may be expected to become deeply involved with their children or to have only distant, formal relationships with them. No single arrangement of important relationships is uniformly preferred across human societies (Ingoldsby, 1995).

Relationships with family and friends both reflect and reinforce the gender stereotypes and roles of a society. They help to define the amount and kinds of influence and power available to men and women, and they shape the quality of people's social lives and their sense of personal well-being. This chapter focuses on the ways close relationships are experienced by women and men, how those experiences are influenced by cultural understandings about gender, and how they are related to the actual and felt control that women and men have in their social environments. We turn first to an examination of close relationships in adulthood: close friendships, couple relationships, and loneliness (the experience of being unable to meet one's relationship needs). Next, we examine the formalization of close relationships in marriage. Finally, we conclude with a discussion of parenthood.

CLOSE RELATIONSHIPS IN ADULTHOOD

Relationships serve important needs for women and men alike. Close relationships fill emotional needs for intimacy and sharing; both close and more casual relationships can fill social needs for companionship, social stimulation, and status. A variety of types of relationships can provide the individual with many forms of social support—everything from comfort in times of deep emotional distress to investment advice to the confidence that someone else will be around to restock the refrigerator when she or he has the flu and cannot venture out. Clearly, such forms of support are important to both women and men, yet the two gender groups have been found to differ somewhat in their expectations of relationships and, to some extent, in who they count on for what.

Same-Sex Friendships

A pervasive stereotype has held that friendships between males are stronger and deeper than those between females. The notion was eloquently expressed by Montaigne: "The ordinary capacity of women is inadequate for the communion and fellowship which is the muse of the sacred bond of friendship, nor does their soul feel firm enough to endure the strain of so tight and durable a knot." In more recent times, anthropologist Lionel Tiger (1969) proposed the hypothesis that men have a genetically based tendency, reinforced by society, to form nonerotic bonds with other males and that these male bonds are stronger and more stable than those formed between females. Despite the credence often given such notions of the superiority of male–male ties, however, research generally has failed to support them. Enduring, passionate friendships between women have been well documented as forming an important support for women as they have challenged societal rules and restrictions on feminine roles (e.g., Faderman, 1981; Lapsley, 1999). Psychological research indicates that men tend to be lower in affiliation motivation and affiliation values than women (Mazur, 1989). Studies indicate that although men may report more same-sex friendships than women, male friendships tend to be less close and less intimate than female friendships (Claes, 1992). College males are more likely to consult with and make intimate self-disclosures to close female friends than to close male friends (Komarovsky, 1976; R. A. Lewis, 1978). Women tend to disclose more about themselves than men do (Dindia & Allen, 1992); however, there is only weak evidence that women self-disclose more than men do to people they like (Collins & Miller, 1994). Older males are less likely than their female counterparts to have intimate same-sex friends and to replace lost friends (Mullins & Mushel, 1992; C. M. Perry & Johnson, 1994); however, the friendships males do have are more likely to be seen as equitable (Roberto & Scott, 1986).

When women and men are questioned about their friendships, strong similarities appear in their responses (Caldwell & Peplau, 1982; Gibbs, Auerbach, & Fox, 1980). However, there are some differences. Women place more emphasis on talking and sharing emotions, and men focus on shared activities (Caldwell & Peplau, 1982). In conversations with their best friends, men are more likely to discuss what is going on in the external world—current events, sports, business—and women are more likely to include discussions of feelings and personal concerns (Davidson & Duberman, 1982). Although the kinds of things women and men do with their friends are different, their reports of subjective satisfaction with such friendship activities are about the same (Mazur, 1989). Some research suggests that women's friendships include less hostility and greater emotional involvement than men's do (R. R. Bell, 1981; Gibbs et al., 1980). Friendship is ranked among the most significant aspects of life by both women and men (Blais, Vallerand, Briere, Gagnon, et al., 1990). The things that are important to young women and men in these relationships may differ, however. One study examined middle adolescents' ranking of the importance of expressions of and desires for companionship, control, and intimacy in relationships. Males ranked the expression of control highest and expression of affection lowest; females reversed the order (Bakken & Romig, 1992).

An in-depth interview study of friendship attitudes among young, middle-aged, and older adults provides some insights into the differences in female and male friendships in adulthood and the ways these differences may change with age (Fox, Gibbs, & Auerbach, 1985). The researchers found that males consistently tended to be more instrumental, or goal-oriented, in their friendships, and females tended to be more expressive, or emotion-centered. This difference was particularly noticeable among the young adults (ages 18 to 22). Young men described their friendships as dating back to childhood, often formed through playing on sports teams together, and as durable in the face of disagreements over dissimilarities or disagreements in attitudes or behavior. They avoided confronting friends who did or said things they didn't like, preferring to preserve the friendship rather than to challenge the friend's behavior. Young women, conversely, described their friendships as less durable and more fragile. They were more willing than males to confront their friends over things that disturbed them, and they felt it was important to express their feelings even if it meant sacrificing the friendship. Thus, it appears, young men were more able to enjoy friendships with people with whom they disagreed, perhaps because, as earlier research showed, their major emphasis was on shared activities rather than shared talk. Young women were much more sensitive to disagreement with their friends, feeling perhaps that their definition of true friendship—emotion sharing—could not be achieved with someone whose beliefs or values differed strongly from their own.

Young men appeared to be less aware than young women of the emotional needs that friendship could fill. They spoke far less than the women did about the role of empathy and altruism in friendship; women, however, stressed the importance of being able to reveal themselves and of accepting their friends' innermost feelings. The authors of the study speculate that the greater intimacy of female friendships may be related to girls' early closeness with their mothers and the absence of a comparable closeness between boys and their fathers. Most of the young women named their mothers as close friends; none of the young men mentioned their fathers.

Among midlife subjects (ages 35 to 55), the instrumental–expressive difference in men's and women's friendship attitudes was still evident. However, men in this age group were more concerned and thoughtful about friendship than younger men were, and the women were more tolerant and less confrontational than younger women. Both sexes expressed a desire to hold on to their friends. Men were negative about too much dependency in friendships, and their concept of need—an instrumental one that included various kinds of concrete help—differed from women's more expressive emphasis on the need to talk, to be comforted, and to share.

Among the older sample (56 and older), both women and men held long-term friendships and were less likely than the midlife sample to be confrontational with their friends. In this age group, men's attitudes toward friendship appeared more idealistic than those of their midlife counterparts. However, men's friendships still differed from those of women in the sense that they tended to originate at work and to focus on shared activities and discussions of such externals as taxes and politics. Women continued to emphasize expressiveness in their friendships.

The authors of this study conclude that major differences exist between women and men in their experience and expression of empathy and altruism in friendship. Women are more likely than men to consider the sharing of feelings a central aspect of friendship. As the authors themselves comment, "Men as well as women defined a friend as someone you could talk to about anything, but when questioned further, the 'anything' for men was sports, politics, and business, and for women was feelings and problems" (Fox et al., 1985, p. 499). Clearly, women and men both have strong needs for friendship, but their friendships differ in the extent to which they provide emotional intimacy.

Various explanations have been suggested for the gender differences in friendship orientation just described. Perhaps men do not need as much emotional intimacy as women do, or perhaps they focus more of these needs on their female friends or partners. A number of authors have discussed the potential barriers to emotional intimacy between men, citing in particular the competitiveness that is socialized into the masculine role (Komarovsky, 1976; R. A. Lewis, 1978). The aura of competition among males makes it difficult for men to be open with other men, to "let down their guard," lest it provide these other men with a competitive advantage. It is seen as safer, perhaps, for a man to disclose his feelings to a female friend or partner—someone who is not perceived as a competitor.

Another barrier to intimacy in male friendships is **homophobia,** negative attitudes toward and fear of homosexuality (R. A. Lewis, 1978; Morin & Garfinkle, 1978). Although data that demonstrate a causal connection are not available, many writers on the subject of male friendship speculate that the fear of being labeled homosexual inhibits the development of emotional intimacy in men's relationships. Still other writers have argued that men *do* achieve emotional intimacy via their friendship style of shared activity. Masculine styles of communicating closeness are simply different—not less intimate—than the more verbally oriented styles favored by women, according to these researchers (Wood & Inman, 1993).

Cross-Sex Friendships

In North America, a strong emphasis is placed on the importance of having an intimate, loving, sexually exclusive relationship with another person: being part of a heterosexual couple. In fact, the pairing of women and men into such intimate relationships is taken so much for granted that people seem to find it difficult to conceive of female–male relationships that do not fit this pattern. Often there is an assumption that any friendly overture from a woman to a man or vice versa is an expression of sexual interest or that any strong bond between a man and woman must have a sexual component. One case in point: When Canadian mountain climber Sharon Wood, the first North American woman to reach the summit of Mount Everest, was interviewed on television, the male interviewer began the session by focusing eagerly on how sleeping arrangements had been managed during the ascent. Had she shared a tent with the men or had she had one to herself? When Wood responded patiently (no doubt she had faced this question before) that she had slept in her sleeping bag, in the same tent as her male co-climbers, who were all her good friends, the interviewer produced a knowing leer. Clearly, he had no conception of the possibility that a woman could live and work closely with a group of men as partners in a challenging expedition without sexuality becoming a big issue—even in the cold, exhausting, oxygen-poor environment of high-altitude climbing.

This tendency to assume a sexual aspect to male–female relationships seems to be stronger in men than women and was illustrated experimentally by Antonia Abbey (1982). Inspired by her own experience and by the anecdotes of other women about having their gestures of friendliness misinterpreted by men as indications of sexual interest, Abbey devised an experiment to see whether the phenomenon was a prevalent one. In the experiment, a series of male–female pairs participated in 5-minute, unstructured conversations in the laboratory, while a hidden female and male observed the interaction. After the interaction, both actors and observers were asked to rate the actors on a number of trait adjectives and to respond to questions about their sexual attraction to and interest in dating the other-sex actor. She found that the college males in her study did indeed show a tendency to misperceive female friendliness as an indication of sexual interest. Male actors and observers rated the female actor as being more promiscuous and seductive than female actors and observers did. Males were also more sexually attracted to the other-sex actor than females were. Surprisingly, males also rated the *male* actor in a more sexualized way than females did, suggesting that men may be more likely than women to view the world in sexual terms. The tendency for men to perceive less friendliness but more "sexiness" in women's behavior than women do has also been demonstrated in a series of three studies that included not only peer interactions but also videotaped exchanges between a male store manager and a female cashier and between a male professor and a female student (Saal, Johnson, & Weber, 1989).

Cross-sex friendships are more likely to be reported by young adults than by middle-aged and older adults, perhaps because marriage makes it practically difficult for individuals to pursue cross-sex relationships except in the context of couple relationships (Fox et al., 1985). Among midlife adults, employed women have more cross-sex friendships than nonemployed women, whereas employment is not related to men's cross-sex friendships (Dickens & Perlman, 1981). Some research suggests that cross-sex friendships are experienced as less satisfactory than same-sex friendships, especially by women (McWilliams & Howard, 1993; Parker & de Vries, 1993). Among a sample of young adults, cross-sex friendships were reported by both men and women as providing less help and loyalty than same-sex friendships, and the women said cross-sex relationships were less accepting and intimate, but provided more companionship, than same-sex ones did (Rose, 1985). Members of one diverse sample of urban adolescent girls reported that they were open and honest with their female peers but felt uncomfortable and nervous about speaking their minds to their male peers (Way, 1995). The girls felt it was dangerous to share their feelings with boys and literally silenced themselves in these cross-sex relationships.

Couple Relationships

For many adults, the most important close relationship is a romantic–sexual one in which two individuals develop strong bonds and think of themselves as a couple. Whether the couple is dating, cohabiting, or married, and whether it is a mixed-gender or same-gender relationship, gender is one of the most important influences on the structure and functioning of the couple relationship.

CHOOSING A PARTNER AND FALLING IN LOVE   Among heterosexuals, both women and men are drawn to partners who are physically attractive. Men tend to place greater value on physical attractiveness than women do (Buss, 1989; Feingold, 1990). Physically attractive men initiate more contact with women and rate these contacts as more meaningful and disclosing than less attractive men do; however, women's physical attractiveness is unrelated to their involvement with men (Reis et al., 1982). This apparent discrepancy may be due to the still prevalent pattern that men take more direct initiatives in making contact with women than vice versa and that they seek out women who, they think, will accept them. A man's chances may indeed be better with a moderately attractive than with a highly attractive woman because, as Reis and his colleagues demonstrated, physically attractive women tend to be less trusting of men.

Social factors seem to affect the way people perceive attractiveness in potentially eligible romantic partners. A study of unattached bar patrons found that men rated the attractiveness of female patrons higher as the evening wore on, and women showed a similar pattern in their ratings of male patrons (Gladue & Delaney, 1990). This effect was unrelated to the amount of alcohol consumed and suggests that people's perceptions of attractiveness are influenced by the availability of a potential partner. The "availability" effect may work in reverse as well: Individuals who are already involved in romantic relationships see other potential partners as less attractive than do individuals who are unattached (Simpson, Gangestead, & Lerma, 1990).

Heterosexual women and men give different responses when asked what characteristics are desirable in a mate. In one study of adult married couples, the women rated the following characteristics as significantly more desirable than the men did: considerate, honest, dependable, kind, understanding, fond of children, well liked by others, good earning capacity, ambitious and career-oriented, good family background, and tall. The men rated these qualities as significantly more desirable for a spouse than the women did: physically attractive, good-looking, good cook, and frugal (Buss et al., 1990). Interestingly, the sexes differ in the way their expressed preference for particular spousal qualities relates to the type of mate with whom they end up. In this study, the wives of husbands who preferred kind-considerate spouses tended to be agreeable, extroverted, and gregarious, whereas husbands of wives who preferred kind-considerate spouses tended to be submissive, unassertive, and socially passive. In a similar vein, wives of men who preferred spouses to be domestic tended to be warm, agreeable, submissive, and feminine, whereas husbands of wives who preferred domestic spouses were low on dominance and ambition but showed no special evidence of warmth and agreeableness. It appears that a trait such as kindness/considerateness can mean different things in women than in men or that the pool of available people seen to possess a particular characteristic is different or more restricted within one gender group than within the other.

There is a widely held stereotype that, in the interpersonal attraction sweepstakes, "nice guys finish last" with women. Supposedly, women want a man who will take charge and be dominant; they are less interested in someone who is kind, caring, and gentle. According to one group of researchers, nothing could be further from the truth. In three successive studies, they found that men who expressed altruism or who were described as considerate, cooperative, kind, and sympathetic were rated by women as more physically and sexually attractive, socially desirable, and desirable as dates than were men who appeared less caring or agreeable. By contrast, men's dominance alone did not affect women's attraction to them, although dominance did interact with men's prosocial qualities to increase attraction under some conditions (Jensen-Campbell, Graziano, & West, 1995).

Once a relationship has begun, the individuals explore the possibilities for increased commitment. The influence of gender on this process can be considerable. For one thing, young men seem more ready to fall in love than their female counterparts—perhaps because the men are focusing on the partners' physical attractiveness and the women are looking more pragmatically at the man's education and earning potential (T. L. Huston & Ashmore, 1986). If men do fall in love more quickly, it may mean that early in the relationship men are more motivated than women to try to make a good impression and to work at maintaining the relationship (T. L. Huston & Ashmore, 1986). At any rate, for both women and men, creating a good impression often involves fulfilling gender-role expectations (Zanna & Pack, 1975).

COMMUNICATING   Although there is a great deal of evidence that women prefer more self-disclosure in intimate relationships than men do, reciprocity may dictate similar levels of disclosure between partners. Thus, the amount of self-disclosure in a relationship may reflect a compromise between the preferences of both partners (Peplau, 1983). When differences do exist, it is usually the woman who discloses more. Gender differences in the content of self-disclosure have been observed by some researchers, with men being more likely than women to reveal strengths and to hide weaknesses.

Gender differences have also been found in the communication patterns of intimate couples. In mixed-gender couples, women provide more support to male speakers than men provide for women. Women ask more questions and use "mm's" and "oh's" more to indicate attention and interest than men do (Fishman, 1978). After analyzing more than 50 hours of spontaneous conversations between the members of three couples, Fishman found that 96% of the topics introduced by males "succeeded" (resulted in a conversation in which they were discussed) but only 36% of those introduced by the females did so. Men frequently did not respond or responded minimally to topics raised by women, but women almost always responded to those raised by men. Perhaps because talking does not always get the results they want, women often turn to nonverbal communication to get their point across. Wives have also been found to be better at sending nonverbal messages to their husbands than vice versa (Noller, 1980).

PERMANENCE/STABILITY AND EXCLUSIVITY   There is little direct evidence as to whether women and men differ in their concern with stability or permanence in intimate relationships. Some research suggests that men are more devastated by breakups of intimate relationships than women are (Nolen-Hoeksema & Girgus, 1994; Z. Rubin et al., 1981).

Comparisons of mixed-gender and lesbian cohabiting couples have found that heterosexuals express greater confidence than lesbians do that their relationship will continue in the future (Schneider, 1986). A factor that may be either a cause or an effect of this difference in confidence is the difference in degree of financial interdependence described by the two sets of couples. Mixed-gender couples were more likely than lesbian couples to have joint bank accounts and to have life insurance and wills naming the partner as beneficiary. Perhaps this difference in confidence about relationship longevity will disappear along with the legal and social barriers to joint financial arrangements between same-sex couples. Some local governments and large companies (for example, the Coors Brewing Company and the Walt Disney Company) have now approved full domestic-partner benefits for the partners of their gay and lesbian employees—meaning, for example, that partners of these employees can be covered by health and pension plans. Among both lesbian and gay male couples, high values placed on dyadic attachment (desire for intimacy in close relationships) are associated with expectations of permanence in the relationship and with willingness to move if necessary to maintain the relationship (Peplau & Cochran, 1981; Peplau, Cochran, Rook, & Padesky, 1978).

It is in the area of exclusivity that a striking difference among the relationships of gay men, lesbians, and mixed-gender couples has appeared in the past. When samples of these three groups were asked whether they had had sex with someone other than their primary partner during the past 2 months, 54% of the gay men said yes, compared to only 13% of the lesbians and 14% of college-age dating men and women (Peplau & Cochran, 1981). In the age of AIDS, awareness of the dangers of casual sex has reduced the number of sexual partners for many gay males. However, in more recent research, gay men still report more sexual contacts outside their primary relationship and more permissive attitudes about such contacts than lesbians do (Peplau & Cochran, 1990). This difference may reflect to some extent gender differences in attitudes toward sexuality, specifically the tendency for men to learn that sexual behavior can be separate from love and intimacy.

RELATIONSHIP QUALITY AND SATISFACTION   One of the qualities related to the success of a close relationship is **trust**—a multifaceted construct that includes faith that one's partner will act in loving ways whatever the future holds and belief in the partner's behavioral predictability and personal dependability (Rempel,

Holmes, & Zanna, 1985). Although trust is seen by both women and men as crucial in close heterosexual relationships, it is viewed somewhat differently by them. For women, the three components of trust are integrally related. For them, trust includes not only faith in the partner's future caring but also belief that the partner is a dependable person, as consistently confirmed by predictable behavioral evidence. For men, conversely, the three components of trust appear to be less integrated; they can, for instance, focus on faith in a partner's future caring without putting too much emphasis on the more pragmatic concerns of dependability and predictability. John Rempel and his colleagues (1985) offer two possible explanations for the gender difference. First, women may be more concerned with the practical aspects of interpersonal behavior because they are often in positions of greater dependency in close relationships. Men, being less dependent, can perhaps afford to take a more romantic viewpoint. Second, and equally plausible, is the possibility that women are more sensitive to relationship issues than men are, and so are more likely to evaluate the future of a relationship with reference to its past and present.

Another aspect of relationship quality that apparently has different implications for women and men in close heterosexual relationships is **intimacy maturity**, which refers to the levels of relationship maturity in terms of other-orientation, caring/concern, sexuality, commitment, and communication that may be found within an intimate relationship (K. M. White, Speisman, Jackson, Bartis, & Costos, 1986). For husbands in the sample studied by Kathleen White and her colleagues (1986), intimacy maturity was significantly and positively related to perceived marital adjustment; for wives there was no relationship between the two scores. Wives' marital adjustment score was predicted by husbands' intimacy maturity, however: The more mature the husbands, the better adjusted the wives. But wives' intimacy maturity was unrelated to husbands' marital adjustment. Clearly, the connections between intimacy and marital adjustment are not the same for the two sexes. These findings may reveal a similar dynamic to those on trust, just discussed. Wives, more oriented to husbands' actual behavior, may be more sensitive to manifestations of their husbands' intimacy maturity, whereas husbands, maintaining a more abstract, idealistic view of their relationships, may be relatively uninfluenced by wives' behavior in their perceptions of marriage.

Some research has compared the relationship quality of couples in mixed-gender, gay, and lesbian relationships (Blumstein & Schwartz, 1983; Kurdek & Schmitt, 1986a, 1986b). Many similarities exist among these different types of couples in the factors that relate to relationship quality. For example, poor relationship quality has been linked in all three groups of couples to arguing about money management, intrusion of work into the relationship, spending much time apart, and nonmonogamy (Blumstein & Schwartz, 1983). Also, love for partner has been linked to the perception of many barriers to leaving the relationship and to high dyadic attachment (Kurdek & Schmitt, 1986b). However, some differences are evident among the different kinds of couples. Reciprocal dependency and equality of power have been found to be particularly important for the relationship quality of lesbian couples, whereas financial equality and similarity of educational level have emerged as especially important for the relationship quality of gay male couples (Blumstein & Schwartz, 1983). In a comparison of married, mixed-gender cohabiting, gay, and lesbian relationships, Kurdek and Schmitt (1986b) found that the four partner types differed both in relationship quality and in the variables that predicted relationship quality. Cohabiting mixed-gender partners had the lowest love for partner and relationship satisfaction scores relative to the other three groups, who were indistinguishable from one another on these scores. Married partners reported the most barriers to leaving the relationship, and cohabiting mixed-gender partners reported the fewest. Gay male partners were more likely than the other groups to believe in "mindreading"—a belief that partners should know each other's thoughts without having to say them out loud. Lesbian couples exceeded all other groups in shared decision making. Gay and lesbian couples perceived less social support from friends and family for the relationship than did either the married or unmarried mixed-gender couples. Despite these differences, however, the major correlates of relationship quality were similar across the different groups of couples. Dyadic attachment was an important predictor of love for each partner type and an important predictor of liking for married, gay, and lesbian partners. For each partner type, relationship satisfaction was predicted by seeing few good alternatives to the relationship, high shared decision making, and few beliefs that disagreement is destructive to the relationship. The authors of this study argue that the results support the existence of a general model of relationship quality, applicable to the various types of intimate couple relationships, that includes dyadic attachment, alternatives to remaining in the relationship, shared decision making, and beliefs regarding the value of disagreement (cf. Sternberg, 1986).

A study of relationship satisfaction in 275 dual-career lesbian couples showed that the strains of pursuing careers and couplehood are not limited to heterosexual couples. In this study, the more role conflict and need for personal autonomy were experienced by individuals, the lower was their satisfaction with the relationship (Eldridge & Gilbert, 1990). Differences between the partners' levels of career commitment were also associated with lower relationship satisfaction. Shared attachment, power, and intimacy were all positively related to satisfaction with the relationship.

Another factor whose influence seems to be similar across all couple groups is gender-role self-concept (Kurdek & Schmitt, 1986a). In gay, lesbian, and mixed-gender couples, androgynous and feminine subjects reported higher relationship quality than did masculine and undifferentiated subjects. Relative to other couples, couples in which one or both partners were androgynous or feminine reported the highest relationship quality, whereas those in which one or both partners were masculine or undifferentiated reported the lowest relationship quality. The reason for these differences may perhaps be found in the characteristics displayed by individuals falling into the four gender-role self-concept categories (Cook, 1985). Both androgynous and feminine individuals appear to have qualities that are conducive to interpersonal relations. Androgynous people are poised, outgoing, concerned about others, likeable, assertive, and self-disclosing. Feminine individuals are submissive and sensitive to expressive cues. Masculine persons, however, have been found to be task-minded, hostile, dominant, egotistical, demanding, and low in nurturance. Undifferentiated people tend to be self-centered, withdrawn, poorly socialized, depressed, and lacking in intimacy—hardly the qualities that would enhance a close relationship. Some research shows that wives' satisfaction tends to be lower in marriages where husbands endorse more undesirable masculine traits, such as arrogance, and fewer desirable masculine traits, such as competitiveness (Bradbury, Campbell, & Fincham, 1995).

Men are more likely than women to be satisfied with their marriages (Fowers, 1991). However, the research on relationship satisfaction within marriage suggests that wives and husbands have a tendency to emphasize different things when determining satisfaction. For example, as a knowledge of traditional gender roles might lead one to expect, husbands' satisfaction is related more strongly to their wives' performance of household activities than it is to how affectionate their wives are; the reverse pattern is found for wives' satisfaction (Huston & Ashmore, 1986). In a similar vein, wives' satisfaction is related to husbands' employment stability and income, but the reverse is not consistently found for husbands' satisfaction (Karney & Bradbury, 1995). Although such findings are likely a direct consequence of gender-role expectations that the husband should be the main provider and the wife the main caretaker of the home, researchers do not seem to have directly tested this question.

Another difference found between husbands and wives is that conflict is more strongly related (negatively) to wives' than to husbands' feelings of love for their partner (Huston, McHale, & Crouter, 1986; Kelly, Huston, & Cate, 1985). Some authors have suggested that this difference is a consequence of the greater power held by men in marriage. Conflict may interfere less with love for the person who generally wins than for the person who generally loses. Research has shown that the perceived use of bullying tactics by one's partner is negatively related to satisfaction with the relationship and to estimates of how long the relationship will last (Howard, Blumstein, & Schwartz, 1986). The issue of power in intimate relationships, and in marriage in particular, is discussed at length later in this chapter.

How do individuals decide how satisfactory their relationship is? Some social psychologists have argued that one of the most powerful standards applied by both women and men in evaluating a relationship is that of fairness or justice. According to this model, the partners ask themselves whether they are getting benefits out of the relationship that are fair with respect to their contributions and to their partner's benefits and contributions. The contributions and benefits that partners put into their implicit equations may include such intangibles as love, understanding, and sympathy, as well as more concrete factors such as money, status, and the performance of needed tasks. The difficulty with studying fairness, however, is that what seems perfectly fair to one person may appear profoundly unjust to someone else. Indeed, many of us have observed close relationships in which the participants seem quite satisfied despite what appears to be a most inequitable arrangement. Nonetheless, researchers have shown that perceived **equity**—the extent to which the ratio of each partner's contributions to rewards is seen to be equal—predicts marital satisfaction for both women and men (Utne, Hatfield, Traupmann, & Greenberger, 1984), and equity theorists argue that it is the participants' weighting of the contributions and benefits that determines perceived equity, not some outside observer's assessment of the situation. Thus, for example, one couple may think it a perfectly fair exchange for the wife to do all the housework and child care while the husband earns all the income and looks after the car. But such an arrangement might appear grossly unjust to another couple. Attitudes about how particular contributions and benefits should be weighted are influenced to some extent by self-interest (e.g., each individual may see the tasks she or he performs as being more important or more difficult than those that the other performs) and by cultural and peer attitudes and expectations (e.g., in a social environment that takes traditional gender roles for granted, the arrangement described in the preceding example would seem more fair than it would in a less traditional environment). Equity may not be the last word on satisfaction, however. One study of premarital couples showed that although perceived equity did predict marital satisfaction it was a less reliable predictor than perceived equality (the view that both partners are giving and getting equal amounts in the relationship) and perceived rewardingness of the relationship (Cate, Lloyd, Henton, & Larson, 1982).

POWER AND INFLUENCE IN INTIMATE RELATIONSHIPS   Even in the most intimate of relationships, both partners do not always want the same thing. Thus, each partner must face the problem of asserting his or her own wishes and of getting the other partner to comply or at least not interfere with them. There are two questions of interest here for students of the psychology of gender: whether gender is related to the relative amount of success one partner has in influencing the other and whether gender is related to the *way* one partner goes about trying to influence the other. These are questions of **interpersonal power:** the ability of one person to get another person to do what the first person wants in the face of resistance from the second person.

As noted in several earlier chapters, men are often seen to hold more status and power, as a group, than women. It might be reasonable to expect that this power asymmetry would be reflected in the intimate relationships between individual women and men and, perhaps, that same-gender intimate relationships would be characterized by greater equality of influence between the partners than would mixed-gender relationships. Furthermore, it might be expected that, given female–male differences in status, access to resources, and learned gender roles, the influence tactics used in intimate relationships might differ for women and men. Are such expectations confirmed by the research? The answer is yes, to some extent—but, as usual, the pattern of gender differences is not as simple as the theory predicts.

Before examining the research findings on power in intimate relationships, we need to look briefly at theories of power in general. One of the basic ideas in this area is that power is based on control of resources (French & Raven, 1959; Raven, 1965) and, thus, on one person's ability to affect the outcomes that occur to the other person (Thibaut & Kelley, 1959). The more resources relevant to another person's life that you control, the more you are able to affect what happens to that person and the more power you have relative to that person. It is important to remember, though, that the translation of power into the ability to influence another is based on both individuals' perceptions of the situation. If the other person does not realize, for instance, how much power you have to affect his or her life, your attempt to influence that person may not work. However, if the other person imagines that you have control over resources or outcomes that you really do not have, that person may give way to your influence despite your objective lack of power. The kinds of resources on which power can be based include various types of rewards and punishments, expertise, legitimacy of position, the ability to inspire identification and liking (referent power), and information (French & Raven, 1959; Raven, 1965). In any intimate relationship, each partner has some resources on which to base power, but one partner may have more than the other. The situation is made even more complex by what social exchange theorists call the **principle of least interest;** that is, the person who is least dependent on the other for rewards—who needs the relationship least—has the most power (Homans, 1974).

In intimate relationships, we might expect that access to bases of power and the amount of interpersonal dependence would affect both the amount of influence and the influence tactics employed by the partners. We might also expect that such issues of power and dependence would be related to the gender of the partners involved—that, for instance, in heterosexual couples, men would be likely to control more resources such as money, expertise, and status by virtue of their privileged position in society. In most mixed-gender couples, the man is also bigger and stronger than the woman—a not insignificant power advantage. Finally, in a patriarchal society, the man is seen, normatively, as the dominant partner or the "head of the house," and this perception endows him with power based on legitimacy. Power based on liking or attraction may well be equally distributed between the partners or may favor the woman. In same-gender couples, there is less reason to expect particular power asymmetries, although particular imbalances may well exist in individual couples.

Toni Falbo and Anne Peplau (1980) examined the influence strategies that members of heterosexual, gay, and lesbian couples reported they used in their intimate relationships. They were able to categorize the strategies along two dimensions: **directness** (direct–indirect) and **interactiveness** (unilateral–bilateral). The directness dimension refers to the openness or obliqueness that characterizes an influence attempt. A straightforward request or order would be a direct influence tactic, for instance, whereas a behind-the-scenes manipulation of the situation to favor one's own preferred outcome would be an indirect tactic. The interactiveness dimension refers to the degree of mutual engagement with the partner required in the influence attempt. An extremely unilateral strategy, such as giving an order or walking out on the other person, involves no mutual engagement at all; a bilateral strategy, such as arguing or bargaining, requires considerable engagement and interchange. Using these dimensions, Falbo and Peplau found that influence strategies varied according to the partners' perceptions of power in the relationship. In heterosexual, gay, and lesbian couples, individuals who preferred and perceived themselves as having more power than their partner reported the use of more direct and bilateral influence strategies. Conversely, those who saw themselves as having less power than their partner reported using more unilateral and indirect tactics to get their way. Finally, as suggested by the intergroup gender differences in power and status, gay and lesbian partners were less likely than were mixed-gender partners to want more power than their partners or to view themselves as having such a power advantage, and women in heterosexual relationships were more likely than men were to feel at a power disadvantage. Across the groups, women showed a greater preference than men did for equal power in their relationships. Further research has confirmed that spouses who see themselves as equal partners are more satisfied with their relationships (Aida & Falbo, 1991).

Perceptions of power are situational and may vary from interaction to interaction for the same couple. One study showed that both wives and husbands were more likely to be demanding (exerting pressure through emotional requests, criticisms, or complaints) when discussing a change that *they* wanted and to be withdrawing (retreating into defensiveness and passive inaction) when discussing a change that the *partner* wanted. On the whole, however, men were more likely than women to withdraw from their spouses during marital conflict (Christensen & Heavey, 1990).

Another study of the connection between gender and power in intimate relationships examined the relative importance of the following on the influence tactics used in same-sex and cross-sex intimate relationships: gender, gender-role orientation, control over structural resources (money, education, age), physical attractiveness, and dependence on the relationship (Howard et al., 1986). Unlike Falbo and Peplau, whose respondents were undergraduates in relationships that were relatively new, these researchers studied a cross-section of adults in long-term relationships. They identified six categories of influence strategies: (1) manipulation (e.g., dropping hints, flattering, behaving seductively), (2) supplication (e.g., pleading, crying, acting ill or helpless), (3) bullying (e.g., threatening, insulting, becoming violent), (4) autocracy (e.g., insisting, claiming greater knowledge, asserting authority), (5) disengagement (e.g., sulking, leaving the scene), and (6) bargaining (e.g., reasoning, offering to compromise). Stereotypically, manipulation and supplication are weak strategies, and bullying and autocracy are strong ones. The researchers expected that the use of the "weak" strategies of manipulation and supplication would be linked to being female, being relatively less masculine and more feminine, having relatively less structural power, and being more dependent on the relationship than one's partner. What they did find was that although the *actor's* gender did not relate to influence tactics, the *partner's* gender did. Both females and males with male partners were more likely to use the weak influence strategies than were females and males with female partners. As the authors suggest, "The power associated with being male thus appears to be expressed in behavior that elicits weak strategies from one's partner" (p. 107). Other aspects of the hypothesis were supported. Having control of fewer resources, such as having less income or seeing oneself as less attractive than one's partner, is linked to greater reported use of supplication and manipulation, as is greater dependence on the relationship. However, these differences in structural power did not themselves account for the effects of gender on influence tactics. In other words, gender was related to power in these intimate relationships above and beyond other forms of power and dependence. Men's capacity to elicit deferential behavior cannot be completely explained by their access to money and expertise; rather, being male in our culture is correlated with so many sources of power (e.g., status, legitimate authority, size, strength) that it would be difficult to measure them all in one study. Moreover, growing up with all these indicators of power, males may develop behavior patterns, perhaps without even realizing it, that tend to elicit deference and "weak" influence strategies from others. There is much yet to learn about the dynamics of interpersonal power and influence, but it is certainly clear that gender and power are linked in intimate relationships—a link that is probably both caused by and supportive of the intergroup gender differences in power and status.

Loneliness

We have seen that gender has implications for both friendship and intimate "couple" relationships. It seems also to have implications for the way perceived scarcity or deficiency in such relationships—loneliness—is experienced. Given the differences that have been noted in males' and females' orientation to close relationships, it might be expected that females would be more likely than males to notice and to be bothered by deficiencies in their relationships and thus to feel lonely. Some researchers have indeed found that women report more loneliness than men do (e.g., Weiss, 1973). However, given the difficulties with intimacy that some researchers have noted among males, it might be expected that males would report more loneliness than females do—and some researchers have found this pattern as well (e.g., Schultz & Moore, 1986). In an effort to make sense of the evidence on this issue, Shelley Borys and

Daniel Perlman (1985) classified the existing studies into those that had used a standard questionnaire measure of loneliness, the UCLA Loneliness Scale (D. Russell, Peplau, & Cutrona, 1980), and those that had used a self-labeling measure of loneliness (responses to questions such as "How often do you feel lonely?"). Although most studies using the UCLA scale showed no gender differences in loneliness, those that did find a difference almost always found males scoring as lonelier than females. However, among the 11 self-labeling studies, 9 showed that women were more apt than men to label themselves as lonely. Borys and Perlman suggest that the incongruent results for the two types of studies derive from the way questions are asked. The UCLA scale asks respondents about the quality of their relationships but does not ask them whether they would label themselves as lonely. Perhaps men, because of social influence pressures, are simply more reluctant than women to admit to being lonely. In support of this explanation, Borys and Perlman (1985) offer the results of their own study indicating that college students are more rejecting of a lonely male than of a lonely female. Their findings suggest that the negative consequences of admitting loneliness are less for women than for men, at least among young adults.

One study (Schultz & Moore, 1986) has shown that there may be qualitative as well as quantitative gender differences in loneliness. These researchers examined the factors that were associated with loneliness for female and male college students. They found that lonely males were more likely than lonely females were to suffer from negative mood and negative self-evaluations—a finding that may mean that males tend to blame loneliness on their own failures, whereas females are more likely to blame it on external circumstances. This study also showed that loneliness was more strongly linked to a reported lack of social risk taking for males than it was for females. This finding is not surprising, the authors suggest, given that gender roles place more of the onus for initiating social contact, especially cross gender contact, on males than on females. Taken together, the two findings suggest that, at least for college students, the relatively greater degree of control over heterosocial relationships that is assigned to the masculine role can backfire on men. Charged with the responsibility for making contacts, men who are hesitant to take social risks may not only feel lonely but also blame their own inadequacies for their loneliness. Women, whose feminine role gives them more support for waiting to be approached, can at least blame some of their loneliness on the social ineptitude of their male acquaintances. In the realm of close relationships, then, it appears that even reactions to the *absence* of such relationships is influenced by gender-related expectations.

AGING, THE LOSS OF RELATIONSHIPS, AND WIDOWHOOD   For both women and men, aging is often associated with the loss of important relationships—a situation that can lead to loneliness. Gender is an important variable here, not only because women outlive men and so are more likely to be widowed but because gender stereotypes and expectations shape the ways elderly people cope with loss and loneliness.

Most studies find that widowers have an advantage over widows in their practical resources, such as income, education, and freedom from health restrictions. They are also more likely than widows to remarry. However, widows seem to have more interpersonal resources and varied sources of support, including close female friends and involved neighbors. Women who have been widowed report greater life satisfaction than their male counterparts do—an effect that goes counter to women's generally greater financial stress and more frequent somatic symptoms (Stevens, 1995). Widowed men are more vulnerable to depression than women are, and the strains associated with widowhood differ for women and men (Siegel & Kuykendall, 1990; Umberson, Wortman, & Kessler, 1992). In general, it appears that widowed men are more likely than widowed women to feel alone and lonely.

Among the elderly in general, women may feel more unhappy about aging and more lonely (Imamoglu, Kuller, Imamoglu, & Kuller, 1993). Both women and men may experience the loss of the work role at retirement as isolating and depressing (Perkins, 1992) and may feel alone and depressed because of physical limitations. In one sample of elderly African Americans, women were more likely than men to report memory problems, and loneliness was found to be the strongest predictor of such self-reports (Bazargan & Barbre, 1992).

For older women, marital status has an important impact on friendship networks and the exchange of social support. Among single, older, childless women, those who have never married report more life satisfaction, even though they do not necessarily have more social contacts (Rice, 1989). In this study, never-married women reported fewer social contacts than widowed women did; however, they were less affected by the absence of such contact. Never-married women are more likely than married women to have pursued careers; their sources of life satisfaction may include a variety of nonrelational factors. Marriage also shapes the ways that older women relate to friends and family. Older married women provide more help and support to family members than widows do; however, widows spend more time and give more practical help to friends than wives do (Gallagher & Gerstel, 1993). Gallagher and Gerstel suggest that marriage "privatizes women's help to others—it provides them with both the resources and opportunity to help those related, while it reduces help—both its breadth and intensity—to those not related" (p. 675). Here again, it appears that relationships are influenced by role expectations.

MARRIAGE: THE INTIMATE ECONOMIC PARTNERSHIP

When an intimate heterosexual relationship is legally formalized through marriage, or acknowledged by the partners to be a permanent living-together arrangement, new issues must be faced. Besides such emotional concerns as love, trust, and satisfaction, the spouses must now confront problems of dividing up the household work, sharing income, and making joint decisions regarding employment, housing, children, and so on. The partnership is more than a close personal relationship: It is an economic and legal one as well. If a couple is formally married or, in some jurisdictions, become common-law spouses simply by living together for a specified length of time, they have agreed, albeit often without realizing it, to abide by the terms of a marriage contract. The terms of the marriage contract are not negotiable by the two partners; they are legal rights and responsibilities spelled out by the government. The terms cover such things as how property is shared during the marriage and divided upon divorce, sexual exclusivity, financial support, inheritance, responsibilities for children, even the woman's right to keep her own name. As Sapiro (1986) notes, the marriage contract is virtually the only one that most people enter without knowing the terms, and that can be changed by a third party (the government) while it is in force and without notification of the involved parties. Moreover, private agreements between a wife and husband that contravene the terms of the marriage contract are not enforceable by law.

Although the marriage contract used to be based on the notion that a woman, upon marriage, came under the more or less complete authority and ownership of her husband, legal changes, such as the introduction of community property laws, have removed some of the inequality built into the marriage contract. However, the idea that women are subordinate to their husbands is still built into the marriage contract in many jurisdictions. For example, in some jurisdictions, the husband has the right to choose where the couple will live. If a wife refuses to move with her husband, she is legally considered as abandoning him—grounds for divorce. In many countries, women's groups are still working to effect changes that would equalize the rights of wives and husbands in marriage. For example, Thai women have been lobbying for passage of legislation that would allow a woman to keep her birth name when she marries instead of being required to take her husband's name ("Thai Women," 1999).

The economic laws and customs surrounding marriage are still largely based on assumptions about family structure and stability that do not fit current social patterns. The core of these assumptions is that women and children will have a man to provide for them. However, instead of a relatively permanent arrangement that includes one employed spouse, one homemaker, and children, families now must often respond to divorce, remarriage, out-of-wedlock births, and the necessity for two incomes. When family-disruptive events such as divorce, job loss, or disability occur, women are more likely than men to experience significant drops in their access to resources and well-being (Burkhauser & Duncan, 1989).

The Division of Labor

Until the 1970s, the basic assumptions of the marital economic arrangement in middle-class urban families were that the husband was responsible for the economic support of the wife and children, and the wife was responsible for most of the domestic labor. It was even suggested that our society measured a man's masculinity by the size of his paycheck (Gould, 1973). The husband's breadwinner role was often considered his most important function by men and women alike, and a survey by Yankelovich (1974) suggested that for about 80% of employed married men the provider role gave purpose and meaning to life and to jobs that were otherwise not very satisfying. The assumption that the man should be the chief breadwinner and the woman his helpmate and homemaker has not disappeared, but it is being widely questioned or rejected outright as women move into the paid work force in large numbers. In fact, what appears to have happened in many cases is that the woman kept most of the domestic role while taking on an increasingly larger share of the breadwinner role.

Studies show that the movement of wives into the paid labor force has not been accompanied by a complementary shift of husbands into greater participation in housework (Baxter, 1992; Biernat & Wortman, 1991; Golding, 1990). Employed married women spend fewer hours doing household tasks than unemployed married women do, but their husbands put in little, if any, time on household chores to compensate for their wives' busier schedule. Most of the housework is done by wives, regardless of their employment situation. In developed regions of the world, two thirds to three quarters of the domestic work is done by women (United Nations, 1995a). Although the gender gap in housework is widest among married persons, women do more housework than men do in every type of family living situation: never married and living with parents, never married and living independently, cohabiting, married, divorced, and widowed. The impact of gender is multigenerational; that is, an adult son living at home increases women's housework whereas an adult daughter living at home decreases housework for both women and men (South & Spitze, 1994).

Various factors affect the relative contributions of women and men to household labor. The number of children increases women's domestic labor, but has no effect for men. Men with liberal gender-role attitudes spend more time on housework, but women's gender-role attitudes have no relationship to the amount of domestic work they do. Economic power also plays a role. The more the husband's earnings exceed those of the wife, the larger is the wife's share of the housework (Baxter, 1992). Cultural and ethnic attitudes and traditions may make the dismantling of gender-typed division of household labor even more difficult. For example, among Mexican American couples, women have been found to do a larger share of the housework than among non-Hispanic White American couples (Golding, 1990). Both African American and Hispanic American men are less likely than Anglo men to view the division of household labor as unfair. However, African American and Anglo women are more likely than their spouses to perceive unfairness (John, Shelton, & Luschen, 1995). It appears that, at least under some conditions, African American men spend more time doing household work than either Hispanic or Anglo men do (Hossain & Roopnarine, 1993; John et al., 1995). Even when a woman is at home full time, the assignment of *all* domestic tasks to her results in a division of labor that burdens her unfairly. One writer (Kaye, as cited in Kome, 1986) has calculated that a full-time homemaker with two preschool children must work 206 hours a week to accomplish necessary chores—more hours than a week actually has!

An obvious explanation for the continuation of a fairly traditional spousal division of household labor in the face of changing ideologies about gender roles is that women and men each feel more skilled at the tasks that fall within their traditional spheres. Beginning in childhood, females and males are assigned tasks on the basis of their gender appropriateness (L. White & Brinkerhoff, 1981), so it is not surprising if men and women each have more confidence in their skill at gender-traditional chores. Indeed, one study showed that men's and women's perceived skill can be a good predictor of the extent to which they perform household tasks traditionally done by members of the other sex (Atkinson & Huston, 1984). However, life repeatedly confronts us with the necessity of learning new activities, and most household tasks are far from impossible for an intelligent adult to master. Why, then, does the traditional division of labor persist? Part of the answer lies in an examination of power inside and outside the marital relationship.

Issues of economics and exchange cannot be separated from issues of power and control, and one factor that slows down the change away from the traditional division of economic responsibilities in marriage is that the change threatens men's "legitimate" power as head of the household. Social norms are such that a man can still feel that his masculinity is impugned if he does too much housework or if he appears too responsive to his wife's demands for sharing in the area of domestic chores. In fact, one comprehensive review of the literature on power in marriage indicated that the lowest marital satisfaction and happiness was reported in couples where the wife was dominant in decision making—perhaps because both partners were acutely conscious of the extent to which their arrangement violated social norms (Gray-Little & Burks, 1983). Moreover, most people will agree that housework is generally not "fun." If a person can get away with letting someone else do it, she or he will. In many marriages, men *can* get away with letting their wives do the housework by using power based on the legitimacy of gender roles ("It's not my job—it's the wife's job") or helplessness ("I can't do it as well as you can"). The assignment of the bulk of household tasks to women is further supported by the imbalance of financial contributions brought to the marriage by each spouse. Even when both spouses are employed, the husband usually earns more than the wife, making her more economically dependent on the relationship and hence more influenceable and more likely to try to maintain equity in the relationship by contributing in nonfinancial ways (Scanzoni, 1972). Increased sharing of domestic chores within a marriage is intricately bound up with changes in gender-related ideology and actual gender equality in the larger society.

If the division of household labor is partially influenced by the degree of financial contribution brought by each spouse to the marriage, it might be expected that a shift in the balance of such contributions would cause a corresponding shift in the division of household labor. Research on couples' reactions to the husband's job loss has shown such a pattern. Couples in which the husband was unemployed reported lower contributions by the wives to household work than did couples in which the husband was employed full time (Aubry, 1986). However, there was no indication that the unemployed husbands took on more household work.

Women do the larger share of the social work in families as well. Not only do women take more of the responsibility for childrearing (Hoffnung, 1995), they also do the bulk of the work of caring for aged parents (Kramer & Kipnis, 1995). This share of family relationship work may be especially large for African American women, who are frequently the central figures and primary sources of socialization in their family units (Wilkinson, 1984).

NONTRADITIONAL FAMILIES   Some families have broken dramatically with tradition in their division of labor. According to some estimates, for instance, there are between 1 million and 2 million men in the United States who have taken on the role of "househusband" (Doyle, 1995). These men stay at home and take the major responsibility for housework and child care, while their wives are employed full time. The few studies of these men that have been done suggest that their role is experienced as a positive one (Beer, 1982). However, for the majority of these men, the househusband role is not taken on by choice but conferred on them by circumstances; not surprisingly, those who have freely chosen the role are most happy with it (Lutwin & Siperstein, 1985). Studies in both the United States (Radin, 1982; Tillitski, 1992) and Australia (G. Russell, 1982) indicate that fathers who become the primary caregivers experience an improved relationship with their children.

Not all families are based on the unions of female–male couples, and laws are slowly beginning to recognize this. For example, in Canada, the Supreme Court recently struck down a definition of "spouse" that included only heterosexual partners, clearing the way for gay and lesbian couples to, for example, apply for alimony from each other if they separate ("Canada Overturns Definition," 1999). In the United

States, legal battles are in progress to allow legal marriages between members of gay and lesbian couples. Legal protections for gay and lesbian couples are necessary, as same-gender couples, like mixed-gender couples, often form permanent relationships, involving economic interdependence and the rearing of children. One such family is described in an article by Lindsy Van Gelder (1991). Two women in a committed lesbian relationship wanted to have a child. They searched for and found a man who was willing to be the biological father of that child. That man, also gay, ended up making a commitment to maintaining a relationship, both emotional and financial, with the child he had fathered. The child, Sarah—a little girl of 6 at the time the article was written—consequently has a family of three adults: Nancy, her mother; Amy, her mother's lover; and Doug, her father. The three adults are good friends, and all share the parenting of Sarah. The arrangement produces some difficulties in terms of explaining the family to the rest of the world, but it has many advantages as well. Three adults rather than two share the responsibilities, and barriers exist that prevent the family from falling into the stereotypical divisions of labor and power often found in more traditional families.

The legal system in the United States has generally been hostile to gay and lesbian parents, often making it difficult for them to retain or gain custody of their children. For this reason, gay- and lesbian-headed families have often, by design, remained relatively invisible. However, estimates of the number of lesbian mothers in the United States range from 1 million to 5 million; those for gay fathers range from 1 million to 3 million. These gay and lesbian parents are raising an estimated 6 million to 14 million children (Patterson, 1992).

Research on such families suggests that there is no psychological justification for the legal reluctance to safeguard lesbians' and gay men's parental rights. One reviewer notes that not a single study has found children of gay or lesbian parents to be disadvantaged in any way relative to the children of heterosexual parents (Patterson, 1992). Children of gay and lesbian parents are no more likely than other children to have difficulty with gender identity or gender-role acquisition, and they are no more likely to be homosexual in their orientation than children of heterosexual parents (Patterson, 1992; Tasker & Golombok, 1995). Children of gay, lesbian, and heterosexual parents show no differences in frequency of emotional disturbance, in self-concept, locus of control, moral maturity, intelligence, peer relations, social relations with adults, or other measures of cognitive functioning and behavioral adjustment (Flaks, Ficher, Masterpasqua, & Joseph, 1995; Patterson, 1992).

Marital Violence

More frequently than we care to admit, coercive power within the marriage relationship is exercised through physical violence. In 29% of all violence against women in the United States, the perpetrator is an intimate (husband, ex-husband, boyfriend, or ex-boyfriend), and women are 6 times more likely than men to be violently assaulted by an intimate. In 1992, 18% of female homicide victims in America were killed by a spouse (U.S. Department of Justice, Office of Justice Programs, 1995). Wives are the most frequent victims of fatal violence in families (Keller, 1999; U.S. Department of Justice, 1994b, 1999). Physical violence in intimate relationships can begin even before marriage. Studies have found that about 30% of courting couples report that physical violence has occurred in their relationships (Arias, Samios, & O'Leary, 1987), and this violence tends to continue as couples progress from dating to marriage (Murphy & O'Leary, 1989).

Domestic violence is a worldwide problem. For example, in one survey of Nicaraguan women, 52% of those who had ever been married reported that they had been physically abused by a partner at some point in their lives (Ellsberg, Caldera, Herrera, Winkvist, & Kullgren, 1999). In Chile, where domestic violence is often called "private violence" or "la violencia privada," one survey suggests that 1 of every 4 women is beaten by her partner (McWhirter, 1999). In Japan, a husband's violence is the second most frequent reason given by women who petition the courts for divorce (Kozu, 1999). In post-Soviet Russia, it is reported that between 14,000 and 16,000 women are killed each year by male partners (Horne, 1999).

Violence within marriage is linked historically to a legal definition of the family that made it acceptable for a man to exercise his authority over his wife by beating her (MacLeod, 1980). From ancient Greece and Rome through to Europe in the Middle Ages, men could beat or kill their wives with impunity. As late as the 19th century, British law books stated that the husband could exercise his power and dominion over his wife by beating her, although the beating must not be cruel and violent! Even in the present day, there is some tendency for judges to avoid "interfering" in wife abuse cases because family matters are supposed to be private. One judge in Nova Scotia was finally suspended after years of complaints from women's groups because he persisted in ordering battered women to "go home and submit to your husband."

Marital violence is usually initiated by the husband, but, as the pattern continues, the wife will often fight back (Saunders, 1986). The violence usually increases in severity over time (Frieze, 1986), becoming so dangerous that in about one third of the cases the victim must seek medical treatment for her injuries (MacLeod, 1980). The female victim often becomes isolated from other people and faces a growing sense of powerlessness and helplessness as she tries and fails to change the situation in some way that will stop the violence (L. E. Walker, 1979). Eventually, the woman may try to leave the relationship but often returns because she has nowhere to go or feels too frightened and inadequate to make it on her own (Frieze, 1986). As the violence becomes even more extreme, she may finally leave because she fears for her life or the lives of her children (Frieze, 1979), or she may actually try to kill her husband. One study of marital homicides in Ontario found that all of the female offenders had been seriously assaulted by their victims (Chimbas, as cited in MacLeod, 1980).

The likelihood that a woman who is being assaulted by her partner will be rescued by the justice system is small. According to one researcher, the probability that wife assault will be detected by the criminal justice system is only 6.5% and, if detected, the probability of an arrest is about 21.2%. Taking all stages of the justice process into account results in the estimate that a man who assaults his wife has only a 0.38% chance of being punished by the courts (Dutton, 1987a).

People who do not know the facts about wife abuse often believe women stay in abusive relationships because they are masochistic. In fact, the reasons for staying in a violent marriage have much more to do with situationally determined issues of power and control in the family than with personality dispositions. The woman who wants to leave an abusive marriage often faces a lack of external resources for doing so: no monetary resources to draw on, no way to protect herself against violent retaliation from her husband if he comes after her, no friends or family who can help her, and no accessible shelter for battered women (Frieze, 1986). Moreover, her sense of self-confidence has been drained by the relationship. Physically abusive husbands are usually verbally abusive as well, and wives often endure long strings of insults about their competence, their appearance, and their sexuality along with the beatings (Walker, 1979). All of these factors conspire to place the abused woman at a huge power disadvantage with respect to her husband. Add to this some common beliefs, such as that all men are violent anyway or that her violent husband needs her, and it becomes easy to see how strong are the pressures on an abused woman to remain in the relationship (Frieze, 1986). However, once a woman has left the relationship temporarily by escaping to a shelter for battered women, her reported exposure to psychological abuse is a better predictor of intentions to leave her spouse than is her reported exposure to physical violence (Arias & Pape, 1999).

When a woman does try to separate from or divorce an abusive partner, she risks further violence. Risks of extreme violence and murder are highest when the victim seeks freedom (Pagelow, 1993), and restraining orders are not always effective. If a wife reveals, during separation or divorce proceedings, that she has been abused by her husband, she may not be able to substantiate her claims because she and her husband have hidden the violence over the years. Thus, the violence-based power dynamics that characterized the marriage may not end with the couple's separation.

Although both men and women may behave violently toward their partners, it is men who inflict the most serious abuse (Holtzworth-Munroe & Stuart, 1994). Moreover, the factors associated with violent behavior toward a spouse or intimate partner are quite different for men and women. Men who have a high need for power are more likely to abuse their partners, but women's need for power is unrelated to abusive behavior (Mason & Blankenship, 1987). Assaultive men are found to be not only high in the need for power but low on verbal assertiveness toward their spouses, suggesting that violence may sometimes stem from the frustration of not having the verbal skills to exert influence (Dutton & Strachan, 1987). Some research indicates that within violent marriages husbands with less power are more physically abusive toward their wives—another indication that violence may sometimes serve as a replacement for other kinds of male power (Babcock, Waltz, Jacobson, & Gottman, 1993; Sagrestano, Heavey, & Christensen, 1999). In line with such findings, researchers have shown that, in dating couples, men who are dissatisfied with the amount of power they have in the relationship are most likely to engage in both psychologically and physically abusive behaviors toward their partners (Ronfeldt, Kimerling, & Arias, 1998). One in-depth interview study of the experiences of nine male batterers suggested that for some men being violent in a domestic relationship comes from their desire to assert a preferred identity—perhaps the identity of being the one in charge or in control—and avoid a devalued identity (Reitz, 1999).

Women who report behaving violently toward their spouses are usually being treated violently by these same spouses; however, men who report being physically or psychologically abusive toward their partners are frequently not receiving the same kind of abuse (Mason & Blankenship, 1987). Lenore Walker (1999) notes that the most frequent type of aggression reported by women in some surveys is biting, "which is obviously used as a defensive strategy to get out of a stronghold" (p. 24). Also, young women's expression of and receipt of violence in adult love relationships appears to be more strongly correlated with having been abused as children than does young men's violent behavior in such relationships (Marshall & Rose, 1990).

Studies of men who repeatedly assault their wives suggest that the men tend to blame their wives or external circumstances for their aggressive behavior. One analysis of wives' reports of their husbands' behavior after a "typical" battering incident showed that only 8% of the men apologized and 80% acted as though nothing had happened (Dobash & Dobash, 1984). A comparison of wives' and husbands' causal attributions for an assault by the husband indicated that the husbands tended to externalize the cause for their behavior by blaming it on their wife's behavior or on alcohol. Wives tended to see the assault as due to their husband's emotional state, personality, or other causes internal to the husband (Shields & Hanneke, 1983). One study of 75 men with histories of repeated wife assault found that about one fifth of them excused their assault as not their responsibility but accepted that the act was wrong. The other four fifths of the men accepted personal responsibility but found ways to justify their actions—by blaming the victim, saying that they had been too angry to control themselves, or claiming that their behavior was in line with the norms of their particular subcultural or ethnic group (Dutton, 1986). In this study, men who blamed their wife for the assault were more likely than other men to minimize the frequency, severity, and consequences of their violence.

Some men who assault their wife may, without realizing it, be trying to face down the specter of abandonment. Research shows that assaultive men become more angry and aroused than other men do when they watch videotaped scenes of male–female arguments in which there is a strong perceived threat of the female leaving the male (Dutton, 1987b). In addition, researchers who have studied *desperate love*—a type of emotional attachment in which the lover feels frantic for contact with the loved one and fearful of being left—have found that in men, but not in women, desperate love is strongly related to an attachment style involving aggressive or destructive impulses (Sperling & Berman, 1991).

The majority of men (about 75%) do not approve of the use of physical violence by a man against his wife (Stark & McEvoy, 1970). However, as seen in Dutton's (1986) research, even men who regard such violence as wrong sometimes engage in it. It appears that men who batter their wives are rewarded in certain ways for this behavior. Dutton and Browning (1983) describe the feelings that are connected with wife assault for some men: power, agency (a sense of taking action), and increased sense of control over aversive stimuli. Among other strategies, then, the clinical treatment of male batterers must include teaching these men not to depend on violence as a source of feelings of power and control (Sonkin, Martin, & Walker, 1986).

General comparisons between violent and nonviolent husbands may sometimes obscure important differences among types of batterers. An understanding of the different types of male batterers may increase the effectiveness of treatment programs. One review suggests that there are three major types: the *family-only batterer*, who focuses his violence on family members and who may have a passive/dependent personality; the *dysphoric/borderline batterer*, who exhibits high levels of depression and anger, whose violence may sometimes extend outside the family, and who may have a borderline personality disorder; and the *generally violent/antisocial batterer,* whose levels of extrafamilial violence and criminal behavior are high, and who has a marked tendency toward alcohol or drug abuse (Holtzworth-Munroe & Stuart, 1994). Another study, based on an examination of 200 seriously violent couples, classified male batterers as either "pit bulls," whose emotions quickly boil over into violence when they are angry, or "cobras," who are cold and methodical in their violence (Jacobson & Gottman, 1998). Different factors may be correlated with violent behavior from men in each group; however, more research is needed to develop interventions that may be useful with the various groups.

It is clear that intimate relationships involve issues of power as much as issues of attachment and caring. Marital relationships exist not in a social vacuum but against a background of social norms and legal rules that encourage or tolerate certain kinds of behavior. As long as those norms continue to encourage inequality between husbands and wives and to tolerate the use of violence as a way of exercising power in these relationships, marital violence, particularly wife abuse, will continue to be a problem.

WOMEN AND MEN AS PARENTS

In the popular imagination, one of the largest assumed gender differences is in parent–child relationships. Many people think of women as naturally nurturant, with a built-in instinct for mothering, and of men as second-class parents, more clumsy and less involved with their children. In fact, the notion that women have an inborn maternal instinct played a large role in shaping the history of psychologists' study of human caregiving behavior (Shields, 1984). Many early psychologists saw motherhood as women's most important function, and, until recently, psychologists concerned with the study of parenting examined only mother–child relationships (Silverstein & Phares, 1996).

Our culture abounds with images of mother nurturance. Anthropologist Ashley Montagu's (1952) comments are representative: "The sensitive relationships which exist between mother and child belong to a unique order of humanity, an order in which the male may participate as a child, but from which he increasingly departs as he leaves childhood behind" (p. 142). Michelle Hoffnung (1995) describes what she calls the "motherhood mystique"—a constellation of romanticized attitudes about motherhood that has influenced women to feel guilty or inadequate if they do not have children or if they do not devote themselves full time to their children. The mystique says that only by having a child can a woman actualize her full potential and achieve the ultimate meaning of her life. Motherhood, according to this myth, is complementary with and does not interfere with the other traditional feminine roles of wife and homemaker. Furthermore, a "good" mother is always patient and content, never resentful, and is available to her child 24 hours a day. This mystique surrounding motherhood, which dates only from the 18th century (B. Harris, 1979), has formed the basis for what Adrienne Rich (1976) calls the institution of motherhood: the set of social prescriptions and norms that limit women's choices in and shape their experience of motherhood. Our society has institutionalized motherhood in such a way that mothers are assumed to have primary responsibility for children, are given little recognition and almost no support in this task, are isolated with their children much of the time, and are expected to experience nothing but fulfillment and a self-sacrificial glow as they live out this role. Rich attempts to convey some of the ambivalence experienced by a woman caught in this institution of motherhood:

> The physical and psychic weight of responsibility on the woman with children is by far the heaviest of social burdens. It cannot be compared with slavery or sweated labor because the emotional bonds between a woman and her children make her vulnerable in ways which the forced laborer does not know; he can hate and fear his boss or master; loathe the toil; dream of revolt or of becoming a boss; the woman with children is a prey to far more complicated, subversive feelings. Love and anger *can* exist concurrently; anger at the conditions of motherhood can become translated into anger at the child, along with the fear that we are not loving"; grief at all we cannot do for our children in a society so inadequate to meet human needs becomes translated into guilt and self-laceration. This "powerless responsibility," as one group of women has termed it, is a heavier burden even than providing a living—which so many mothers have done, and do, simultaneously with mothering—because it is recognized in some quarters, at least, that economic forces, political oppression, lie behind poverty and unemployment; but the mother's very character, her status as a woman, are in question if she has "failed" her children. (pp. 35–36)

The motherhood role may be institutionalized differently in different cultures. In Japan, for example, traditionally the role of mother has been associated with independence and power. Mothers have had almost complete control over childrearing, have directed their children's education, and have been able to influence government and community leaders when speaking as guardians of the new generation. Japanese women have perhaps been able to gain status, respect, and a personal sense of self-worth from their role as mothers (Bankart, 1989). As the options open to women in Japan increase, however, young women appear to be very realistic about the amount of work involved in motherhood and reluctant to accept motherhood as their sole route to fulfillment.

One of the goals of the feminist movement has been to gain for women the right to choose or refuse motherhood. Although the advent of effective contraception and safe access to abortion has made it much easier than it used to be for women to put off or avoid motherhood, the social expectations that continue to surround motherhood still make it difficult for women to combine motherhood with other goals. Whereas men rarely face a choice between career and parenthood, that choice is still a painful reality for many women. Women with paid jobs face this conflict starkly with their first pregnancy. For those who cannot afford sufficient maternity leave, depression stemming from overload is a real risk (Hyde, 1995). Greater child-care responsibility is associated with lower well-being and greater psychological distress among professional women who have just had their first child (Ozer, 1995). Immediately after the birth of a first child, trying to balance family and occupational roles can be overwhelming if a woman does not have practical help and support from a spouse or other family members, and institutional support from her employer. Many women cannot count on such support, however. As Betty Friedan (1981), who has argued persuasively that feminism must not deny or devalue the human importance of love, parenthood, and family, notes:

> The price of motherhood is still too high for most women; the stunting of abilities and earning power is a real fear, because professions and careers are still structured in terms of the lives of men whose wives took care of the parenting and other details

of life. The point is that *equality*—the rights for which women have been fighting for over a century—was, is, necessary, for women to be able to affirm their own personhood, and in the fullest sense of choice, motherhood. The point is, the movement to equality and the personhood of women isn't finished until motherhood is a fully free choice. (p. 87)

As women approach motherhood, they are not oblivious to the problems associated with it. Among first-time expectant parents, age and duration of marriage are positively linked to good feelings about the pregnancy for men, but not for women (Lips, 1983). Apparently, the older and more established in her life a woman is, the more she knows she will have to give up in becoming a mother. The older the woman in this sample, the more likely she was to agree that she could have a fulfilling life without children. Despite this awareness, however, women were more likely than men to link having children with fulfillment of their gender roles and with having a satisfying life.

All of the preceding is not to say that parenthood is not a potential source of joy and transformation for both mothers and fathers. Expectant and new parents—female and male—often report strong feelings of happiness, hope for the future, and a change in their concept of relationship from "couple" to "family" (Lips, 1982c; Lips & Morrison, 1986). Yet, in general, the behavioral correlates of these attitudes are quite different for mothers and fathers. Despite claims that father nurturance is on the rise, recent studies have estimated the amount of time fathers spend with children at 12 minutes a day (Lamb, 1987), 26 minutes a day (Gottfried & Gottfried, 1988), 36 minutes a day (Robinson, Andreyenkov, & Patrushev, 1988), 1.7 hours a day (Sanik, 1990), and just over 2 hours a day (Hossain & Roopnarine, 1993). Even in the latter case, a study of infant care in dual-earner African American families, mothers spent far more time than fathers in caring for children.

Fathers are more likely to play with and to engage in caregiving behaviors with their infants if they view fatherhood as a self-enriching experience (Levy-Shiff & Israelashvili, 1988) and if they are not overwhelmed with other life concerns (De Luccie & Davis, 1991). From the beginning of the baby's life, fathers are more likely to be found playing with the baby, and mothers are more likely to be found feeding, changing, dressing, or cleaning him or her. In fact, regardless of the espousal of egalitarian ideals by couples, or of social class or dual- or single-earner status, the birth of a baby is the occasion for a shift toward a gender-traditional division of roles (Arbeit, 1975; Cowan, Cowan, Coie, & Coie, 1978; Lewis & Cooper, 1988; Moss, Bolland, Foxman, & Owen, 1987). This shift is associated with more stress and dissatisfaction among mothers than fathers.

There is some evidence that the amount of time fathers spend with their children increases as the children grow older. This increase has been noted especially in the case of male children, with whom fathers often become involved in particularly "masculine" aspects of socialization such as sporting activities (Starrels, 1994). Like mothers, fathers may feel inadequate in their parental role because they give their children less attention and care than they think they should. There are also some indications that fathers' involvement with children is increasing. For example, Meg Luxton (1980), studying the changes in women's work in the home across three generations of women in a northern Canadian town, noted a distinct change across generations in the amount of father participation in child care reported by these women. Women in the youngest generation, those with small children at the time of the study, were the envy of the older women because of the amount of help their husbands gave them. The older women claimed that during their childbearing years their husbands had refused all involvement with pregnancy, childbirth, and child care; the younger women felt they had a right to expect help from their husbands in this sphere. However, the husband's participation was still viewed as "helping out," and there was little thought that he should or could be an equal participant in the job of raising the children.

Division of child-care work is an issue for gay and lesbian couples too. Lesbian parents report more satisfaction with their relationship when involvement in child care is more evenly divided (Patterson, 1995). Gay male parents, like heterosexual parents, report euphoria when the baby first arrives, followed by stress as they try to redesign their relationship to accommodate the demands on time and energy associated with a new baby (Silverstein, 1996). Parents of all persuasions must "learn on the job," and they become more skilled with practice (Lamb, 1987). Perhaps parents in nontraditional families sometimes try harder to develop the appropriate skills. One study showed lesbian couples to have more parenting awareness skills than heterosexual parents (Flaks et al., 1995).

Despite the "motherhood mystique" and the lack of adequate child-care participation by fathers, mothers of young children have entered the paid labor force in large numbers. These "working mothers" often experience a great deal of conflict and guilt about the possible harm they may be doing to their children by not being more available to them. However, research on the effects of maternal employment on children indicates that schoolage children suffer no emotional or intellectual deprivation as a result of maternal employment (Hoffman, 1974), that preschoolers often benefit socially and intellectually from child care outside the home (Clarke-Stewart, 1991), and that some women are better mothers when they are employed (Schubert, Bradley-Johnson, & Nuttal, 1980). One recent large-scale study, which followed thousands of children, found that children whose mothers worked during the first 3 years of their lives were not significantly different from children whose mothers were not employed during their first 3 years on the outcome variables of the study: obedience, behavior problems, cognitive development, self-esteem, and academic achievement (Harvey, 1999). Even infants do not seem to be adversely affected by being cared for extensively by caregivers other than the mother (Mott, 1991). Of course, the impact of maternal employment must vary with the kind of child-care arrangements mothers are able to make (Scarr, 1998), as well as with such variables as the mother's attitude toward employment and the support she gets from her partner. When women are given the same supports that men are for working—the knowledge that their children are being well cared for in their absence and that their paid work is valued by other family members—maternal employment is apparently a positive, rewarding choice for women and their families. However, only a lucky minority of women have access to such support.

The gender differences in parental behavior, like so many other gender differences, can be at least partially understood with reference to learned social roles, ongoing social expectations, and access to power. First, the socialization process tends to strengthen the female's and minimize the male's attachment to children; the feminine and masculine roles have a strong influence on responsiveness to the young (Silverstein, 1996). Second, the social arrangements that support these feminine and masculine roles—the unavailability of paternity leave, the demand that "work" take place from 9 to 5 each day—make it difficult for people to be flexible, even if they are so inclined. In a study of new parents, Susan McHale and Ted Huston (1984) found that the extent of involvement in child-oriented activities was predicted by involvement in the paid labor force for women but not for men, and by perceived skill at child-care tasks for men but not for women. Also, fathers' involvement with their children was more related to their own and their spouses' attitudes than mothers' involvement was. In concrete terms, the more the mother worked outside the home, the less central was the child to her activities when she was at home, and the more competent and interested a man was in child care before becoming a father, the more he actually did with his child later on. As the authors of the study note, these findings can be explained as stemming from social norms that give mothers little leeway with respect to child care and fathers little freedom of choice with respect to employment. In other words, individual differences in attitude are more likely to influence behavior when the person is free to decide whether or not to engage in the behavior.

The McHale and Huston (1984) study has some practical implications for increasing fathers' involvement in child care. The strong correlations they found between fathers' perceived skill at child-care tasks before their babies' birth and these fathers' later involvement in child care, which are in line with other studies, suggest that giving fathers practice or training in child-care activities may increase their participation in the care of their infants. The researchers also found that the extent to which the mothers were nontraditional in their gender-role attitudes and role preferences was positively related to their spouses' involvement in child care—suggesting, perhaps, that "women must be willing to step back from the role of primary caregiver if fathers are to become more involved in caring for their sons and daughters" (p. 1360). Women may be unwilling to step back, however, if they feel that child care is their major sphere of influence and expertise in the family. Moreover, the "motherhood mystique" ensures that a woman will feel guilty at first for giving up any aspect of the traditional mothering role, no matter how competent and willing her partner is.

Although most of the research on parenting has focused on women and men in two-parent, heterosexual families, parenting obviously takes place in a variety of family contexts (e.g., see Hanson, 1985; Nieva, 1985). Besides dual-earner and wife-as-sole-earner families—the more commonly acknowledged variations on the traditional family—parenting takes place in stepfamilies and single-parent families, by parents who do not live with their children and see them only on weekends, and by gay fathers and lesbian mothers. All of these groups encounter special difficulties, but perhaps their greatest shared problem is their invisibility. We continue to think of families in traditional terms and to assume that families that differ from the "normal," two-biological-parent model generate problems for their members. Such an assumption has, for example, been behind the notion that the 48% of African American families that are headed by women have problems that stem from the way the family is structured rather than, as seems more likely, from the fact that female-headed families are much more likely than are two-parent families to be living below the poverty line (Kemp, 1995). Similarly, the assumption that families should conform to the "man as provider, woman as nurturer" model has been responsible over past decades for the insistence that Native American groups abandon their own family traditions and conform to those of the dominant White culture (Almquist, 1995). Even in the European American middle-class population, however, there is much more diversity among families than existed two decades ago. For example, the number of single-parent families has risen dramatically in recent years. Our vision of the family and our research have not kept pace with these changes.

SUMMARY

The influence of gender on peer and family relationships is rooted in our socialization into feminine and masculine patterns of behavior and maintained by social arrangements that favor these patterns. Girls learn at an early age that intimate, self-disclosing friendships are rewarding and socially approved. Boys learn equally early that too much intimacy with another male is often regarded with suspicion in a society influenced by competitive and homophobic attitudes. The narrow emphasis on sexuality in female–male relationships makes it unlikely that cross-sex friendships will develop, and the separation of males and females into different kinds of jobs and even different domestic roles contributes further to this situation.

Intimate sexual/affectional relationships between women and men share many features with intimate sexual/affectional relationships between men or between women. However, a major difference between same-gender and mixed-gender intimate relationships is that there tends to be more emphasis on equality between the partners in lesbian and gay relationships than in heterosexual relationships. This difference probably derives from the difficulty mixed-gender couples have in separating their relationship from a social context in which men are accorded more status and have access to more bases of power than women do. The influence of this context is particularly apparent in the institution of marriage, where the authority of husband over wife is legally entrenched in some respects. The impact of assumptions about gender differences and the man's right to have authority over the woman can be seen in the problems that beset many male–female couples: inequitable division of household labor and the use of violence by men against their partners.

Relationships between parents and their children are also conditioned by gender-role ideology and the power differences between women and men. Women are supposed to be naturally interested in and good at parenting, by virtue of their sex. The motherhood mystique encourages them to feel guilty if they find motherhood uninteresting or problematic, or if they try to combine it with other goals. Men, in contrast, are not expected to be particularly interested or involved in child care, although there is some evidence that these expectations are slowly changing.

Changes in families over the past two decades—the increase in employment among mothers and the rise in single-parent families—have led to fears that the family is disintegrating. Some have even accused the feminist movement of destroying the family. Perhaps what is being destroyed is the monolithic conception of the family as a patriarchal structure in which the husband is the breadwinner and head, the wife is the caregiver and supporter, and the children grow up lacking all but the most superficial contact with adults other than their parents. According to Betty Friedan (1981), the family is a "feminist frontier"—an institution that must be not destroyed but changed to accommodate the full personhood of both women and men. Such an accommodation would no doubt mean, in part, that many different kinds of families would be considered "normal" and that, within such families, women and men would not be locked into expectations of submission and dominance, caregiver and bread-winner, as they have been in the past. Although some movement in this direction has certainly happened, it remains to be seen how readily this particular "feminist frontier" can be crossed.

KEY TERMS

polygyny	trust	principle of least interest
polyandry	intimacy maturity	directness
serial monogamy	equity	interactiveness
homophobia	interpersonal power	

FOR ADDITIONAL READING

Ehrenreich, Barbara. (1983). *The hearts of men: American dreams and the flight from commitment.* Garden City, NY: Anchor. The author examines the ways ideas about masculinity have changed and how those changes relate to changes in the marriage relationship.

Hewlitt, Barry S. (1991). *Intimate fathers: The nature and context of Aka pygmy paternal care.* Ann Arbor: University of Michigan Press. The author examines fatherhood from a cross-cultural perspective, focusing on a hunter-gatherer group in which fathers spend almost half their day in close contact with their infants.

Lapsley, Hilary. (1999). *Margaret Mead and Ruth Benedict: The kinship of women.* Amherst, MA: University of Massachusetts Press. This is the story of the lifelong friendship and love between two extraordinary women.

Nardi, Peter M. (Ed.). (1992). *Men's friendships.* Newbury Park, CA: Sage. The contributors to this volume present a variety of different perspectives on how gender and social forces shape friendships.

Tannen, Deborah. (1990). *You just don't understand: Women and men in conversation.* New York: Morrow. A linguist writes about the complexities of female–male communication. She argues that women and men have different underlying goals in much of their communication: connection for women and status seeking for men.

CHAPTER *12*

Economic &
Political Life

Power, Status, & Achievement

A common retort to advocates of equality between the sexes is, "If women are as capable as men, why are there so few great women artists? Where are the eminent women novelists, composers, philosophers, economists, chemists, politicians?" Writer Virginia Woolf would have provided a swift and decisive answer to such questions. In her haunting essay, *A Room of One's Own* (1929/1957), she describes the obstacles of prejudice and economic hardship that beset women would-be writers until the 20th century. What, she muses, would have become of a sister to William Shakespeare, a sister whose talent rivaled that of the famous bard?

> It seemed to me that any woman born with a great gift in the sixteenth century would certainly have gone crazed, shot herself, or ended her days in some lonely cottage outside the village, half witch, half wizard, feared and mocked at. For it needs little skill in psychology to be sure that a highly gifted girl who had tried to use her gift for poetry would have been so thwarted and hindered by other people, so tortured and pulled asunder by her own contrary instincts, that she must have lost her health and sanity to a certainty. (p. 51)

Woolf is only one of many individuals who have argued persuasively that women's invisibility relative to men in terms of recognized achievements is due not to a lack of talent but to barriers imposed by discrimination and other external factors.

It is clear that in most fields few women relative to men have managed to achieve positions of eminence and power. Although they make up half the world's enfranchised population, women's parliamentary representation is less than 40% in every country except Sweden—and it is a great deal lower than that in most regions of the world. By 1994, only 5.7% of the world's cabinet ministers were women, and women held no ministerial positions in 59 countries (United Nations, 1995a). Women make up an extremely low percentage of the conductors of major orchestras, the directors of major motion pictures, the members of the National Academy of Sciences, or the recipients of the Nobel Prize. When Nadine Gordimer was awarded the Nobel Prize for literature in 1991, she became the first woman novelist in a quarter of a century to receive this honor. (Two women, Toni Morrison and Wislawa Szymborska, have won this prize since 1991.) Men received almost 98% of the Nobel prizes in science areas and 99% of the prestigious awards in mathematics during the 20th century. The Nobel Prize for literature has been awarded to men rather than women at a ratio of greater than 9.5 to 1, and other prestigious literary prizes show a pattern of male dominance that is almost as strong (Lips, 1999). Awarding the 1991 Nobel Peace Prize to a woman, Myanmar's (formerly Burma) imprisoned opposition leader Aung San Suu Kyi, was also highly unusual. In a somewhat encouraging development, two more women, Rigoberta Menchú and Jody Williams, have been honored with this prize since 1991. Women of color, often the targets of double discrimination, have even less representation in the ranks of the eminent than do their ethnic majority counterparts. For instance, the first Ph.D. in mathematics awarded to an African American woman, Evelyn Boyd Collins, was granted in 1946; the first African American woman to earn a Ph.D. in physics, Shirley Jackson, received it in 1976; and only in 1987 did the NASA astronaut training program select its first African American female astronaut, Dr. Mae Jemison (V. L. Thomas, 1989).

Although women have made considerable progress in gaining access to the labor force in recent years, they have been relegated mainly to traditionally feminine occupations or to the lower ranks of male-dominated occupations. As organizational sociologist Carolyn Dexter (1985) puts it, "Regardless of the type of work or the type of organization involved, women's employment is characterized by limited power over their own and others' activities, few economic or symbolic rewards, and low prestige" (p. 240).

An understanding of the large gender gap in positions of eminence, prestige, and influence requires that we examine the psychological and social issues surrounding power and achievement. In earlier chapters, we noted that females and males are socialized differently with respect to achievement, that males are often automatically accorded more status than females, and that women and men frequently differ in their access to the resources on which power is based. This chapter will focus on the ways such differences are translated into a social structure in which men occupy a disproportionate number of the positions of prestige and eminence and dominate most aspects of economic and political activity. It begins with an examination of a typical, personality-based explanation for the gender differences in economic and political power: "Women aren't as motivated as men are to get to the top." This section will show that, in fact, there is no evidence that women and men differ in the strength of their motivation to achieve success or power. The next section delves into the question of what power and achievement mean to women and men. Do the two genders satisfy their needs for power and achievement in different ways? Gender roles and a society structured to maintain those roles often make it easier for women to seek achievement and power vicariously or indirectly and for men to seek them directly. The very definitions of "success" and "power" may thus differ for men and women. The third section looks at social influences on the access that men and women have to bases of power and at the impact of this differential access on the influence strategies women and men use. This is followed by an examination of the ways power is gained and maintained in politics and in organizational settings and the reasons women so often find themselves at a disadvantage in those arenas. The chapter concludes with a discussion of the self-perpetuating nature of power: how power transforms its users and how people in a hierarchical power relationship maintain the power difference through their behavior.

MOTIVATION: THE DRIVING FORCE?

Many psychological theories are based on the assumption that individuals differ in the strength of their motives—their tendencies to need and to seek particular outcomes. Both the achievement motive and the power motive have been studied energetically by psychologists looking for clues to explain individual differences in behavior. The **achievement motive** is defined as a general personality disposition to strive for success in any situation where standards of excellence are applied (McClelland et al., 1953). The **power motive** is defined as the tendency to strive to feel that one is having an impact on others (Winter, 1973). Both motives are measured using the Thematic Apperception Test (TAT), a projective test in which the respondent is asked to tell stories about a series of pictures (Murray, 1937). The stories are then scored for the presence of themes indicating an orientation toward or concern with achievement or power.

The Achievement Motive

Almost all of the original research on the achievement motive was done with male respondents. David McClelland and his colleagues (1953) found that for men achievement motivation could be shown to relate to performance in competitive situations in the lab as well as to later career performance. They also found that men's achievement motivation scores tended to rise, often dramatically, when men were given "achievement-involving" task instructions—that is, instructions that stressed that their performance would reflect their intelligence, organizational ability, or leadership capacity. These relationships did not hold for female respondents, however. McClelland and his colleagues summarized their findings on gender differences in achievement motivation as follows: (1) Women get higher achievement motive scores than men do under neutral conditions. (2) Women do not show an increase in achievement motive scores when given achievement-involving instructions. (3) Women's achievement motive scores relate to their performance in the same way that men's do (p. 178).

The finding that women's achievement motivation did not seem to be easily aroused by the instructions that researchers had found to be achievement-involving for men was interpreted by many people to mean that women simply had less need for achievement than men did. This interpretation fit nicely with the observation that women did indeed appear to be achieving less than men in many fields of endeavor and reinforced the assumption that women did not have great achievements because they weren't particularly interested. Because achievement appeared to be mainly a male preserve, researchers focused on males. John Atkinson's (1958) classic work on achievement motivation mentions women in only a single footnote, and McClelland's book, *The Achieving Society* (1961), omits any mention of women. It was only in the context of interest generated by the feminist movement that researchers again turned their attention to achievement orientation in females.

When researchers finally tackled the problem of why women, who seemed to have the same basic amount of achievement motivation as men, did not pursue achievement in many situations, they zeroed in on the differing rewards attached to success for women and men. They began to realize, for example, that women and men might each attach higher value to performing well in gender-appropriate than in gender-inappropriate areas of achievement. Thus, for instance, two psychologists who reviewed the literature on achievement socialization in females noted that in contrast to intellectual, artistic, mechanical, and athletic skills social skills are somewhat unique in being viewed as "feminine" in our culture—and women tend to respond with increased achievement arousal when given achievement-involving instructions emphasizing social skills (Stein & Bailey, 1973). The research that brought the most attention to how people's motivation to achieve might be affected by their awareness of the gender-linked consequences of success focused on a motive that was labeled **fear of success.**

FEAR OF SUCCESS   According to a widely accepted analysis of achievement motivation (Atkinson & Feather, 1966), the motivation to achieve that is aroused in a given situation depends on three things: the strength of the person's underlying achievement motivation, the probability of success, and the incentive or reward value of success in that situation. Using this approach, it can be seen that, even if a person has a very strong motivation to achieve, this motivation might not be aroused in a particular situation if, for example, the person perceives that the consequences of such success would be negative (that is, if the incentive value of success is low).

Matina Horner (1968) hypothesized that because achievement in many areas is considered inappropriate, or at least unusual, for women, a woman achieving in one of these areas might feel she was losing some aspect of her femininity. Thus, success for a woman would be an ambivalent experience, having both the positive consequences of self-respect and external recognition and the negative consequences of the real or imagined disapproval of others for being unfeminine. If the negative consequences appeared to outweigh the positive ones, motivation to achieve in a given situation would be low.

Horner's theory arose from her own observations that successful career women often seemed to feel a need to demonstrate that besides being successful in their vocational sphere they were also successful as "real" women—that they were loving mothers, devoted wives, marvelous cooks, and impeccable housekeepers. These women perceived that society found it unacceptable for a woman to be outstandingly successful at her career if that success led her to give short shrift to her "proper" feminine role. Such observations led Horner to postulate that for women the negative consequences in terms of loss of femininity would often outweigh the positive consequences of success, leading to a situation where the woman developed a motive to *avoid* success. Because success for a man rarely implies any loss of masculinity, Horner predicted that a motive to avoid success would appear much less frequently in men than in women.

Horner began testing her predictions on a group of University of Michigan students by giving them a projective test that she hoped would measure fear of success (the anticipation of negative consequences for success). In the test, female students were asked to complete a story beginning with the following sentence: "After first-term finals, Anne finds herself at the top of her medical school class" (Horner, 1970, p. 59). Males completed a similar story about a medical student named John. As Horner had predicted, many of the women (65%) told stories that incorporated either negative consequences of Anne's success (social rejection, anxiety over her normality or femininity) or denied the possibility of that success by attributing it to an error in marking, cheating, and so on. A common theme in many of the stories was that Anne's success threatened her relationship with the man in her life or with men in general. In contrast, fewer than 10% of the men told stories in which any negative consequences came to John because of his success.

Horner's findings at first appeared to support her theory that because of their gender-role socialization women and men had acquired different amounts of the motivation to avoid success. The theory struck a chord with the popular media, and magazine articles glibly explained that the reason women so seldom achieved eminence was that they had a basic flaw: They were afraid of success. The ready acceptance of the theory was not surprising in an era when discrimination against women in many areas was just beginning to be seriously questioned. After all, it blamed women in large part for their failure to make an impact. However, the acceptance turned out to be premature, as researchers who followed up on Horner's work were quick to discover (Condry & Dyer, 1976; Tresmer, 1976).

Some critics argued that, first, there was no certainty that Horner's projective test actually tapped a stable internal motive (Sancho & Hewitt, 1990). Perhaps the negative consequences described in the stories represent not a personal fear of success but simply an awareness that negative consequences can result from success, particularly for women (Pfost & Fiore, 1990). This argument gains support from the finding that male students given the opportunity to tell a story about Anne instead of John also tend to include many negative consequences for her success. Similarly, women as well as men tend more often to complete the story about John without negative consequences (Monahan, Kuhn, & Shaver, 1974). Thus, the results of this type of test may reflect a cultural stereotype that success is often aversive for women, instead of (or as well as) an actual motive to avoid success. Research does show that successful individuals, male or female, are described as more masculine than unsuccessful individuals (Gerber, 1984). In addition, women are apparently more sensitive than men to others' evaluations of their performance (Roberts, 1991), making it likely that they will be bothered by any negative reactions others might have.

Second, it was argued that the gender difference in fear of success was more apparent than real. In a summary of 64 studies, Paludi (1984) found that the proportion of females showing fear of success ranged from 6% to 93%, with a median of 49%, whereas for males the proportions ranged from 7% to 95%, with a median of 45%. The reason for the wide variation may lie partly in the story cues used. Cherry and Deaux (1978) found that men indicated more fear of success when writing about John in nursing school than in medical school, whereas the reverse was true for women writing about Anne. They concluded that although both women and men have an awareness and perhaps a fear of the negative consequences of succeeding in a "gender-inappropriate" situation, there is little reason to believe that women fear success in general more than men do. Research using African American female and male graduate students also supports the interpretation that fear of success represents a flight from inappropriate situations (Fleming, 1982). Both the men and the women in Fleming's sample showed fear of success that could be interpreted as motivation to avoid subjectively role-inappropriate behaviors. Women who showed fear of success were trying to develop career interests compatible with a strong commitment to home and husband, and the men who showed fear of success "seemed to be reacting to negative racial stereotypes and attempting to live up to a new image of the black male" (p. 339). Fear of success, then, may be a situational rather than a motivational variable, with women or men showing more fear depending on the particular situation described. In fact, when no situation is described and subjects are merely told that "Anne (or John) succeeded," no difference in fear of success is seen between male and female stories (Gravenkemper & Paludi, 1983).

If the fear of success stories are really reflections of a realistic appraisal of the negative consequences that might arise from success in gender-inappropriate situations, it might be reasonable to predict that the more traditional an individual is, the more that person's achievement-related feelings and behavior might be affected by situational variables. Some researchers have found fear of success scores to be associated with low "masculinity" scores and feminine gender-typing (Cano, Solomon, & Holmes, 1984; Mulig, Haggerty, Carballosa, Cinnick, & Madden, 1985; Wong, Kettlewell, & Sproule, 1985). However, this relationship seems to hold for men as well as women, so it seems to be a low level of instrumentality, the quality most clearly measured by the masculinity scales on gender-typing questionnaires, rather than adherence to traditional roles, that is, related to fear of success scores.

In summary, there is no reason to believe women and men differ in the strength of their basic motivations toward success. However, the research stimulated by the fear of success concept has shown clearly that individuals are sensitive to the social consequences of their achievement behavior and that such consequences are perceived to be different for women and men in particular situations. Perceived institutional and social barriers rather than internal motivational ones are responsible for the different achievement behaviors of women and men.

The Power Motive

Research on the power motive has followed much the same pattern as that for achievement. Early research was conducted on males, but when females were eventually studied, it was found that the two gender groups did not differ in their power motive scores under neutral conditions. Also, both women and men responded with increased power motivation scores to power-arousing procedures (Stewart & Winter, 1976; Winter & Stewart, 1978). For both women and men, a high need for power is associated with acquiring formal institutionalized power through leadership roles or offices and with choosing careers that involve having direct, legitimate interpersonal power over others (Winter & Stewart, 1978). Once again, then, it appears that the difference in men's and women's ascendance to positions of prestige and influence cannot be attributed to gender differences in motivational variables.

DEFINING ACHIEVEMENT AND POWER

Some research suggests that women and men may differ in the way they define *achievement* and *power*, and, thus, in the ways they find to satisfy these needs. For example, for women more than for men, success at social relationships may be experienced as an achievement because the area of social relations is one in which it is acceptable for females to excel (Stein & Bailey, 1973). Congruent with this idea, women who are oriented toward the traditional feminine role show high achievement motivation only under conditions designed to arouse affiliation, whereas women who accept achievement behavior as part of the feminine role respond to the same kinds of achievement-arousing conditions that men do (Gralewski & Rodgon, 1980).

The definition of achievement used in most psychological measures of motivation is likely too narrow, tapping only the traditional, male-oriented factors of direct, competitive achievement. People view not only public mastery situations but also personal and interpersonal events in achievement terms (Travis, Phillippi, & Henley, 1991). In fact, when separate components of the achievement motive are studied, males have been found to score higher than females on the drive to compete with and be better than others, and females have been found to outscore males on orientation to work for its own sake (Spence & Helmreich, 1978). Another difference between the two gender groups may be that, following the dictates of and barriers imposed by their gender role, more women than men may try to satisfy their achievement needs vicariously through the successes of their spouses, children, or bosses, rather than directly through their own achievements (Lipman-Blumen & Leavitt, 1976). This pattern may be true for the satisfaction of power needs as well.

Where differences do exist between women and men in the outlets they find for their achievement needs, such differences may be due not so much to definition as to opportunity and self-confidence. We have seen that people are quite sensitive to the social approval or disapproval that their achievement behavior elicits. Women trying to achieve in a masculine-oriented arena hold overly negative self-evaluations (Beyer, 1990). No doubt many women have found that they face fewer negative and more positive consequences for achievement when they avoid competition with men and when they support the achievement efforts of their families rather than themselves. Certainly, many women in professional and managerial careers have experienced the negative responses and exclusion that sometimes accompany competition with men. For example, in a recent survey of top-level female executives in the Unites States, a majority of the respondents said that an important factor in their success was adjusting their personal style so they would not threaten male executives. One respondent to the survey summed up the narrow path she saw as necessary for a women in her position: "Don't be attractive. Don't be too smart. Don't be assertive. Pretend you're not a woman" (Grimsley, 1996, p. C1). Men may discover that competition and winning is a core aspect of the masculine role and that such an approach to achievement gains them more points than does a strictly task-oriented approach. Among women, however, achievement satisfaction often comes from the intrinsic satisfaction of task accomplishment, the vicarious satisfaction of helping others to reach their goals, and from exerting influence (Offermann & Beil, 1992). Thus, differing styles of achievement for women and men reflect, to some extent, a reaction to social expectations imposed by gender roles. However, constraints are forged by more than simple approval or disapproval. A woman who is at home caring for children may find few opportunities for achievement other than through her husband; a secretary may find it more practical to bask in the satisfaction of her boss's successes than to find any source of public recognition for herself.

The stereotypically masculine and feminine patterns of meeting achievement needs can both be problematic. The early literature of the feminist movement is filled with examples of women's dissatisfaction with the expectation that they limit their achievement drives to achieving social success or to achieving through the lives of those they nurture (e.g., Bernard, 1974; Friedan, 1963). For men, however, the emphasis on competition and the material rewards of achieving can be the source of considerable stress and can interfere with personal relationships and the exploration of less prestigious but potentially more satisfying lifestyles. An interesting perspective on the male side of the problem can be gleaned from an examination of the "fear of success" stories told by males. Although the stories told by females tend to stress fear of social rejection as a result of success, those told by males often involve discovering the emptiness of success (Basow, 1986).

Women and men may also differ in the way they define and experience power. Some theorists have suggested that women and men may conceive of and seek power differently: men by dominating others and women by developing a sense of their own abilities and strengths (J. B. Miller, 1977; Rich, 1976). Research has shown, though, that when asked explicitly about what power means to them, college women and men do not differ in the proportions of each group that include themes of influence over others and achievement/self-worth in their definitions (Lips, 1985a). However, certain types of experiences were more linked to feelings of power for men than for women: having material possessions, being physically strong, and participating in sports. One study has shown that women tend to define power for themselves most often as "personal authority" and that they perceive society as defining power most often as "control over others" (Miller & Cummins, 1992). Other researchers have noted that men and women may satisfy their power motives differently, according to how the two gender groups are expected to behave (McClelland, 1975). The expression of a need for power is somewhat more likely to be tempered by socialization toward responsibility in females than in males (Winter & Barenbaum, 1985).

Women in the United States may have a more difficult time than men imagining themselves as holders of powerful positions. Two studies asked college students to imagine themselves in turn as "a person with power," a president of a major corporation, an important political leader, and the director of a major scientific research center (Lips, 2000; Lips & Rogers, 1999). Females tended to view the possibilities as both less positive and less possible than males did. However, parallel gender differences did not appear in samples of college students in Spain or Argentina (Back, Diaz Zuniga, & Lips, 1996; Lips, de Verthelyi, & Gonzalez, 1996).

In considering gender differences in the way needs for achievement and power are expressed, it is important to remember that the value and prestige assigned to particular positions and accomplishments are not decreed by some absolute authority but are decided by social consensus. That consensus in a male-centered culture reflects a tendency to value traditionally masculine accomplishments more than feminine ones. Thus, in our society, becoming a corporation president, writing a best-selling novel, reaching the million mark in record sales, hitting a record number of home runs, or getting a large research grant are considered achievements; raising three children is not. The popular definition of achievement has emerged in such a way that success in the traditionally feminine domain of home and family is simply taken for granted rather than treated as an accomplishment. When asked what she does, the woman who is a full-time homemaker has learned to answer diffidently that she is "just a house-wife," although her job may well involve more work and higher levels of skill than many others that are more prestigious.

Perhaps nowhere can the disregarding of traditional feminine achievements be seen more clearly than in the difficult quest for the history of women. A reading of traditional history books might well give one the impression that women had not even been present during most major historical events or at least that they had made no noticeable impact on the way things turned out. In North American history, one reads references to "the pioneer and his wife" (is the wife not also a pioneer?) with the realization that even when working against terrible odds and under the most difficult and dangerous conditions a woman devoting herself to her home and family is considered merely to be doing her duty rather than accomplishing anything special. Thus, although men and women are encouraged to pursue achievement and power in different ways, these ways are neither equally visible nor equally valued.

ACCESS TO RESOURCES

Power and achievement merge to some extent into a single concept when power is conceptualized as the ability to get things done (Goodchilds, 1979). As noted in Chapter 11, the exercise of power depends on access to certain types of resources: the capacity to reward or punish others, credentials of expertise, legitimacy of authority or position, being identified with or liked by others, and information (French & Raven, 1959). Within these categories fall such specific resources as money, education, employment, physical health and strength, status, legal rights, and time. Individuals differ widely in their access to resources, but the group differences between women and men are consistent: In almost every category of resource, men have more access and control than women do. In addition, when women try to increase their access to these resources, their efforts are often regarded as illegitimate because they are violating established norms. In North America, employed women earn about 74% of what men earn. One national study has shown that if working women were paid the same as men working in comparable jobs the poverty rate for U.S. families would drop by more than 50% (Institute for Women's Policy Research, 1999). Although the majority of women are in the labor force, they are clustered in low-status jobs with little chance for advancement. Women also do considerably more unpaid household labor than men do, a situation that puts women at a disadvantage with respect to the precious personal resources of time and energy to accomplish other things (Lips, 1986b). Women are much more likely than men are to live below the poverty line; this is especially true for women of color. In the United States, among African Americans, about 20% of all men and 32% of all women fall below the poverty line, as compared to 7.8% of European American men and 11.7% of European American women (Kemp, 1995). In Canada, Native women and Central and South American women have the lowest incomes of all groups. Although Canadian women have made substantial inroads into male-dominated, high-status jobs, their earnings in these jobs were only 71% of men's at the beginning of the 1990s. In other countries, women fare even less well. In Guam, Japan, and Korea, for instance, women's wages in manufacturing are about half those of men (United Nations, 1995a). Women have less access to political power than men do. Of the 11 oldest democracies in the world, 10 waited until the 20th century to give women the right to vote, ending with Switzerland in 1971. Women are underrepresented in political decision-making positions. In the United States in 1998, men outnumbered women 91 to 9 in the Senate, and women made up only 12.9% of the House of Representatives. In fact, over the life of the United States, less than 1.5% of the persons elected to the Senate and less than 2% of those elected to the House of Representatives have been women. In Canada, women held only 19.6% of the seats in the federal Parliament by 1999. A continuing increase in women's political power is far from assured. In the countries of Eastern Europe, where women once held a significant number of legislative positions, the collapse of the Communist system resulted in a dramatic decline in women's parliamentary representation. Between 1987 and 1990, the percentage of parliamentary seats held by women declined from 30 to 6 in Czechoslovakia, from 21 to 9 in Bulgaria, from 21 to 7 in Hungary, from 34 to 4 in Romania, and from 34 to 4 in Poland's Lower House (United Nations, 1991).

Females' and males' access to schools is about equal in North America; however, from a world perspective, the situation with respect to education is less egalitarian. There are more illiterate women than men in every part of the world. In sub-Saharan Africa and southern and western Asia, more than 50% of women age 15 or over cannot read or write, and girls' enrollment in school lags behind boys' in these regions (United Nations, 1995a). These statistics could go on for pages, but the ones already listed make the point: Men as a group have more access than women do to the resources on which power is based. Yet women who complain about these inequities are still frequently treated as if they are being unreasonable, and those who have pioneered women's entry into the many arenas that have been closed to them have been, at every stage, the subject of disapproval and ridicule. Sometimes this disapproval has come, and continues to come, from other women. While the British suffragists were struggling to gain the vote for women, they were being opposed by Queen Victoria herself, who was, she said, "most anxious to enlist everyone to join in checking this mad wicked folly of Women's Rights, with all its attendant horrors" (as quoted in Nunes & White, 1973, p. 10). While North American feminists have been struggling to improve women's access to resources, they have been vigorously opposed by an antifeminist women's movement in the United States (Marshall, 1995) and by the REAL (Realistic, Equal, Active for Life) women in Canada (Dubinsky, 1985; Eichler, 1986).

A conflict theory perspective on the opposition to the feminist movement suggests that such opposition stems from the fact that certain groups benefit while others are systematically deprived under the traditional pattern of gender relations. Those who benefit are more likely to be men than women, but many women may be convinced that a system in which males hold most of the authority is ultimately beneficial for all concerned. In fact, it has been argued that for a group to exert effective control over a society that group must not merely secure power but must also establish, in the eyes of subordinate groups, its *right* to wield such power (Weber, 1965). In Max Weber's words, the group needs to "legitimate" its power, thus achieving authority over—or the right to dominate—subordinate groups. It appears that men have been, and remain, quite successful at convincing women that male dominance of society is legitimate. Weber's analysis, which lists three basic sources for legitimizing power, offers some clues as to how male authority became so entrenched. Authority can stem from tradition (ruling groups may rule because they have always done so), from charisma (leaders of ruling groups have personal magnetism or charm that induces others to follow them), or from rational means (the use of legal and judicial mechanisms). Male authority certainly has tradition on its side, and, once in authority, it is easier to have access to the legal and judicial mechanisms to reinforce that authority. Even charisma, which might reasonably be expected to be evenly distributed between women and men, may lie more strongly with men because men more than women are taught to be assertive and to expect others to follow them. Thus, all three sources of authority can be seen to work to make male dominance of society appear legitimate. Furthermore, as Weber also notes, once a group is in power, it can maintain its legitimacy in the eyes of subordinate groups partly through the control and dissemination of ideas—and we have already noted the difficulties that have traditionally greeted women writers, politicians, and other activists. Once in place, the dominance of one group by another is reinforced by so many factors that it is extremely difficult to dismantle, and the pattern of differential access to resources is not easily changed.

Women's and men's differential access to resources has implications on both the group and the individual levels. It affects the capacity that each group has to make an impact, and it affects the chances female and male individuals have to achieve particular goals. For example, a female politician, even if she does not want to be identified with so-called women's issues, must deal with the fact that she is in a minority position and that this position will color her acceptance by others and affect her ability to be effective in her job. As Agnes Macphail, the first woman elected to the Canadian House of Commons, recalled about her 14 years as the lone woman in that institution,

> I found that I couldn't quietly do my job without being ballyhooed like the bearded lady. . . . I couldn't open my mouth to say the simplest thing without it appearing in the papers. I was a curiosity, a freak. And you know the way the world treats freaks. (as quoted in Cochrane, 1977, p. 42)

Men, too, cannot evade the implications of their gender group membership when it comes to achievement and power. In mixed-sex situations, men are more likely than women are to be assigned leadership roles, whether they seek them or not (Lockheed & Hall, 1976; Nyquist & Spence, 1986), and unsuccessful men are subject to more negative evaluations than unsuccessful women are (Fogel & Paludi, 1984). Perhaps because more resources are assigned to men, more is expected of them. Thus, both genders carry the weight of their intergroup differences in access to resources when they are in situations involving power and achievement. These differences influence not only what women and men can accomplish but how they try to accomplish it and how their accomplishments are evaluated by themselves and others. As described in the following section, the strategies women and men employ to gain influence and make an impact are shaped by the fact that women, more often than men, are operating from a position of weakness in terms of resources and that people tend to see efforts to change the accepted distribution of resources as illegitimate and threatening.

Strategies of Influence

People use a bewildering array of strategies in their attempts to use the resources they have to exert influence and to acquire more resources. Psychologists have made various attempts to categorize these strategies (e.g., Falbo, 1977; Kipnis, Castell, Gergen, & Mauch, 1976) and to examine the relationship between the resources a person controls and the particular interpersonal influence strategies she or he favors. Persons who operate from positions of relative strength (that is, who control more resources) tend to use "strong" authoritative influence techniques, whereas those in weak positions rely on "weaker" tactics based on accommodation and dependency (Howard et al., 1986; Kipnis, 1984). Furthermore, those who control more resources or who are in initially dominant positions tend to use a greater variety of influence strategies than do those with less power (Kipnis, Schmidt, & Wilkinson, 1980).

The extent to which such findings on interpersonal influence would generalize to intergroup influence is not certain. However, when groups are in a hierarchical power relationship, as men and women are, group membership itself becomes a resource for interpersonal influence. Not surprisingly, then, researchers have examined the relationship between gender and influence tactics.

Paula Johnson (1976), a pioneer in research on gender and power, suggests that there are three major dimensions on which the use of power to exert influence is affected by gender stereotypes: **directness, concreteness,** and **competence.** According to her analysis, gender norms dictate that men's influence styles can be direct, concrete, and competent, but women's should be indirect, personal, and based on helplessness or dependence.

INDIRECT VERSUS DIRECT INFLUENCE   Direct influence is demonstrated when a person uses power openly, by giving an order or making a request. Indirect influence is exercised when the individual obtains the desired outcome while trying to keep the other person unaware of the influence. Indirect influence is often called "manipulation." Johnson (1976) suggests that in our society there are many constraints against directness by women and that, consequently, women more than men tend to rely on indirect influence. Many feminist writers have noted that a woman who uses direct power is quickly labeled "unfeminine," "castrating,"and "bitchy." Furthermore, even a casual perusal of the popular magazines devoted to advising women about interpersonal relationships indicates that women are actually instructed to use manipulative rather than direct strategies to get what they want ("Let him think it was his idea").

The use of indirect influence, although potentially effective in the short run, may have negative long-term consequences for the user. When the source of influence is concealed, the person wielding it may not be regarded as powerful, may be kept in a subordinate position, and is not likely to see herself or himself as a strong person. A person who is actually wielding a good deal of influence indirectly may get little credit for it. Being the "power behind the throne" or the woman behind the successful man may have its gratifications, but probably not as many as being *on* the throne or claiming the success for oneself.

PERSONAL VERSUS CONCRETE RESOURCES   An individual's attempt to exercise influence is given weight by the amount and nature of resources that person controls. The implied threat in any influence attempt is that a refusal will be met by invoking the resources at the power holder's command to induce compliance. Johnson (1976) suggests that resources can be divided into two categories: those that depend on personal relationships, such as liking and approval, and those that are concrete and independent of relationships, such as money, knowledge, and physical strength. She argues that in our society, men have considerably more control over concrete resources than women do (an argument borne out by the statistics given at the beginning of this section) and that women therefore rely on personal resources more than men do.

Personal resources are certainly not unimportant. The threat of a denial of love, affection, or sex can be a very powerful way to induce cooperation from a person to whom that denial matters deeply. Nonetheless, as Johnson points out, this type of influence is effective only in the context of a personal relationship. Also, it has the disadvantage of leaving the influencer highly dependent on others. Although a woman may hold great personal power in an individual relationship, it is often not the sort that generalizes beyond the relationship or holds up in a court of law. For example, a woman may hold a great deal of power based on personal resources such as affection and sexuality with respect to her husband, easily gaining his compliance to her wishes. However, if the affection between the spouses wanes, this same woman could find herself fighting in court for child support or an equal share of the couple's financial resources. Her power is based on the affection her husband holds for her; when that disappears, her power disappears as well.

HELPLESSNESS VERSUS COMPETENCE   It is sometimes possible to get others to do things for us either by acting competent, taking charge, and giving orders or by acting incompetent and helpless and throwing ourselves on their mercy. A major theme in our gender stereotypes is that men are strong and competent, women weak and helpless—a theme that is reinforced in everything from children's stories about the handsome prince rescuing the damsel in distress to television serials in which, week after week, fearless male heroes save hapless women from pursuit by crazed killers or international terrorists. Johnson (1976) suggests that because women are often in situations where they are not regarded as or do not feel competent they tend to rely on helplessness as a mode of influence more than men do. By acting helpless, women can get men to take on responsibilities and do tasks for them, particularly those tasks that fit society's expectations for the masculine role. It should be mentioned, though, that men are not above using helplessness themselves as an influence tactic, as many women have discovered when they first asked their spouse to do laundry, cook supper, or change the baby's diaper.

Johnson suggests that helplessness, though effective in the short run, does not establish its users as strong influencers and may contribute to both low status and low self-esteem.

Do Women and Men Really Use Power Differently?

Johnson's (1976) research on people's reactions to power use in a hypothetical situation (one student trying to get another to change his or her opinion on a legal case) suggested that men and women are *expected* to use power in different ways. Given a list of 15 different methods of influence in the hypothetical situation, respondents were asked to indicate whether the influencer was male or female. Results showed that co-ercion based on concrete resources, competence based on legitimacy or expertise, and the direct use of informational power were expected more of male influencers, whereas the use of reward based on personal resources and sexuality was seen as significantly more characteristic of females. Johnson suggested that men are allowed to use many different forms of influence, depending on the situation, but women are more severely restricted to the less aggressive types. This finding is reminiscent of the finding by Kip-nis and his colleagues (1980), cited earlier in this chapter, that persons operating from strong positions use a greater variety of influence tactics than do those whose positions are weaker. If men really are allowed to use more kinds of influence strategies than women are, perhaps it is no wonder that some women resist the changes in gender roles advocated by feminists. These women may fear that if they are "liberated" their tradi-tional feminine modes of influence may no longer be effective (e.g., if women are rec-ognized as being as competent as men are, they can't get their way by acting helpless). Yet these women do not anticipate being comfortable with, good at, or allowed to use the more direct, competent tactics. Consequently, they may foresee a "liberation" that results in a net loss, rather than a net gain, of power for women.

Although Johnson's (1976) research addressed the question of what influence styles are stereotypically associated with women and men, it did not answer the ques-tion of whether women and men actually do use power differently. Earlier research by Johnson herself and more recent studies by other researchers do indicate, however, that different influence strategies tend to be favored by the two gender groups and that the target of the influence makes a difference as to the choice of strategy (Cowan, Drinkard, & McGavin, 1984; J. W. White, 1988). Paula Johnson (1974) gave male and female group leaders a choice of six influence messages to persuade their group to work faster at a task. The male leaders often chose the persuasive message that stressed their own expertise, whereas female leaders avoided it. The female leaders were more likely to use the persuasive message that emphasized their own helplessness and de-pendency on the workers—a strategy that male leaders, without exception, rejected. In a study using a simulated organizational setting, another group of researchers placed women and men in positions of equal power and investigated whether they would use different strategies to influence their subordinates (Instone, Major, & Bunker, 1983). They found that, relative to males, females made fewer influence at-tempts, used fewer types of influence strategies, and relied more on coercion and less on reward. These differences seemed to be mediated by lower self-confidence among the women than the men. Other organizational research also shows that males are more likely to use direct, assertive strategies, whereas females are more likely to use in-direct, submissive ones (Ansari, 1989; Fairhurst, 1985; Goodyear, 1990). Certainly, women are more likely than men to *report* using more obliging and compromising and less assertive supervisory styles (Goh, 1991; Korabik, Baril, & Watson, 1993). How-ever, in at least one laboratory study (Korabik et al., 1993), such gender differences in self-reports did not match any observed differences in supervisory behavior. And the gender difference in self-reported influence styles may be sensitive to context. One study of employees in a business environment found that men were more likely than women to report that they relied on charm, manipulation, and appearance to achieve personal and organizational objectives (DuBrin, 1989).

Although the frequency with which women and men report using various strategies differs, women and men do not seem to differ overall in their order of preference for particular strategies. For both men and women, the influence strategy ranked highest in order of preference is "use reason and logic," followed by "simply state my desires," "offer to compromise," and "convince, persuade, and coax" (J. W. White & Roufail, 1989). Yet, in terms of absolute frequency of reported use, men are more likely than women to use high-pressure tactics such as arguing and yelling, threatening force, and forceful assertion as first-choice strategies; women are more likely than men to report using negative emotion (pleading, crying, acting cold, getting angry and demanding) as their first choice. Furthermore, some differences in the use of influence strategies may begin when people are quite young. One study of Israeli eighth-graders found that the boys reported that they would use *all* types of influence strategies more than girls did—obviously feeling justified in using whatever methods were necessary to exert their influence (Schwarzwald & Koslowsky, 1999).

One reason for a gender difference in influence strategies may well be the impact of social expectations for women and men. As Linda Carli (1999) points out, a wealth of research shows that women are less likely than men to be perceived as competent experts, making them less able to use competence-based influence strategies. Furthermore, she notes, even when women are perceived as competent, they are often not perceived as having legitimate authority, and their efforts to exert influence in a directive manner are viewed as illegitimate and often resisted. Direct, assertive influence attempts by women often engender social disapproval in a way that similar strategies by men do not (Eagly et al., 1992; Gervasio & Crawford, 1989), and assertive, self-promoting women produce reactions of distaste in some situations (Rudman, 1998). Thus, gender-role expectations produce real differences in the amount of initial power, in the form of expertise and legitimacy, available to women and men. Add these differences to those in such concrete resources as money and position and it is not at all surprising that women and men differ in the way they approach certain influence situations. In fact, gender is so strongly linked to power and status that it is impossible to understand how gender relates to the use of influence strategies without considering how women and men differ in their power and status (Lips, 1991; Sagrestano, 1992a).

What happens when women violate the expectation that they will be generally agreeable and will use mainly personal, subtle, indirect influence strategies? Linda Carli (1998) explored this question in an experiment in which she paired participants with confederates who were trained to express either agreements or direct disagreements during group discussions. She found that participants increased their own disagreements when confronted with a partner who disagreed with them. However, this increased disagreement was much more pronounced when the partner was female than male and participants expressed more open hostility toward the disagreeing woman than the disagreeing man. As Carli (1999) notes, these "results indicate that as long as a woman behaves in the expected manner, that is, pleasantly and agreeable, people use pleasant influence tactics when interacting with her. However, if she appears direct and resistant to their ideas, they react with much more direct and aggressive influence strategies than they would use with a man" (p. 92).

When researchers manipulate the situation so that women hold as much or more power than men, the gender differences in influence strategies tend to be obscured by power differences. People who hold more power use more direct influence strategies (Sagrestano, 1992b). An interesting case in point revolves around the resource of legitimacy. In many cultures, including our own, men hold more of the positions of authority than women do—positions that give them a legitimate right to make decisions and command obedience. In fact, in a culture that tends to ascribe higher status to males than to females and to consider that the man is the head of the family, even men who are not in formal positions of authority are still viewed as having some rights to exert authority over women. Obviously, a position of authority lends considerable force to any attempt to exercise influence directly. As Rosaldo (1974) notes, however, a person who tries to exercise a significant amount of influence independent of authority is regarded as manipulative, disruptive, and troublesome and is generally not taken seriously as a powerful person. Thus, women must be cautious about open attempts to exercise influence from subordinate positions in organizations, and the woman who allows her power in the marriage relationship to show in public may risk an unflattering label (Bernard, 1972).

Legitimacy may vary according to the situation, of course, and with it the acceptability of certain kinds of influence tactics for females and males. Johnson and Goodchilds (1976) found that in a dating situation where the issue of sexual intimacy occurs men are seen as using direct methods to influence a woman to have sexual intercourse, and women are perceived as being capable of equal directness in turning a man down. In a reversal of this situation, however, participants suggested that a woman would be quite indirect in her efforts to seduce a man, and the man would be correspondingly indirect in refusing her. The researchers use these results to suggest that a person engaging in an out-of-role influence attempt is likely to be less direct than someone operating within his or her role expectations. A more general explanation might be, however, that the more legitimate a person perceives his or her demands to be, the more direct will be the mode of influence used.

Pat Mainardi's (1970) essay on the politics of housework provides a good example of the way the perceived legitimacy of a person's argument can affect the influence tactics that are used. In it, she outlines the helpless and indirect tactics her husband used in his attempts to avoid doing his share of the housework. Of course, as a man, he was well within the rights of the traditional masculine role in refusing to do many household chores. However, in the course of the marriage, he had acknowledged the legitimacy of his wife's argument that housework should be shared, and this acknowledgment disallowed him the use of direct means of influence such as flat refusal. The arguments that he did use were as indirect ("Housework is too trivial to even talk about"), irrelevant ("Women's liberation isn't really a political movement"), and helpless ("I don't mind doing the housework, but I don't do it very well") as one might ever hope to find.

If it is indeed the case that the legitimacy of one's position increases one's capacity to use direct modes of influence, it would seem that the feminist attempts to legitimize the demands of women for equal rights will eventually make it easier for women to exercise direct power in a wide range of situations. However, because a challenge to men's authority is a challenge to a system that is considered by many to be not only normative but natural, such attempts may have trouble commanding the resource of legitimacy. They are bound to be regarded by some as merely disruptive, troublesome, and annoying. In fact, research shows that it can be extraordinarily difficult for a woman to gain legitimacy in certain situations. Janice Yoder and her colleagues (1998) devised a laboratory experiment in which women were placed in leadership positions with all-male groups on a masculine-stereotyped task. This procedure was meant to simulate the position in which women find themselves when they acquire leadership positions in male-dominated organizations. In all three experimental conditions, group members were told that the woman had been randomly appointed by the experimenters to lead the group. In two of the three conditions, the women leaders received special pre-task training to give them expertise on the group task. However, in one of these two conditions, the women were told *not* to reveal that they had been trained, whereas in the other condition a male experimenter informed the group that the woman who would be leading them had come in early for special training and that she had information that could be useful to the group as they made their decisions. Thus, the experiment compared the group outcomes for an appointed-only leader, an appointed and trained leader, and an appointed, trained, and "legitimated as credible" leader. Results showed that only the women who had been appointed and trained and were legitimated as credible by the male experimenter were effective in influencing the performance of their all-male groups. Women who had been simply appointed leaders tended to be relegated to secretarial roles in their groups. Women who had been appointed and trained but not introduced by the experimenter as experts were continually frustrated in their attempts to share their expertise with their groups: "these women's added expertise gave them the background to influence the group without the power base from which to do it effectively. They interrupted in vain to try to make relevant points; they pleaded for acknowledgment using tag questions, yet they went unheeded" (p. 219). The women who had been trained but had not had legitimacy bestowed on them externally were apparently seen by the male group members as ineffectual and contributing little to the group. The researchers argue, based on these findings, that no matter how competent they are women in male-dominated organizations often cannot overcome the stereotype that women are not expected to be leaders unless they are empowered by an external endorsement from the organization.

SOME IMPLICATIONS OF THE DIFFERENCES   The definition of power implicitly includes some freedom to decide how to act. Powerlessness implies a situation in which one is not free to decide or to act. When a person feels free to behave in a certain way, and then senses a threat to that freedom, the reaction is predictable: what psychologists label reactance (Brehm, 1966). **Reactance** is basically an effort to protect or regain the behavioral freedom that is threatened. It can manifest itself as anger and hostility toward the individual or institution that is doing the threatening. Because a threat to a person's freedom to behave in a particular way often comes from an influence attempt that is directed at that person, reactance is an important concept for understanding the effects of different influence tactics.

When a person is the target of influence based on coercion or expertise, he or she may feel a threat to behavioral freedom and be motivated to regain control by resisting the influence attempt (Rodin & Janis, 1979). However, when persons do comply with expert, coercive, or reward-based influence, they tend to attribute their compliance to external reasons and to suffer some loss of their sense of control. Both these patterns are helpful in understanding the impact of stereotypically masculine and feminine influence styles on their users and targets. Women, operating from a weaker power base, often cannot afford to provoke reactance in their influence targets. They use more subtle, indirect influence strategies that are less likely to make the target feel threatened. Men frequently have access to more resources with which to back their influence attempts and can be direct enough to arouse anger, hostility, and resistance. In a male–female relationship, if the woman uses an indirect and personal style of influence and the man tends to be more direct and concrete, it is likely that the two people will attribute their compliance to very different causes. When the woman complies with the man's wishes, she will attribute her behavior to pressure from him, and she may feel little sense of control over or responsibility for her behavior. When the man complies with the woman, however, he may not even view his behavior as compliance. Instead, he may be responding to a manipulation that allows him to see his behavior as stemming from his own decision. He is thus able to maintain a sense of control and responsibility, and the couple's initial difference in the sense of power is reinforced. It is possible, then, that under certain conditions gender differences in influence styles can become a self-perpetuating cycle.

RESOURCES, STRATEGIES, AND POLITICAL POWER

For some people, the word *power* is synonymous with politics. Can the psychological analysis of power differences between women and men be applied to their behavior in the political arena? The answer to this question must begin with an examination of gender differences in political behavior.

In a democracy, one of the most basic political behaviors is voting in elections. In most countries, women have had to fight for the right to vote. Among half the countries responding to a survey of embassies by the World Priorities organization, the average delay between men's and women's suffrage was 47 years. In the United States and Canada, women have had the right to vote since 1920. When suffrage for women was new, some women still felt that voting was inappropriate, and women's participation in elections lagged behind men's. In addition, women tended to be less educated than men, and studies show that education is related to political participation. However, the gender differences in voter turnout disappeared years ago in both countries (Brodie & Vickers, 1982; Klein, 1984), and women's voting rates have exceeded those of men in every U.S. presidential election since 1984 (Mandel, 1995). Women are also now as active as men in grassroots-level politics; both groups do a lot of campaigning and behind-the-scenes work for political parties. At the citizen level, then, there is little difference between the political participation levels of women and men. Politics is still seen as a "masculine" endeavor by many people (Rosenwasser & Dean, 1989), however, and female (but not male) high school political activists see future family life as limiting the possibility of their involvement in politics in adulthood (Romer, 1990).

At levels of politics above the grassroots level, gender differences are quite dramatic. Women make up only a small percentage of the holders of public office and are less likely than men to be in leadership or elected governmental positions (Mandel, 1995). Within political parties, there used to be a tendency for women to be assigned the supportive and "housekeeping" tasks (Brodie & Vickers, 1982). Some changes are evident, however. In Canada in 1991, the New Democratic Party became the first major party in North America to decide that women would make up half its nominations for federal elected office. In recent years, two of the three major political parties in Canada have been headed, at least for a time, by women. Canada's first female prime minister, Kim Campbell, held office briefly in 1993. Neither the U.S. nor Canada, however, can match the political advances made by women in New Zealand, where currently both the prime minister and the leader of the opposition are women.

A power analysis of the situation described here suggests many reasons why women's and men's relatively equal participation in citizen-level politics does not translate into more equal participation at the higher levels. First, gender ideology and custom still give men more legitimacy than women as leaders, political or otherwise (Butler & Geis, 1990; Porter & Geis, 1981). Specifically in the realm of politics, male candidates are still perceived as more electable than female candidates, and men are less likely than women to say they would vote for a woman (Ogletree, Coffee, & May, 1992). Many voters tend to shy away from female candidates unless they are clearly better qualified than their male opposition (Basler, 1984; Sigelman, Thomas, Sigelman, & Ribich, 1986). A recent poll commissioned by financial services firm Deloitte & Touche reveals that 16% of respondents would not vote for a woman for president and that there is not a single issue on which a majority of respondents say that most people would favor a female candidate (Mann, 2000). In fact, respondents were twice as likely to say that people would expect a male president to perform better than a female president.

Women also tend to have less access than men to the power base of expertise. They rate their understanding of politics lower than men do their own, although research does not support this perceived difference (Sapiro, 1983). Within political parties, women used to be much less likely than men to be chosen to perform strategic leadership tasks—tasks that are often the first step toward building the expertise and the loyal support that are crucial for seeking public office (Brodie & Vickers, 1982). However, women running for office are now increasingly likely to have backgrounds in elective, appointive, or political staff positions (Mandel, 1995). When women do run for office, they are often hampered by a lack of access to funds, a concrete resource that is now the *sine qua non* of an effective campaign. Elizabeth Dole's run for the presidency of the United States was cut short in 1999, not because she did not appeal to voters but because she could not raise enough funds to mount an effective challenge against her rivals for the nomination. Moreover, there are often few structural opportunities for women to gain office. In the United States, incumbents are rarely defeated, so there are relatively few openings for new faces at high levels. The campaigns that women wage are, more often than for men, for "lost cause" seats. For years, female candidates were the sacrificial lambs in elections, gaining their parties' nominations most easily for races they had little realistic expectation of winning (Brodie & Vickers, 1982).

Despite the disadvantages under which women have labored in the political arena, there are signs that female candidates and female holders of high political office are gaining more legitimacy. In both the United States and Canada, more women are running as candidates in elections than ever before. During the 1980s, Americans had their first opportunity to vote for a female vice presidential candidate, Geraldine Ferraro, on the ticket of a major party. The 1980s and 1990s have also seen the election of female governors in a number of states, including Texas, stereotypically a bastion of male power. Canadians have seen the roles of Speaker of the House of Commons, governor general, provincial premier, and prime minister filled by women for the first time. In both countries, women have gained some power during election campaigns as a special interest group. In Canada, the 1985 federal election saw, for the first time, the leaders of the three major parties stage a televised debate specifically on "women's issues." Beyond North America, too, changes can be seen. For instance, in France, where women did not get the vote until 1944 and where, until 1964, a woman had to have her husband's permission to open a bank account or get a passport, an outspoken feminist woman, Edith Cresson, was appointed premier in 1991. In Ireland, a strong feminist woman, Mary Robinson, was elected president in 1990. Turkey's first female prime minister, Tansu Ciller, took office in 1993.

It is no accident that political parties have started to put somewhat more emphasis on women as an interest group. Over the past two decades, women have organized to increase their power as a pressure group—by increasing their political skills and expertise, setting up funds to support women candidates or to lobby for specific issues, and by organizing mutually supportive coalitions among groups of women. Women's caucuses within the political parties push for the adoption of policies important to women as platform planks. Nonpartisan organizations such as the League of Women Voters in the United States and the National Action Committee on the Status of Women in Canada keep these issues visible both during and after the elections. The political system is still largely dominated by men, but women are building the power to make an increasing impact.

POWER IN ORGANIZATIONS AND INSTITUTIONS

As was indicated in the preceding discussion of political power, even when women's and men's access to particular institutions is nominally equal, or almost so, women are more likely than men to be relegated to marginal positions within the institution and to wield relatively less power. Sometimes it is suggested that men have more of "what it takes" to hold leadership positions than women do. However, the reasons for the gender differences in organizational power are more complex than that. They are built into the structure of the organizations themselves and into the social context in which these organizations exist.

Research within organizations shows that particular constraints and requirements in the way organizations run affect the power available to individuals within them. For instance, Rosabeth Moss Kanter's (1975) research, which began as an attempt to isolate the variables that separate women from career success in organizations, showed that the leadership behavior of individuals was more strongly related to the position they held than to their gender. Poor leadership and success skills were found among people in token positions, people in dead-end jobs, and people in positions of nominal leadership that carried no real power. People in these positions were characterized by rigidity and hostility toward outsiders and powerful superiors, and they appeared to have more concern for socializing than for advancement. It appears that the organizational context of relative powerlessness combined with responsibility (or "blameability") may produce these unproductive behavior patterns. Unfortunately for women, women tended to hold more of these problematic positions than men did. Kanter concluded that the stereotypes about women being poor managers were based on women's relegation to powerless organizational positions.

One thing researchers have found to be an important determinant of an individual's power and success in an organization is that person's access to informal networks of communication and exchange. Managers must coordinate the activities of many people within a work group, as well as negotiate with members of other groups or organizations. In performing these functions, managers cannot rely solely on the formal power that goes with their positions. They must also use informal power based on reciprocation of favors and sharing of information. Doing this successfully requires maintaining a large number of good relationships. However, for a number of reasons, the maintenance of such networks may be more difficult for women than for men. First, the woman is often in a minority or token status and so does not easily fit in to the informal networks of her male colleagues. In fact, in what Bernard (1976) has called the "stag effect," women may find that the most important informal meeting places for their male colleagues are off limits, or at least unwelcoming, to women. Second, women are more likely than men to be doing double duty as homemakers and businesspersons, and so simply have less time for informal discussions after work or other "optional" activities. Third, informal organizational networks are often based on male modes of communication and shared experiences, making it more difficult for women, with less background in common, to fit in (Hennig & Jardim, 1977). For these and perhaps some additional reasons, women often lack access to the networks that foster organizational power. Within organizations, men are more likely than women to form strong same-gender ties across many networks. Women too, form same-gender ties, but they are more likely to use these networks for support and friendship and to rely on their ties with men to obtain access to resources (Ibarra, 1992). Perhaps because they are more likely than men to see interpersonal bonds as friendship-oriented rather than business-oriented, women are less tolerant than men of politically manipulative behavior in the workplace (Drory & Beaty, 1991). However, both women and men are more tolerant of such behavior from a member of their own gender and toward a member of the other gender.

Women's relative lack of access to informal networks within and outside an organization limits their influence. They may have more trouble obtaining rewards for their subordinates, for instance. Such a situation can become a vicious circle, as subordinates may lose respect for a manager who appears powerless, thus further diminishing her power (Kanter, 1979; Ragins & Sundstrom, 1989). In addition, a lack of access to informal networks can hinder a woman's chances of being hired or promoted. For example, Dexter (1985) notes that women have difficulty achieving partnerships in major accounting firms, largely because of their lack, relative to men, of third-party relationships. Partners are expected to bring business into the firm, and they fulfill this function by maintaining large networks of relationships with community and business leaders through formal and informal organizations. Many businesses are headed by men, and the organizations in which the socializing takes place are restricted to men or at least are extremely male dominated. Therefore, women have many fewer opportunities than men do to contact other business leaders. Making a woman a partner in the firm is thus viewed as a risk to the profitability of the firm.

In looking at the larger culture that provides the setting for organizations, it is not difficult to see how the ideology surrounding gender contributes to the maintenance of male dominance of them. As Barbara Polk (1974) notes in an article on the sources of male power, because men have shaped society's institutions, they tend to fit the value structure of such institutions. For example, the masculine gender role matches certain professional and business roles (lawyer, business executive, university president) better than the feminine gender role does. In a pattern that would be comic if it were not so aggravating, women trying to fit their behavior to the requirements of such roles are sometimes accused of acting masculine.

Certain institutions are imbued so strongly with the notion of male dominance that women are barred from even trying to fit into leadership roles. Many religions, for example, are built on the idea of a male god ruling the universe from outside. Such an image serves to legitimize male control of worldly institutions and acts very specifically as a barrier to women's participation in such formal and ceremonial leadership positions as priest, minister, rabbi, or ayatollah. Many feminists have argued that the pervasive image of "God the Father" runs deeply in our culture, affecting even people who have consciously rejected religious dogmas, and that such imagery must be replaced if the culture is to develop a new vision of women and men (e.g., Daly, 1973; Ruether, 1983; Starhawk, 1979). Certainly, religion has a large impact on people's values and their conceptions of what is right and wrong. The pervasive acceptance of male dominance within major institutional religions is not a trivial matter for women and men.

MAINTAINING THE STATUS QUO: HOW HIERARCHIES PERPETUATE THEMSELVES

Although many people, female and male, say that they believe in equality between the sexes, male dominance is not easily banished from most situations. Many of women's and men's habits of thought and behavior act to perpetuate the power difference between them. Learned patterns of verbal and nonverbal behavior perpetuate status distinctions. Implicit stereotypes bias perceptions before they even register in awareness, and the metamorphic effects of holding power have sometimes caused men to justify their dominance by inflating their sense of their own worth and devaluing that of women.

Verbal and Nonverbal Behavior

In an earlier chapter, the role played by language in maintaining the status difference between females and males was noted. The habitual use of "he" to mean any person, of "man" to mean people, makes people feel as if females are exceptions. Women who have changed their linguistic habits to avoid the generic "he" actually think more easily of females in response to sex-indefinite cues than do those who use traditional linguistic forms (Khosroshahi, 1989). The terms of address used for males and females also help to reinforce the status difference. Men are men, but women are girls or gals, chicks or broads. It is not uncommon to hear 50-year-old women referred to as "the girls" or to hear a male manager refer to his middle-aged secretary as "my girl." Even a woman's name often incorporates her marital status (Miss or Mrs.), and when a woman marries she is still generally expected to take her husband's name rather than vice versa. Finally, the use of the term "ladies," with its implied delicacy, for adult females is incompatible with the idea of those adult females holding jobs as construction workers, police officers, perhaps even politicians.

Dominance is also conveyed by the degree to which one can control a conversation: how successfully one can interrupt another speaker and how much attention and response one is able to draw from others. Researchers have found that men talk more than women and that they maintain this difference partly by interrupting women and by not listening or responding to them (Makri-Tsilipakou, 1994; Malamuth & Thornhill, 1994). Such tactics, commonly used by males in cross-gender conversations, tend to discourage females and subdue their efforts at participation, allowing the males conversational control. These patterns of verbal participation tend to reinforce status differences between females and males. The conversational dominance patterns are so well ingrained that when women interrupt men they are seen as rude and disrespectful—as if their behavior is undermining established power relations (LaFrance, 1992).

Communication involves more than words, however, and psychologist Nancy Henley (1977; see also Henley & Freeman, 1995) was one of the first to suggest that nonverbal communication is even more influential than language in maintaining the power differential between women and men. Henley noted that much of the nonverbal communication that characterized male–female relationships followed a pattern parallel to that characterizing superior–subordinate relationships. Subordinates and women, for example, tend to show controlled, circumspect nonverbal behavior, to contract into a small amount of space, and to be touched by other people. Men and powerful people tend to be more relaxed and expansive in their nonverbal behavior and to "touch downward" in the status hierarchy. Henley further suggested that when women break these rules by staring, touching men, or loosening their demeanor their actions are interpreted not as power plays, which are unexpected in females, but as sexual invitations.

For several reasons, nonverbal behavior may pose a particularly resistant barrier to change in gender power relations (Mayo & Henley, 1981). First, a great deal of nonverbal behavior lies outside of awareness, so people often do not realize they are communicating power-related cues. Even if they do realize it, the habits are so strong and so routinized that they are very difficult to break. Second, much nonverbal behavior is learned through socialization by family, friends, and media and is based on norms that are extremely slow to change. Third, women tend to be nonverbally adaptive. That is, they are more partner-oriented than men in their nonverbal behavior. Studies of movement show that when men communicate dominance their female partners tend to respond with low-power gestures; men, however, tend not to show similar nonverbal accommodation to high-power moves by women (M. Davis & Weitz, 1981). This tendency for women to adapt to men's behavior may slow down behavioral change for both genders. Finally, nonverbal behavior is particularly effective at communicating covert power messages. All types of nonverbal behaviors—gesture, touch, use of space, movement, gaze, facial expression—can be used to communicate power differentials. Moreover, they can be used even in situations where a power differential is verbally unacknowledged, or even denied. Thus, even in a male–female dyad in which both persons say their status is equal, nonverbal behavior may reveal male dominance.

If nonverbal behavior is so potentially important to gender power relations, perhaps women and men should work hard at trying to change their nonverbal behavior. In fact, there is mixed evidence about how effective such a strategy would be. Some research shows that because of gender stereotypes the same nonverbal cues that communicate power for men may not work for women. Porter and Geis (1981) found that a man sitting at the head of the table is associated with being viewed as the leader of the group, but this same cue had no impact on the perception of a woman as the leader in mixed-sex groups. They suggest that nonconscious gender stereotypes bias people's perceptions, making it difficult to "see" women as leaders, even when they engage in the very same nonverbal behavior that has helped men establish leadership. Other research shows that the way a person delivers a persuasive message—using a nonverbal style that is task-oriented, social, submissive, or dominant—has more impact on the degree to which participants are influenced than the speaker's gender does (Carli, LaFleur, & Loeber, 1995). However, when the audience is male, likeableness is a more important determinant of influence for female than for male speakers. Thus, when trying to influence men, women's adoption of a task-oriented style is not necessarily effective.

On the positive side, some research indicates that conscious manipulation of nonverbal cues can sometimes affect power-related aspects of the way a person is viewed and treated. Both female and male observers can accurately interpret different levels of visual dominance displayed by a woman who is interacting with either a man or another woman, rating her as more powerful in the conditions where her use of visual dominance cues is high (Ellyson, Dovidio, & Fehr, 1981). Thus, with some nonverbal behaviors at least, it may be possible to change the perception of one's status by changing one's nonverbal behavior. Nonverbal communication, then, can act either as a barrier to or facilitator of change in the power relationship between females and males (Mayo & Henley, 1981).

The Metamorphic Effects of Power

One more factor that tends to perpetuate status hierarchies is the effect of power on the power holder. According to a model developed by David Kipnis (1972; Kipnis et al., 1976), if power holders use strong, controlling means of influence to gain compliance, they tend to believe they have caused the other person's compliance. This belief leads them to devalue the other person, take credit for that person's performance, and try to increase social and psychological distance from that person. A powerful person, gaining a lot of compliance and a lot of (perhaps false) feedback that his or her ideas are good, easily develops an inflated sense of self-worth. Kipnis's model can readily be applied to the male–female situation. In many situations, men hold power over women, and women are taught to build up men's egos to keep them happy. In such a situation, it is quite likely that men develop an exaggerated sense of superiority with respect to women—a feeling that has the potential to become addictive. One of the reasons the cycle of power differences between women and men is difficult to break, then, is that the very existence of a power difference probably has a tendency to make men feel they are superior to women. The converse of this pattern is that women, having so frequently been given second-class status, may learn to accept it as a true reflection of their worth. It appears that the power difference between men and women will not easily be wiped out, even when many people consciously see it as anachronistic. Narrowing the gender gap in power requires reshaping many habits of thought and behavior.

SUMMARY

There is a large difference in the visibility of women and men in positions of eminence and power. Research has established that no gender differences in basic achievement or power motivation account for these differences in visibility. Research shows, however, that social barriers against achievement and power are often different for women and men and that both sexes are sensitive to these barriers and tend to adjust their behavior accordingly. Consequently, attempts to change patterns of gender-related achievement without altering the social structure in which these patterns are embedded will probably not be very effective at getting more women into positions of visible eminence or power.

Power comes in many forms, and women and men may tend to use it differently. Men hold more of the concrete resources, such as wealth, than women do. Thus, men have more opportunities than women to wield power that involves threats or rewards based on these resources and to wield that power openly and directly. Women often find themselves in positions where the only way they can exert influence is through subtle manipulation or an appeal to personal, relationship-based resources. However, there is not necessarily any built-in gender difference in styles of influence. Rather, the difference is a result of a social structure that awards men higher status and stereotypes them as more competent than women. When women are in positions of authority or are making a demand that is perceived as legitimate, they can more easily use strong, direct influence styles.

It is no small task to make a dramatic increase in the proportion of women holding positions of authority or eminence. The male–female status differences tend to be self-perpetuating, not only because of stereotyping but also because of women's relative exclusion from the "old boy" networks of influence in business, politics, and the professions and because of habits of thought and behavior that frequently place women and men in complementary submissive–dominant roles. Such subtleties as who touches whom, who controls the conversation, and which pronoun is used to refer to humans in general all help to create a climate where power differences between women and men go unquestioned.

Status hierarchies, power differentials, and dominance–submission are not necessarily "natural" aspects of the human condition. As Erich Fromm (1973) noted in his classic work on human destructiveness, many so-called primitive hunting-gathering societies have been characterized by an absence of dominance or even permanent leadership associated with high-status qualities or skills. He suggested that the social structure adopted by a group of people determines, in large measure, their need for power differences and status hierarchies among themselves and that the psychology of dominance–submission is an adaptation to a social order rather than a natural human condition that generates a particular social structure. Fromm's point is a good one to keep in mind when contemplating the kind of future society that might emerge in the course of women's struggle for a society in which *female* is not automatically associated with lower status than *male*. Men themselves now sometimes complain that the traditional masculine role, with its built-in authority, can be restrictive and burdensome. Perhaps, in the process of making changes in the power relationship between the sexes, the social structure will be altered in ways that make the dominance aspect of power less important.

KEY TERMS

achievement motive   directness   competence

power motive   concreteness   reactance

fear of success

FOR ADDITIONAL READING

Cantor, Dorothy W., & Bernay, Toni, with Stoess, Jean. (1992). *Women in power: The secrets of leadership*. Boston: Houghton Mifflin. The authors profile 25 American women in politics and develop a model of the processes that support women's emergence as leaders.

Higonnet, Anne. (1990). *Berthe Morisot*. New York: Harper & Row. This book tells the story of one woman's achievements: how she became a "great woman artist" though deprived of the encouragement, training, and rewards that were available to her male counterparts.

Lips, Hilary M. (1991). *Women, men, and power*. Mountain View, CA: Mayfield. A wide-ranging examination of the relationship between gender and power, including chapters on images of power, interpersonal power, and power in family, work, and politics.

Russell, Diana E. H. (1989). *Lives of courage: Women for a new South Africa*. New York: Basic Books. A sociologist provides firsthand portraits of the achievements of 24 women activists who were part of the struggle to end apartheid.

CHAPTER 13

Issues in the Workplace

Hilary Lips and Nina Colwill

In 1990, Houston's chief of police, Elizabeth Watson, only 3 months into her new job, discovered that she was pregnant. As she prepared to leave her position, she braced herself for what she felt would be the inevitable flood of comments along the lines of, "That's what you get when you put a woman in the job." Instead, to her surprise, her announcement was greeted with arguments that she should *not* quit—strong promises of support from the mayor, her five-member board of assistant chiefs, community members, and her husband. She stayed in the job, becoming probably the first American big-city police chief to have a baby during her tenure (Ryan, 1992).

Chief Watson's case is noteworthy because it is still unusual, not only for a woman to be so visibly successful in a male-dominated line of work, but also for that woman to receive so much encouragement and support for combining career and family responsibilities in such a position. Women have always worked, even in male-dominated fields, but rarely has their work achieved the same status and recognition as men's, and they have frequently been penalized for trying to "have it all."

To work, to be judged as competent in one's line of endeavor, to be recognized as a contributing member of society—these are important ingredients of the self-concept.

Employment forms such a critical part of an individual's identity that it is common practice to ask new acquaintances to disclose their occupation within seconds of being introduced to them. This question often takes the form "What do you do?", indicating that it is a basic question, the answer to which will classify the speaker. This very question provides a clue to the impact of gender stereotypes on social attitudes about work, for it is more likely to be addressed to a man than to a woman. Women are sometimes asked "Do you work?" or "What does your husband do?"—questions that reveal an expectation that women are unlikely to be in the workforce. Such an expectation is based on ignorance of the facts. About 67% of single and 62% of married American women over the age of 16 are employed outside the home or are actively looking for a job, and women make up about 46% of the paid labor force in the United States and Canada. Among women ages 25 to 34, the percentage of employed women rises to over 70%. Almost 65% of women with children younger than age 6 were in the labor force in 1997, and women with children under the age of 3 made up almost 7% of the labor force in 1998 (U.S. Bureau of Labor Statistics, 1999). The frequency with which women are asked "Do you work?" also reveals a pervasive bias in the way work is defined. No activity can be counted as work unless one gets paid for it. Unpaid work in the home, an activity to which many women devote a significant portion of their time and energy, is not granted the status of "real" work.

Because work defines an individual's place in society—social standing, lifestyle, prestige, and respect—it is not surprising that many of the battles for liberation from traditional gender roles have been fought in the workplace. The reasons for these battles are many. Historically, women have been kept out of many areas of employment. In the 1990s, the average full-time employed woman over the age of 25 continued to earn only 74% of what the average full-time employed man earned (Institute for Women's Policy Research, 1999). Women earn less than men in nearly every occupation. The earning ratio of female to male attorneys is 76%; that of female to male office clerks is 84%; that of female to male psychologists is 71%; that of female to male surveyors, architects, and engineers is 69%; and that of female to male insurance sales agents is 65% (American Federation of Labor, 1999). Even among staffers who work for the U.S. Senate, women make only 88% of what their male colleagues make ("Women Still Earn Less," 1999). Women in top corporate positions do not escape the gender pay gap: they make about 69.6% of men's earnings in similar positions (Mann, 1999). De facto vertical and horizontal occupational segregation of the workforce keeps most women in a few low-paid occupations, while men have access to a wider variety of jobs. Occupations with a high percentage of women and minority workers are likely to have a high percentage of low-wage workers (people whose hourly wages are not sufficient to maintain them above the poverty line). In the United States, women are 54% more likely than men to be poor, and that likelihood varies across ethnic groups. Among European Americans, women are 50% more likely than men to be poor, and that number rises to 61% among African Americans (Kemp, 1995).

This chapter examines some of the issues facing men and women in the workplace. It begins with an examination of the division of labor by sex—what has come to be the "men's work" and the "women's work" of our society—and the changes that are being wrought in this familiar system. It then addresses the discrimination faced by women and men as they try to disassemble the division of labor by sex. From there we move to the inevitable conflict facing every person who has a life outside the work-place—the stress of combining work and family—and we look at how those stresses differ for women and men. And finally we examine sexuality in the workplace in its romantic as well as its coercive forms.

DIVISION OF LABOR BY SEX

Women's Entry Into Male-Dominated Professions

How quickly are changes in the gender composition of the professional and managerial labor force taking place? Most of the research that addresses this question has been directed at women. In 1975, for instance, Bennett and Loewe (1975) argued that it would be fully a century at the rate of change that was taking place in the 1970s before women would be represented in management in the same proportion that they were represented in the workforce. There is some possibility that women may gain equal representation in management more quickly than predicted, however, because more women are now entering professional schools than even the most optimistic forecaster would have predicted in the early 1970s.

Let us look at some recent U.S. figures. In 1982, women hit the majority point in the college population at 52%, and that year they earned 49% of all bachelor degrees and 51% of all master's degrees. Between 1972 and 1982, women more than doubled, and in some cases tripled or quadrupled, their representation in architecture, medicine, economics, law, accounting, and pharmacy. Women's participation in business programs has more than quadrupled since 1970, when their representation was 10%, and by the 1980s women were earning 30% of four-year computer degrees—up from 0% in the early 1970s ("The feminization,"1986). However, the latter number has now dropped back down to 17% (National Science Foundation, 1999), and women still account for less than 1 in 3 scientists and only 9.7% of engineers (U.S. Bureau of Labor Statistics, 1999). The representation is lower among minority women; however, minority women are doing better than minority men in terms of science degrees. The most recent statistics available show that African American women are receiving 21% of all doctoral degrees in engineering awarded to African Americans—a higher percentage than any other female/ethnic group (National Science Foundation, 1998). However, because African Americans earn very few of the doctoral degrees in engineering, this translates into less than 0.5% of such degrees.

Women entering male-dominated professions regularly encounter what some have termed a **glass ceiling.** What is a glass ceiling? It is a barrier that keeps people from rising past a certain point—but a barrier that is transparent and therefore virtually invisible until the person crashes into it. Glass ceiling is an apt label for the phenomenon faced by women who aspire to positions of leadership. In 1997, women made up just 2.5% of the top earners in Fortune 500 companies and held only 5.3% of the line corporate officer positions (positions with profit/loss responsibilities that traditionally lead to the top executive positions). They held 10.6% of the total board seats in Fortune 500 companies and 2 of the CEO positions (Catalyst, 1998). In Canada, women hold 12 of the CEO positions in the Financial Post 500 companies (*Women in Management,* 1999). Minority women are underrepresented at the top, even in comparison to European American women. Asian, Hispanic, and African American women make up 10% of the U.S. work-force but hold only 5.6% of management jobs in private companies, and 60% of women of color managers are clustered in three of the lowest-paying industries: retail trade; professional-related services; and finance, insurance, and real estate (Catalyst, 1998).

Even women who do make it past the glass ceiling into top executive positions apparently do not reach a place where gender equity is the norm. A recent study of executives in one multinational corporation showed that the women who had reached this level faced a *second* glass ceiling (Lyness & Thompson, 1997). These women made the same pay and received the same bonuses as their male counterparts. However, they managed fewer people, were given fewer stock options, and obtained fewer overseas assignments than the men did. They had reached the same level as the men, but being in the same position does not necessarily imply having the same level of status and clout in the organization. When surveyed, the women reported more obstacles and less satisfaction than the men did with their future career opportunities. Clearly, they had gotten the message that they had moved up as far as they could in their company, whereas the men were more likely to see new opportunities ahead. The differences in the ways the two groups were rewarded were subtle, but they apparently signaled to men that they were valued for the long term and to women that they were not.

Women in management jobs are all too aware of gender discrepancies in compensation. A survey of managers and executives by the American Management Association and the Business and Professional Women's Foundation (AMA/BPW, 1999) shows that women are less likely than men to view their compensation as fair and equitable and as equivalent to that of others doing essentially the same work.

Given the problems women encounter when they enter male-dominated professions, what incentives are likely to attract them? Responses to the AMA/BPW survey indicated that women were more likely than men to work for companies that offered a variety of benefits such as parental leave, flexible work hours, and child care assistance, that they placed a higher value on these benefits than men did, and that they were more likely than men to take advantage of the benefits. Ironically, however, women felt that the use of these benefits carried negative career fallout. For example, over 38% of the women, but less than 26% of the men, said that using unpaid leave would have a negative impact on their status or career advancement within the company.

If women continue to enroll in programs that train them for the male-dominated professions, the gender composition of business, law, medicine, and architecture will soon change, but that of engineering, mathematics, and the physical sciences have further to go. The male-dominated professions control much of the power in society and thus have a strong impact that extends beyond a narrow occupational sphere, but they employ a minority of North American men and women. Perhaps more telling to those who study the division of labor by sex is the fact that women are not entering male-dominated blue-collar occupations and that men are not entering any of the female-dominated occupations fast enough to warrant our notice.

The Forgotten People

Although there have been millions, probably billions, of words written about gender-role issues in the workplace over the past 25 years, most of these words have been addressed to two visible but small groups of people: women in management and male-dominated professions and the people who study them. Hundreds of articles have reported research on female professionals and female managers. Dozens of books have advised them on their clothing, their family lives, and their sex lives. They have dissected their ambition, their past, and their probable future. Yet relatively little attention has been paid to the women who enter male-dominated blue-collar jobs or to the men who enter female-dominated occupations. Even more surprising, researchers' and the media's seemingly insatiable interest in employed women has rarely extended itself to the majority of employed women who work in female-dominated occupations.

WOMEN IN FEMALE-DOMINATED OCCUPATIONS   Nurses, home economists, nursery-school teachers, secretaries, typists, and switchboard operators—most of these people share a common characteristic: their femaleness. These are the women who work in female-dominated occupations, the women who are doing "women's work." They do not enjoy the prestige that their formal education, on-the-job training, and responsibility would suggest; their pay is lower and their opportunities for advancement fewer than those in male-dominated occupations. Yet every year young women enter the female-dominated occupations in large numbers. More than 70% of women are employed in the following six occupations: secretary, bookkeeper, registered nurse, cashier, elementary school teacher, and waitress—and each of these categories is more than 80% female (Thornborrow & Sheldon, 1995; U.S. Bureau of the Census, 1995). There has been surprisingly little public relations aimed at improving the image of these occupations and surprisingly little effort aimed at lowering their female domination by recruiting men.

Women in female-dominated occupations cluster into two groups: those who are in such female-dominated professions as nursing, social work, elementary school teaching, home economics, and librarianship and those who are in clerical and "pink-collar" jobs such as secretarial positions, bookkeeping, sales, and food service. As we shall see, research shows that the reasons for selecting and remaining in the female-dominated occupations vary between these two groups of women workers.

The female-dominated professions are sometimes called "semi-professions" because, although to some extent they require advanced education and credentials, they tend to lack the authority, independence, and monopoly over a knowledge base that characterizes such professions as law or medicine (Fox & Hesse-Biber, 1984). What are the characteristics of women in female-dominated professions? In one study in which female nurses and businesswomen were matched for age, education, and managerial level, nurses tended to be less achievement-oriented, less production-oriented, and less likely to see themselves as having characteristics ascribed to managers or to men (Moore & Rickel, 1980). Nurses had more children and considered the domestic role to be more important, although the two groups did not differ in the importance they attached to their career or in their perceptions of their husbands' attitudes. Because this study focused specifically on nurses, it is difficult to know whether these are characteristics that one might expect to find among women in other female-dominated fields or whether these are characteristics specific to nurses. Furthermore, it is difficult to know whether women with particular characteristics seek out female-dominated professions or whether there are different effects of working in female-dominated and male-dominated fields that cause the differences reported in the study. Perhaps the women who choose these professions are balancing their desire for a professional career against the perceived obstacles to a family life associated with the more prestigious, male-dominated professions. Educational data do indicate that women who enter the female-dominated professions have planned their choice; they tend to follow gender-typed patterns of preparation and entry. The educational choices that many women make at the college level (for example, their disproportionate representation among degree recipients in education, health, and library science) suggest that they anticipate entry into one of the female-dominated professions (Fox, 1995). Furthermore, many women entering female-dominated professions say they expect their careers to be interrupted by childrearing.

It has been noted that high school girls who plan to enter male-dominated fields tend to attribute their successes to ability and their failures to lack of ability, as men are usually found to do, and that females who plan to enter female-dominated fields are more likely to attribute their failures to lack of effort and interest and their successes somewhat to effort, but more strongly to luck (Wergers & Frieze, 1977). In addition, qualities of assertiveness and self-efficacy are positively related to college women's willingness to engage in nontraditional, but not traditional, career activities (Nevill & Schlecker, 1988). Although these findings suggest that a self-selection factor propels some women into male-dominated and others into female-dominated occupations, the extent to which these young women actually followed nontraditional or traditional career paths is not known.

Not just individual but also structural factors act to guide women into the female-dominated professions. Women are more likely than men to be deterred from attending college because of financial concerns (Mcqueen, 1999). Gender stereotyping of academic areas such as mathematics and science may channel female students away from courses needed to pursue the male-dominated professions. The perceived lack of availability of parental leave and child-care alternatives may discourage women from pursuing careers that require a 60-hour workweek, as some of the male-dominated professions do. The very male domination of some professions means that a woman needs an extra dose of courage just to claim her place in that world. Sex discrimination, both blatant and subtle, still blocks women's entry into some professions. All of these structural factors are discussed in more detail later in this chapter.

The vast majority of women who do not enter the female-dominated professions enter the labor force as clerical workers. These women tend to work for reasons of income and to maintain an identity separate from their family roles, just as their counterparts in the professions do. They also find work important as a way of forming and maintaining social connections and as a way of structuring their time and feeling useful (Glenn & Feldberg, 1995). They tend to be committed to working, although not necessarily to their specific jobs. Some research shows that women may choose clerical jobs even though they find them boring because they see few options for themselves and because they do not expect to be in the workforce for an extended period of time (Gaskell, 1981).

More than one quarter of the female workforce in both Canada and the United States is employed in the clerical sector (Glenn & Feldberg, 1995; Statistics Canada, 1995). A full 98.4% of today's secretaries, 94% of typists, 95.5% of receptionists, and 82% of data entry clerks are female (U.S. Bureau of Labor Statistics, 1999), and although some have predicted that a severe shortage of good secretaries will eventually cause a crisis in the workplace (Colwill, 1985), secretaries are often unappreciated, laboring invisibly in a world in which all eyes are on their sisters in management. North American organizations are still reaping the secretarial benefits from the days when women seldom extended their occupational choices beyond nurse, teacher, and secretary, and managers have come to expect highly talented people to fill top-level secretarial positions. However, the stereotype of a secretary as a bright young woman temporarily marking time in a job while she waits to get married is no longer (if it ever was) accurate. The average secretary is 35 years old, married, and economically responsible for children (Spalter-Roth & Hartmann, 1990). Although often highly skilled, she is undercompensated for those skills, particularly over a long tenure in the workforce. This future is not an attractive one for young women currently making occupational choices. More than 40% of clerical workers have some college education (Glenn & Feldberg, 1995). As more and more highly intelligent, highly motivated women enter male-dominated fields where they can expect to be better paid for their efforts, recognized for their talents, and given opportunities for advancement, however, a critical shortage of good secretaries may threaten the job market. At the same time, advanced technology is changing the face of secretarial work. It is difficult to predict the changes this shortage will engender, but one optimistic possibility is that to attract first-rate secretarial help, top management of large organizations will begin to envision the secretarial position as a training ground for management and offer secretaries with some management training or secretaries who are prepared to gain management training the opportunities for advancement that have always been offered to entry-level men. The secretarial position requires many skills required of middle managers—skills such as independence, organization, the ability to take orders, and the ability to gain satisfaction from the accomplishments of others. It also offers an ideal location to learn the workings of the organization, and a case could be made for establishing the secretarial position as a common route into management for women and men (Colwill, 1985).

WOMEN IN BLUE-COLLAR JOBS   It is no accident that more women are entering male-dominated professions than are entering male-dominated blue-collar jobs. Women have long benefited from a gender-role stereotype that labels them as good students, and women who enter occupations based largely on "book learning," even though they may be considered "uppity," can take advantage of this stereotype. But technical, spatial, and mechanical abilities and physical strength—the characteristics deemed necessary for male-dominated blue-collar work, particularly the trades—are characteristics that women are seen to be lacking (Colwill & Colwill, 1985). Furthermore, as Walshok (1981) has argued, professional women come to their jobs equipped with degrees that serve as recognized proof of their competence—degrees they earned in an atmosphere in which everyone else was equally naive. Because a blue-collar woman learns most of her visible skills on the job rather than in the classroom, she must undergo her training in an extremely vulnerable situation, often as the only neophyte in the group. Thus, there are few visible skills by which the entry-level female blue-collar worker can be assessed. In situations such as this, where there are few cues available to evaluate ability, evaluators tend to rely more heavily on external characteristics, such as gender, as a means for judging a worker's competence.

Given these problems, it's not surprising that blue-collar women have remained in lower-paying female-dominated industries. Women are the textile workers, making just over minimum wage, rather than the highly paid construction workers (U.S.

Bureau of the Census, 1995), and when they do enter the higher-paying industries, it is often into different and lower-paying jobs than men have traditionally occupied. For example, men hold 99% of the automobile mechanic positions, and women hold 24% of the less lucrative occupations, such as assembling small electronic components. In the United States, women make up only 0.7% of plumbers and pipefitters, 1% of carpenters, 1.7% of crane and tower operators, 2.1% of electricians, 6.5% of precision metalworkers, 6.9% of construction vehicle operators, and 11% of motor vehicle operators (Cantrell, 1996). On the whole, only 2.2% of women are employed in the precision production, craft, and repair occupations that have traditionally been termed "blue collar," whereas almost 19% of men are employed in these jobs (U.S. Bureau of Labor Statistics, 1999).

When a woman does venture into a male-dominated trade, her sense of isolation resembles that of the top-level female executive. She is unlikely to have a female peer and even less likely to have a female boss (Cantrell, 1996; Colwill & Colwill, 1985). As a recent hire, her advancement, which is probably based solely on seniority, will be slow, her potential for layoff high (O'Farrell, 1995). In addition, virtually every study of women in the trades shows some evidence of resentment among coworkers and first-line supervisors; these women were subjected to practical jokes, threats of violence, sexual harassment, and actual violence—although few men actually participated in these activities (Colwill & Colwill, 1985; O'Farrell, 1995). The woman who enters a male-dominated blue-collar job when a woman before her has failed at that job is particularly likely to experience the resentment of this small minority of male coworkers.

Brigid O'Farrell (1995) argues that the slow pace of integration is due in large part not to the choices of individual women but to employer resistance, organizational barriers, government policies, and lack of opportunities. During World War II, when women were needed for factory work, the government did not simply suggest that companies lift previous restrictions on hiring women. Rather, they undertook a massive recruitment drive and established child-care centers for women workers. When such opportunities were clearly made available, women were responsive to them. Under current conditions, the opportunities for women in blue-collar jobs are neither aggressively marketed nor even clearly supported in many companies. However, a small but determined group of women is making some inroads. The number of women employed in construction, machine, electrical, and repair-shop trades almost doubled, from 5.4% to 9.3%, between 1974 and 1994 (Cantrell, 1996).

MEN IN FEMALE-DOMINATED OCCUPATIONS   There is no doubt that women in male-dominated occupations suffer discrimination from people who feel that their reach exceeds their grasp, and women in female-dominated occupations suffer from association with that which is female, and therefore low in prestige. But do the few men who enter the female-dominated occupations—nurses, child-care workers, home economists, and secretaries—sometimes have an even tougher row to hoe? To emulate one's status superiors, as women do when they enter male-dominated occupations, is a forgivable deviation from the norm in an achieving society, but to emulate one's status inferiors, as men do when they enter female-dominated occupations, gives cause for alarm. There is evidence that people tend to attribute homosexuality to males, but not to females, who do not conform to gender-role stereotypes (Deaux & Lewis, 1984). More specifically, Levinson's (1975) research indicates that men are less likely than women to be considered for an occupation nontraditional for their sex and that their sexual orientation may be called into question.

The situation is far from bleak for men in most female-dominated occupations, however. Regardless of the occupation, from clerical work to such professions as nursing and librarianship, men are represented disproportionately for their numbers in senior and administrative positions (Spalter-Roth & Hartmann, 1990; Kaufman, 1995). In nursing, a field that is 94% female, many of the small number of men hold administrative positions, and the usually female chief nursing executives are rarely tapped for top hospital administration positions (Borman & Biordi, 1992). Similarly, although women numerically dominate the field of education, they tend to occupy lower-prestige-level jobs and are severely underrepresented in administrative positions (M. F. Fox, 1995; Kaufman, 1995). Although women make up the vast majority of elementary school teachers, 95% of school superintendents and 72% of school principals are men (Jordan, 1992). Similar patterns are found in social work and librarianship. Moreover, the tendency for men to make more money than women do carries over into female-dominated occupations. Even among clerical workers, males get paid more than their female counterparts with similar education and job qualifications (Spalter-Roth & Hartmann, 1990). It appears that even when men do enter female-dominated occupations, the division of labor along gender lines is maintained through the clustering of men in the higher status, higher paid segments of these occupations.

One researcher who studied the career progress of men in the female-dominated occupations of nursing, librarianship, elementary school teaching, and social work found what she termed a **glass escalator**—a systematic set of hidden advantages for men in such occupations. In her interviews with men in these positions, Christine Williams (1992) found that they experienced discrimination in hiring but that it was usually a positive discrimination, a *preference* for hiring men, because men were in such short supply in those occupations. The men also reported that they faced subtle pressures to "move up" in their professions. For example, one talented kindergarten teacher who loved teaching was continually encouraged to consider administration or to teach at a higher level, and one librarian had to struggle to remain in his preferred field of children's collections while his supervisors told him that he was not aiming high enough. In contrast to women in token positions, the men were likely to be supervised by someone of their own sex, because males are disproportionately represented among supervisors in these occupations. This meant that it was sometimes easier for the token men than for their female colleagues to form bonds of friendship with supervisors—another reason they were often tapped for advancement.

The main problem with discrimination faced by men in female-dominated professions came from the public. For instance, male elementary school teachers encountered suspicion about their interest in children and had to monitor their behavior carefully to guard against charges of sexual abuse. One librarian reported that "Some of the people . . . complained that they didn't want to have a man doing the storytelling scenario. And I got transferred here to the central library in an equivalent job" (p. 295). These men also encountered negative stereotypes about their competence and motivation, particularly from other men. An elementary school teacher reported, "If I tell men that I don't know, that I'm meeting for the first time, that that's what I do . . . sometimes there's a look on their faces that, you know, 'Oh, couldn't get a real job?' " (p. 294).

The division of labor by sex will not subside until men enter female-dominated occupations in large numbers. Currently, men are entering female-dominated jobs at a faster rate than women are entering male-dominated jobs (Ott, 1989), with the unfortunate result that some women will be denied jobs in their traditional strongholds, even as some men are now denied jobs in their traditional strongholds because of increased female competition. If history repeats itself, men's entry into female-dominated occupations will raise the status of the jobs and the salaries of the incumbents, but not without pain for the men who are treated as gender-role deviants and for the women whose jobs are lost. Only when this transition is complete—only when jobs cease to be identified as "men's work" and "women's work"—will it be possible to objectively evaluate the contribution to the labor market made by any particular occupation.

SEX DISCRIMINATION

Pay Equity

In the not too distant past, it was considered perfectly acceptable to pay females less than males for the same work. Anyone arguing against the unfairness of such a system was told that supporting a family was the primary responsibility of the man of the house and that even single men must prepare financially for that responsibility. There were, of course, single women with children; there were women who supported their husbands and their children; and there were single men and women who never married or had children. The social conscience of North America was not easily activated by gender-role issues in those days, however, and social policy was rarely affected by deviations from the norm.

In more recent times, society's collective conscience has been activated by gender inequalities, and two new concepts have been introduced into the workplace. The first was the notion that women and men should be paid the same wage for the same work. Although this concept, known as **equal pay for equal work,** is supported by legislation, it has yet to become reality for all women and men throughout the labor force. Another idea, the widespread acceptance of which was begun only in the 1980s and 1990s, has also been considered: the notion that the work traditionally done by women and that traditionally done by men can be considered equal in value and should be remunerated accordingly. Implementation of this idea requires that the value—the composite of skill, effort, responsibility, and working conditions—of jobs normally filled by women and jobs normally filled by men within the same organization be established and compared. For example, how does the value of the work of a mail clerk (usually male) compare with that of a secretary (usually female)? How does the work of a grocery store shelving clerk (usually male) compare in value to the work of a cashier (usually female) in the same store? If the values of the jobs are determined to be similar, the salaries should be similar, according to the principle of **comparable worth** or equal pay for work of equal value.

There is an increasing amount of legislation and increasing social pressure to support the second as well as the first of these principles, but these two facets of the same problem of pay equity—that men and women should be paid the same for the same work and that men and women should be paid the same for jobs of comparable worth—are far from being resolved. It has been argued, for instance, that employers will react to the pressures to pay women for the real worth of their work by refusing to hire women at all. This argument is based on the unspoken assumption that any employer would, given the choice, prefer a male to a female employee, and it points to the need for a broader approach to this issue. Although the concept of equal pay for work of equal value is considered to be an economic issue, it has been argued that it is merely a symptom of a much broader social psychological phenomenon that manifests itself in the devaluation of women and that which women do (Colwill, 1984). Because women and men are valued differently, work that is gender-labeled "masculine" has a different connotation attached to it than work that has been gender-labeled "feminine." It is extremely difficult, if not virtually impossible, for anyone who has been conventionally socialized in North American society to evaluate the worth of an occupation independent of the gender labeling of that occupation (Baron & Newman, 1990; Steel & Lovrich, 1987). Thus, Canadian and American employers, union leaders, legislators, and policymakers face a monumental task as they attempt to come to grips with the concept of equal pay for work of equal value. To tackle that issue is to tackle the most basic tenets of our gender-role socialization, the most basic assumptions behind sex discrimination.

Discrimination in Hiring and Evaluation

Although sex discrimination in the workplace has been illegal for over 20 years, researchers continue to find evidence of its existence. Most of this discrimination is directed at women, who are more likely than men to be seen as stepping out of their "place." One particularly telling area of study is discrimination within the working of unions; the primary function of unions is to protect their worker-members, yet women and minorities are underrepresented in the top levels of virtually all unions (Roby, 1995; J. White, 1980) and rarely find their way into union executive positions unless they belong to a union in which women form a clear majority (Chaison & Andrappan, 1982).

One basis for sex discrimination in evaluation is a general tendency to devalue the things that women typically do. In a series of studies, men and women were given an advantage when they employed the power strategies typically used by men (Colwill, Perlman, & Spinner, 1983) or when they were identified as being in a male-dominated (engineering) rather than a female-dominated (home economics) profession (Colwill, Pollock, & Sztaba, 1986). Furthermore, Colwill and Sztaba's (1986) research indicates that both women and men are seen as less effective when they speak in the traditionally feminine manner: using superlatives ("the most wonderful"), qualifiers ("This product is, perhaps, the best on the market"), tag questions ("You will, won't you?"), and highly descriptive and explicit words such as *mauve, ecru,* and *lovely.*

In any case, sex discrimination against women and sex discrimination against men seem to take different forms. Women tend to be the recipients of prejudice and discrimination in situations in which their competence and credibility, particularly to do malelike things, are at stake. Men, conversely, tend to have discriminatory attitudes and behaviors directed at them when they incur the hostility of others by doing femalelike things that are considered to be beneath them. Thus, as suggested earlier, women are punished as incompetents for trying to emulate their social superiors, and men are punished as deviants for trying to emulate their social inferiors. This difference was probably best demonstrated in Levinson's (1975) field study, in which men who applied for traditionally female jobs were often told that the job was too simple, too dull, or too low-paying. Women applying for "men's jobs" were more likely to be told that the job was too difficult or that it required too much strength or time commitment for a woman.

But haven't prejudice and discrimination been reduced dramatically in the years since 1975, when Levinson's research was published? Few longitudinal data examine this question directly, but in one study of MBA students' attitudes toward female executives done in 1975 and again in 1983, males' attitudes toward women as managers remained consistently negative, and females' attitudes remained significantly more positive than those of their male counterparts did (Dubnos, 1985). Surveys show that negative attitudes toward female managers persist, especially among men (Frank, 1988; Wiley & Eskilson, 1990) and especially if the female manager uses a stereotypically masculine, "directive" leadership style (Eagly et al., 1992).

Data concerning the career paths of managers continue to show that women in high-status male-dominated occupations are the targets of prejudice and discrimination (Cox & Harquail, 1991). One study of 1000 top female and male managers at the top 20 U.S. companies showed that even when women had the same qualifications as men—the same education, similar levels of job tenure, equivalent work experience in the same industries and job areas, similar willingness and ability to relocate—they received smaller salary increases and fewer opportunities to relocate over a 5-year period. Over that 5-year period, women received pay increases and bonuses averaging 54% of their salaries, compared to 65% for men (Stroh, Brett, & Reilly, 1996). A more recent survey of top executives by the American Management Association and the Business and Professional Women's Foundation (1999) showed that, among this group of high-level managers, women's base compensation averaged less than 70% of men's. Moreover, the gender discrepancy was greatest at the highest levels. Women at the top (CEO) level of management made 60.8% of what their male counterparts made, whereas women in the next two levels made 68.7% of male earnings, and women at the fourth and fifth levels of management made 71% and 74.4% of male earnings, respectively.

Women are still underrepresented in top positions. The final report of the U.S. government's Glass Ceiling Commission in 1995 noted that the nation's boardrooms remain "overwhelmingly" White and male: 95% of the senior-level managers in the Fortune 1000 industries and Fortune 500 companies are men, and 97% are White (Swoboda, 1995). Among managers and executives, women are considerably less likely than men to hold strategic, policymaking positions (American Management Association, 1999). Recent research finds that, relative to men, women in higher positions receive fewer promotions than women in lower positions—further evidence of a glass ceiling effect (Lyness & Judiesch, 1999).

It appears that the strongest prejudice against women in a traditionally male occupation is likely to occur when people are considering hypothetical situations, among men who have had little exposure to women in that particular job, or in situations in which people are lacking data that would help them make an informed decision about the worth of a woman's work. It is known, for example, that women and men who have been managed by women have fewer negative stereotypes about female managers (Ezell, Odewahn, & Sherman, 1981; Wheeless & Berryman-Fink, 1985) and that discrimination against women is more likely to occur if managers are given insufficient information to make a personnel decision based on competence, as Gerdes and Garber's (1983) study of engineers has demonstrated.

There has been a tendency in the past for both men and women to show prejudice against women, leading many people to believe everyone prefers to work with and for men. However, numerous studies now show that women are more accepting of female managers than men are (Die, Debbs, & Walker, 1990; Stevens & DeNisi, 1980; Wheeless & Berryman-Fink, 1985). In one such study, female employees expressed a preference for female coworkers (Haefner, 1977), and in another, female managers evaluated managerial women more positively than they evaluated comparably qualified men (Jabes, 1980). Female managers in the latter study were judged as being more intelligent, more likeable, more successful, and more able than their male counterparts, and the future of female managers was seen as more satisfying. Similarly, the MBA women in Mikalachki and Mikalachki's (1984) study gave more favorable ratings to female than to male managers. Finally, in a study that shows pro-female biases may sometimes benefit women, D. R. Dalton and Todor (1985) found that union grievances were 50% more likely to be settled in favor of female plaintiffs and that this effect was maintained even when the researchers controlled for severity of grievance or the level at which the case was settled. (There were five possible levels, from meeting with first-level supervisors to arbitration.)

Whether gender-role stereotypes favor women or men, the consequence is an inequitable workplace, because stereotypes almost invariably lead to discrimination. There is increasing evidence that stereotypes may have other deleterious effects. They may actually motivate the stereotyped person to behave in a manner consistent with the stereotype. This process, known as the **self-fulfilling prophecy,** was demonstrated in a study by von Baeyer, Sherk, and Zanna (1981), in which women were interviewed by men whom they were led to believe held either traditional or nonstereotypical views about women. Women who were interviewed by the "traditional" men dressed for the interview in a more "feminine" manner and were more likely to wear jewelry, scarf, and makeup than were women who were interviewed by the "nontraditional" men. In addition, women who thought they were being interviewed by men with traditional attitudes were more likely to adopt subservient nonverbal gestures: to stare at the interviewer when he was talking and to look away when they answered his questions.

Stereotypes may create a vicious circle. We have certain attitudes about a person, she or he becomes aware of these attitudes and behaves in a manner consistent with our stereotypes, and our stereotypes are reinforced. The von Baeyer, Sherk, and Zanna (1981) study demonstrated the link between perceived stereotypes and the stereotyped person's behavior. A second study by Towson, MacDonald, and Zanna (1981) demonstrated the reinforcement of the stereotyper's original attitudes. In this study, the researchers had male actors conduct interviews with female actors playing one of two roles: the role of a "feminine" woman (jewelry, scarf, makeup, and subservient nonverbal communication) or the role of a "nonfeminine" woman (same clothing, but no jewelry, scarf, or makeup, and she looked at the interviewer when he *and* she were speaking). In addition, the feminine woman said that she would quit work to raise her family; the nonfeminine woman said that if she were to get married and have children she would organize her life so that family commitments and career advancement would not conflict. Videotapes of these interviews were shown to men who had been tested as having either traditional or nontraditional gender-role attitudes. Men with traditional attitudes were less likely to predict job success for any of the female applicants. Furthermore, feminine women were seen as being better fitted for jobs in female-dominated occupations, and nonfeminine women were judged as being more appropriate candidates for traditionally male jobs.

Sex discrimination is apparently still with us and will not be easily banished. Women and men are readily classified into two groups, and the myriad stereotypes about these two groups, which are inextricably intertwined with sexual mores, religious teachings, and family roles, cannot help but affect workplace attitudes. Sex discrimination helps us to preserve the status quo, and the status quo, whatever its shortcomings and whatever its unfairness, has the advantage of familiarity. Perhaps because of this familiarity, or perhaps because they cannot bear to face the reality of its unfairness, women tend to underrate the amount of sex discrimination that is visited on them personally, even when they are quite aware that women in general experience sex discrimination. This phenomenon is known as **denial of personal discrimination** (Crosby, 1984). Women, and probably all people who are the objects of discrimination, adopt cognitive strategies that protect them from feeling deprived, using reference groups similar to themselves (other women in similar situations) rather than facing the incongruity associated with comparisons to more privileged groups (Abbondanza, 1982, 1983). Clearly, people prefer to protect themselves from feelings that they are being treated unfairly.

Despite their lower salaries, women are less likely than men to report dissatisfaction with their pay (Jackson, 1989; Steel & Lovrich, 1987; Summers, 1988). When given the opportunity to compare their pay with that of other workers, participants in one study chose to see the pay of the same-sex and same-job group first (Major & Forcey, 1985). The same study also showed that both men and women assigned to a "feminine" job expected less pay and rated their obtained pay as fairer than those in "masculine" jobs did. In addition, women thought they deserved less pay for their work than men did, regardless of their job assignment. People are apparently so used to evaluating their own and others' pay expectations by making implicit same-sex comparisons that they do not question the fairness or appropriateness of restricting their comparisons in this way. Interestingly, for women at least, looking beyond one's own sex for comparison purposes may be linked to discontent. One study of professional women indicated that women with male reference groups perceived a greater gap between what they had and wished to have, were more pessimistic about their futures, and were more dissatisfied than were their counterparts who compared themselves to other women (Zanna, Crosby, & Loewenstein, 1987).

We can do little to eliminate the fact that women and men belong to two identifiable groups and are thus susceptible to sex discrimination. We can do even less to overcome sex discrimination based on the fact that gender-role change disturbs the status quo. We can, however, through education, particularly education directed at the women and men who believe they are not personally the targets of sex discrimination, help to break down one of the barriers to social change: the denial of personal discrimination. This process is particularly important in the lives of men and women who find themselves in token positions, for they are especially vulnerable to discrimination.

Minorities and Tokenism

Women and men in occupations nontraditional for their sex often find themselves holding **token positions**—positions in which they are treated as symbols or representatives of their sex. Kanter (1977) makes a clear distinction between tokens and minority members. She argues that in skewed groups, where there is a large preponderance of one sex over the other (a ratio of 85 to 15, for example), the minority members are truly tokens or symbols of their group. It is only when their proportions rise to a ratio of, say, 65 to 35, that we can speak of *minorities* and *majorities* rather than of *tokens* and *dominants,* for only then do the minority members have the opportunity to be seen as individuals, differentiated from one another. At this point, they can form coalitions and have the opportunity to affect the group culture.

Kanter's sociological study of "Indsco," a pseudonymous company in which she conducted research in the 1970s, has provided a great deal of information about people in token positions. From her research, it has become clear that tokens tend to be perceived as members of the outgroup rather than as individuals. Their every action tends to be seen either as typical outgroup behavior or as behavior that is unusual for a member of the outgroup, rather than as the action of one unique person.

The token status places one in a particularly visible, and thus vulnerable, position, and both male and female tokens may find it difficult to relax and do their jobs as competently as they would under less adverse circumstances. In a study that attempted to duplicate the situation in which tokens find themselves, participants believed they were interacting, via television screen, with three other people, discussing opinions on several noncontroversial topics (Lord & Saenz, 1985). In reality, they were being videotaped giving their opinions, but were watching prerecorded videotapes of three confederates. In the nontoken condition of this experiment, the confederates were the same sex as the participant; in the token condition, the three confederates were the other sex. The results indicated that tokens seemed to exhibit a memory deficit. Even in this relatively nonthreatening situation of expressing opinions on everyday topics, and even though they were treated no differently than nontokens, they could not remember as well as nontokens what they had said or what the three others had said. In a second part of the experiment, participants serving as observers watched the four videotapes—the three videotapes watched by the participant plus a videotape of the participant him- or herself. These observers were more likely to remember the opinions of the token than they were to remember the opinions of the nontokens or confederates. The authors argue that the tokens' memory difficulties resulted from the feeling of being scrutinized by an audience of other-sex peers. If this phenomenon generalizes to the work situation, and there is no reason to believe it does not, the token is in a particularly vulnerable position: She or he is unable to remember the details of interactions that take place in a situation in which she or he is obviously the center of attention, and a memorable one at that. Moreover, if tokenism alone is enough to cause cognitive difficulties, the added pressure of differential treatment in the workplace may well compound the problem.

Because most of the tokens at Indsco were women, Kanter's (1977) research has focused mainly on the roles that token women find themselves playing in organizational settings in which they are seen primarily as "women" rather than "workers":

- The *mother* to men in the group—the comforter, the button-sewer, the emotional specialist
- The *seductress* or sex object—the object of sexual competition or male "protection" from the sexual advances of other men
- The *pet* or mascot of the organization—the good-humored cheerleader whose competencies are fussed over as being exemplary performance for a woman
- The *iron maiden* who expects full rights of group membership—the "women's libber" for whom no passages are smoothed

These four roles share two commonalities: They are blatant caricatures of the female gender role, and they rob the role players of the chance to be seen in their worker role. Thus, Kanter argues, every effort should be made not to introduce lone employees into a work situation in which they are surrounded solely by members of the other sex. Although that is undoubtedly the ideal, it is equally important that managers not postpone the integration of their organization until the day when they can introduce two or more employees into nontraditional work situations, for there is evidence that mere exposure to a token can create more positive attitudes toward the group to which the minority member belongs. In one particularly dramatic study, Shomer and Centers (1970) found more positive attitudes toward feminism among men in a group with one woman than among men in an all-male group, even though group members did not have the opportunity to talk to one another.

The workplace stresses associated with token experiences are numerous because the token position contains several dilemmas and contradictions. Tokens are treated as representatives of their group, yet as exceptions to their group; they are visible, yet backstage; they stand apart, yet are stereotyped; they can relax least in "relaxing" situations in which formal organizational roles are dropped (Kanter, 1977).

Either women or men can be tokens in a workplace setting dominated by the other group. Is the token experience the same for men as it is for women? Two studies suggest it is not—that, in fact, for men gender stereotypes act to ameliorate the negative aspects of being a token. In the first, a study of young concession stand workers, findings revealed that the token man did not experience the negative consequences—high visibility, contrast, and assimilation—that the token woman did. Rather, token men identified with (male) supervisors and advanced more quickly than nontoken men and women did (Yoder & Sinnett, 1985). In the second study, a comparison of the experiences of female police officers and male nurses, the female, but not the male, tokens reported that they did not feel accepted by their peers, that they felt extremely visible, and that they had been sexually harassed (Ott, 1989). Another study suggests that male nurses do not have to play the subordinate role to physicians to the same extent that female nurses do (Floge & Merrill, 1986). Male nurses interacted more with male physicians and were more likely to voice their opinions and have those opinions accepted than female nurses were. However, tokens of either gender can experience some disadvantages. Both male nurses and female physicians reported that they were excluded from conversations among the dominant group.

One thing that tokens, minority members, or new members of a group may do to reduce stress is to search for solidarity among themselves. They may isolate themselves from majority group members, interacting more frequently and positively with one another than with more established members of the group (Schein, 1968). Although such solidarity can be helpful, it also has a major drawback: It can slow down the process by which newcomers are assimilated into the group (Moreland, 1985). This finding underlines the dilemma inherent in the position of women or men entering an occupation or workplace in which their sex is underrepresented. Not only must they cope with the many problems associated with token or minority status, but even their attempts to seek support from others in the same position may present a danger to their ultimate acceptance. The brave souls who persevere in such situations surely deserve the label *pioneers*. These pioneers are not the only people who experience workplace stress, however. Let us turn now to an examination of the stresses inherent in the interface between work and family.

TWO SPHERES IN CONTACT: THE INTERACTION OF FAMILY AND EMPLOYMENT ISSUES

How simple (and how dull) life would be for the average working person if the only responsibilities he or she faced were those connected with the job. For most of us, however, a job represents only one of the sets of tasks and sources of worry, pride, frustration, and fulfillment that fill our lives. No serious examination of gender-related issues in the workplace can ignore the fact that when women and men leave the workplace and head for home they are faced with different amounts and kinds of responsibilities.

Combining Job and Family: Stresses and Rewards

It used to be expected that women would set aside their own work and achievement needs to provide support for those of their husbands. Consider the comments, made in 1972, of one of the gifted women from Terman's longitudinal study of high-IQ individuals:

> A person of Henry's talent and drive desperately needs a partner to take care of family, home and all of the social needs and other involvement. . . . My husband's multifaceted career has been the central factor in my life. Ours has been a partnership in many ways, as I have carried most of the home, family, and social responsibilities. This has enabled him to devote full time to his creative work, his teaching, etc. I wish I could have achieved creatively myself, but what small talent I might have had was absorbed in his great gifts. (as quoted in Tomlinson-Keasey, 1990, p. 217)

Traditional gender roles, by assigning women to the home and men to the working world, have allowed a certain amount of separation between the employment and family spheres. The entry of women in large numbers into the labor force now means that the tidy separation is crumbling. For women, especially, this new situation is likely to result in increased stress. Mothers who work outside the home usually find themselves faced with another full-time job in their "off" hours: cooking, cleaning, and caring for children. Even in dual-career families, mothers continue to assume the major responsibility for the care and socialization of young children and for housework (Bielby & Bielby, 1988; Hoffnung, 1995; South & Spitze, 1994). Employed women report more absences from work due to personal or family responsibilities than men do (Statistics Canada, 1995), and they also report that a major source of stress is the conflicting set of demands generated by work and family roles (Canadian Mental Health Association, 1984; Duxbury & Higgins, 1991; Koberg & Chusmir, 1989). Women garment workers interviewed in one study reported that worry over finding adequate day care for their children was more stressful than the unhealthy working conditions at their plant (de Koninck, 1984). Studies of some populations show that women are more likely than men to report work–family role conflict (Mashal & Kalin, 1985; Wiersma, 1990).

However, as women and men increasingly share employment responsibilities, they may also begin to share more family-related stress. Research now shows that parent-role stress and negative parent–child relationships are equally likely to be associated with psychological distress among employed mothers and employed fathers (Barnett, Brennan, & Marshall, 1994). Furthermore, for both women and men, a positive family climate is associated with less work–family conflict. A positive family climate, including a readiness to talk things out, provide moral support, and do things together, also correlates with less time spent on domestic chores by women and less free time spent on career-related activities by men (Wiersma & Van den Berg, 1991). Sharing household tasks is associated with lower levels of role strain for women, and many employed women expect their husbands to adjust to a higher level of participation in domestic work. One study of Mexican American women in dual-earner couples, for example, found that these women perceived themselves as coproviders (Herrera & DelCampo, 1995). They did not subscribe to the myth that they should be "superwomen"—able to work full time and manage all aspects of the housework and child care. Even among women at the very top levels of management in Fortune 1000 companies, stress is ameliorated by adjustments in the family. In a Catalyst survey of female executives who earned an average of $248,000 a year, three quarters of the married women were their family's primary breadwinner. These women noted the importance of having a supportive husband (Grimsley, 1996).

In recent years, a new load has been added to the domestic side of women's double burden by an emerging demographic phenomenon: increasing longevity and the concomitant demand that middle-aged people spend years caring for their elderly parents. The people called on to be the caregivers in this situation are usually women, as are most of the dependent elderly, because women live longer than men (Kramer & Kipnis, 1995). These female caregivers who are also mothers have been characterized as "women in the middle" by gerontologist Elaine Brody (1981), not only because their age places them in the position of being expected to care for both their parents and their children but also because they are juggling so many competing demands on their time and energy: job, husband, health problems, and children. According to Brody's research, three fifths of these heavily burdened women felt guilty about not doing enough for their mothers.

Stress among employed women comes not only from the burden of unpaid, unrecognized domestic work added to their outside employment but also from conditions on the job. Women are more likely than men to face pay inequities (Institute for Women's Policy Research, 1999), underutilization of skills (Belanger, 1984; de Koninck, 1984), sex discrimination in performance evaluation and promotion (Cox & Harquail, 1991), and tokenism (Kanter, 1977)—all of which, along with work–family role conflict, have been related to negative physical and psychological stress symptoms (Greenglass, 1985a, 1985b, 1991).

If the strain of combining work and family responsibilities is so great for women, what is there to be said in favor of doing it, other than the obvious financial payoff? It is clear that women can reap psychological and physical, as well as economic, benefits from the effort of juggling two roles, particularly if they have support from family and friends (Amatea & Fong, 1991; Epstein, 1983). In fact, employed women appear to be happier and healthier than homemakers, except when they have infants to care for (L. O. Walker & Best, 1991). One study of women in the 40-to-59 age range found that work outside the home may play an important role in the psychological well-being of middle-aged women. Employed women at midlife had higher self-esteem and less psychological anxiety than homemakers did, and they also reported being in better physical health (Coleman & Antonucci, 1983). Taken alone, these correlational data do not prove that holding jobs caused women to feel happier, healthier, more self-confident, and less anxious; perhaps happy, healthy, self-confident, calm women are simply more likely to seek and find jobs. However, in the Coleman and Antonucci study, employment was the only significant predictor of self-esteem in midlife women, in contrast to income, education, marital status, and family life-cycle stage—none of which predicted self-esteem. This finding led the researchers to speculate that employment in and of itself may affect women's well-being. They suggest that the stabilizing impact of employment enables women to avoid some of the possible negative effects of family-role loss that occur at midlife: empty-nest syndrome, feelings of inadequacy, and loss of purpose. They further suggest that working outside the home may have a similar stabilizing influence at other crucial transition periods of the life cycle, such as early parenthood, divorce, or death of a spouse. Perhaps it simply helps to keep life in perspective when one can look at it from the viewpoints of two very different roles. This suggestion receives support from Crosby's (1990) study of divorce and work life among women managers. She noted that work was explicitly recognized by the women managers as a source of pride and repair to damaged self-esteem.

For men, stress in the workplace has long been recognized as a problem. The early research on Type A behavior—a hard-driving, job-devoted behavioral style characterized by excessive competitive striving, time urgency, and aggressiveness that has been linked to coronary heart disease (Friedman & Rosenman, 1959)—was concerned only with men. The Jenkins Activity Survey, which measures Type A behavior, was developed for men (Jenkins, Rosenman, & Friedman, 1967) and was only later adapted for use with women (C. Davis & Cowles, 1985). Although Type A behavior is more common among men than among women (Waldron, 1976), it seems to be related more to gender role than to sex. When employment or college status is controlled for, the Type A personality shows up equally often in women and men (DeGregorio & Carver, 1980; Waldron, 1978), and Type A behavior correlates significantly with masculinity but not femininity scale scores (DeGregorio & Carver, 1980; Grimm & Yarnold, 1985). Many of the correlates of Type A behavior are similar for the two sexes (Heilbrun, Friedberg, & Wydra, 1989).

Some research indicates that a major source of stress for men may be that, because of expectations linked to the masculine role, they rely too heavily on their job and their breadwinner role for their sense of identity. When this role is threatened through unemployment, men may show increased symptoms of stress, such as ulcers, heart attacks, elevated blood pressure, and strokes (Liem & Rayman, 1982). Moreover, these negative effects of unemployment are not limited to the out-of-work men themselves; stress and ill health are common among the wives of men who have lost their jobs (Grayson, 1983). Perhaps, then, the benefits of combining two roles are not limited to women who add employment to their traditional domestic tasks. Perhaps men can also gain from dividing their commitment more evenly between the spheres of work and family. Certainly there is a good deal of evidence that men who increase their involvement with parenting find the experience to be a positive and rewarding one, as discussed in Chapter 11. It is quite likely that, given mutual support, both men and women can benefit by not putting all their eggs in one basket—by finding sources of identity and satisfaction in both job and family.

Dual-Career Couples: Finding a New Job–Family Balance

For the growing number of families in which the two adult partners are pursuing careers, many of the traditional expectations about the division of household tasks, the supportive role played by the wife for the husband, and family mobility to accommodate the career moves of the male partner become unworkable. Even in the absence of any ideology about female–male equality, the pressures on a two-career couple force them in the direction of a more equitable division of family tasks. As this type of family structure has become more common, the male members of these couples have discovered firsthand two of the major difficulties that have traditionally plagued career women: (1) the limitations imposed on career accomplishment by the necessity to perform such survival activities as shopping, cooking, cleaning, and laundry; and (2) the frequent assumption by employers that anyone who takes family responsibilities seriously lacks career commitment.

A well-worn assumption in the corporate world has been that men bring two people to their jobs, but women bring less than one (Kanter, 1977). According to this assumption, men come equipped with wives, whose unpaid work enhances men's productivity on the job. Furthermore, wives not only free their husbands from the necessity of spending energy on daily concerns such as clean shirts and school lunches, but also help host business associates and maintain smooth social relations among the husbands' colleagues and coworkers. Although expectations are changing somewhat, the average female employee rarely has anyone doing these things for her and, indeed, is often trying to do them for someone else. Clearly, a single man, or one whose partner spends her energy on her own career rather than on supporting his, is at a disadvantage similar to that faced by most women. Although he is not likely to be in the desperate situation faced by many married career women, who juggle employment and the greater share of domestic responsibilities, he is still denied the opportunity to focus all his energy on his career and leave the details of daily living to someone else.

When men do try to take on a serious share of family duties, they may run into trouble at work. Although an employer may show some understanding and flexibility in making adjustments to accommodate a female employee whose work and family responsibilities conflict, a man experiencing similar conflicts can expect a less sympathetic response—and a lower salary (Schneer & Reitman, 1993). Traditionally, people who have allowed family considerations to "distract" them from their jobs have been judged to be less than serious about their work and have been passed over for promotions and raises. In fact, women have often been stereotyped as having less "commitment" to their careers simply because they were married and had children, and some companies and employees have identified such stereotypes as the main obstacles to women's advancement (Grimsley, 1996; Shellenbarger, 1995). Some companies, in an attempt to erase stereotypes about the interference of family responsibilities with work, have made flexible work arrangements available to all employees who need to manage "multiple commitments" and speak of a "life outside work" instead of work–family conflict. Such programs counter the notion that an employee must have a completely single-minded focus on his or her career to be successful and undermine the idea that women need a special "mommy track." Some organizations are recognizing that fewer and fewer of their employees can make career decisions independent of family considerations or can blithely leave all family responsibilities in the hands of a spouse.

A Catalyst (1998b) study of dual-career couples in the United States finds that the majority say that the chief benefit of having two earners is higher income. However, they also cited personal fulfillment, intellectual equality, and emotional support as important advantages, and most said they would continue working even if the financial need to do so was not there. Both members of such dual-career couples said that their top choice for benefits they would look for if they were switching companies was flexibility: the freedom to arrange their own day-to-day schedules. They also said they would like the option to customize the pace of their career advancement—being able to slow down when family responsibilities were very pressing without hurting their chances for eventual success.

The concern about work–family balance is not surprising for couples engaged in a two-career lifestyle. Such couples must wrestle with questions of whether and when to have children; they face enormous challenges each time one spouse is asked to relocate; and they sometimes spend years in long-distance "commuter" relationships. Because some of the differences in salary levels between men and women with the same educational background seem to be explained by geographical relocations based on the husband's career (Felmlee, 1995), the option of living apart is seen as preferable to relocation by some couples. This solution is still considered a drastic departure from society's expectations about marriage, and couples who adopt it may have to face the disapproval of family and friends along with the inevitable difficulties of the separation. However, studies of these couples reveal some advantages to this difficult lifestyle: The suspension of spousal-role demands allows individuals to devote long hours to their work; the absence of a better-established spouse allows the other to begin a career without relying on or being overshadowed by him or her; and individuals find opportunities for personal growth and development independent of their spouse (Douvan & Pleck, 1978; Farris, 1978; Gross, 1980). The disadvantages, though, are equally compelling: loneliness, the expense of maintaining two residences, long-distance phone calls, commuting, and the lack of a partner with whom to share domestic responsibilities (Green & Zenisek, 1983). When couples do not make such drastic compromises, however, it is often the woman's career that suffers. In the Catalyst (1998b) survey cited above, fully one third of the men in the dual-career couples viewed their careers as primary in the household, whereas only 6% of the women said their own careers were primary.

Career Paths of Women and Men

In past decades, the pattern of labor force participation for North American women has been quite different from that of men. Although men have tended to enter the workplace and continue employment until they retire, women's participation has shown a sharp dip during childbearing years, followed by a rise as women whose children are grown return to work. Because of its shape on the graph and its significance, this pattern has sometimes been labeled the M curve—M for mother (Farley, 1980). With each passing year, however, the M curve has been disappearing; fewer women are leaving the labor force during their childrearing years, and the so-called women's pattern of employment participation is becoming increasingly like men's (Treiman, 1985). Between 1975 and 1991, White married women with children under age 6 increased their participation rate in the labor force from just over 34% to 59%. For African American women in the same category, the participation rate rose from just under 55% to over 73%. In fact, the majority of wives with children age 1 year or younger now participate in the labor force. From 1975 to 1992, White women in this group increased their labor force participation from just over 29% to almost 55%, and African American women's participation rose from 50% to almost 70% (Thornborrow & Sheldon, 1995). The current labor force participation rate for women with children under the age of 6 is 65% (U.S. Bureau of Labor Statistics, 1999).

For women who do leave the workforce, the break is a costly one. Labor force discontinuity is one of the factors responsible for the salary and status differentials between employed women and men (Felmlee, 1995). According to one estimate, earnings forgone in the year of birth (or adoption) and in the two subsequent years amount to $14,400 (in 1986 dollars) per woman (Institute for Women's Policy Research, 1990). Not only does the discontinuity limit a woman's opportunity to build experience and seniority, it places her in a poor bargaining position when she wishes to reenter the job market. She is likely to find, despite her experience, that her opportunities are limited to entry-level jobs (Treiman, 1985). Research supports a link between labor force discontinuity and job advancement. Women without children tend to be in the labor force continuously and experience more upward mobility in occupational status (Felmlee, 1995). Even women with continuous labor force participation do not achieve upward mobility levels comparable to those of men, however, so this variable alone cannot account for the female–male differences (Cox & Harquail, 1991).

In recent years, despite a minor flurry of cautionary tales in the popular press about the dangers for women of trying to "have it all," the trend of women combining family and employment shows no sign of slowing down. Indeed, for many families, losing the wife's income, even for a few years, would mean the impossibility of adequate housing, occasional family vacations, and college education for the children. Moreover, should marriage breakdown occur, as it does in one third to one half of cases in Canada and the United States, the woman who has been out of the labor force is at an extreme economic disadvantage. Researchers have found that after a divorce the woman's standard of living typically drops about 30%, but the man's rises about 10% (Peterson, 1996, as cited in Webster, 1996). Finally, the choice of staying home with children rarely means being in a completely ideal setting, with adequate resources and an available, supportive male partner. For most people, the home comes no closer to perfection than the workplace does; if both were restructured to accommodate the needs of people who are seriously committed to both family and employment responsibilities, women and men would have less stress and more time with their children and each other.

What if solutions could be found to all the dilemmas faced by women and men in trying to fulfill both work and family roles? Would sex and gender no longer be important issues in the workplace? The answer is no, for there is at least one other major arena in which gender expectations can interact with work roles: sexuality.

WORK, SEXUALITY, AND POWER

One of the traditional concerns about integrating women and men in the workplace has been that sexuality will interfere with job performance. In 1978, the assignment of women to work alongside men on U.S. Navy ships at sea caused a public outcry, fueled by the specter of sailors having romantic liaisons when they should be swabbing the decks. Husbands and wives of male and female managers may feel stabs of jealousy when business meetings last late into the evening or when their mates take business trips with a member of the other sex. Because changes in the gender composition of the workplace have most frequently involved the addition of women to a previously all-male preserve, these worries about sexuality have most commonly been used as arguments for keeping women out. However, the issue of sexuality in the workplace is not a simple matter of women's presence turning men's fancy to thoughts of romance. Men and women have learned ritualized ways of relating to one another, often adopting reciprocal gender roles based partially on sexuality, and these roles are not easily shed at the entrance to the workplace. Who, for example, has not encountered the man or woman who cannot seem to relate to members of the other sex without flirting? And who has not observed a change come over a group of men or women at coffee when they are joined by a single member of the other sex? It would be extremely naive to ignore the impact that sexuality can have on our perceptions of and responses to the people with whom we work.

Sexuality has implications for both women's and men's power and achievement in the workplace, and also for the smooth functioning of the workplace itself. An individual can use sexuality as a power resource for influence or advancement at work or, coercively, as a weapon to keep others in line. The intimate bonds that can form in noncoercive sexual relationships at work, although sometimes good for individuals' morale and motivation, can promote the formation of coalitions that interfere with group decision making in the workplace. Moreover, public awareness of the existence of such a relationship has a variety of implications for the participants. Let us look briefly at the implications of both coercive and noncoercive sexuality in the workplace.

Coercive Sexuality: Sexual Harassment on the Job

In 1991, one of the first female neurosurgeons, Dr. Frances Conley, a professor at Stanford University School of Medicine, shocked students and colleagues when she announced her resignation. The 51-year-old physician had established an outstanding reputation over the 17 years of her career. Why was she leaving? She said that she had endured a career-long pattern of sexual harassment from her medical colleagues and superiors. She was tired of being asked, for effect, in jest, to go to bed with her colleagues. She was tired of being called "honey" by male doctors in front of her patients. She was tired of the constant sexual innuendos and putdowns to remind her that she was not a real member of the "club" ("A Surgeon Cuts to the Heart," 1991).

Sexual harassment, now recognized as a major problem in the workplace, can take two forms. In the first, commonly labeled **quid pro quo,** an individual is pressured to submit to unwelcome sexual advances or other unwelcome sexual conduct as a condition of employment, or employment decisions that affect the individual, such as promotion or raises, are based on her or his submission to or rejection of such conduct. The second form of sexual harassment involves the creation of a **hostile environment:** making unwelcome sexual advances or engaging in other conduct of a sexual nature that unreasonably interferes with an individual's work performance or creates an intimidating, hostile, or offensive atmosphere. Although both female and male workers can be sexually harassed, females are the most frequent victims. The U.S. Merit Systems Protection Board (1981) found that 42% of women workers, as compared to 15% of men workers, reported experiencing sexual harassment. According to a 1983 survey by the Canadian Human Rights Commission, 1.2 million women and 300,000 men say they have been sexually harassed at work. This harassment is not limited to any particular employment sector. A study by the American Medical Association found that 55% of the women in a sample of 3rd-year medical students reported being sexually harassed by residents, interns, and faculty (Friend, 1990). A survey of United Methodist clergywomen revealed that 77% of them had experienced incidents of sexual harassment—41% of them by colleagues or other pastors ("Women Clerics," 1990). And, in the aftermath of law professor Anita Hill's testimony charging Supreme Court nominee Clarence Thomas with sexual harassment, a flood of anecdotes by women working on Capitol Hill has illustrated that working for an elected representative of the people is no guarantee of safety from unwanted, often humiliating, sexual attention (Sharpe, 1992).

Although gender is by far the best predictor of sexual harassment, other factors also seem to play a part. White women in their 30s who are living with a man to whom they are not married report the most instances of harassment (Gutek & Nakamura, 1983). However, women from virtually every age, racial, and marital status group report sexual harassment to some extent; one review of 18 studies of sexual harassment indicated that about 42% of women report being sexually harassed (Gruber, 1990). Another review suggests that about half of women in workplaces and universities have experienced sexual harrassment (Fitzgerald & Shullman, 1993). The people doing the harassing are preponderantly male: 95% of the female victims and 22% of the male victims in a large survey of federal employees in the United States reported harassment by males only (Tangri, Burt, & Johnson, 1982). In both the United States and Canada, sexual harassment is now recognized as a form of sex discrimination.

Reports by women who are pioneers in male-dominated jobs suggest that they may be at special risk for sexual harassment. Studies of blue-collar women, mentioned earlier, indicate that they face resentment from coworkers and supervisors—resentment that is manifested in practical jokes, threats, violence, and sexual harassment (Cantrell, 1996; Colwill & Colwill, 1985). And six female members of the Royal Canadian Mounted Police (RCMP) caused a sensation with complaints to the press about years of being propositioned and victimized by crude sex jokes. As one woman who quit the force after 5 years commented, "I got tired of being propositioned by senior officers who thought you were a lesbian if you didn't or a slut if you did" ("RCMP Accused," 1986). Not surprisingly, RCMP records at the time showed that the resignation rate for women was 5 times higher than that of their male counterparts.

The consequences of sexual harassment can be serious, both in terms of the victim's personal well-being and her or his job performance and advancement. Gutek and Nakamura (1983) report that 17.3% of the women and 4.8% of the men in their samples had quit a job because of sexual harassment; 7.1% of the women and 2.4% of the men had missed work for the same reason. In another study, 96% of the victims of sexual harassment reported emotional stress manifested in nervousness, fear, anger, or sleeplessness; 63% developed physical reactions such as headaches, nausea, and weight losses and gains (Crull, 1980). Quid pro quo sexual harassment, with its implicit message that noncompliance will lead to reprisals, creates an intimidating and unhealthy work environment for the victim. In a precedent-setting decision, the Workers Compensation Board in Quebec ruled that extreme stress, depression, and physical symptoms caused by sexual harassment from a coworker during working hours is a work-related injury for which compensation should be paid (Lipovenko, 1985).

For victims of sexual harassment, the economic consequences may be as severe as the emotional ones. Noncompliance with the quid pro quo harasser or lodging a complaint may lead to retaliation: workloads increased, raises and promotions withheld, jobs lost, and references jeopardized. Victims who are fired or leave their jobs report that prospective employers tend to be skeptical when they cite sexual harassment as their reason for leaving previous jobs, and some have even been refused unemployment benefits (Crull, 1980). One study shows that persons who used confrontation to cope with the harassment tended to experience worse job outcomes than did others (Stockdale, 1998).

Governments, unions, and researchers acknowledge that sexual harassment is a serious problem for workers, but there is still disagreement about the kinds of behaviors that should be included as sexual harassment. Behaviors reported as harassment include actual or attempted rape or sexual assault; unwanted letters, phone calls, or materials of a sexual nature; unwanted pressure for sexual favors or for dates; unwanted deliberate touching, leaning over, cornering, or pinching; unwanted sexually suggestive looks or gestures; and unwanted sexual teasing, jokes, remarks, or questions (Tangri et al., 1982). The U.S. Equal Employment Opportunity Commission (1980) defined sexual harassment as follows:

> Unwelcome sexual advances, requests for sexual favors, and other verbal or physical conduct of a sexual nature constitutes sexual harassment when (1) submission to such conduct is made either explicitly or implicitly a term or condition of an individual's employment, (2) submission to or rejection of such conduct by an individual is used

as the basis for employment decisions affecting such individual, or (3) such conduct has the purpose or effect of unreasonably interfering with an individual's work performance or creating an intimidating, hostile, or offensive work environment. (p. 746)

Despite the presence of this and other "official" definitions of sexual harassment, however, individuals may disagree about whether a specific incident constitutes harassment, and victims of unambiguous harassment are reluctant to report it. Research findings provide some explanations of why sexual harassment is often unrecognized by anyone but the victim and why the whole problem has been ignored for so long. In one study (Cohen & Gutek, 1985), college students who were interpreting a possible case of sexual harassment placed little emphasis on variables directly related to the sexual and harassing nature of the incident (relative power of the individuals, appropriateness of the behavior) and paid more attention to the personal aspects of the incident (the degree to which the behavior in question was friendly, complimentary, or insulting) and the interpersonal relationship (amount of liking and respect) between the two parties. Furthermore, they focused on the positive aspects of the incident and tended to ignore the problematic aspects. It seems also that behavior is most likely to be labeled as sexual harassment when it violates the ordinary expectations of the actor's social role—expectations that often include the perceived power of the actor over the target. Thus, participants in a study by Pryor (1985) rated the same comment as more harassing when made by a professor than when made by a fellow student. In addition, if the actor behaved consistently toward the target over time and similarly toward other women, Pryor's research showed that participants had a greater tendency to label the behavior sexual harassment. Finally, one study shows that the frequency of the behavior is related to its perceived offensiveness, which is, in turn, related to the likelihood of reporting the harasser (Brooks & Perot, 1991). Taken together, these studies show that observers (and victims) are reluctant to conclude that sexual harassment is taking place. However, people are most likely to notice and label it harassment when the behavior seems out of role or surprising, when it is performed consistently by a particular individual, and when it occurs with more than one target person. Almost everyone perceives sexual bribery, explicit propositions, unwanted touching, or pressure for sexual activity as harassment (Frazier, Cochran, & Olson, 1995). There is more disagreement about behaviors such as sexist comments, suggestive looks, sexual jokes, and coarse language; however, these behaviors too are perceived as sexually harassing by many individuals.

Some have argued that women and men perceive incidents differentially as sexually harassing, and this argument has led to the adoption of a "reasonable woman" (as opposed to a "reasonable person") standard in the courts for determining whether a work environment is hostile enough to warrant legal action. In other words, is the work environment sufficiently hostile that a reasonable woman would find it hostile or abusive? Research shows little difference in the ways women and men define sexual harassment (Frazier et al., 1995; Gutek & O'Connor, 1995), so the reasonable woman standard may not be particularly useful.

Some people have argued that sexual harassment is simply a normal result of biology: Put women and men together in the workplace, and what can you expect? Tangri, Burt, and Johnson (1982) examined the responses of a stratified random sample of more than 20,000 federal employees to questions about their experience of sexual harassment in an effort to assess the adequacy of three explanations for its widespread existence:

- Natural social–sexual attraction
- The hierarchical way organizations are structured
- The way society stratifies power and status between women and men

They concluded that sexual harassment was not a single, unitary phenomenon and that each of the explanations was probably applicable, alone or in combination, to certain cases. The fact that women who sexually harass men are likely to be young, single, and subordinate suggests that the first explanation, social–sexual attraction, is operating in many of these cases. The fact that for both sexes being a "pioneer" in the job, being young, and needing the job badly are related to being sexually harassed supports the second explanation. Finally, the fact that women are, so much more often than men, the victims of sexual harassment lends support to the third explanation. The authors conclude that sexual harassment of women conforms more to an intimidation explanation, whereas that of men conforms more to an attraction explanation.

Other researchers have suggested that sexual harassment stems from ambivalent attitudes and stereotypes about gender that pervade many workplaces (Fiske & Glick, 1995). They note that women often encounter male coworkers whose attitudes combine **hostile sexism** (dominance-oriented paternalism, the notion that women are inferior, and hostile, dominance-oriented heterosexuality) and **benevolent sexism** (protective paternalism, the notion that women and men are different and complementary, and heterosexual intimacy motives). These attitudes, discussed in Chapter 1, can both promote harassment, albeit of different kinds. These attitudes are reinforced by organizational contexts that emphasize a masculine culture in the workplace, a scarcity of information about women, power asymmetries between women and men in the workplace, and the entry of women on a one-at-a-time, solo basis into the workforce. Each of these contextual problems can be addressed by an organization that is serious about reducing sexual harassment.

There is a popular myth that coercive and exploitative sexuality is not limited to sexual harassment but is widespread in another area: women deliberately exploiting and "selling" their sexuality for gain. Women are said to be able to reap huge professional and financial rewards by "sleeping their way to the top." One cannot help suspecting that this idea owes its popularity to a reluctance to attribute competence to women. Certainly some women *and* some men depend on their sexuality as a source of power and advancement at work. As Backhouse and Cohen (1978) point out, however, the penalties for this behavior make it a dangerous one. Not only do people who obtain their promotions, raises, and so on through sexual payoffs experience self-doubts about their own abilities but they are frequently the objects of vicious office gossip and sabotage. Moreover, for a person in this position, the end of the affair may also mean the end of the job. It appears that sexuality is only a temporary passport to power in the workplace.

Noncoercive Sexuality: Romance at Work

Fewer than 2% of top male executives in one U.S. study reported having had an affair with a woman in the office (H. J. Johnson, 1974). We have seen no comparable data on women or on nonoffice work environments. Although the actual number of "office romances" is difficult to determine, the amount of concern generated by the possibility of such liaisons is great (Mainiero, 1986, 1989). Some authors, in fact, have argued that the fear of sexual entanglements can lead to such extreme interpersonal vigilance that normal friendly relationships between female and male coworkers cannot develop (Bradford, Sargent, & Sprague, 1975; Eyler & Baridon, 1992).

Not surprisingly, proximity is a major factor in the development of romantic relationships at work (Quinn, 1977). People whose work throws them together have more opportunities to develop intimate relationships with each other. Motivation also plays a role. Robert Quinn's research shows that observers attribute office romances to three types of motives: ego (excitement, adventure, conquest), job security or advancement, or love. Three kinds of relationships were described most frequently: (1) the "fling," characterized by ego motives on the part of both participants; (2) the "utilitarian relationship," in which the female was pursuing job-related goals while the male was seeking ego satisfaction; and (3) true love, in which both participants had sincere feelings for each other.

The impact of romance in the workplace is not limited to the participants. Observers are quick with stories of how the participants in workplace romances changed for better or for worse—becoming, for example, more efficient and competent or less available than previously (Quinn, 1977). Such changes have a ripple effect on other relationships in the workplace, sometimes with disastrous results. Quinn argues that the disasters typically result from a distortion of the power and reward system created by the new relationship. He reports several cases of romances involving a male superior and a female subordinate in which the male informally increased the female's power, ignored complaints about her, and became inaccessible except through her. Coworkers who found such situations frustrating and unfair felt powerless and demoralized and resorted to tactics ranging from complaining and ostracizing to blackmailing and quitting. Some of the hostility in such cases stems from the perception that a lower ranking person has unfairly been given authority to interfere with people who are technically her superiors. Resentment may also flare when coworkers perceive that their confidences have been violated by one of the romantic partners—that, because of the special relationship, one partner is privy to information that other employees do not or should not have. The situation is fraught with potential not only for ruining employee morale but also for torpedoing the career of the subordinate in question. Apparently viewed as more dispensable, the female, who is usually subordinate, is twice as likely to be fired as the male.

Even when the office romance is between two equals, it may generate problems. It may cause traditional superior–subordinate gender roles to interfere with the equality that has been established in the workplace between, say, two vice presidents—a female and male. The sexual double standard may cause the woman to lose status and respect in the eyes of coworkers, and the man may feel angry and out of control because of his inability to protect her from slurs and vicious gossip (E. Collins, 1983).

It is with a view to dangers such as these that Margaret Mead (1980) proposed a new taboo on sex at work: "You don't make passes at or sleep with the people you work with" (p. 55). Arguing that ruling out coworkers as potential sexual partners would enable women and men to develop honest, respectful working relationships, Mead suggested that giving up sex in the workplace was an important step toward developing true equality between women and men. Whether or not her solution is correct, Mead's article clearly summarized the problem: As long as women and men relate to each other mainly in sexual terms, their attempts to work together will be filled with tension.

SUMMARY

Although both women and men have always worked, the traditional division of labor in industrialized societies has mandated that they work in different spheres: women in the private sphere of the home, men in the public (and paid) sphere of employment outside the home. Until recently, when women ventured into the world of paid employment, they were automatically relegated to low-status, low paid jobs. Although vertical and horizontal segregation of the workforce by gender still keeps most women in a few clerical and service occupations, a significant minority of women are now entering male-dominated professions. By contrast, there is a much less noticeable influx of men into female-dominated occupations.

A strong factor in the maintenance of the division of labor along gender lines has been discrimination. Sex discrimination has been manifested in a tendency to pay women less than men for the same or comparable work, to evaluate women's work performance less highly than men's, and to give preference to men over women when hiring. Some research shows that men also can sometimes be the victims of sex discrimination in evaluation and hiring when the job is defined specifically as female-appropriate. Legislation has been introduced to counteract sex discrimination in hiring and to promote pay equity between women and men. Although these legislative approaches have solved some problems (for instance, by making it more difficult for employers to practice obvious sex discrimination), they have opened the door to others. Controversies now rage about the extent to which male-dominated and female-dominated jobs are comparable in worth, and women who have been hired into male-dominated occupations find themselves dealing with all the pressures that go with token or minority status.

A second factor that helps to maintain gender-based occupational segregation is the assignment of most homemaking and child-care tasks to women, even in dual-career families. Many employed women carry a double burden of responsibility; the consequent stress, fatigue, and time pressure may well limit their capacity to take the steps necessary to move out of female-dominated occupations. However, research indicates that both women and men benefit when they take on a balance of occupational and family responsibilities. A small but growing minority of two-career couples are dividing family tasks more equitably and trying to place equal priority on the careers of both partners. Under pressure from such people, some employers are beginning to make structural changes that acknowledge and allow for the family responsibilities of their employees.

A third barrier to gender equality in the workplace has been the emphasis on sexuality in male–female relationships. Concern over the development of sexual liaisons at work has been the reason sometimes voiced for resistance to the integration of women into male-dominated occupations. Some people have little practice relating to members of the other gender on an equal footing in ways that are task-oriented and businesslike, and they fear the necessity of doing so. When sexual liaisons *do* develop between people at work, problems sometimes result—and those problems can lead to job loss for the member of the couple who has the least seniority (usually the woman). Moreover, sexual harassment is a common problem in the workplace, especially for women, and even more especially for women in token or "pioneer" positions. Such harassment can serve to keep the gender-based division of labor in place by forcing the victims from their jobs or interfering with their job performance.

Despite the barriers to gender equality in the workplace, significant steps in the direction of equality have been and continue to be achieved. Perhaps the most important change has been recognition and questioning of the barriers—a process that may eventually transform the work situation for women and men.

KEY TERMS

glass ceiling

glass escalator

equal pay for equal work

comparable worth

self-fulfilling prophecy

denial of personal
    discrimination

token positions

quid pro quo

hostile environment

hostile sexism

benevolent sexism

FOR ADDITIONAL READING

Barkalow, Cpt. Carol, with Raab, Andrea. (1990). *In the men's house: An inside account of life in the army by one of West Point's first female graduates.* New York: Poseidon. Captain Barkalow's story of her career in the army offers insights into the difficulties faced by women who try to make a place for themselves in institutions that are profoundly sexist.

Clayton, Susan D., & Crosby, Faye J. (1992). *Justice, gender, and affirmative action.* Ann Arbor: University of Michigan Press. Research on relative deprivation led these authors to the conclusion that affirmative action, which operates without the necessity for victims of discrimination to come forward on their own behalf, is a necessary policy.

Cohen, Sherry Suib. (1989). *Tender power: A revolutionary approach to work and intimacy.* Reading, MA: Addison-Wesley. The author discusses the ways the entry of women into management positions may influence how power is wielded by both women and men at high corporate levels.

England, Paula. (1992). *Comparable worth: Theories and evidence.* Hawthorne, NY: Aldine de Gruyter. Here is an overview of research on such controversial questions as how comparable worth can be decided, the economic and legal aspects of its implementation, and whether such strategies are justified.

Lowman, Margaret D. (1999). *Life in the treetops: Adventures of a woman in field biology.* New Haven, CT: Yale University Press. The author, a biologist, has been among the first to study rainforest canopies. The book tells the story of her entry into science, the way she has handled conflicts between her career and family, and her delight in her work.

Williams, Christine L. (Ed.) (1993). *Doing "women's work": Men in nontraditional occupations.* Newbury Park, CA: Sage. A provocative series of articles examines the experiences of men who work in jobs traditionally considered feminine.

CHAPTER 14

Justice, Equity, & Social Change

J ustice is often depicted in the form of a woman—a blindfolded woman holding the scales on which human deeds are balanced by their outcomes. The image says a lot about society's dominant conception of justice: the equity-based notion that people deserve outcomes (rewards or punishments) in proportion to their actions. However, the depiction of justice as a woman is more than a little ironic. A long history of pronouncements by male "experts" assert that women are morally inferior to men and less able to develop a strong, clear sense of justice unclouded by personal emotional biases. In the field of psychology, this tradition began with Sigmund Freud (1925/1974), who argued that women's weaker superego made them less capable than men of impersonal justice. Echoes of this attitude have appeared in some of the most widely accepted psychological theories of moral development.

There is another sense in which the depiction of justice as a woman is ironic. Society's formal institutions of justice—the laws and the judicial system—have been developed and dominated by men. Most lawyers and judges are still men. Women have had to struggle to be considered equal with men under the law, and many of those struggles are still under way. In Canada, women were not legally considered "persons" until 1929. In the United States, it has proved impossible so far to amend the Constitution with the words "Equality of rights under the law shall not be denied or abridged by the United States or any state on account of sex." Although 165 countries have ratified the United Nations Convention on the Elimination of All Forms of Discrimination Against Women, some nations have not yet agreed to it. It appears that, as Florynce Kennedy (1970) once noted, justice really is blind—blind to the existence of sexism.

This chapter examines various issues of justice as they pertain to gender. It begins with an overview of research on gender differences and similarities in the perception and actualization of justice. Included here is a discussion of the ways the desire to see the world as fair and just shapes people's perceptions of social arrangements, helping them to rationalize the treatment of women and men as equal even when it is clearly not. A section on gender and the law then examines some concrete results of the formal application of the justice system to women and men. Finally, the chapter closes with a discussion of the social change that might result from the challenges posed by the feminist movement to society's traditional notions of justice.

GENDER AND CONCEPTIONS OF JUSTICE

Two streams of research within the field of psychology have examined the relationship between gender and conceptions of justice: studies of reward allocation and studies of moral development. Both areas reveal evidence for both differences and similarities between women and men.

Reward Allocation and Personal Entitlement: Equity or Equality?

Differences between women and men in the way they allocate rewards to themselves and to others have been found consistently. In general, women tend to pay themselves less than men do when dividing rewards between themselves and others (Kahn, O'Leary, Krulewitz, & Lamm, 1980; Major, 1987; Major & Deaux, 1982). Women report as much satisfaction with their jobs as men do, despite the fact that they tend to hold jobs that are lower status and more poorly paid than men's (American Management Association, 1999; Cox & Harquail, 1991). In fact, Brenda Major (1994) notes that many women experience a "paradoxical contentment": They report being satisfied with their situation and seemingly do not regard as illegitimate any gender inequalities they may notice. In addition, there is a tendency for women to favor an equality norm in the distribution of rewards for task performance, allocating the same degree of reward to each participant, whereas men tend to favor an equity norm, allocating rewards differentially according to task performance (Major & Adams, 1983). Also, men report more satisfaction than women do with an exchange relationship that is equitable (Brockner & Adsit, 1986). It has sometimes been argued that these differences in reward allocation stem from the socialization of women to be more interpersonally oriented than men are, so that women place more emphasis on maintaining good relationships with their coworkers than on getting a fair share of the reward (Kahn et al., 1980). A second possible explanation is that women and men differ in their own personal feelings of entitlement—of what is a fair reward for their efforts (Major, 1987; Major, McFarlin, & Gagnon, 1984).

Studies have shown that women's standards of what is fair pay for themselves are lower than those of men (Callahan-Levy & Messe, 1979; Major et al., 1984). When women and men are asked to work on a task for a period of time and then to assign themselves fair pay for their performance, women pay themselves significantly less money than men pay themselves, and they also report that less money is fair pay for their work. This happens even when men and women do not differ in their evaluations of their own performance. Moreover, when asked to do as much work as they think is fair for a given amount of money, women work longer, do more work, and perform more correctly and efficiently than men do (Major et al., 1984). Many plausible explanations have been offered for these findings. Perhaps women have lower expectations for pay because of the history of wage discrimination against them. Or perhaps women tend to compare themselves to other women—a lower reference group standard than men because women typically are paid less than men. A third possibility is that women and men may place different values on rewards. Women may value money less and interpersonal relationships more than men do. Yet another perspective is that women are more likely than men to devalue their own work and hence to underreward it, or, conversely, that men overvalue and overreward their own work. Finally, it has been suggested that gender-role socialization leads women to see a weaker connection than men do between their work and pay.

All of these explanations may have some merit in particular situations, and several have received some experimental support. Major and her colleagues (1984) found that gender differences in personal entitlement did not occur when information was available about the pay of other people—a finding that suggests that women are no more likely than men to pay themselves less than others whom they see as comparable. These researchers did find evidence, however, that when no obviously appropriate comparison group was available people tended to use generalized same-sex comparisons. People seemed to match their behavior to what they thought others of their own sex would do—and both women and men thought women would pay themselves less than men for the same work and that women would work longer than men given the same pay.

This study also provides evidence that women tend to undervalue and men to overvalue their own work. Although women did more and better work than men for the specified amount of pay, men and women did not differ in the value they assigned to their own work or in their satisfaction with their pay. However, no evidence was found to support the notion that men value money more than women do; there were no gender differences in the importance ascribed to the money earned.

Finally, this research also shows that gender differences, not only in personal entitlement but also in interpersonal orientation, may have something to do with women's and men's allocation of rewards to themselves. Women, but not men, worked longer when they knew they were being observed by the experimenter—a finding that suggests that women's balancing of work inputs with pay outcomes was more influenced by concerns about making a good impression or pleasing the experimenter than men's was. However, the fact that women overworked or underpaid themselves relative to men in all conditions, even when not being observed, indicates that gender differences in interpersonal orientation are not enough to explain the tendency for men to allocate more rewards to themselves than women do.

Continuing research in this area has shown that people tend to prefer same-sex wage comparison information when deciding whether or not they are being paid fairly. In one study, even when the disadvantaged status of their own gender group was made clear, and when wage comparison information for both females and males were equally available (and equally unavoidable), women were more influenced by same-sex than by cross-sex comparisons in deciding the amount they thought they should be paid, how well they thought they had performed, and how satisfied they were with their pay (Bylsma & Major, 1994). However, there are apparently some limits to the tendency to rely on same-gender comparisons. When participants in one study were led to believe wage allocation procedures were biased, their entitlement beliefs were weighted more heavily by their perceptions of their own performance than by comparisons with other women (Bylsma, Major, & Cozzarelli, 1995).

The tendency for women and men, when not provided with any comparison information, to think that they deserve differing amounts of pay for the same work apparently does not have a single cause, but many. Most of these causes, however, are probably traceable to a social structure that has traditionally provided fewer tangible rewards to women than to men for their work. If there is a norm, accepted by both sexes, that women expect less pay than men do for the same amount of work, that norm did not emerge in a vacuum but from many generations of social consensus.

Gender differences in reward allocation extend beyond individuals' allocations to themselves. Researchers have found that, at least under some conditions, men and women differ in the way they distribute rewards to other people, such as coworkers and subordinates. Gender differences in this behavior are not always found, but when they do appear they show men favoring a distribution system in which people are rewarded in proportion to their work inputs (equity) and women favoring a system in which people are rewarded equally, regardless of differences in work inputs (equality). The most popular explanation for this difference has been that women have been socialized to be more concerned with interpersonal relations than men have, and so they distribute rewards in ways that will maintain interpersonal harmony rather than emphasize differences in performance. This explanation has received some support. However, situational factors are also apparently very important in determining the way women and men distribute rewards. For example, Major and Adams (1983) found that even when men and women were equivalent in their scores on a questionnaire measure of interpersonal orientation women still tended to allocate rewards more equally than men did. Zanna and Bowden (1977) showed that both women and men allocated rewards equally when relating to others as persons, but equitably when relating to others as positions or roles. Nevertheless, when the situation was ambiguous, traditional males allocated equitably and traditional females allocated equally. Another study showed that when pressured to improve their group's productivity males, but not females, allocated rewards more equitably; when pressured to improve worker relationships, females, but not males, tended to allocate rewards more equally (Stake, 1985). Finally, Major and Adams (1984) showed that under certain conditions women relied more heavily on equity, distributing rewards more in proportion to merit, than men did. The crucial factor was whether people were dividing a shared reward between themselves and their partner or whether they were allocating independent rewards to themselves and their partner (that is, when the allocation they made to themselves did not affect the allocation to their partner, and vice versa). Both women and men divided the reward more equally when asked to divide a joint reward than when asked to allocate independent rewards to themselves and their partner. Surprisingly, however, when participants were allocating rewards separately to themselves and their partners, women allocated the rewards more in proportion to merit than men did. The researchers speculate that women do not ignore merit or different levels of performance when giving out rewards; rather, they are uncomfortable when rewarding themselves for better performance means their partner will receive less. When some of the stigma of taking more for the self is removed by making the two allocations independent, women are more comfortable differentiating between their performance and that of their partner by giving themselves a larger reward. The study does not explain *why* women should be more sensitive than men to the negative connotations of taking more for oneself at the expense of someone else, even in the case where this can be justified by better performance. It does, however, point to the importance of such situational factors as the privacy of allocation decisions, the expectation of future interactions with the partner, and the nature of the reward on the justice decisions of both men and women. It may well be that situational factors in reward allocation settings provide cues about what behavior is appropriate for both genders. When researchers have identified all of these cues, we may be in a better position to explain the gender differences in reward allocation.

Regardless of the reasons for gender differences in justice decisions, the existence of such differences in certain situations has some interesting possible implications. In the workplace, for example, what might the implications be if male and female managers favored equity and equality, respectively, in dealing with the performance of their subordinates? Perhaps the subordinates of the female manager would be more cooperative with one another and less inclined to compete than the subordinates of the male manager would. Or perhaps the subordinates of the female manager would be demoralized and resentful, knowing that their less competent coworkers were being rewarded equally with themselves. Without knowing more about the specific organizational context and the people involved, it is impossible to predict the outcome. As yet, however, there is very little evidence from such field situations about whether, in fact, male and female managers do differ in their preference for equity or equality when dealing with subordinates. Most of the research on reward allocation has been done in laboratory situations using college students as participants, and one study that has focused specifically on justice in manager–subordinate relations is no exception. In this study, Dobbins (1986) asked students to play the role of a manager who must choose what corrective action should be taken toward an employee who demonstrated poor performance by making two serious shipping errors. He found that the males relied solely on equity to decide what corrective action should be taken, responding most harshly when poor performance appeared to be caused by the employee's disposition rather than by situational factors. Females, however, used a mixture of equity and equality in their corrective action decisions. Although they too were harshest with the employee when the error appeared to be that individual's fault, they were also, in contrast to the men, more influenced in their decisions by the likeableness and gender of the employee. Female "managers" were less harsh when the employee was female or likeable; male "managers" were not influenced by these factors. This study has many limitations. The participants had no real management experience, the situation was hypothetical, and there was no actual contact with a subordinate but only a written description of the subordinate's behavior. It cannot be used to draw conclusions about the behavior of real male and female managers, but it raises some issues worthy of further investigation.

On the whole, research on the way females and males allocate rewards to themselves and others shows that men and women have learned to take different perspectives toward distributive justice in particular situations. The differences in behavior may reflect differences in the sense of personal entitlement or deserving, differences in interpersonal orientation, or differential sensitivity to particular social cues—but what these latter differences reflect is not yet clear. Major and her colleagues' (1984) argument that the gender differences stem from individuals' attempts to match their behavior with their awareness of norms for their own sex is a persuasive one—and, as long as it is normative to reward women at lower rates than men, it signals real, not theoretical, problems for women. Research shows that initial expectations for pay tend to be self-confirming; that is, expecting and requesting a high salary tends to be associated with *receiving* a higher salary (Major, Vanderslice, & McFarlin, 1984). Women, expecting lower salaries, may keep on getting exactly what they expect.

GENDER INEQUALITY AND THE PERCEPTION OF JUSTICE   The finding that both women and men tend to subscribe to norms that women will be rewarded less for their work or will do more work for less pay is congruent with many of the other findings discussed in this book. There appears to be a great deal of acceptance and rationalization of situations that amount to sex discrimination. How are people able to square their acceptance of such situations with their notions of justice?

If there is one general principle that cognitive social psychology has demonstrated, it is that human beings are capable of Olympic feats of rationalization. When people see a situation that they either cannot or do not wish to change, they are extremely good at thinking up reasons that situation is fair. For example, research has shown that people have a need to believe the world is a just place where people generally get what they deserve (Lerner, 1970, 1974). Individuals often seem to satisfy this need by seeing victims as, by definition, deserving of the harm inflicted on them. Such a general tendency may provide a partial explanation for accepting discrimination against women. Men and women may justify discrimination by believing women's work is less valuable than men's, that women are less competent, need money less, or are less interested in their work than men are. As long as people can think of reasons women *deserve* less than men, their belief in a just world can coexist comfortably with their awareness of sex discrimination.

A parallel explanation for the acceptance of female subordination stems from the study of the relationship between power and justice. As noted in Chapter 12, the group with the most power in a hierarchy not only gains control of more resources than other groups but also evolves a social philosophy that supports its right to monopolize these resources (Walster & Walster, 1975). According to equity theory, this philosophy will tend to become accepted by the entire community as justification for the status quo; if the entire group accepts the status quo, everyone avoids the discomfort of a relationship viewed as inequitable or unfair. Research has shown that both exploiters and victims can and frequently do convince themselves that even the most unbalanced of exchanges is perfectly fair (Walster, Berscheid, & Walster, 1973). The ideology of dominance tends to be self-perpetuating: The more power a group obtains, the more its members convince themselves and others that such power is deserved and stems from superiority. For many people, recognizing that a system that

discriminates against women is unfair is tantamount to admitting that their own decisions and actions have been unfair or that they have been victims of unfair treatment—
possibilities that, according to equity theory, can result in considerable discomfort for
individuals on both sides of the equation.

The Perceived In/Justice of Affirmative Action

If women feel uncomfortable taking more reward for themselves, even when their performance is better, how do they respond to a system that gives them any form of special treatment just because they are women? If people have learned to rationalize a
situation in which men dominate the positions that are highest in status and pay by
thinking that men are more competent, more ambitious, and more suitable for leadership than women, how do they react to a system that is explicitly designed to wear
down such gender inequalities? Researchers who have studied the social psychology of
affirmative action have found a complex set of answers to these questions.

Affirmative action refers to a set of strategies to increase the proportion of
women and minorities hired by organizations or admitted into universities, particularly in fields from which they have traditionally been excluded. Such strategies may
include special outreach programs and recruitment efforts and special opportunities
for training directed at underrepresented groups. The programs are designed to bring
the level of opportunity for underrepresented groups up to the level that it has historically been for well-represented groups.

Not surprisingly, research shows that the men who are most likely to be supportive of affirmative action for women are those who are aware of and unhappy about the
discrimination directed at women (Tougas & Veilleux, 1989). However, these men do
not support all affirmative action programs equally. They are more supportive of programs in which the main goals involve elimination of systematic barriers against
women than of those that involve preferential hiring or promotion.

At least one study shows that, despite years of sex discrimination, women are
less comfortable than men are with accepting the preferential treatment implied by
affirmative action. In this laboratory study, women and men were told that they had
been selected as task leaders either on the basis of merit or preferentially on the basis of their gender (Heilman, Simon, & Repper, 1987). Women's, but not men's
self-perceptions and self-evaluations were negatively affected by the gender-based
preferential selection method in comparison to the merit-based method. When told
they had been selected as leaders because of their gender, women devalued their
leadership performance, took less credit for success, described themselves as more
deficient in leadership skills, and reported less interest in continuing as leader. Men
were plagued by no such self-doubts when told they had been selected on the basis of their gender.

Women are the largest group to benefit from affirmative action, yet they are often not vocal in their support of it. One explanation for this silence is suggested by
the study just described. Perhaps women, who have been socialized to have more
doubts about their competence than men, are especially vulnerable to the adverse
effects of preferential selection based on non-work-related criteria because they want
and need the assurance and self-confidence that come with the knowledge that they

have been selected or promoted on their merits. Other possible explanations may lie in women's lower sense of entitlement and their preference for equality-based rather than equity-based reward distribution. It appears that one key factor lies in whether or not women are aware that they themselves and women as a group are targets of discrimination.

Faye Crosby (1984) has argued that women often engage in a **denial of personal discrimination**: the perception by individual women that they themselves are being treated fairly, even though they may acknowledge the existence of discrimination against women as a group. There are a number of possible reasons for this denial, including the lack of relevant comparison information, such as the salaries and work histories of comparable male employees, and the unwillingness to believe that a well-regarded supervisor has supported or tolerated discriminatory treatment. However, if a woman is confronted with the necessary information, she may experience **personal relative deprivation**: a sense of dissatisfaction stemming from a comparison with others who are being more highly rewarded. She may also, if she has not already done so, experience a sense of **collective relative deprivation**: a feeling of dissatisfaction due to perceived inequities between one's own and a more advantaged group (Runciman, 1966).

Research shows that women who feel personally and collectively deprived relative to men are likely to support affirmative action policies (Beaton & Tougas, 1997; Tougas, Brown, Beaton, & St-Pierre, 1999; Tougas & Veilleux, 1988). What leads to this sense of deprivation? Women who identify strongly with women as a group are more likely to feel a sense of collective relative deprivation (Tougas & Veilleux, 1988), as are women who have been in organizations where affirmative action policies that have been in place for some time have still not produced significant progress in women's representation (Beaton & Tougas, 1997). Finally, the experience of personally encountering discriminatory barriers when trying to move into nontraditional jobs or higher level positions leads to the experience of collective relative deprivation, which leads, in turn, to support for affirmative action (Tougas et al., 1999).

Women often resist seeing the injustices of discriminatory treatment directed against them, and they may also resist remedies for these injustices that, because they involve preferential treatment, may themselves appear unjust. Yet women's tendency to be more than fair to others and their caution about taking "more than they deserve" is modified when they are confronted with clear instances of personal or group discrimination. Under such circumstances, women become more likely to view affirmative action policies as legitimate mechanisms for rectifying injustices toward women.

Moral Development and Moral Reasoning

Several psychological theories have postulated that males and females differ in the way they develop moral reasoning, the ability to make judgments about right and wrong. Freud's (1925/1974) psychoanalytic theory suggested that because of differences in the resolution of the Oedipal complex (see Chapter 2) males develop a superego that is more internalized, rigid, and demanding than that of females, with the consequence that the moral character of men is more strongly defined than is that of women. Piaget's (1965) cognitive developmental theory of morality posited a similar belief in male moral superiority. He argued that equity, which involves taking into account the personal circumstances of each individual, was a more useful and advanced form of justice than equality, and Piaget noted that boys prefer equity and girls prefer equality.

Perhaps the best known theory of moral development was elaborated by Lawrence Kohlberg (1964, 1984). This theory proposes that moral development progresses through three levels in six stages, the highest of which is not reached until adulthood, or may never be reached. Individuals progress from basing moral judgments on fear of consequences to themselves, to basing them on concern for social approval, harmony, and law and order, to basing them on abstract principles of universal rights for all persons. Kohlberg indicates that most women and men develop at least to the middle, conventional level of moral reasoning, but that, within this level, women prefer Stage 3 reasoning based on good intentions and social approval and men prefer the more advanced Stage 4 reasoning based on maintaining the social order. Furthermore, men are more likely than women to reach the highest level of moral reasoning; women supposedly do not reach these top two stages unless they take on occupational positions similar to men's. Otherwise, "while girls are moving from high school or college to motherhood, sizeable proportions of them are remaining at Stage 3, while their male agemates are dropping Stage 3 in favor of the stages above it. Stage 3 morality is a functional morality for housewives and mothers; it is not for businessmen and professionals" (Kohlberg & Kramer, 1969, p. 108).

Kohlberg's theory reflects some strong biases, not only about males and females and the moral requirements of their respective roles but also about the superiority of certain kinds of moral reasoning. The possibility that different forms of moral reasoning might be equally useful and valid is not acknowledged in his theory. Furthermore, the theory was developed using data only from males; thus, males provide the standard for what is humanly normal. Psychologist Carol Gilligan (1982) proposed a new cognitive developmental theory of morality in an effort to correct the masculine bias of this and other theories.

GILLIGAN'S THEORY: TWO MORAL PRINCIPLES   When Gilligan analyzed the responses made by girls and women to questions about morality, she did not limit herself to looking for the kinds of themes that would indicate stages of moral development according to Kohlberg's theory. Rather, she tried to find out whether there were themes in women's moral reasoning that had been missed by Kohlberg's scoring system. Her research led her to suggest that besides the principle of rights that had emerged as the basis of moral reasoning in Kohlberg's work another principle was frequently invoked as her respondents struggled to explain why a particular decision was right or wrong: the principle of caring and responsibility. Moral judgments based on the principle of caring stressed the necessity to be responsible in one's relationships, to be sensitive to the needs of others, and to avoid giving hurt. Gilligan's research led her to conclude that there were stages in the development of the care orientation to morality just as there were stages in the development of the rights orientation. Individuals moved from an initial stage of caring only for the self, to a middle stage of trying to be "good" by caring for others (sometimes called maternal morality by Gilligan because it is the type of morality that is urged on women in their maternal role), to a mature stage of caring for truth, which involves achieving a balance of care for the self and others.

Although both the **rights orientation** and the **care orientation** can be found in the moral reasoning of women and men, Gilligan argues that men tend to place more emphasis on rights, and women place more emphasis on care. The difference in emphasis, she suggests, is due to the different goals of development for women and men: attachment and relationship for women, separation and achievement for men. The goals are different because the problems and challenges faced by females are different from those faced by men, partly because society expects different things from them and partly because their biological differences make them vulnerable to different experiences in the area of reproduction. Gilligan argues, however, that neither the rights orientation nor the care orientation represents a superior type of moral reasoning. Rather, they are different, in some sense complementary, orientations: "two disparate modes of experience that are in the end connected. . . . In the representation of maturity, both perspectives converge in the realization that just as inequality adversely affects both parties in an unequal relationship, so too violence is destructive for everyone involved" (p. 174).

Many people have found Gilligan's theory appealing, but others have criticized it for reifying the stereotype that women are emotional and nurturant and men are logical and clearheaded. Although agreeing that her contribution has been immense in drawing attention to the dimension of care and responsibility in moral judgments, many investigators have been more cautious in accepting her claim that women and men differ in their reliance on this orientation. In recent years, careful investigations have been made of both Kohlberg's and Gilligan's theories with respect to gender differences.

L. J. Walker (1984) performed a meta-analysis of studies on moral reasoning as measured by Kohlberg's interview method in 106 samples of children, adolescents, and adults. Of all these samples, only 8 clearly indicated significant differences favoring males. Moreover, several of these 8 were inconclusive because gender was confounded with occupational–educational differences. Walker suggests that rather than arguing over the extent to which gender bias is inherent in Kohlberg's theory it would be more appropriate to ask why, in the face of so little evidence, the myth persists that males are more advanced in Kohlberg's levels of moral reasoning than females are. He concludes that, in fact, the moral reasoning of men and women is remarkably similar, especially given publication and reporting biases that make differences more likely to be reported.

The failure to find empirical confirmation for the notion that males operate at higher levels of moral reasoning than females do is echoed in a meta-analysis of 56 samples including over 6000 subjects (Thoma, 1986). The findings showed that at every age and educational level small but reliable gender differences appeared—with females scoring significantly higher than males on moral reasoning.

Another review of the literature on moral development, this one including not only studies using Kohlberg's measure but also those using a variety of other measures, found that 60% of the studies found no differences between males and females with respect to moral development (Lifton, 1985). Among the studies that did report a significant male–female difference in moral development, most used Kohlberg's measure, and the differences sometimes favored females, particularly for children. In his own research, Lifton (1985) found no evidence of male–female differences in moral development among adolescents or adults, using either Kohlberg's measure of moral judgment or his own measure of moral character. He did, however, find significant differences in stage of moral judgment between masculine and feminine persons of both sexes, suggesting that Kohlberg's measure may favor masculine over feminine persons.

Researchers who have taken a longitudinal approach to the development of moral and prosocial reasoning among adolescents suggest that gender differences in maturity may be mistaken for differences in moral reasoning (Eisenberg, Miller, Shell, McNalley, & Shea, 1991). When they followed a sample of adolescents over an 11-year period, they found that girls used other-oriented, self-reflective modes of reasoning earlier than boys did, but within 2 years the boys had caught up. Girls did show a higher level of moral reasoning overall, a finding the researchers attribute partly to the tendency of high school boys to use more hedonistic reasoning and to make fewer socially responsible choices than girls at this age.

Some researchers have tried specifically to evaluate Gilligan's theory that an ethic of care is more prevalent among women and an ethic of rights is more prevalent among men. Gilligan and Attanucci (1988), using real-life dilemmas, found that women and men used both care and justice orientations. But care-focus dilemmas were more likely to be presented by women, and justice-focus dilemmas were more likely to be presented by men. Stiller and Forrest (1990) also found that men emphasized justice and women emphasized care in their moral reasoning. Similar findings have been reported by Yacker and Weinberg (1990) using hypothetical childhood dilemmas. Skoe and Diessner (1994) found that use of the ethic of care was more strongly related to identity for women than for men. However, another study by Skoe and her colleagues found that gender-role orientation was a better predictor of care-oriented moral reasoning than gender was (Sochting, Skoe, & Marcia, 1994). Other studies that have examined individuals' moral reasoning about competitive athletic encounters (Crown & Heatherington, 1989) and interpersonal relationships (Pratt, Pancer, & Hunsberger, 1990) have found no gender differences in such reasoning. One study investigated moral reasoning among African American working class adolescents and adults found no evidence for a gender difference in care and rights orientations (Stack, 1997).

Ford and Lowery (1986) conducted a study specifically designed to compare women and men on their use of the principles of rights and care in their moral judgments. They asked male and female undergraduates to describe three important moral conflicts in their lives and to rate the importance of those conflicts and the degree of difficulty they experienced in deciding what to do. Next, the students read summary descriptions of the rights and care orientations to moral judgment and rated, on a 7-point scale, the degree to which each orientation was a part of their own approach to the conflicts they had described. They also completed a measure of gender-role orientation and a scale evaluating the two moral orientations along good–bad, powerful–weak, and active–passive dimensions. The results of the study offered some, but not overwhelming, support for Gilligan's theory. Men and women did not differ significantly in the degree to which they used the rights and care orientations. However, women were more consistent from one conflict to the next in their use of the care orientation than in their use of the rights orientation; men were more consistent in their use of the rights than of the care orientation. Interestingly, for both female and male participants, the importance and difficulty ratings for the conflict situations were significantly associated with care ratings but not with rights ratings. For this college student sample, the most important and difficult moral decisions encountered so far had been related more to issues of care than to issues of rights. A later study (Friedman, Robinson, & Friedman, 1987), which also found a lack of support for Gilligan's hypothesis that gender is related to differences in moral judgments, similarly suggests that Gilligan is correct in her proposal that care is a distinct and important dimension of moral reasoning.

One longitudinal study that examined the possibility of gender differences in care and responsibility orientations suggests that, for most individuals, there is little consistency in these orientations over time (L. J. Walker, 1989). This study, in which persons ages 5 to 63 were interviewed twice, 2 years apart, revealed no gender differences in justice and care orientations for children and adolescents, and none at any age using standard moral dilemmas. The only gender difference found was among adults using real-life dilemmas—for whom there was a tendency for women to use the care orientation more frequently. This gender difference in orientation appeared to be confounded with a gender difference in the content of the real-life dilemmas recalled by the respondents. Women were more likely to recall personal, as opposed to impersonal, real-life moral dilemmas—and, for both women and men, personal dilemmas were strongly associated with the use of the care orientation.

In the Ford and Lowery (1986) study, although females and males did not differ significantly in their use of the care and rights orientations, both groups rated the care orientation as a feminine response and the rights orientation as a masculine response. It appears that the belief in different styles of moral judgment for women and men existed even in this sample where only minimal evidence for such female–male differences could be found. This finding brings us back to the question posed by L. J. Walker (1984): Why does the belief in gender differences in moral reasoning persist so strongly in the face of such weak or contradictory evidence? Brabeck (1983) addresses the question of why so many people find an intuitive appeal to Gilligan's theory, despite its lack of clear empirical support. She notes that stereotypes about gender differences in morality abound; for instance, studies have found that girls and boys develop different reputations for altruism, even when their actual behavior is very similar (Shigetomi, Hartmann, & Gilford, 1981). In some way, she suggests, a belief that males and females are morally different meets our cultural and emotional needs—but it does so by distorting our vision of human beings:

> There is an essential tension between autonomy and interdependence, between the requirements of justice and the demands of mercy, between absolute moral principles and situation specific moral action, between reason and affect. To resolve this tension by assigning half to males and half to females when evidence does not support that division is to reduce the complexity of morality, to cloud truth with myth, to do an injustice to the capacities of both sexes and to lose an opportunity to revise and modify our theories of morality. (Brabeck, 1983, p. 287)

Although the last word is certainly not in on the possibility of gender differences in moral orientation (for example, it may be that the situations men experience as moral conflicts are more likely to involve rights and those women experience as conflicts are more likely to involve care), the evidence to date suggests that women and men are unlikely to bring very different principles of moral judgment to any particular moral dilemma. The controversy continues to stimulate research, and thus far it has had the effect of broadening our understanding of moral reasoning and of conferring new respect on a dimension of morality that, whether it actually differentiates the sexes or not, has always been trivialized because it was stereotyped as feminine.

GENDER AND THE LAW

Social notions of justice are formalized into a legal system of laws and courts that, in the tradition of justice as "blind," are supposed to treat everyone with equal favor, regardless of economic, social, or political status. Not surprisingly, however, this formal justice system reflects and even perpetuates the prevalent stereotypes and prejudices about gender. Such biases are evident in the induction of lawyers and judges into the system, in laws concerning the rights of women and men, and in the treatment of male and female criminals and victims who come into contact with the legal system.

Participation in the Legal System: Lawyers and Judges

Early in this century, when women in Canada were petitioning for the opportunity to become lawyers, one judge ruled that their exclusion was perfectly reasonable. His rationale: a "lady lawyer" would have to subject her delicate ears to courtroom testimony concerning rape—a subject about which no woman should have to hear (L. Smith, 1987). In 1873, a woman named Myra Bradwell was barred from practicing law in Illinois because, the judge said, woman's natural place was in the home (Agate & Meacham, 1977) and also because the state restricted the right of married women to make legally binding contracts. No client would want to deal with an attorney who could not be held accountable for the agreements she signed. The law in this case placed women in a frustrating double bind: first, by limiting their accountability for their actions, and second, by acting to protect others from the consequences of this lack of accountability.

Although women have now been admitted to the practice of law, they are still hampered by the stereotype that women are more emotional and less rational than men in their orientation toward justice. Women are still a definite minority among lawyers and judges, although their numbers are increasing. In 1990, 21% of U.S. lawyers and judges combined were women (Kaufman, 1995). By 1997, women were 24% of the lawyers in the United States, 19% of federal judges, 14% of partners in law firms, 8% of law school deans, and 19% of full professors in law schools (American Bar Association, 1998). In both the United States and Canada, there are two women justices on the Supreme Court.

The gender distribution of positions in the legal profession is changing; 44% of law school students in the United States are women. However, female lawyers face different career patterns than their male colleagues. They tend to be clustered in the less prestigious areas of the law: family law, trust and estates, and tax law (Kaufman, 1995). In addition, they face discrimination, gender disparagement, and sexual harassment on the job (Rosenberg, Perlstadt, & Phillips, 1993). Female lawyers report feeling marginalized by behavior that emphasizes their "token" status in the profession: receiving compliments for their appearance but not for their handling of a case, hearing sexist jokes and remarks from judges and attorneys, and being patronized, called by their first names, and asked whether they are lawyers (MacCorquodale & Jensen, 1993). In addition, one study shows that more than a quarter of the difference in earnings of female and male lawyers can be attributed to gender discrimination (Hagan, 1990).

Reports show that all is not yet clear sailing for women in law school. McIntyre (1987), in a searching and painful description of her first year on the faculty of a prestigious Canadian law school, describes experiences of hostility and harassment from male students and colleagues in response to her feminist views. Particularly instructive, in view of the issues of power already discussed in this book, is her description of how female law students were silenced and intimidated when they tried to articulate feminist arguments or when they challenged traditional legal approaches to particular problems. For example, two women in her seminar on labor law expressed discomfort with the assumptions of adversarial relations and conflict built into the working model of labor law and labor relations that the class was using. They were interrupted, contradicted, and shouted down by male students:

> I . . . asked the class to reflect on what had just happened. Two usually silent women had spoken and explained why they had trouble participating. One was interrupted and called "wrong"; then the subject was changed; then their contribution was characterized as non-law. I suggested their contributions introduced an alternative model of law and labor relations which we might try to explore. Again there was an uproar. I was shouted down by the left-wing male and denounced as a "bourgeois feminist". . . . I proposed we draw up two models for a first contract: one under the working model premised on conflict, power, inequality, and private property; the other premised on codetermination, communal interests, and equality. . . . About five male students put down their pens, pulled back their chairs and glared at me, refusing to participate. No one invited the two women who had advanced an alternative model to articulate what their vision might include. They went silent. A few men ventured some possibilities, but were met with open anger from other men who interrupted, laughed, or talked over them. (p. 8)

This example illustrates just how difficult it can be for female students, even with the support of a female professor, to challenge the structure or built-in assumptions of a legal system that has always been articulated and dominated by men.

Such difficulties are not unique to law schools, of course, but they may be aggravated in the law school atmosphere of adversarial justice. A reading of McIntyre's article makes it painfully clear that women who survive law school may have had much of their interest in questioning established legal assumptions and priorities ground out of them in the process. And progress since her article appeared has been slow. In 1994/95 hearings at 58 law schools, the American Bar Association's Commission on Women in the Profession found persistent reports of gender stereotyping, sexual harassment, and hostile and disrespectful behavior toward female faculty. They heard descriptions of a male faculty member calling his female students "little girl" and "sweetie" and stories of male students calling female faculty members inadequate and bitchy and testing them with repeated interruptions (American Bar Association, 1998). It appears that women entering the legal profession, although increasing in numbers, still face considerable resistance.

Sex, Gender, and Legal Rights

In 1986, the Ontario Court of Appeal in Canada ruled that Justine Blainey, a 12-year-old girl who had been chosen to play on a first-class hockey team in Toronto but had been barred from play by the Ontario Hockey Association, could legally play on the team. This was the first sex equality case to be decided by an appeal court under Canada's then new *Charter of Rights and Freedoms,* and it is one highly publicized example of how sex discrimination can be fought by legal means (Brodsky, 1986).

Several years later, in a decision with far-reaching implications, the U.S. Supreme Court ruled that companies may not use "fetal protection" as a reason to bar women of childbearing age from jobs that pose reproductive hazards (Marcus, 1991). The case involved a Milwaukee-based battery manufacturer that barred female employees from jobs that exposed them to high levels of lead. (Lead can damage a developing fetus.) The legal action was brought on behalf of a 50-year-old divorced woman who was transferred from her position and another who chose to be sterilized to keep her job. The Court held that it was illegal for a company to force a woman to decide between having a child and having a job and noted that discrimination on the basis of a person's ability to become pregnant amounted simply to a form of sex discrimination.

In recent years, we have seen an escalation of efforts, international in scope, to achieve equal rights under the law for women and men. A major push has been made toward the adoption by all countries of the United Nations Convention on the Elimination of All Forms of Discrimination Against Women (CEDAW). This convention includes, among other things, the assurance that women and men will be equal before the law, including laws governing property and contracts, have equal rights to family benefits and bank credit, have the same rights and responsibilities during marriage and its dissolution, and have equal pay for work of equal value. At this writing, 165 countries, including Canada but not including the United States, have ratified this convention (United Nations, 1999). By ratifying the convention, a country makes a commitment to pass legislation and promote policies congruent with the treaty's conditions and to submit periodic progress reports on the status of women and the implementation of the treaty. Canada ratified this treaty in 1981; the most recent countries to ratify it are Niger and Tuvalu, in October of 1999. The United States signed, but did not ratify, the treaty in 1980. By this action, this country agreed to do nothing in contravention of the treaty's terms, but did *not* agree to actively implement the treaty. The other countries that have signed, but refused to ratify, the treaty are Afghanistan and Sao Tome and Principe.

Within North America, attempts to promote equality under the law for men and women have frequently foundered on arguments about what definition of "equality" is most appropriate. This argument turns on the perception of justice: Although a group of individuals may agree that women and men should be treated the same way under the law in many circumstances, they may disagree about which legal distinctions between the sexes, if any, should be preserved. The problem is a difficult one, because, as discussed earlier in this chapter, perceptions of fairness are so often conditioned by what we are used to and by "the way things have always been." As an illustration of this point, consider the following list of situations in which the law, in certain jurisdictions, discriminates on the basis of sex:

- Certain social service benefits are available to mothers who stay home with their children but not to fathers who do the same thing.
- The child of a married couple can be given the father's surname but not the mother's.
- The father of a child born out of wedlock can be sued by the mother for the support of the child; however, a father who has custody of a child born out of wedlock cannot initiate similar proceedings against the mother.

- "Protective" labor laws in some jurisdictions establish a maximum number of hours a woman may work.
- Proposed legislation in several states would deny custodial single parents, 95% of whom are women, increases in welfare benefits if they have additional children and would allow married couples to retain more of their earnings than single-parent families.

For years such laws have seemed so "natural" that few people considered them unfair, despite their discrimination on the basis of sex. It is only in consciously stepping back from traditional assumptions about sex differences and gender roles that people become aware of the arbitrariness of laws such as these.

Within the legal system, a debate is still going on about how gender equality should be defined under the law. There are at least three perspectives (Lahey, 1984). The first is *absolute equality,* which would require legislation to be sex-blind and gender-neutral and to deny the existence of any meaningful differences between women and men, with the exception of reproductive differences. A feminist-inspired variation on this perspective is the *sex-specific/gender-neutral* approach, which would try to achieve equality by drafting legislation specifically geared to the needs of women as a disadvantaged group, but written using such neutral terms as "parent" and "spouse" so that protections and benefits would be available to both women and men. A second alternative is the *gender-specific* approach, which acknowledges biological, social, and economic differences between the sexes and recognizes women as a disadvantaged group. This approach would strike down legislation that was detrimental to women but would retain provisions that were beneficial to women to redress the inequalities between women and men. The third possibility is *equality with recognition of real differences.* This would involve a standard in which equal treatment is the norm, but strong statistical evidence that women and men are in unequal positions can be used to uphold unequal treatment. This third standard reflects the current reasoning applied by the U.S. Supreme Court.

All of these approaches to gender equality have potential pitfalls. The problem with a gender-specific approach to equality is that gender-specific legislation can be used in the service of inequality as well as equality. For example, the recognition that women as a group are physically weaker than men has in the past been used to construct gender-specific legislation that "protected" women from being hired for jobs that required lifting heavy loads. The sex-specific/gender-neutral approach, despite its neutral language, could possibly reinforce existing gender stereotypes. For instance, laws designed to meet the needs of employed mothers may reinforce the stereotype that child care is "naturally" women's work, even though the actual wording of the legislation is in terms of "parental" rather than "maternal" leave. Even the absolute equality approach has its share of potential problems. Absolute equality denies male–female differences but does so in the context of a legal system that was designed with males in mind, so that females and female experiences end up being judged according to a male standard. An example of how ludicrous this "gender-neutral" approach to justice can become in the hands of an unsympathetic judge can be found in the ruling on a sexual assault case in Canada. A young woman had been approached by a man who, against her will, grabbed and fondled her breasts. The man was charged with sexual assault. The court ruled, however, that because breasts are female secondary sex characteristics, just as beards are male secondary sex characteristics, for a man to fondle a woman's breasts was no more a case of sexual assault than it would be for a woman to stroke a man's beard (L. Smith, 1987). This ruling was eventually overturned by the Supreme Court of Canada. However, it is clear that attempts to make the law treat both sexes fairly can backfire against either women or men and that, because laws are interpreted in courts by judges, gender bias can be a factor in the justice system even when the laws themselves are unbiased.

Gender and Crime

An important aspect of society's concern with justice has to do with preventing and punishing criminal behavior. In this area as well, gender has an impact on justice. Women and men differ in their criminal behavior, in which of their behaviors are considered criminal, and in the way their crimes are punished. Women and men also differ in their experiences as victims of crime.

WOMEN AND MEN AS CRIMINALS   Men commit more crimes than women, and men's crimes tend to be more serious and violent than women's crimes. Women account for only 15% of those arrested for violent crimes and 28% of those arrested for property crimes (American Bar Association, 1998). The reported incidence of crimes by women, particularly property crimes, have increased at a faster rate than those of men in recent years, but all over the world most crimes, especially violent ones, are still committed by men.

It is difficult to evaluate how well the statistics on crime reflect gender differences in criminal behavior, because there are gender biases in the criminal justice system's treatment of offenders. Among adolescents, females, but not males, tend to be charged with so-called status offenses, such as promiscuity or running away from home (Figueira-McDonough, 1987). These behaviors are violations of social norms for young women; it is hard to imagine a male being detained on the grounds of "promiscuity." Also, a female juvenile can apparently sometimes be detained because her behavior is "unladylike."

Among adults, women have traditionally been less likely to be arrested and have tended to be given more lenient treatment than their male counterparts (Weisberg, 1982), perhaps because gender stereotypes support the notion that women can't really be as "bad" as men. The stereotypes can backfire for women accused of particularly unfeminine crimes, however; these women sometimes receive particularly punitive sentences (Chesney-Lind, 1987). Most evidence now suggests that when women receive lesser sentences it is because they have fewer and less violent previous convictions (Mauer & Huling, 1995). However, women face new laws that criminalize their behavior. The use of illegal drugs by pregnant women has been deemed a delivery of controlled substances to the unborn child, and women have begun to be arrested and prosecuted for this offense (Cooper, 1992). In addition, poor and homeless women and men now frequently become entangled in the criminal justice system as many cities pass laws prohibiting begging or sleeping in public places.

Recent years have seen a dramatic increase in the number of women who are imprisoned. Between 1986 and 1991, the number of women in prison increased by 75%, and the number of men increased by 53% (American Bar Association, 1998). Women are less likely than men to be imprisoned for violent offenses and more likely to be imprisoned for drug-related crimes. One significant difference between women and men in prison is that the women are more likely than men to have children of whom they have custody. More than three quarters of the women in prison have children; two thirds have children under the age of 18.

For many female prisoners, incarceration is only the latest in a string of problems. More than 40% of women in prison say that they have been abused; three quarters of these were sexually abused (American Bar Association, 1998). According to one study, nearly half of women prisoners had run away from home as girls (American Correctional Association, 1990).

Certain criminal laws discriminate directly on the grounds of sex. For example, in some jurisdictions, both statutory rape and homosexual acts are legally considered crimes only when performed by males, whereas, in others, prostitution is an exclusively female crime. Other laws, for the most part now changed, were based on the double standard with respect to sexuality in marriage. For example, in some jurisdictions, murder was considered a justifiable reaction for a man who found his wife in bed with another man, but not for a wife who found her husband in bed with another woman. Clearly, criminal law as well as civil law contains built-in inequalities with respect to gender, and these inequalities are related to social stereotypes about women and men.

An aspect of the criminal law that has been the target of much criticism for its inequitable treatment of women and men is that surrounding prostitution: the selling of sex for money. Most prostitutes are women, although there are gay male prostitutes and there are also men who sell sex and companionship to women—but not usually on the street. Although the law in most jurisdictions defines soliciting or prostitution as a crime, not all the participants in the crime are usually charged, or even liable to be charged. Generally, the woman who sells sex is charged with breaking the law if she is caught; the man purchasing her services is not. For example, in Toronto, a jurisdiction where both prostitutes and their customers are liable for prosecution, over a 4-year period from 1979 to 1982, 71% of the charges for soliciting as prostitutes or customers were laid against women, only 29% were laid against men (Canadian Advisory Council on the Status of Women, 1984). A study of prostitution-related arrests in Buffalo, New York, between 1977 and 1979 showed a similar pattern: only 12.9% of the female prostitutes, but 73% of the men arrested for patronizing them, were released after the arrest to await trial (Bernat, 1984). According to one estimate, the average pattern of prostitution arrests in U.S. cities is 70% female prostitutes, 20% male prostitutes, and 10% customers (Prostitutes Education Network, 1999).

The sex discrimination shown in applying the law on prostitution has always been very blatant, perhaps because it fits so well with the double standard of sexual behavior (discussed in Chapter 7) and with the established power differences between women and men. The following comment, made in a 1914 report on prostitution in Europe, reflects a sentiment that has changed little in the intervening years:

> The professional prostitute being a social outcast may be periodically punished without disturbing the usual course of society. . . . The man, however, is something more than a partner in an immoral act: he discharges important social and business relations, is as father and brother responsible for the maintenance of others, has commercial or industrial duties to meet. He cannot be imprisoned without deranging society. (Flexner, 1914, p. 108)

The existence of prostitution, and its lopsided gender distribution and punishment, is to some extent a symptom of the inequality between the sexes. In one version of a gender-equal society, women and men would be equally likely to be prostitutes and customers, to sell and purchase sex. In another version, prostitution would not exist at all because there would be no market or social support for impersonal, commercialized sexual relations. However, prostitution will continue to be the path of least resistance for a large number of women until the economic and social pressures that disadvantage women are changed. Women's poverty and low socioeconomic status with respect to men, and the gender-role socialization of both sexes, make prostitution one of the very few alternatives for some women. The impact of these pressures is highlighted by the difficulties women encounter when they try to get out of prostitution and get a "respectable" job:

> The prostitute who can generally set her own hours of work and who lives in a world of cash exchanges, whose money may come as easily and quickly as it goes, and who is not linked firmly to the "disciplines" of work in a bureaucratic setting, is likely to find it very difficult to make the transition to that new world. A woman who has spent a significant portion of her early adult life in a marginal or even "outlaw" occupation is unlikely to have the skills and knowledge required for most standard jobs. Nor is she likely to have contacts to help her find a job in the regular working world. Aside from these difficulties, there is the distinct possibility that jobs in the "straight" world will be unappealing and low paying. An ex-prostitute is faced with the fact that the jobs which she can get, like the jobs most women hold, are neither as interesting nor as well-paid as the jobs any man, even if equally marginal, is able to get. (Canadian Advisory Council on the Status of Women, 1984, p. 94)

Traditional gender-role socialization with respect to work does not help the situation. Many young women still expect that their employment, whatever it is, will be an unimportant and temporary stage in their lives before they take on their "real" job as mothers. The young women who go into prostitution are no exceptions. As one 15-year-old Winnipeg prostitute said wistfully when asked in a television interview what she would ideally like to do with her life, "I want to have children, and a husband to look after me." This is a fantasy that is supported by myths and fairy tales and movies such as *Pretty Woman*.

Clearly, prostitution is one area of the law where justice is not meted out equally to women and men. However, the inequality in the law has roots that stretch deeply into other, even more basic inequalities between women and men.

VICTIMS OF CRIME   On December 6, 1989, in a tragedy that has since become known as the "Montreal Massacre," Marc Lepine rampaged through the school of engineering at the University of Montreal with an assault rifle, killing 14 women and wounding 9 other women and 4 men. The preponderance of females among Lepine's victims was no coincidence. He ordered men out of the way and rounded up women to be shot, screaming at his victims that they were "all fucking feminists." Found among his belongings after he turned his gun on himself were a suicide note blaming all his failures on women, as well as a "hit list" of prominent Canadian women (Caputi & Russell, 1990). This terrible incident reflects the disastrous intersection of three destructive forces: a bitter, angry, troubled individual; the availability of an automatic weapon to such an individual; and a cultural context that often legitimizes attitudes of male superiority and the notion that women who challenge traditional roles or male authority deserve to be victimized.

Despite the horror of the Montreal Massacre, and despite what some experts argue are increasing levels of viciousness in crimes against women (Caputi & Russell, 1990), homicide statistics show no increase in the murder rate for women (American Bar Association, 1998). Across countries, time, and age groups, studies show that men are more often victimized by crime than women are, but women express greater fear of being victimized than men do—perhaps because the crimes of which women are victims are more likely to be personal ones such as sexual assault or violent attacks by known assailants (American Bar Association, 1998; Statistics Canada, 1995; U.S. Department of Justice, 1995). Women are more than twice as likely as men to say that being victimized has made it difficult or impossible to carry out their normal activities, and many more women than men report that they feel unsafe walking alone in their neighborhood after dark or being home alone at night (Statistics Canada, 1995). Women's greater fear may stem from their socialization that they are incapable of protecting themselves, but it probably also relates to the type of crimes to which women are most vulnerable. Women are considerably more likely than men to live in fear of physical violence from a person in their own household. Women are most likely to be killed by people they know intimately and are more likely to be murdered in their own homes than anywhere else. Victimization surveys also show that women are 7 times as likely as men to experience a sexual assault. Not only are such victimization experiences especially traumatic in themselves, but reporting them tends to expose the victim to stigmatization. Women who have been raped or who have been beaten by their husbands are often assumed to have done something to encourage or provoke their attacker. The possibility of encountering such attitudes often causes a female victim to not report the crime. Estimates are that only 1 of every 4 rapes and 1 of every 10 incidents of wife assault are reported; the Canadian national Violence Against Women Survey indicated that only 14% of cases of wife assault or nonspousal physical or sexual assault were reported to police, and 22% of the victimized women had told no one about their experience (Statistics Canada, 1995).

Gender prejudice has played an important role in the legal treatment of victims of rape and wife assault. For many years, a wife was considered the property of her husband, and it was legally permissible for him to beat her (see Chapter 11). Rape of a wife by her husband was considered a contradiction in terms: A husband had the right to have sex with his wife with or without her consent. The latter law has now been changed in North America and in many of the world's nations.

The assumption that a female rape victim had enticed her attacker, or had actually consented to have intercourse with him, was built into the rules of evidence for rape trials. It used to be routine for the victim's prior sexual history to be brought up in court to establish that she was promiscuous and therefore had probably consented to the intercourse. New laws made such evidence inadmissible in most U.S. and Canadian jurisdictions; however, this legislation was struck down in Canada in 1991 on the ground that it might deny a fair trial to the accused (Fulton, 1991). A newer "rape-shield" law was proposed in Canada that would place the burden of proof for the woman's consent to sexual relations on the man, rather than making it incumbent on the rape victim to prove that she did *not* consent. The so-called no-means-no legislation required an explicit voluntary agreement, in words or action, by the woman to engage in sexual activity.

If a female victim kills her attacker while defending herself against rape, she is often regarded as having used unnecessary force and is sometimes jailed, whereas men who have killed while protecting themselves from rape by another man have generally been acquitted (Sapiro, 1986). One half of this pattern may reflect a lack of understanding about how traumatic and dangerous rape can be for the female victim. As one person is reported to have commented during the 1977 trial of Inez Garcia, a woman who killed her rapist, "You can't kill someone for trying to give you a good time" (as quoted in Sapiro, 1986). The other half of the pattern may relate to homophobia: A man defending himself against homosexual rape may be seen as defending himself from something unnatural, whereas heterosexual rape, in some people's perceptions, falls within the range of normal heterosexual experience.

A final twist on the gender bias that affects the treatment of victims is that on the relatively rare occasions when men find themselves the victims of sexual assault or physical abuse by women they are likely to receive very unsympathetic treatment if they report the incident. A man who cannot successfully defend himself against a woman is not much of a man according to the prevailing norms of masculinity, and the male victim of female violence is more likely to be the target of jokes than sympathy.

In summary, gender ideology plays a large part in the justice system's treatment of victims, particularly when the crime is related to sexuality or male–female relationships. Some changes in the direction of increased sensitivity and fairness have begun to occur, such as better training for police officers who must handle rape and spousal assault cases. However, it may be many years yet before the criminal justice system is equally responsive to the needs of female and male victims.

SOCIAL CHANGE: JUSTICE FOR ALL?

The Feminist Movement and Legislative Change

The past three decades have seen the emergence of a strong movement for social change in the situation of women and the relations between women and men. The feminist movement has included small local groups of activists and broadly based national organizations such as the National Organization for Women (NOW) in the United States and the National Action Committee on the Status of Women (NAC) in Canada. Active women's caucuses have formed within most professional organizations and political parties. On college campuses, feminist students, faculty, and staff have pooled their efforts to establish women's resource centers and programs labeled "women's studies" or "feminist studies." This mobilization of energy in the feminist movement has generated the power to produce significant changes in the laws governing the treatment of the sexes in work, education, and the allocation of resources. In Canada, a national coalition of feminist groups lobbied successfully to have gender equality under the law built into the new Charter of Rights and Freedoms. Section 15 of the Charter, which took effect on April 17, 1985 (fondly referred to by Canadian feminists as "a date with equality"), guarantees equality under the law to women and men and is currently providing the basis for challenging a number of discriminatory statutes and practices. In the United States, some important legislation has made sex discrimination more difficult in several areas. An example of the difference that such legislation can make can be seen in the impact of Title IX of the Education Amendments of 1972, which prohibited sex discrimination in federally funded educational institutions. Before this legislation came into effect, girls and women could routinely be excluded from certain educational programs on the basis of their gender, and there was no requirement that equal resources and facilities be available to both genders.

Before the passage of Title IX, educational institutions routinely discriminated against women students and faculty. Female students were excluded from certain courses or were subject to a quota system for admission into certain programs. Female faculty members were often excluded from faculty clubs and encouraged to join faculty wives clubs instead. Female teachers were often forced to resign or take unpaid leave when they were pregnant. Colleges could, and did, require higher test scores for female than for male applicants to gain admission. Young women had a very difficult time finding athletic scholarships to support their university education.

Since the implementation of Title IX, there have been many dramatic changes. The number of female high school graduates going on to college rose from 43% in 1972 to 63% in 1997 (American Bar Association, 1998). Dramatic effects have been seen in the influx of girls and women in two previously male-dominated areas: sports and certain vocational education programs. Research by Carl Ojala shows that the number of American high school girls participating in sports rose from 300,000 participants in 14 sports in 1970/71, just before Title IX was passed, to more than 1.7 million participants in 33 sports in 1984 ("Title IX Cited," 1987). Women now make up about 37% of athletes in college—up from 15% in 1972 (Marklein, 1997). This unprecedented growth in girls' sports participation is attributable in large part to Title IX's requirement that colleges put equivalent money into women's and men's sports, thus making it possible for more high school girls to aspire to college sports scholarships.

Title IX also provided the impetus for large changes in vocational education. Females could no longer be excluded from particular vocational programs and, as provided by a later law (Title II of the Education Amendments of 1976), each state appointed a full-time sex equity coordinator to work on broadening the range of vocational education opportunities for women. In the 10 years between 1972 and 1982, both the number and the percentage of female students increased in the traditionally male programs of agriculture, technical, and trade and industry. Within programs training students for office occupations, women now constitute over half the students in the supervisory and management programs, whereas in 1971 only about one quarter of these students were women (Vetter & Hickey, 1985). Women's share of the enrollment in the supervision and management sections of trade and industry programs increased by more than 20%. At the same time, male student enrollment is up in two traditionally female programs: home economics and office occupations.

Although Title IX has had a large effect in promoting gender equity in education, its force was blunted considerably in 1984, when the Supreme Court ruled that the law applied only to the actual programs that were directly receiving federal money within an institution, not to entire institutions ("Supreme Court," 1984). The Civil Rights Restoration Act, passed by Congress in 1988 broadened the definition of "program," however, so that it applied to the whole institution. The lesson is clear: Although much positive change can be generated through good legislation, vigilance is necessary to make sure the legislation survives and works well.

Clearly, feminism as a social movement has already had a large impact on the way females and males are treated in North America. Many instances of unfairness remain, however, and, as the following discussion will show, supporters of feminist social change do not always agree on the best way to rectify them.

How should the situation in which resources are distributed unfairly between the sexes, and in which the law often supports that unfairness, be rectified? How might we come up with a society that meets the ideals of justice held by both women and men? A variety of perspectives has been offered in response to such questions. Some have suggested that change will come faster if we recognize differences between women and men rather than denying them. Others have argued that what is needed is a deemphasis on gender as an organizing principle in society. Still others have stressed the importance of making people aware of the existence of sex discrimination and its impact on themselves. Finally, it has been argued that tinkering with the reward structure is not enough: There must be a transformation of social values and the institutions that represent them so that society's rewards are linked less strongly to competition and more strongly to behavior that emphasizes interpersonal harmony and cooperation. Let's look in turn at examples of each of these arguments.

Recognizing Differences

There is and has been a continuing debate among feminist legal scholars about whether it is good for women to have complete equality under the law (e.g., Chesney-Lind, 1995). One participant in this debate, Alice Kessler-Harris (1985), in an examination of the historical failure to achieve equality in the workplace for women, argues that the major reason these attempts have failed is that they assume women must adjust to the male-structured workplace. If women are to achieve equal status with men, the assumption has been, they must be prepared to make it in a man's world. Kessler-Harris suggests that, whether for reasons of preference or necessity, many women are not prepared to make this kind of adjustment in their priorities. If we want gender equality in the workplace, she says, we must make some accommodations in the workplace for women. Such accommodations may benefit both women and men by making the workplace more amenable to the special needs of all.

The following example is given by Kessler-Harris as a strategy that acknowledges gender-related differences but encompasses them in a policy that extends rights to all workers. In 1984, the Women's Rights Project of the American Civil Liberties Union (ACLU) filed a brief opposing Montana's Maternity Leave Act—an act that granted pregnant women the right to unpaid leave for a time before and after the birth of a child. The ACLU argued that such a law would place women in a special category, making them less attractive to employers as workers. The ACLU proposed instead that the law be extended to cover health-related unpaid leave for all workers. In this way, an act that was potentially discriminatory could be turned into a gain for all workers, and the special needs of women with respect to pregnancy could still be met. (This example also fits the "sex-specific/gender-neutral" approach to equality under the law discussed earlier in this chapter.) In 1987, in the *California Federal S. & L. v. Guerre* decision, the U.S. Supreme Court rejected the ACLU position in favor of a stance that it is permissible for states to treat women workers equally with men by establishing a maternity leave policy (an example of the "equality plus real differences" approach discussed earlier).

The main aspect of the approach advocated by Kessler-Harris is that the work that has traditionally been done by women—child care and the maintenance of home and family life—is important work that, in the quest for gender equality, must be publicly recognized and shared. Issues that have previously been considered private must be placed on the public stage. Family and relationship responsibilities are recognized as a necessary adjunct to the wage–work process, for men as well as women, and it is essential to consider family issues when designing the workplace:

> At its most optimistic, this approach is nothing less than a belief that gender equality will be achieved only when the values of the home (which have previously been assumed to keep women out of the workplace or to assign them to inferior places within it) are brought to the workplace where they can transform work itself. It opens the possibility that an ethic of compassion or tolerance, a sense of group responsibility to the world at large (instead of to self) might in fact penetrate the workplace. (p. 157)

A Nongendered Social Order

Although it is currently necessary to draw attention to the issue of gender to combat it as a discriminative status, some people have argued that such strategies are likely to be effective only in the short term. At least one writer (Lorber, 1986) has argued that the long-term goal of feminism should be to eradicate gender as an organizing principle in society. As long as we continue to make gender an important category and to view women and men as essentially different, gender will be used to make distinctions— between workers, voters, political candidates, criminals, and so on.

Judith Lorber tries to articulate what our society might be like if restructured to deemphasize gender. Policies regarding families would change, for instance. Each adult would be treated as a single unit for purposes of income, taxation, and legal responsibilities. Family and kinship would not be based on gender; groups of differing size and gender composition would make up households. Parenting would not be gender-linked; women and men would be equally likely to take responsibility for dependent children. There would be no support for a division of labor along sexual lines within the family. The wage structure for workers would not discriminate on the basis of workers' gender or of the gender linkage of certain jobs; thus, the man would not automatically be the main financial support of the family. All adults would receive support allowances for themselves and their dependents, and professional caretaking of children would no longer be treated and paid as a low-status occupation but would be compensated according to its skill level. Women would no longer be kept out of positions of power and authority by a sex-stratified occupational structure or by powerful men's perception of them as "different."

Lorber (1986) argues that drastic steps to change the gender structuring of society are necessary because political and legal equality between women and men will not necessarily ensure social equality:

> In my mind, gender equality is too limited a goal. Unless women and men are seen as socially interchangeable, gender equality does not challenge the concept of sex differences that leads to separate spheres in the family and marketplace division of labor, which in turn results in women's lesser access to control of valued resources and positions of power. Scrupulous equality of categories of people considered essentially different needs constant monitoring. I would question the very concept of gender itself, and ask why, if women and men are social equals in all ways, there needs to be two encompassing social statuses at all. (p. 577)

Lorber's argument is based on the idea that our notions of gender are socially constructed and that the differences between women and men are largely a product of the emphasis we as a society place on gender. Her proposal is not likely to be put into effect in the near future, so we cannot be sure of the extent to which her basic premise is correct. Yet, as discussed at many points in this book, research shows that social expectations about gender have a strong impact on male–female differences in many areas of behavior. Deemphasizing gender as a relevant category in the way society is structured is no doubt a necessary aspect of weakening those social expectations.

Raising Awareness of Discrimination

Lucy Stone, a 19th-century American suffragist and abolitionist, declared passionately in a speech delivered in 1885: "In education, in marriage, in religion, in everything disappointment is the lot of women. It shall be the business of my life to deepen this disappointment in every woman's heart until she bows down to it no longer."

Stone's recognition that a deep and clear awareness of injustice must precede action to correct the injustice is a well-accepted one. Before society can get very far with grand schemes for equality between women and men, individuals within society must be made aware of the fact that gender inequalities exist and affect them personally. People are simply more likely to mobilize for change if they feel that the current system is unjust, particularly if it is seen as disadvantageous to themselves. Yet researchers have found that people often do not recognize sex discrimination and that even among women who recognize that discrimination against women in general exists there is little recognition that they have personally been affected by it (Crosby, 1982; Unger & Sussman, 1986).

Some researchers have concentrated on the question of how best to raise awareness of discrimination (Crosby, Clayton, Alksnis, & Hemker, 1986). What they have found is that, at least some of the time, the failure to recognize discrimination is linked to the format in which information is presented. Crosby and her colleagues presented information about women and men in a fictitious corporation to male college students. Half the time, the information was presented in aggregated form, providing students with an overall picture of the situation in the company; the rest of the time, students were shown case-by-case comparisons of women and men in particular departments. The researchers suggest that the first type of presentation is comparable to learning about discrimination through the media, whereas the second is more like what occurs when we hear of a particular case or consider our own situation relative to that of another person.

The results of this study confirmed the researchers' hypothesis that the perception of discrimination was influenced by information processing considerations. Apparently, it was easier to see patterns of discrimination when many cases were presented together, perhaps because the quantity of data was more compelling or because, when information was aggregated, irrelevant differences among departments were averaged out, making the salary difference between women and men more obvious.

The results of this study indicate clearly that when trying to demonstrate that sex discrimination exists in a particular setting it is more effective to present an overall view than a trickle of case comparisons. The findings also demonstrate that cognitive factors, the way human beings process information, can have an impact above and beyond such attitudinal factors as prejudice or misogyny or the desire to see the world as a just place on people's readiness to see discrimination. Attempts to rectify sex discrimination must take this factor into account.

Transformation of Institutions

Many feminists have argued that society's institutions must be fundamentally transformed rather than simply made more open to women's participation. They argue that the hierarchical, competitive, and individualistic values that permeate most institutions are fundamentally opposed to designing a system that would stress equality among groups. For instance, some groups of women have tried to challenge the male dominance of the health-care system, not by getting more women into medical school but by a variety of tactics that question the doctor's place at the top of a medical hierarchy. Some groups have fought for the legalization of midwifery. Others have challenged traditional physician–nurse power relationships that make it impossible for a nurse to question a doctor's instructions with respect to a patient. Still others have started self-care clinics or information services to make people less dependent on medical experts for their health.

Other institutions have also felt the brunt of this approach. For example, in many universities, the introduction of women's studies courses has meant not just a new content area but a questioning of the way things are done in academia as well as in the outside world. As Roberta Hamilton (1985) notes, feminists in the academy tend to be political subversives: "They have challenged not only the structure of the university, and the limited place of women within it, but also the very parameters of what constitutes knowledge, and many of the assumptions underlying the traditional academic disciplines" (p. 3).

The transformational approach to social change is based on the idea that gender bias may be present even in areas where it has not yet been recognized: in the way we think about issues that have no obvious connection to gender. It thus forces a scrutiny of the status quo that goes beyond even that encouraged by the other approaches cited here. It is a difficult and often uncomfortable approach to social change, but, as Hamilton (1985) notes, "Students of society surely deserve challenge, not consolation, and this is especially true . . . in the questions that we pose about those aspects of human relationships that we have hitherto taken for granted" (p. 20).

SUMMARY

We have seen that strong prescriptive stereotypes exist that women and men should rely on different standards of justice and morality and that women's and men's experiences tend to push them in the direction of those stereotypes. For example, the power differences between women and men often mean that women have fewer resources than men, and the very prevalence of this situation may lead people to accept it as normal. As a result, women may come to believe that they *deserve* less, and men to believe that *they* deserve more. This difference in feelings of personal entitlement may cause what appears to be a gender difference in selfishness: Women stress equality, take less for themselves and give more to others, and men stress equity and are ready to reward themselves at the expense of others. Research shows, however, that such differences are ephemeral. If the situation is changed by giving individuals an appropriate comparison group, if the situation is deliberately structured to emphasize either interpersonal concerns or task concerns, if individuals can reward their own superior performance without penalizing others, the traditional gender differences disappear. It appears that in the area of justice behavior, as in so many other areas discussed in this book, males and females are sensitive to situational cues about what behavior is appropriate, that these cues often differ for the two sexes, and that the difference relates to the power difference between women and men.

Studies of the way females and males actually think about justice and morality do not unequivocally support the idea that females emphasize equality and interpersonal concerns and males stress equity and rights. However, both the manner in which that field of inquiry has developed and the findings of the studies themselves indicate that there is a pervasive belief in the existence of the gender difference just described. Women are expected to emphasize care and interpersonal concerns, men to emphasize rights. A reading of the early psychological writings on justice and morality leaves no doubt that the stereotypically feminine morality of care and interpersonal responsibility has been devalued. Perhaps this devaluation has acted in a circular fashion to cause the dissociation of such an orientation from men and thus to ensure that it would continue to be devalued in a society that assigns more status to men than to women.

The idea that women and men differ in their tendency to be emotional or rational with respect to justice has been reflected in the male dominance of the judicial system and is entrenched, along with other gender stereotypes, in the fabric of the law itself. For years, civil laws gave men authority over women, even within the family; some of these laws have yet to be changed. These laws have restricted women's legal and political rights and their access to economic resources, thus maintaining a power difference between women and men that, in turn, helped to maintain behavioral differences. In criminal law as well, gender stereotypes, particularly those concerning sexuality and marital roles, have made for inequities between women and men, both as criminals and as victims. The law itself, supposedly the embodiment of justice, sometimes perpetuates injustice on the basis of gender.

Many approaches have been offered as directions for social change that would redress the unbalanced distribution of resources and other injustices based on gender. These approaches range from practical suggestions about how to educate people with respect to sex discrimination to attempts to develop the best possible vision of the ultimate goals of change. They include strategies for how to make the system work for women and strategies for a radical transformation of that system. All of them have in common a basis of passionate concern for gender justice. Although the debate goes on about the relative merits of these various approaches to social transformation, it advances, through a series of small changes, the notion that the real needs of both sexes must weigh equally in any consideration of justice.

KEY TERMS

affirmative action	personal relative	rights orientation
denial of personal	deprivation	care orientation
discrimination	collective relative	
	deprivation	

FOR ADDITIONAL READING

Backhouse, Constance. (1991). *Petticoats and prejudice: Women and the law in nineteenth-century Canada.* Toronto, Ontario: Women's Press. This legal history, filled with interesting vignettes, describes how Canadian law treated courtship and marriage, rape, abortion, infanticide, divorce, child custody, and prostitution.

Boxer, Marilyn Jacoby. (1998). *When women ask the questions: Creating women's studies in America.* Baltimore: Johns Hopkins University Press. The author tells the story of how the discipline of women's studies has transformed U.S. institutions of higher education.

Collins, Patricia Hill. (1990). *Black feminist thought: Knowledge, consciousness, and the politics of empowerment.* Boston: Unwin Hyman. This book provides an analysis of the intellectual and social activism of African American women as they have struggled to develop a perspective that is "both emancipatory and reflective."

Kimmel, Michael S., & Mosmiller, Thomas E. (Eds.). (1992). *Against the tide: Pro-feminist men in the United States 1776–1990.* Boston: Beacon. When the editors first mentioned the possibility of this book to their feminist women friends, one scoffed that a book about pro-feminist men would surely be the shortest book in history! Actually, this book provides over 500 pages of information about, and statements by, men who made their voices heard on behalf of gender justice.

Unger, Rhoda K. (1998). *Resisting gender: Twenty-five years of feminist psychology.* Thousand Oaks, CA: Sage. This book provides an interesting and thought-provoking history of how the introduction of a feminist perspective has changed psychology.

The Ties That Bind

The Future of Sex & Gender

Sex and gender together have formed one of the most important distinctions human beings have made about one another. Awareness of another person's femaleness or maleness shapes our reactions to that person from the moment she or he is born. We judge ourselves and others according to the degree to which we and they fit the expectations of femininity and masculinity; most of us cannot imagine what it would be like to have the body of the other sex or the role expectations and identity of the other gender.

As distinctions go, however, there is something unique about the one based on sex and gender. Although we insist on the division, on the importance of the distinction between female and male, feminine and masculine, we tend to argue not that the two genders should be kept separate but that they should go together—that they complement and complete each other. We speak of situations needing a "woman's touch" or a "man's hand," and, as a society, we espouse one ideal of intimacy that involves a shared, lifelong commitment between a woman and a man. Despite the talk about how different men and women are and how little they understand each other, a large number of North American adults would count their closest, most important relationship as one with a spouse or partner of the other gender.

The gender division is somewhat unique, then, in that the two genders, though divided, are thought to "go together." But, both as individuals and as groups, women and men have tended to go together not as equal partners but as participants in a hierarchical arrangement, with men holding the top positions. Our culture's ideas about male–female differences reflect this hierarchy. Stereotypes of femininity and masculinity split up human qualities between females and males. The qualities assigned to females are devalued—a devaluation that is linked to females' subordinate position in the gender hierarchy. Interestingly, a quality that is stereotyped as feminine may in fact be equally prevalent in both women and men, but because it is associated with femininity it may be devalued and thus unacknowledged in men. A clear example of this phenomenon comes from the research on moral reasoning discussed in Chapter 14. An ethic of care and responsibility, ignored in previous male-centered research on moral reasoning, was proposed as a principle that was especially characteristic of women's moral reasoning (Gilligan, 1982). However, as researchers began to include this hitherto ignored element of morality in their studies of moral reasoning, most found to their surprise that it was prevalent among both women and men. Why had no one noticed it before? The tendency to base decisions on concern for relationships is stereotyped as feminine. Perhaps male researchers and research participants were not noticing or acknowledging this tendency in themselves, and females were simply accepting men's definition of the situation. The hierarchical social context in which women and men perceive and relate to each other makes it impossible for us to be completely clear-eyed about what gender similarities and differences exist. Yet, when we try to nail down such differences and similarities, we are confronted with the realization that gender is socially constructed and is, to some extent, a figment of our expectations and our imagination. The more carefully we do our research, the more it appears that women and men share, or have the potential to share under conditions of social equality, most qualities.

The realization that we need not be limited to present cultural definitions of femininity and masculinity can be an empowering one for both women and men. However, it can also be a frightening one. Social change is now occurring at such a rapid rate that individuals or whole societies may freeze in "future shock" rather than adapt comfortably to new possibilities. Part of this inability or refusal to adapt may well involve holding on with grim determination to traditional gender roles. And there are, of course, good reasons for not discarding the qualities that are associated with traditional gender roles. As Joan Rabin (1987) argued, under conditions of rapid social change, we human beings are especially in need of the communal qualities usually associated with women to maintain a sense of comfort and connection—to ensure our survival as a social species. Indeed, traditions form important anchors in a rapidly changing world, and they often help us maintain our sense of meaning and connection with one another. Women, whose communal, family roles often implicate them as the guardians of tradition and social bonds, may feel especially guilty as they redefine their roles and cannot devote as much energy to activities that bring family and friends together. Yet such feelings of guilt are based on the assumption that only women can fulfill these functions—an assumption that is simply wrong. As a society, we may finally come to the realization that the functions and qualities stereotypically associated with each gender are valuable and necessary—and much more interchangeable and shareable than we used to think.

Glossary

achievement motive a general personality disposition to strive for success in any situation where standards of excellence are applied

acquired immunodeficiency syndrome (AIDS) a condition caused by the human immunodeficiency virus (HIV), characterized by destruction of the immune system and consequent vulnerability to life-threatening diseases

adrenogenital syndrome (AGS)) genetically transmitted syndrome in which the adrenal glands of the fetus malfunction, resulting in a release of excess androgens from the prenatal period onward

affirmative action a set of strategies to increase the proportion of women and minorities hired by organizations or admitted to universities, particularly in fields from which they have traditionally been excluded

agoraphobia a persistent, irrational fear of being in public places from which escape might be difficult or in which help might be unavailable in case of sudden incapacitation

alpha bias a tendency toward exaggerating differences between women and men

anal stage the second of Freud's psychosexual stages, in which pleasure is linked to defecation

androcentric norms use of male behavior as the norm against which to measure females

androcentric centered on men and shaped by masculine values

androgen insensitivity syndrome (AIS) genetically transmitted disorder in which cells are partially or completely unable to respond to androgens

androgyny a blend of stereotypically feminine and masculine qualities in a person

andropause a transition experienced by men in their 70s and 80s that is characterized by a thinning of the ejaculate, a reduction of ejaculatory pressure, and a decrease in the levels of FSH and LH

anorexia nervosa a mental disorder that involves self-starvation in an effort to maintain an unrealistically low body weight, characterized by an intense fear of becoming obese and by a disturbed body image—a tendency to "feel fat" even when severely underweight

anthropomorphism the tendency to interpret animal behavior in terms of human customs and ideology

antisocial personality disorder a mental disorder characterized by a lack of ethical or moral sensitivity and the absence of guilt or anxiety about hurting others

benevolent sexism a type of sexism that includes protective paternalism, idealization of women, and desire for intimate relations, measured by the Ambivalent Sexism Inventory

beta bias an inclination to ignore or minimize differences between women and men

bisexual a person who can be sexually and/or emotionally attracted to partners of either sex

bulimia a mental disorder characterized by an obsession with food and with body weight, involving a pattern of "binge" overeating followed by self-induced "purging" through a variety of means, including dieting, vomiting, or laxatives

care orientation stresses the necessity to be responsible in one's relationships, to be sensitive to the needs of others, and to avoid giving hurt

case history method involves gathering many details about one or several individuals, usually through interviews, to support, develop, or refine a particular explanation of behavior

cerebral cortex the outermost part of the brain, divided into lobes (or sections), that fulfill different sensory and motor functions

cognitive developmental theory proposes that gender, like other concepts, cannot be learned until a child reaches a particular stage of intellectual development

collective relative deprivation a feeling of dissatisfaction due to perceived inequities between one's own and a more advantaged group

comparable worth the principle that persons should earn equal pay for work of equal value, even when their jobs are not identical

competence a dimension on which influence styles are described that refers to the degree to which a person tries to gain compliance by acting knowledgeable and confident, as opposed to helpless

components of gender stereotypes distinct aspect of gender stereotypes that can be identified, such as personality traits, role behaviors, occupations, and physical appearance

concreteness a dimension on which influence styles are described that refers to the degree to which the resources on which influence attempts are based is independent of relationships

consciousness (or conscious mind) according to Freudian theory, the part of the mind available to awareness that contains the thoughts and feelings people know they have

constricting interaction style style in which participants in an interaction are more likely to interrupt one another, command and threaten, boast, refuse to comply, or give information

corpus callosum a mass of nerve fibers that connects the two hemispheres of the cerebral cortex

correlational method method capable of showing that two things are related to each other, or go together, but that cannot show that either one caused the other

couvade rituals used in some cultures to express father involvement in the birth process and to protect the mother and infant

couvade syndrome syndrome in which expectant fathers suffer from physical symptoms during their wife's pregnancy or labor

cross-sequential method incorporates cross-sectional comparisons of different age groups tested at one time period, longitudinal comparisons of the same individuals tested repeatedly over time, and time-lag comparisons of same-age samples at different time periods

cumulative continuity the process through which an individual, beginning in childhood, selects and creates environments that fit her or his preferred forms of behavior; these selected environments, in turn, reinforce and sustain that behavior

denial of personal discrimination tendency for women to underrate the amount of sex discrimination visited on them personally, even when they are quite aware that women in general experience sex discrimination

dependent variable the variable that is measured in an experiment

depression a mental illness signaled by feelings of extreme sadness and hopelessness and by a loss of interest in most activities

devaluation according to Karen Horney, one of two major environmental dangers to a child's development: parents' lack of respect for the child as a unique and worthwhile individual

directness a dimension on which influence strategies are categorized that refers to the openness or obliqueness that characterizes an influence attempt

discourse analysis analysis of the language in various texts, such as interview responses, discussions, and essays

distribution frequency with which certain responses or scores are obtained when a group of individuals is studied

double standard use of two different standards of acceptable sexual behavior, one for women and one for men

dysmenorrhea pain and discomfort during menstruation

effect size amount of variation in a criterion variable that is attributable to a particular treatment or category variable (such as gender) in one study or a group of studies

ego according to Freudian theory, the rational part of the personality structure that handles transactions between an individual's subjective needs and the objective world of reality

Electra complex according to Freud, in the phallic stage girls realize they cannot have a penis and replace this wish for a penis with a wish for a child, focusing on father as a love object and on mother as a rival

enabling interaction style interactants seem most interested in sustaining social relationships and are likely to say they agree with another speaker, acknowledge points made by other speakers, and pause to allow another to speak

entity approach to ability notion that each individual has a fixed amount of ability, which is revealed by her or his performance

equal pay for equal work principle that women and men should be paid the same salaries when they perform the same jobs

equity in relationships, the extent to which the ratio of each partner's contributions to rewards is seen to be equal

essentialism the idea that gender differences in behavior stem from qualities that are resident in, or possessed by, women and men

ethnocentrism tendency to interpret observations of another culture or group in terms of our own culture

evolutionary theory argues that human nature (including human sex differences) has evolved in certain ways because of pressures to adapt and survive as a species

excitement phase the first phase of sexual response, according to Masters and Johnson's model, characterized by the onset of vasocongestion

experiment research method in which the researcher directly manipulates (that is, sets at different levels) one variable, called the **independent variable,** while measuring its effects on another variable, the **dependent variable**

expressiveness an orientation toward emotion and relationships

fear of success the anticipation of negative consequences of success, such as social disapproval

follicular phase first phase of the menstrual cycle, in which the pituitary secretes follicle-stimulating hormone (FSH), stimulating a follicle in one of the ovaries to secrete estrogen and to bring an egg to maturity

G-spot area on the anterior wall of the vagina that some researchers think is especially sensitive to sexual stimulation

gay an alternative for the term **homosexual,** often used to describe a lifestyle rather than just sexuality

gender refers to the nonphysiological aspects of being female or male inculcated in cultural expectations for femininity and masculinity

gender-aschematic having a weak gender schema

gender constancy an understanding that a person's gender is fixed and cannot be altered by a change in hairstyle, dress, or name, achieved by a child, according to cognitive developmental theory, sometime between the ages of 3 and 5

gender dysphoria unhappiness or dissatisfaction with one's given gender or sexual identity

gender identity individual's private experience of the self as female or male

gender role set of behaviors socially defined as appropriate for one's sex

gender roles as developmental pathways suggests that the *process* of acquiring gender roles, not just the *content* of these roles, may differ for males and females on the dimensions of rigidity, simplicity, internal consistency, and continuity

gender-role strain difficulty in conforming to expected gender roles because such roles are often contradictory and inconsistent

gender schema theory proposes that children early on develop a network of cognitive associations (schema) for gender based on the degree to which the gender dichotomy is emphasized during socialization and use this to organize incoming information about themselves and others

gender-schematic having a strong gender schema and having a tendency to spontaneously sort people, characteristics, and behaviors into masculine and feminine categories

genital stage the fifth of Freud's psychosexual stages, that of mature sexuality, beginning at puberty

glass ceiling an invisible barrier that keeps women from advancing into high-level positions in organizations

glass escalator a systematic set of hidden advantages for men in female-dominated occupations

gonadotropins hormones that stimulate the gonads (sex glands) to activity

group socialization theory postulates that children become socialized primarily by identifying with their peer group and taking on that group's norms for attitudes and behavior

gynocentric literally, centered on the female womb or female-centered

heterosexism tendency to view heterosexuality as the norm and to ignore or render invisible the alternatives of homosexuality and bisexuality

heterosexual a person who prefers sexual and affectional partners of the other sex

homophobia negative attitudes toward and fear of homosexuality

homosexual a person who prefers sexual and affectional partners of the same sex

hostile environment form of sexual harassment that involves making unwelcome sexual advances or engaging in other conduct of a sexual nature that unreasonably interferes with an individual's work performance

or creates an intimidating, hostile, or offensive atmosphere

hostile sexism a type of sexism that includes dominance-oriented paternalism, derogatory beliefs about women, and heterosexual hostility as measured by the Ambivalent Sexism Inventory

human immunodeficiency virus (HIV) virus that produces AIDS, damaging the immune system and leaving the body open to opportunistic diseases

hysteria (from the Greek word meaning uterus) a mysterious "disease of the uterus" often diagnosed in women until early in the 20th century, marked by fainting or fits and a variety of symptoms such as loss of voice or partial paralysis, with no apparent physical cause

id according to Freudian theory, the part of the personality structure that includes the individual's biological heritage and sexual and aggressive instincts and provides a reservoir of psychic energy that powers the other two systems

identity the significance and qualitative meaning that individuals attribute to their membership with a particular group (such as a gender or ethnic or racial group) within their self-concept

independent variable variable that is manipulated in an experiment

instrumentality an orientation toward action, accomplishment, and leadership

interactional continuity two-way transactions between the person and the social environment in which the person's behavior elicits reactions from others, and those reactions promote continuity in the original behavior through reinforcement, confirmation of expectations, and confirmation of the person's self-concept

interactive model of gender-related behavior built on the proposition that an individual's gender-related behaviors in a given social interaction are influenced by what others expect, what the individual believes about her- or himself, and situational cues

interactiveness a dimension on which influence strategies are categorized that refers to the degree of mutual engagement with the partner required in the influence attempt

interpersonal power the ability of one person to get another person to do what the first person wants, in the face of resistance from the second person

intersexed individuals people whose sexual differentiation was disrupted *in utero* by hormonal imbalance, and who are born with some biological indicators of both sexes

intimacy maturity levels of relationship maturity in terms of other-orientation, caring/concern, sexuality, commitment, and communication that may be found in an intimate relationship

late luteal phase dysphoric disorder earlier label for **premenstrual dysphoric disorder,** a formal diagnosis included in an appendix of the *Diagnostic and Statistical Manual of the American Psychiatric Association,* which lists a set of psychological symptoms that may occur during the week prior to menstruation

latency phase the fourth phase of psychosexual development, according to Freud, during which erotic impulses are repressed until just before puberty

lateralization (or cerebral lateralization or hemispheric lateralization) the degree to which particular functions are localized in one side of the brain

lesbian a woman who is sexually and affectionally attracted to other women

logical positivism approach to knowledge that assumes reality is independent of the knower and can be discerned "objectively" under the proper conditions

longitudinal study following the same research participants over an extended period of time, usually years, and obtaining data from them repeatedly during that time

luteal phase third phase of the menstrual cycle, in which the luteinizing hormone stimulates the follicle to turn into a glandular mass of cells called the corpus luteum, which in turn manufactures progesterone

maternal feminisms feminist viewpoints strongly supportive of women's rights that emphasized the differences between women and men and the importance of motherhood for women and for society

menarche a girl's first menstrual period

menopause the cessation of a woman's menstrual periods during middle age

menstrual cycle the cyclic pattern of sex hormone levels in women, maintained through a negative feedback system involving the hypothalamus, the pituitary gland, and the ovaries

menstruation final phase of the menstrual cycle when the inner uterine lining (the endometrium) is shed and flows out through the cervix and the vagina

mental rotation a type of spatial ability that involves being able to quickly visualize objects from different perspectives than the one shown

meta-analysis using statistical methods to combine the findings of a large number of different studies of the same behavior to evaluate the overall pattern of findings

misogyny hatred of women

modern sexism a constellation of attitudes characterized by a denial that women are still targets of discrimination, antagonism toward women's demands, and a lack of support for policies designed to improve women's status

Müllerian ducts primitive ducts in the human embryo that eventually, in females, become the fallopian tubes, uterus, and vagina

myotonia one of the physiological processes in sexual response: the contraction of muscles

narrative approach gathering a lot of information from a single individual and allowing the research participant the opportunity to react to the meanings and interpretations the researcher gives to the participant's life story

naturalistic observation research method in which a researcher spends a lot of time watching individuals in their normal setting, keeping track of the number and type of certain kinds of behaviors displayed

neosexism a constellation of attitudes characterized by a denial that women are still targets of discrimination, antagonism toward women's demands, and a lack of support for policies designed to improve women's status

Oedipus complex a system of feelings and stage of development, named by Freud for the mythical Greek character who unwittingly killed his own father and married his own mother, during which boys develop an intense attachment for mother and begin to see father as a rival

oral stage the first of Freud's psychosexual stages, in which pleasure is centered in the mouth and sucking

orgasm third phase of human sexual response, according to Masters and Johnson, in which arousal reaches a critical point and triggers orgasm, a series of involuntary rhythmic contractions of the pelvic organs

ovulation second phase of the menstrual cycle, in which the follicle ruptures to release the mature egg

penis envy theorized by Freud to be experienced by girls during the phallic stage when they realize they lack a penis and develop a sense of inferiority and contempt for their own sex

personal relative deprivation a sense of dissatisfaction stemming from a comparison with others who are being more highly rewarded

phallic stage the third of Freud's psychosexual stages, in which erotic pleasure is obtained from the penis for boys and the clitoris for girls

phallocentric literally, centered on the male penis or male-centered

phenomenological method oriented toward understanding behavior from the perspective of the person being studied, often based on in-depth, subjective information collected in interviews

phobia persistent, irrational fear of and desire to avoid specific objects, activities, or situations

plateau phase second phase of human sexual response, according to Masters and Johnson's model, in which a peak level of

vasocongestion is reached and the rate of breathing, pulse rate, and blood pressure increase further

polyandry one wife having several husbands at the same time

polygyny one husband having several wives at the same time

postpartum depression mild to serious negative emotions experienced by women in the days, weeks, or months after childbirth

posttraumatic stress disorder (PTSD) a disorder caused by a traumatic event that is characterized by anxiety, depression, flashbacks, nightmares, and somatic symptoms

power motive the tendency to strive to feel that one is having an impact on others

prejudice the negative evaluation of persons or their activities because they belong to a particular group

premenstrual dysphoric disorder (PMDD) a formal diagnosis included in an appendix of the *Diagnostic and Statistical Manual of the American Psychiatric Association,* which lists a set of psychological symptoms that may occur during the week prior to menstruation

premenstrual syndrome (PMS) period of high tension, depression, irritability, and assorted physical symptoms that is said to occur during the days immediately preceding the onset of menstruation

principle of least interest in a relationship the person who is least dependent on the other for rewards—who needs the relationship least—has the most power

prostaglandins hormonelike substances from the lining of the uterus that cause excessive contractions in the uterine muscles, decreased blood flow, and increased sensitivity to pain, all of which contribute to menstrual cramps

prototypical traits traits associated with the clearest examples of a particular category

pseudocyesis pseudopregnancy, characterized by physical symptoms similar to those associated with pregnancy: menstrual disturbance, abdominal enlargement, swelling and tenderness of the breasts, softening of the cervix, enlargement of the uterus, nausea and vomiting, and weight gain

psychoanalytic theory theory first developed by Sigmund Freud that emphasized the importance of unconscious motivations in personality development

quid pro quo form of sexual harassment in which an individual is pressured to submit to unwelcome sexual advances or other unwelcome sexual conduct as a condition of employment or employment decisions that affect the individual, such as promotion or raises, are based on her or his submission to or rejection of such conduct

rape forcing sexual relations on someone against that person's choice

reactance a reaction to a perceived threat to a behavioral freedom, constituting an effort to protect or regain the freedom that is threatened and manifested as resistance, anger, and hostility toward the individual or organization viewed as threatening

refractory period a period lasting from a few minutes to 24 hours after **orgasm,** during which a man typically cannot be restimulated to erection and **orgasm**

resolution phase fourth phase of human sexual response, according to Masters and Johnson's model, in which muscular tension is relaxed and blood is released from the engorged blood vessels

rights orientation to morality stresses an attention to principles and questions what choices are legitimate in particular situations

schema a cognitive structure (a network of associations or set of interrelated ideas) that guides and organizes the way an individual processes and makes sense of information

self-fulfilling prophecy process in which the presence of a stereotype may actually motivate the stereotyped person to behave in a manner consistent with the stereotype

self-in-relation the sense of oneself as a relational being, someone who is developing and growing in the ability to connect with and relate to others

serial monogamy an individual having a series of mates, one at a time

sex a person's biological maleness or femaleness

sex chromosomes the 23rd pair of chromosomes in humans: if the individual is female, the sex chromosomes are represented as XX; if male, the pair is designated as XY

sex-limited traits traits carried on genes that are not on either of the sex chromosomes but are, nonetheless, generally manifest in only one sex because they require the presence of certain levels of male or female sex hormones to appear

sex-linked traits traits for which the genes are carried partially or totally on one of the sex (X or Y) chromosomes

sex-of-experimenter effects effects produced as a result of using a female or male experimenter to carry out research because people react differently to men and women

sex roles as rules theory the acquisition of gender roles is similar to the process of pattern recognition in vision and speech, which grows out of an interaction between the child's built-in ability to generalize, discriminate, and form categories of all kinds and the specific sex-related associations that pervade the environment

sex stereotypes socially shared beliefs that certain qualities can be assigned to individuals, based on their membership in the female or male half of the human race

sexism prejudice based on a person's sexual category

sexual orientation an individual's preference for sexual and affectional partners of the same or other sex

sexualization according to Karen Horney, one of two major environmental dangers to a child's development: a sexual approach to the child, an emotional "hothouse" atmosphere

social cognitive theory a modification of social learning theory that suggests that although children may initially learn gender roles through external rewards and punishments, as they mature they begin to regulate their own actions through internal rewards and punishments

social constructionism approach to knowledge that assumes researchers do not discover independently existing facts through objective observation; rather, they construct knowledge that is influenced by the social context of their inquiry

social learning theory states that the child develops both gender identity and gender role through a learning process that involves modeling, imitation, and reinforcement

social role theory states that differential role occupancy by women and men is mediated by the formation of gender roles in which persons of each sex are expected to have qualities that equip them for the tasks typically carried out by that group

social structure theories state that female–male differences in behavior are driven by the ways societies are organized, in particular by gender differences in power and status and the division of labor by sex

sociobiology states that sex differences in human behavior have evolved because of different reproductive strategies adopted by males and females to maximize the chances that their genes will be passed on to future generations

spatial perception a type of spatial performance that involves determining spatial relationships with respect to one's own body orientation despite distracting information

spatial visualization a type of spatial performance that involves complicated, multistep mental manipulations of spatial information such as being asked to "disembed" a simple figure from a complex background or to imagine how a piece of paper would look when folded a certain way

spatiotemporal ability a type of spatial ability that involves making judgments about moving visual displays, such as predicting when a moving object will reach a particular spot

spermarche a boy's first ejaculation

statistically significance the probability a particular result could occur by chance alone, based on tests that consider sample size and variability; by convention, if the probability of the result occurring by chance alone is less than 5%, the finding is accepted as statistically significant

stereotype threat awareness that one may be judged by or may self-fulfill negative stereotypes about one's group

straight an alternative term for **heterosexual**

stressors external events or conditions that are appraised as threatening by an individual and thus are the source of upset, worry, discomfort, and general distress

superego according to Freudian theory, this part of the personality structure acts as the moral aspect of the personality, striving for perfection rather than pleasure, and persuading the **ego** to substitute moralistic goals for realistic ones

survey methods methods of data collection that use a standardized questionnaire or interview to collect information from a large number of people

theory a formalized set of ideas about how and why things happen and used in science to guide research and generate hypotheses (propositions) that can be tested against observed reality

token positions when individuals are treated as symbols or representatives of their sex, race, or other underrepresented group

transformationism an approach to understanding the way biology and environment work together, with neither being more fundamental than the other to an organism's development but combining to transform the organism so that it responds differently to other concurrent or subsequent biological or environmental influences

transgendered community people who refuse to live within a particular set of gender expectations and who, in various ways, are transgressing gender boundaries

transgenders people who live all or part of the time in the identity of the other sex, but who have no intention of having surgery to change their bodies

transsexuals people whose gender identity does not match their biological sex and who have had or want to have surgery to change their bodies to match those of the other sex

transvestites (cross-dressers) people who enjoy dressing in the clothing of the other sex

trust in intimate relationships, a multifaceted construct that includes faith that one's partner will act in loving ways whatever the future holds and a belief in the partners behavioral predictability and personal dependability

unconscious (or unconscious mind) according to Freudian theory, the part of the mind that contains the unacceptable urges, passions, ideas, and feelings that people do not know they have and cannot acknowledge, which can be explored only indirectly through dreams, free association, symptoms, mistakes (now sometimes called "Freudian slips"), or other "leaks" of the unconscious into conscious awareness

vasocongestion a physiological process in sexual response that allows accumulation of blood in the blood vessels of a particular region

Wolffian ducts primitive duct system in the human embryo that eventually, in males, develops into the vas deferens, seminal vesicle, epididymides, urethra, and prostate

References

Abbey, A. (1982). Sex differences in attributions for friendly behavior: Do males misperceive females' friendliness? *Journal of Personality and Social Psychology, 42*(5), 830–838.

Abbondanza, M. (1982, July). *Categorization, identification and feelings of deprivation: A multidimensional study of homemaker and employed mothers' social perceptions.* Paper presented at the 20th International Congress of Applied Psychology, Edinburgh.

Abbondanza, M. (1983, June). *Cognitive barriers to intergroup equality between the sexes.* Paper presented at the Section on Social Psychology graduate student awards session, 44th annual convention of the Canadian Psychological Association, Winnipeg, Manitoba.

Abplanalp, J. M. (1983). Premenstrual syndrome: A selective review. *Women & Health, 8*(2/3), 107–123.

Abramowitz, S., & Herrera, H. R. (1981). On controlling for patient psychopathology in naturalistic studies of sex bias: A methodological demonstration. *Journal of Consulting and Clinical Psychology, 49,* 597–603.

Adams, C. G., & Turner, B. F. (1985). Reported change in sexuality from young adulthood to old age. *Journal of Sex Research, 21*(2), 126–141.

Adams, D. O., Johnson, T. C., Cole, S. P., Matthiasson, H., et al. (1990). Physical fitness in relation to amount of physical exercise, body image, and locus of control among college men and women. *Perceptual and Motor Skills, 70*(3), 1347–1350.

Adams, K. A. (1980). Who has the final word? Sex, race and dominance behavior. *Journal of Personality and Social Psychology, 38,* 1–8.

Adams, K. A. (1983). Aspects of social context as determinants of Black women's resistance to challenges. *Journal of Social Issues, 39,* 69–78.

Adler, N. E. (1975). Emotional responses of women following therapeutic abortion. *American Journal of Orthopsychiatry, 45*(3), 446–454.

Adler, T. (1990). NIH opens office on women's issues. *APA Monitor, 21*(12), 5.

Agate, C., & Meacham, C. (1977). Women's equality: Implications of the law. In A. Sargent (Ed.), *Beyond sex roles* (pp. 434–450). St. Paul: West.

Ahlgren, A. (1983). Sex differences in the correlates of cooperative and competitive school attitudes. *Developmental Psychology, 19*(6), 881–888.

Aida, Y., & Falbo, T. (1991). Relationships between marital satisfaction, resources, and power strategies. *Sex Roles, 24*(1/2), 43–56.

Alan Guttmacher Institute. (1998). *Facts in brief: Induced abortion* [On-line]. Available: www. agi-usa.org/pubs/

Alan Guttmacher Institute. (1999). *Facts in brief: Teen sex and pregnancy* [On-line]. Available: www.agiusa.org/pubs/

Allen, B. P. (1995). Gender stereotypes are not accurate: A replication of Martin (1987) using diagnostic vs. self-report and behavioral criteria. *Sex Roles, 32*(9/10), 583–600.

Allen, L. S., Richey, M. F., Chai, Y. M., & Gorski, R. A. (1991). Sex differences in the corpus callosum of the living human being. *Journal of Neuroscience, 11*(4), 933–942.

Allen, P. G. (1986). *The sacred hoop: Recovering the feminine in American Indian traditions.* Boston: Beacon.

Allport, G. W. (1954). *The nature of prejudice.* Reading, MA: Addison-Wesley.

Almquist, E. M. (1995). The experiences of minority women in the United States: Intersections of race, gender, and class. In J. Freeman (Ed.), *Women: A feminist perspective* (pp. 573–606). Mountain View, CA: Mayfield.

Alzate, H., & Hoch, Z. (1986). The "G spot" and "female ejaculation": A current appraisal. *Journal of Sex and Marital Therapy, 12,* 211–220.

Amaro, H., Beckman, L., & Mays, V. (1987). A comparison of Black and White women entering alcoholism treatment. *Journal of Studies on Alcohol, 48*(3), 220–228.

Amatea, E. S., & Fong, M. L. (1991). The impact of role stressors and personal resources on the stress experience of professional women. *Psychology of Women Quarterly, 15*(3), 419–430.

American Bar Association. (1998). *Facts about women and the law* [On-line]. Available: www.abanet.org/media/ factbooks/womenlaw.pdf

American Correctional Association. (1990). *The female offender: What does the future hold?* Washington, DC: St. Mary's Press.

American Federation of Labor. (1999). *Equal pay by occupation* [On-line]. Available: www.aflcio.org/women

American Management Association, and Business and Professional Women's Foundation. (1999). *1999 AMA/BPW survey. Compensation and benefits: A focus on gender* [On-line]. Available: http://www.amanet.org

American Psychiatric Association. (1994). *Diagnostic and Statistical Manual of Mental Disorders* (4th ed.). Washington, DC: Author.

American Psychological Association. (1975). Report of the Task Force on Sex Bias and Sex-Role Stereotyping in Psychotherapeutic Practice. *American Psychologist, 30,* 1169–1175.

American Psychological Association. (1978). Guidelines for therapy with women. *American Psychologist, 13,* 1122–1123.

American Psychological Association. (1994). *Ph.D. recipients in psychology from U.S. universities by sex and subfield: 1920–1993.* Compiled by the Research Office, APA. Washington, DC: Author.

Amott, T., & Matthaei, J. (1991). *Gender and work: A multicultural economic history of women in the United States.* Boston: South End Press.

Anastasi, A. (1958a). *Differential psychology: Individual and group differences in behavior.* New York: Macmillan. (Original work published 1937)

Anastasi, A. (1958b). Heredity, environment, and the question "how?" *Psychological Review, 65,* 197–208.

Anastasi, A. (1981). Sex differences: Historical perspectives and methodological implications.

Developmental Review, 1, 187–206.

Andersson, B. (1979). Developmental trends in reaction to social pressure from adults versus peers. *International Journal of Behavior Development, 2,* 269–286.

Andrew, W. K. (1985). The phenomenological foundations for empirical methodology I: The method of optional variations. *Journal of Phenomenological Psychology, 16*(2), 1–29.

Andrew, W. K. (1986). The phenomenological foundations for methodology II: Experimental phenomenological psychology. *Journal of Phenomenological Psychology, 17*(1), 77–97.

Angier, N. (1990, July 20). Scientists find sex differentiation gene. *International Herald Tribune,* p. 3.

Angier, N. (1999). *Woman: An intimate geography.* Boston: Houghton Mifflin.

Angold, A., & Rutter, M. (1992). Effects of age and pubertal status on depression in a large clinical sample. *Development and Psychopathology, 4*(1), 5–28.

Ansari, M. A. (1989). Effects of leader sex, subordinate sex, and subordinate performance on the use of influence strategies. *Sex Roles, 20*(5/6), 283–293.

Antill, J. K., & Cunningham, J. D. (1982). Sex differences in performance on ability tests as a function of masculinity, femininity and androgyny. *Journal of Personality and Social Psychology, 42,* 718–728.

Arbeit, S. A. (1975). *A study of women during their first pregnancy.* Unpublished doctoral dissertation, Yale University.

Archer, J. (1979). *Animals under stress.* London: Edward Arnold.

Archer, J. (1984). Gender roles as developmental pathways. *British Journal of Social Psychology, 23,* 245–256.

Archer, J., & Lloyd, B. (1985). *Sex and gender.* Cambridge: Cambridge University Press.

Archer, J., & Westeman, K. (1981). Sex differences in the aggressive behavior of schoolchildren. *British Journal of Social Psychology, 20,* 31–61.

Arias, I., & Pape, K. T. (1999). Psychological abuse: Implications for adjustment and commitment to leave violent partners. *Violence and Victims, 14*(1), 55–67.

Arias, I., Samios, M., & O'Leary, K. D. (1987). Prevalence and correlates of physical aggression during courtship. *Journal of Interpersonal Violence, 2,* 82–90.

Aries, E. (1976). Interaction patterns and themes of male, female, and mixed groups. *Small Group Behavior, 7*(1), 7–18.

Armitage, K. J., Schneiderman, L. J., & Bass, R. A. (1979). Response of physicians to medical complaints in men and women. *Journal of the American Medical Association, 241*(20), 2186–2187.

Aronson, J., Lustina, M. J., Good, C., Keough, K., Steele, C. M., & Brown, J. (1999). When White men can't do math: Necessary and sufficient factors in stereotype threat. *Journal of Experimental Social Psychology, 35*(1), 29–46.

Ashton, E. (1983). Measures of play behavior: The influence of sex-role stereotyped children's books. *Sex Roles, 9,* 43–47.

Astin, A. W. (1985, January 16). Freshman characteristics and attitudes. *Chronicle of Higher Education,* pp. 15–16.

Astrachan, A. (1989). Dividing lines. In M. S. Kimmel & M. A. Messner (Eds.), *Men's lives* (pp. 63–73). New York: Macmillan.

Atkinson, J., & Huston, T. L. (1984). Sex role orientation and division of labor early in marriage. *Journal of Personality* and Social Psychology, 46(2), 330–345.

Atkinson, J. W. (Ed.). (1958). *Motives in fantasy, action and society*. Princeton, NJ: Van Nostrand.

Atkinson, J. W., & Feather, N. T. (1966). *A theory of achievement motivation*. New York: Wiley.

Aubry, T. (1986). *Marital relations in the context of the unemployment of the husband*. Unpublished master's thesis, University of Manitoba.

Aubuchon, P. G., & Calhoun, K. S. (1985). Menstrual cycle symptomatology: The role of social expectancy and experimental demand characteristics. *Psychosomatic Medicine, 47*(1), 35–45.

Aulin, K. P. (1995). Gender-specific issues. *Journal of Sports Sciences, 13,* S35–S39.

Avis, N. E., & McKinlay, S. M. (1991). A longitudinal analysis of women's attitudes toward the menopause: Results from the Massachusetts Women's Health Study. *Maturitas, 13,* 65–69.

Awiakta, M. (1993). Anorexia bulimia speaks from the grave. In M. Awiakta, *Selu* (pp. 193–194). Golden, CO: Fulcrum.

Azar, B. (1998, October). Sex differences may not be set at birth. *APA Monitor, 29*(10), 25.

Babcock, J. C., Waltz, J., Jacobson, N. S., & Gottman, J. M. (1993). Power and violence: The relation between communication patterns, power discrepancies, and domestic violence. *Journal of Consulting and Clinical Psychology, 61*(1), 40–50.

Baber, K. M., & Monaghan, P. (1988). College women's career and motherhood expectations: New options, old dilemmas. *Sex Roles, 19,* 189–203.

Baca Zinn, M. (1989). Chicano men and masculinity. In M. S.

Kimmel & M. A. Messner (Eds.), *Men's lives* (pp. 87–97). New York: Macmillan.

Bachu, A. (1999). *Trends in marital status of U.S. women at first birth*. Technical Working Paper 20, U.S. Census Bureau, Population Division, Fertility and Family Statistics Branch.

Back, S., Diaz Zuniga, C., & Lips, H. M. (1996, March). *Spanish university students' perceptions of their possible powerful selves*. Paper presented at the annual meeting of the Southeastern Psychological Association, Norfolk, VA.

Backhouse, C., & Cohen, L. (1978). *The secret oppression: Sexual harassment of working women*. Toronto: Macmillan of Canada.

Bacon, M. (1974). The dependency-conflict hypothesis and the frequency of drunkenness: Further evidence from a cross-cultural study. *Quarterly Journal of Studies on Alcohol, 35,* 863–876.

Badagliacco, J. M. (1990). Gender and race differences in computing attitudes and experience. *Social Science Computer Review, 8*(1), 42–63.

Baenninger, M., & Newcombe, N. (1989). The role of experience in spatial test performance: A meta-analysis. *Sex Roles, 20*(5/6), 327–344.

Bailey, J. M., Pillard, R. C., Neale, M. C., & Agyci, Y. (1993). Heritable factors influence sexual orientation in women. *Archives of General Psychiatry, 50,* 217–223.

Baker, M. (1985). *"What will tomorrow bring? . . . " A study of the aspirations of adolescent women*. Ottawa: Canadian Advisory Council on the Status of Women.

Baker, S. W. (1980). Biological influences on human sex and gender. *Signs: Journal of Women in Culture and Society, 6,* 80–96.

Bakken, L., & Romig, C. (1992). Interpersonal needs in middle adolescents: Companionship, leadership and intimacy. *Journal of Adolescence, 15*(3), 301–316.

Bandura, A. (1973). *Aggression: A social learning analysis*. Englewood Cliffs, NJ: Prentice-Hall.

Bandura, A. (1977). *Social learning theory*. Englewood Cliffs, NJ: Prentice-Hall.

Bandura, A. (1986). *Social foundations of thought and action: A social cognitive theory*. Englewood Cliffs, NJ: Prentice-Hall.

Bankart, B. (1989). Japanese perceptions of motherhood. *Psychology of Women Quarterly, 13,* 59–76.

Barash, D. (1979). *The whisperings within*. New York: Harper & Row.

Barbach, L. G. (1976). *For yourself: The fulfillment of female sexuality*. Garden City, NY: Anchor Books.

Barbarino, T. L. (1991). *Effects of viewing rock videos on women's acceptance of rape myths*. Unpublished master's thesis, Radford University.

Barbee, A. P., Cunningham, M. R., Winstead, B. A., Derlega, V. J., et al. (1993). Effects of gender role expectations on the social support process. *Journal of Social Issues, 19*(3), 175–190.

Barclay, R. I., & Barclay, M. L. (1976). Aspects of the normal psychology of pregnancy: The midtrimester. *American Journal of Obstetrics and Gynecology, 125,* 207.

Bardwick, J. (1971). *The psychology of women: A study of bio-cultural conflicts*. New York: Harper & Row.

Barer, B. M. (1994). Men and women aging differently. *International Journal of Aging and Human Development, 38*(1), 29–40.

Barfield, A. (1976). Biological influences on sex differences in behavior. In M. S. Teitelbaum (Ed.), *Sex differences: Social and biological perspectives* (pp. 62–121). Garden City, NY: Anchor Books.

Barglow, P., & Brown, E. (1972). Pseudocyesis. To be and not to be pregnant: A psychosomatic question. In J. G. Howells (Ed.), *Modern perspectives in psycho-obstetrics* (pp. 53–67). New York: Brunner/Mazel.

Barnett, R. C., Brennan, R. T., & Marshall, N. L. (1994). Gender and the relationship between parent role quality and psychological distress. *Journal of Family Issues, 15*(2), 229–252.

Baron, J. N., & Newman, A. E. (1990). For what it's worth: Organizations, occupations, and the value of work done by women and nonwhites. *American Sociological Review, 55*(2), 155–175.

Bart, P. (1971). Depression in middle-aged women. In V. Gornick & B. Moran (Eds.), *Women in sexist society.* New York: Basic Books.

Bart, P. (1980, March). *Socialization and rape avoidance: How to say no to Storaska and survive.* Paper presented at the National Conference on Feminist Psychology, Santa Monica, CA.

Bart, P. (1993). Protean women: The liquidity of female sexuality and the tenaciousness of lesbian identity. In S. Wilkinson & C. Kitzinger (Eds.), *Heterosexuality: A feminism and psychology reader* (pp. 246–252). London: Sage.

Baruch, G. K. (1972). Maternal influences upon college women's attitudes toward women and work. *Developmental Psychology, 6,* 32–37.

Baruch, G. K., Barnett, R., & Rivers, C. (1983). *Lifeprints: New patterns of love and work for today's women.* New York: McGraw-Hill.

Basler, B. (1984, February 12). Study finds sex stereotypes affect voters at polls. *New York Times,* p. 4.

Basow, S. A. (1986). *Gender stereotypes: Traditions and alternatives.* Pacific Grove, CA: Brooks/Cole.

Baumgartner, A. (1983). *"My daddy might have loved me": Student perceptions of differences between being male and being female.* Denver: Institute for Equality in Education.

Baumrind, D. (1979, March). *Sex-related socialization effects.* Paper presented at the meeting of the Society for Research in Child Development, San Francisco.

Baxter, J. (1992). Power attitudes and time: The domestic division of labour. *Journal of Comparative Family Studies, 13*(2), 165–179.

Bayley, N., & Oden, M. (1955). The maintenance of intellectual ability in gifted adults. *Journal of Gerontology, 10,* 91–107.

Bazargan, M., & Barbre, A. R. (1992). Self-reported memory problems among the Black elderly. *Educational Gerontology, 18*(1), 71–82.

Bazin, N. T., & Freeman, A. (1974). The androgynous vision. *Women's Studies, 2*(2), 185–215.

Bazzini, D. G., McIntosh, W. D., Smith, S. M., Cook, S., et al. (1997). The aging women in popular film: Underrepresented, unattractive, unfriendly, and unintelligent. *Sex Roles, 36*(7/8), 531–543.

Beaton, A. M., & Tougas, F. (1997). The representation of women in management: The more the merrier? *Personality and Social Psychology Bulletin, 23*(7), 773–782.

Beaton, A. M., Tougas, F., & Joly, S. (1996). Neosexism among male managers: Is it a matter of numbers? *Journal of Applied Social Psychology, 26,* 2189–2203.

Becker, B. J., & Hedges, L. N. (1984). Meta-analysis of cognitive gender differences: A comment on an analysis by Rosenthal and Rubin. *Journal of Educational Psychology, 76,* 583–587.

Becker, B. J., & Hedges, L. N. (1988). The effects of selection and variability in studies of gender differences. *Behavioral and Brain Sciences, 11*(2), 183–184.

Bee, H. L., Mitchell, S. K., Barnard, K. E., Eyres, S. J., & Hammond, M. A. (1984). Predicting intellectual outcomes: Sex differences in response to early environmental stimulation. *Sex Roles, 10,* 783–803.

Beer, W. (1982). *Househusbands: Men and housework in American families.* New York: Praeger.

Belanger, S. (1984). Women and technology. *Canada's Mental Health, 32*(3), 17–18.

Bell, A. P., & Weinberg, M. S. (1978). *Homosexualities.* New York: Simon & Schuster.

Bell, A. P., Weinberg, M. S., & Hammersmith, S. K. (1981). *Sexual preference.* Bloomington: Indiana University Press.

Bell, D. (1983). *Daughters of the dreaming.* Melbourne, Australia: McPhee Gribble.

Bell, I. P. (1989). The double standard: Age. In J. Freeman (Ed.), *Women: A feminist perspective* (4th ed., pp. 236–244). Mountain View, CA: Mayfield.

Bell, L. (1999, November 9). Hispanic mothers face risks. *Washington Post,* Health section, p. 21.

Bell, R. R. (1981). Friendships of women and men. *Psychology of Women Quarterly, 5,* 402–417.

Belle, D. (1984). Inequality and mental health: Low income and minority women. In L. Walker (Ed.), *Women and mental health policy* (pp. 135–150). Beverly Hills, CA: Sage.

Belle, D., & Goldman, N. (1980). Patterns of diagnoses received by men and women. In M. Guttentag, S. Salasin, & D. Belle (Eds.), *The mental health of women* (pp. 21–30). New York: Academic Press.

Bellinger, D. C., & Gleason, J. B. (1982). Sex differences in parental directives to young children. *Sex Roles, 8,* 1123–1139.

Belote, B. (1976). Masochistic syndrome, hysterical personality, and the illusion of a healthy woman. In S. Cox (Ed.), *Female psychology: The emerging self* (pp. 335–348). Chicago: Science Research Associates.

Bem, S. L. (1974). The measurement of psychological androgyny. *Journal of Consulting and Clinical Psychology, 42,* 155–162.

Bem, S. L. (1975). Sex-role adaptability: One consequence of psychological androgyny. *Journal of Personality and Social Psychology, 31,* 634–643.

Bem, S. L. (1981). Gender schema theory: A cognitive account of sex typing. *Psychological Review, 88,* 354–364.

Bem, S. L. (1985). Androgyny and gender schema theory: A conceptual and empirical integration. In T. B. Sonderegger (Ed.), *Nebraska Symposium on Motivation: Psychology of gender* (pp. 179–226). Lincoln: University of Nebraska Press.

Bem, S. L. (1993). *The lenses of gender.* New Haven, CT: Yale University Press.

Bem, S. L., & Lenney, E. (1976). Sex-typing and the avoidance of cross-sex behavior. *Journal of Personality and Social Psychology, 33*(1), 48–54.

Bem, S. L., Martyna, W., & Watson, C. (1976). Sex-typing and androgyny: Further exploration of the expressive domain. *Journal of Personality and Social Psychology, 34,* 1016–1023.

Benbow, C. P. (1986). Physiological correlates of extreme intellectual precocity. *Neuropsychologia, 24,* 719–725.

Benbow, C. P. (1988). Sex differences in mathematical reasoning ability in intellectually talented preadolescents: Their nature, effects, and possible causes. *Behavioral and Brain Sciences, 11*(2), 169–232.

Benbow, C. P., & Stanley, J. C. (1980). Sex differences in mathematical ability: Fact or artifact? *Science, 210,* 1262–1264.

Benbow, C. P., & Stanley, J. C. (1982). Consequences in high school and college of sex differences in mathematical reasoning ability: A longitudinal perspective. *American Educational Research Journal, 19,* 598–622.

Benbow, C. P., & Stanley, J. C. (1983). Sex differences in mathematical reasoning ability: More facts. *Science, 222,* 1029–1031.

Bennett, J. E., & Loewe, P. M. (1975). *Women in business: A shocking waste of human resources.* Toronto: Maclean-Hunter.

Berenbaum, S. A., & Hines, M. (1992). Early androgens are related to childhood sex-typed toy preferences. *Psychological Science, 3,* 203–206.

Berganza, C. E., Peyre, C. A., & Aguilar, G. (1989). Sexual attitudes and behavior of Guatemalan teenagers: Considerations for prevention of adolescent pregnancy. *Adolescence, 24,* 327–337.

Berman, P. W. (1976). Social context as a determinant of sex differences in adults' attraction to infants. *Developmental Psychology, 12,* 365–366.

Berman, P. W. (1980). Are women more responsive than men to the young? A review of developmental and situational variables. *Psychological Bulletin, 88,* 668–695.

Bernard, J. (1972). *The future of marriage.* New York: World.

Bernard, J. (1974). *The future of motherhood.* New York: Dial Press.

Bernard, J. (1976). Where are we now? Some thoughts on the current scene. *Psychology of Women Quarterly, 1*(1), 21–37.

Bernat, F. P. (1984). Gender disparity in the setting of bail: Prostitution offenses in Buffalo, NY, 1977–1979. *Journal of Offender Counseling, Services and Rehabilitation, 9*(1/2), 21–47.

Berndt, T. J., & Hoyle, S. G. (1985). Stability and change in childhood and adolescent friendships. *Developmental Psychology, 21*(6), 1007–1015.

Bernstein, L., Henderson, B. E., Hanisch, R., Sullivan-Halley, J., & Ross, R. K. (1994). Physical exercise and breast cancer in young women. *Clinical Journal of Sports Medicine, 5*(2), 144.

Berry, J. W. (1966). Temne and Eskimo perceptual skills. *International Journal of Psychology, 1,* 207–229.

Berzins, J., Welling, M., & Wetter, R. (1975). *The PRF Andro scale user's manual.* Unpublished manual, University of Kentucky.

Betz, N. E., & Fitzgerald, L. E. (1987). *The career psychology of women.* New York: Academic Press.

Betz, N. E., & Hackett, G. (1983). The relationship of mathematics self-efficacy expectations to the selection of science-based college majors. *Journal of Vocational Behavior, 23,* 329–345.

Beuf, A. (1974). Doctor, lawyer, household drudge. *Journal of Communication, 24*(2), 142–145.

Beyer, S. (1990). Gender differences in the accuracy of self-evaluations of performance. *Journal of Personality and Social Psychology, 59*(5), 960–970.

Bibring, G. (1959). Some considerations of the psychological process of pregnancy. In *The psychoanalytic study of the child* (Vol. 14, pp. 113–121). New York: International Universities Press.

Bickman, L. (1974). Sex and helping behavior. *Journal of Social Psychology, 93*(1), 43–53.

Bidwell, R. J., & Deisher, R. W. (1991). Adolescent sexuality: Current issues. *Pediatric Annals, 20,* 293–302.

Bielby, D. D., & Bielby, W. T. (1988). She works hard for the money: Household responsibilities and the allocation of work effort. *American Journal of Sociology, 83*(5), 1031–1059.

Biernat, M., & Wortman, C. B. (1991). Sharing of home responsibilities between professionally employed women and their husbands. *Journal of Personality and Social Psychology, 60*(6), 844–860.

Binion, V. (1990). Psychological androgyny: A Black female perspective. *Sex Roles, 22,* 487–507.

Bishop, P., Cureton, K., Conerly, M., & Collins, M. (1989). Sex difference in muscle cross-sectional area of athletes and non-athletes. *Journal of Sport Sciences, 7,* 31–39.

Black breast-cancer deaths not just a matter of health-care access. (1998, April 2). *Roanoke Times,* p. A7.

Black, S. L., & Koulis-Chitwood, A. (1990). The menstrual cycle and typing skill: An ecologically-valid test of the "raging hormones" hypothesis. *Canadian Journal of Behavioural Science, 22*(4), 445–455.

Blais, M. R., Vallerand, R. J., Briere, N. M., Gagnon, A., et al. (1990). Significance, structure, and gender differences in life domains of college students. *Sex Roles, 22*(3/4), 199–212.

Blanchard, R. (1985). Gender dysphoria and gender reorientation. In B. W. Steiner (Ed.), *Gender dysphoria: Development, research, management* (pp. 227–257). New York: Plenum Press.

Blanchard, R., Steiner, B. W., & Clemmensen, L. H. (1985). Gender dysphoria, gender reorientation, and the management of transsexualism. *Journal of Consulting and Clinical Psychology, 53*(3), 295–304.

Bleier, R. (1984). *Science and gender: A critique of biology and its theories on women.* New York: Pergamon Press.

Block, J. H. (1973). Conceptions of sex roles: Some cross-cultural and longitudinal perspectives. *American Psychologist, 28,* 512–526.

Block, J. H. (1984). *Sex role identity and ego development.* San Francisco: Jossey-Bass.

Blough, P. M., & Slavin, L. K. (1987). Reaction time assessments of gender differences in visual-spatial performance. *Perception and Psychophysics, 41*(3), 276–281.

Blumstein, P., & Schwartz, P. (1976). Bisexual women. In J. P. Wiseman (Ed.), *The social psychology of sex.* New York: Harper & Row.

Blumstein, P., & Schwartz, P. (1983). *American couples.* New York: Morrow.

Bock, D. R., & Kolakowski, D. (1973). Further evidence of a sex-linked major-gene influence on human spatial visualizing ability. *American Journal of Human Genetics, 25,* 1–14.

Bohan, J. S. (1992). Contextual history: A framework for replacing women in the history of psychology. In J. S. Bohan (Ed.), *Re-placing women in psychology: Readings toward a more inclusive history* (pp. 44–56). Dubuque, IA: Kendall/Hunt.

Bohan, J. S. (1996). *Psychology and sexual orientation: Coming to terms.* New York: Routledge.

Bohan, J. S. (1997). Regarding gender: Essentialism, constructionism, and feminist psychology. In M. M. Gergen & S. N. Davis (Eds.). *Toward a new psychology of gender* (pp. 31–48). New York: Routledge.

Bonen, A. (1994). Exercise-induced menstual cycle changes: A functional, temporary adaptation to metabolic stress. *Sports Medicine, 17*(6), 373–392.

Booth, A., & Dabbs, J. M. (1993). Testosterone and men's marriages. *Social Forces, 72*(2), 463–477.

Boring, E. (1929). *A history of experimental psychology* (Vol. 1). New York: Appleton-Century.

Borman, J., & Biordi, D. (1992). Female nurse executives: Finally, at an advantage? *Journal of Nursing Administration, 22*(9), 37–41.

Bornstein, K. (1994). *Gender outlaw: On men, women, and the rest of us.* New York: Vintage Books.

Bornstein, R. A. (1984). Unilateral lesions and the Wechsler Adult Intelligence Scale–Revised: No sex differences. *Journal of Consulting and Clinical Psychology, 52,* 604–608.

Borowy, T., & Goebel, R. (1976). Cerebral lateralization of speech: The effects of age, sex, race, and socioeconomic class. *Neuropsychologia, 14,* 363–370.

Borys, S., & Perlman, D. (1985). Gender differences in loneliness. *Personality and Social Psychology Bulletin, 11*(1), 63–74.

Boskind-White, M. (1985). Bulimarexia: A sociocultural perspective. In S. W. Emmett (Ed.), *Theory and treatment of anorexia nervosa and bulimia: Biomedical, sociocultural, and psychological perspectives* (pp. 113–126). New York: Brunner/Mazel.

Boswell, H. (1997). The transgender paradigm shift toward free expression. In B. Bullough & V. L. Bullough (Eds.), *Gender blending* (pp. 53–57). New York: Prometheus Books.

Boswell, S. L. (1985). The influence of sex-role stereotyping on women's attitudes and achievement in mathematics. In S. F. Chipman, L. R. Brush, & D. M. Wilson (Eds.), *Women and mathematics: Balancing the equation* (pp. 175–198). Hillsdale, NJ: Erlbaum.

Bouchard, T. J., Lykken, D. T., McGue, M., Segal, N. L., & Tellegen, A. (1990). Sources of human psychological differences: The Minnesota study of twins reared apart. *Science, 25,* 223–228.

Bowen, D. J., & Grunberg, N. E. (1990). Variations in food preference and consumption across the menstrual cycle. *Physiology and Behavior, 47*(2), 287–291.

Boy still meets girl—but not at the computer. (1987, January/February). *NEA Today, 5*(5), 17.

Boyd, N. (1979). Black families in therapy: A study of clinicians' perceptions. *Sandoz Psychiatric Spectator, 11*(7), 21–25.

Boylan, C. R., Hill, D. M., Wallace, A. R., & Wheeler, A. E. (1992). Beyond stereotypes. *Science Education, 76*(5), 465–476.

Brabeck, M. (1983). Moral judgment: Theory and research on differences between males and females. *Developmental Review, 3,* 274–291.

Bradbury, T. N., Campbell S. M., & Fincham, F. D. (1995). Longitudinal and behavioral analysis of masculinity and femininity in marriages. *Journal of Personality and Social Psychology, 68*(2), 328–341.

Bradford, D. L., Sargent, A. G., & Sprague, M. S. (1975). The executive man and woman: The issue of sexuality. In F. E. Gordon & M. H. Strober (Eds.), *Bringing women into management.* New York: McGraw-Hill.

Bradley, C. F. (1983). Psychological consequences of intervention in the birth process. *Canadian Journal of Behavioral Science, 15*(4), 422–438.

Brandon, P. R. (1991). Gender differences in young Asian Americans' educational attainment. *Sex Roles, 25*(1/2), 45–61.

Brannock, J. C., & Chapman, B. E. (1990). Negative sexual experiences with men among heterosexual women and lesbians. *Journal of Homosexuality, 19*(1), 105–110.

Brannon, R. (1976). The male sex role: Our culture's blueprint for manhood and what it's done for us lately. In D. David & R. Brannon (Eds.), *The forty-nine percent majority.* Reading, MA: Addison-Wesley.

Breathnach, C. S. (1990). The secondary sexual characteristics of the brain. *Irish Journal of Psychological Medicine, 7*(1), 59–63.

Brehm, J. W. (1966). *A theory of psychological reactance.* New York: Academic Press.

Brehony, A. (1982). Women and agoraphobia: A case for the etiological significance of the feminine sex role stereotype. In V. Franks & E. Rothblum (Eds.), *Sex role stereotypes and women's mental health.* New York: Springer.

Brehony, K. A., & Geller, E. S. (1981). Relationship between psychological androgyny, social conformity and perceived locus of control. *Psychology of Women Quarterly, 6,* 204–217.

Bretl, D. J., & Cantor, J. (1988). The portrayal of men and women in U.S. television commercials: A recent content analysis and trends over 15 years. *Sex Roles, 18*(9/10), 595–609.

Bridges, J. S. (1987). College females' perception of adult roles and occupational fields for women. *Sex Roles, 16,* 591–604.

Bridges, J. S. (1988). Sex differences in occupational performance expectations. *Psychology of Women Quarterly, 12*(1), 75–90.

Bridges, J. S. (1993). Pink or blue: Gender-stereotypic perceptions of infants as conveyed by birth congratulations cards. *Psychology of Women Quarterly, 17*(2), 193–206.

Briere, J., Corne, S., Runta, M., & Malamuth, N. (1984, August). *The rape arousal inventory: Predicting actual and potential sexual aggression in a university population.* Paper presented at the meeting of the American Psychological Association, Toronto.

Briere, J., & Malamuth, N. (1983). Self-reported likelihood of sexually aggressive behavior: Attitudinal versus sexual explanations. *Journal of Research in Personality, 17,* 315–323.

Brockner, J., & Adsit, L. (1986). The moderating impact of sex on the equity-satisfaction relationship: A field study. *Journal of Applied Psychology, 71*(4), 585–590.

Brodie, M. J., & Vickers, J. M. (1982). *Canadian women in politics: An overview.* Ottawa: Canadian Research Institute for the Advancement of Women.

Brodsky, G. (1986, Fall). LEAF's legal cases: an update. *LEAF Letter,* p. 4.

Brody, E. M. (1981). "Women in the middle" and family help to older people. *Gerontologist, 21,* 471–479.

Bronstein, P. (1984). Differences in mothers' and fathers' behaviors toward children: A cross-cultural comparison. *Developmental Psychology, 20*(6), 995–1003.

Bronstein, P., Black, L., Pfenning, J., & White, A. (1986). Getting academic jobs: Are women equally qualified and equally successful? *American Psychologist, 41,* 318–322.

Brooks, J., Ruble, D. N., & Clarke, A. E. (1977). College women's attitudes and expectations concerning menstrual-related changes. *Psychosomatic Medicine, 39*(5), 288–298.

Brooks, L., & Perot, A. R. (1991). Reporting sexual harassment: Exploring a predictive model. *Psychology of Women Quarterly, 15*(1), 31–48.

Brooks-Gunn, J., Burrow, C., & Warren, M. P. (1988). Attitudes toward eating and body weight in different groups of female adolescent athletes. *International Journal of Eating Disorders, 7,* 749–757.

Brooks-Gunn, J., & Ruble, D. (1980). Menarche. In A. J. Dan, E. A. Graham, & C. P. Beecher (Eds.), *The menstrual cycle* (Vol. 1). New York: Springer.

Brooks-Gunn, J., & Ruble, D. N. (1983). Dysmenorrhea in adolescence. In S. Golub (Ed.), *Menarche: The transition from girl to woman* (pp. 251–261). Lexington, MA: Lexington Books.

Broverman, I. K., Broverman, D. M., Clarkson, F. E., Rosenkrantz, P. S., & Vogel, S. R. (1970). Sex role stereotypes and clinical judgments of mental health. *Journal of Consulting and Clinical Psychology, 34*(1), 1–7.

Broverman, I. K., Vogel, S. R., Broverman, D. M., Clarkson, F. E., & Rosenkrantz, P. S. (1972). Sex-role stereotypes: A current appraisal. *Journal of Social Issues, 28*(2), 59–78.

Brown, A., Larsen, M. B., Rankin, S. A., & Ballard, R. A. (1980). Sex differences in information processing. *Sex Roles, 6,* 663–673.

Brown, D. (1992, May 22). Smoking deaths seen climbing. *Washington Post,* pp. A1, A6.

Brown, J. D. (1985). Race and gender in rock video. *Social Science Newsletter, 70*(2), 82–86.

Brown, J. D., Childers, K. W., & Waszak, C. S. (1990). Television and adolescent sexuality. *Journal of Adolescent Health Care, 11*(1), 62–70.

Brown, L. S. (1989). New voices, new visions: Toward a lesbian/gay paradigm for psychology. *Psychology of Women Quarterly, 13*(4), 445–458.

Brown, L. S., & Root, M. P. P. (Eds.). (1990). *Diversity and complexity in feminist therapy.* Binghamton, NY: Haworth Press.

Brown, M., Amoroso, D. M., & Ware, E. E. (1976). Behavioral effects of viewing pornography. *Journal of Social Psychology, 98,* 235–245.

Brown, W. B., Bhrolchain, M., & Harris, T. (1975). Social class and psychiatric disturbance among women in an urban population. *Sociology, 9*(2), 225–254.

Brownell, K. D., & Rodin, J. (1994). The dieting maelstrom: Is it possible and advisable to lose weight? *American Psychologist, 49,* 781–791.

Brownmiller, S. (1975). *Against our will: Men, women, and rape.* New York: Simon & Schuster.

Brownmiller, S. (1984). *Femininity.* New York: Fawcett Columbine.

Bryan, A. D., Aiken, L. S., & West, S. G. (1999). The impact of males proposing condom use on perceptions of an initial sexual encounter. *Personality and Social Psychology Bulletin, 25*(3), 275–286.

Bryden, M. P., & Vrbancic, M. I. (1988). Dichotic lateralization, cognitive ability, and age at puberty. *Developmental Neuropsychology, 4*(2), 169–180.

Buchanan, M., & Robbins, C. (1990). Early adult psychological consequences for males of adolescent pregnancy and its resolution. *Journal of Youth and Adolescence, 19*(4), 413–424.

Budoff, P. W. (1980). *No more menstrual cramps and other good news.* New York: Putnam.

Burchardt, C. J., & Serbin, L. A. (1982). Psychological androgyny and personality adjustment in college and psychiatric populations. *Sex Roles, 8,* 835–851.

Burlew, A. K. (1982). The experiences of Black females in traditional and nontraditional professions. *Psychology of Women Quarterly, 6*(3), 312–326.

Burns, R. B. (1977). Male and female perceptions of their own and the other sex. *British Journal of Social and Clinical Psychology, 16,* 213–220.

Busby, L. (1974). Defining the sex-role standard in commercial network television programs directed toward children. *Journalism Quarterly, 51,* 690–696.

Buss, D. M. (1989). Sex differences in human mate preferences: Evolutionary hypotheses tested in 37 countries. *Behavioral and Brain Sciences, 12,* 1–49.

Buss, D. M. (1994). *The evolution of desire: Strategies of human mating.* New York: Basic Books.

Buss, D. M. (1995). Psychological sex differences: Origins through sexual selection. *American Psychologist, 50,* 164–168.

Buss, D. M., et al. (1990). International preferences in selecting mates: A study of 37 cultures. *Journal of Cross-Cultural Psychology, 21,* 5–47.

Bussey, K., & Bandura, A. (1984). Influence of gender constancy and social power on sex-linked modeling. *Journal of Personality and Social Psychology, 47,* 1292–1302.

Bussey, K. & Bandura, A. (1992). Self-regulatory mechanisms governing gender development. *Child Development, 63,* 1236–1250.

Bussey, K., & Perry, D. G. (1982). Same-sex imitation: The avoidance of cross-sex models or the acceptance of same-sex models? *Sex Roles, 8,* 773–784.

Butler, D., & Geis, F. L. (1990). Nonverbal affect responses to male and female leaders: Implications for leadership evaluations. *Journal of Personality and Social Psychology, 58*(1), 48–59.

Butler, S., & Wintram, C. (1991). *Feminist groupwork.* Newbury Park, CA: Sage.

Bylsma, W. H., & Major, B. (1994). Social comparisons and contentment: Exploring the psychological costs of the gender wage gap. *Psychology of Women Quarterly, 18*(2), 241–249.

Bylsma, W. H., Major, B., & Cozzarelli, C. (1995). The influence of legitimacy appraisals on the determinants of entitlement beliefs. *Basic and Applied Social Psychology, 17*(1/2), 223–237.

Byne, W., Bleier, R., & Houston, L. (1988). Variations in human corpus callosum do not predict gender: A study using magnetic resonance imaging. *Behavioral Neuroscience, 102*(2), 222–227.

Cabaj, R. P. (1988). Gay and lesbian couples: Lessons on human intimacy. *Psychiatric Annals, 18,* 21–25.

Cafferata, G. L., & Meyers, S. M. (1990). Pathways to psychotropic drugs: Understanding the basis of gender differences. *Medical Care, 28*(4), 285–300.

Caldera, Y. M., Huston, A. C., & O'Brien, M. (1989). Social interactions and play patterns of parents and toddlers with feminine, masculine, and neutral toys. *Child Development, 60,* 70–76.

Caldwell, M. A., & Peplau, L. A. (1982). Sex differences in same-sex friendships. *Sex Roles, 8,* 721–732.

Callahan-Levy, C. M., & Messe, L. A. (1979). Sex differences in the allocation of pay. *Journal of Personality and Social Psychology, 37,* 433–446.

Calloni, J. C., & Handal, P. J. (1992). Differential parental attachment: Empirical support for the self-in-relation model. *Perceptual and Motor Skills, 75*(3, Pt. 1), 904–906.

Campbell, A., & Muncer, S. (1987). Models of anger and aggression in the social talk of women and men. *Journal for the Theory of Social Behavior, 17,* 489–511.

Campbell, J. R. (1991). The roots of gender inequity in technical areas. *Journal of Research in Science Teaching, 28*(3), 251–264.

Canada overturns definition of 'spouse' as heterosexual (1999, May 21). *New York Times,* p. A10.

Canadian Advisory Council on the Status of Women. (1984). *Prostitution in Canada.* Ottawa: Author.

Canadian Human Rights Commission. (1983). *Unwanted sexual attention and sexual harassment: Results of a survey of Canadians.* Ottawa: Author.

Canadian Mental Health Association. (1984). *Work and well-being: The changing realities of employment.* Toronto: Author.

Canadian Psychological Association. (1980). *Guidelines for therapy and counselling with women.* Ottawa: Author.

Canadian Psychological Association. (1982). *Therapy and counselling with women: A handbook on educational materials.* Ottawa: Author.

Cann, A., & Garnett, A. K. (1984). Sex stereotype impacts on competence ratings by children. *Sex Roles, 11,* 333–343.

Cannon, L. W., Higginbotham, E., & Leung, M. L. A. (1991). Race and class bias in qualitative research on women. In J. Lorber & S. A. Farrell (Eds.), *The social construction of gender* (pp. 237–248). Newbury Park, CA: Sage.

Cano, L., Solomon, S., & Holmes, D. S. (1984). Fear of success: The influence of sex, sex-role identity, and components of masculinity. *Sex Roles, 10,* 341–346.

Cantrell, P. (1996, January/February). Blue-collar workers: Breaking through the brick ceiling. *Ms., 6*(4), 34–38.

Caplan, P. J. (1993). Premenstrual syndrome DSM-IV diagnosis: The coalition for a scientific and responsible DSM-IV. *Psychology of Women: Newsletter of Division 35, 20*(3), 4–5, 13.

Caplan, P. J., & Eichler, M. (1989). *A proposal for the delusional dominating personality disorder.* Toronto: Authors.

Caplan, P. J., MacPherson, G. M., & Tobin, P. (1985). Do sex-related differences in spatial ability exist? A multilevel critique with new data. *American Psychologist, 40*(7), 786–799.

Caputi, J., & Russell, D. E. H. (1990, September/October). "Femicide": Speaking the unspeakable. *Ms., 1*(2), 34–37.

Carbonell, J. L. (1984). Sex roles and leadership revisited. *Journal of Applied Psychology, 53,* 377–382.

Carli, L. L. (1990). Gender, language, and influence. *Journal of Personality and Social Psychology, 59*(5), 941–951.

Carli, L. L. (1998, June). *Gender effects in social influence.* Paper presented at the meeting of the Society for the Study of Social Issues, Ann Arbor, MI.

Carli, L. L. (1999). Gender, interpersonal power, and social influence. *Journal of Social Issues, 55*(1), 81–99.

Carli, L. L., LaFleur, S. J., & Loeber, C. C. (1995). Nonverbal behavior, gender, and influence. *Journal of Personality and Social Psychology, 68*(6), 1030–1041.

Carlson, A. (1991, March). When is a woman not a woman? *Women's Sports & Fitness,* pp. 24–29.

Carlson, B. E., & Videka-Sherman, L. (1990). An empirical test of androgyny in the middle years: Evidence from a national survey. *Sex Roles, 23*(5/6), 305–324.

Carroll, J., Volk, K. D., & Hyde, J. S. (1985). Differences between males and females in motives for engaging in sexual intercourse. *Archives of Sexual Behavior, 14,* 131–139.

Carunungan-Robles, A. (1986). Perceptions of parental nurturance, punitiveness and power by selected Filipino primary school children. *Philippine Journal of Psychology, 19,* 18–28.

Carver, C. S., & de la Garza, N. H. (1984). Schema-guided information search in stereotyping of the elderly. *Journal of Applied Social Psychology, 14*(1), 69–81.

Cash, T. F., Gillen, B., & Burns, D. S. (1977). Sexism and "beautyism" in personnel consultant decision making. *Journal of Applied Psychology, 62,* 301–310.

Cash, T. F., & Henry, P. E. (1995). Women's body images: The results of a national survey in the U.S.A. *Sex Roles, 33*(1/2), 19–28.

Cash, T. F., Winstead, B. W., & Janda, L. H. (1986). The great American shape-up: Body image survey report. *Psychology Today, 20*(4), 30–37.

Caspi, A., Bem, D., & Elder, G. H. Jr. (1989). Continuities and consequences of interactional styles across the life course. *Journal of Personality, 57*(2), 375–406.

Cass, V. C. (1979). Homosexual identity formation: A theoretical model. *Journal of Homosexuality, 4,* 219–235.

Cass, V. C. (1984). Homosexual identity formation: Testing a theoretical model. *Journal of Sex Research, 20,* 143–167.

Catalyst (1998a, November 9). Equal pay and highest executive ranks still elude women [Online]. Press release. Available: www.catalystwomen.org/press/

Catalyst (1998b, March 10). NBC breakfast addresses work/life balancing act [On-line]. Press release. Available: www.catalyst-women.org/press/

Cate, R. M., Lloyd, S., Henton, J. M., & Larson, J. (1982). Fairness and reward level as predictors of relationship satisfaction. *Social Psychology Quarterly, 45,* 177–181.

Cattell, J. M. (1903). A statistical study of eminent men. *Popular Science Monthly, 62,* 359–377.

Cazenave, N. A. (1984). Race, socioeconomic status, and age:

The social context of American masculinity. *Sex Roles, 11*(7/8), 639–656.

Cazenave, N. A., & Leon, G. H. (1987). Men's work and family roles and characteristics: Race, gender, and class perceptions of college students. In M. S. Kimmel (Ed.), *Changing men: New directions in research on men and masculinity* (pp. 244–262). Newbury Park, CA: Sage.

Ceballo, R. (1999). Negotiating the life narrative: A dialogue with an African American social worker. *Psychology of Women Quarterly, 23*(2), 309–322.

Cejka, M. A., & Eagly, A. H. (1999). Gender-stereotypic images of occupations correspond to the sex segregation of employment. *Personality and Social Psychology Bulletin, 25*(4), 413–423.

Centers for Disease Control and Prevention. (1998a). National data on HIV prevalence among disadvantaged youth in the 1990s. *CDC Update,* September, pp. 1–2.

Centers for Disease Control and Prevention. (1998b). *HIV/AIDS surveillance report, 10*(2).

Chaison, G. N., & Andrappan, P. (1982). Characteristics of female union officers in Canada. *Industrial Relations, 37*(4), 765–778.

Chavez, D. (1985). Perpetuation of gender inequality: A content analysis of comic strips. *Sex Roles, 13*(1/2), 93–102.

Chernin, K. (1981). *The obsession: Reflections on the tyranny of slenderness.* New York: Harper & Row.

Cherry, F., & Deaux, K. (1978). Fear of success versus fear of gender-inappropriate behavior. *Sex Roles, 4,* 97–101.

Chertok, L. (1969). *Motherhood and personality.* London: Tavistock.

Chesler, P. (1971). Patient and patriarch: Women in the psychotherapeutic relationship.

In V. Gornick & B. Moran (Eds.), *Women in sexist society: Studies in power and powerlessness* (pp. 251–275). New York: Basic Books.

Chesler, P. (1972). *Women and madness.* New York: Doubleday.

Chesney-Lind, M. (1987). Female offenders: Paternalism reexamined. In L. Crites & W. Hepperle (Eds.), *Women, the courts, and equality.* Newbury Park, CA: Sage.

Chesney-Lind, M. (1995). Rethinking women's imprisonment: A critical examination of trends in female incarceration. In B. R. Price & N. Sokoloff (Eds.), *Women, crime, and criminal justice.* New York: McGraw-Hill.

Chino, A. F., & Funabiki, D. (1984). A cross-validation of sex differences in the expression of depression. *Sex Roles, 11,* 175–187.

Chodorow, N. (1978). *The reproduction of mothering: Psychoanalysis and the sociology of gender.* Berkeley: University of California Press.

Chodorow, N. (1989). *Feminism and psychoanalytic theory.* New Haven, CT: Yale University Press.

Chrisler, J. C., Johnston, I. K., Champagne, N. M., & Preston, K. E. (1994). Menstrual joy: The construct and its consequences. *Psychology of Women Quarterly, 18*(3), 375–388.

Chrisler, J. C., & Levy, K. B. (1990). The media construct a menstrual monster: A content analysis of PMS articles in the popular press. *Women and Health, 16*(2), 89–104.

Christensen, A., & Heavey, C. L. (1990). Gender and social structure in the demand/withdraw pattern of marital conflict. *Journal of Personality and Social Psychology, 59*(1), 73–81.

Christiansen, K., & Knussman, R. (1987). Androgen levels and components of aggressive behavior in men. *Hormones and Behavior, 21,* 170–180.

Cicchetti, D., & Toth, S. L. (1998). The development of depression in children and adolescents. *American Psychologist, 53*(2), 221–241.

Claes, M. E. (1992). Friendship and personal adjustment during adolescence. *Journal of Adolescence, 15*(1), 39–55.

Clark, C. (1972). Race, identification, and television violence. In G. A. Comstock, E. A. Rubenstein, & J. P. Murray (Eds.), *Television and social behavior: Vol. 5. Television's effects: Further explorations.* Washington, DC: U.S. Government Printing Office.

Clark, M. L., & Ayers, M. (1991). Friendship similarity during early adolescence: Gender and racial patterns. *Journal of Psychology, 126*(4), 393–405.

Clark, R., & Hatfield, E. (1989). Gender differences in receptivity to sexual offers. *Journal of Psychology and Human Sexuality, 2*(1), 39–55.

Clarke, E. (1873). *Sex in education; or, a fair chance for girls.* Boston: Osgood and Co.

Clarke-Stewart, K. A. (1991). A home is not a school: The effects of child care on children's development. *Journal of Social Issues, 47*(2), 105–124.

Clinton, J. F. (1987). Physical and emotional responses of expectant fathers throughout pregnancy and the early postpartum period. *International Journal of Nursing Studies, 24*(1), 59–68.

Clum, G. A., & Knowles, S. (1991). Why do some people with panic disorders become avoidant?: A review. *Clinical Psychology Review, 11,* 295–313.

Coats, S., & Smith, E. R. (1999). Perception of gender subtypes: Sensitivity to recent exemplar activation and in-group/out-group differences. *Personality and Social Psychology Bulletin, 25*(4), 515–526.

Cobb, N. J., Stevens-Long, J., & Goldstein, S. (1982). The influence of televised models on toy preference in children. *Sex Roles, 8,* 1075–1080.

Cochran, S. D., & Peplau, L. A. (1985). Value orientations in heterosexual relationships. *Psychology of Women Quarterly, 9*(4), 477–488.

Cochrane, J. (1977). *Women in Canadian politics.* Toronto: Fitzhenry & Whiteside.

Cohen, A. G., & Gutek, B. A. (1985). Dimensions of perceptions of social-sexual behavior in a work setting. *Sex Roles, 13*(5/6), 317–328.

Cohen, D., & Wilkie, F. (1979). Sex-related differences in cognition among the elderly. In M. A. Wittig & A. C. Petersen (Eds.), *Sex-related differences in cognitive functioning: Developmental issues* (pp. 145–159). New York: Academic Press.

Cohen, L. L., & Swim, J. K. (1995). The differential effect of gender ratios on women and men: Tokenism, self-confidence, and expectations. *Personality and Social Psychology Bulletin, 21,* 876–884.

Coker, D. R. (1984). The relationship among concepts and cognitive maturity in preschool children. *Sex Roles, 10,* 19–31.

Colapino, J. (1997, December 11). The true story of John/Joan. *Rolling Stone,* pp. 55–73, 92, 94–97.

Coleman, A., & Coleman, L. (1971). *Pregnancy: The psychological experience.* New York: Seabury.

Coleman, B. G. (1999, June 1). *Study: Andro may grow breasts* [On-line]. Associated Press. Available: http://search. washingtonpost.com/wp-srv /WAPO/ 19990601/V000907- 060199-idx.html

Coleman, L. M., & Antonucci, T. C. (1983). Impact of work on women at midlife. *Developmental Psychology, 19*(2), 290–294.

Coley, R. L., & Chase-Lansdale, P. (1998). Adolescent pregnancy and parenthood: Recent evidence and future directions. *American Psychologist, 53*(2), 152–166.

Collaer, M. L., & Hines, M. (1995). Human behavioral sex differences: A role for gonadal hormones during early development? *Psychological Bulletin, 118*(1), 55–107.

Collin, C. A., Di Sano, F., & Malik, R. (1994). Effects of confederate and subject gender on conformity in a color classification task. *Social Behavior and Personality, 22*(4), 355–364.

Collins, E. G. C. (1983, September/October). Managers and lovers. *Harvard Business Review,* pp. 142–153.

Collins, N. L., & Miller, L. C. (1994). Self-disclosure and liking: A meta-analytic review. *Psychological Bulletin, 116*(3), 457–475.

Collins, P. H. (1991). *Black feminist thought: Knowledge, consciousness, and the politics of empowerment.* Boston: Unwin Hyman.

Collis, B. (1985). Psychosocial implications of sex differences in attitudes toward computers: Results of a survey. *International Journal of Women's Studies, 8*(3), 207–213.

Colwill, N. L. (1984, November). Direction for future research. *Proceedings of Colloquium on the Economic Status of Women in the Labour Market.* Ottawa: Economic Council of Canada.

Colwill, N. L. (1985). The secretarial crisis: Toward evolution or extinction? *Business Quarterly, 50*(1), 12–14.

Colwill, N. L., & Colwill, H. D. (1985). Women with blue collars: The forgotten minority. *Business Quarterly, 50*(2), 15–17.

Colwill, N. L., & Lips, H. M. (1978). Masculinity, femininity, and androgyny: What have you done for us lately? In H. M. Lips & N. L. Colwill, *The psychology of sex differences* (pp. 125–144). Englewood Cliffs, NJ: Prentice-Hall.

Colwill, N. L., Perlman, D., & Spinner, B. (1983, June). *"Masculine" and "feminine" power styles of female secretaries and regional managers: An in-basket task*. Paper presented at the 44th annual convention of the Canadian Psychological Association, Winnipeg.

Colwill, N. L., Pollock, M., & Sztaba, T. I. (1986). Power in home economics: An individual and personal issue. *Canadian Home Economics Journal, 36*(2), 59–61.

Colwill, N. L., & Sztaba, T. I. (1986). Organizational gender-lect: The problem of two different languages. *Business Quarterly, 51*(2), 64–66.

Comas-Díaz, L., & Greene, B. (1994). Overview: Gender and ethnicity in the healing process. In L. Comas-Díaz & B. Greene (Eds.), *Women of color: Integrating ethnic and gender identities in psychotherapy* (pp. 185–193). New York: Guilford Press.

Condon, J. T. (1987). Psychological and physical symptoms during pregnancy: A comparison of male and female expectant parents. *Journal of Reproductive and Infant Psychology, 5*(4), 207–219.

Condry, J., & Condry, S. (1976). Sex differences: A study of the eye of the beholder. *Child Development, 47*, 812–819.

Condry, J., & Ross, D. (1985). Sex and aggression: The influence of gender label on the perception of aggression in children. *Child Development, 56*, 225–233.

Condry, S. M., & Dyer, S. (1976). Fear of success: Attribution of cause to the victim. *Journal of Social Issues, 32*(3), 63–83.

Connor, J. M., & Serbin, L. A. (1985). Visual-spatial skill: Is it

important for mathematics? Can it be taught? In S. Chipman, L. Brush, & D. Wilson (Eds.), *Women and mathematics: Balancing the equation* (pp. 151–174). Hillsdale, NJ: Erlbaum.

Connor-Greene, P. A. (1988). Gender differences in body weight perception and weight-loss strategies of college students. *Women and Health, 14*(2), 27–42.

Constantinople, A. (1973). Masculinity-femininity: An exception to a famous dictum? *Psychological Bulletin, 80*(3), 389–407.

Constantinople, A. (1979). Sex-role acquisition: In search of the elephant. *Sex Roles, 5*, 121–133.

Cook, E. P. (1985). *Psychological androgyny*. New York: Pergamon Press.

Cooper, E. B. (1992). When being ill is illegal: Women and the criminalization of HIV. *Health/PAC Bulletin*, Winter, 10–14.

Cooper, K. L., & Guttmann, D. L. (1987). Gender identity and ego mastery style in middle-aged pre- and post-empty nest women. *Gerontologist, 27*, 347–352.

Cornell, E. H., & Strauss, M. S. (1973). Infants' responsiveness to compounds of habituated visual stimuli. *Developmental Psychology, 2*, 73–78.

Corrigan, E., & Butler, S. (1991). Irish alcoholic women in treatment: Early findings. *International Journal of the Addictions, 26*(3), 281–292.

Costello, C. B., Miles, S., & Stone, A. J. (1998). *The American woman 1999–2000*. New York: W. W. Norton & Company.

Cotton, N. S. (1979). The familial incidence of alcoholism: A review. *Journal of Studies on Alcohol, 40*(1), 89–116.

Cowan, C. P., Cowan, P. A., Coie, L., & Coie, J. D. (1978). Becoming a family: The impact of a first child's birth on the

couple's relationship. In W. B. Miller & L. F. Newman (Eds.), *The first child and family formation*. Chapel Hill, NC: Carolina Population Center.

Cowan, G., Drinkard, J., & MacGavin, L. (1984). The effects of target, age, and gender in the use of power strategies. *Journal of Personality and Social Psychology, 47*, 1391–1398.

Cox, T. H., & Harquail, C. V. (1991). Career paths and career success in the early career stages of male and female MBAs. *Journal of Vocational Behavior, 39*, 54–75.

Crabb, P. B., & Bielawski, D. (1994). The social representation of material culture and gender in children's books. *Sex Roles, 30*(1/2), 69–79.

Craig, R. S. (1992). Women as home caregivers: Gender portrayal in OTC drug commercials. *Journal of Drug Education, 22*(4), 303–312.

Craig, T. J., & Lin, S. P. (1984). Sex differences in mortality rate among long-stay psychiatric inpatients. *Sex Roles, 10*, 725–732.

Cramer, R. E., Dragna, M., Cupp, R. G., & Stewart, P. (1991). Contrast effects in the evaluation of the male sex role. *Sex Roles, 24*(3/4), 181–193.

Crandall, V. C. (1969). Sex differences in expectancy of intellectual and academic reinforcement. In C. P. Smith (Ed.), *Achievement-related motives in children* (pp. 11–45). New York: Russell Sage Foundation.

Crandall, V. C., Katkovsky, W., & Preston, A. A. (1960). A conceptual foundation for some research on children's achievement development. *Child Development, 31*, 787–797.

Crews, D. (1993). The organizational concept and vertebrates without sex chromosomes. *Brain Behavior and Evolution, 42*, 202–214.

Crocker, L., Schmitt, A., & Tang, L. (1988, January). Test anxiety and standardized achievement test performance in the middle school years. *Measurement and Evaluation in Counseling and Development, 20*(4), 149–157.

Crohan, S. E., Antonucci, T. C., Adelmann, P. K., & Coleman, L. M. (1989). Job characteristics and well-being at midlife: Ethnic and gender comparisons. *Psychology of Women Quarterly, 13*(2), 223–236.

Crooks, R., & Bauer, K. (1987). *Our sexuality* (3rd ed.). Menlo Park, CA: Benjamin/Cummings.

Crosby, F. J. (1982). *Relative deprivation and working women*. New York: Oxford.

Crosby, F. J. (1984). The denial of personal discrimination. *American Behavioral Scientist, 27*(3), 371–386.

Crosby, F. J. (1990). Divorce and work life among women managers. In H. Y. Grossman & N. L. Chester (Eds.), *The experience and meaning of work in women's lives* (pp. 121–142). Hillsdale, NJ: Erlbaum.

Crosby, F. J., Clayton, S., Alksnis, O., & Hemker, K. (1986). Cognitive biases in the perception of discrimination: The importance of format. *Sex Roles, 14*(11/12), 637–646.

Crown, J., & Heatherington, L. (1989). The costs of winning? The role of gender in moral reasoning and judgments about competitive athletic encounters. *Journal of Sport and Exercise Psychology, 11*(3), 281–289.

Crull, P. (1980). The impact of sexual harassment on the job: A profile of the experiences of 92 women. In D. A. Neugarten & J. M. Shafritz (Eds.), *Sexuality in organizations: Romantic and coercive behaviors at work* (pp. 67–71). Oak Park, IL: Moore.

Cutrona, C. E. (1982). Nonpsychotic postpartum depression: A review of recent research.

Clinical Psychology Review, 2, 487–503.

Dabbs, J. M. Jr. (1992). Testosterone measurements in social and clinical psychology. *Journal of Social and Clinical Psychology, 11*(3), 302–321.

Dabbs, J. M. Jr., Alford, E. C., & Fielden, J. A. (1998). Trial lawyers and testosterone: Blue-collar talent in a white-collar world. *Journal of Applied Social Psychology, 28*, 84–94.

Dabbs, J. M. Jr., Frady, R. L., Carr, T. S., & Besch, N. F. (1987). Saliva testosterone and criminal violence in young adult prison inmates. *Psychosomatic Medicine, 49*, 174–182.

Dabbs, J. M. Jr., & Hargrove, M. F. (1997). Age, testosterone, and behavior among female prison inmates. *Psychosomatic Medicine, 59*, 477–480.

Dabbs, J. M. Jr., de La Rue, D., & Williams, P. M. (1990). Testosterone and occupational choice: Actors, ministers, and other men. *Journal of Personality and Social Psychology, 39*(6), 1261–1265.

Dabbs, J. M. Jr., & Morris, R. (1990). Testosterone, social class, and antisocial behavior in a sample of 4,462 men. *Psychological Science, 1*(3), 209–211.

Dabrow, A., & Ameci, G. (1991, August). What you should know about pregnancy and the law. *Management Review*, pp. 38–40.

Dalton, D. R., & Todor, W. D. (1985). Gender and workplace justice: A field assessment. *Personnel Psychology, 38*, 133–151.

Dalton, H. (1989). AIDS in blackface. *Daedalus, 118*, 205–277.

Dalton, K. (1964). *The premenstrual syndrome*. Springfield, IL: Thomas.

Daly, M. (1973). *Beyond God the Father*. Boston: Beacon Press.

Dan, A. J. (1976). Patterns of behavioral and mood variations in men and women: Variability

and the menstrual cycle. *Dissertation Abstracts International, 37*(6-B), 3145–3146.

Dan, A. J. (1979). The menstrual cycle and sex-related differences in cognitive variability. In M. A. Wittig & A. C. Petersen (Eds.), *Sex-related differences in cognitive functioning: Developmental issues* (pp. 241–260). New York: Academic Press.

Danek, M. M. (1992). The status of women with disabilities revisited. *Journal of Applied Rehabilitation Counseling, 23*(4), 7–13.

Daniluk, J. C. (1993). The meaning and experience of female sexuality: A phenomenological analysis. *Psychology of Women Quarterly, 17*, 53–69.

Dankoski, M. E., Penn, C. D., Carlson, T. D., & Hecker, L. L. (1998). What's in a name? A study of family therapists' use and acceptance of the feminist perspective. *American Journal of Family Therapy, 26*, 95–104.

Darley, J. M., & Fazio, R. H. (1980). Expectancy confirmation processes arising in the social interaction sequence. *American Psychologist, 35*, 867–881.

Darwin, C. (1967). *The descent of man*. New York: Modern Library. (Original work published 1871)

Davidson, C. V., & Abramowitz, S. (1980). Sex bias in clinical judgement: Later empirical returns. *Psychology of Women Quarterly, 4*, 377–395.

Davidson, J. K., & Moore, N. B. (1994). Masturbation and premarital sexual intercourse among college women: Making choices for sexual fulfillment. *Journal of Sex and Marital Therapy, 20*, 178–199.

Davidson, J. M. (1989). Sexual emotions, hormones, and behavior. *Advances, 6*(2), 56–58.

Davidson, L. R., & Duberman, L. (1982). Friendship: Communication and interactional patterns in same-sex dyads. *Sex Roles, 8,* 809–822.

Davies, D. R. (1989/90). The effects of gender-typed labels on children's performance. *Current Psychology: Research and Reviews, 8,* 267–272.

Davies, M. (1975). Women's place is at the typewriter: The feminization of the clerical work force. In R. C. Edwards, M. Reich, & D. Gordon (Eds.), *Labor market segmentation* (pp. 279–296). Lexington, MA: Heath.

Davis, A. (1981). *Women, race and class.* New York: Random House.

Davis, A. J. (1984). Sex-differentiated behaviors in nonsexist picture books. *Sex Roles, 11,* 1–16.

Davis, C., & Cowles, M. (1985). Type A behaviour assessment: A critical comment. *Canadian Psychology, 26*(1), 39–42.

Davis, D. M. (1990). Portrayals of women in prime-time network television: Some demographic characteristics. *Sex Roles, 23*(5/6), 325–332.

Davis, F. (1996, February). The estrogen question. *Working Women,* pp. 50–53, 73–75.

Davis, M., & Weitz, S. (1981). Sex differences in body movements and positions. In C. Mayo & N. M. Henley (Eds.), *Gender and nonverbal behavior* (pp. 81–92). New York: Springer-Verlag.

Davis, M. D., & Kennedy, E. L. (1990). Oral history and the study of sexuality in the lesbian community: Buffalo, New York, 1940–1960. In E. C. DuBois & V. L. Ruiz (Eds.), *Unequal sisters: A multicultural reader in U.S. women's history* (pp. 387–399). New York: Routledge.

Davis, S. (1990). Men as success objects and women as sex objects: A study of personal advertisements. *Sex Roles, 23*(1/2), 43–50.

Davis, S. F., Byers, R. H., Lindegren, M. L., Caldwell, M. B., Karon, J. M., & Gwinn, M. (1995). Prevalence and incidence of vertically acquired HIV infection in the United States. *Journal of the American Medical Association, 274*(12), 952–955.

Dawson, D., Hendershot, G., & Fulton, J. (1987, June 10). *Aging in the eighties: Functional limitations of individuals age 65 years and over.* Advance Data No. 133. Hyattsville, MD: National Center for Health Statistics.

Deaux, K. (1977). Sex differences. In T. Blass (Ed.), *Personality variables in social behavior* (pp. 357–378). Hillsdale, NJ: Erlbaum.

Deaux, K. (1984). From individual differences to social categories: Analysis of a decade's research on gender. *American Psychologist, 39*(2), 105–116.

Deaux, K., & Emswiller, T. (1974). Explanations of successful performance on sex-linked tasks: What's skill for the male is luck for the female. *Journal of Personality and Social Psychology, 29,* 80–85.

Deaux, K., & Lewis, L. L. (1984). Structure of gender stereotypes: Interrelationships among components and gender label. *Journal of Personality and Social Psychology, 46*(5), 991–1004.

Deaux, K., & Major, B. (1987). Putting gender into context: An interactive model of gender-related behavior. *Psychological Review, 94*(3), 369–389.

De Cecco, J. P., & Shively, M. G. (1983/84). From sexual identity to sexual relationships: A contextual shift. *Journal of Homosexuality, 9*(2/3), 1–26.

DeGregorio, E., & Carver, C. S. (1980). Type A behavior pattern, sex role orientation, and psychological adjustment. *Journal of Personality and Social Psychology, 39,* 286–293.

de Koninck, M. (1984). Double work and women's health. *Canada's Mental Health, 32*(3), 28–31.

de Lacoste-Utamsing, C., & Holloway, R. L. (1982). Sexual dimorphism in the human corpus callosum. *Science, 216,* 1431–1432.

Delaney, J., Lupton, M. J., & Toth, E. (1987). *The curse: A cultural history of menstruation* (rev. ed.). Urbana: University of Illinois Press.

De Lisi, R., & Soundranayagam, L. (1990). The conceptual structure of sex role stereotypes in college students. *Sex Roles, 23* (11/12), 593–611.

De Luccie, M. F., & Davis, A. J. (1991). Do men's adult life concerns affect their fathering orientations? *Journal of Psychology, 125*(2), 175–188.

Demaré, D., Briere, J., & Lips, H. M. (1988). Violent pornography and self-reported likelihood of sexual aggression. *Journal of Research in Personality, 22,* 140–153.

Demaré, D., Lips, H. M., & Briere, J. (1993). Violent pornography, anti-women attitudes, and sexual aggression: A structural equation model. *Journal of Research in Personality, 27,* 285–300.

Denmark, F. L. (1998). Women and psychology: An international perspective. *American Psychologist, 53*(4), 465–473.

Deutsch, H. (1945). *The psychology of women* (Vol. 2). New York: Grune & Stratton.

De Wolf, V. A. (1981). High school mathematics preparation and sex differences in quantitative abilities. *Psychology of Women Quarterly, 5,* 555–567.

Dexter, C. R. (1985). Women and the exercise of power in organizations: From ascribed to achieved status. In L. Larwood, A. H. Stromberg, & B. A. Gutek (Eds.), *Women and work: An annual review* (Vol. 1, pp. 239–258). Beverly Hills, CA: Sage.

Diamond, M., & Sigmundson, H. K. (1997). Sex reassignment at birth: Long-term review and clinical implications. *Archives of Pediatric Medicine, 151*(3), 298–304.

Dickason, A. (1976). Anatomy and destiny: The role of biology in Plato's views of women. In C. C. Gould & M. W. Wartofsky (Eds.), *Women and philosophy: Toward a theory of liberation* (pp. 45–53). New York: Putnam.

Dickens, W. J., & Perlman, D. (1981). Friendship over the life cycle. In S. Duck & R. Gilmour (Eds.), *Personal relationships: Vol. 2. Developing personal relationships* (pp. 91–122). London: Academic Press.

Die, A. H., Debbs, T. Jr., & Walker, J. L. Jr. (1990). Managerial evaluations by men and women managers. *Journal of Social Psychology, 130*(6), 763–769.

Dindia, K., & Allen, M. (1992). Sex differences in self-disclosure: A meta-analysis. *Psychological Bulletin, 112*(1), 106-124.

Dinnerstein, D. (1976). *The mermaid and the minotaur: Sexual arrangements and human malaise.* New York: Harper Colophon.

DiPietro, J. A. (1981). Rough and tumble play: A function of gender. *Developmental Psychology, 17,* 50–58.

Dittmar, M. L. (1994). Relations among depression, gender, and television viewing of college students. *Journal of Social Behavior and Personality, 9*(2), 317–328.

Dobash, R. E., & Dobash, R. P. (1984). The nature and antecedents of violent events. *British Journal of Criminology, 24,* 269–288.

Dobbins, G. H. (1986). Equity vs equality: Sex differences in leadership. *Sex Roles, 15*(9/10), 513–525.

Dodge, H. H. (1995). Movements out of poverty among elderly widows. *Journal of Gerontology-B-Psychol-Sci-Soc-Sci, 50*(4), S240–249.

Dodril, C. (1979). Sex differences on the Halsted-Reitan Neuropsychological Battery and on other neuropsychological measures. *Journal of Clinical Psychology, 35,* 236–241.

Dodson, B. (1974). *Liberating masturbation: A meditation on self love.* (Available from Bodysex Designs, P.O. Box 1933, New York, NY 10001).

Doering, C. H., Brodie, H. K. H., Kraemer, H. C., Becker, H. B., & Hamburg, D. A. (1974). Plasma testosterone levels and psychological measurements in men over a 2-month period. In R. C. Friedman, R. M. Richart, & R. L. Vande Wiele (Eds.), *Sex differences in behavior* (pp. 413–421). New York: Wiley.

Donnerstein, E. (1980). Aggressive-erotica and violence against women. *Journal of Personality and Social Psychology, 3,* 269–277.

Donnerstein, E. (1983). Erotica and human aggression. In R. Green & E. Donnerstein (Eds.), *Aggression: Theoretical and empirical reviews* (Vol. 2). New York: Academic Press.

Doty, R. L., & Silverthorne, C. (1975). Influence of the menstrual cycle on volunteering behavior. *Nature, 254,* 139–140.

Doucette, J. (1986). Violent acts against disabled women. In *The future is now* (Appendix A). Report of the conference of the Ontario Disabled Women's Network. (Available from D.A.W.N., 122 Galt Ave., Toronto, Ontario, Canada, M4M 2Z3).

Douvan, E., & Adelson, J. (1966). *The adolescent experience.* New York: Wiley.

Douvan, E., & Pleck, J. (1978). Separation as support. In R. Rapoport & R. N. Rapoport (Eds.), *Working couples* (pp. 138–146). New York: Harper Colophon.

Dovidio, J. F. E., Ellyson, S. L., Keating, C. F., Heltman, K., & Brown, C. E. (1988). The relationship of social power to visual displays of dominance between men and women. *Journal of Personality and Social Psychology, 54,* 233–242.

Downs, A. C. (1983). Letters to Santa Claus: Elementary school-age children's sex-typed toy preferences in a natural setting. *Sex Roles, 9,* 159–163.

Doyal, L. (1995). *What makes women sick: Gender and the political economy of health.* New Brunswick, NJ: Rutgers University Press.

Doyle, J. A. (1995). *The male experience* (3rd ed.). Madison, WI: Brown & Benchmark.

Driver, 65, beaten, slain. (1991, August 24). *Washington Post,* pp. A1, A10.

Drory, A., & Beaty, D. (1991). Gender differences in the perception of organizational influence tactics. *Journal of Organizational Behavior, 12*(3), 249–258.

Dubinsky, K. (1985). *Lament for a "patriarchy lost"? Anti-feminism, anti-abortion, and R.E.A.L. women in Canada.* Ottawa: Canadian Research Institute for the Advancement of Women.

Dubnos, P. (1985). Attitudes toward women executives: A longitudinal approach. *Academy of Management Journal, 28*(1), 235–239.

DuBrin, A. J. (1989). Sex differences in endorsement of influence tactics and political behavior tendencies. *Journal of Business and Psychology, 4*(1), 3–14.

Duckert, F. (1989). The treatment of female problem drinkers. In Nordic Council for Alcohol and Drug Research, *Women, alcohol and drugs in the Nordic countries.* Helsinki: NAD.

Duffy, A., & Momirov, J. (1997). *Family violence: A Canadian introduction.* Toronto: James Lorimer & Company.

Dugger, K. (1991). Social location and gender-role attitudes: A comparison of Black and White women. In J. Lorber & S. A. Farrell (Eds.), *The social construction of gender* (pp. 38–59). Newbury Park, CA: Sage.

Duke, L. (1991, August 19). Military's last social taboo: Homosexuality. *Washington Post,* pp. A1, A8.

Dukes, R. L., & Martinez, R. (1994). The impact of ethgender on self-esteem among adolescents. *Adolescence, 29*(113), 105–115.

Dumas, M. C., Calliet, L. L., Tumblin, I. G., & King, A. R. (1984). Menstrual cycle influence on alcohol consumption among Blacks. *Journal of Black Psychology, 11*(1), 9–18.

Dunkle, J. H., & Francis, P. L. (1990). The role of facial masculinity/femininity in the attribution of homosexuality. *Sex Roles, 23*(3/4), 157–167.

Durkin, K. (1985). Television and sex-role acquisition. 1. Content. *British Journal of Social Psychology, 24,* 101–113.

Dutton, D. G. (1986). Wife assaulters' explanations for assault: The neutralization of self-punishment. *Canadian Journal of Behavioural Science, 18*(4), 381–390.

Dutton, D. G. (1987a). The criminal justice response to wife assault. *Law and Human Behavior, 11*(3), 189–206.

Dutton, D. G. (1987b). Wife assault: Social psychological contributions to criminal justice policy. *Applied Social Psychology Annual, 7,* 238–261.

Dutton, D. G., & Browning, J. J. (1983). *Violence in intimate relationships.* Paper presented at the International Society for Research on Aggression, Victoria, British Columbia.

Dutton, D. G., & Strachan, C. E. (1987). Motivational needs for power and spouse-specific assertiveness in assaultive and nonassaultive men. *Violence and Victims 2*(3), 145–156.

Duxbury, L. E., & Higgins, C. A. (1991). Gender differences in work-family conflict. *Journal of Applied Psychology, 76*(1), 60–74.

Dweck, C. S. (1975). The role of expectations and attributions in the alleviation of learned helplessness. *Journal of Personality and Social Psychology, 31,* 674–685.

Dweck, C. S. (1999). *Self-theories: Their role in motivation, personality, and development.* Philadelphia, PA: Psychology Press.

Dweck, C. S., Davidson, W., Nelson, S., & Enna, B. (1978). Sex differences in learned helplessness. II. The contingencies of evaluative feedback in the classroom. III. An experimental analysis. *Developmental Psychology, 14,* 268–276.

Dweck, C. S., Goetz, T. E., & Strauss, N. L. (1980). Sex differences in learned helplessness. IV. An experimental and naturalistic study of failure generalization and its mediators. *Journal of Personality and Social Psychology, 38,* 441–452.

Dweck, C. S., & Leggett, E. L. (1988). A social-cognitive approach to motivation and personality. *Psychological Review, 95,* 256–273.

Dye, E., & Roth, S. (1990). Psychotherapists' knowledge about and attitudes toward sexual assault victim clients. *Psychology of Women Quarterly, 14*(2), 191–212.

Eagly, A. H. (1983). Gender and social influence: A social psychological analysis. *American Psychologist, 38,* 971–981.

Eagly, A. H. (1987). *Sex differences in social behavior: A social-role interpretation.* Hillsdale, NJ: Erlbaum.

Eagly, A. H. (1995). The science and politics of comparing women and men. *American Psychologist, 50*(3), 145–158.

Eagly, A. H., & Carli, L. L. (1981). Sex of researchers and sex-typed communications as determinants of

sex differences in influenceability: A meta-analysis of social influence studies. *Psychological Bulletin, 90,* 1–20.

Eagly, A. H., & Crowley, M. (1986). Gender and helping behavior: A meta-analytic review of the social psychological literature. *Psychological Bulletin, 100,* 283–308.

Eagly, A. H., & Johnson, B. T. (1990). Gender and leadership style: A meta-analysis. *Psychological Bulletin, 108,* 233–256.

Eagly, A. H., & Karau, S. J. (1991). Gender and the emergence of leaders: A meta-analysis. *Journal of Personality and Social Psychology, 60*(5), 685–710.

Eagly, A. H., Makhijani, M. G., & Klonsky, B. G. (1992). Gender and the evaluation of leaders: A meta-analysis. *Psychological Bulletin, 11*(1), 3–22.

Eagly, A. H., & Mladinic, A. (1989). Gender stereotypes and attitudes toward women and men. *Personality and Social Psychology Bulletin, 15*(4), 543–558.

Eagly, A. H., & Mladinic, A. (1994). Are people prejudiced against women? Some answers from research on attitudes, gender stereotypes, and judgments of competence. In W. Stroebe & M. Hewstone (Eds.), *European review of social psychology* (Vol. 5, pp. 1–35). New York: Wiley.

Eagly, A. H., Mladinic, A., & Otto, S. (1991). Are women evaluated more favorably than men? An analysis of attitudes, beliefs, and emotions. *Psychology of Women Quarterly, 15,* 203–216.

Eagly, A. H., & Steffen, V. J. (1984). Gender stereotypes stem from the distribution of women and men into social roles. *Journal of Personality and Social Psychology, 46*(4), 735–754.

Eagly, A. H., & Steffen, V. J. (1986). Gender and aggressive behavior: A meta-analytic review of the social psychological literature. *Psychological Bulletin, 100,* 309–330.

Eagly, A. H., & Wood, W. (1982). Inferred sex differences in status as a determinant of gender stereotypes about social influence. *Journal of Personality and Social Psychology, 43,* 915–928.

Eagly, A. H., & Wood, W. (1985). Gender and influenceability: Stereotype versus behavior. In V. O'Leary, R. Unger, & B. Wallston (Eds.), *Women, gender, and social psychology* (pp. 225–256). Hillsdale, NJ: Erlbaum.

Eagly, A. H., & Wood, W. (1991). Explaining sex differences in social behavior: A meta-analytic perspective. *Personality and Social Psychology Bulletin, 17*(3), 306–315.

Eagly, A. H., & Wood, W. (1999). The origins of sex differences in human behavior: Evolved dispositions versus social roles. *American Psychologist, 54*(6), 408–423.

Eagly, A. H., Wood, W., & Fishbaugh, L. (1981). Sex differences in conformity: Surveillance by the group as a determinant of male nonconformity. *Journal of Personality and Social Psychology, 40,* 384–394.

Eals, M., & Silverman, I. (1994). The hunter-gatherer theory of spatial sex differences: Proximate factors mediating the female advantage in recall of object arrays. *Ethology and Sociobiology, 15*(2), 95–105.

Eaton, W. O., & Enns, L. R. (1986). Sex differences in human motor activity level. *Psychological Bulletin, 100*(1), 19–28.

Eccles, J. (1985). Sex differences in achievement patterns. In T. B. Sonderegger (Ed.), *Psychology and gender. Nebraska Symposium on Motivation, 1984* (pp. 97–132). Lincoln: University of Nebraska Press.

Eccles, J. (1987). Gender roles and women's achievement-related decisions. *Psychology of Women Quarterly, 11*(2), 135–172.

Eccles, J. S. (1989). Bringing young women to math and science. In M. Crawford & M. Gentry (Eds.), *Gender and thought: Psychological perspectives* (pp. 36–58). New York: Springer-Verlag.

Eccles, J. S. (1994). Understanding women's educational and occupational choices: Applying the Eccles et al. model of achievement-related choices. *Psychology of Women Quarterly, 18*(4), 585–610.

Eccles (Parsons), J., Adler, T. F., Futterman, R., Goff, S. B., Kaczala, C. M., Meece, J. L., & Midgley, C. (1983). Expectations, values and academic behaviors. In J. T. Spence (Ed.), *Achievement and achievement motives* (pp. 75–146). San Francisco: W. H. Freeman.

Edwards, J. R., & Williams, J. E. (1980). Sex-trait stereotypes among young children and young adults: Canadian findings and cross-national comparisons. *Canadian Journal of Behavioural Science, 12,* 210–220.

Efron, R. (1990). *The decline and fall of hemispheric specialization.* Hillsdale, NJ: Erlbaum.

Ehrenreich, B. (1983). *The hearts of men: American dreams and the flight from commitment.* Garden City, NY: Anchor.

Ehrenreich, B., & English, D. (1979). *For her own good: 150 years of the experts' advice to women.* Garden City, NY: Anchor.

Ehrhardt, A. A. (1985). Gender differences: A biosocial perspective. In T. Sonderegger (Ed.), *Nebraska Symposium on Motivation: Psychology of gender* (pp. 37–57). Lincoln: University of Nebraska Press.

Ehrhardt, A. A., & Baker, S. W. (1974). Fetal androgens, human central nervous system differentiation, and behavior sex differences. In R. M. Richart & R. L. Vande Wiele (Eds.), *Sex differences in behavior* (pp. 33–52). New York: Wiley.

Ehrhardt, A. A., & Baker, S. W. (1976). *Prenatal androgens and future adolescent behavior.* Paper presented at the International Conference of Sexology, Montreal.

Eichler, A., & Parron, D. L. (1987). *Women's mental health: An agenda for research.* Rockville, MD: National Institute of Mental Health.

Eichler, M. (1983). *Sexism in research and its policy implications.* Ottawa: Canadian Research Institute for the Advancement of Women.

Eichler, M. (1986). *The pro-family movement: Are they for or against families?* Ottawa: Canadian Research Institute for the Advancement of Women.

Eichler, M., & Lapointe, J. (1985). *On the treatment of the sexes in research.* Ottawa: Social Sciences and Humanities Research Council of Canada.

Eisenberg, N., & Lennon, R. (1983). Sex differences in empathy and related capacities. *Psychological Bulletin, 94*(1), 100–131.

Eisenberg, N., Miller, P. A., Shell, R., McNalley, S., & Shea, C. (1991). Prosocial development in adolescence: A longitudinal study. *Developmental Psychology, 27*(5), 849–857.

Eisenstock, B. (1984). Sex-role differences in children's identification with counterstereotypic televised portrayals. *Sex Roles, 10,* 417–430.

Eldridge, N. S., & Gilbert, L. A. (1990). Correlates of relationship satisfaction in lesbian couples. *Psychology of Women Quarterly, 14*(1), 43–62.

Elias, M. (1981). Serum cortisol, testosterone and testosterone-binding globulin responses to competitive fighting in human males. *Aggressive Behavior, 7,* 215–224.

Eliason, M. J. (1995). Accounts of sexual identity formation in heterosexual students. *Sex Roles, 32*(11/12), 821–834.

Eliason, M. J., Donelan, C., & Randall, C. (1992). Lesbian stereotypes. *Health Care for Women International, 13*(2), 131–144.

Elliott, E. S., & Dweck, C. S. (1988). Goals: An approach to motivation and achievement. *Journal of Personality and Social Psychology, 54,* 5–12.

Ellis, L. (1982). Developmental androgen fluctuations and the dimensions of mammalian sex (with emphasis upon the behavioral dimension and the human species). *Ethology and Sociobiology, 3,* 171–179.

Ellis, L., & Ames, M. A. (1987). Neurohormonal functioning and sexual orientation. *Psychological Bulletin, 101*(2), 233–258.

Ellis, L., Burke, D., & Ames, M. A. (1987). Sexual orientation as a continuous variable: A comparison between the sexes. *Archives of Sexual Behavior, 16*(6), 523–529.

Ellsberg, M., Caldera, T., Herrera, A., Winkvist, A., & Kullgren, G. (1999). Domestic violence and emotional distress among Nicaraguan women. *American Psychologist, 54*(1), 30–36.

Ellyson, S. L., Dovidio, J. F., & Fehr, B. J. (1981). Visual behavior and dominance in women and men. In C. Mayo & N. M. Henley (Eds.), *Gender and nonverbal behavior* (pp. 63–79). New York: Springer-Verlag.

Elsner, C. W., Buster, J. E., Schindler, R. A., Nessim, S. A., & Abraham, G. E. (1980). Bromocryptine in the treatment of premenstrual tension syndrome. *Obstetrics and Gynecology, 56,* 723–726.

Elstad, J. I. (1996). Inequalities in health related to women's marital, parental, and employment status: A comparison between the early 70s and the late 80s, Norway. *Social Science and Medicine, 42*(1), 75–89.

Entwisle, D. R., & Baker, D. P. (1983). Gender and young children's expectations for performance in arithmetic. *Developmental Psychology, 19*(2), 200–209.

Epstein, C. F. (1983, April). The new total woman. *Working Woman,* pp. 100–103.

Erickson, B. E., Lund, E. A., Johnson, B. C., & O'Barr, W. M. (1978). Speech style and impression formation in a court setting: The effects of "powerful" and "powerless" speech. *Journal of Experimental Social Psychology, 14,* 266–279.

Erikson, E. (1950). *Childhood and society.* New York: Norton.

Eron, L. D., Huesmann, L. R., Brice, P., Fischer, P., & Mermelstein, R. (1983). Age trends in the development of aggression, sex typing, and related television habits. *Sex Roles, 19*(1), 71–77.

Espín, O. M. (1987). Issues of identity in the psychology of Latina lesbians. In The Boston Lesbian Psychologies Collective (Eds.), *Lesbian psychologies* (pp. 35–55). Urbana: University of Illinois Press.

Espín, O. M. (1997). *Latina realities: Essays on healing, migration, and sexuality.* Boulder, CO: Westview.

Estimate of rape victims is quintupled (1992, April 24). *Washington Post,* p. A11.

Etaugh, C. (1974). Effects of maternal employment on children: A review of recent research. *Merrill Palmer Quarterly, 20,* 71–98.

Etaugh, C., & Duits, T. (1990). Development of gender discrimination: Role of stereotypic and counterstereotypic gender cues. *Sex Roles, 23*(5/6), 215–222.

Etaugh, C., & Kasley, H. C. (1981). Evaluating competence: Effects of sex, marital status, and parental status. *Psychology of Women Quarterly, 6,* 196–203.

Etaugh, C., Levine, D., & Mennella, A. (1984). Development of sex biases in children: 40 years later. *Sex Roles, 10,* 913–924.

Ethington, C. A., & Wolfle, L. M. (1984). Sex differences in a causal model of mathematics achievement. *Journal for Research in Mathematics Education, 15,* 361–377.

Eyler, D. R., & Baridon, A. P. (1992, Winter). Managing sexual attraction in the workplace. *Business Quarterly,* pp. 19–26.

Ezell, H. F., Odewahn, C. A., & Sherman, J. D. (1981). The effects of having been supervised by a woman on perceptions of female managerial competence. *Personnel Psychology, 34*(2), 291–299.

Fabes, R. A., & Martin, C. L. (1991). Gender and age stereotypes of emotionality. *Personality and Social Psychology Bulletin, 17*(5), 532–540.

Faderman, L. (1981). *Surpassing the love of men: Romantic friendship between women from the Renaissance to the present.* New York: Morrow.

Fagot, B. I. (1984). Teacher and peer reactions to boys' and girls' play styles. *Sex Roles, 11,* 691–702.

Fagot, B. I. (1985). Beyond the reinforcement principle: Another step toward understanding sex role development. *Developmental Psychology, 21*(6), 1097–1104.

Fagot, B. I., & Hagan, R. (1985). Aggression in toddlers: Responses to the assertive acts of boys and girls. *Sex Roles, 12*(3/4), 341–351.

Fagot, B. I., & Leinbach, M. D. (1993). Gender-role development in young children: From discrimination to labeling. *Developmental Review, 13,* 205–224.

Fairhurst, G. T. (1985). Male–female communication on the

job: Literature review and commentary. In M. McLaughlin (Ed.), *Communication Yearbook* (Vol. 9, pp. 83–115). Beverly Hills, CA: Sage.

Fairweather, H. (1976). Sex differences in cognition. *Cognition, 4,* 231–280.

Fairweather, H., & Hutt, S. J. (1972). Sex differences in a perceptual motor skill in children. In C. Ounsted & D. C. Taylor (Eds.), *Gender differences: Their ontogeny and significance.* Edinburgh: Churchill Livingstone.

Falbo, T. (1977). Multidimensional scaling of power strategies. *Journal of Personality and Social Psychology, 35,* 537–547.

Falbo, T., & Peplau, L. A. (1980). Power strategies in intimate relationships. *Journal of Personality and Social Psychology, 38,* 618–628.

Fallon, A. E., & Rozin, P. (1985). Sex differences in perceptions of desirable body shape. *Journal of Abnormal Psychology, 94*(1), 102–105.

Farley, J. (1980). Worklife problems for both women and men. In D. A. Neugarten & J. M. Shafritz (Eds.), *Sexuality in organizations: Romantic and coercive behaviors at work* (pp. 29–37). Oak Park, IL: Moore.

Farrell, M., & Rosenberg, S. (1981). *Men at midlife.* Boston: Auburn House.

Farris, A. (1978). Commuting. In R. Rapoport & R. N. Rapoport (Eds.), *Working couples* (pp. 100–107). New York: Harper Colophon.

Fausto-Sterling, A. (1992). *Myths of gender* (rev. ed.). New York: Basic Books.

Fausto-Sterling, A., & English, L. A. (1986, January). Women and minorities in science: An interdisciplinary course. *Radical Teacher,* pp. 16–20.

Favreau, O. E. (1977). Sex bias in psychological research.

Canadian Psychological Review, 18(1), 56–65.

Favreau, O. E. (1993). Do the Ns justify the means? Null hypothesis testing applied to sex and other differences. *Canadian Psychology, 34*(1), 64–78.

Fedigan, L. M. (1982). *Primate paradigms: Sex roles and social bonds.* Montreal: Eden Press.

Fehr, S. C. (1992, January 14). Dramatic increase in traffic fatality rate for women puzzles analysts. *Washington Post,* p. A7.

Feingold, A. (1988). Cognitive gender differences are disappearing. *American Psychologist, 43*(2), 95–103.

Feingold, A. (1990). Gender differences in effects of physical attractiveness on romantic attraction: A comparison across five research paradigms. *Journal of Personality and Social Psychology, 59*(5), 981–993.

Feingold, A. (1993). Cognitive gender differences: A developmental perspective. *Sex Roles, 29*(1/2), 91–112.

Feingold, A. (1994a). Gender differences in personality: A meta-analysis. *Psychological Bulletin, 116*(3), 429–456.

Feingold, A. (1994b). Gender differences in variability in intellectual abilities: A cross-cultural perspective. *Sex Roles, 30*(1/2), 81–92.

Feldman, S. S., & Nash, S. C. (1978). Interest in babies during young adulthood. *Child Development, 49,* 617–622.

Feldman, S. S., Nash, S. C., & Cutrona, C. (1977). The influence of age and sex on responsiveness to babies. *Developmental Psychology, 13,* 675–676.

Felmlee, D. H. (1995). Causes and consequences of women's employment discontinuity, 1967–1973. *Work and Occupations, 22*(2), 167–187.

The feminization of the professional workforce. (1986, February 17). *Business Week,* p. 21.

Fenelon, J., & Megargee, E. (1971). Influence of race on the manifestation of leadership. *Journal of Applied Psychology, 55,* 353–358.

Fennema, E., Peterson, P. L., Carpenter, T. P., & Lubinski, C. A. (1990). Teachers' attitudes and beliefs about girls, boys, and mathematics. *Educational Studies in Mathematics, 21,* 55–69.

Fennema, E., & Sherman, J. (1977). Sex-related differences in mathematics achievement, spatial visualization and affective factors. *American Educational Research Journal, 14,* 51–71.

Fennema, E., & Tartre, L. A. (1985). The use of spatial visualization in mathematics by girls and boys. *Journal for Research in Mathematics Education, 16*(3), 184–206.

Fidell, L. S. (1982). Gender and drug use and abuse. In I. Al-Issa (Ed.), *Gender and psychopathology* (pp. 221–236). New York: Academic Press.

Field, T., Sandberg, D., Garcia, R., Vega-Lahr, N., Goldstein, S., & Guy, L. (1985). Pregnancy problems, postpartum depression, and early mother–infant interaction. *Developmental Psychology, 21*(6), 1152–1156.

Figueira-McDonough, J. (1987). Discrimination or sex differences? Criteria for evaluating the juvenile justice system's handling of minor offenses. *Crime and Delinquency, 33*(3), 403–424.

Filardo, E. K. (1996). Gender patterns in African American and White adolescents' social interactions in same-race, mixed-gender groups. *Journal of Personality and Social Psychology, 71*(1), 71–81.

Fine, M. (1991, March). *Women with disabilities.* Paper presented at the national conference of the Association for Women in Psychology, Hartford, CT.

Fine, M., & Asch, A. (1981). Disabled women: Sexism

without the pedestal. *Journal of Sociology and Social Welfare, 8,* 233–248.

Fink, D. (1983, April 19). The sexes agree more about sex. *USA Today,* pp. 1D–2D.

Finkelhor, D. (1986). *A sourcebook on child sexual abuse.* Beverly Hills, CA: Sage.

Finn, J. D. (1980). Sex differences in educational outcomes: A cross-national study. *Sex Roles, 6,* 9–26.

Fischbein, S. (1990). Biosocial influences on sex differences for ability and achievement test results as well as marks at school. *Intelligence, 14*(1), 127–139.

Fish, M. C., Gross, A. L., & Sanders, J. S. (1986). The effect of equity strategies on girls' computer usage in school. *Computers in Human Behavior, 2*(2), 127–134.

Fishbein, J. (1988, December). Teenage girls know about AIDS, but don't act accordingly. *The Nation's Health, 18*(12).

Fisher, T. D., Pollack, R. H., & Malatesta, V. J. (1986). Orgasmic latency and subjective ratings of erotic stimuli in male and female subjects. *Journal of Sex Research, 22,* 85–93.

Fishman, P. M. (1978). Interaction: The work women do. *Social Problems, 25,* 397–406.

Fisk, W. R. (1985). Responses to "neutral" pronoun presentations and the development of sex-biased responding. *Developmental Psychology, 21*(3), 481–485.

Fiske, S. T., & Glick, P. (1995). Ambivalence and stereotypes cause sexual harassment: A theory with implications for organizational change. *Journal of Social Issues, 51*(1), 97–115.

Fitzgerald, L. F. (1980). Nontraditional occupations: Not for women only. *Journal of Counseling Psychology, 27,* 252–259.

Fitzgerald, L. F., & Cherpas, C. C. (1985). On the reciprocal relationship between gender and

occupation: Rethinking the assumptions concerning masculine career development. *Journal of Vocational Behavior, 27,* 109–122.

Fitzgerald, L. F., & Shullman, S. L. (1993). Sexual harassment: A research analysis and agenda for the 1990s. *Journal of Vocational Behavior, 42,* 5–27.

Flaks, D. K., Ficher, I., Masterpasqua, F., & Joseph, G. (1995). Lesbians choosing motherhood: A comparative study of lesbian and heterosexual parents and their children. *Developmental Psychology, 31*(1), 105–114.

Fleischer, R. A., & Chertkoff, J. M. (1986). Effects of dominance and sex on leader selection in dyadic work groups. *Journal of Personality and Social Psychology, 50*(1), 94–99.

Fleming, J. (1982). Fear of success in Black male and female graduate students: A pilot study. *Psychology of Women Quarterly, 6*(3), 327–341.

Fleming, J. (1983a). Black women in Black and White college environments: The making of a matriarch. *Journal of Social Issues, 39*(3), 41–54.

Fleming, J. (1983b). Sex differences in the educational and occupational goals of Black college students: Continued inquiry into the Black matriarchy theory. In M. S. Horner, M. Notman, & C. Nadelson (Eds.), *The challenge of change.* New York: Plenum.

Flexner, A. (1914). *Prostitution in Europe.* New York: Century.

Floge, L., & Merrill, D. M. (1986). Tokenism reconsidered: Male nurses and female physicians in a hospital setting. *Social Forces, 64*(4), 925–947.

Fogel, R., & Paludi, M. A. (1984). Fear of success and failure, or norms for achievement? *Sex Roles, 10,* 431–443.

Foot, H. C., Chapman, A. J., & Smith, J. R. (1977). Friendship and social responsiveness in boys and girls. *Journal of Personality*

and *Social Psychology, 35,* 401–411.

Ford, M. R., & Lowery, C. R. (1986). Gender differences in moral reasoning: A comparison of the use of justice and care orientations. *Journal of Personality and Social Psychology, 50*(4), 777–783.

Foushee, H. C., Davis, M. H., & Archer, R. L. (1979). Empathy, masculinity, and femininity. *JSAS Catalogue of Selected Documents in Psychology, 9,* 85. (Ms. no. 1974).

Foushee, H. C., Helmreich, R. L., & Spence, J. T. (1979). Implicit theories of masculinity and femininity: Dualistic or bipolar? *Psychology of Women Quarterly, 3,* 259–269.

Fowers, B. J. (1991). His and her marriage: A multivariate study of gender and marital satisfaction. *Sex Roles, 24*(3/4), 209–221.

Fox, L. H. (1976). Career education for gifted pre-adolescents. *Gifted Child Quarterly, 20,* 262–273.

Fox, L. H. (1981). *The problem of women and mathematics.* New York: Ford Foundation.

Fox, M., Gibbs, M., & Auerbach, D. (1985). Age and gender dimensions of friendship. *Psychology of Women Quarterly, 9,* 489–502.

Fox, M. F. (1995). Women and higher education: Gender differences in the status of students and scholars. In J. Freeman (Ed.), *Women: A feminist perspective* (5th ed., pp. 220–237). Mountain View, CA: Mayfield.

Fox, M. F., & Hesse-Biber, S. (1984). *Women at work.* Palo Alto, CA: Mayfield.

Franceschi, S., Dal Maso, L., La Vecchia, C., Negri, E., & Serraino, D. (1994). AIDS incidence rates in Europe and the United States. *AIDS, 8*(8), 1173–1177.

Frank, E. J. (1988). Business students' perceptions of women in management. *Sex Roles, 19*(1/2), 107–118.

Frank, R. T. (1931). The hormonal causes of premenstrual tension. *Archives of Neurological Psychiatry, 26,* 1053.

Frankel, M. T., & Rollins, H. A. Jr. (1983). Does Mother know best? Mothers and fathers interacting with preschool sons and daughters. *Developmental Psychology, 19*(5), 694–702.

Franken, M. (1983). Sex role expectations in children's vocational aspirations and perceptions of occupations. *Psychology of Women Quarterly, 8,* 59–68.

Franklin, C. W. II. (1984). *The changing definition of masculinity.* New York: Plenum.

Franklin, C. W. II. (1988). *Men and society.* Chicago: Nelson-Hall.

Franklin, U. M. (1985). *Will women change technology or will technology change women?* Ottawa: Canadian Research Institute for the Advancement of Women.

Franzoi, S. L., Anderson, J., & Frommelt, S. (1990). Individual differences in men's perceptions of and reactions to thinning hair. *Journal of Social Psychology, 130*(2), 209–218.

Frazier, P. A., Cochran, C. C., & Olson, A. M. (1995). Social science research on lay definitions of sexual harassment. *Journal of Social Issues, 51*(1), 21–38.

Fredrickson, B. L., Roberts, T., Noll, S. M., Quinn, D. M., & Twenge, J. M. (1998). That swimsuit becomes you: Sex differences in self-objectification, restrained eating, and math performance. *Journal of Personality and Social Psychology, 75*(1), 269–284.

Freedman, R. (1986). *Beauty bound.* Lexington, MA: Heath.

Freedman, R. R. (1989). Laboratory and ambulatory monitoring of menopausal hot flashes. *Psychophysiology, 26*(5), 573–579.

Freedman, S. A., & Lips, H. M. (1993, March). *Articulating feminist identities against a backdrop of heterosexuality: Six voices.* Paper presented at the annual meeting of the Association for Women in Psychology, Atlanta.

Freedman, S. A., & Lips, H. M. (1996). A response latency investigation of the gender schema. In R. Crandall, (ed.), Handbook of gender research [Special issues]. *Journal of Social Behavior and Personality, 11*(5), 41–53.

Freeman, E. W., Rickels, K., Sondheimer, S. J., and Polansky, M. (1990, July 18). Ineffectiveness of progesterone suppository treatment for premenstrual syndrome. *Journal of the American Medical Association, 264*(3), 349–353.

Freiberg, P. (1991a). Self-esteem gender gap widens in adolescence. *APA Monitor, 22*(4), 29.

Freiberg, P. (1991b). Women's health office in ADAMHA proposed. *APA Monitor, 22*(5), 39.

French, J. R. P. Jr., & Raven, B. H. (1959). The bases of social power. In D. Cartwright (Ed.), *Studies in social power* (pp. 150–167). Ann Arbor: University of Michigan Press.

Freud, S. (1960). *A general introduction to psychoanalysis.* (J. Riviere, Trans.). New York: Washington Square Press. (Original work published 1924)

Freud, S. (1961). *Letters of Sigmund Freud, 1873–1939.* (E. L. Freud, Ed.). London: Hogarth Press.

Freud, S. (1974). Some psychical consequences of the anatomical distinction between the sexes. In J. Strachey (Ed. and Trans.), *The standard edition of the complete psychological works of Sigmund Freud* (Vol. 19, pp. 241–260). London: Hogarth Press and the Institute of Psycho-Analysis.

(Original work published 1925)

Frey, K. A. (1981). Middle-aged women's experience and perceptions of menopause. *Women and Health, 6*(1/2), 25–36.

Fried, R., & Major, B. (1980). *Self-presentation of sex-role attributes to attractive others.* Paper presented at the meeting of the Eastern Psychological Association, Hartford, CT.

Friedan, B. (1963). *The feminine mystique.* New York: Dell.

Friedan, B. (1981). *The second stage.* New York: Summit Books.

Friederich, M. A. (1983). Dysmenorrhea. *Women and Health, 8*(2/3), 91–106.

Friedman, A. (1987). Getting powerful with age: Changes in women over the life cycle. *Israel Social Science Research, 5,* 76–86.

Friedman, H. S., Tucker, J. S., Schwartz, J. E., Tomlinson-Keasey, C., Martin, L. R., Wingard, D. L., & Criqui, M. H. (1995). Psychosocial and behavioral predictors of longevity: The aging and death of the "Termites." *American Psychologist, 50*(2), 69–78.

Friedman, L. (1989). Mathematics and the gender gap: A meta-analysis of recent studies on sex differences in mathematical tasks. *Review of Educational Research, 59*(2), 185–213.

Friedman, M., & Rosenman, R. H. (1959). Association of specific overt behavior patterns with blood and cardiovascular findings. *Journal of the American Medical Association, 169,* 1286–1296.

Friedman, R. C., Hurt, S. W., Arnoff, M. S., & Clarkin, J. (1980). Behavior and the menstrual cycle. *Signs: Journal of Women in Culture and Society, 5,* 719–738.

Friedman, W. J., Robinson, A. B., & Friedman, B. L. (1987). Sex differences in moral judgments? A test of Gilligan's theory. *Psychology of Women Quarterly, 11*(1), 37–46.

Friend, T. (1990, January 26). Abuse in med school 'common'. *USA Today*, p. 1.

Frieze, I. H. (1979). Perceptions of battered wives. In I. H. Frieze, D. Bar-Tal, & J. S. Carroll (Eds.), *New approaches to social problems: Applications of attribution theory* (pp. 79–108). San Francisco: Jossey-Bass.

Frieze, I. H. (1983). Causes and consequences of marital rape. *Signs: Journal of Women in Culture and Society, 8*, 532–553.

Frieze, I. H. (1986, August). *The female victim: Rape, wife battering, and incest.* American Psychological Association Master Lecture, presented at the annual meeting of the American Psychological Association, Washington, DC.

Frodi, A., & Lamb, M. (1978). Sex differences in responsiveness to infants: A developmental study of psychophysiological and behavioral responses. *Child Development, 49*, 1182–1188.

Frodi, A., Macaulay, J., & Thome, P. R. (1977). Are women always less aggressive than men? A review of the experimental literature. *Psychological Bulletin, 84*, 634–660.

Fromm, E. (1973). *The anatomy of human destructiveness.* Greenwich, CT: Fawcett.

Frueh, T., & McGhee, P. (1975). Traditional sex role development and amount of time spent watching television. *Developmental Psychology, 11*, 109.

Fujita, F., Diener, E., & Sandvik, E. (1991). Gender differences in negative affect and well-being: The case for emotional intensity. *Journal of Personality and Social Psychology, 61*(3), 427–434.

Fulkerson, K. F., Furr, S., & Brown, D. (1983). Expectations and achievement among third-, sixth-, and ninth-grade Black and White males and females. *Developmental Psychology, 19*(2), 231–236.

Fulton, E. K. (1991, September 2). Rape and the court. *Maclean's,* p. 45.

Fulton, S. A., & Sabornie, E. J. (1994). Evidence of employment inequality among females with disabilities. *Journal of Special Education, 28*(2), 149–165.

Funk and Wagnalls Corporation. (1994). *The world almanac and book of facts: 1995.* New York: St. Martin's.

Furey, E. M. (1994). Sexual abuse of adults with mental retardation: Who and where. *Mental Retardation, 32*(3), 173–180.

Furomoto, L., & Scarborough, E. (1986). Placing women in the history of psychology: The first women psychologists. *American Psychologist, 4*(1), 35–42.

Futuyma, D. J., & Risch, S. J. (1984). Sexual orientation, sociobiology, and evolution. *Journal of Homosexuality, 9*(2/3), 157–168.

Gaddis, A., & Brooks-Gunn, J. (1985). The male experience of pubertal change. *Journal of Youth and Adolescence, 14*(1), 61–69.

Gallagher, S. K., & Gerstel, N. (1993). Kin keeping and friend keeping among older women: The effect of marriage. *Gerontologist, 33*(5), 675–681.

Gammell, D. J., & Stoppard, J. M. (1999). Women's experiences of treatment of depression: Medicalization or empowerment? *Canadian Psychology, 40*(2), 112–128.

Gandelman, R. (1983). Gonadal hormones and sensory function. *Neuroscience and Biobehavioral Reviews, 7*, 1–17.

Gannon, L., & Ekstrom, B. (1993). Attitudes toward menopause: The influence of sociocultural paradigms. *Psychology of Women Quarterly, 17*(3), 275–288.

Garcia, A. M. (1991). The development of Chicana feminist discourse. In J. Lorber & S. A. Farrell (Eds.), *The social construction of gender* (pp. 269–287). Newbury Park, CA: Sage.

Garfinkle, E. M., & Morin, S. F. (1978). Psychotherapists' attitudes toward homosexual psychotherapy clients. *Journal of Social Issues, 34*(3), 101–112.

Garrison, D. (1981). Karen Horney and feminism. *Signs: Journal of Women in Culture and Society, 6*(4), 672–691.

Gaskell, J. (1981). Sex inequalities in education for work: The case of business education. *Canadian Journal of Education, 6*(2), 54–72.

Gaskell, J. (1985, November). *Young women choose paths to the future.* Paper presented at the annual meeting of the Canadian Research Institute for the Advancement of Women, Saskatoon.

Gastil, J. (1990). Generic pronouns and sexist language: The oxymoronic character of masculine generics. *Sex Roles, 23*(11), 629–643.

Gavey, N., & McPhillips, K. (1999). Subject to romance: Heterosexual passivity as an obstacle to women initiating condom use. *Psychology of Women Quarterly, 23*(2), 349–368.

Geffner, D. S., & Hochberg, I. (1971). Ear laterality performance of children from low and middle socioeconomic levels on a verbal dichotic listening task. *Cortex, 7*, 193–203.

Gehlmann, S., Wicherski, M., & Kohout, J. (1995). *Characteristics of graduate departments of psychology: 1993–1994.* Washington, DC: American Psychological Association.

Gelb, S. A. (1989). Language and the problem of male salience in early childhood classroom environments. *Early Childhood Research Quarterly, 4*(2), 205–215.

Gerber, G. L. (1984). Attribution of feminine and masculine traits to opposite-sex dyads. *Psychological Reports, 55*(3), 907–918.

Gerdes, E. P., & Garber, D. M. (1983). Sex bias in hiring: Effects of job demands and applicant competence. *Sex Roles, 9*(3), 307–319.

Geringer, W. M., Marks, S., Allen, W. J., & Armstrong, K. A. (1993). Knowledge, attitudes, and behavior related to condom use and STDs in a high-risk population. *Journal of Sex Research, 30,* 75–83.

Gervasio, A. H., & Crawford, M. (1989). Social evaluations of assertiveness: A critique and speech act reformulation. *Psychology of Women Quarterly, 13*(1), 1–26.

Geschwind, N., & Behan, P. (1982). Left-handedness: Association with immune disease, migraine, and developmental learning disorder. *Proceedings of the National Academy of Sciences, 79,* 5097–5100.

Geschwind, N., & Galaburda, A. M. (1985). Cerebral lateralization: Biological mechanisms, associations, and pathology. I. A hypothesis and a program for research. *Archives of Neurology, 42,* 428–459.

Gibbs, M., Auerbach, D., & Fox, M. (1980). A comparison of male and female same-sex friendships. *International Journal of Women's Studies, 3*(3), 261–272.

Gilbert, L. A., Lee, R. N., & Chiddix, S. (1981). Influence of presenter's gender on students' evaluations of presenters discussing sex fairness in counseling: An analogue study. *Journal of Counseling Psychology, 28,* 258–264.

Gilligan, C. (1982). *In a different voice: Psychological theory and women's development.* Cambridge, MA: Harvard University Press.

Gilligan, C. (1990). Teaching Shakespeare's sister: Notes from the underground of female adolescence. In C. Gilligan, N. P. Lyons, & T. J. Hanmer (Eds.), *Making connections* (pp. 6–29). Cambridge, MA: Harvard University Press.

Gilligan, C., & Attanucci, J. (1988). Two moral orientations: Gender differences and similarities. *Merrill Palmer Quarterly, 34*(3), 223–237.

Ginorio, A. B., Gutiérrez, L., Cauce, A. M., & Acosta, M. (1995). Psychological issues for Latinas. In H. Landrine (Ed.), *Bringing cultural diversity to feminist psychology: Theory, research, practice* (pp. 241–263). Washington, DC: American Psychological Association.

Ginsburg, F. (1996, January 26). The anthropology of abortion activism. *Chronicle of Higher Education,* p. A48.

Gjerdingen, D. K., Froberg, D. G., & Kochevar, L. (1991). Changes in women's mental and physical health from pregnancy through six months postpartum. *Journal of Family Practice, 32*(2), 161–166.

Gladue, B. (1990, November). Adolescents' sexual practices: Have they changed? *Medical Aspects of Human Sexuality,* pp. 53–54.

Gladue, B. A., Boechler, M., & McCaul, K. D. (1989). Hormonal response to competition in human males. *Aggressive Behavior, 15,* 409–422.

Gladue, B. A., & Delaney, H. J. (1990). Gender differences in perception of attractiveness of men and women in bars. *Personality and Social Psychology Bulletin, 16*(2), 378–391.

Gladue, B. A., Green, R., & Hellman, R. E. (1984). Neuroendocrine response to estrogen and sexual orientation. *Science, 225,* 1469–1499.

Gladwell, M. (1990, November 26). Public health experts turn to economic ills. *Washington Post,* p. A3.

Glass, J., & Fujimoto, T. (1994, June). Housework, paid work, and depression among husbands and wives. *Journal of Health and Social Behavior, 35,* 179–191.

Glassner, B. (1989). Men and muscles. In M. S. Kimmel & M. A. Messner (Eds.), *Men's lives* (pp. 310–320). New York: Macmillan.

Glenn, E. N., & Feldberg, R. L. (1995). Clerical work: The female occupation. In J. Freeman (Ed.), *Women: A feminist perspective* (5th ed., pp. 262–286). Mountain View, CA: Mayfield.

Glick, P. (1991). Trait-based and sex-based discrimination in occupational prestige, occupational salary, and hiring. *Sex Roles, 25*(5/6), 351–378.

Glick, P., Diebold, J., Bailey-Werner, B., & Zhu, L. (1997). The two faces of Adam: Ambivalent sexism and attitudes toward women. *Personality and Social Psychology Bulletin, 32*(12), 1323–1334.

Glick, P., & Fiske, S. T. (1997). Hostile and benevolent sexism: Measuring ambivalent sexist attitudes toward women. *Psychology of Women Quarterly, 21*(1), 119–135.

Glick, P., Wilk, K., & Perreault, M. (1995). Images of occupations: Components of gender and status in occupational stereotypes. *Sex Roles, 32*(9/10), 565–582.

Go, C. G., Brustrom, J. E., Lynch, M. F., & Aldwin, C. M. (1995). Ethnic trends in survival curves and mortality. *Gerontologist, 35*(3), 318–326.

Goh, S. C. (1991). Sex differences in perceptions of interpersonal work style, career emphasis, supervisory mentoring behavior, and job satisfaction. *Sex Roles, 24*(11/12), 701–710.

Gold, A. R., & Adams, D. B. (1981). Motivational factors affecting fluctuations of female sexual activity at menstruation. *Psychology of Women Quarterly, 5,* 670–680.

Gold, D., Crombie, G., & Noble, S. (1987). Relations between teachers' judgments of girls' and boys' compliance and intellectual competence. *Sex Roles, 16*(7/8), 351–358.

Gold, R. (1981). Women entering the labor force draw attention to reproductive hazards for both sexes. *Family Planning/Population Reporter, 10*(1), 10–13.

Goldberg, D. C., Wipple, B., Fishkin, R. E., Waxman, H., Fink, P. J., & Weisberg, M. (1983). The Grafenberg spot and female ejaculation: A review of initial hypotheses. *Journal of Sex and Marital Therapy, 9,* 27–37.

Goldberg, P. H. (1968). Are women prejudiced against women? *Trans-action, 5,* 28–30.

Golden, C. (1987). Diversity and variability in women's sexual identities. In The Boston Lesbian Psychologies Collective (Eds.), *Lesbian psychologies* (pp. 18–34). Urbana: University of Illinois Press.

Golding, J. M. (1988). Gender differences in depressive symptoms. *Psychology of Women Quarterly, 12*(1), 61–74.

Golding, J. M. (1990). Division of household labor, strain, and depressive symptoms among Mexican Americans and non-Hispanic Whites. *Psychology of Women Quarterly, 14,* 103–117.

Golub, S. (1976). The effect of premenstrual anxiety and depression on cognitive function. *Journal of Personality and Social Psychology, 34,* 99–104.

Golub, S. (1983). Menarche: The beginning of menstrual life. *Women and Health, 8*(2/3), 17–36.

Golub, S., & Catalano, J. (1983). Recollections of menarche and women's subsequent experiences with menstruation. *Women and Health, 8,* 49–61.

Gomberg, E. S. L. (1982). Historical and political perspective: Women and drug use. *Journal of Social Issues, 38*(2), 9–23.

Good, P. R., & Smith, B. D. (1980). Menstrual distress and sex-role attributes. *Psychology of Women Quarterly, 4,* 482–491.

Goodchilds, J. D. (1979). Power: A matter of mechanics? *Society for the Advancement of Social Psychology Newsletter, 5*(3), 3.

Goodman, E. (1999, May 30). TV arrived in Fiji in 1995, and the islands' women changed forever. *Arizona Daily Star,* p. F2.

Goodyear, R. K. (1990). Gender configurations in supervisory dyads: Their relation to supervisee influence strategies and skill evaluations of the supervisee. *Clinical Supervisor, 8*(2), 67–79.

Gooren, L. (1990). The endocrinology of transsexualism. A review and commentary. *Psychoneuroendocrinology, 15,* 3–14.

Gordon, H. W., & Lee, P. A. (1986). A relationship between gonadotropins and visuospatial function. *Neuropsychologia, 24*(4), 563–576.

Gornick, V. (1990). *Women in science.* New York: Simon & Schuster.

Gottfried, A. E., & Gottfried, A. W. (1988). *Maternal employment and children's development.* New York: Plenum.

Gouchie, C., & Kimura, D. (1991). The relationship between testosterone levels and cognitive ability patterns. *Psychoneuroendocrinology, 16,* 323–334.

Gould, R. M. (1973). Measuring masculinity by the size of a paycheck. *Ms., 1*(12), 18–21.

Gould, S. (1981). *The mismeasure of man.* New York: Norton.

Gove, W. R., Style, C. B., & Hughes, M. (1990). The effect of marriage on the well-being of adults: A theoretical analysis. *Journal of Family Issues, 11,* 4–35.

Gove, W. R., & Tudor, J. F. (1973). Adult sex roles and mental illness. *American Journal of Sociology, 78,* 812–832.

Goy, R. W. (1968). Organizing effects of androgen on the behavior of rhesus monkeys. In R. P. Michael (Ed.), *Endocrinology and human behaviour* (pp. 12–31). London: Oxford University Press.

Goy, R. W. (1970). Experimental control of psychosexuality. In G. W. Harris & R. G. Edwards (Eds.), *A discussion on the determination of sex.* London: Philosophical Transactions of the Royal Society.

Graham, K., Wilsnack, R., Dawson, D., & Vogeltanz, N. (1998). Should alcohol consumption measures be adjusted for gender differences? *Addiction, 93*(8), 1137–1147.

Gralewski, C., & Rodgon, M. M. (1980). Effect of social and intellectual instruction on achievement motivation as a function of role orientation. *Sex Roles, 6,* 301–309.

Grant, L. (1984). Black females' "place" in desegregated classrooms. *Sociology of Education, 57,* 98–111.

Gravenkemper, S. A., & Paludi, M. A. (1983). Fear of success revisited. Introducing an ambiguous cue. *Sex Roles, 9,* 897–900.

Gray-Little, B., & Burks, N. (1983). Power and satisfaction in marriage: A review and critique. *Psychological Bulletin, 93,* 513–538.

Grayson, J. P. (1983). The effects of a plant closure on the stress levels and health of workers' wives: A preliminary analysis. *Journal of Business Ethics, 2,* 221–225.

Green, D. H., & Zenisek, T. J. (1983). Dual career couples. Individual and organizational implications. *Journal of Business Ethics, 2,* 171–184.

Green, R. (1974). *Sexual identity conflict in children and adults.* Baltimore: Penguin Books.

Greene, B. (1994a). African American women. In L. Comas-Díaz & B. Greene (Eds.), *Women of color: Integrating ethnic and gender identities in psychotherapy* (pp. 10–29). New York: Guilford Press.

Greene, B. (1994b). Lesbian women of color: Triple jeopardy. In L. Comas-Díaz & B. Greene (Eds.), *Women of color: Integrating ethnic and gender identities in psychotherapy* (pp. 389–427). New York: Guilford Press.

Greene, E. (1987, January 28). Too many women? That's the problem at Chapel Hill, say some trustees. *Chronicle of Higher Education*, pp. 27–28.

Greenglass, E. R. (1976). *After abortion*. Toronto: Longman Canada.

Greenglass, E. R. (1985a). An interactional perspective on job-related stress in managerial women. *Southern Psychologist, 2,* 42–48.

Greenglass, E. R. (1985b). Psychological implications of sex bias in the workplace. *Academic Psychology Bulletin, 1,* 227–240.

Greenglass, E. R. (1991). Burnout and gender: Theoretical and organizational implications. *Canadian Psychology, 32*(4), 562–572.

Greenough, W. T., Black, J. E., & Wallace, C. S. (1987). Experience and brain development. *Child Development, 58,* 539–559.

Greenspan, M. (1983). *A new approach to women and therapy.* New York: McGraw-Hill.

Griffitt, W. (1987). Females, males, and sexual responses. In K. Kelley (Ed.), *Females, males and sexuality* (pp. 156–173). Albany: State University of New York Press.

Grimm, L., & Yarnold, P. R. (1985). Sex typing and the coronary-prone behavior pattern. *Sex Roles, 12,* 171–178.

Grimsley, K. D. (1996, February 28). From the top: The women's view. *Washington Post*, pp. C1, C4.

Gross, H. E. (1980). Dual-career couples who live apart: Two

types. *Journal of Marriage and the Family, 42,* 567–576.

Grossman, F. K., Eichler, L. S., & Winickoff, S. A. (1980). *Pregnancy, birth, and parenthood*. San Francisco: Jossey-Bass.

Gruber, J. E. (1990). Methodological problems and policy implications in sexual harassment research. *Population Research and Policy Review, 9,* 235–254.

Gupta, A. (1991). Gender stereotypes and self-concepts in college students. *Psychological Studies, 36*(3), 180–186.

Gurwitz, S. B., & Dodge, K. A. (1975). Adults' evaluation of a child as a function of sex of adult and sex of child. *Journal of Personality and Social Psychology, 32,* 822–828.

Gutek, B., & Nakamura, C. (1983). Gender roles and sexuality in the world of work. In E. R. Allgeier & N. B. McCormick (Eds.), *Changing boundaries: Gender roles and sexual behavior* (pp. 182–201). Palo Alto, CA: Mayfield.

Gutek, B. A., & O'Connor, M. (1995). The empirical basis for the reasonable woman standard. *Journal of Social Issues, 51*(1), 151–166.

Guthrie, R. V. (1976). *Even the rat was white: An historical view of psychology.* New York: Harper & Row.

Gutierres, S. E., Kenrick, D. T., & Goldberg, L. (1983, August). *Adverse effect of popular erotica on judgments of one's mate.* Paper presented at the meeting of the American Psychological Association, Anaheim, CA.

Gutmann, D. (1972). Ego psychological and developmental approaches to the "retirement crisis" in men. In F. M. Carp (Ed.), *Retirement* (pp. 267–305). New York: Behavioral Publications.

Haddock, G., & Zanna, M. P. (1994). Preferring "housewives" to "feminists." Categorization and the favorability of attitudes

toward women. *Psychology of Women Quarterly, 18*(1), 25–52.

Haefner, J. E. (1977). Sources of discrimination among employees: A survey investigation. *Journal of Applied Psychology, 62*(3), 265–270.

Hagan, J. (1990). The gender stratification of income inequality among lawyers. *Social Forces, 68*(3), 835–855.

Hall, J. A. (1978). Gender effects in decoding nonverbal cues. *Psychological Bulletin, 85,* 845–875.

Hall, J. A. (1984). *Nonverbal sex differences: Communication accuracy and expressive style.* Baltimore: Johns Hopkins University Press.

Halpern, D. F. (1992). *Sex differences in cognitive abilities* (2nd ed.). Hillsdale, NJ: Erlbaum.

Halpern, D. F. (1997). Sex differences in intelligence: Implications for education. *American Psychologist, 52,* 1091–1102.

Hamburg, D. A., Moos, R. H., & Yalom, I. D. (1968). Studies of distress in the menstrual cycle and the postpartum period. In R. P. Michael (Ed.), *Endocrinology and human behaviour* (pp. 94–116). London: Oxford University Press.

Hamilton, D. L. (1979). A cognitive-attributional analysis of stereotyping. *Advances in Experimental Psychology, 12,* 53–81.

Hamilton, J. A., & Gallant, S. J. (1990). Problematic aspects of diagnosing premenstrual phase dysphoria: Recommendations for psychological research and practice. *Professional Psychology Research and Practice, 2*(1), 60–68.

Hamilton, J. A., Gallant, S. A., & Lloyd, C. (1989). Evidence for a menstrual-linked artifact in determining rates of depression. *Journal of Nervous and Mental Disease, 177*(6), 359–365.

Hamilton, R. (1985). Feminists in the academy: Intellectuals or political subversives? *Queen's Quarterly, 92*(1), 3–20.

Hammond, D., & Dingley, J. (1989). Sex differences in career preferences of lower sixth formers in Belfast grammar schools. *Journal of Occupational Psychology, 62*, 263–264.

Hampson, E. (1990a). Estrogen-related variations in human spatial and articulatory-motor skills. *Psychoneuroendocrinology, 15*(2), 97–111.

Hampson, E. (1990b). Variations in sex-related cognitive abilities across the menstrual cycle. *Brain and Cognition, 14*(1), 26–43.

Hampson, J. L., & Hampson, J. G. (1961). The ontogenesis of sexual behavior in man. In W. C. Young (Ed.), *Sex and internal secretions* (Vol. 1, pp. 1401–1432). Baltimore: Williams and Wilkins.

Hanna, W. J., & Rogovsky, E. (1991). Women with disabilities: Two handicaps plus. *Disability, Handicap and Society, 6*(1), 49–63.

Hanna, W. J., & Rogovsky, E. (1992). On the situation of African American women with physical disabilities. *Journal of Applied Rehabilitation Counseling, 23*(4), 39–45.

Hansen, C. H., & Hansen, R. D. (1988). How rock music videos can change what is seen when boy meets girl: Priming stereotypic appraisal of social interactions. *Sex Roles, 19*, 287–316.

Hanson, S. M. H. (1985). Fatherhood: Contextual variations. *American Behavioral Scientist, 29*(1), 55–77.

Harding, J. J. (1989). Postpartum psychiatric disorders: A review. *Comprehensive Psychiatry, 30*, 109–112.

Hardman, A. E., & Hudson, A. (1994). Brisk walking and serum lipid and lipoprotein variables in previously sedentary women: Effect of 12 weeks of regular brisk walking followed by 12 weeks of detraining. *British Journal of Sports Medicine, 28*(4), 261–266.

Hare-Mustin, R. (1983). An appraisal of the relationship between women and psychotherapy: 80 years after the case of Dora. *American Psychologist, 38*, 593–601.

Hare-Mustin, R. T., & Maracek, J. (1990). Gender and the meaning of difference: Postmodernism and psychology. In R. T. Hare-Mustin & J. Maracek (Eds.), *Making a difference: Psychology and the construction of gender* (pp. 22–64). New Haven, CT: Yale University Press.

Hargreaves, D. J., Bates, H. M., & Foot, J. M. C. (1985). Sex-typed labelling affects task performance. *British Journal of Social Psychology, 24*, 153–155.

Harris, B. (1979). Careers, conflict, and children. In A. Roland & B. Harris (Eds.), *Career and motherhood* (pp. 55–86). New York: Human Sciences Press.

Harris, J. F. (1991, October 19). Va. to drop its ban on gay bars. *Washington Post*, p. C1.

Harris, J. R. (1995). Where is the child's environment? A group socialization theory of development. *Psychological Review, 102*(3), 458–489.

Harris, L. J. (1992). Left-handedness. In I. Rapin & S. J. Segalowitz (Eds.), *Handbook of neuropsychology* (pp. 145–208). Amsterdam: Elsevier Science.

Harris, S. M. (1993). The influence of personal and family factors on achievement needs and concerns of African-American and Euro American college women. *Sex Roles, 29*(9/10), 671–689.

Harris, S. M. (1994). Racial differences in predictors of women's body image attitudes. *Women and Health, 2*, 89–104.

Harris, S. M. (1995). Family, self, and sociocultural contributions to body-image attitudes of African-American women.

Harrison, J. (1978). Warning: The male sex role may be dangerous to your health. *Journal of Social Issues, 34*(1), 65–86.

Harry, B., & Balcer, C. M. (1987). Menstruation and crime: A critical review of the literature from the clinical criminology perspective. *Behavioral Sciences and the Law, 5*(3), 307–321.

Hartup, W. W. (1983). The peer system. In P. Mussen & E. Heatherington (Eds.), *Handbook of child psychology* (4th ed., Vol. 4, pp. 103–196). New York: Wiley.

Harvey, E. (1999). Short-term and long-term effects of early parental employment on children of the National Longitudinal Survey of Youth. *Developmental Psychology, 35*(2), 445–459.

Harvie, K., Marshal-McCaskey, J., & Johnston, L. (1998). Gender-based biases in occupational hiring decisions. *Journal of Applied Social Psychology, 28*(18), 1698–1711.

Hatcher, R. A., Trussell, J., Stewart, F., Stewart, G., et al. (1994). *Contraceptive technology.* New York: Irvington.

Hatchett, S. J., & Quick, A. D. (1983). Correlates of sex-role attitudes among Black men and women: Data from a national survey of Black Americans. *Urban Research Review, 9*(2), 1–3, 11.

Hatfield, E. (1983). What do women and men want from love and sex? In E. R. Allgeier & N. B. McCormick (Eds.), *Changing boundaries: Gender roles and sexual behavior* (pp. 106–134). Palo Alto, CA: Mayfield.

Hatfield, E., Sprecher, S., Pillemer, J. T., & Greenberger, D. (1988). Gender differences in what is desired in the sexual relationship. *Journal of Psychology and Human Sexuality, 1*(2), 39–52.

Psychology of Women Quarterly, 19(1), 129–145.

Havemann, J. (1999, April 29). Birth rate of teens is down. *Washington Post*, p. A3.

Hazzard, W. R. (1986). Biological basis of the sex differential in longevity. *Journal of the American Geriatric Society, 34*(6), 455–471.

Healey, S. (1993). The common agenda between old women, women with disabilities and all women. *Women and Therapy, 14*(3/4), 65–77.

Heilbrun, A. B. Jr. (1984). Sex-based models of androgyny: A further cognitive elaboration of competence differences. *Journal of Personality and Social Psychology, 46*, 216–229.

Heilbrun, A. B., Friedberg, L., & Wydra, D. (1989). Personality underlying motivation for Type A behavior in late adolescents. *Journal of Youth and Adolescence, 18*(4), 311–319.

Heilbrun, C. (1973). *Toward a recognition of androgyny.* New York: Harper & Row.

Heilman, M. E., Martell, R. F., & Simon, M. C. (1988). The vagaries of sex bias: Conditions regulating the undervaluation, equivaluation, and overvaluation of female job applicants. *Organizational Behavior and Human Decision Processes, 41*, 98–110.

Heilman, M. E., Simon, M. C., & Repper, D. P. (1987). Intentionally favored, unintentionally harmed? Impact of sex-based preferential selection on self-perception and self-evaluations. *Journal of Applied Psychology, 72*(1), 62–68.

Heiman, J. R. (1977). A psychophysiological exploration of sexual arousal patterns in females and males. *Psychophysiology, 14*, 266–274.

Heise, L., Pitanguy, J., & Germain, A. (1993). *Violence against women: The hidden health burden.* Washington, DC: World Bank.

Heiser, P., & Gannon, L. (1984). The relationship of sex-role stereotypes to anger expression and the report of psychosomatic symptoms. *Sex Roles, 10*, 601–611.

Helms, J. E. (Ed.). (1993). *Black and White racial identity: Theory, research, and practice.* Westport, CT: Praeger.

Helson, R., & Mitchell, V. (1990). Women's prime of life: Is it the fifties? *Psychology of Women Quarterly, 14*, 451–470.

Helson, R., & Picano, J. (1990). Is the traditional role bad for women? *Journal of Personality and Social Psychology, 59*(2), 311–320.

Henderson, N., & Baker, P. (1990, February 2). For VMI cadets, it's still 'better dead than coed'. *Washington Post*, pp. B1, B7.

Hendrick, S., Hendrick, C., Slapion-Foote, M. J., & Foote, F. H. (1985). Gender differences in sexual attitudes. *Journal of Personality and Social Psychology, 48*(6), 1630–1642.

Henley, N. (1973). Power, sex and nonverbal communication. *Berkeley Journal of Sociology, 18*, 1–26.

Henley, N. (1977). *Body politics: Power, sex, and nonverbal communication.* Englewood Cliffs, NJ: Prentice-Hall.

Henley, N., & Freeman, J. (1995). The sexual politics of interpersonal behavior. In J. Freeman (Ed.), *Women: A feminist perspective* (5th ed., pp. 79–91). Mountain View, CA: Mayfield.

Henley, N., & LaFrance, M. (1984). Gender as culture: Difference and dominance in nonverbal behavior. In A. Wolfgang (Ed.), *Nonverbal behavior: Perspectives, applications, intercultural insights* (pp. 351–372). New York: C. J. Hogrefe.

Hennig, M., & Jardim, A. (1977). *The managerial woman.* New York: Doubleday.

Hepburn, C. (1985). Memory for the frequency of sex-typed versus neutral behaviors: Implications for the maintenance of sex stereotypes. *Sex Roles, 12*(7/8), 771–776.

Herdt, G. (1989). Introduction: Gay and lesbian youth, emergent identities, and cultural scenes at home and abroad. In G. Herdt (Ed.), *Gay and lesbian youth* (pp. 1–42). New York: Harrington Park Press.

Herek, G. M. (1988). Heterosexuals' attitudes toward lesbians and gay men: Correlates and gender differences. *Journal of Sex Research, 25*(4), 451–477.

Herek, G. M. (1993). Documenting prejudice against lesbians and gay men on campus: The Yale sexual orientation survey. *Journal of Homosexuality, 25*(4), 15–28.

Herman, J. L. (1981). *Father-daughter incest.* Cambridge MA: Harvard University Press.

Herrera, R. S., & DelCampo, R. L. (1995). Beyond the superwoman syndrome: Work satisfaction and family functioning among working-class, Mexican American women. *Hispanic Journal of Behavioral Sciences, 17*(1), 49–60.

Herring, S., & Reitan, R. M. (1984, August). *Sex similarities in neuropsychological sequelae of lateralized cerebral lesions.* Paper presented at the meeting of the American Psychological Association, Toronto, Ontario.

Herrmann, D. J., Crawford, M., & Holdsworth, M. (1992). Gender-linked differences in everyday memory performance. *British Journal of Psychology, 83*(2), 221–231.

Herscher, E. (1999, January 15). Health Institute confirms need for lesbian studies/Doctors in the dark about gay women's medical needs. *San Francisco Chronicle*, p. A2.

Herz, E. J., & Reis, J. S. (1987). Family life education for young inner-city teens: Identifying needs. *Journal of Youth and Adolescence, 16*(4), 361–377.

Herzog, A., & Detre, T. (1976). Psychotic reactions associated with childbirth. *Diseases of the Nervous System, 37*, 229–235.

Hibbard, J. H., & Pope, C. R. (1993). The quality of social roles as predictors of morbidity and mortality. *Social Science and Medicine, 36*(3), 217–225.

Hill, C. T., Rubin, Z., & Peplau, L. A. (1976). Breakups before marriage: The end of 103 affairs. *Journal of Social Issues, 32*, 147–168.

Hines, M. (1982). Prenatal gonadal hormones and sex differences in human behavior. *Psychological Bulletin, 92*, 56–80.

Hines, M. (1990). Gonadal hormones and human cognitive development. In J. Balthazart (Ed.), *Hormones, brain and behavior in vertebrates. Vol. 1. Sexual differentiation, neuroanatomical aspects, neurotransmitters and neuropeptides* (pp. 51–63). Basel: Karger.

Hines, M., & Shipley, C. (1984). Prenatal exposure to diethylstilbestrol (DES) and the development of sexually dimorphic cognitive abilities and cerebral lateralization. *Developmental Psychology, 20*(1), 81–94.

Hirsch, K. (1990, September/October). Fraternities of fear. *Ms., 1*(2), 52–56.

Hiscock, M., Inch, R., Jacek, C., Hiscock-Kalil, C., & Kalil, K. M. (1994). Is there a sex difference in human laterality? I. An exhaustive survey of auditory laterality studies from six neuropsychology journals. *Journal of Clinical and Experimental Neuropsychology, 16*, 423–435.

Hiscock, M., Israelian, M., Inch, R., Jacek, C., & Hiscock-Kalil, C. (1995). Is there a sex difference in human laterality? II. An exhaustive survey of visual laterality studies from six neuropsychology journals. *Journal of Clinical and Experimental Neuropsychology, 17*, 590–610.

Hite, S. (1976). *The Hite report.* New York: Macmillan.

Hite, S. (1981). *The Hite report on male sexuality.* New York: Knopf.

Ho, D. D., Schooley, R. T., Rota, T. R., Kaplan, J. C., Flynn, T., Salahuddin, S. Z., Gonda, M. A., & Hirsch, M. (1984). HTLV-III in the semen and blood of a healthy homosexual man. *Science, 226*(4673), 451–453.

Hoffman, J. C. (1982). Biorhythms in human reproduction: The not-so-steady states. *Signs: Journal of Women in Culture and Society, 7*(4), 829–844.

Hoffman, L. W. (1972). Early childhood experiences and women's achievement motives. *Journal of Social Issues, 29*(2), 120–155.

Hoffman, L. W. (1974). Effects of maternal employment on the child: A review of the research. *Developmental Psychology, 10*, 204–228.

Hoffman, L. W., & Kloska, D. D. (1995). Parents' gender-based attitudes toward marital roles and child rearing: Development and validation of new measures. *Sex Roles, 32*(5/6), 273–295.

Hoffnung, M. (1995). Motherhood: Contemporary conflict for women. In J. Freeman (Ed.), *Women: A feminist perspective* (5th ed., pp. 162–181). Mountain View, CA: Mayfield.

Hokanson, J. E., & Edelman, R. (1966). Effects of three social responses on vascular processes. *Journal of Personality and Social Psychology, 3*, 442–447.

Hokanson, J. E., Willers, K. R., & Koropsak, E. (1968). The modification of autonomic responses during aggressive interchange. *Journal of Personality, 36*, 386–404.

Hollingworth, L. (1914). *Functional periodicity: An experimental study of the mental and motor abilities of women during menstruation.* New York: Teachers College, Columbia University.

Hollingworth, L. (1916). Sex differences in mental traits. *Psychological Bulletin, 13*, 377–385.

Hollingworth, L. (1918). Comparison of the sexes in mental traits. *Psychological Bulletin, 25*, 427–432.

Hollingworth, L. (1922). Differential action upon the sexes of forces which tend to segregate the feebleminded. *Journal of Abnormal Psychology and Social Psychology, 17*, 35–57.

Hollingworth, L., & Montague, H. (1914). The comparative variability of the sexes at birth. *American Journal of Sociology, 20*, 335–370.

Holms, V. (1985). *Factors related to career motivation among female adolescents.* Unpublished master's thesis, University of Manitoba.

Holtzworth-Munroe, A., & Stuart, G. L. (1994). Typologies of male batterers: Three subtypes and the differences among them. *Psychological Bulletin, 116*(3), 476–497.

Homans, G. C. (1974). *Social behavior: The elementary forms.* New York: Harcourt Brace Jovanovich.

Hong, J., & Seltzer, M. M. (1995). The psychological consequences of multiple roles: The non-normative case. *Journal of Health and Social Behavior, 36*, 386–398.

Hooker, E. (1957). The adjustment of the male overt homosexual. *Journal of Projective Techniques, 21*, 18–31.

Hooker, E. (1993). Reflections of a 40-year exploration: A scientific view on homosexuality. *American Psychologist, 48*(4), 450–453.

Hopkins, H. R., & Klein, H. A. (1993). Multidimensional self-perception: Linkages to parental nurturance. *Journal of Genetic Psychology, 154*(4), 165–173.

Hopkins, J., Marcues, M., & Campbell, S. B. (1984). Postpartum depression: A critical review. *Psychological Bulletin, 95,* 498–515.

Horne, S. (1999). Domestic violence in Russia. *American Psychologist, 54*(1), 55–61.

Horner, M. (1968). *Sex differences in achievement motivation and performance in competitive and noncompetitive situations.* Unpublished doctoral dissertation, University of Michigan.

Horner, M. (1970). Femininity and successful achievement: A basic inconsistency. In J. Bardwick, E. Douvan, M. Horner, & D. Guttman (Eds.), *Feminine personality and conflict* (pp. 45–76). Pacific Grove, CA: Brooks/Cole.

Horney, K. (1939). *The neurotic personality of our time.* New York: Norton.

Horney, K. (1973). The flight from womanhood. In J. B. Miller (Ed.), *Psychoanalysis and women* (pp. 5–20). Baltimore: Penguin Books. (Original work published 1926).

Horowitz, M. J., Schaefer, C., & Cooney, P. (1974). Life event scaling for recency of experience. In E. K. E. Gunderson & R. H. Rahe (Eds.), *Life stress and illness* (pp. 125–133). Springfield, IL: Charles C. Thomas.

Hort, B. E., Fagot, B. I., & Leinbach, M. D. (1990). Are people's notions of maleness more stereotypically framed than their notions of femaleness? *Sex Roles, 23*(3/4), 197–212.

Horwitz, E. L. (1990, October). For your health's sake. *AAUW Outlook,* p. 5.

Hossain, Z., & Roopnarine, J. L. (1993). Division of household labor and child care in dual-earner African-American families with infants. *Sex Roles, 29*(9/10), 571–583.

Houston, M. (1991, May 7). Girls opt for pink ghetto. *Winnipeg Free Press,* pp. 1, 4.

Howard, J. A., Blumstein, P., & Schwartz, P. (1986). Sex, power, and influence tactics in intimate relationships. *Journal of Personality and Social Psychology, 51*(1), 102–109.

Howes, C., & Phillipsen, L. (1992). Gender and friendship: Relationships within peer groups of young children. *Social Development, 1*(3), 230–242.

Hoyenga, K. B., & Hoyenga, K. T. (1993). *Gender-related differences: Origins and outcomes.* Boston: Allyn & Bacon.

Hrdy, S. B. (1981). *The woman that never evolved.* Cambridge, MA: Harvard University Press.

Hsu, L. K. G. (1987). Are the eating disorders becoming more common in Blacks? *International Journal of Eating Disorders, 6,* 113–124.

Huang, J. (1993). An investigation of gender differences in cognitive abilities among Chinese high school students. *Personality and Individual Differences, 15*(6), 717–719.

Hubbard, R. (1990). *The politics of women's biology.* New Brunswick, NJ: Rutgers University Press.

Hudgens, G. A., Fatkin, L. T., Billingsley, P. A., & Mazurczak, J. (1988). Hand steadiness: Effects of sex, menstrual phase, oral contraceptives, practice, and handgun weight. *Human Factors, 30*(1), 51–60.

Huesmann, L. R., Guerra, N. G., Zelli, A., & Miller, L. (1992). Differing normative beliefs about aggression for boys and girls. In K. Bjorkqvist & P. Niemela (Eds.), *Of mice and women: Aspects of female aggression* (pp. 77–87). New York: Academic Press.

Humphreys, A. P., & Smith, P. K. (1987). Rough and tumble friendship and dominance in school children: Evidence for continuity and change with age

in middle childhood. *Child Development, 58,* 201–212.

Hunt, M. (1974). *Sexual behavior in the 1970s.* Chicago: Playboy Press.

Hunter, M. S. (1990). Psychological and somatic experiences of the menopause: A prospective study. *Psychosomatic Medicine, 52,* 357–367.

Huston, A. C., Greer, D., Wright, J. C., Welch, R., & Ross, R. (1984). Children's comprehension of televised formal features with masculine and feminine connotations. *Developmental Psychology, 20*(4), 707–716.

Huston, T. L., & Ashmore, R. D. (1986). Women and men in personal relationships. In R. D. Ashmore & F. K. Del Boca (Eds.), *The social psychology of female–male relations* (pp. 167–210). Orlando, FL: Academic Press.

Huston, T. L., McHale, S. M., & Crouter, A. C. (1986). When the honeymoon is over: Changes in the marriage relationship over the first year. In R. Gilmour & S. Duck (Eds.), *The emerging field of personal relationships* (pp. 109–132). Hillsdale, NJ: Erlbaum.

Hyde, J. S. (1981). How large are cognitive gender differences? A meta-analysis using ω^2 and d. *American Psychologist, 36,* 892–901.

Hyde, J. S. (1984a). Children's understanding of sexist language. *Developmental Psychology, 20*(4), 697–706.

Hyde, J. S. (1984b). How large are gender differences in aggression? A developmental meta-analysis. *Developmental Psychology, 20,* 722–736.

Hyde, J. S. (1986). *Understanding human sexuality.* New York: McGraw-Hill.

Hyde, J. S. (1994). Should psychologists study gender differences? Yes, with some guidelines. *Feminism and Psychology, 4*(4), 507–512.

Hyde, J. S. (1995). Women and maternity leave: Empirical data and public policy. *Psychology of Women Quarterly, 19*(3), 299–314.

Hyde, J. S., & Ashby Plant, E. (1995). Magnitude of psychological gender differences: Another side to the story. *American Psychologist, 50*(3), 159–161.

Hyde, J. S., Fennema, E., & Lamon, S. J. (1990a). Gender differences in mathematics performance: A meta-analysis. *Psychological Bulletin, 107*(2), 139–155.

Hyde, J. S., Fennema, E., Ryan, M., Frost, L., & Hopp, C. (1990). Gender comparisons of mathematics attitudes and affect. *Psychology of Women Quarterly, 14,* 299–324.

Hyde, J. S., & Linn, M. C. (1988). Gender differences in verbal ability: A meta-analysis. *Psychological Bulletin, 104*(1), 53–69.

Hyde, J. S., Rosenberg, B. G., & Behrman, J. (1974). *Tomboyism: Implications for theories of female development.* Paper presented at the annual convention of the Western Psychological Association, San Francisco.

Hynie, M., & Lydon, J. E. (1995). Women's perceptions of female contraceptive behavior. *Psychology of Women Quarterly, 19*(4), 563–581.

Ibarra, H. (1992). Homophily and differential returns: Sex differences in network structure and access in an advertising firm. *Administrative Science Quarterly, 37*(3), 422–447.

Imamoglu, E. O., Kuller, R., Imamoglu, V., & Kuller, M. (1993). The social psychological worlds of Swedes and Turks in and around retirement. *Journal of Cross Cultural Psychology, 24*(1), 26–41.

Imperato-McGinley, J., Guerrero, L., Gautier, T., & Peterson, R. E. (1974). Steroid 5-alpha-reductase deficiency in man: An inherited form of male pseudo-hermaphroditism. *Science, 186,* 1213–1215.

Imperato-McGinley, J., Miller, M., Wilson, J. D., Peterson, R. E., Shackleton, C., & Gajdusek, D. C. (1991). A cluster of male pseudohermaphrodites with 5-alpha-reductase deficiency in Papua New Guinea. *Clinical Endocrinology, 34,* 293–298.

Imperato-McGinley, J., Peterson, R. E., Gautier, T., & Sturla, E. (1979). Androgens and the evolution of male gender identity among male pseudohermaphrodites with a 5-alpha-reductase deficiency. *New England Journal of Medicine, 310,* 839–840.

Ingoldsby, B. B. (1995). Marital structure. In B. B. Ingoldsby & S. Smith (Eds.), *Families in multicultural perspective* (pp. 117–137). New York: Guilford Press.

Ingrassia, M. (1994, October 17). Virgin cool. *Newsweek,* pp. 59–69.

Institute for Women's Policy Research. (1990). *Unnecessary losses* (Research-in-Brief fact sheet). Washington, DC: Author.

Institute for Women's Policy Research. (1999, February). *Employment, earnings and economic change* [On-line]. Available: www.iwpr.org/RESEARCH.HTM

Instone, D., Major, B., & Bunker, B. B. (1983). Gender, self-confidence, and social influence strategies: An organizational simulation. *Journal of Personality and Social Psychology, 44,* 322–333.

Irvine, J. J. (1986). Teacher–student interactions: Effects of student race, sex, and grade level. *Journal of Educational Psychology, 78*(1), 14–21.

Jabes, J. (1980). Causal attributions and sex-role stereotypes in the perceptions of women managers. *Canadian Journal of Behavioural Science, 12*(1), 52–63.

Jacklin, C. N. (1985, June). *Stalking the development of sex differences.* Invited address to the Canadian Psychological Association, Halifax, Nova Scotia.

Jacklin, C. N., Maccoby, E. E., & Doering, C. H. (1983). Neonatal sex-steroid hormones and timidity in 6–18-month-old boys and girls. *Developmental Psychobiology, 16*(3), 163–168.

Jacklin, C. N., Maccoby, E. E., Doering, C. H., & King, D. R. (1984). Neonatal sex steroid hormones and muscular strength of boys and girls in the first three years. *Developmental Psychobiology, 17*(3), 301–310.

Jackson, L. A. (1989). Relative deprivation and the gender wage gap. *Journal of Social Issues, 45*(4), 117–133.

Jackson, L. A., Sullivan, L. A., & Rostker, R. (1988). Gender, gender role, and body image. *Sex Roles, 19,* 429–443.

Jacobsen, F. M. (1994). Psychopharmacology. In L. Comas-Díaz & B. Greene (Eds.), *Women of color: Integrating ethnic and gender identities in psychotherapy* (pp. 319–338). New York: Guilford Press.

Jacobson, N., & Gottman, J. (1998). *When men batter women: New insights into ending abusive relationships.* New York: Simon & Schuster.

James, W. (1890). *The principles of psychology.* New York: Holt.

Janus, S. S., & Janus, C. L. (1993). *The Janus report on sexual behavior.* New York: Wiley.

Jazzman Billy Tipton revealed as a woman. (1989, February 1). *Tucson Citizen,* p. 3A.

Jemelka, J. R., & Downs, C. (1991). The social support construct in an experimental context: A reexamination. *Psychology: A Journal of Human Behavior, 28*(3), 35–46.

Jenkin, N., & Vroegh, K. (1969). Contemporary concepts of masculinity and femininity. *Psychological Reports, 25,* 679–697.

Jenkins, C. D., Rosenman, R. H., & Friedman, M. (1967). Development of an objective psychological test for the determination of the coronary-prone behavior pattern in employed men. *Journal of Chronic Disease, 20,* 371–379.

Jensen, J. M. (1990). Native American women and agriculture: A Seneca case study. In E. C. DuBois & V. L. Ruiz (Eds.), *Unequal sisters: A multicultural reader in U.S. women's history* (pp. 51–65). New York: Routledge.

Jensen-Campbell, L. A., Graziano, W. G., & West, S. G. (1995). Dominance, prosocial orientation, and female preferences: Do nice guys really finish last? *Journal of Personality and Social Psychology, 68*(3), 427–440.

Jobson, S., & Watson, J. S. (1984). Sex and age differences in choice behaviour: The object-person dimension. *Perception, 13*(6), 719–724.

John, D., Shelton, B. A., & Luschen, K. (1995). Race, ethnicity, gender, and perceptions of fairness. *Journal of Family Issues, 16*(3), 357–379.

Johnson, C., & Engelhard, G. (1992). Gender, academic achievement, and preference for cooperative, competitive, and individualistic learning among African-American adolescents. *Journal of Psychology, 126*(4), 385–392.

Johnson, H. J. (1974). *Executive life styles: A Life Extension Institute report on alcohol, sex and health.* New York: Crowell.

Johnson, H. L., Johnson, P. B., Nusbaum, B. J., Glassman, M. B., Bejarano, A., & Rosen, T. S. (1999). Depressive symptomatology in African-American, Dominican, Irish-Amerian, and Puerto Rican women. *Journal of Gender, Culture, and Health, 4*(1), 49–60.

Johnson, P. (1974). *Social power and sex role stereotypes.* Paper presented at the meeting of the Western Psychological Association, San Francisco.

Johnson, P. (1976). Women and power: Toward a theory of effectiveness. *Journal of Social Issues, 32,* 99–110.

Johnson, P., & Goodchilds, J. D. (1976, October). How women get their way. *Psychology Today,* pp. 69–70.

Jones, J. C., & Barlow, D. H. (1990). Self-reported frequency of sexual urges, fantasies and masturbatory fantasies in heterosexual males and females. *Archives of Sexual Behavior, 19*(3), 269–279.

Jordan, M. (1992, February 12). Wide gender gap found in schools. *Washington Post,* pp. A1, A8.

Jordan, P. L. (1990). Laboring for relevance: Expectant and new fatherhood. *Nursing Research, 39*(1), 11–16.

Joseph, C. A., McKay, T., & Joseph, C. R. (1982). Sex effects on free recall and recognition of orally presented nouns into imagery form. *Journal of General Psychology, 106,* 213–217.

Kaats, G., & Davis, K. (1971). Effects of volunteer biases in studies of sexual behavior and attitudes. *Journal of Sex Research, 7,* 26–34.

Kagan, J., & Lewis, M. (1965). Studies of attention in the human infant. *Merrill-Palmer Quarterly, 11,* 95–127.

Kahana, B., & Kahana, E. (1970). How different generations view each other. *Geriatric Focus, 9*(10), 1–13.

Kahn, A. S., O'Leary, V., Krulewitz, J. E., & Lamm, H. (1980). Equity and equality: Male and female means to a just end. *Basic and Applied Social Psychology, 1,* 173–197.

Kahn, A. S., & Yoder, J. D. (1989). The psychology of women and conservatism: Rediscovering social change. *Psychology of Women Quarterly, 13*(4), 417–432.

Kaij, L., & Nilsson, A. (1972). Emotional and psychotic illness following childbirth. In J. G. Howells (Ed.), *Modern perspectives in psycho-obstetrics* (pp. 364–384). London: Oliver & Boyd.

Kalin, R., Stoppard, J. M., & Burt, B. (1980). Sex-role ideology and sex bias in judgements of occupational suitability. In C. Stark-Adamec (Ed.), *Sex roles: Origins, influences, and implications for women* (pp. 89–99). Montreal: Eden Press Women's Publications.

Kane, P. (1991). *Women's health.* New York: St. Martin's.

Kanter, R. M. (1975). Women and the structure of organizations: Explorations in theory and behavior. In M. Millman & R. M. Kanter (Eds.), *Another voice* (pp. 34–74). Garden City, NY: Anchor.

Kanter, R. M. (1976). Why bosses turn bitchy. *Psychology Today, 9*(2), 56–59, 88–91.

Kanter, R. M. (1977). *Men and women of the corporation.* New York: Basic Books.

Kanter, R. M. (1979). Power failure in management circuits. *Harvard Business Review, 57,* 65–75.

Kantner, J. F., & Zelnick, M. (1972). Sexual experience of young unmarried women in the United States. *Family Planning Perspectives, 4*(4), 9–18.

Kaplan, A. G. (1980). Human sex-hormone abnormalities viewed from an androgynous perspective: A reconsideration of the work of John Money. In J. E. Parsons (Ed.), *The psychobiology of sex differences and sex roles* (pp. 81–94). Washington, DC: Hemisphere Publishing.

Kaplan, A. G., & Surrey, J. L. (1984). The relational self in women: Developmental theory and public policy. In L. E. Walker (Ed.), *Women and mental health policy* (pp. 79–94). Beverly Hills, CA: Sage.

Kaplan, B. J. (1986). A psychobiological review of depression during pregnancy. *Psychology of Women Quarterly, 10,* 35–38.

Kaplan, H. S. (1974). *The new sex therapy.* New York: Brunner/Mazel.

Kaplan, H. S., & Sager, C. (1971, June). Sexual patterns at different ages. *Medical Aspects of Human Sexuality, 5,* 10–23.

Kaplan, M. (1983). A woman's view of the DSM-III. *American Psychologist, 38*(7), 786–792.

Karabenick, S. A. (1983). Sex-relevance of content and influenceability: Sistrunk & McDavid revisited. *Personality and Social Psychology Bulletin, 9,* 243–252.

Karney, B. R., & Bradbury, T. N. (1995). The longitudinal course of marital quality and stability: A review of theory, method, and research. *Psychological Bulletin, 118*(1), 3–34.

Kaschak, E. (1992). *Engendered lives: A new psychology of women's experience.* New York: Basic Books.

Katz, E. J., & Madden, J. M. (1984). Using policy capturing to measure prejudicial attitudes of women toward women. *Bulletin of the Psychonomic Society, 22,* 90–91.

Katz, J. B. (1977). *I am the fire of time: The voices of Native American women.* New York: E. P. Dutton.

Katz, P. A. (1986). Gender identity: Development and consequences. In R. D. Ashmore & F. K. Del Boca (Eds.), *The social psychology of female–male relations* (pp. 21–67). Orlando, FL: Academic Press.

Katz, P. A., & Boswell, S. L. (1984). Sex-role development and the one-child family. In T. Falbo (Ed.), *The single-child family* (pp. 63–116). New York: Guilford Press.

Kaufman, D. R. (1995). Professional women: How real are the recent gains? In J. Freeman (Ed.), *Women: A feminist*

perspective (5th ed., pp. 287–305). Mountain View, CA: Mayfield.

Kay, B., & Neeley, J. N. (1982). Sexuality and aging: A review of current literature. *Sexuality and Disability, 5*(1), 38–46.

Keller, E. F. (1985). *Reflections on gender and science.* New Haven, CT: Yale University Press.

Keller, S. (1999, Summer). The purpose and potential of public health surveillance of family and intimate homicide. *In Our Vision: Biannual newsletter of Virginians Against Domestic Violence,* pp. 11–12.

Kelly, C., Huston, T. L., & Cate, R. M. (1985). Premarital relationships correlates of the erosion of satisfaction in marriage. *Journal of Social and Personal Relationships, 2*(2), 167–178.

Kelly, K. R., & Cobb, S. J. (1991). A profile of the career development characteristics of young gifted adolescents: Examining gender and multicultural differences. *Roeper Review, 13*(4), 202–206.

Keltikangas-Jarvinen, L. (1990). The stability of self-concept during adolescence and early adulthood: A six-year follow-up study. *Journal of General Psychology, 117*(4), 361–368.

Kemp, A. A. (1995). Poverty and welfare for women. In J. Freeman (Ed.), *Women: A feminist perspective* (5th ed., pp. 458–480). Mountain View, CA: Mayfield.

Kennedy, D. (1993). Nonsexist language: A progress report. *Canadian Journal of Education, 18*(3), 223–238.

Kennedy, F. (1970). Institutionalized oppression vs. the female. In R. Morgan (Ed.), *Sisterhood is powerful* (pp. 438–446). New York: Vintage Books.

Kessler, S. J. (1990). The medical construction of gender: Case management of intersexed infants. *Signs: Journal of Women*

in Culture and Society, 16(1), 3–26.

Kessler-Harris, A. (1985). The debate over equality for women in the workplace: Recognizing differences. In L. Larwood, A. H. Stromberg, & B. Gutek (Eds.), *Women and work: An annual review* (Vol. 1, pp. 141–161). Beverly Hills, CA: Sage.

Khosroshahi, F. (1989). Penguins don't care, but women do: A social identity analysis of a Whorfian problem. *Language in Society, 18*(4), 505–525.

Kilianski, S. E., & Rudman, L. A. (1998). Wanting it both ways: Do women approve of benevolent sexism? *Sex Roles, 39*(5/6), 333–352.

Kim, J. (1981). *The process of Asian-American identity development: A study of Japanese American women's perceptions of their struggle to achieve positive identities.* Unpublished doctoral dissertation, University of Massachusetts.

Kimball, M. M. (1989). A new perspective on women's math achievement. *Psychological Bulletin, 105,* 198–214.

Kimball, M. M. (1995). *Feminist visions of gender similarities and differences.* Binghamton, NY: Haworth.

Kimble, C. E., Yoshikawa, J. C., & Zehr, H. D. (1981). Vocal and verbal assertiveness in same-sex and mixed-sex groups. *Journal of Personality and Social Psychology, 40,* 1047–1054.

Kimura, D. (1985, November). Male brain, female brain: The hidden difference. *Psychology Today,* pp. 50–52, 54, 56–58.

Kimura, D. (1987). Are men's and women's brains really different? *Canadian Psychology, 28*(2), 133–147.

Kimura, D. (1993). Sex differences in the brain. In *Mind and brain: Readings from Scientific American magazine* (pp. 79–89). New York: W. H. Freeman.

Kimura, D., & Hampson, E. (1994). Cognitive pattern in men and women is influenced by fluctuations in sex hormones. *Current Directions in Psychological Science, 3,* 57–61.

Kinsey, A. C., Pomeroy, W. B., & Martin, C. E. (1948). *Sexual behavior in the human male.* Philadelphia: Saunders.

Kinsey, A. C., Pomeroy, W. B., Martin, C. E., & Gebhard, P. H. (1953). *Sexual behavior in the human female.* Philadelphia: Saunders.

Kipnis, D. (1972). Does power corrupt? *Journal of Personality and Social Psychology, 24,* 33–41.

Kipnis, D. (1984). The use of power in organizations and in interpersonal settings. In S. Oskamp (Ed.), *Applied social psychology annual* (Vol. 5, pp. 179–210). Beverly Hills, CA: Sage.

Kipnis, D., Castell, P. J., Gergen, M., & Mauch, D. (1976). Metamorphic effects of power. *Journal of Applied Psychology, 61,* 127–135.

Kipnis, D., Schmidt, S. M., & Wilkinson, I. (1980). Intraorganizational influence tactics: Explorations in getting one's way. *Journal of Applied Psychology, 65,* 440–452.

Kissane, B. V. (1986). Selection of mathematically talented students. *Educational Studies in Mathematics, 17,* 221–241.

Kite, M. E., Deaux, K., & Miele, M. (1991). Stereotypes of young and old: Does age outweigh gender? *Psychology and Aging, 6,* 19–27.

Kitzinger, C., & Wilkinson, S. (1995). Transition from heterosexuality to lesbianism: The discursive production of lesbian identities. *Developmental Psychology, 31*(1), 95–104.

Klein, E. (1984). *Gender politics.* Cambridge, MA: Harvard University Press.

Klein, M. (1960). *The psychoanalysis of children.* New York: Grove Press. (Original work published 1932).

Klerman, G. L., & Weissman, M. M. (1980). Depressions among women: Their nature and causes. In M. Guttentag, S. Salasin, & D. Belle (Eds.), *The mental health of women* (pp. 57–92). New York: Academic Press.

Klohn, L. S., & Rogers, R. W. (1991). Dimensions of the severity of a health threat: The persuasive effects of visibility, time of onset, and rate of onset on young women's intentions to prevent osteoporosis. *Health Psychology, 10*(5), 323–329.

Klonoff, E. A., & Landrine, H. (1995). The Schedule of Sexist Events: A measure of lifetime and recent sexist descrimination in women's lives. *Psychology of Women Quarterly, 19*(4), 439–472.

Knight, G. P., & Chao, C. (1989). Gender differences in cooperative, competitive, and individualistic social values of children. *Motivation and Emotion, 13*(2), 125–141.

Knussman, R., Christiansen, K., & Couwenbergs, C. (1986). Relations between sex hormone levels and sexual behavior in men. *Archives of Sexual Behavior, 15*(5), 429–445.

Koberg, C. S., & Chusmir, L. H. (1989). Relationship between sex role conflict and work-related variables: Gender and hierarchical differences. *Journal of Social Psychology, 129*(6), 779–791.

Koeske, R. K., & Koeske, G. F. (1975). An attributional approach to moods and the menstrual cycle. *Journal of Personality and Social Psychology, 31,* 474–478.

Koff, E., Rierdan, J., & Stubbs, M. L. (1990). Conceptions and misconceptions of the menstrual cycle. *Women and Health, 16*(3/4), 119–136.

Kohlberg, L. (1964). Development of moral character and moral ideology. In M. Hoffman & L. Hoffman (Eds.), *Review of child development research* (Vol. 1, pp. 383–431). New York: Russell Sage Foundation.

Kohlberg, L. (1966). A cognitive-developmental analysis of children's sex-role concepts and attitudes. In E. E. Maccoby (Ed.), *The development of sex differences* (pp. 82–173). Stanford, CA: Stanford University Press.

Kohlberg, L. (1984). *The psychology of moral development.* San Francisco: Harper & Row.

Kohlberg, L., & Kramer, R. (1969). Continuities and discontinuities in childhood and adult moral development. *Human Development, 12,* 93–120.

Kohlberg, L., & Ullian, D. Z. (1974). Stages in the development of psychosexual concepts and attitudes. In R. C. Friedman, R. M. Richart, & R. L. Vande Wiele (Eds.), *Sex differences in behavior* (pp. 209–222). New York: Wiley.

Komarovsky, M. (1976). *Dilemmas of masculinity: A study of college youth.* New York: Norton.

Kome, P. (1986, July 24). Feminism in the home [Letter to the editor]. *Toronto Globe and Mail,* p. A6.

Koop, C. E. (1989, March 16). Testimony before the Human Resources and Intergovernmental Relations Subcommittee on Government Operations, House of Representatives. In *Medical and psychological impact of abortion* (pp. 193–203, 218, 223–250). Washington, DC: U.S. Government Printing Office.

Korabik, K., Baril, G. L., & Watson, C. (1993). Managers' conflict management style and leadership effectiveness: The moderating effects of gender. *Sex Roles, 29*(5/6), 405–420.

Kortenhaus, C. M., & Demarest, J. (1993). Gender role stereotyping in children's literature: An update. *Sex Roles, 28*(3/4), 219–232.

Koss, M. P. (1993). Detecting the scope of rape: A review of prevalence research methods. *Journal of Interpersonal Violence, 8,* 98–122.

Koss, M. P., Gidycz, C. A., & Wisniewski, N. (1987). The scope of rape: Incidence and prevalence of sexual aggression and victimization in a national sample of higher education students. *Journal of Consulting and Clinical Psychology, 55,* 162–170.

Koss, M. P., Heise, L., & Russo, N. F. (1994). The global health burden of rape. *Psychology of Women Quarterly, 18*(4), 509–537.

Kozu, J. (1999). Domestic violence in Japan. *American Psychologist, 54*(1), 50–54.

Kramer, B. J., & Kipnis, S. (1995). Eldercare and work-role conflict: Toward an understanding of gender differences in caregiver burden. *Gerontologist, 35*(3), 340–348.

Krasner, L., & Houts, A. C. (1984). A study of the "value" systems of behavioral scientists. *American Psychologist, 39,* 840–850.

Kreuz, L. E., & Rose, R. M. (1972). Assessment of aggressive behavior and plasma testosterone in a young criminal population. *Psychosomatic Medicine, 34,* 321.

Kreuz, L. E., Rose, R. M., & Jennings, J. R. (1972). Suppression of plasma testosterone levels and psychological stress. *Archives of General Psychiatry, 26,* 479–482.

Kristiansen, C. M. (1984, August). *Women and health behavior: For ourselves or others?* Paper presented at the annual convention of the American Psychological Association, Toronto.

Krupnick, C. G. (1985, May). Women and men in the classroom: Inequality and its remedies. *On Teaching and Learning: The Journal of the Harvard-Danforth Center,* pp. 18–25.

Kuczynski, A. (1998, July 12). Plastic surgeons: Why so few women? *New York Times,* Section 9, p. 1.

Kuhn, D., Nash, S. C., & Brucken, L. (1978). Sex-role concepts of two- and three-year olds. *Child Development, 49,* 445–451.

Kurdek, L. A., & Schmitt, J. P. (1986a). Interaction of sex role self-concept with relationship quality and relationship beliefs in married, heterosexual cohabiting, gay, and lesbian couples. *Journal of Personality and Social Psychology, 51*(2), 365–370.

Kurdek, L. A., & Schmitt, J. P. (1986b). Relationship quality of partners in heterosexual married, heterosexual cohabiting, and gay and lesbian relationships. *Journal of Personality and Social Psychology, 51*(4), 711–720.

Lacoursiere, R. (1972). Fatherhood and mental illness: A review and new material. *Psychiatric Quarterly, 46,* 105–124.

Laessle, R. G., Tuschl, R. J., Schweiger, U., & Pirke, K. M. (1990). Mood changes and physical complaints during the normal menstrual cycle in healthy young women. *Psychoneuroendocrinology, 15*(2), 131–138.

LaFrance, M. (1992). Gender and interruptions: Individual infraction or violation of the social order. *Psychology of Women Quarterly, 16*(4), 497–512.

Lafromboise, T. D., Berman, J. S., & Sohi, B. K. (1994). American Indian women. In L. Comas-Díaz & B. Greene (Eds.), *Women of color: Integrating ethnic and gender identities in psychotherapy* (pp. 30–71). New York: Guilford Press.

Lahey, K. (1984). *Equality and specificity in feminist thought.* Paper presented to the Charter of Rights Educational Fund Statute Audit Project of Ontario. (Summarized in the *Newsletter of the National Association of Women and the Law, 5*(8), 24–25)

Lamb, M. (1987). The emergent American father. In M. Lamb (Ed.), *The father's role: Cross-cultural perspectives* (pp. 3–25). Hillsdale, NJ: Erlbaum.

Lamb, M. E., Owen, M. T., & Chase-Lansdale, L. (1979). The father daughter relationship: Past, present, and future. In C. B. Kopp (Ed.), *Becoming female: Perspectives on development* (pp. 89–112). New York: Plenum.

Lancaster, J. B. (1975). *Primate behavior and the emergence of human culture.* New York: Holt, Rinehart & Winston.

Landrine, H. (1985). Race x class stereotypes of women. *Sex Roles, 13*(1/2), 65–75.

Landrine, H. (1987). On the politics of madness: A preliminary analysis of the relationship between social roles and psychopathology. *Psychology Monographs, 113,* 341–406.

Landrine, H. (1989). The politics of personality disorder. *Psychology of Women Quarterly, 13*(3), 325–340.

Landrine, H., Klonoff, E. A., & Brown-Collins, A. (1995). Cultural diversity and methodology in feminist psychology: Critique, proposal, empirical example. In H. Landrine (Ed.), *Bringing cultural diversity to feminist psychology: Theory, research, and practice* (pp. 55–75). Washington, DC: American Psychological Association.

Landrine, H., Klonoff, E. A., Gibbs, J., Manning, V., & Lund, M. (1995). Physical and psychiatric correlates of gender discrimination: An application of the Schedule of Sexist Events. *Psychology of Women Quarterly, 19*(4), 473–492.

Lang-Takac, E., & Osterwell, Z. (1992). Separateness and

connectedness: Differences between the genders. *Sex Roles, 27*(5/6), 277–289.

Lapsley, H. (1999). *Margaret Mead and Ruth Benedict: The kinship of women.* Amherst, MA: University of Massachusetts Press.

Laqueur, T. (1990). *Making sex: Body and gender from the Greeks to Freud.* Cambridge, MA: Harvard University Press.

Laumann, E. O., Michael, R. T., Gagnon, J. H., & Michaels, S. (1994). *Social organization of sexuality.* Chicago: University of Chicago Press.

Lavine, H., Sweeney, D., & Wagner, S. H. (1999). Depicting women as sex objects in television advertising: Effects on body dissatisfaction. *Personality and Social Psychology Bulletin, 25*(8), 1049–1058.

Law, D. J., Pellegrino, J. W., & Hunt, E. B. (1993). Comparing the tortoise and the hare: Gender differences and experience in dynamic spatial reasoning tasks. *Psychological Science, 4,* 35–40.

Leacock, E. (1983). Ideologies of male dominance as divide and rule politics: An anthropologist's view. In M. Lowe & R. Hubbard (Eds.), *Woman's nature: Rationalizations of inequality* (pp. 111–122). New York: Pergamon Press.

Leahy, R. L., & Shirk, S. R. (1984). The development of classificatory skills and sex-trait stereotypes in children. *Sex Roles, 10,* 281–292.

Lebrun, C. M., McKenzie, D. C., Prior, J. C., & Taunton, J. E. (1995). Effects of menstrual cycle phase on athletic performance. *Medicine and Science in Sports and Exercise, 27*(3), 437–444.

Leder, G. (1990). Teacher/student interactions in the mathematics classroom: A different perspective. In E. Fennema & G. C. Leder, (Eds.), *Mathematics and gender* (pp. 149–168). New York: Teachers College Press.

Lehne, G. K. (1976). Homophobia among men. In D. S. David & R. Brannon (Eds.), *The forty-nine percent majority* (pp. 66–88). Reading, MA: Addison-Wesley.

Lehrke, R. G. (1972). A theory of X-linkage of major intellectual traits. *American Journal of Mental Deficiency, 76,* 611–619.

Leifer, M. (1980). *Psychological effects of motherhood: A study of first pregnancy.* New York: Praeger.

Leitenberg, H., Detzer, M. J., & Srebnik, D. (1993). Gender differences in masturbation and the relation of masturbation experience in preadolescence and/or early adolescence to sexual behavior and sexual adjustment in young adulthood. *Archives of Sexual Behavior, 22,* 87–98.

Leitenberg, H., & Henning, K. (1995). Sexual fantasy. *Psychological Bulletin, 117*(3), 469–496.

Lennane, K. J., & Lennane, R. J. (1973). Alleged psychogenic disorders in women: A possible manifestation of sexual prejudice. *New England Journal of Medicine, 288,* 288–292.

Lenney, E. (1977). Women's self-confidence in achievement settings. *Psychological Bulletin, 84,* 1–13.

Lennon, M. C. (1987). Is menopause depressing? An investigation of three perspectives. *Sex Roles, 17*(1/2), 1–16.

Lennon, M. C. (1994). Women, work, and well-being: The importance of work conditions. *Journal of Health and Social Behavior, 35,* 235–247.

Leon, A. C., Klerman, G. L., & Wickramaratne, P. (1993). Continuing female predominance in depressive illness. *American Journal of Public Health, 83*(5), 754–757.

Lerner, M. J. (1970). The desire for justice and reactions to victims. In J. Macaulay & L. Berkowitz (Eds.), *Altruism and helping behavior* (pp. 205–230). New York: Academic Press.

Lerner, M. J. (1974). Social psychology of justice and interpersonal attraction. In T. L. Huston (Ed.), *Foundations of interpersonal attraction* (pp. 331–351). New York: Academic Press.

LeVay, S. (1991). A difference in hypothalamic structure between heterosexual and homosexual men. *Science, 253,* 1034–1037.

Levin, R. J., & Levin, A. (1975, October). The *Redbook* report on premarital and extramarital sex. *Redbook,* p. 38.

Levine, S. (1966). Sex differences in the brain. *Scientific American, 214*(4), 84–90.

Levinson, D. J. (1978). *The seasons of a man's life.* New York: Ballantine.

Levinson, R. M. (1975). Sex discrimination and employment practices: An experiment with unconventional job inquiries. *Social Problems, 22*(4), 533–543.

Levy, J. (1972). Lateral specialization of the human brain: Behavioral manifestations and possible evolutionary basis. In J. A. Kiger (Ed.), *The biology of behavior* (pp. 159–180). Corvallis: Oregon State University Press.

Levy-Shiff, R., & Israelashvili, R. (1988). Antecedents of fathering: Some further exploration. *Developmental Psychology, 24*(3), 434–440.

Lewin, M. (1984). "Rather worse than folly?" Psychology measures femininity and masculinity, 1: From Terman and Miles to the Guilfords. In M. Lewin (Ed.), *In the shadow of the past: Psychology portrays the sexes* (pp. 155–178). New York: Columbia University Press.

Lewis, M. (1969). Infants' response to facial stimuli during the first year of life. *Developmental Psychology, 1,* 75–86.

Lewis, M., & Weinraub, M. (1979). Origins of early sex-role development. *Sex Roles, 5,* 135–153.

Lewis, R. A. (1978). Emotional intimacy among men. *Journal of Social Issues, 34*(1), 108–121.

Lewis, R. J., Winstead, B. A., & Derlega, V. J. (1989). Gender differences in volunteering for friendship research. *Journal of Social Behavior and Personality, 4*(5), 623–632.

Lewis, S. N., & Cooper, C. L. (1988). The transition to parenthood in dual-earner couples. *Psychological Medicine, 18*(2), 477–486.

Libby, M. N., & Aries, E. (1989). Gender differences in preschool children's narrative fantasy. *Psychology of Women Quarterly, 13*, 293–306.

Liem, R., & Rayman, P. (1982). Health and social costs of unemployment: Research and policy considerations. *American Psychologist, 37*, 1116–1123.

Lifton, P. D. (1985). Individual differences in moral development: The relation of sex, gender, and personality to morality. *Journal of Personality, 53*(2), 306–334.

Lii, S., & Wong, S. (1982). A cross-cultural study on sex-role stereotypes and social desirability. *Sex Roles, 8*(5), 481–491.

Linn, M. C. (1985). Gender equity in computer learning environments. *Computers and the Social Sciences, 1*(1), 19–27.

Linn, M. C., & Petersen, A. C. (1985). Emergence and characterization of gender differences in spatial ability: A meta-analysis. *Child Development, 56*, 1479–1498.

Linz, D., Donnerstein, E., & Penrod, S. (1984). The effects of multiple exposure to filmed violence against women. *Journal of Communications, 34*(3), 130–147.

Lipman-Blumen, J. (1984). *Gender roles and power*. Englewood Cliffs, NJ: Prentice-Hall.

Lipman-Blumen, J., & Leavitt, H. (1976). Vicarious and direct achievement patterns in adulthood. *Counseling Psychologist, 6*, 26–32.

Lipovenko, D. (1985, April 11). Compensation decision sets precedent: Sexual harassment ruled work injury. *Toronto Globe and Mail*, pp. 1–2.

Lippa, R., & Beauvais, C. (1983). Gender jeopardy: The effects of gender, assessed femininity and masculinity and false success/failure feedback on performance in an experimental quiz game. *Journal of Personality and Social Psychology, 44*, 344–353.

Lips, H. M. (1980, March). *Pregnancy as a stimulus factor in the perception of women's moods and their causal attribution*. Paper presented at the Seventh Annual Conference on Feminist Psychology, Santa Monica, CA.

Lips, H. M. (1982a). Somatic and emotional aspects of the normal pregnancy experience: The first five months. *American Journal of Obstetrics and Gynecology, 142*(5), 524–529.

Lips, H. M. (1982b, June). *Symptom-reporting among expectant fathers: A new look at the couvade syndrome*. Paper presented at the annual meeting of the Association for Birth Psychology, Halifax, Nova Scotia.

Lips, H. M. (1982c, June). *Themes of the pregnancy experience: A content analysis of personal reports*. Paper presented at the Institute of the Section on Women and Psychology, Canadian Psychological Association meeting, Montreal.

Lips, H. M. (1983). Attitudes toward childbearing among women and men expecting their first child. *International Journal of Women's Studies, 6*(2), 119–129.

Lips, H. M. (1984, September). *University women's causal attributions for participation in math and science*. Paper presented at the annual meeting of the American Psychological Association, Toronto.

Lips, H. M. (1985a). Gender and the sense of power: Where are we and where are we going? *International Journal of Women's Studies, 8*(5), 483–489.

Lips, H. M. (1985b). A longitudinal study of the reporting of emotional and somatic symptoms during and after pregnancy. *Social Science and Medicine, 21*(6), 631–640.

Lips, H. M. (1986a). *Self-schema theory and gender-related behaviours: Research on some correlates of university women's participation in mathematics, science and athletic activities*. (ERIC Document ED 263517, ERIC Clearinghouse on Counseling and Personnel Services)

Lips, H. M. (1986b). Women and power in the workplace. In G. Hoffman Nemiroff (Ed.), *Interdisciplinary readings on gender* (pp. 403–415). Toronto: Fitzhenry & Whiteside.

Lips, H. M. (1991). *Women, men and power*. Mountain View, CA: Mayfield.

Lips, H. M. (1992). Gender and science-related attitudes as predictors of college students' academic choices. *Journal of Vocational Behavior, 40*, 62–81.

Lips, H. M. (1996). Predicting university women's participation in mathematics and science: A causal model. *Journal of Women and Minorities in Science and Engineering, 2*(4), 193–206.

Lips, H. M. (1998, June). *Gendered possibilities: Young women's and men's visions of their future power and competence*. Invited address, Canadian Psychological Association convention, Edmonton, Alberta.

Lips, H. M. (1999, February). *Awards, rewards, and gender: The invisibility of women's achievements*. Invited address, University of Auckland, Auckland, NZ.

Lips, H. M. (2000). College students' visions of power and possibility as mediated by gender. *Psychology of Women Quarterly, 24*(1), 37–41.

Lips, H. M., & Asquith, K. (1995). Students' possible selves as scientists. *GATES: An International Journal Promoting Greater Access to Technology, Engineering, and Science, 2*(1), 1–7.

Lips, H. M., & Freedman, S. A. (1992). Heterosexual feminist identities: Private boundaries and shifting centers. *Feminism & Psychology, 2*(3), 441–444.

Lips, H. M., & Morrison, A. (1986). Changes in the sense of family among couples expecting their first child. *Journal of Social and Personal Relationships, 3*(3), 393–400.

Lips, H. M., & Rogers, M. (1999, March). *Powerful roles and relationships: An uneasy combination?* Paper presented at the annual meeting of the Southeastern Psychological Association, Savannah, GA.

Lips, H. M., & Temple, L. (1990). Majoring in computer science: Causal models for women and men. *Research in Higher Education, 31*(1), 99–113.

Lips, H. M., de Verthelyi, R. F., & Gonzalez, M. (1996, August). *Gender and students' possible powerful selves: A cross-cultural study.* Paper presented at the meeting of the International Congress of Psychology, Montreal.

Littig, L. W., & Branch, D. (1993). Exposure frequencies and sensation-seeking: No novelty effect but an unexpected experimenter–subject sex interaction. *Social Behavior and Personality, 21*(1), 25–31.

Lock, M. (1993). *Encounters with aging: Mythologies of menopause in Japan and North America.* Berkeley: University of California Press.

Lockheed, M. E. (1985). Sex and social influence: A meta-analysis guided by theory. In J. Berger & M. Zelditch Jr. (Eds.), *Status, rewards, and influence: How expectations organize behavior* (pp. 406–429). San Francisco: Jossey-Bass.

Lockheed, M. E., & Hall, K. P. (1976). Conceptualizing sex as a status characteristic: Applications to leadership training strategies. *Journal of Social Issues, 32*(3), 111–124.

Lockwood, D. (1980). *Prison sexual violence.* New York: Elsevier.

Loeber, R., & Stouthamer-Loeber, M. (1998). Development of juvenile aggression and violence: Some common misconceptions and controversies. *American Psychologist, 53*(2), 242–259.

Logothetis, M. L. (1991). Women's decisions about estrogen replacement therapy. *Western Journal of Nursing Research, 13*(4), 458–474.

Long, B. (1989). Sex-role orientation, coping strategies, and self-efficacy of women in traditional and nontraditional occupations. *Psychology of Women Quarterly, 13,* 307–324.

Long, L. S., & Simon, R. J. (1974). The roles and statuses of women on children's and family programs. *Journalism Quarterly, 51,* 107–110.

Long, P. (1991, March/April). A woman's heart. *In Health, 5*(2), 53–58.

Long, V. O. (1991). Masculinity, femininity, and women scientists' self-esteem and self-acceptance. *Journal of Psychology, 125*(3), 263–270.

Lorber, J. (1986). Dismantling Noah's Ark. *Sex Roles, 14*(11/12), 567–580.

Lord, C. G., & Saenz, D. S. (1985). Memory deficits and memory surfeits: Differential cognitive consequences of tokenism for tokens and observers. *Journal of Personality and Social Psychology, 49*(4), 918–926.

Loring, M., & Powell, B. (1988). Gender, race and DSM-III: A study of the objectivity of psychiatric diagnostic behavior. *Journal of Health and Social Behavior, 29,* 1–22.

Lott, B. (1985). The devaluation of women's competence. *Journal of Social Issues, 41*(4), 43–60.

Lott, B. (1989). Sexist discrimination as distancing behavior. II. Primetime television. *Psychology of Women Quarterly, 13*(3), 341–355.

Lowe, M. (1983). The dialectic of biology and culture. In M. Lowe & R. Hubbard (Eds.), *Woman's nature: Rationalizations of inequality* (pp. 39–62). New York: Pergamon Press.

Lubinski, D., & Humphreys, L. G. (1990). Assessing spurious "moderator effects": Illustrated substantively with the hypothesized ("synergistic") relation between spatial and mathematical ability. *Psychological Bulletin, 107*(3), 385–393.

Lubinski, D., Tellegen, A., & Butcher, J. N. (1981). The relationship between androgyny and subjective indicators of emotional well-being. *Journal of Personality and Social Psychology, 40,* 722–730.

Luker, K. (1984). *Abortion and the politics of motherhood.* Berkeley: University of California Press.

Lummis, M., & Stevenson, H. W. (1990). Gender differences in beliefs and achievement: A cross-cultural study. *Developmental Psychology, 26*(2), 254–263.

Lurie, N., Slater, J., McGovern, P., Ekstrum, J., et al. (1993). Preventive care for women: Does the sex of the physician matter? *New England Journal of Medicine, 329*(7), 478–482.

Lutter, J. M., Lee, V., & Cushman, S. (1984). Fetal outcomes of women who ran while pregnant: A preliminary report. *Melpomene Report, 3*(3), 6–8.

Lutwin, D. R., & Siperstein, G. N. (1985). Househusband fathers. In S. M. H. Hanson & F. W.

Bozett (Eds.), *Dimensions of fatherhood* (pp. 269–287). Beverly Hills, CA: Sage.

Luxton, M. (1980). *More than a labour of love: Three generations of women's work in the home.* Toronto: Women's Press.

Lyness, K. S., & Judiesch, M. K. (1999). Are women more likely to be hired or promoted into management positions? *Journal of Vocational Behavior, 54*(1), 158–173.

Lyness, K. S., & Thompson, D. (1997). Above the glass ceiling? A comparison of matched samples of female and male executives. *Journal of Applied Psychology, 82*(3), 359–375.

Lynn, D. B. (1966). The process of learning parental and sex-role identification. *Journal of Marriage and the Family, 28,* 466–470.

Lynn, D. B. (1979). *Daughters and parents: Past, present, and future.* Pacific Grove, CA: Brooks/Cole.

Lyons, R. D. (1983, October 4). Sex in America. *New York Times,* p. C1.

Lyson, T. A. (1986). Race and sex differences in sex role attitudes of Southern college students. *Psychology of Women Quarterly, 10,* 421–428.

Lytton, H., & Romney, D. M. (1991). Parents' differential socialization of boys and girls: A meta-analysis. *Psychological Bulletin, 109*(2), 267–296.

Maccoby, E. E. (1966). Sex differences in intellectual functioning. In E. E. Maccoby (Ed.), *The development of sex differences* (pp. 25–55). Stanford, CA: Stanford University Press.

Maccoby, E. E. (1990). Gender and relationships: A developmental account. *American Psychologist, 45*(4), 513–520.

Maccoby, E. E. (1992). The role of parents in the socialization of children: An historical overview. *Developmental Psychology, 28*(6), 1006–1017.

Maccoby, E. E. (1998). *The two sexes: Growing up apart, coming together.* Cambridge, MA: Harvard University Press.

Maccoby, E. E., Doering, C. H., Jacklin, C. N., & Kraemer, H. (1979). Concentrations of sex hormones in umbilical cord blood: Their relation to sex and birth order. *Child Development, 50*(3), 632–642.

Maccoby, E. E., & Jacklin, C. N. (1974). *The psychology of sex differences.* Stanford, CA: Stanford University Press.

Maccoby, E. E., Snow, M. E., & Jacklin, C. N. (1984). Children's dispositions and mother–child interaction at 12 and 18 months: A short-term longitudinal study. *Developmental Psychology, 20*(3), 459–472.

MacCorquodale, P., & Jensen, G. (1993). Women in the law: Partners or tokens? *Gender and Society, 7*(4), 582–593.

Macfarlane, J., Allen, L., & Honzik, M. A. (1974). *Developmental study of the behavioral problems of normal children.* Berkeley: University of California Press.

MacLean, P. A. (1991, April). Tee'd off. *Women's Sports and Fitness, 13*(3), 40, 44–46, 48.

MacLeod, L. (1980). *Wife battering in Canada: The vicious circle.* Hull, Quebec: Canadian Government Publishing Centre.

Macy, C. (1986). Psychological factors in nausea and vomiting in pregnancy: A review. *Journal of Reproductive and Infant Psychology, 4*(1/2), 23–55.

Maffeo, P. A., Ford, T. W., & Lavin, P. F. (1990). Gender differences in depression in an employment setting. *Journal of Personality Assessment, 55*(1/2), 249–262.

Magazanik, M. (1991, August 9). Rape trauma less for prostitute, says judge. *The Age* (Melbourne, Australia), p. 1.

Mainardi, P. (1970). The politics of housework. In R. Morgan (Ed.), *Sisterhood is powerful*

(pp. 447–454). New York: Vintage Books.

Mainiero, L. A. (1986). A review and analysis of power dynamics in organizational romances. *Academy of Management Review, 11*(4), 750–762.

Mainiero, L. A. (1989). *Office romance.* New York: Rawson Associates/Macmillan.

Major, B. (1987). Women and entitlement. *Women and Therapy, 6*(3), 3–19.

Major, B. (1994). From social inequality to personal entitlement: The role of social comparisons, legitimacy appraisals, and group membership. In M. P. Zanna (Ed.), *Advances in experimental social psychology* (Vol. 6, pp. 293–335). San Diego: Academic Press.

Major, B., & Adams, J. B. (1983). The role of gender, interpersonal orientation and self-presentation in distributive justice behavior. *Journal of Personality and Social Psychology, 45,* 598–608.

Major, B., & Adams, J. B. (1984). Situational moderators of gender differences in reward allocations. *Sex Roles, 11*(9/10), 869–880.

Major, B., & Cozzarelli, C. (1992). Psychosocial predictors of adjustment to abortion. *Journal of Social Issues, 48*(3), 121–142.

Major, B., & Deaux, K. (1982). Individual differences in justice behavior. In J. Greenberg & R. L. Cohen (Eds.), *Equity and justice in social behavior* (pp. 43–76). New York: Academic Press.

Major, B., & Forcey, B. (1985). Social comparisons and pay evaluations: Preferences for same-sex and same-job wage comparisons. *Journal of Experimental Social Psychology, 21,* 393–405.

Major, B., McFarlin, D. B., & Gagnon, D. (1984). Overworked and underpaid: On the nature of gender differences in personal entitlement. *Journal of Personality and Social Psychology, 47*(6), 1399–1412.

Major, B., Schmidlen, A. M., & Williams, L. (1990). Gender patterns in social touch: The impact of setting and age. *Journal of Personality and Social Psychology, 58,* 634–643.

Major, B., Spencer, S., Schmader, T., Wolfe, C., & Crocker, J. (1998). Coping with negative stereotypes about intellectual performance: The role of psychological disengagement. *Personality and Social Psychology Bulletin, 24*(1), 34–50.

Major, B., Vanderslice, V., & McFarlin, D. B. (1984). Effects of pay expected on pay received: The confirmatory nature of initial expectations. *Journal of Applied Social Psychology, 14*(5), 399–412.

Majors, R. (1989). Cool pose: The proud signature of Black survival. In M. S. Kimmel & M. A. Messner (Eds.), *Men's lives* (pp. 83–87). New York: Macmillan.

Makosky, V. P. (1980). Stress and the mental health of women: A discussion of research and issues. In M. Guttentag, S. Salasin, & D. Belle (Eds.), *The mental health of women* (pp. 111–128). New York: Academic Press.

Makri-Tsilipakou, M. (1994). Interruption revisited: Affiliative vs. disafilliative intervention. *Journal of Pragmatics, 21*(4), 401–426.

Malamuth, N. M. (1981). Rape proclivity among males. *Journal of Social Issues, 37*(4), 138–157.

Malamuth, N. M. (1984). Aggression against women: Cultural and individual causes. In N. Malamuth & E. Donnerstein (Eds.), *Pornography and sexual aggression* (pp. 19–52). New York: Academic Press.

Malamuth, N. M. (1996). The confluence model of sexual aggression: Feminist and evolutionary perspectives. In D. M. Buss & N. M. Malamuth (Eds.), *Sex, power, conflict: Evolutionary and feminist perspectives* (pp. 269–295). New York: Oxford University Press.

Malamuth, N. M., & Check, J. V. P. (1981). The effects of mass media exposure on acceptance of violence against women: A field experiment. *Journal of Research in Personality, 15,* 436–446.

Malamuth, N. M., Haber, S., & Feshbach, S. (1980). Testing hypotheses regarding rape: Exposure and sexual violence, sex differences and the "normality" of rapists. *Journal of Research in Personality, 14*(1), 121–137.

Malamuth, N. M., & Thornhill, N. W. (1994). Hostile masculinity, sexual aggression, and gender-biased domineeringness in conversations. *Aggressive Behavior, 20*(3), 185–193.

Male hormones key to math. (1986, May 28). *Winnipeg Free Press,* p. 38.

Maloiy, G. M. O., Heglund, N. C., Prager, L. M., Cavagna, G. A., & Taylor, C. R. (1986, February). Energetic costs of carrying loads: Have African women discovered an economic way? *Nature, 319*(6055), 668–669.

Maltz, D. N., & Borker, R. A. (1983). A cultural approach to male–female miscommunication. In J. A. Gumperz (Ed.), *Language and social identity* (pp. 195–216). New York: Cambridge University Press.

Mamiya, T. (1984). Aging and sex. *Japanese Psychological Review, 27*(3), 295–306.

Mancini, J. A., & Orthner, D. K. (1978). Recreational sexuality preferences among middle-class husbands and wives. *Journal of Sex Research, 14*(2), 96–106.

Mandel, R. B. (1995). A generation of change for women in politics. In J. Freeman (Ed.), *Women: A feminist perspective* (5th ed., pp. 405–429). Mountain View, CA: Mayfield.

Manley, R. O. (1977). Parental warmth and hostility as related to sex differences in children's achievement orientation. *Psychology of Women Quarterly, 1*(3), 229–246.

Mann, J. (1999, July 6). Things could be better for women at the top. *Washington Post,* p. C10.

Mann, J. (2000, January 28). Who says a woman can't be president? We do. *Washington Post,* p. C11.

Mann, V. A., Sasanuma, S., Sakuma, N., & Masaki, S. (1990). Sex differences in cognitive abilities: A cross-cultural perspective. *Neuropsychologia, 28*(10), 1063–1077.

Mansfield, P. K., Hood, K. E., & Henderson, J. (1989). Women and their husbands: Mood and arousal fluctuations across the menstrual cycle and days of the week. *Psychosomatic Medicine, 51*(1), 66–80.

Manson, S., Shore, J., Baron, A., Ackerson, L., & Neligh, G. (1992). Alcohol abuse and dependence among American Indians. In J. E. Helzer & G. J. Canimo (Eds.), *Alcoholism in North America, Europe, and Asia* (pp. 113–130). Oxford, England: Oxford University Press.

Maracek, J. (1978). Psychological disorders in women: Indices of role strain. In I. Frieze, J. Parsons, P. Johnson, D. Ruble, & G. Zellman (Eds.), *Women and sex roles* (pp. 255–276). New York: Norton.

Marcus, R. (1991, March 21). "Fetal protection" plan ruled biased. *Washington Post,* pp. A1, A14, A15.

Margolin, L. (1992). Beyond maternal blame: Physical child abuse as a phenomenon of gender. *Journal of Family Issues, 13*(3), 410–423.

Markides, K. S. (1989). Consequences of gender differentials in life expectancy for Black and Hispanic Americans.

International Journal of Aging and Human Development, 29(2), 95–102.

Marklein, M. B. (1997, June 17). Title IX also aided women academically. *USA Today,* p. 1A.

Marks, B. L., Ward, A., Morris, D. H., Castellani, J., & Rippe, J. M. (1995). Fat-free mass is maintained in women following a moderate diet and exercise program. *Medicine and Science in Sports and Exercise, 27*(9), 1243–1251.

Markush, R., & Favero, R. (1974). Epidemiologic assessment of stressful life events, depressed mood, and psychophysiological symptoms: A preliminary report. In B. P. Dohrenwend & B. S. Dohrenwend (Eds.), *Stressful life-events: Their nature and effects* (pp. 171–190). New York: Wiley.

Marshall, D. S. (1971). Sexual behavior on Mangaia. In D. S. Marshall & R. C. Suggs (Eds.), *Human sexual behavior* (pp. 103–162). New York: Basic Books.

Marshall, L. L., & Rose, P. (1990). Premarital violence: The impact of family of origin on violence, stress, and reciprocity. *Violence and Victimology, 5*(1), 51–64.

Marshall, S. E. (1995). Keep us on the pedestal: Women against feminism in twentieth-century America. In J. Freeman (Ed.), *Women: A feminist perspective* (5th ed., pp. 547–560). Mountain View, CA: Mayfield.

Martel, R. F., Lane, D. M., & Emrich, C. (1996). Male–female differences: A computer simulation. *American Psychologist, 51,* 157–158.

Martin, C. L. (1987). A ratio measure of gender stereotyping. *Journal of Personality and Social Psychology, 52,* 489–499.

Martin, C. L. (1989). Children's use of gender-related information in making social judgments. *Developmental Psychology, 25,* 80–88.

Martin, C. L. (1990). Attitudes and expectations about children with nontraditional and traditional gender roles. *Sex Roles, 22*(3/4), 151–165.

Martin, C. L. (1993). New directions for investigating children's gender knowledge. *Developmental Review, 13,* 184–204.

Martin, C. L., & Halverson, C. F. (1981). A schematic processing model of sex typing and stereotyping in children. *Child Development, 52,* 1119–1134.

Martin, C. L., & Halverson, C. F. Jr. (1983). Gender constancy: A methodological and theoretical analysis. *Sex Roles, 9,* 775–790.

Martin, C. L., & Little, J. K. (1990). The relation of gender understanding to children's sex-typed preferences and gender stereotypes. *Child Development, 61,* 1427–1439.

Martin, C. L., Wood, C. H., & Little, J. K. (1990). The development of gender stereotype components. *Child Development, 61*(6), 1891–1904.

Martin, D. S., & Huang, M. (1984). Effects of time and perceptual orientation on actors' and observers' attributions. *Perceptual and Motor Skills, 58,* 23–30.

Martin, E. (1987). *The woman in the body: A cultural analysis of reproduction.* Boston: Beacon Press.

Martin, H. P. (1991). The coming-out process for homosexuals. *Hospital and Community Psychiatry, 42,* 158–162.

Martin, J. A., Maccoby, E. E., & Jacklin, C. N. (1981). Mother's responsiveness to interactive bidding and nonbidding in boys and girls. *Child Development, 52*(3), 1064–1067.

Martz, D. M., Handley, K. B., & Eisler, R. M. (1995). The relationship between feminine gender role stress, body image, and eating disorders. *Psychology of Women Quarterly, 19*(4), 493–508.

Mashal, M. M. S., & Kalin, R. (1985, June). *The development of an interrole strain measure for dual-worker couples.* Paper presented at the 46th Annual Convention of the Canadian Psychological Association, Halifax, Nova Scotia.

Masica, D., Money, J., & Ehrhardt, A. A. (1971). Fetal feminization and female gender identity in the testicular feminizing syndrome of androgen insensitivity. *Archives of Sexual Behavior, 1*(2), 131–142.

Maslow, A., & Sakoda, J. (1952). Volunteer-error in the Kinsey study. *Journal of Abnormal and Social Psychology, 47,* 259–267.

Mason, A., & Blankenship, V. (1987). Power and affiliation motivation, stress, and abuse in intimate relationships. *Journal of Personality and Social Psychology, 52*(1), 203–210.

Masson, J. (1984, December). The persecution and expulsion of Jeffrey Masson. *Mother Jones,* pp. 34–37, 42–47.

Masters, B. A. (1991, May 18). A rite of passage, a matter of rights. *Washington Post,* pp. B1, B7.

Masters, W. H., & Johnson, V. (1966). *Human sexual response.* Boston: Little, Brown.

Masters, W. H., & Johnson, V. (1970). *Human sexual inadequacy.* Boston: Little, Brown.

Mathes, E. W., Brennan, S. M., Haugen, P. M., & Rice, H. B. (1985). Ratings of physical attractiveness as a function of age. *Journal of Social Psychology, 125*(2), 157–168.

Matsui, T., Ohsawa, T., & Onglatco, M. (1995). Work–family conflict and the stress-buffering effects of husband support and coping behavior among Japanese married working women. *Journal of Vocational Behavior, 47,* 178–192.

Matthews, G. F. (1985). Mirror, mirror: Self-image and disabled women. *Resources for Feminist Research, 14*(1), 47–50.

Mauer, M., & Huling, T. (1995). *Young Black Americans and the criminal justice system five years later*. Washington, DC: The Sentencing Project.

Mauthner, N. S. (1999). "Feeling low and feeling really bad about feeling low": Women's experiences of motherhood and postpartum depression. *Canadian Psychology, 40*(2), 143–161.

Mayes, S., & Valentine, K. (1979). Sex-role stereotyping in Saturday morning cartoon shows. *Journal of Broadcasting, 23*, 41–50.

Mayo, C., & Henley, N. M. (1981). Nonverbal behavior: Barrier or agent for sex role change? In C. Mayo & N. M. Henley (Eds.), *Gender and nonverbal behavior* (pp. 3–13). New York: Springer-Verlag.

Mazur, A., Booth, A., & Dabbs, J. M. (1992). Testosterone and chess competition. *Social Psychology Quarterly, 55*(1), 70–77.

Mazur, A., & Lamb, T. A. (1980). Testosterone, status, and mood in human males. *Hormones and Behavior, 14*, 236–246.

Mazur, E. (1989). Predicting gender differences in same-sex friendships from affiliation motive and value. *Psychology of Women Quarterly, 13*, 277–291.

McArthur, L. Z., & Eisen, S. V. (1976). Achievements of male and female storybook characters as determinants of achieving behavior by boys and girls. *Journal of Personality and Social Psychology, 33*, 467–473.

McAuley, E., Courneya, K. S., & Lettunich, J. (1991). Effects of acute and long-term exercise on self-efficacy responses in sedentary, middle-aged males and females. *Gerontologist, 31*(4), 534–542.

McCall, R. B., & Kagan, J. (1970). Individual differences in the infant's distribution of attention to stimulus discrepancy. *Developmental Psychology, 2*, 90–98.

McClelland, D. C. (1961). *The achieving society*. Princeton, NJ: Van Nostrand.

McClelland, D. C. (1975). *Power: The inner experience*. New York: Irvington.

McClelland, D. C., Atkinson, J. W., Clark, R. A., & Lowell, E. L. (1953). *The achievement motive*. New York: Appleton.

McClelland, D. C., Davis, W. N., Kalin, R., & Wanner, E. (1972). *The drinking man*. New York: Free Press.

McCormack, A. (1985). The sexual harassment of students by teachers: The case of students in science. *Sex Roles, 13*(1/2), 21–32.

McCormick, N. B. (1994). *Sexual salvation: Affirming women's sexual rights and pleasure*. Westport, CT: Praeger.

McCray, C. A. (1980). The Black woman and family roles. In L. Rodgers-Rose (Ed.), *The Black woman* (pp. 67–78). Beverly Hills, CA: Sage.

McDonnell, K. (1984). *Not an easy choice: A feminist re-examines abortion*. Toronto: Women's Press.

McEwan, C. (1985). Crying the blues: Male postpartum depression explained. *Great Expectations, 14*(3), 56, 59.

McFarland, C., Ross, M., & DeCourville, N. (1989). Women's theories of menstruation and biases in recall of menstrual symptoms. *Journal of Personality and Social Psychology, 57*(3), 522–531.

McFarlane, J., Martin, C. L., & Williams, T. M. (1988). Mood fluctuations: Women versus men and menstrual versus other cycles. *Psychology of Women Quarterly, 12*(2), 201–223.

McFarlane, J., & Williams, T. M. (1990). The enigma of premenstrual syndrome. *Canadian Psychology, 31*, 95–108.

McFarlane, J., & Williams, T. M. (1994). Placing premenstrual syndrome in perspective. *Psychology of Women Quarterly, 18*, 339–373.

McGhee, P. E., & Frueh, T. (1980). Television viewing and the learning of sex-role stereotypes. *Sex Roles, 6*, 179–188.

McGlone, J. (1980). Sex differences in human brain asymmetry: A critical survey. *Behavioral and Brain Sciences, 3*, 215–263.

McGuinness, D. (1972). Hearing: Individual differences in perceiving. *Perception, 1*, 465–473.

McGuinness, D. (1976). Away from a unisex psychology: Individual differences in visual perception. *Perception, 5*, 279–294.

McGuinness, D. (1985). Sensorimotor biases in cognitive development. In R. L. Hall (Ed.), *Male–female differences: A biocultural perspective*. New York: Praeger.

McGuinness, D. (1988). Socialization versus biology: Time to move on. *Behavioral and Brain Sciences, 11*(2), 203–204.

McGuinness, D., & Courtney, A. (1983). Sex differences in visual and phonetic search. *Journal of Mental Imagery, 7*(1), 95–104.

McGuinness, D., & McLaughlin, L. (1982). An investigation of sex differences in visual recognition and recall. *Journal of Mental Imagery, 6*(1), 203–212.

McGuinness, D., & Pribram, K. (1979). The origins of sensory bias in the development of gender differences in perception and cognition. In M. Bortner (Ed.), *Cognitive growth and development: Essays in honor of Herbert G. Birch* (pp. 3–56). New York: Brunner/Mazel.

McGuinness, D., & Symonds, J. (1977). Sex differences in choice behaviour: The object–person dimension. *Perception, 6*, 691–694.

McHale, S. M., & Huston, T. L. (1984). Men and women as parents: Sex role orientations, employment, and parental roles with infants. *Child Development, 55,* 1349–1361.

McHugh, M. D., Koeske, R. D., & Frieze, I. H. (1986). Issues to consider in conducting nonsexist psychological research: A guide for researchers. *American Psychologist, 41,* 879–890.

McIntyre, S. (1987). Gender bias in a Canadian law school. *Canadian Association of University Teachers Bulletin, 34*(1), 7–11.

McKee, J. P., & Sherriffs, A. C. (1957). The differential evaluation of males and females. *Journal of Personality, 25,* 356–371.

McKinlay, J. B., McKinlay, S. M., & Brambilla, D. (1987). The relative contributions of endocrine changes and social circumstances to depression in mid-aged women. *Journal of Health and Social Behavior, 28*(4), 345–363.

Mcqueen, A. (1999, June 10). *Debt blocks some women from college* [On-line]. Available: search.washingtonpost.com/wp-srv/WAPO/19990610/V000122-061099-idx.html

McWhirter, P. T. (1999). La violencia privada: Domestic violence in Chile. *American Psychologist, 54*(1), 37–40.

McWilliams, S., & Howard, J. A. (1993). Solidarity and hierarchy in cross-sex friendships. *Journal of Social Issues, 49*(3), 191–202.

Mead, M. (1935). *Sex and temperament in three primitive societies.* New York: Morrow.

Mead, M. (1980). A proposal: We need taboos on sex at work. In D. A. Neugarten & J. M. Shafritz (Eds.), *Sexuality in organizations: Romantic and coercive behaviors at work* (pp. 53–56). Oak Park, IL: Moore.

Megargee, E. (1969). Influence of sex roles on the manifestation of

leadership. *Journal of Applied Psychology, 53,* 377–382.

Melges, F. T. (1968). Postpartum psychiatric syndromes. *Psychosomatic Medicine, 30,* 95–108.

Meredith, N. (1984, January). The gay dilemma. *Psychology Today,* pp. 56–62.

Messenger, J. C. (1971). Sex and repression in an Irish folk community. In D. S. Marshall & R. C. Suggs (Eds.), *Human sexual behavior* (pp. 3–37). New York: Basic Books.

Messner, M. A., Duncan, M. C., & Jensen, K. (1993). Separating the men from the girls: The gendered language of televised sports. *Gender and Society, 7*(1), 121–137.

Meyer-Bahlburg, H. F. L. (1980). Homosexual orientation in women and men: A hormonal basis? In J. Eccles Parsons (Ed.), *The psychobiology of sex differences and sex roles* (pp. 105–130). Washington, DC: Hemisphere.

Meyer-Bahlburg, H. F. L., Boon, D. A., Sharma, M., & Edwards, J. A. (1974). Aggressiveness and testosterone measures in man. *Psychosomatic Medicine, 36,* 267–274.

Micciolo, R., Zimmerman-Tansella, C., Williams, P., & Tansella, M. (1989). Seasonal variation in suicide: Is there a sex difference? *Psychological Medicine, 19*(1), 199–203.

Michael, R. T., Gagnon, J. H., Laumann, E. O., & Kolata, G. (1994). *Sex in America.* Boston: Little, Brown.

Mikalachki, D., & Mikalachki, A. (1984). MBA women: The new pioneers. *Business Quarterly, 49*(1), 110–115.

Miller, C. L., & Cummins, A. G. (1992). An examination of women's perspectives on power. *Psychology of Women Quarterly, 16,* 415–428.

Miller, C. T., & Downey, K. T (1999). A meta analysis of heavyweight and self-esteem.

Personality and Social Psychology Review, 3(1), 68–84.

Miller, J. B. (1977). *Toward a new psychology of women.* Boston: Beacon Press.

Miller, W. E., & Friedman, S. (1988). Male and female sexuality during pregnancy: Behavior and attitudes. *Journal of Psychology and Human Sexuality, 1*(2), 17–37.

Mirande, A., & Enriquez, E. (1979). *La Chicana: The Mexican-American woman.* Chicago: University of Chicago Press.

Mischel, W. (1970). Sex-typing and socialization. In P. H. Mussen (Ed.), *Carmichael's manual of child psychology* (Vol. 2, pp. 3–72). New York: Wiley.

Mishkind, M. E., Rodin, J., Silberstein, L. R., & Striegel-Moore, R. H. (1987). The embodiment of masculinity: Cultural, psychological, and behavioral dimensions. In M. S. Kimmel (Ed.), *Changing men: New directions in research on men and masculinity* (pp. 37–52). Newbury Park, CA: Sage.

Moir, A., & Jessel, D. (1991, May 5). A test. How female is your brain? *Washington Post,* p. K3.

Monahan, L., Kuhn, D., & Shaver, P. (1974). Intrapsychic versus cultural explanations for the "fear of success" motive. *Journal of Personality and Social Psychology, 29,* 60–64.

Money, J., & Daley, J. (1977). Hyperadrenocortical 46 XX hermaphroditism with penile urethra: Psychological studies in seven cases, three reared as boys, four as girls. In P. A. Lee et al. (Eds.), *Congenital adrenal hyperplasia* (pp. 433–446). Baltimore: University Park Press.

Money, J., & Ehrhardt, A. A. (1972). *Man and woman, boy and girl.* Baltimore: Johns Hopkins University Press.

Money, J., & Mathews, D. (1982). Prenatal exposure to virilizing progestins: An adult follow-up study on 12 young women. *Archives of Sexual Behavior, 11,* 73–83.

Money, J., & Ogunro, B. (1974). Behavioral sexology: Ten cases of genetic male intersexuality with impaired prenatal and pubertal androgenization. *Archives of Sexual Behavior, 3*(3), 181–205.

Money, J., & Schwartz, M. (1977). Dating, romantic and nonromantic friendships, and sexuality in 17 early-treated adrenogenital females, aged 16–25. In P. A. Lee et al. (Eds.), *Congenital adrenal hyperplasia* (pp. 419–431). Baltimore: University Park Press.

Money, J., Schwartz, M., & Lewis, V. G. (1984). Adult erotosexual status and fetal hormonal masculinization and demasculinization: 46,XX congenital virilizing adrenal hyperplasia and 46,XX androgen-insensitivity syndrome compared. *Psychoneuroendocrinology, 9,* 405–414.

Monk, T. H., Moline, M. L., Fookson, J. E., & Peetz, S. M. (1989). Circadian determinants of subjective alertness. *Journal of Biological Rhythms, 4*(4), 393–404.

Montagu, A. (1952). *The natural superiority of women.* New York: Macmillan.

Montaigne, M. de (1580). *Essays* I. Chapter 27—Of friendship. Quoted in M. Gibbs, D. Auerbach, & M. Fox, A comparison of male and female same-sex friendships. *International Journal of Women's Studies, 3*(3), 270.

Moore, C. L. (1985). Another psychobiological view of sexual differentiation. *Developmental Review, 5,* 18–55.

Moore, D. P. (1984). Evaluating in-role and out-of-role performers. *Academy of Management Journal, 27,* 603–618.

Moore, L. M., & Rickel, A. U. (1980). Characteristics of women in traditional and non-

traditional managerial roles. *Personnel Psychology, 33,* 317–322.

Moore, T. (1996, January/February). Willow Farey: For believing in the right of girls to be treated with honesty and respect. *Ms., 6*(4), 58–60.

Morawski, J. G. (1994). *Practicing feminisms, reconstructing psychology: Notes on a liminal science.* Ann Arbor: University of Michigan Press.

Moreland, J. (1980). Age and change in the adult male sex role. *Sex Roles, 6,* 807–818.

Moreland, R. L. (1985). Social categorization and the assimilation of "new" group members. *Journal of Personality and Social Psychology, 48*(5), 1173–1190.

Morgan, B. (1998). A three generational study of tomboy behavior. *Sex Roles, 39*(9/10), 787–800.

Morgan, M. (1982). Television and adolescents' sex role stereotypes: A longitudinal study. *Journal of Personality and Social Psychology, 43,* 947–955.

Morin, S. F., & Garfinkle, E. M. (1978). Male homophobia. *Journal of Social Issues, 34*(1), 29–47.

Morokoff, P. J. (1985). Effects of sex guilt, repression, sexual "arousability," and sexual experience on female sexual arousal during erotica and fantasy. *Journal of Personality and Social Psychology, 49*(1), 177–187.

Morrell, M. J., Dixen, J. M., Carter, S., & Davidson, J. M. (1984). The influence of age and cycling status on sexual arousability in women. *American Journal of Obstetrics and Gynecology, 148,* 66–71.

Morris, J. (1974). *Conundrum.* New York: Harcourt Brace Jovanovich.

Morris, S. (1978, May). Do men *need* to cheat on their women? A new science says YES: Darwin and the double standard. *Playboy,* pp. 109ff.

Moser, D., & Dracup, P. K. (1993). Gender differences in treatment-seeking delay in acute myocardial infarction. *Progress in Cardiovascular Nursing, 8*(1), 6–12.

Moss, P., Bolland, G., Foxman, R., & Owen, C. (1987). The division of household work during the transition to parenthood. *Journal of Reproductive and Infant Psychology, 5*(2), 71–86.

Mott, F. L. (1991). Developmental effects of infant care: The mediating role of gender and health. *Journal of Social Issues, 47*(2), 139–158.

Moyer, K. E. (1974). Sex differences in aggression. In R. C. Friedman, R. M. Richart, & R. L. Vande Wiele (Eds.), *Sex differences in behavior* (pp. 149–163). New York: Wiley.

Moynihan, D. (1967). The Negro family: The case for national action (1965). In L. Rainwater & W. Yancey (Eds.), *The Moynihan report and the politics of controversy* (pp. 39–124). Cambridge, MA: MIT Press.

Muir, J. G. (1993, March 31). Homosexuals and the 10 percent fallacy. *Wall Street Journal,* p. A14.

Mulig, J. C., Haggerty, M. E., Carballosa, A. B., Cinnick, W. J., & Madden, J. M. (1985). Relationships among fear of success, fear of failure, and androgyny. *Psychology of Women Quarterly, 9*(2), 284–287.

Muller, C. F. (1990). *Health care and gender.* New York: Russell Sage.

Mullins, L. C., & Mushel, M. (1992). The existence and emotional closeness of relationships with children, friends, and spouses: The effect of loneliness among older persons. *Research on Aging, 14,* 448–470.

Mulvey, A., & Dohrenwend, B. S. (1984). The relation of stressful life events to gender. In A. U. Rickel, M. Gerrard, & I. Iscoe

(Eds.), *Social and psychological problems of women*. Washington, DC: Hemisphere.

Munroe, R. H., Shimmin, H. S., & Munroe, R. L. (1984). Gender understanding and sex role preference in four cultures. *Developmental Psychology, 20,* 673–682.

Murphy, C. M., & O'Leary, K. D. (1989). Psychological aggression predicts physical aggression in early marriage. *Journal of Consulting and Clinical Psychology, 57,* 579–582.

Murray, B. (1998, October). Survey reveals concerns of today's girls. *APA Monitor, 29*(10), 12.

Murray, H. A. (1937). Techniques for a systematic investigation of fantasy. *Journal of Psychology, 3,* 115–143.

Murrell, A. J., Frieze, I. H., & Frost, J. L. (1991). Aspiring to careers in male- and female-dominated professions: A study of Black and White college women. *Psychology of Women Quarterly, 15*(1), 103–126.

Myers, A. M., & Gonda, G. (1982). Utility of the masculinity-femininity construct: Comparison of traditional and androgyny approaches. *Journal of Personality and Social Psychology, 43,* 514–523.

Nagia, S. A., & Bennett, S. J. (1992). Postmenopausal women: Factors in osteoporosis preventive behaviors. *Journal of Gerontological Nursing, 18*(12), 23–32.

Narrow, W. E., Rae, D. S., Moscicki, E. K., Locke, B. Z., & Regier, D. A. (1990). Depression among Cuban Americans. The Hispanic Health and Nutrition Examination Survey. *Social Psychiatry and Psychiatric Epidemiology, 25*(5), 260–268.

Nash, S. C., & Feldman, S. S. (1981). Sex-role and sex-related attributions: Constancy and change across the family life cycle. In M. E. Lamb & A. L. Brown (Eds.), *Advances in developmental psychology* (Vol. 1, pp. 1–36). Hillsdale, NJ: Erlbaum.

National Academy of Sciences. (1999). *Membership directories* [On-line]. Available: http://www.nationalacademies.org/directories

National Cancer Institute. (1999, May 10). *Course of breast cancer treatment differs for Black and White women* [On-line]. [Press release]. Available: http://rex.nci.nih.gov/ massmedia/ pressreleases/coursc.html

National Center for Health Statistics. 1998. *Health, United States, 1998.* Washington, DC: Author.

National Center for Health Statistics. (1999a). *Fastats* [On-line]. Available: www.cdc.gov/nchswww/datawh/statab

National Center for Health Statistics. (1999b, April 29). *Teen birth rate down in all states* [On-line]. [Press release.] Available: www.cdc.gov/nchswww/releases/99news

National Institutes of Health. (1997, April 23). *Risks of cigarette smoking for women on the rise* [On-line]. [Press release]. Available: www.os.dhhs.gov/cgi-bin/wai

National Science Foundation. (1998). *Women, minorities, and persons with disabilities in science and engineering: 1994.* Arlington, VA (NSF-99-338).

Neft, N., & Levine, A. D. (1997). *Where women stand: An international report on the status of women in 140 countries, 1997–1998.* New York: Random House.

Nesselroade, J. R., & Thompson, W. W. (1995). Selection and related threats to group comparisons: An example comparing factorial structures of higher and lower ability groups of adult twins. *Psychological Bulletin, 117*(2), 271–284.

Neugarten, B. L., & Kraines, R. J. (1965). "Menopausal symptoms" in women of various ages. *Psychosomatic Medicine, 27,* 266.

Nevill, D. D., & Schlecker, D. I. (1988). The relation of self-efficacy and assertiveness to willingness to engage in traditional/nontraditional career activities. *Psychology of Women Quarterly, 12*(1), 91–98.

Newcomb, M. D. (1984, August). *Notches on the bedpost: Correlates of sexual experience.* Paper presented at the annual convention of the American Psychological Association, Toronto.

Newcombe, N. (1987, April). *A longitudinal study of predictors of spatial ability in adolescent females.* Paper presented at the meeting of the Society for Research in Child Development, Baltimore.

Newcombe, N., & Bandura, M. M. (1983). Effect of age at puberty on spatial ability in girls: A question of mechanism. *Developmental Psychology, 19*(2), 213–224.

Newcombe, N., Bandura, M. M., & Taylor, D. G. (1983). Sex differences in spatial ability and spatial activities. *Sex Roles, 9,* 377–386.

Newton, E. (1984). The mythic mannish lesbian: Radclyffe Hall and the new woman. *Signs: Journal of Women in Culture and Society, 9,* 557–575.

Newton, N. (1971). Trebly sensuous woman. *Psychology Today, 5,* 68–71, 98–99.

Nichols, M. (1990). Lesbian relationships: Implications for the study of sexuality and gender. In D. McWhiter, S. A. Sanders, & J. Reinisch (Eds.), *Homosexuality/heterosexuality: Concepts of sexual orientation* (pp. 350–364, Kinsey Institute Series). New York: Oxford University Press.

Nicholson, J. (1984). *Men and women: How different are they?* Oxford: Oxford University Press.

Nicolson, P. (1999). Loss, happiness and postpartum depression: The ultimate paradox. *Canadian Psychology, 40*(2), 162–178.

Nieva, V. F. (1985). Work and family linkages. In L. Larwood, A. H. Stromberg, & B. Gutek (Eds.), *Women and work: An annual review* (Vol. 1). Beverly Hills, CA: Sage.

Nolen-Hoeksema, S. (1987). Sex differences in unipolar depression: Evidence and theory. *Psychological Bulletin, 101*(2), 259–282.

Nolen-Hoeksema, S. (1990). *Sex differences in depression.* Stanford, CA: Stanford University Press.

Nolen-Hoeksema, S., & Girgus, J. S. (1994). The emergence of gender differences in depression during adolescence. *Psychological Bulletin, 115*(3), 424–443.

Noller, P. (1980). Misunderstandings in marital communication: A study of couples' nonverbal communication. *Journal of Personality and Social Psychology, 39*, 1135–1148.

Norman, R. L., & Spies, H. G. (1986). Cyclic ovarian function in a male macaque: Additional evidence for a lack of sexual differentiation in the physiological mechanisms that regulate the cyclic release of gonadotrophins in primates. *Endocrinology, 118*, 2608–2610.

Nowakowski, R. S. (1987). Basic concepts of CNS development. *Child Development, 58*, 568–595.

Nowell, A., & Hedges, L. V. (1998). Trends in gender differences in academic achievement from 1960 to 1994: An analysis of differences in mean, variance, and extreme scores. *Sex Roles, 39* (1/2), 21–43.

Nunes, M., & White, D. (1973). *The lace ghetto.* Toronto: New Press.

Nyborg, H. (1983). Spatial ability in men and women: Review and a new theory. *Advances in Behaviour Research and Therapy, 5*, 89–140.

Nyquist, L., & Spence, J. (1986). Effects of dispositional dominance and sex role expectations on leadership behaviors. *Journal of Personality and Social Psychology, 50*(1), 377–382.

Oakes, R. (1984). Sex patterns in DSM III: Bias or basis for theory development [Letter to the editor]. *American Psychologist, 39*, 1320–1322.

Oden, M. H. (1968). The fulfillment of promise: 40-year follow-up of the Terman gifted group. *Genetic Psychology Monographs, 77*, 3–93.

O'Farrell, B. (1995). Women in blue-collar occupations: Traditional and nontraditional. In J. Freeman (Ed.), *Women: A feminist perspective* (5th ed., pp. 238–261). Mountain View, CA: Mayfield.

Offermann, L. R., & Beil, C. (1992). Achievement styles of women leaders and their peers: Toward an understanding of women and leadership. *Psychology of Women Quarterly, 16*(1), 37–56.

Ogletree, S. M., Coffee, M. C., & May, S. A. (1992). Perceptions of female/male presidential candidates: Familial and personal situations. *Psychology of Women Quarterly, 16*(2), 201–208.

Ogur, B. (1986). Long day's journey into night: Women and prescription drug abuse. *Women and Health, 11*, 99–115.

O'Hagan, F. T., Sale, D. G., MacDougall, J. D., & Garner, S. H. (1995). Response to resistance training in young women and men. *International Journal of Sports Medicine, 16*, 314–321.

O'Hara, M. W. (1985). Depression and marital adjustment during pregnancy and after delivery. *American Journal of Family Therapy, 13*(4), 49–55.

O'Hara, M. W. (1997). The nature of postpartum depressive disorders. In L. Murray, P. J. Cooper, et al. (Eds.), *Postpartum depression and child development* (pp. 3–31). New York: Guilford Press.

O'Hara, M. W., & Swain, A. M. (1996). Rates and risk of postpartum derpession: A meta-analysis. *International Review of Psychiatry, 8*(1), 37–54.

O'Heron, C. A., & Orlofsky, J. L. (1990). Stereotypic and nonstereotypic sex role trait and behavior orientations, gender identity, and psychological adjustment. *Journal of Personality and Social Psychology, 58*(1), 134–143.

O'Keefe, E. S. C., & Hyde, J. S. (1983). The development of occupational sex-role stereotypes: The effects of gender stability and age. *Sex Roles, 39*, 481–492.

O'Kelly, C. G., & Carney, L. S. (1986). *Women and men in society: Cross-cultural perspectives on gender stratification.* Belmont, CA: Wadsworth.

Okorodudu, C. (1999, April). Statement of the task force on mental health of the NGO committee on the status of women. *SPSSI Newsletter, 208*, 14–15.

Oldenburg, D. (1994, November 29). The electron gender gap. *Washington Post*, p. D5.

O'Leary, V. E., & Harrison, A. O. (1975, September). *Sex role stereotypes as a function of race and sex.* Paper presented at the annual convention of the American Psychological Association, Chicago.

Olian, J. D., Schwab, D. P., & Haberfeld, Y. (1988). The impact of applicant gender compared to qualifications on hiring recommendations: A meta-analysis of experimental studies. *Organizational Behavior and Human Decision Processes, 41,* 180–195.

Oliver, M. B., & Hyde, J. S. (1993). Gender differences in sexuality: A meta-analysis. *Psychological Bulletin, 114*(1), 29–51.

Oppenheimer, V. K. (1970). *The female labor force in the United States: Demographic and economic factors governing its growth and changing composition* (Population Monograph Series No. 5). Berkeley: University of California.

Ortmeyer, L. E. (1979). The female's natural advantage? Or, the unhealthy environment of males?: The status of sex mortality differentials. *Women and Health, 4*(2), 121–133.

Ostertag, P. A., & McNamara, J. R. (1991). "Feminization" of psychology: The changing sex ratio and its implications for the profession. *Psychology of Women Quarterly, 15*(3), 349–370.

Ott, E. M. (1989). Effects of the male–female ratio at work: Policewomen and male nurses. *Psychology of Women Quarterly, 13*(1), 41–58.

Ozer, E. M. (1995). The impact of childcare responsibility and self-efficacy on the psychological health of professional working mothers. *Psychology of Women Quarterly, 19*(3), 315–336.

Padgett, V. R., Brislin Slutz, J. A., & Neal, J. A. (1989). Pornography, erotica, and attitudes toward women: The effects of repeated exposure. *Journal of Sex Research, 26,* 479–491.

Pagelow, M. D. (1993). Justice for victims of spouse abuse in divorce and child custody cases. *Violence and Victims, 8*(1), 69–83.

Paige, K. E. (1971). The effects of oral contraceptives on affective fluctuations associated with the menstrual cycle. *Psychosomatic Medicine, 33,* 515–537.

Paige, K. E. (1973). Women learn to sing the menstrual blues. *Psychology Today, 7*(4), 41–46.

Paikoff, R. L., & Savin-Williams, R. C. (1983). An exploratory study of dominance interactions among adolescent females at a summer camp. *Journal of Youth and Adolescence, 12,* 419–433.

Pajntar, M. (1972). Obstetrical complications: Personality changes and emotional tension during pregnancy. In N. Morris (Ed.), *Psychosomatic medicine in obstetrics and gynecology* (Third International Congress, London, 1971). Basel: Karger.

Paludi, M. A. (1984). Psychometric properties and underlying assumptions of four objective measures of fear of success. *Sex Roles, 10,* 765–781.

Paludi, M. A., & Strayer, L. A. (1985). What's in an author's name? Differential evaluations of performance as a function of author's name. *Sex Roles, 12*(3/4), 353–362.

Pantony, K., & Caplan, P. J. (1991). Delusional dominating personality disorder: A modest proposal for identifying some consequences of rigid masculine socialization. *Canadian Psychology, 32*(2), 120–135.

Papini, D. R., Farmer, F. F., Clark, S. M., Micka, J. C., & Barnett, J. K. (1990). Early adolescent age and gender differences in patterns of emotional self-disclosure to parents and friends. *Adolescence, 25,* 959–976.

Paralyzed woman in beauty pageant. (1987, January 17). *Winnipeg Free Press,* p. 73.

Parke, R. D. (1981). *Fathers.* Cambridge, MA: Harvard University Press.

Parke, R. D., & Sawin, D. B. (1976). The father's role in infancy: A reevaluation. *Family Coordinator, 25,* 365–371.

Parker, S., & de Vries, B. (1993). Patterns of friendship for women and men in same- and cross-sex relationships. *Journal of Social and Personal Relationships, 10*(4), 617–626.

Parlee, M. B. (1973). The premenstrual syndrome. *Psychological Bulletin, 80,* 454–465.

Parlee, M. B. (1974). Stereotypic beliefs about menstruation: A methodological note on the Moos menstrual distress questionnaire and some new data. *Psychosomatic Medicine, 36,* 229–240.

Parlee, M. B. (1982). Changes in moods and activation levels during the menstrual cycle in experimentally naive subjects. *Psychology of Women Quarterly, 7,* 119–131.

Parlee, M. B. (1983). Menstrual rhythms in sensory processes: A review of fluctuations in vision, olfaction, audition, taste, and touch. *Psychological Bulletin, 93,* 539–548.

Parsons, J. E., Adler, T. F., & Kaczala, C. M. (1982). Socialization of achievement attitudes and beliefs: Parental influences. *Child Development, 53,* 310–321.

Parsons, T., & Bales, R. F. (1955). *Family, socialization, and interaction process.* Glencoe, IL: Free Press.

Patterson, C. J. (1992). Children of lesbian and gay parents. *Child Development, 63,* 1025–1042.

Patterson, C. J. (1995). Families of the baby boom: Parents' division of labor and children's adjustment. *Developmental Psychology, 31*(1), 115–123.

Paul, J. P. (1985). Bisexuality: Reassessing our paradigms of sexuality. *Journal of Homosexuality, 10*(3/4), 21–34.

Paulsen, K., & Johnson, M. (1983). Sex role attitudes and mathematical ability in 4th-, 8th-, and 11th-grade students from a high socioeconomic area. *Developmental Psychology, 19*(2), 210–214.

Pauly, I. (1968). The current status of the change of sex operation.

Journal of Nervous and Mental Disorders, 147, 460–471.

Pearlin, L. (1975). Sex roles and depression. In N. Datan & L. Ginsberg (Eds.), *Life-span developmental psychology: Normative life crises* (pp. 191–207). New York: Academic Press.

Pearlin, L., & Johnson, J. (1977). Marital status, life-strains and depression. *American Sociological Review, 42,* 704–715.

Pearson, J. C., & West, R. (1991). An initial investigation of the effects of gender on student questions in the classroom: Developing a descriptive base. *Communication Education, 40*(1), 22–32.

Pennebaker, J. W. (1982). *The psychology of physical symptoms.* New York: Springer-Verlag.

Pepe, M. V., Sanders, D. W., & Symons, C. W. (1993). Sexual behaviors of university freshman and the implications for sexuality educators. *Journal of Sex Education and Therapy, 19,* 20–30.

Peplau, L. A. (1981, March). What homosexuals want in relationships. *Psychology Today, 15*(3), 28–38.

Peplau, L. A. (1983). Roles and gender. In H. H. Kelley, E. Berscheid, A. Christensen, J. H. Harvey, T. L. Huston, G. Levinger, E. McClintock, L. A. Peplau, & D. R. Peterson (Eds.), *Close relationships* (pp. 221–264). New York: W. H. Freeman.

Peplau, L. A., & Amaro, H. (1982). Understanding lesbian relationships. In W. Paul, J. D. Weinrich, J. C. Gonsiorek, & M. E. Hotvedt (Eds.), *Homosexuality: Social, psychological, and biological issues* (pp. 233–247). Beverly Hills, CA: Sage.

Peplau, L. A., & Cochran, S. D. (1981). Value orientations in the intimate relationships of gay

men. *Journal of Homosexuality, 6*(3), 1–19.

Peplau, L., & Cochran, S. D. (1990). A relationship perspective on homosexuality. In D. P. McWhirter, S. A. Sanders, & J. M. Reinisch (Eds.), *Homosexuality/heterosexuality: Concepts of sexual orientation* (pp. 321–349). New York: Oxford University Press.

Peplau, L. A., Cochran, S., Rook, K., & Padesky, C. (1978). Loving women: Attachment and autonomy in lesbian relationships. *Journal of Social Issues, 34*(3), 7–27.

Peplau, L. A., & Conrad, E. (1989). Beyond nonsexist research: The perils of feminist methods in psychology. *Psychology of Women Quarterly, 13*(4), 379–400.

Percival, E. (1991). *Thinking about gender similarities and differences: A discussion paper.* Paper presented at the annual meeting of the Association for Women in Psychology, Hartford, CT.

Perkins, K. (1992). Psychosocial implications of women and retirement. *Social Work, 37*(6), 526–532.

Perry, C. M., & Johnson, C. L. (1994). Families and support networks among African American oldest-old. *International Journal of Aging and Human Development, 38*(1), 41–50.

Perry, D. G., & Bussey, K. (1979). The social learning theory of sex differences: Imitation is alive and well. *Journal of Personality and Social Psychology, 37,* 1699–1712.

Perry, D. G., Perry, L. C., & Weiss, R. J. (1989). Sex differences in the consequences children anticipate for aggression. *Developmental Psychology, 25,* 312–319.

Perry, J. D., & Whipple, B. (1981). Pelvic muscle strength of female ejaculators: Evidence in support of a new theory of orgasm.

Journal of Sex Research, 17, 22–39.

Pesmen, C. (1991, November). Love and sex in the '90s: Our national survey. *Seventeen,* pp. 63–68.

Peters, M., Servos, P., & Day, R. (1990). Marked sex differences on a fine motor skill task disappear when finger size is used as covariate. *Journal of Applied Psychology, 75*(1), 87–90.

Petersen, A. C. (1976). Physical androgyny and cognitive functioning in adolescence. *Developmental Psychology, 12,* 524–533.

Petersen, A. C., & Wittig, M. A. (1979). Sex-related differences in cognitive functioning: An overview. In M. A. Wittig & A. C. Petersen (Eds.), *Sex-related differences in cognitive function: Developmental issues* (pp. 1–17). New York: Academic Press.

Petersen, A. E. (1983). Menarche: Meaning of measures and measuring meaning. In S. Golub (Ed.), *Menarche.* Lexington, MA: D. C. Heath.

Peterson, D. L., & Pfost, K. S. (1989). Influence of rock videos on attitudes to violence against women. *Psychological Reports, 64,* 319–322.

Peterson, G. H., Mehl, L. E., & Leiderman, P. H. (1979). The role of some birth-related variables in father attachment. *American Journal of Orthopsychiatry, 40,* 330–338.

Peterson, S. B., & Lach, M. A. (1990). Gender stereotypes in children's books: Their prevalence and influence on cognitive and affective development. *Gender and Education, 2*(2), 185–197.

Pettigrew, T. (1964). *A profile of the Negro American.* Princeton, NJ: Van Nostrand.

Pfost, K. S., & Fiore, M. (1990). Pursuit of nontraditional occupations: Fear of success or fear of not being chosen. *Sex Roles, 23*(1/2), 15–24.

Phillips, R. D., & Gilroy, F. D. (1985). Sex-role stereotypes and clinical judgements of mental health: The Brovermans' findings reexamined. *Sex Roles, 12,* 179–193.

Phillis, D. E., & Gromko, M. H. (1985). Sex differences in sexual activity: Reality or illusion? *Journal of Sex Research, 21*(4), 437–448.

Phinney, J. S. (1989). Stages of ethnic identity in minority group adolescents. *Journal of Early Adolescence, 9,* 34–49.

Phinney, J. S. (1990). Ethnic identity in adolescents and adults: Review of research. *Psychological Bulletin, 108*(3), 499–514.

Phoenix, C., Goy, R. W., & Resko, J. A. (1968). Psychosexual differentiation as a function of androgenic stimulation. In M. Diamond (Ed.), *Reproduction and sexual behavior.* Bloomington: Indiana University Press.

Piaget, J. (1954). *The construction of reality in the child.* New York: Basic Books.

Piaget, J. (1965). *The moral judgment of the child.* New York: Free Press. (Original work published 1932).

Pidano, A. E., & Tennen, H. (1985). Transient depressive experiences and their relationship to gender and sex-role orientation. *Sex Roles, 12,* 97–110.

Piliavin, J. A., & Unger, R. K. (1985). The helpful but helpless female: Myth or reality? In V. O'Leary, R. Unger, & B. Wallston (Eds.), *Women, gender, and social psychology* (pp. 149–189). Hillsdale, NJ: Erlbaum.

Pillard, R. C., & Bailey, J. M. (1991). A genetic study of male sexual orientation. *Archives of General Psychiatry, 48,* 1089–1096.

Pillard, R. C., & Weinrich, J. D. (1986). Evidence of familial nature of male homosexuality. *Archives of General Psychiatry, 43*(8), 800–812.

Pingree, S. (1978). The effects of nonsexist TV commercials and perceptions of reality on children's attitudes about women. *Psychology of Women Quarterly, 2,* 262–277.

Pleck, J. H. (1981). *The myth of masculinity.* Cambridge, MA: MIT Press.

Pleck, J. H. (1995). The gender role strain paradigm: An update. In R. F. Levant & W. S. Pollock (Eds.), *A new psychology of men* (pp. 11–32). New York: Basic Books.

PMS defense successful in Va. drunken driving case. (1991, June 7). *Washington Post,* p. A1.

Polk, B. B. (1974). Male power and the women's movement. *Journal of Applied Behavioral Science, 10*(3), 415–431.

Pomerleau, A., Bolduc, D., Malcuit, G., & Cossette, L. (1990). Pink or blue: Environmental gender stereotypes in the first two years of life. *Sex Roles, 22*(5/6), 359–367.

Popenow, D., & Whitehead, B. D. (1999). *The state of our unions: The social health of marriage in America.* Rutgers, NJ: The National Marriage Project, Rutgers University.

Porter, N., & Geis, F. (1981). Women and nonverbal leadership cues: When seeing is not believing. In C. Mayo & N. Henley (Eds.), *Gender and nonverbal behavior* (pp. 39–59). New York: Springer-Verlag.

Poulin-Dubois, D., Serbin, L. A., Kenyon, B., & Derbyshire, A. (1994). Infants' intermodal knowledge about gender. *Developmental Psychology, 30*(3), 436–442.

Poussaint, A. F. (1982, August). What every Black woman should know about Black men. *Ebony,* pp. 36–40.

Powell, G. N. (1987). The effects of sex and gender on recruitment. *Academy of Management Review, 12,* 731–743.

Powlishta, K. K. (1990). *Children's biased views of male and female traits.* Paper presented at the second annual convention of the American Psychological Society, Dallas.

Prather, J. E. (1971). When the girls move in: A sociological analysis of the feminization of the bank teller's job. *Journal of Marriage and the Family, 33*(4), 777–782.

Prather, J. E., & Fidell, L. S. (1978). Drug use and abuse among women: An overview. *International Journal for the Addictions, 13,* 863–885.

Pratt, M. W., Pancer, M., & Hunsberger, B. (1990). Reasoning about the self and relationships in maturity: An integrative complexity analysis of individual differences. *Journal of Personality and Social Psychology, 59*(3), 575–581.

Pratto, F., Sidanius, J., & Siers, B. (1997). The gender gap in occupational role attainment: A social dominance approach. *Journal of Personality and Social Psychology, 72*(1), 37–53.

Price, W. H., & Whatmore, P. B. (1967a). Behavior disorders and pattern of crime among XYY males identified at a maximum security prison. *British Medical Journal, 1,* 533–536.

Price, W. H., & Whatmore, P. B. (1967b). Criminal behavior and the XYY male. *Nature, 213,* 815.

Prostitutes' Education Network (1999). *Prostitution in the United States: The statistics.* Available at http:// [On-line]. www.bayswan.org/stats.html

Pryor, J. B. (1985). The lay person's understanding of sexual harassment. *Sex Roles, 13*(5/6), 273–286.

Ptacek, J. T., Smith, R. E., & Zanas, J. (1992). Gender, appraisal, and coping: A longitudinal analysis. *Journal of Personality, 60,* 747–770.

Pugliesi, K. (1995). Work and well-being: Gender differences in the psychological consequences of employment. *Journal of Health and Social Behavior, 36,* 57–71.

Pursell, P., & Stewart, L. (1990). Dick and Jane in 1989. *Sex Roles, 22*(3/4), 177–185.

Pyke, S. (1979). Cognitive templating: A technique for feminist (and other) counselors. *Personnel and Guidance Journal, 57*(6), 315–318.

Quill, T. E., Lipkin, M., & Lamb, G. S. (1984). Health-care seeking by men in their spouse's pregnancy. *Psychosomatic Medicine, 46*(3), 277–283.

Quinn, R. E. (1977). Coping with Cupid: The formation, impact, and management of romantic relationships in organizations. *Administrative Science Quarterly, 22,* 30–45.

Rabasca, L. (1999, February). Women addicts vulnerable to trauma. *APA Monitor,* p. 32.

Rabin, J. S. (1987, March). *Adaptation across the lifespan: Evolution, sex roles, and social change.* Paper presented at the Conference of the Association for Women in Psychology, Denver, CO.

Rabin, J. S. (1998, March). *Using developmental-interactionist and feminist perspectives in teaching ethology and comparative psychology.* Paper presented at the annual national conference of the Association for Women in Psychology, Baltimore, MD.

Radin, N. (1982). Primary caregiving and role-sharing fathers. In M. E. Lamb (Ed.), *Nontraditional families: Parenting and child development* (pp.

173–204). Hillsdale, NJ: Erlbaum.

Radloff, L. S. (1980). Risk factors for depression: What do we learn from them? In M. Guttentag, S. Salasin, & D. Belle (Eds.), *The mental health of women* (pp. 93–109). New York: Academic Press.

Ragins, B. R., & Sundstrom, E. (1989). Gender and power in organizations: A longitudinal perspective. *Psychological Bulletin, 105*(1), 51–88.

Rajecki, D. W., Dame, J. A., Creek, K. J., Barrickman, P. J., et al. (1993). Gender casting in television toy advertisements: Distributions, message content analysis, and evaluations. *Journal of Consumer Psychology, 2*(3), 307–327.

Ramey, E. (1972). Men's cycles. *Ms., 1*(8), 8, 11–12, 14–15.

Randall, D. M. (1985). Women in toxic work environments: A case study and examination of policy impact. In L. Larwood, A. H. Stromberg, & B. A. Gutek (Eds.), *Women and work: An annual review* (Vol. 1, pp. 259–281). Beverly Hills, CA: Sage.

Rapist husband. (1991, September 14). *The Times,* p. 14.

Raskin, P. A., & Israel, A. C. (1981). Sex-role imitation in children: Effects of sex of child, sex of model, and sex-role appropriateness of modeled behavior. *Sex Roles, 7,* 1067–1077.

Rauhala, A. (1987, April 2). Religion is key for anti-abortionists, study finds. *Toronto Globe and Mail,* pp. A1, A5.

Rauramo, L. (1986). A review of study findings of the risks and benefits of estrogen therapy in the female climacteric. *Maturitas, 8,* 177–186.

Ravelli, G., Stein, Z., & Susser, M. (1976). Obesity in young men after famine exposure *in utero* and early infancy. *New England*

Journal of Medicine, 295, 349–353.

Raven, B. H. (1965). Social influence and power. In I. D. Steiner & M. Fishbein (Eds.), *Current studies in social psychology* (pp. 371–381). New York: Holt, Rinehart & Winston.

Rawlings, E. I., & Carter, D. K. (1977). *Psychotherapy for women: Treatment toward equality.* Springfield, IL: Charles C. Thomas.

Raymond, J. (1979). *The transsexual empire: The making of the she-male.* Boston: Beacon Press.

RCMP accused of sexual abuses. (1986, January 20). *Winnipeg Free Press,* p. 20.

Reddy, M. A. (Ed.). (1994). *Statistical abstract of the world.* Detroit, MI: Gale.

Redman, S., Webb, G. R., Hennrikus, D. J., & Sanson-Fisher, R. W. (1991). The effects of gender upon diagnosis of psychological disturbance. *Journal of Behavioral Medicine, 14,* 527–540.

Reid, P., & Finchilescu, G. (1995). The disempowering effects of media violence against women. *Psychology of Women Quarterly, 19*(3), 397–411.

Reid, P. T. (1993). Poor women in psychological research: Shut up and shut out. *Psychology of Women Quarterly, 17,* 133–150.

Reinisch, J. (1981). Prenatal exposure to synthetic progestins increases potential for aggression in humans. *Science, 211,* 1171–1173.

Reis, E., Frick, U., & Schmidtbleicher, D. (1995). Frequency variations of strength training sessions triggered by the phases of the menstrual cycle. *International Journal of Sports Medicine, 16,* 545–550.

Reis, H. T., Wheeler, L., Spiegel, N., Kernis, M. H., Nezlek, J., & Perri, M. (1982). Physical attractiveness in social interaction: II. Why does appearance affect social experience? *Journal of Personality and Social Psychology, 43,* 979–996.

Reis, H. T., & Wright, S. (1982). Knowledge of sex-role stereotypes in children aged 3 to 5. *Sex Roles, 8,* 1049–1056.

Reitz, R. R. (1999). Batterers' experiences of being violent: A phenomenological study. *Psychology of Women Quarterly, 23,* 143–165.

Rempel, J. K., Holmes, J. G., & Zanna, M. P. (1985). Trust in close relationships. *Journal of Personality and Social Psychology, 49*(1), 95–112.

Reviere, R., & Eberstein, I. W. (1992). Work, marital status, and heart disease. *Health Care for Women International, 13*(4), 393–399.

Rheingold, H., & Cook, K. (1975). The contents of boys' and girls' rooms as an index of parents' behaviors. *Child Development, 46,* 459–463.

Rice, S. (1989). Single, older childless women: Differences between never-married and widowed women in life satisfaction and social support. *Journal of Gerontological Social Work, 13*(3/4), 35–47.

Rich, A. (1976). *Of woman born.* New York: Norton.

Richards, M. H., Gitelson, I. B., Petersen, A. C., & Hurtig, A. L. (1991). Adolescent personality in girls and boys: The role of mothers and fathers. *Psychology of Women Quarterly, 15,* 65–81.

Richardson, J. T. (1989). Student learning and the menstrual cycle: Premenstrual symptoms and approaches to studying. *Educational Psychology, 9*(3), 215–238.

Richman, J. A., Raskin, V. D., & Gaines, C. (1991). Gender roles, social support, and postpartum depressive symptomatology. The benefits of caring.

Journal of Nervous and Mental Disorders, 179(3), 139–147.

Ricketts, M. (1989). Epistemological values of feminists in psychology. *Psychology of Women Quarterly, 13*(4), 401–416.

Riddle, D. I., & Sang, B. (1978). Psychotherapy with lesbians. *Journal of Social Issues, 34*(3), 84–100.

Rigby, D. N., & Sophie, J. (1990). Ethical issues and client sexual preference. In H. Lerman & N. Porter (Eds.), *Feminist ethics in psychotherapy* (pp. 165–175). New York: Springer.

Robbins, M. B., & Jensen, G. D. (1977). Multiple orgasm in males. In R. Gemme & C. C. Wheeler (Eds.), *Progress in sexology* (pp. 323–334). New York: Plenum.

Roberto, K. A., & Scott, J. P. (1986). Friendships of older men and women: Exchange patterns and satisfaction. *Psychology and Aging, 1*(2), 103–109.

Roberts, T. (1991). Gender and the influence of evaluations on self-assessments in achievement settings. *Psychological Bulletin, 109*(2), 297–308.

Robinson, G. E., & Garfinkel, P. E. (1990). Problems in the treatment of premenstrual symptoms. *Canadian Journal of Psychiatry, 35*(3), 199–206.

Robinson, J. P., Andreyenkov, V. G., & Patrushev, V. D. (1988). *The rhythm of everyday life: How Soviet and American citizens use time.* Boulder, CO: Westview.

Robinson, J. P., & Godbey, G. (1993). Sport, fitness, and the gender gap. *Leisure Sciences, 15,* 291–307.

Roby, P. A. (1995, Fall). Becoming shop stewards: Perspectives on gender and race in ten trade unions. *Labor Studies Journal,* pp. 65–82.

Rodin, J., & Janis, I. (1979). The social power of health-care prac-

titioners as agents of change. *Journal of Social Issues, 35*(1), 60–81.

Rodin, J., Silberstein, L., & Striegel-Moore, R. (1985). Women and weight: A normative discontent. In T. B. Sonderegger (Ed.), *Psychology and gender: Proceedings of the Nebraska Symposium on Motivation, 1984* (pp. 267–307). Lincoln: University of Nebraska Press.

Rodin, J., & Striegel-Moore, R. H. (1984, September). *Predicting attitudes toward body weight and food intake in women.* Paper presented at the 14th Congress of the European Association of Behavior Therapy, Brussels.

Roe, K. V., Drivas, A., Karagellis, A., & Roe, A. (1985). Sex differences in vocal interaction with mother and stranger in Greek infants: Some cognitive implications. *Developmental Psychology, 21*(2), 373–377.

Romer, N. (1990). Is political activism still a "masculine" endeavor? Gender comparisons among high school political activists. *Psychology of Women Quarterly, 14*(2), 229–244.

Ronfeldt, H. M., Kimerling, R., & Arias, I. (1998). Satisfaction with relationship power and the perpetration of dating violence. *Journal of Marriage and the Family, 60,* 70–78.

Root, M. P. P. (1990). Disordered eating in women of color. *Sex Roles, 22,* 525–536.

Rosaldo, M. Z. (1974). Woman, culture and society: A theoretical overview. In M. Z. Rosaldo & L. Lamphere (Eds.), *Woman, culture and society* (pp. 1–16). Stanford, CA: Stanford University Press.

Rose, R. M. (1969). Androgen excretion in stress. In P. G. Bourne (Ed.), *The psychology and physiology of stress* (pp. 117–147). New York: Academic Press.

Rose, S. M. (1985). Same-sex and cross-sex friendships and the psychology of homosociality. *Sex Roles, 12,* 63–74.

Rose, S. M. (1995). Women's friendships. In J. C. Chrisler & A. Huston Hemstreet (Eds.), *Variations on a theme: Diversity and the psychology of women* (pp. 79–105). Albany: State University of New York Press.

Rosenberg, J., Perlstadt, H., & Phillips, W. R. (1993). Now that we are here: Discrimination, disparagement, and harassment at work and the experience of women lawyers. *Gender and Society, 7*(3), 415–433.

Rosenberg, R. (1982). *Beyond separate spheres: Intellectual origins of modern feminism.* New Haven, CT: Yale University Press.

Rosenthal, R. (1966). *Experimental effects in behavioral research.* New York: Appleton-Century-Crofts.

Rosenthal, R. (1990). How are we doing in soft psychology? *American Psychologist, 45,* 775–777.

Rosenthal, R., Archer, D., DiMatteo, M. R., Kowumaki, J. H., & Rogers, P. O. (1974, September). Body talk and tone of voice: The language without words. *Psychology Today, 8,* 64–68.

Rosenthal, R., & DePaulo, B. M. (1979). Sex differences in eavesdropping on nonverbal cues. *Journal of Personality and Social Psychology, 37,* 273–285.

Rosenthal, R., Persinger, G. W., Mulry, R. C., Vikan-Kline, L., & Grothe, M. (1964). Changes in experimental hypotheses as determinants of experimental results. *Journal of Projective Techniques and Personality Assessment, 28,* 465–469.

Rosenthal, R., & Rubin, D. B. (1982). Further meta-analytic procedures for assessing cognitive gender differences. *Journal of Educational Psychology, 74,* 708–712.

Rosenwasser, S. M., & Dean, N. G. (1989). Gender role and political office: Effects of perceived masculinity/femininity of candidate and political office. *Psychology of Women Quarterly, 13*(1), 77–86.

Rosenweig, S. (1933). The experimental situation as a psychological problem. *Psychological Review, 40,* 337–354.

Rosewater, L. B. (1984). Feminist therapy: Implications for practitioners. In L. E. Walker (Ed.), *Women and mental health policy* (pp. 267–280). Beverly Hills, CA: Sage.

Rosewater, L. B., & Walker, L. E. (Eds.). (1985). *Handbook of feminist therapy: Women's issues in psychotherapy.* New York: Springer.

Ross, S. I., & Jackson, J. M. (1991). Teachers' expectations for Black males' and Black females' academic achievement. *Personality and Social Psychology Bulletin, 17*(1), 78–82.

Rosser, P. (1982, December). Do schools teach computer anxiety? *Ms.,* p. 15.

Rossi, A. S., & Rossi, P. E. (1977). Body time and social time: Mood patterns by menstrual cycle phase and day of week. *Social Science Research, 6,* 273–308.

Rossi, J. D. (1983). Ratios exaggerate gender differences in mathematical ability. *American Psychologist, 38,* 348.

Rothert, M., Rovner, D., Holmes, M., Schmitt, N., Talarczyk, G., Kroll, J., & Gogate, J. (1990). Women's use of information regarding hormone replacement therapy. *Research in Nursing and Health, 13,* 355–366.

Rothman, B. K. (1982). *In labor: Women and power in the birthplace.* New York: Norton.

Rotkin, K. F. (1972). The phallacy of our sexual norm. *RT: A Journal of Radical Therapy, 3*(11). Reprinted in A. G. Kaplan & J. D. Bean (Eds.) (1976), *Beyond sex-role stereotypes: Readings toward a psychology of androgyny* (pp. 154–162). Boston: Little, Brown.

Rousso, H. (1986, March). Confronting the myth of asexuality: The networking project for disabled women and girls. *SIECUS Report,* pp. 4–6.

Rozin, P., & Fallon, A. E. (1988). Body image, attitudes to weight and misperceptions of figure preferences of the opposite sex: A comparison of men and women in two generations. *Journal of Abnormal Psychology, 97,* 342–345.

Rubin, D. L., Greene, K., & Schneider, D. (1994). Adopting gender-inclusive language reforms: Diachronic and synchronic variation. *Journal of Language and Social Psychology, 13*(2), 91–114.

Rubin, J., Provenzano, F., & Luria, Z. (1974). The eye of the beholder: Parents' views on sex of newborns. *American Journal of Orthopsychiatry, 44,* 512–519.

Rubin, L. B. (1976). *Worlds of pain.* New York: Basic Books.

Rubin, L. B. (1979). *Women of a certain age: The mid-life search for self.* New York: Harper & Row.

Rubin, L. B. (1991). *Erotic wars: What happened to the sexual revolution?* New York: Harper Perennial.

Rubin, R. T., Reinisch, J. M., & Haskett, R. F. (1981). Postnatal gonadal steroid effects on human behavior. *Science, 211,* 1318–1324.

Rubin, Z., Peplau, L. A., & Hill, C. T. (1981). Loving and leaving: Sex differences in romantic attachments. *Sex Roles, 7,* 821–835.

Ruble, D. N. (1977). Premenstrual symptoms: A reinterpretation. *Science, 197,* 291–292.

Ruble, D. N., Greulich, F., Pomerantz, E. M., & Gochberg, B. (1993). The role of gender-related processes in the development of sex differences in self-evaluation and depression. *Journal of Affective Disorders, 29*(2/3), 97–128.

Ruddick, S. (1989). *Maternal thinking: Toward a politics of peace.* New York: Ballantine.

Rudman, L. A. (1998). Self-promotion as a risk factor for women: The costs and benefits of counter-stereotypical impression management. *Journal of Personality and Social Psychology, 74,* 629–645.

Ruether, R. R. (1983). *Sexism and god-talk: Toward a feminist theology.* Boston: Beacon Press.

Runciman, W. G. (1966). *Relative deprivation and social justice: A study of attitudes to social inequality in twentieth-century England.* Berkeley: University of California Press.

Rush, F. (1980). *The best kept secret: Sexual abuse of children.* New York: McGraw-Hill.

Russell, D., Peplau, L. A., & Cutrona, C. E. (1980). The revised UCLA loneliness scale: Concurrent and discriminant validity evidence. *Journal of Personality and Social Psychology, 39,* 472–480.

Russell, D. E. H. (1983a). The incidence and prevalence of intrafamilial and extrafamilial sexual abuse of female children. *Child Abuse and Neglect, 7,* 133–146.

Russell, D. E. H. (1983b). *Rape in marriage.* New York: Macmillan.

Russell, D. E. H. (1984). *Sexual exploitation: Rape, child sexual abuse and workplace harassment.* Beverly Hills, CA: Sage.

Russell, D. E. H., & Howell, N. (1983). The prevalence of rape in the United States revisited. *Signs: Journal of Women in Culture and Society, 8,* 688–695.

Russell, G. (1982). Shared-care-giving families: An Australian study. In M. E. Lamb (Ed.), *Nontraditional families: Parenting and child development.* Hillsdale, NJ: Erlbaum.

Russell, G. M., & Bohan, J. S. (1999). Hearing voices: The uses of research and the politics of change. *Psychology of Women Quarterly, 23*(2), 403–418.

Russell, K., Wilson, M., & Hall, R. (1992). *The color complex: The politics of skin color among African Americans.* New York: Harcourt Brace Jovanovich.

Russell, S. (1985). Social dimensions of disability: Women with MS. *Resources for Feminist Research, 14*(1), 56–58.

Russo, N. F., Amaro, H., & Winter, M. (1987). The use of inpatient mental health services by Hispanic women. *Psychology of Women Quarterly, 11*(4), 427–441.

Russo, N. F., Horn, J. D., & Schwartz, R. (1992). U.S. abortion in context: Selected characteristics and motivation of women seeking abortions. *Journal of Social Issues, 48*(3), 183–202.

Russo, N. F., & Sobel, S. B. (1981). Sex differences in the utilization of mental health facilities. *Professional Psychology, 12,* 7–19.

Ryan, M. (1992, January 5). Don't quit on us. *Parade,* pp. 8–9.

Saal, F. E., Johnson, C. B., & Weber, N. (1989). Friendly or sexy? It may depend on whom you ask. *Psychology of Women Quarterly, 13,* 263–276.

Sadker, M., & Sadker, D. (1985, March). Sexism in the school-room of the '80s. *Psychology Today,* pp. 54–57.

Saghir, M. T., & Robins, E. (1973). *Male and female homosexuality.* Baltimore: Williams & Wilkins.

Sagrestano, L. M. (1992a). The use of power and influence in a gendered world. *Psychology of Women Quarterly, 16*(4), 439–447.

Sagrestano, L. M. (1992b). Power strategies in interpersonal relationships: The effects of expertise and gender. *Psychology of Women Quarterly, 16*(4), 481–495.

Sagrestano, L. M., Heavey, C. L., & Christensen, A. (1999). Perceived power and physical violence in marital conflict. *Journal of Social Issues, 55*(1), 65–79.

Sales, E., & Frieze, I. H. (1984). Women and work: Implications for mental health policy. In L. E. Walker (Ed.), *Women and mental health policy* (pp. 229–246). Beverly Hills, CA: Sage.

Sancho, A. M., & Hewitt, J. (1990). Questioning fear of success. *Psychological Reports, 67*(3, Pt. 1), 803–806.

Sanday, P. R. (1981a). *Female power and male dominance: On the origins of sexual inequality.* Cambridge: Cambridge University Press.

Sanday, P. R. (1981b). The socio-cultural context of rape: A cross-cultural study. *Journal of Social Issues, 37,* 5–27.

Sanders, B., & Soares, M. P. (1986). Sexual maturation and spatial ability in college students. *Developmental Psychology, 22*(2), 199–203.

Sanger, M. (1938). *Margaret Sanger: An autobiography.* New York: Dover.

Sanik, M. M. (1990). Parents' time use: A 1967–1986 comparison. *Lifestyles: Family and Economic Issues, 11*(3), 299–316.

Sapiro, V. (1983). *The political integration of women: Roles, socialization, and politics.* Urbana: University of Illinois Press.

Sapiro, V. (1986). *Women in American society.* Palo Alto, CA: Mayfield.

Sarrel, P., & Masters, W. (1982). Sexual molestation of men by women. *Archives of Sexual Behavior, 11,* 117–132.

Saunders, D. G. (1986). When battered women use violence: Husband-abuse or self-defense? *Victims and Violence, 1,* 47–60.

Savage, R. M., & Gouvier, D. D. (1992). Rey Auditory-Verbal Learning Test: The effects of age and gender, and norms for delayed recall and story recognition trials. *Archives of Clinical Neuropsychology, 7,* 407–414.

Scamarella, T. J., & Brown, W. A. (1978). Serum testosterone and aggressiveness in hockey players. *Psychosomatic Medicine, 40,* 262–265.

Scanzoni, J. (1972). *Sexual bargaining: Power politics in the American marriage.* Englewood Cliffs, NJ: Prentice-Hall.

Scarf, M. A. (1979). The more sorrowful sex. *Psychology Today, 12*(11), 44–52, 89–90.

Scarr, S. (1988). How genotypes and environments combine: Development and individual differences. In N. Bolger, A. Caspi, G. Downey, & M. Moorhouse (Eds.), *Persons in context: Developmental processes* (pp. 217–244). Cambridge: Cambridge University Press.

Scarr, S. (1991, February 25). *How genes and environments work together.* Colloquium presentation at Radford University, Radford, VA.

Scarr, S. (1998). American child care today. *American Psychologist, 53*(2), 95–108.

Schacter, S., & Singer, J. E. (1962). Cognitive, social, and physiological determinants of emotional state. *Psychological Review, 69,* 379–399.

Schein, E. H. (1968). Organizational socialization and the profession of management. *Industrial Management Review, 9,* 1–15.

Schneer, J. A., & Reitman, F. (1993). Effects of alternate family structures on managerial career paths. *Academy of Management Journal, 36*(4), 830–843.

Schneider, F. W., & Coutts, L. M. (1985). Person orientation of male and female high school students: To the educational disadvantage of males? *Sex Roles, 13*(1/2), 47–63.

Schneider, M. S. (1986). The relationships of cohabiting lesbian and heterosexual couples: A comparison. *Psychology of Women Quarterly, 10*(3), 234–239.

Schnellmann, J., & Gibbons, J. L. (1984, August). *The perception by women and minorities of trivial discriminatory actions in the classroom.* Paper presented at the annual meeting of the American Psychological Association, Toronto.

School rapes common: Head. (1991, July 25). *The News,* (Adelaide, Australia), p. 8.

Schubert, J. B., Bradley-Johnson, S., & Nuttal, J. (1980). Mother–infant communication and maternal employment. *Child Development, 51*(1), 246–249.

Schultz, N. R., & Moore, D. (1986). The loneliness experience of college students: Sex differences. *Personality and Social Psychology Bulletin, 12*(1), 111–119.

Schwartz, J. (1998, April 3). Teens are lighting up in increasing numbers. *Washington Post,* p. A2.

Schwartz, J. M., & Abramowitz, S. I. (1975). Value-related effects on psychiatric judgment. *Archives of General Psychiatry, 32*(2), 1525–1529.

Schwarzwald, J., & Koslowsky, M. (1999). Gender, self-esteem, and focus of interest in the use of power strategies by adolescents in conflict situations. *Journal of Social Issues, 55*(1), 15–32.

Scientists identify sex of 3-day-old embryos. (1990, April 19). *New York Times,* p. B7.

Scott, W. B., & Webster, S. K. (1984, August). *Gender differences in the attributional effect of videotape self-observation.* Paper presented at the annual meeting of the American Psychological Association, Toronto.

Segura, D. A., & Pesquera, B. M. (1995). Chicana feminisms: The political context and contemporary expressions. In J. Freeman (Ed.), *Women: A feminist perspective* (5th ed., pp. 617–631). Mountain View, CA: Mayfield.

Selgado de Snyder, V. N., Cervantes, R. C., Padilla, A. M. (1990). Gender and ethnic differences in psychosocial stress and generalized distress among Hispanics. *Sex Roles, 22*(7/8), 441–453.

Selkow, P. (1984, August). *Maternal employment: Effects on daughters' and sons' early career aspirations.* Paper presented at the annual meeting of the American Psychological Association, Toronto.

Sellers, R. M., Smith, M. A., Shelton, J. N., Rowley, S. A. J., & Chavous, T. M. (1998). Multidimensional model of racial identity: A reconceptualization of African American racial identity. *Personality and Social Psychology Review, 2*(1), 18–39.

Serbin, L., & O'Leary, K. (1975). How nursery schools teach girls to shut up. *Psychology Today, 9*(7), 56–58ff.

Serbin, L. A., Powlishta, K. K., & Gulko, J. (1993). The development of sex typing in middle childhood. *Monographs of the Society for Research in Child Development, 58*(2, Serial No. 232), 1–73.

Serbin, L. A., Zelkowitz, P., Doyle, A. B., Gold, D., & Wheaton, B. (1990). The socialization of sex-differentiated skills and academic performance: A mediational model. *Sex Roles, 23,* 613–628.

Seymour, E. (1995). The loss of women from science, mathematics, and engineering undergraduate majors: An explanatory account. *Science Education, 79*(4), 437–473.

Shapiro, J. L. (1987, January). The expectant father. *Psychology Today, 21*(1), 36–42.

Sharpe, R. (1992, January/February). Capitol Hill's worst

kept secret: Sexual harassment. *Ms., 2*(4), 28–31.

Shashaani, L. (1994). Gender differences in computer experience and its influence on computer attitudes. *Journal of Educational Computing Research, 11*(4), 347–367.

Sheffield, C. J. (1995). Sexual terrorism. In J. Freeman (Ed.), *Women: A feminist perspective* (5th ed., pp. 1–21). Mountain View, CA: Mayfield.

Shellenbarger, S. (1995, December 20). Work and family: Shedding light on women's records dispels stereotypes. *Wall Street Journal,* p. B1.

Sherfey, M. J. (1966). The evolution and nature of female sexuality in relation to psychoanalytic theory. *Journal of the American Psychoanalytic Association, 14,* 28–128.

Sherman, B. L., & Dominick, J. R. (1986). Violence and sex in music videos: TV and rock'n' roll. *Journal of Communication, 36*(1), 79–93.

Sherman, J. A. (1982). Mathematics, the critical filter: A look at some residues. *Psychology of Women Quarterly, 6,* 428–444.

Sherman, J. A., & Fennema, E. (1977). The study of mathematics by high school girls and boys: Related variables. *American Educational Research Journal, 14,* 159–168.

Sherman, J. A., Koufacos, C., & Kenworthy, J. A. (1978). Therapists: Their attitudes and information about women. *Psychology of Women Quarterly, 2,* 299–313.

Sherwin, B. B. (1988). A comparative analysis of the role of androgen in human male and female sexual behavior: Behavioral specificity, critical thresholds, and sensitivity. *Psychobiology, 16*(4), 416–425.

Shields, N. M., & Hanneke, C. R. (1983). Attribution processes in violent relationships: Perceptions of violent husbands and their wives. *Journal of Applied Social Psychology, 13,* 515–527.

Shields, S. A. (1975). Functionalism, Darwinism and the psychology of women: A study in social myth. *American Psychologist, 30*(7), 739–754.

Shields, S. A. (1984). "To pet, coddle, and 'do for' ": Caretaking and the concept of maternal instinct. In M. Lewin (Ed.), *In the shadow of the past: Psychology portrays the sexes* (pp. 256–273). New York: Columbia University Press.

Shigetomi, C. C., Hartmann, D. P., & Gilford, D. M. (1981). Sex differences in children's altruistic behavior and reputations for helpfulness. *Developmental Psychology, 17*(4), 434–437.

Shively, M. G., Jones, C., & De Cecco, J. P. (1983/84). Research on sexual orientation: Definitions and methods. *Journal of Homosexuality, 9*(2/3), 127–136.

Shomer, R. W., & Centers, R. (1970). Differences in attitudinal responses under conditions of implicitly manipulated group salience. *Journal of Personality and Social Psychology, 15*(2), 125–132.

Shortridge, K. (1989). Poverty is a woman's problem. In J. Freeman (Ed.), *Women: A feminist perspective* (4th ed., pp. 422–501). Mountain View, CA: Mayfield.

Shusterman, L. R. (1976). The psychosocial factors of the abortion experience: A critical review. *Psychology of Women Quarterly, 1*(1), 79–106.

Shute, V. J., Pellegrino, J. W., Hubert, L., & Reynolds, R. W. (1983). The relationship between androgen levels and human spatial abilities. *Bulletin of the Psychonomic Society, 21,* 465–468.

Sidanuis, J., Pratto, F., & Rabinowitz, J. L. (1994). Gender, ethnic status, and ideological asymmetry: A social dominance interpretation. *Journal of Cross Cultural Psychology, 25*(2), 194–216.

Siegel, J. M., & Kuykendall, D. H. (1990). Loss, widowhood, and psychological distress among the elderly. *Journal of Consulting and Clinical Psychology, 58*(5), 519–524.

Sigelman, C. K., Thomas, D. B., Sigelman, L., & Ribich, F. D. (1986). Gender, physical attractiveness and electability: An experimental investigation of voter bias. *Journal of Applied Social Psychology, 16*(3), 229–248.

Signorella, M., Bigler, R. S., & Liben, L. (1993). Developmental differences in children's gender schemata about others: A meta-analytic review. *Developmental Review, 13*(2), 147–183.

Signorielli, N., McLeod, D., & Healy, E. (1994). Gender stereotypes in MTV commercials: The beat goes on. *Journal of Broadcasting and Electronic Media, 38*(1), 91–101.

Silverman, L. K. (1989). It all began with Leta Hollingworth: The story of giftedness in women. *Journal for the Education of the Gifted, 12*(2), 86–98.

Silverstein, L. B. (1996). Fathering is a feminist issue. *Psychology of Women Quarterly, 20*(1), 3–38.

Silverstein, L. B., & Auerbach, C. F. (1999). Deconstructing the essential father. *American Psychologist, 54*(6), 397–407.

Silverstein, L. B., & Phares, V. (1996). Expanding the mother–child paradigm: An examination of dissertation research 1986–1994. *Psychology of Women Quarterly, 20*(1), 39–54.

Simmons, R. G., Blyth, D. A., Van Cleave, E. F., & Bush, D. M. (1979). Entry into early adolescence: The impact of school structure, puberty, and early dating on self-esteem. *American*

Sociological Review, 44, 948–967.

Simon, B., Glässner-Bayerl, B., & Stratenwerth, I. (1991). Stereotyping and self-stereotyping in a natural intergroup context: The case of heterosexual and homosexual men. *Social Psychology Quarterly, 54*(3), 252–266.

Simon, R. W. (1995). Gender, multiple roles, role meaning, and mental health. *Journal of Health and Social Behavior, 36,* 182–194.

Simpson, J. A., Gangestead, S. W., & Lerma, M. (1990). Perception of physical attractiveness: Mechanisms involved in the maintenance of romantic relationships. *Journal of Personality and Social Psychology, 59*(6), 1192–1201.

Sistrunk, F., & McDavid, J. W. (1971). Sex variables in conforming behavior. *Journal of Personality and Social Psychology, 17,* 200–207.

Six, B., & Eckes, T. (1991). A closer look at the complex structure of sex stereotypes. *Sex Roles, 24*(1/2), 57–71.

Skaalvik, E. M., & Rankin, R. J. (1994). Gender differences in mathematics and verbal achievement, self-perception and motivation. *British Journal of Educational Psychology, 64*(3), 419–428.

Skinner, P. H., & Shelton, R. L. (1985). *Speech, language, and hearing: Normal processes and disorders* (2nd ed.). New York: Wiley.

Skoe, E. E., & Diessner, R. (1994). Ethic of care, justice, identity, and gender: An extension and replication. *Merrill Palmer Quarterly, 40*(2), 272–289.

Skrypnek, B. J., & Snyder, M. (1982). On the self-perpetuating nature of the stereotypes about women and men. *Journal of Experimental Social Psychology, 18,* 277–291.

Slaby, R. G., & Frey, K. S. (1975). Development of gender constancy and selective attention to same-sex models. *Child Development, 46,* 849–856.

Slater, B. & Rabin, J. (in preparation). Developmental patterns in lesbians.

Sloane, E. (1993). *The biology of women* (3rd ed.). Albany, NY: Delmar.

Smith, A., & Stewart, A. J. (1983). Approaches to studying racism and sexism in Black women's lives. *Journal of Social Issues, 39*(3), 1–15.

Smith, E. J. (1982). The Black female adolescent: A review of the educational, career, and psychological literature. *Psychology of Women Quarterly, 6*(3), 261–288.

Smith, J. E., Waldorf, V. A., & Trembath, D. L. (1990). "Single White male looking for thin, very attractive . . . " *Sex Roles, 23*(11/12), 675–685.

Smith, L. (1987, January). *A feminist approach to legal research.* Paper presented at the conference on the Effects of Feminist Approaches on Research Methodologies, Calgary Institute for the Humanities, Calgary, Alberta.

Smith, M. (1980). Sex bias in counseling and psychotherapy. *Psychological Bulletin, 87,* 392–407.

Smith, P. A., & Midlarsky, E. (1985). Empirically derived conceptions of femaleness and maleness: A current view. *Sex Roles, 12,* 313–328.

Smith, P. B., Chacko, M. R., & Bermudez, A. (1989). Contraceptive and sexuality knowledge among inner-city middle school students from minority groups. *School Counselor, 37*(2), 103–108.

Smith-Rosenberg, C., & Rosenberg, C. (1976). The female animal: Medical and biological views of women. In C. Rosenberg, *No other gods: On science and American social thought* (pp. 54–70). Balti-more: Johns Hopkins University Press.

Snodgrass, S. E. (1985). Women's intuition: The effect of subordinate role upon interpersonal sensitivity. *Journal of Personality and Social Psychology, 49,* 146–155.

Snodgrass, S. E. (1992). Further effects of role versus gender on interpersonal sensitivity. *Journal of Personality and Social Psychology, 62,* 154–158.

Snow, J. T., & Harris, M. B. (1989). Disordered eating in Southwestern Pueblo Indians and Hispanics. *Journal of Adolescence, 12,* 329–336.

Snow, M. E., Jacklin, C. N., & Maccoby, E. E. (1981). Birth-order differences in peer sociability at thirty-three months. *Child Development, 52*(2), 589–595.

Snow, W. G., & Sheese, S. (1985). Lateralized brain damage, intelligence, and memory: A failure to find sex differences. *Journal of Consulting and Clinical Psychology, 33*(6), 940–941.

Sochting, I., Skoe, E. E., & Marcia, J. E. (1994). Care-oriented moral reasoning and prosocial behavior: A question of gender or sex-role orientation. *Sex Roles, 31*(3/4), 131–147.

Sommer, B. (1973). The effect of menstruation on cognitive and perceptual-motor behavior: A review. *Psychosomatic Medicine, 35,* 515–534.

Sommer, B. (1975). *Mood and the menstrual cycle.* Paper presented at the annual meeting of the American Psychological Association, Chicago.

Sommer, B. (1983). How does menstruation affect cognitive competence and psychophysiological response? *Women and Health, 8*(2/3), 53–90.

Sommer, B. (1984, August). PMS in the courts: Are all women on trial? *Psychology Today,* pp. 36–38.

Sommer, B. (1992). Cognitive performance and the menstrual cycle. In J. T. E. Richardson

(Ed.), *Cognition and the menstrual cycle* (pp. 39–66). New York: Springer-Verlag.

Sommers-Flanagan, R., Sommers-Flanagan, J., & Davis, B. (1993). What's happening on Music Television? A gender role content analysis. *Sex Roles, 28*(11/12), 745–753.

Sonkin, D. J., Martin, D., & Walker, L. E. A. (1986). *The male batterer: A treatment approach.* New York: Springer.

Sorenson, R. C. (1973). *Adolescent sexuality in contemporary America.* New York: World.

South, S. J., & Spitze, G. (1994). Housework in marital and nonmarital households. *American Sociological Review, 59,* 327–347.

Spalter-Roth, R., & Hartmann, H. (1990). *Raises and recognition: Secretaries, clerical workers and the union wage premium.* Washington, DC: Institute for Women's Policy Research.

Spence, J. T., & Helmreich, R. L. (1978). *Masculinity and femininity: The psychological dimensions, correlates and antecedents.* Austin: University of Texas Press.

Spence, J. T., Helmreich, R., & Stapp, J. (1974). The personal attributes questionnaire: A measure of sex-role stereotypes and masculinity-femininity (Ms. no. 617). JSAS *Catalog of Selected Documents in Psychology, 4,* 43.

Spencer, S. J., Steele, C. M., & Quinn, D. M. (1999). Stereotype threat and women's math performance. *Journal of Experimental Social Psychology, 31*(1), 4–28.

Spender, D. (1980). *Man made language.* London: Routledge & Kegan Paul.

Sperling, M. B., & Berman, W. H. (1991). An attachment classification of desperate love. *Journal of Personality Assessment, 56*(1), 45–55.

Sperry, R. (1982). Some effects of disconnecting the cerebral hemi-spheres. *Science, 217,* 1223–1226.

Spigelman, M., & Schultz, K. (1981, June). *Attitudes toward obesity.* Paper presented at the annual convention of the Canadian Psychological Association, Toronto.

Springer, S. P., & Deutsch, G. (1998). *Left brain, right brain* (5th ed.). New York: Freeman.

St. Lawrence, J. S., & Joyner, D. J. (1991). The effects of sexually violent rock music on males' acceptance of violence against women. *Psychology of Women Quarterly, 15*(1), 49–64.

Stack, C. B. (1997). Different voices, different visions: Gender, culture, and moral reasoning. In M. Baca Zinn, P. Hondagneu-Sotelo, & M. Messner (Eds.), *Through the prism of difference: Readings on sex and gender* (pp. 51–57). Boston: Allyn & Bacon.

Stafford, R. E. (1961). Sex differences in spatial visualization as evidence of sex-linked inheritance. *Perceptual and Motor Skills, 13,* 428.

Stake, J. E. (1985). Exploring the basis of sex differences in third-party allocations. *Journal of Personality and Social Psychology, 48*(6), 1621–1629.

Stake, J., & Lauer, M. L. (1987). The consequences of being over-weight: A controlled study of gender differences. *Sex Roles, 17,* 31–47.

Stallings, J. (1985). School, classroom, and home influences on women's decisions to enroll in advanced mathematics courses. In S. F. Chipman, L. R. Brush, & D. M. Wilson (Eds.), *Women and mathematics: Balancing the equation* (pp. 199–223). Hillsdale, NJ: Erlbaum.

Staples, R. (1978). Masculinity and race: The dual dilemma of Black men. *Journal of Social Issues, 34*(1), 169–183.

Starhawk. (1979). *The spiral dance.* New York: Harper & Row.

Stark, R., & McEvoy, J. (1970). Middle-class violence. *Psychology Today, 4,* 107–112.

Stark-Adamec, C., & Kimball, M. (1984). Science free of sexism: A guide to the conduct of nonsexist research. *Canadian Psychology, 25*(1), 23–34.

Starrels, M. E. (1994). Gender differences in parent–child relations. *Journal of Family Issues, 15*(1), 148–165.

Statistics Canada. (1995). *Women in Canada: A statistical report* (3rd ed.). Ottawa, Canada: Author.

Steel, B. S., & Lovrich, N. P. (1987). Comparable worth: The problematic politicization of a public personnel issue. *Public Personnel Management, 16*(1), 23–36.

Steele, C. M. (1997). A threat in the air: How stereotypes shape intellectual identity and performance. *American Psychologist, 52,* 613–629.

Stein, A. H., & Bailey, M. M. (1973). The socialization of achievement orientation in females. *Psychological Bulletin, 80*(5), 345–366.

Steinbacher, R., & Gilroy, F. (1990). Sex selection technology: A prediction of its use and effect. *Journal of Psychology, 124*(3), 283–288.

Steinem, G. (1983). *Outrageous acts and everyday rebellions.* New York: Holt, Rinehart and Winston.

Steinhauer, J. (1999, March 1). For women in medicine, a road to compromise, not perks. *New York Times,* p. A1.

Stellman, J. M. (1977). *Women's work, women's health.* New York: Pantheon.

Stellman, J. M. (1978). Forum on women's occupational health: Medical, social and legal implications. Occupational health hazards of women: An overview. *Preventive Medicine, 7,* 281–293.

Sternberg, R. J. (1986). A triangular theory of love. *Psychological Review, 93,* 119–135.

Sternglanz, S. H., & Serbin, L. A. (1974). Sex-role stereotyping in children's television programs. *Developmental Psychology, 10,* 710–715.

Stevens, G. E., & DeNisi, A. S. (1980). Women as managers: Attitudes and attributions for performance by men and women. *Academy of Management Journal, 23*(2), 355–360.

Stevens, N. (1995). Gender and adaptation to widowhood in later life. *Ageing and Society, 15,* 37–58.

Stevenson, H. W., Lee, S., & Stigler, J. (1986, February 14). Mathematics achievement of Chinese, Japanese, and American children. *Science,* pp. 693–699.

Stewart, A. J., & Ostrove, J. M. (1998). Women's personality and middle age: Gender, history, and midcourse corrections. *American Psychologist, 53*(11), 1185–1194.

Stewart, A. J., & Salt, P. (1981). Life stress, life-styles, depression and illness in adult women. *Journal of Personality and Social Psychology, 40*(6), 1063–1069.

Stewart, A. J., & Winter, D. G. (1976). Arousal of the power motive in women. *Journal of Consulting and Clinical Psychology, 44*(3), 495–496.

Stewart, D. E. (1989). Positive changes in the premenstrual period. *Acta Psychiatrica Scandinavica, 79*(4), 400–405.

Stewart, M. W., Verstraate, C. D., & Fanslow, J. L. (1990). Sexist language and university academic staff: Attitudes, awareness and recognition of sexist language. *New Zealand Journal of Educational Studies, 25*(2), 115–125.

Stiller, N. J., & Forrest, L. (1990). An extension of Gilligan and Lyon's investigation of morality: Gender differences in college students. *Journal of College Student Development, 31*(1), 54–63.

Stockard, J., & Johnson, M. (1979). The social origins of male dominance. *Sex Roles, 5*(2), 199–218.

Stockard, J., Schmuck, P. A., Kempner, K., Williams, P., Edson, S. K., & Smith, M. A. (1980). *Sex equity in education.* New York: Academic Press.

Stockdale, M. S. (1998). The direct and moderating influences of sexual harassment pervasiveness, coping strategies, and gender on work-related outcomes. *Psychology of Women Quarterly, 22,* 521–535.

Stoltzman, S. M. (1986). Menstrual attitudes, beliefs, and symptom experiences of adolescent females, their peers, and their mothers. *Health Care for Women International, 7,* 97–114.

Storms, M. D. (1973). Videotape and the attribution process: Reversing actors' and observers' points of view. *Journal of Personality and Social Psychology, 27,* 165–175.

Storms, M. D. (1980). Theories of sexual orientation. *Journal of Personality and Social Psychology, 38,* 783–792.

Stroh, L. K., Brett, J. M., & Reilly, A. H. (1996). Family structure, glass ceiling, and traditional explanations for the differential rate of turnover of female and male managers. *Journal of Vocational Behavior, 49*(1), 99–118.

Strommen, E. A. (1977). Friendship. In E. Donelson & J. Gullahorn (Eds.), *Women: A psychological perspective* (pp. 154–167). New York: Wiley.

Studies show women 50% more likely to die of heart attacks than men (1998, April 2). *Roanoke Times,* p. A6.

Stuenkel, C. A. (1989). Menopause and estrogen replacement therapy. *Psychiatric Clinics of North America, 12*(1), 133–152.

Sulloway, F. J. (1979). *Freud, biologist of the mind.* New York: Basic Books.

Summers, T. P. (1988). Examination of sex differences in expectations of pay and perceptions of equity in pay. *Psychological Reports, 62*(2), 491–496.

Sun, S. W., & Lull, J. (1986). The adolescent audience for music videos and why they watch. *Journal of Communication, 29*(1), 116–124.

Super, D. L. (1951). Vocational adjustment: Implementing a self concept. *Occupations, 30,* 88–92.

Suplee, C. (1991, August 30). Brain may dictate sexuality. *Washington Post,* pp. A1, A13.

Supreme Court delivers mixed decisions on key cases. (1984, May). *NEA Today, 2*(7), 23.

A surgeon cuts to the heart of the matter. (1991, October 28). *People,* p. 50.

Surrey, J. L., Scott, L., & Phillips, E. L. (1975). Menstrual cycle and the decision to seek psychological services. *Perceptual and Motor Skills, 40,* 886.

Susman, E. J., Inoff-Germain, G., Nottlemann, E. D., Loriaux, D. L., Cutler, G. B., & Chrousos, G. P. (1987). Hormones, emotional dispositions, and aggressive attributes in young adolescents. *Child Development, 58,* 1114–1134.

Swaab, D. F., & Hofman, M. A. (1988). Sexual differentiation of the human hypothalamus: Ontogeny of the sexually dimorphic nucleus of the preoptic area. *Developmental Brain Research, 44*(2), 314–318.

Swardson, A. (1991, June 18). Women and the sporting life. *Washington Post,* p. D3.

Swartzman, L. C., Edelberg, R., & Kemmann, E. (1990). The menopausal hot flush: Symptom reports and concomitant physiological changes. *Journal of Behavioral Medicine, 13*(1), 15–30.

Sweeney, J., & Bradbard, M. R. (1988). Mothers' and fathers' changing perceptions of their male and female infants over the course of pregnancy. *Journal of Genetic Psychology, 149*(3), 393–404.

Swim, J. K. (1994). Perceived versus meta-analytic effect sizes: An assessment of the accuracy of gender stereotypes. *Journal of Personality and Social Psychology, 66*(1), 21–36.

Swim, J. K., Aikin, K. J., Hall, W. S., & Hunter, B. A. (1995). Sexism and racism: Old-fashioned and modern prejudices. *Journal of Personality and Social Psychology, 68*(2), 199–214.

Swim, J., Borgida, E., Maruyama, G., & Myers, D. G. (1989). Joan McKay versus John McKay: Do gender stereotypes bias evaluations? *Psychological Bulletin, 105*, 409–425.

Swim, J. K., Cohen, L. L., & Hyers, L. L. (1998). Experiencing everyday prejudice and discrimination. In J. K. Swim & C. Stangor (Eds.), *Prejudice: The target's perspective* (pp. 37–60). San Diego: Academic Press.

Swim, J. K., Ferguson, M. J., & Hyers, L. L (1999). Avoiding stigma by association: Subtle prejudice against lesbians in the form of social distancing. *Basic and Applied Social Psychology, 21*(1), 61–68.

Swim, J. K., & Hyers, L. L. (1999). Excuse me—What did you just say?!: Women's public and private responses to sexist remarks. *Journal of Experimental Social Psychology, 35*(1), 68–88.

Swoboda, F. (1995, November 25). Law, education failing to break glass ceiling. *Washington Post,* pp. C1, C2.

Symons, D. (1979). *The evolution of human sexuality.* Oxford: Oxford University Press.

Szymanski, L. A., & Chrisler, J. C. (1990/1991). Eating disorders, gender-role, and athletic activity. *Psychology, 27*(4) & *28*(1), 20–29.

Tamir, L. M. (1982). *Men in their forties: The transition to middle age.* New York: Springer.

The Tampax Report. (1981). (Available from Ruder, Finn & Rotman, 110 E. 59th Street, New York, NY 10022).

Tangri, S., Burt, M. R., & Johnson, L. B. (1982). Sexual harassment at work: Three explanatory models. *Journal of Social Issues, 38*(4), 33–54.

Tasker, F., & Golombok, S. (1995). Adults raised as children in lesbian families. *American Journal of Orthopsychiatry, 65*(2), 203–215.

Tauber, M. A. (1979). Parental socialization techniques and sex differences in children's play. *Child Development, 50,* 225–234.

Taylor, S. E., & Langer, E. J. (1977). Pregnancy: A social stigma? *Sex Roles, 3,* 27–35.

Teahan, J. E. (1974). The effect of sex and predominant socioeconomic class school climate on expectations of success among Black students. *Journal of Negro Education, 43,* 245–255.

Tennov, D. (1975). *Psychotherapy: The hazardous cure.* New York: Abelard-Schuman.

Teri, L. (1982). Effects of sex and sex-role style on clinical judgement. *Sex Roles, 8,* 639–649.

Terman, L. M. (1925). *Genetic studies of genius: Vol. 1. Mental and physical traits of a thousand gifted children.* Stanford, CA: Stanford University Press.

Terman, L. M. (1951). Correlates of orgasm adequacy in a group of 556 wives. *Journal of Psychology, 32,* 115–172.

Terman, L. M., & Miles, C. C. (1936). *Sex and personality: Studies in masculinity and femininity.* New York: McGraw-Hill.

Terman, L. M., & Oden, M. (1947). *The gifted child grows up.*

Stanford, CA: Stanford University Press.

Terman, L. M., & Oden, M. (1959). *The gifted group at midlife.* Stanford, CA: Stanford University Press.

Terrelonge, P. (1989). Feminist consciousness and Black women. In J. Freeman (Ed.), *Women: A feminist perspective* (4th ed., pp. 556–566). Mountain View, CA: Mayfield.

Tersman, Z., Collins, A., & Eneroth, P. (1991). Cardiovascular responses to psychological and physiological stressors during the menstrual cycle. *Psychosomatic Medicine, 53*(2), 185–197.

Testa, R. J., Kinder, B. N., & Ironson, G. (1987). Homosexual bias in the perception of loving relationships of gay males and lesbians. *Journal of Sex Research, 23*(2), 163–172.

Thai women want to keep maiden name (1999, June 12) [Online]. Available:http://search. washingtonpost.com/wp-srv/WAPO/19990612

Thibaut, J., & Kelley, H. (1959). *The social psychology of groups.* New York: Wiley.

Thoma, S. J. (1986). Estimating gender differences in the comprehension and preference of moral issues. *Developmental Review, 6*(2), 165–180.

Thomas, J. R., & French, K. E. (1985). Gender differences across age in motor performance: A meta-analysis. *Psychological Bulletin, 98*, 260–282.

Thomas, V. G., & Miles, S. E. (1995). Psychology of Black women: Past, present, and future. In H. Landrine (Ed.), *Bringing cultural diversity to feminist psychology: Theory, research, practice* (pp. 303–330). Washington, DC: American Psychological Association.

Thomas, V. L. (1989). Black women engineers and technologists. *Sage: A Scholarly Journal on Black Women, 6*(2), 24–32.

Thompson, A. P. (1983). Extramarital sex: A review of the research literature. *Journal of Sex Research, 19,* 1–22.

Thompson (Woolley), H. B. (1903). *The mental traits of sex: An experimental investigation of the normal mind in men and women.* Chicago: University of Chicago Press.

Thompson, T. L., & Zerbinos, E. (1995). Gender roles in animated cartoons: Has the picture changed in 20 years? *Sex Roles, 32*(9/10), 651–673.

Thornborrow, N. M., & Sheldon, M. B. (1995). Women in the labor force. In J. Freeman (Ed.), *Women: A feminist perspective* (5th ed., pp. 197–219). Mountain View, CA: Mayfield.

Thorndike, E. L. (1910). *Educational psychology* (2nd ed.). New York: Columbia University, Teacher's College.

Tiefer, L. (1995). *Sex is not a natural act and other essays.* Boulder, CO: Westview.

Tiger, L. (1969). *Men in groups.* New York: Random House.

Tillitski, C. J. (1992). Fathers and child custody: Issues, trends, and implications for counseling. *Journal of Mental Health Counseling, 14*(3), 351–361.

Tinsley, E. G., Sullivan-Guest, S., & McGuire, J. (1984). Feminine sex role and depression in middle-aged women. *Sex Roles, 11,* 25–32.

Title IX cited for fivefold increase in girls playing high school sports. (1987, June 17). *Arizona Daily Star,* p. 9C.

Tobias, S. (1982, January). Sexist equations. *Psychology Today,* pp. 14–17.

Tolman, D. L., & Szalacha, L. A. (1999). Dimensions of desire: Bridging qualitative and quantitative methods in a study of female adolescent sexuality. *Psychology of Women Quarterly, 23*(1), 7–39.

Tomlinson-Keasey, C. (1990). The working lives of Terman's gifted women. In H. Y. Grossman & N. L. Chester (Eds.), *The experience and meaning of work in women's lives* (pp. 213–240). Hillsdale, NJ: Erlbaum.

Tonkinson, R. (1974). *The Jigalong Mob: Aboriginal victors of the desert crusade.* Menlo Park, CA: Cummings.

Top, T. J. (1991). Sex bias in the evaluation of performance in the scientific, artistic, and literary professions: A review. *Sex Roles, 24*(1/2), 73–106.

Tosi, H. L., & Einbender, S. W. (1985). The effects of the type and amount of information in sex discrimination research: A meta-analysis. *Academy of Management Journal, 28,* 712–723.

Tougas, F., Brown, R., Beaton, A. M., & Joly, S. (1995). Neosexism: Plus ça change, plus c'est pareil. *Personality and Social Psychology Bulletin, 21,* 842–849.

Tougas, F., Brown, R., Beaton, A. M., & St-Pierre, L. (1999). Neosexism among women: The role of personally experienced social mobility attempts. *Personality and Social Psychology Bulletin, 25*(12), 1487–1497.

Tougas, F., & Veilleux, F. (1988). The influence of identification, collective relative deprivation, and procedure of implementation on women's response to affirmative action: A causal modeling approach. *Canadian Journal of Behavioral Science, 20,* 16–29.

Tougas, F., & Veilleux, F. (1989). Who likes affirmative action: Attitudinal processes among men and women. In F. A. Blanchard & F. Crosby (Eds.), *Affirmative action in perspective.* Boston: Springer-Verlag.

Touhey, J. C. (1974). Effects of additional women professionals on ratings of occupational prestige and desirability. *Journal of Personality and Social Psychology, 29,* 86–89.

Towson, S. M. J., MacDonald, G., & Zanna, M. P. (1981, June). *Confirming sex-role stereotypes in the job interview: Payoffs and pitfalls.* Paper presented at the annual convention of the Canadian Psychological Association, Montreal.

Trahan, D. E., & Quintana, J. W. (1990). Analysis of gender effects upon verbal and visual memory performance in adults. *Archives of Clinical Neuropsychology, 5,* 325–334.

Travis, C. B. (1988). *Women and health psychology: Mental health issues.* Hillsdale, NJ: Erlbaum.

Travis, C. B., Phillippi, R. H., & Henley, T. B. (1991). Gender and causal attributions for mastery, personal, and interpersonal events. *Psychology of Women Quarterly, 15,* 233–249.

Tredinnick, M. G., & Fowers, B. J. (1997). Gender bias and individualism: Responses to case vignettes among psychologists, professors, and students. *Current Psychology: Developmental, Learning, Personality, Social, 15*(4), 291–299.

Treffke, H., Tiggemann, M., & Ross, M. (1992). The relationship between attitude, assertiveness, and condom use. *Psychology and Health, 6,* 45–52.

Treiman, D. J. (1985). The work histories of women and men: What we know and what we need to find out. In A. S. Rossi (Ed.), *Gender and the life course* (pp. 213–232). New York: Aldine.

Trepanier, M. L., & Romatowski, J. A. (1985). Attributes and roles assigned to characters in children's writing: Sex differences and sex-role perceptions. *Sex Roles, 13*(5/6), 263–272.

Trescott, J. (1991, August 17). Anthology of a mother's grief. *Washington Post,* pp. C1, C5.

Tresmer, D. (1976). Do women fear success? *Signs: Journal of Women in Culture and Society, 1*(4), 863–874.

Trethowan, W. H. (1972). The couvade syndrome. In J. G. Howells (Ed.), *Modern perspectives in psycho-obstetrics* (pp. 68–93). New York: Brunner/Mazel.

Trobst, K. K., Collins, R. L., & Embree, J. M. (1994). The role of emotion in social support provision: Gender, empathy and expressions of distress. *Journal of Social and Personal Relationships, 11*(1), 15–62.

Tuck, R. (1975). The relationship between a mother's menstrual status and her response to illness in her child. *Psychosomatic Medicine, 37*, 388–394.

Tucker, L. A. (1982). Relationship between perceived somatotype and body cathexis of college males. *Psychological Reports, 50*, 1055–1061.

Turell, S. C., Armsworth, M. W., & Gaa, J. P. (1990). Emotional responses to abortion: A critical review of the literature. *Women and Therapy, 9*(4), 49–68.

Turkle, S., & Papert, S. (1990). Epistemological pluralism: Styles and voices within the computer culture. *Signs: Journal of Women in Culture and Society, 16*(1), 128–157.

Tyler, L. (1965). *The psychology of human differences.* New York: Appleton-Century-Crofts. (Original work published 1947)

Umberson, D., Wortman, C. B., & Kessler, R. C. (1992). Widowhood and depression: Explaining long-term gender differences in vulnerability. *Journal of Health and Social Behavior, 33*, 10–24.

Unger, R. (1979). Toward a redefinition of sex and gender. *American Psychologist, 34*, 1085–1094.

Unger, R., & Crawford, M. (1993). Commentary: Sex and gender: The troubled relationship between terms and concepts. *Psychological Science 4*(2), 122–124.

Unger, R. K., & Sussman, L. E. (1986). "I and thou": Another barrier to societal change? *Sex Roles, 14*(11/12), 629–636.

United Nations. (1991). *The world's women 1970–1990: Trends and statistics.* Social statistics and indicators, Series K, no. 8. New York: Author.

United Nations. (1995a). *The world's women 1995: Trends and statistics.* New York: Author.

United Nations. (1995b). *Statistical yearbook for Asia and the Pacific.* New York: Author.

United Nations. (1999). *Convention on the elimination of all forms of discrimination against women. States that have signed, ratified, acceded or succeeded to the Convention* [On-line]. Available: www.un.org/womenwatch/daw/cedaw/ratifica.htm

U.S. Bureau of the Census. (1994). *Statistical abstracts of the United States 1994* (114th ed.). Washington, DC: U.S. Government Printing Office.

U.S. Bureau of the Census. (1995). *Statistical abstract of the United States 1995* (115th ed.). Washington, DC: U.S. Government Printing Office.

U.S. Bureau of the Census. (1998). *Statistical abstract of the United States 1998* (118th ed.). Washington, DC: U.S. Government Printing Office.

U.S. Bureau of Labor Statistics. (1999). *Labor force statistics from the current population survey* [On-line]. Available: http://stats.bls.gov

U.S. Department of Health and Human Services. (1988). *National household survey on drug abuse: Main findings 1988.* Bethesda, MD: Alcohol, Drug Abuse and Mental Health Administration.

U.S. Department of Health and Human Services. (1995). *Health, United States, 1994.* Hyattsville, MD: Author.

U.S. Department of Health and Human Services. (1998, September). Trends in sexual risk behaviors among high school students—United States, 1991–1997. *Morbidity and Mortality Weekly Report, 47*(36), 749–752.

U.S. Department of Justice. (1994a, June 22). Half of women raped during 1992 were younger than 18 years old. [Press Release]. Washington, DC: Author.

U.S. Department of Justice. (1994b, July 10). Wives are the most frequent victims in family murders. [Press Release]. Washington, DC: Author.

U.S. Department of Justice. (1995, August 16). Women usually victimized by offenders they know. [Press Release]. Washington, DC: Author.

U.S. Department of Justice, Bureau of Justice Statistics. (1998). *Homicide trends in the U.S. Age, gender and race* [On-line]. Available: http://www.ojp.usdoj.gov/bjs/homicide/ageracesex.htm

U.S. Department of Justice, Bureau of Justice Statistics. (1999, July). *Criminal victimization 1998. Changes 1997–98 with trends 1993–98.* Washington DC: Author.

U.S. Department of Justice, Federal Bureau of Investigation. (1997). *Uniform crime reports for the United States, 1997.* Washington, DC: Author.

U.S. Department of Justice, Federal Bureau of Investigation. (1999a, May). *Uniform crime reports: 1998 preliminary annual release.* Washington, DC: Author.

U.S. Department of Justice, Federal Bureau of Investigation. (1999b). *The structure of family violence: An analysis of selected incidents.* Washington DC: Author.

U.S. Department of Justice, Office of Justice Programs. (1995). *Violence against women: Estimates from the redesigned survey, August 1995.* Washington, DC: Author.

U.S. Equal Opportunity Commission. (1980). Guidelines on discrimination because of sex. *Federal Register, 45*(219), 74676–74677.

U.S. Merit Systems Protection Board. (1981). *Sexual harassment in the federal workplace: Is it a problem?* Washington, DC: U.S. Government Printing Office.

U.S. National Institutes of Health. (1992). *Opportunities for research on women's health* (NIH Publication no. 92–3457). Washington, DC: U.S. Department of Health and Human Services.

Utne, M. K., Hatfield, E., Traupmann, J., & Greenberger, D. (1984). Equity, marital satisfaction, and stability. *Journal of Social and Personal Relationships, 1,* 323–332.

Valois, R. F., & Waring, K. A. (1991). An analysis of college students' anonymous questions about human sexuality. *Journal of American College Health, 39*(6), 263–268.

Vance, E. B., & Wagner, N. N. (1976). Written descriptions of orgasm: A study of sex differences. *Archives of Sexual Behavior, 5,* 87–98.

Vandenberg, S. G. (1987). Sex differences in mental retardation and their implications for sex differences in ability. In J. M. Reinisch, L. A. Rosenblum, & S. A. Sanders (Eds.), *Masculinity/femininity: Basic perspectives* (pp. 157–171). New York: Oxford University Press.

Van Gelder, L. (1985). The strange case of the electronic lover: A real-life story of deception, seduction, and technology. *Ms., 14*(4), 94–95, 99, 101–104, 117, 123–124.

Van Gelder, L. (1991, March/April). A lesbian family revisited. *Ms., 1*(5), 44–47.

Van Preagh, P. (1982). The Hamilton birth control clinic: In response to need. *News/Nouvelles, Journal of the Planned Parenthood Federation of Canada, 3*(1), 2.

Verbrugge, L. (1979). Female illness rates and illness behavior: Testing hypotheses about sex differences in health. *Women and Health, 4,* 61–79.

Verbrugge, L. (1982a). Sex differences in legal drug use. *Journal of Social Issues, 38*(2), 59–76.

Verbrugge, L. (1982b). Work satisfaction and physical health. *Journal of Community Health, 7*(4), 262–282.

Verbrugge, L. (1983, March). Multiple roles and physical health of women and men. *Journal of Health and Social Behavior, 24,* 16–30.

Verbrugge, L., & Madans, J. H. (1985, March). Women's roles and health. *American Demographics, 7*(3), 36–39.

Vergano, D. (1999, May 27). *Pumping iron lowers women's cholesterol* [On-line]. Medical Tribune News Service. Available: www.drkoop.com/healthnews/latest/may/strong_women.html

Veroff, J., Douvan, E., & Kulka, A. (1981). *The inner American: A self-portrait from 1957–1976.* New York: Basic Books.

Vetter, L., & Hickey, D. R. (1985, October). Women in vocational education: Changes since Title IX. *Vocational Education Journal, 60,* 26–29.

Viss, D. C., & Burn, S. M. (1992). Divergent perceptions of lesbians: A comparison of lesbian self-perceptions and heterosexual perceptions. *Journal of Social Psychology, 132*(2), 169–177.

Voda, A. M., & Eliasson, M. (1983). Menopause: The closure of menstrual life. *Women and Health, 8*(2/3), 137–156.

Vollmer, F. (1984). Sex differences in personality and expectancy. *Sex Roles, 11,* 1121–1139.

von Baeyer, C. L., Sherk, D. L., & Zanna, M. P. (1981). Impression management in the job interview. When the female applicant meets the male "chauvinist" interviewer. *Personality and Social Psychology Bulletin, 7,* 45–51.

Voyer, D., Voyer, S., & Bryden, M. P. (1995). Magnitude of sex differences in spatial abilities: A meta-analysis and consideration of critical variables. *Psychological Bulletin, 117*(2), 250–270.

Vrbancic, M. I., & Mosley, J. L. (1988). Sex-related differences in hemispheric lateralization: A function of physical maturation. *Developmental Neuropsychology, 4*(2), 151–167.

Waber, D. (1977). Sex differences in mental abilities, hemispheric lateralization, and rate of physical growth at adolescence. *Developmental Psychology, 13,* 29–38.

Waber, D. P., Bauermeister, M., Cohen, C., Ferber, R., & Wolff, P. H. (1981). Behavioral correlates of physical and neuromotor maturity in adolescents from different environments. *Developmental Psychobiology, 14,* 513–522.

Waber, D. P., Mann, M. B., Merola, J., & Moylan, P. M. (1985). Physical maturation rate and cognitive performance in early adolescence: A longitudinal examination. *Developmental Psychology, 21*(4), 666–681.

Wada, J. A., Clark, R., & Hamm, A. (1975). Cerebral hemisphere asymmetry in humans. *Archives of Neurology, 32,* 239–246.

Wade, R. (1978). *For men, about abortion.* (Available from Roger C. Wade, P.O. Box 4748, Boulder, CO, 80306).

Waldron, I. (1976). Why do women live longer than men? *Social Science and Medicine, 10,* 349–362.

Waldron, I. (1978). Type A behavior pattern and coronary heart disease in men and women. *Social Science and Medicine, 12,* 167–170.

Waldron, I. (1983). Employment and women's health: An analysis of causal relationships. In E. Fee (Ed.), *Women and health: The politics of sex and medicine* (pp. 119–138). Farmingdale, NY: Baywood.

Waldron, I., & Herold, J. (1984, May). *Employment, attitudes toward employment, and women's health.* Paper presented at the meeting of the Society for Behavioral Medicine, Philadelphia.

Walker, E., Bettes, B. A., Kain, E. L., & Harvey, P. (1985). Relationship of gender and marital status with symptomatology in psychotic patients. *Journal of Abnormal Psychology, 94,* 42–50.

Walker, L. E. (1979). *The battered woman.* New York: Harper & Row.

Walker, L. E. (1984). Introduction. In L. E. Walker (Ed.), *Women and mental health policy* (pp. 7–19). Beverly Hills, CA: Sage.

Walker, L. E. (1999). Psychology and domestic violence around the world. *American Psychologist, 54*(1), 21–29.

Walker, L. J. (1984). Sex differences in the development of moral reasoning: A critical review. *Child Development, 55,* 677–691.

Walker, L. J. (1989). A longitudinal study of moral reasoning. *Child Development, 60,* 157–166.

Walker, L. O., & Best, M. A. (1991). Well-being of mothers with infant children: A preliminary comparison of employed women and homemakers. *Women and Health, 17*(1), 71–89.

Walkerdine, V., & The Girls and Mathematics Unit. (1989). *Counting girls out.* London: Virago Press.

Wallen, J., Waitzkin, H., & Stoeckle, J. D. (1979). Physician stereotypes about female health and illness: A study of patients' sex and the informative process during medical interviews. *Women and Health, 4,* 135–146.

Wallston, B. S., DeVellis, B. M., & Wallston, K. (1983). Licensed practical nurses' sex role stereotypes. *Psychology of Women Quarterly, 7,* 199–208.

Walshok, M. L. (1981). *Blue-collar women: Pioneers on the male frontiers.* Garden City, NY: Doubleday.

Walster, E. (1974). Passionate love. In Z. Rubin (Ed.), *Doing unto others* (pp. 150–162). Englewood Cliffs, NJ: Prentice-Hall.

Walster, E., Berscheid, E., & Walster, G. W. (1973). New directions in equity research. *Journal of Personality and Social Psychology, 25,* 151–176.

Walster, E., & Walster, G. W. (1975). Equity and social justice. *Journal of Social Issues, 31*(3), 21–43.

Walters, V., Avotri, J. Y., & Charles, N. (1999). "Your heart is never free": Women in Wales and Ghana talking about distress. *Canadian Psychology, 40*(2), 129–142.

Wardle, M. G. (1976). Women's physiological reactions to physically demanding work. *Psychology of Women Quarterly, 1*(2), 151–159.

Washington, V. (1982). Racial differences in teacher perceptions of first and fourth grade pupils on selected characteristics. *Journal of Negro Education, 51,* 60–72.

Watkins, P. L., & Lee, J. (1997). A feminist perspective on panic disorder and agoraphobia: Etiology and treatment. *Journal of Gender, Culture, and Health, 2*(1), 65–87.

Watts-Jones, D. (1990). Toward a stress scale for African-American women. *Psychology of Women Quarterly, 14*(2), 271–276.

Wauchope, B., & Straus, M. (1990). Age, gender and class differences in physical punishment and physical abuse of American children. In M. Straus & R. J. Gelles (Eds.), *Physical violence in American families: Risk factors and adaptations in 8,145 families* (pp. 133–148). New Brunswick, NJ: Transaction.

Waxman, B. F. (1994). Up against eugenics: Disabled women's challenge to receive reproductive health services. *Sexuality and Disability, 12*(2), 155–171.

Way, N. (1995). "Can't you see the courage, the strength that I have?" Listening to urban adolescent girls speak about their relationships. *Psychology of Women Quarterly, 19*(1), 107–128.

Webb, N. M., & Kenderski, C. M. (1985). Gender differences in small-group interaction and achievement in high- and low-achieving classes. In L. C. Wilkinson & C. B. Marrett (Eds.), *Gender influences in classroom interactions* (pp. 209–236). Orlando, FL: Academic Press.

Weber, M. (1965). *The Protestant ethic and the spirit of capitalism.* London: Unwin.

Weber, R., & Crocker, J. (1983). Cognitive processes in the revision of stereotypic beliefs. *Journal of Personality and Social Psychology, 45,* 961–977.

Webster, K. (1996, May 17). New analysis disproves oft-quoted divorce statistic. *Roanoke Times,* p. A5.

Weideger, P. (1977). *Menstruation and menopause.* New York: Dell.

Weidner, G., & Helmig, L. (1990). Cardiovascular stress reactivity and mood during the menstrual cycle. *Women and Health, 16*(3/4), 5–21.

Weinstein, S., & Sersen, E. A. (1961). Tactual sensitivity as a function of handedness and laterality. *Journal of Comparative and Physiological Psychology, 54,* 665–669.

Weis, D. L. (1983). Affective reactions of women to their

initial experiences of coitus. *Journal of Sex Research, 19,* 209–237.

Weisberg, D. K. (Ed.). (1982). *Women and the law: The social historical perspective: Vol. 1. Women and the criminal law.* Cambridge, MA: Schenkman.

Weiss, R. S. (1973). *Loneliness: The experience of emotional and social isolation.* Cambridge, MA: MIT Press.

Weisstein, N. (1971). *Psychology constructs the female or, the fantasy life of the male psychologist.* Boston: New England Free Press.

Weitz, R. (1989). What price independence? Social reactions to lesbians, spinsters, widows, and nuns. In J. Freeman (Ed.), *Women: A feminist perspective* (4th ed., pp. 446–456). Mountain View, CA: Mayfield.

Weitz, S. (1976). Sex differences in nonverbal communication. *Sex Roles, 2*(2), 175–184.

Weitzman, N., Birns, B., & Friend, R. (1985). Traditional and nontraditional mothers' communication with their daughters and sons. *Child Development, 56,* 894–898.

Welch, R., Huston-Stein, A. C., Wright, J. C., & Plehal, R. (1979). Subtle sex-role cues in children's commercials. *Journal of Communication, 29,* 202–209.

Wentworth, D. K., & Anderson, L. R. (1984). Emergent leadership as a function of sex and task type. *Sex Roles, 11,* 513–524.

Wergers, R. M., & Frieze, I. H. (1977). Gender, female traditionality, achievement level and cognitions of success and failure. *Psychology of Women Quarterly, 2,* 125–137.

Westkott, M. (1986). *The feminist legacy of Karen Horney.* New Haven, CT: Yale University Press.

Wexler, J. G. (1985). Role style of women police officers. *Sex Roles, 12*(7/8), 749–755.

Weyant, R. G. (1979). The relationship between psychology and women. *International Journal of Women's Studies, 2*(4), 358–385.

Wheeler, A., Lee, E. S., & Loe, H. (1983). Employment, sense of well-being, and use of professional services among women. *American Journal of Public Health, 73*(8), 908–911.

Wheeless, V. E., & Berryman-Fink, C. (1985). Perceptions of women managers and their communicator competencies. *Communication Quarterly, 33*(2), 137–148.

Whelan, C. I., & Stewart, D. E. (1990). Pseudocyesis: A review and report of six cases. *International Journal of Psychiatry in Medicine, 20,* 97–108.

Whitbeck, C. (1976). Theories of sex difference. In C. C. Gould & M. W. Wartofsky (Eds.), *Women and philosophy: Toward a theory of liberation* (pp. 54–80). New York: Putnam.

White, J. (1980). *Women and unions.* Ottawa: Canadian Advisory Council on the Status of Women.

White, J. W. (1988). Influence tactics as a function of gender, insult, and goal. *Sex Roles, 18,* 433–448.

White, J. W., & Kowalski, R. M. (1994). Deconstructing the myth of the nonaggressive woman: A feminist analysis. *Psychology of Women Quarterly, 18,* 487–508.

White, J. W., & Roufail, M. (1989). Gender and influence strategies of first choice and last resort. *Psychology of Women Quarterly, 13*(2), 175–189.

White, K. M., Speisman, J. C., Jackson, D., Bartis, S., & Costos, D. (1986). Intimacy maturity and its correlates in young married couples. *Journal of Personality and Social Psychology, 50*(1), 152–162.

White, L., & Brinkerhoff, D. (1981). The sexual division of labor: Evidence from childhood. *Social Forces, 60,* 170–181.

White, S. A. (1991). Effects of gender and competitive coaction on motor perform-

ance. *Perceptual and Motor Skills, 73*(2), 581–582.

Whitehead, T. (1981). Sex hormone treatment of prisoners. In P. Brain & D. Benton (Eds.), *Multidisciplinary approaches to aggression research* (pp. 503–511). Amsterdam: Elsevier.

Whiten, A., Goodall, J., McGrew, W. C., Nishida, T., Reynolds, V., Sugiyama, Y., Tutin, C. E. G., Wrangham, R. W., & Boesch, C. (1999). Cultures in chimpanzees. *Nature, 399,* 682–685.

Whiting, B., & Edwards, C. P. (1973). A cross-cultural analysis of sex differences in the behavior of children aged three through eleven. *Journal of Social Psychology, 91* (second half), 171–188.

Whitley, B. E. Jr., & Kite, M. E. (1995). Sex differences in attitudes toward homosexuality: A comment on Oliver and Hyde (1993). *Psychological Bulletin, 117*(1), 146–154.

Wickrama, K., Conger, R. D., & Lorenz, F. O. (1995). Work, marriage, lifestyle, and changes in men's physical health. *Journal of Behavioral Medicine, 18*(2), 97–111.

Wiersma, U. J. (1990). Gender differences in job attribute preferences: Work–home role conflict and job level as mediating variables. *Journal of Occupational Psychology, 63,* 231–243.

Wiersma, U. J., & Van den Berg, P. (1991). Work–home role conflict, family climate, and domestic responsibilities among men and women in dual-earner families. *Journal of Applied Social Psychology, 21,* 1207–1217.

Wiggins, J. S., & Holzmuller, A. (1981). Further evidence on androgyny and interpersonal flexibility. *Journal of Research in Personality, 15,* 67–80.

Wikan, U. (1977). Man becomes woman: Transsexualism in Oman as a key to gender roles. *Man, 12,* 304–319.

Wilbur, J., Dan, A., Hedricks, C., & Holm, K. (1990). The relationship among menopausal status, menopausal symptoms, and physical activity in midlife women. *Family and Community Health, 13*(3), 67–78.

Wilder, G., Mackie, D., & Cooper, J. (1985). Gender and computers: Two surveys of computer-related attitudes. *Sex Roles, 13*(3/4), 215–228.

Wildman, B. G., & White, P. A. (1986). Assessment of dysmenorrhea using the Menstrual Symptom Questionnaire: Factor structure and validity. *Behaviour Research and Therapy, 24,* 547–551.

Wiley, M. G., & Eskilson, A. (1990). What price success? Evaluations of male and female managers. *Sociological Focus, 23*(2), 115–127.

Wilkinson, D. Y. (1984). Afro-American women and their families. *Marriage and Family Review, 7*(3/4), 125–142.

Wilkinson, L. C., Lindow, J., & Chiang, C. P. (1985). Sex differences and sex segregation in students' small-group communication. In L. C. Wilkinson & C. B. Marrett (Eds.), *Gender influences in classroom interaction* (pp. 185–207). Orlando, FL: Academic Press.

Will, J., Self, P., & Datan, N. (1976). Maternal behavior and perceived sex of infant. *American Journal of Orthopsychiatry, 46,* 135–139.

Williams, C. L. (1992). The glass escalator: Hidden advantages for men in the "female" professions. *Social Problems, 39*(3), 253–267. Reprinted in M. S. Kimmel & M. A. Messner (Eds.) (1998). *Men's lives.* Boston: Allyn & Bacon.

Williams, D. A., & King, P. (1980, December 15). Do males have a math gene? *Newsweek,* p. 73.

Williams, J. B., & Spitzer, R. L. (1983). The issue of sex bias in DSM-III. *American Psychologist, 38,* 793–798.

Williams, J. E., & Bennett, S. M. (1975). The definition of sex stereotypes via the adjective check list. *Sex Roles, 1,* 327–337.

Williams, J. E., & Best, D. L. (1982). *Measuring sex stereotypes: A thirty-nation study.* Beverly Hills, CA: Sage.

Williams, J. E., & Best, D. L. (1990). *Measuring sex stereotypes: A multination study.* Newbury Park, CA: Sage.

Williams, L. R. (1983). Beliefs and attitudes of young girls regarding menstruation. In S. Golub (Ed.), *Menarche.* Lexington, MA: D. C. Heath.

Williams, S. W., Ogletree, S. M., Woodburn, W., & Raffeld, P. (1993). Gender roles, computer attitudes, and dyadic computer interaction performance in college students. *Sex Roles, 29*(7/8), 515–525.

Willis, S. L., & Schaie, K. W. (1988). Gender differences in spatial ability in old age: Longitudinal and intervention findings. *Sex Roles, 18*(3/4), 189–203.

Wilmoth, G. H. (1992). Abortion, public health policy, and informed consent legislation. *Journal of Social Issues, 48*(3), 1–17.

Wilmoth, G. H., de Alteriis, M., & Bussell, D. (1992). Prevalence of psychological risks following legal abortion in the U.S.: Limits of the evidence. *Journal of Social Issues, 48*(3), 37–66.

Wilsnack, S. C., Vogeltanz, N. D., Klassen, A. D., & Harris, T. R. (1997). Childhood sexual abuse and women's substance abuse: National survey findings. *Journal of Studies on Alcohol, 58*(3), 264–271.

Wilson, E. O. (1975). *Sociobiology: The new synthesis.* Cambridge, MA: Harvard University Press.

Win O'Brien, M. (1980). Law in conflict: Another view. *Journal of Occupational Medicine, 22*(8), 509–510.

Winter, D. G. (1973). *The power motive.* New York: Free Press.

Winter, D. G., & Barenbaum, N. B. (1985). Responsibility and the power motive in women and men. *Journal of Personality, 53*(2), 335–355.

Winter, D. G., & Stewart, A. J. (1978). Power motivation. In H. London & J. Exner (Eds.), *Dimensions of personality* (pp. 391–448). New York: Wiley.

Witkin, H. A., Mednick, S. A., Schulsinger, F., Bakkestrom, E., Christiansen, K. O., Goodenough, D. R., Hirschhorn, K., Lundsteen, C., Owen, D. R., Philip, J., Rubin, D. B., & Stocking, M. (1976). Criminality in XYY and XXY men. *Science, 193,* 547–555.

Wittig, M. A. (1979). Genetic influences of sex-related differences in intellectual performance: Theoretical and methodological issues. In M. A. Wittig & A. C. Petersen (Eds.), *Sex-related differences in cognitive functioning: Developmental issues* (pp. 21–66). New York: Academic Press.

Wittig, M. A. (1985). Metatheoretical dilemmas in the psychology of gender. *American Psychologist, 40*(7), 800–811.

Wolfson, S. L. (1981). Sex, dependency and volunteering. *British Journal of Social Psychology, 20,* 293–294.

Wollman, N., Griggs, G., & Stouder, R. (1990). The effects of bystander sex and visibility of victim on intended helping. *Imagination, Cognition and Personality, 9*(2), 141–146.

Women clerics find sexual harassment. (1990, December 1). *Washington Post,* p. C12.

Women in Management. (1999, January). Women leaders in corporate Canada: Twelve women head *Financial Post 500* companies (p. 8). London,

Ontario: The University of Western Ontario.

Women still earn less than men. Study looks at female, male Senate staff pay. (1999, November 15). *Roanoke Times,* p. A8.

Women's intuition linked to thicker nerves in brain. (1986, July 24). *Winnipeg Free Press,* p. 34.

Wong, M. W., & Csikszentmihalyi, M. (1991). Affiliation motivation and daily experience: Some issues on gender differences. *Journal of Personality and Social Psychology, 60*(1), 154–164.

Wong, P. T. P., Kettlewell, G., & Sproule, C. F. (1985). On the importance of being masculine: Sex role, attribution, and women's career achievement. *Sex Roles, 12,* 757–769.

Wood, J. T., & Inman, C. C. (1993). In a different mode: Masculine styles of communicating closeness. *Journal of Applied Communication Research, 21*(3), 279–295.

Wood, W., Rhodes, N., & Whelan, M. (1989). Sex differences in positive well-being: A consideration of emotional style and marital status. *Psychological Bulletin, 106*(2), 249–264.

Wooley, S. C., & Wooley, O. W. (1985). Intensive outpatient and residential treatment for bulimia. In D. M. Garner & P. E. Garfinkel (Eds.), *Handbook of psychotherapy for anorexia and bulimia* (pp. 391–430). New York: Guilford Press.

Woolf, V. (1957). *A room of one's own.* New York: Harcourt, Brace & World. (Original work published 1929)

World Health Organization. (1998). *AIDS epidemic update: December 1998.* New York: Joint United Nations Programme on HIV/AIDS.

Worrell, J., & Remer, P. (1992). *Feminist perspectives in therapy: An empowerment model for women.* Chichester, England: Wiley.

Wu, J. H., & Eichmann, M. A. (1988). Fetal sex identification and prenatal bonding. *Psychological Reports, 63*(1), 199–202.

Yacker, N., & Weinberg, S. L. (1990). Care and justice moral orientation: A scale for its assessment. *Journal of Personality Assessment, 55*(1/2), 18–27.

Yahr, P. (1988). Sexual differentiation of behavior in the context of developmental psychobiology. *Handbook of behavioral neurobiology* (pp. 197–243). New York: Plenum.

Yalom, I., Green, R., & Fisk, N. (1973). Prenatal exposures to female hormones: Effect on psychosexual development in boys. *Archives of General Psychiatry, 28,* 554–561.

Yankelovich, D. (1974). The meaning of work. In J. Rosow (Ed.), *The worker and the job* (pp. 19–48). Englewood Cliffs, NJ: Prentice-Hall.

Yee, D. K., & Eccles, J. S. (1988). Parent perceptions and attributions for children's math achievement. *Sex Roles, 19*(5/6), 317–333.

Yengoyan, A. (1982, Spring). Transvestitism and the ideology of gender. *Newsletter of the Committee for Gender Research* (no. 1), pp. 1, 3, 6–7.

Yi, K. Y. (1989, April). Symptoms of eating disorders among Asian-American college female students as a function of acculturation. *Dissertation Abstract International, 50,* 10.

Yoder, J. D. (1991). Rethinking tokenism: Looking beyond numbers. *Gender and Society, 5*(2), 178–192.

Yoder, J. D. (1994). Looking beyond numbers: The effects of gender status, job prestige, and occupational gender-typing on tokenism processes. *Social Psychology Quarterly, 57*(2), 150–159.

Yoder, J. D., Schleicher, T. L., & McDonald, T. W. (1998). Empowering token women leaders: The importance of organizationally legitimated credibility. *Psychology of Women Quarterly, 22,* 209–222.

Yoder, J. D., & Sinnett, L. M. (1985). Is it all in the numbers? A case study of tokenism. *Psychology of Women Quarterly, 9*(3), 413–418.

Zaner, A. R., Levee, R. F., & Gunta, R. R. (1968). The development of auditory perceptual skills as a function of maturation. *Journal of Auditory Research, 8,* 313–322.

Zanna, M., & Bowden, M. (1977, June). *Influence of interpersonal relationships on justice.* Paper presented at the annual convention of the Canadian Psychological Association, Vancouver.

Zanna, M., Crosby, F., & Loewenstein, G. (1987). Male reference groups and discontent among female professionals. In B. A. Gutek & L. Larwood (Eds.), *Women's career development* (pp. 18–41). Beverly Hills, CA: Sage.

Zanna, M. P., & Pack, S. J. (1975). On the self-fulfilling nature of apparent sex differences in behavior. *Journal of Experimental Social Psychology, 11,* 583–591.

Zarbatany, L., Hartmann, D. P., Gelfand, D. M., & Vinciguerra, P. (1985). Gender differences in altruistic reputation: Are they artifactual? *Developmental Psychology, 21,* 97–101.

Zellman, G. L., & Goodchilds, J. D. (1983). Becoming sexual in adolescence. In E. R. Allgeier & N. B. McCormick (Eds.), *Changing boundaries: Gender roles and sexual behavior* (pp. 49–63). Mountain View, CA: Mayfield.

Zelnick, M., & Kantner, J. (1977). Sexual and contraceptive experiences of young unmarried women in the United States, 1976 and 1971. *Family Planning Perspectives, 9,* 55–71.

Zelnick, M., & Kantner, J. (1980). Sexual activity, contraceptive use, and pregnancy among metropolitan-area teenagers: 1971–1979. *Family Planning Perspectives, 12,* 230–237.

Zemach, T., & Cohen, A. A. (1986). Perception of gender equality on television and in social reality. *Journal of Broadcasting and Electronic Media, 30,* 427–444.

Zern, D. S. (1984). Relationships among selected child-rearing variables in a cross-cultural sample of 110 societies. *Developmental Psychology, 20*(4), 683–690.

Zickmund, W. G., Hitt, M. A., & Pickens, B. A. (1978). Influence of sex and scholastic performance on reactions to job applicant résumés. *Journal of Applied Psychology, 63,* 252–254.

Ziegler, R., Scheidt-Nave, C., & Scharla, S. (1995). Pathophysiology of osteoporosis: Unresolved problems and new insights. *Journal of Nutrition, 125*(7 Supplement), 2033S–2037S.

Zilbergeld, B. (1978). *Male sexuality.* Boston: Little, Brown.

Zillman, D., & Weaver, J. B. (1989). Pornography and men's sexual callousness toward women. In D. Zillman & J. Bryant (Eds.), *Pornography: Research advances and policy considerations* (pp. 95–125). Hillsdale, NJ: Erlbaum.

Zimet, G. D., Bunch, D. L., Anglin, T. M., Lazebnik, R., et al. (1992). Relationship of AIDS-related attitudes to sexual behavior changes in adolescents. *Journal of Adolescent Health, 13*(6), 493–498.

Zimmerman, D. H., & West, C. (1975). Sex roles, interruptions and silence in conversation. In B. Thorne & N. Henley (Eds.), *Language and sex: Difference and dominance* (pp. 105–129). Rowley, MA: Newbury House.

Zorza, V. (1986, September 1). Wife-sharing works in the remote Himalayas. *Toronto Globe and Mail,* p. A7.

Zuckerman, D. (1981). Family background, sex-role attitudes, and life goals of technical college and university students. *Sex Roles, 7,* 1109–1126.

Zussman, J. U., Zussman, P. P., & Dalton, K. (1975). *Postpubertal effects of prenatal administration of progesterone.* Paper presented at the meeting of the Society for Research in Child Development, Denver.

Subject Index

Author Index

Credits, continued from copyright page

Chapter 1

Page 19, Fig. 1.1: From Costello, Miles, and Stone, *American Women, 1999–2000: A Century of Change—What's Next?*. 1998, p. 294. Reprinted with permission from Women's Research & Education Institute.

Page 33, Table 1.3: From J. K. Swim and L. L. Myers, "Excuse Me—What Did You Just Say?!: Women's Public and Private Responses to Sexist Remarks," *Journal of Experimental Social Psychology*, 1999, 35(1), 68-88. Copyright © 1999 by Academic Press. Reproduced by permission of the publisher.

Chapter 2

Page 76, Fig. 2.1: From K. Deaux and B. Major, "Putting Gender into Context: An Interactive Model of Gender-Related Behavior," 1987, *Psychological Review,* 94(3), p. 372. Copyright © 1987 by the American Psychological Association. Reprinted with permission.

Chapter 5

Page 142, Fig. 5.1: Copyright © 1965 Ciba-Geigy Corporation. Reproduced with permission from The Ciba Collection of Medical Illustrations by Fred H. Netter, M. D. All rights reserved.

Chapter 6

Page 176, Fig. 6.1: From J. S. Hyde, E. Fennema, and S. J. Lamon, "Gender Differences in Mathematics Performance: A Meta-Analysis," *Psychological Bulletin*, 107(2), p. 149. Copyright © 1990 by the American Psychological Association. Reprinted with permission. Page 179, Fig. 6.2: From W. D. Ellis, ed., *A Source Book of Gestalt Psychology.* Reprinted by permission of Routledge & Kegan Paul.

Page 184, Fig. 6.3: From Richard M. Restak, *The Brain: The Last Frontier*, p. 190. Copyright © 1979 by Richard M. Restak. Used by permission of Doubleday, a division of Random House, Inc.

Chapter 7

Pages 202, 203, Figs. 7.1, 7.2: From Janet S. Hyde, *Understanding Human Sexuality, Third Edition,* pp. 200, 201. Reproduced by permission of The McGraw-Hill Companies.

Chapter 8

Page 243, Fig. 8.1: From Vander et al., *Human Physiology: The Mechanics of Body Functions, Sixth Edition* and Janet S. Hyde, *Understanding Human Sexuality, Third Edition*. Reproduced by permission of The McGraw-Hill Companies.

Chapter 9

Page 294: Reprinted with permission from the poem "Anorexia Bulimia Speaks from the Grave," from the book *Selu: Seeking the Corn-Mother's Wisdom* by Marilou Awiakta. Copyright © 1993 Fulcrum Publishing, Inc., Golden, Colorado USA. All rights reserved.